SOCIAL PSYCHOLOGY AND HUMAN SEXUALITY

Key Readings in Social Psychology

General Editor: ARIE W. KRUGLANSKI, University of Maryland at College Park

The aim of this series is to make available to senior undergraduate and graduate students key articles in each area of social psychology in an attractive, user-friendly format. Many professors want to encourage their students to engage directly with research in their fields, yet this can often be daunting for students coming to detailed study of a topic for the first time. Moreover, declining library budgets mean that articles are not always readily available, and course packs can be expensive and time-consuming to produce. **Key Readings in Social Psychology** aims to address this need by providing comprehensive volumes, each one of which will be edited by a senior and active researcher in the field. Articles will be carefully chosen to illustrate the way the field has developed historically as well as current issues and research directions. Each volume will have a similar structure, which will include:

- An overview chapter, as well as introductions to sections and articles,
- Questions for class discussion,
- Annotated bibliographies,
- Full author and subject indexes.

Published Titles

The Self in Social Psychology	Roy F. Baumeister
Stereotypes and Prejudice	Charles Stangor
Motivational Science	E. Tory Higgins and Arie W. Kruglanski
Emotions in Social Psychology	W. Gerrod Parrott
Intergroup Relations	Michael Hogg and Dominic Abrams

Titles in Preparation

Social Psychology	Arie W. Kruglanski and E. Tory Higgins
Social Cognition	David Hamilton
Close Relationships	Harry Reis and Caryl Rusbult
Group Processes	John Levine and Richard Moreland
Language and Communication	Gün R. Semin
Attitudes and Persuasion	Richard E. Petty, Shelly Chaiken, and Russell Fazio
The Social Psychology of Culture	Hazel Markus and Shinobu Kitayama
The Social Psychology of Health	Peter Salovey and Alexander J. Rothman

SOCIAL PSYCHOLOGY AND HUMAN SEXUALITY

Essential Readings

Edited by

Roy F. Baumeister

USA	Publishing Office:	PSYCHOLOGY PRESS *A member of the Taylor & Francis Group* 325 Chestnut Street Philadelphia, PA 19106 Tel: (215) 625-8900 Fax: (215) 625-2940
	Distribution Center:	PSYCHOLOGY PRESS *A member of the Taylor & Francis Group* 7625 Empire Drive Florence, KY 41042 Tel: 1-800-634-7064 Fax: 1-800-248-4724
UK		PSYCHOLOGY PRESS *A member of the Taylor & Francis Group* 27 Church Road Hove E. Sussex, BN3 2FA Tel: +44 (0)1273 207411 Fax: +44 (0)1273 205612

SOCIAL PSYCHOLOGY AND HUMAN SEXUALITY: Essential Readings

1 2 3 4 5 6 7 8 9 0

Printed by Sheridan Books, Ann Arbor, MI, 2001.
Cover design by Ellen Seguin.

A CIP catalog record for this book is available from the British Library.
∞The paper in this publication meets the requirements of the ANSI Standard Z39.48-1984 (Permanence of Paper).

Library of Congress Cataloging-in-Publication Data

Social psychology and human sexuality / edited by Roy F. Baumeister
p. cm. — (Key readings in social psychology)
Includes bibliographical references and index.
ISBN 1-84169-018-X (alk. paper) — ISBN 1-84169-019-8 (pbk. : alk. paper)
1. Sex—Social aspects. 2. Social exchange. 3. Sex (Psychology) I. Baumeister, Roy F. II. Series.

HQ23 .S63 2001
306.7—dc21 00-046027

ISBN: 1-84169-018-X (case)
ISBN: 1-84169-019-8 (paper)
ISSN: 1531-2569

Dedicated in gratitude to my parents,
Rudolf and Donna Baumeister,
on the occasion of their fiftieth wedding anniversary.

Contents

About the Editor

Roy F. Baumeister holds the Elsie B. Smith Chair in the Liberal Arts at Case Western Reserve University. He received his Ph.D. in 1978 from Princeton and then had a postdoctoral fellowship at the University of California at Berkeley. He has worked at Case Western Reserve University since 1979 and has had visiting fellowships at the University of Virginia, the University of Texas, and the Max-Planck-Institute in Munich, Germany. Roy F. Baumeister has authored over 200 scientific publications. His research and writing span a range of topics in social psychology, including self-esteem, self-control, performance under pressure, reactions in emergencies, guilt, sexuality, emotion, decision-making, taking risks, and trying to make a good impression.

Acknowledgements

The Authors and Publishers are grateful to the following for permission to reproduce the articles in this book:

Reading 1: M. Oliver and J. Hyde, Gender differences in sexuality: a meta-analysis. Psychological Bulletin, Vol. 114, No. 1, 29–51. Copyright © 1993 by the American Psychological Association. Reprinted with permission.

Reading 2: R. Clark and E. Hatfield, Gender differences in receptivity to sexual offers. Journal of Psychology & Human Sexuality, Vol. 2 (1), 39–55. Copyright © 1989 by Haworth Press, Inc. Reprinted with permission.

Reading 3: D. Buss and D. Schmitt, Sexual Strategies Theory: an evolutionary perspective on human mating. Psychological Review, Vol. 100, No. 2., 204-232, Copyright © 1993 by the American Psychological Association. Reprinted with permission.

Reading 4: R. Baumeister, Gender differences in erotic plasticity: the female sex drive as socially flexible and responsive. Psychological Bulletin, Vol. 126, No. 3, 347–374, Copyright © 2000 by the American Psychological Association. Reprinted with permission.

Reading 5: S. Sprecher, A. Barbee, & P. Schwartz, "Was it good for you, too?": gender differences in first sexual intercourse experiences. The Journal of Sex Research, Vol. 32, No. 1, 3–15. Copyright ©1995 by the Society for the Scientific Study of Sexuality. Reprinted with permission.

Reading 6: J. Billy and J. Udry, Patterns of adolescent friendship and effects on sexual behavior. Social Psychology Quarterly, Vol. 48, No. 1, 27–41. Copyright © 1985 by the American Sociological Association. Reprinted with permission.

Reading 7: E. Maticka-Tyndale, E. Herold, & D. Mewhinney, Casual sex on spring break: intentions and behaviors of Canadian students. The Journal of Sex Research, Vol. 35, No. 3, 254–264. Copyright © 1998 by the Society for the Scientific Study of Sexuality. Reprinted with permission.

Reading 8: D. Bem, Exotic becomes erotic: a developmental theory of sexual orientation. Psychological Review, Vol. 103, No. 2, 320–335. Copyright © 1996 by the American Psychological Association. Reprinted with permission.

Reading 9: H. Adams, L. Wright, & B. Lohr, Is homophobia associated with homosexual arousal? Journal of Abnormal Psychology, Vol. 105, No. 3, 440–445. Copyright © 1996 by the American Psychological Association. Reprinted with permission.

Reading 10: C. Palmer, Twelve reasons why rape is not sexually motivated: a skeptical examination. The Journal of Sex Research, Vol. 25, No. 4, 521–530. Copyright © 1988 by the Society for the Scientific Study of Sexuality. Reprinted with permission.

Reading 11: E. Kanin, Date rapists: differential sexual socialization and relative deprivation. Archives of Sexual Behavior, Vol. 14, No. 3, 219–231. Copyright © 1985 by Kluwer Academic/Plenum Publishers. Reprinted with permission.

Reading 12: C. Buf Meyer and S. Taylor, Adjustment to rape. Journal of Personality and Social Psychology, Vol. 50, No. 6, 1226–1234. Copyright © 1986 by the American Psychological Association. Reprinted with permission.

Reading 13: J. Bargh, P. Raymond, J. Pryor, & F. Strack, Attractiveness of the underling: an automatic power—sex association and its consequences for sexual harassment and aggression. Journal of Personality and Social Psychology, Vol. 68, No. 5, 768–781. Copyright © 1995 by the American Psychological Association. Reprinted with permission.

Reading 14: D. Buss, R. Larsen, D. Western, & J. Semmelroth, Sex differences in jealousy: evolution, physiology and psychology. Psychological Science, Vol. 3, No. 4, 251–255. Copyright © 1992 by Blackwell Publishers, Ltd. Reprinted with permission.

Reading 15: G. Hansen, Extradyadic relations during courtship, Brief Reports, 383–390. Copyright © 1986. Reprinted with permission.

Reading 16: R. Baumeister, Masochism as escape from self. The Journal of Sex Research, Vol. 25, No. 1, 28–59. Copyright © 1988 by the Society for the Scientific Study of Sexuality. Reprinted with permission.

Reading 17: W. Fisher and D. Byrne, Sex differences in response to erotica?: love versus lust. Journal of Personality and Social Psychology, Vol. 36, No. 2, 117–125. Copyright © 1978 by the American Psychological Association. Reprinted with permission.

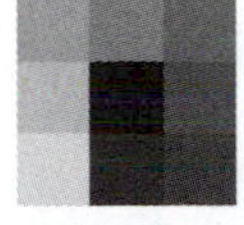

VOLUME OVERVIEW

Social Psychology, Social Exchange, and Sexuality

Roy F. Baumeister

The study of human sexuality has advanced only by fits and starts, and even today it has won only partial and grudging respect from the scientific community at large. Research on sex is a hodge podge of diverse methods, fragmentary theories, and intriguing findings that are often subject to competing explanations. Many scientists remain skeptical of sexuality research for a variety of reasons. The federal granting agencies remain reluctant to support research into sexuality even though many major national problems are associated with sexuality, including teen pregnancy and unwanted pregnancy, AIDS and other venereal diseases, and sexual victimization and coercion.

Despite these handicaps, a lively and devoted core of sexuality researchers has steadily contributed a growing volume of research findings. One need only to compare how well sex is understood in the year 2000 with the state of knowledge a century earlier to see how far we have come.

Perhaps ironically, social psychology has played only a minor part in the growth of sexuality research, at least until recently. One need only glance through any of the major textbooks on sexuality to verify that most of the coverage is devoted to biological aspects of sexuality, clinical aspects such as sexual problems, and technical matters. Our field looks upon sex as a natural, biological function that sometimes suffers from disturbances, and as a set of skills to perform.

Although biological, clinical, and technical aspects of sex are important, it is also helpful to examine sex as a social phenomenon: As a group of behavior patterns that people engage in together, under the influence of social pressures, and indeed as ways that people relate to one another. In particular, it is subject to many of the main principles that regulate other forms of sexual behavior. Put down your sexuality textbook and look instead at a textbook in social psychology, and you can quickly see that many of the chapters in that book—attitudes, relationships, self, aggression, influence, prejudice, decision-making—are potentially quite relevant to sex.

However, the link between social psychology and sex remains in large part a matter of unfulfilled potential. A variety of research has begun to rely on specific ideas or approaches within social psychology to explain sexual behavior, but this merger remains in its infancy. This book contains an assortment of that kind of work, but there is as yet no general or systematic attempt to build this understanding into a coherent whole.

Thus, this reader makes no pretense of trying to offer an overview of research on sexuality. It is devoted specifically to the links between social psychology and sexuality. It offers a sample of how social psychologists have begun to look into the area of sexuality to extend and test their theories.

We are not the first to call for more attention to the social dimension of sex. The authors of the influential "Sex in America" survey, the NHSLS (Laumann, Gagnon, Michael, & Michaels, 1994) argued forcefully that a better understanding of the *social* factors affecting sex was the most pressing need. Their research is widely regarded as the most important and useful contribution to American sexuality in the last decade and perhaps even since Kinsey's pioneering work, and so their opinions are worth noting. In their view, the biggest gap in current knowledge about sex was something that social psychology seems well poised to fill.

Sexual Science Today

Let us take a broad look at the field of sexuality today, as a research enterprise. What do our studies tell us about sex? To appraise any field of study, it is necessary to consider several factors. Foremost among them are the ideas or theories and the methods.

The field of sexuality is weak on theories and ideas. This was the clear conclusion of a special issue of the *Journal of Sex Research* in 1998 devoted to assessing the status of theory in sexual science. Most telling was an article by Weis (1998). He went through the field's two most prominent journals, article by article, and examined the state of theorizing. He concluded that three quarters of them just reported data with little or no discussion of theoretical meaning. Indeed, a large number of them did not even make a pretense of having ideas to test: They merely described their methods and results.

It would be rash to say that there are no major theories or ideas in the field of sexuality. There are some. But these have to some extent polarized the field without providing a strong basis for progress in knowledge. Another article in that special issue of the *Journal of Sex Research*, by the highly esteemed husband-and-wife research team of John DeLamater and Janet Hyde (1998), described how two large theoretical approaches have dominated thinking about sexuality. Every student of sexuality should have a basic grasp of these two approaches.

One of these views is described as "social constructionist." The term social constructionism came into broad use after the publication, in 1967, of Berger and Luckmann's book *The Social Construction of Reality*. This book rebelled against the common view that reality consisted ultimately of atoms and molecules and other phenomena that are the province of the natural sciences. They emphasized that social processes also create a form of reality and indeed one that is much more important to people's everyday experiences. In particular, the social construction of reality depends on language and on the shared understandings that language makes possible. Berger and Luckmann certainly recognized the existence of physical reality, of chemicals and physical particles, but they also emphasized the importance of shared meanings.

Applied to sex, this approach has emphasized that sexuality is largely something that is learned and shaped by culture, socialization, and situational influences. What people do sexually, and even what they desire, is regarded as something that is heavily dependent on the social context. This approach emphasizes differences between different cultures or different historical eras to argue that culture exerts a strong influence on sex. It is not surprising that social constructionism dominated the study of sex in the decade following Berger and Luckmann's book, because that decade coincided with the height of the sexual revolution—and the sexual revolution seemed to provide dramatic evidence that cultural, historical events could produce sweeping changes in sexual behaviors and attitudes.

Feminists in particular were drawn into the social constructionist camp, partly because the dramatic changes of the sexual revolution were most apparent in female sexuality. Feminists undertook an interpretation of a broad range of social behavior as reflecting men's oppression of women, and sex fit right into this analysis. They saw feminism as including the need to liberate female sexuality from the exploitative, oppressive influence of male-dominated society.

Ranged against the social constructionist approaches are what DeLamater and Hyde (1998) called "essentialist" views. These views have treated sexuality as an innate part of the human being, emphasizing biological and evolutionary determinants. The role of culture was downplayed. Genes, hormones, and other biological processes are regarded as central determinants of human sexuality.

The essentialist approach to sex has gained considerable clout and excitement with the application of evolutionary theory (e.g., Buss, 1994; Symons, 1979). Central to this approach is that human beings are descended from those ancestors who were most successful in passing on their genes by reproducing. Crucially, the argument emphasizes that human sexual motivation today reflects the natural selection in bygone millennia: The forms of sexual desire and sexual behavior that produced the most successful offspring are the ones that dominate the human gene pool (and the human psyche) today. Gender differences in sex drive are linked to the differences in reproduction that demand more prudence and responsibility from women than men, insofar as women cannot produce a viable offspring with zero effort or contribution beyond the first five minutes of pleasure.

The contrast between the two approaches can be easily appreciated in the ongoing debate about the causal roots of homosexuality. Are homosexuals born that way, such as by having a "gay gene," or does homosexual orientation derive from socializing and influential experiences (or even personal choice)? Essentialists will lean toward the former explanation; social constructionists toward the latter. Many other aspects of sexuality, such as promiscuity, deviant tastes such as fetishism, and so-called sex addiction, are likewise susceptible to either essentialist or constructionist interpretations.

With two large theoretical approaches, one might think that the field of sexuality would be relatively well off. Yet these two approaches do not function the way theories do in most fields. They are quite difficult to prove or disprove. Many findings can be fit into either theory. Certainly there is some interesting work that attempts to test predictions based on one or the other theory. But for many researchers and many topics, the broad nature–culture debate is not focused enough to offer specific predictions that can be tested with the methods currently available.

That brings us to methods. Research on sexuality has come a long way since the early part of the 20th century, when almost no systematic information was available and a handful of clinical case studies were the main source of knowledge. Undoubtedly the greatest single step forward was the research by Alfred Kinsey and his group (Kinsey, Pomeroy, & Martin, 1948; Kinsey, Pomeroy, Martin, & Gebhard, 1953). Kinsey himself was a biology professor who had spent most of his career studying wasps. When he was asked to teach a course on (human) marriage and sexuality at Indiana University in the late 1930s, he was shocked at how little scientific evidence was available about the topic. To remedy this, he began asking his students systematic questions about their experiences, and soon he proceeded to conduct in-depth interviews with people from all walks of life about their sexual histories, including both behaviors and feelings. Kinsey was not able to assemble a sample that would resemble the American population as a whole, but he obtained detailed information from thousands of people. The reports he published in human sexuality created a sensation. The first one sold more than 200,000 copies in its first two months. The long-awaited second one, whose release on "K-Day" made front-page news, reached 200,000 sales in a few weeks. Both drew criticism from all sides, including Congressional hearings to ascertain whether Kinsey was part of a Communist plot. He died shortly thereafter, "an exhausted and broken man" (Petersen, 1999, p. 228).

Some of Kinsey's numbers are now recognized as misleading, insofar as he did not collect a systematic sample. For example, he concluded that a third of men had reached orgasm through homosexual contact at least once, but this high number probably reflects the fact that he actively sought out homosexuals to interview (because their experiences were especially unknown to science). Still, the approach he championed—that we should find out the facts and report them with as little moralizing and evaluative judging as possible—has been an inspiration to generations of sexuality researchers ever since.

Today there is a steady flow of scientific information about sexuality, including several major journals devoted entirely to research on that topic. Still, the quality of the work and the soundness of its findings are not uniformly high. Research is hampered by a lack of federal funding, by pragmatic difficulties such as the reluctance of research participants to disclose personal material or perform sex acts in the laboratory, and the rising tendency of research watchdogs to prevent researchers from studying anything that might upset people or intrude into their private doings.

Sex is therefore not on the same par as other social behaviors, in terms of research possibilities. Helping, aggression, first impressions, prejudice, cooperation, task performance, intelligence, and most other topics can be studied without great difficulty and with great precision in laboratory work. Sex is much more difficult. Hardly any studies include overt sexual behavior that is directly measured or observed.

Three levels of research methods have therefore become used in the sexuality area. The first involves hypothetical questions: Would you have sex with a certain person under certain circumstances? Would you object if your partner performed a certain act with someone else? Would you expect to have sex with someone if this or that criterion were met, or after a certain amount of time? Would you rather do this or that?

These hypothetical methods furnish intriguing findings but must be regarded with extreme caution. People are often unable to furnish accurate guesses about what they would actually do. Outside the sexual realm, several researchers have compared actual versus hypothetical responses, and at least on some occasions the differences are large. Milgram (1963) found that people were much more willing in reality than hypothetically to obey instructions to deliver painful and dangerous electric shocks to another person. West and Brown (1975) found that people were vastly more generous and helpful in their hypothetical answers than in actual behavior.

The second level of work relies on self-report. Interviews and questionnaires ask people what sexual behaviors they have performed. In some cases people are asked to keep a diary to report on their sexual acts or feelings on a daily basis.

The self-report method is probably the most commonly used one in sexuality research, and its popularity is likely to continue. It is certainly better than the hypothetical method, because asking people what they have done is closer to reality than asking them what they might do under some imaginary circumstance.

Yet self-report suffers from a variety of flaws too. Self-reports are not entirely reliable, especially when one is dealing with such powerful material as sex. People selectively forget sexual behaviors they regret having performed (Downey, Ryan, Roffman, & Kulich, 1995). They may inflate or undercount certain activities simply because they want to conform to the societal standard of what is good and desirable. (For example, on nearly all surveys men report having had more sex partners and more sex than women—but this is not logically possible.) Surveys can also run into trouble by relying on volunteers, because people who refuse to volunteer for sex research are generally different (in particular, they tend to have less sexual experience) than people who do volunteer. Ask yourself: Would you be willing to respond to a long series of personal questions about your sex life and experiences? Your level of willingness probably tells something about yourself, including how comfortable you are with your own sexuality.

The third level consists of objective information, based on observations of sexual behavior that are not dependent on self-report. A broad range of methods is included in this category. Research may explore whether people actually engage in sexual behavior with someone. It may measure people's physical responses while watching erotica (such as by means of electrodes on the genitals). It may examine how they respond to a sexually inappropriate remark.

The objective, behavioral measures do not guarantee good science, but they are generally superior to hypothetical questions and self-reports. Their main drawbacks are practical. Researchers may want to learn about the causes of rape, for example, but it is unrealistic to expect that full-fledged rape can actually be studied in the laboratory. Self-report and hypothetical questions are a much more viable way to learn about rape, despite their drawbacks.

For the present, all these methods are likely to continue to be used. Any social science can be judged by the strength and diversity of its methods. The study of sex could certainly be improved by more and better research methods, but for now it is likely to continue with what it has been using. The important thing is for people who read the research reports to keep in mind what the limitations of these methods are and to think about how solid the conclusions can be.

A Social Exchange Theory of Sex

As we have seen, the field of sexuality could benefit from new ideas and new theories. This section will offer one such theory. It takes a basic approach from social psychology and spells out implications of applying this to sex. This must be recognized as a preliminary effort, and so these conclusions should not be mistaken for proven truths or established facts. Rather, the goal is to offer a way of thinking about the social nature of sex. This approach can then be contrasted with others and can be adjusted according to research findings. In plain terms, it is offered here in the spirit of "playing with ideas." As you read the articles in the rest of this book, you may ask yourself from time to time whether this approach could explain the findings in the articles.

The basis for this theory is *social exchange theory*, a style of analysis developed by sociologists and psychologists around the middle of the 20th century. Homans (1950, 1961) and Blau (1964) analyzed human interactions in terms of the costs and benefits that each participant derives. People may interact because they seek benefits such as help, money, friendship, social support, protection, or a few laughs. They may avoid interactions because they fear costs such as physical harm, exploitation, embarrassment, rejection, or anxiety. What two people say or do together may reflect their respective pursuit of various rewards. Ideally, both people gain more benefits than rewards from an interaction.

A crucial point of social exchange theory is that supply and demand principles regulate social behavior. For example, people may desire praise, and their pursuit of praise will be different depending on how easily they can obtain praise. A given person's praise also varies in value as a function of how rare it is: Someone who almost never says a kind word to anyone can get a strong reaction with a simple compliment, whereas someone who routinely compliments everybody cannot easily produce such a strong response. Beyond praise, even simple human contact can be either scarce or abundant. People who walk the streets of New York city, for example, have often developed habits of avoiding eye contact or any sort of interactions, simply because the amount of social interaction with so many different people would be overwhelming if you allowed yourself to be open to it. In contrast, prisoners in solitary confinement have been known to speak into toilets (the water in the pipes transmits the sound waves to other cells, where other prisoners can hear and reply) or to tap Morse code messages on walls, simply to have any shred of communication with another human being.

Social exchange analyses were applied to love and sex by Waller and Hill (1951). They proposed the "principle of least interest," which means that whoever is less in love has more power in the relationship. If you have been in a relationship where you loved the other person far more than that person loved you, you probably recall that you were willing to do and put up with a great deal. In contrast, if you were the one who was less in love, you most likely would have been far less accommodating, and the other person would be the one to do what you wanted.

A more recent social exchange analysis of sex by Baumeister and Tice (2000) emphasized another key point: Sex is a resource that women give to men. Put another way, men have a strong desire for sex, and women control the men's opportunities to get it, so men must offer women other resources in order to obtain sex. Sex is a *female resource*. It is something women have and men want, and so men must offer women something in exchange for it.

The view that women give sex to men is consistent with Waller and Hill's (1951) principle of least interest—if we assume that men want sex more than women. By this view, women may desire sex, but men desire it more, and so ultimately the woman is doing something for the man (or giving something to him) in the act of sex. Hence to make the social exchange work, he has to give her something in return. If women wanted sex more than men, then the men would be doing the women a favor by having sex with them, and the women would owe the men something in exchange.

Claiming that women give sex to men entails that the two genders are not really equal partners in bed. This may seem contrary to recent political and ideological views that have sought to depict male and female sexuality as essentially the same. By the social exchange view, when a man and a woman make love, even if they both perform the same acts (e.g., oral sex) and both enjoy orgasms, the transaction is not quite an equitable sharing. Instead, she has given him something of value, to a much greater extent than what he has given her.

To be sure, this social exchange approach is compatible with aspects of both evolutionary and feminist (or constructionist) thought, and so it is not a rival theory that will require people to choose one or the other. Evolutionary analyses emphasize that males desire to copulate with many females and must often offer them something in return (e.g., Symons, 1979). Moreover, the female orgasm is a relatively recent development in evolution, raising the suspicion that males in most species desire and enjoy sex more than women. Evolutionary analyses also emphasize the principle of "female choice," which holds that males of many species have a broad range of sexual desire but the female is the one who ultimately decides whether sex takes place or not. The principle of female choice dramatizes how males must offer the female something to induce her to change her initially skeptical or negative attitude into a positive one, so that the couple can have sex.

Despite these compatibilities with evolutionary thinking, the social exchange theory is essentially a social and cultural theory rather than an evolutionary one. It emphasizes current social conditions, such as supply and demand and a fluctuating set of norms and standards for how much sexual activity the woman will permit the man in exchange for what degree of commitment or expenditure he offers her.

The social exchange approach can also be integrated with important aspects of feminist thought. Feminists have long sought to regard sex in the broader context of "gender politics," which means the power relations between men and women. The social exchange analysis of sex offers a compelling reason that men may have sought to oppress women in political, economic, legal, and other spheres: The more desperate women are for such basic resources, the more they would presumably be willing to exchange sex for them. In plain terms, a needy woman will be more likely to offer a man sex at bargain rates. For example, at many points in history some women have been willing to be a kept mistress of a married man. By that arrangement, he would pay her rent and other expenses, in exchange for which he would be permitted to have sex with her from time to time. Such arrangements are probably more common when women are prevented by job discrimination and other barriers from supporting themselves. In contrast, when women can earn good money and support themselves by regular work, the supply of potential kept mistresses is probably much reduced.

Despite these convergences, the social exchange theory does differ from feminist approaches in some crucial respects. For feminists, men use sex along with other things to pursue their ultimate goal of keeping power over women. In other words, power is the goal, and sex is only a means. In contrast, this social exchange analysis emphasizes sex as the uppermost thing men want from women, and gaining power is a strategy men will use to try to improve their access to sex. Thus, sex is the goal, and power is the means.

What is it that women want in exchange for sex? There is certainly more than one answer. Men may offer a woman money, status, respect, or other resources. Simply being permitted to interact with elite individuals is a resource that many people covet, and women can gain such access by offering sex. The phenomenon of groupies, for example, consists of young women who are able to interact with famous celebrity musicians—who otherwise would be far out of the women's reach—by having sex with them. More generally, women can interact with men of a higher social status if the women offer sex.

Commitment may be another important thing that men can offer women in exchange for sex. Throughout much of history, men's main opportunity for regular sex was through marriage, and it was necessary to marry in order to obtain sex. Marriage entailed a lifetime commitment to share the man's possessions, home, and earnings with the woman (and not with anyone else outside their family). To be sure, sex was not all the woman brought to a marriage. By and large, wives have done the majority of housework and child care, and in many societies women have contributed a greater share of the food than the men. Still, unmarried men can usually pay someone to do their housework, whereas paying for sex has a variety of drawbacks including high expense and risks. Hence sex becomes a major reason that men get married. Grandmother was right: If he can get the milk for free, he is less eager to buy the cow.

Another interesting and relevant question is whether the woman really gives up anything of value by having sex. The transaction appears one-sided: She gets something from him but gives up nothing. If anything, she gains too, insofar as she gets sexual pleasure and the satisfaction of her own sexual desires.

Yet there does seem to be a sense of giving something up. (Indeed, the phrase "give it up" is sometimes used to describe women's participation in sex.) Also, women sometimes feel exploited or used in sex, and this implies that they have taken some loss in the transaction, as opposed to simply having failed to get the best possible price. It would be interesting to know what it is about bad sexual experiences that makes them bad.

As already noted, the original social exchange theorists claimed that social rewards lose their value whenever they are given out too freely. So the woman's capacity to command a high price for sex is a limited resource, in a sense, and the more lovers she has, the less value there is. In that sense, she does give up something of value each time she goes to bed with a new partner. No single partner makes much of a difference (well, beyond the first), but as they accumulate they collectively make her sexual favors less of a compliment.

Furthermore, a woman's sex appeal is limited in time, even if it does not obviously diminish by being used by her to get what she wants, or even by being given away freely. She is young and beautiful for only a short part of her life. So in that sense she needs to be getting a good bargain for sex, because in reality she only makes a relatively small number of deals. By the time she reaches the age of fifty, or perhaps even forty, she gets fewer offers.

Women's situation thus pushes them in both directions, or perhaps more precisely away from both extremes: A woman who never has sex has failed to capitalize on a major asset, but a woman who has sex too frequently and freely depreciates her asset's value. As we shall see, the social exchange analysis will suggest several other ways in which women are pulled or pushed in opposite directions in terms of sex, and so the net result is likely to be that adult women maintain a profound ambivalence about sex and will have widely mixed feelings about it.

Is this social exchange analysis a useful theory for analyzing sexual behavior? One way to evaluate it is to see how well it fits an assortment of sexual behaviors. The next few sections will explore some of them.

Prostitution

The most obvious form of social exchange of sex occurs in prostitution. The essence of prostitution is that one person gives another money and gets sex in return. Although in some parts of the world (and even some U.S. cities) prostitutes accept credit cards, cash is still probably the most common form of payment. In any case, the exchange is clear: Money transfers from one person to another, as a condition of having sex. The two people may never see each other again, but in theory each has gotten something of value.

It is probably not very controversial to analyze prostitution in exchange terms, because that is its very nature. It is however worth pointing out that there is a severe gender imbalance. Women hardly ever pay men for sex. Men pay female prostitutes for sex. Male prostitutes also cater mainly to male customers.

This one-sided pattern supports the view of sex as something that men obtain from women, rather than the reverse. Some women can earn a living, even perhaps a pretty good one, by giving men sex in exchange for money. In contrast, hardly any men are able to earn money by having women pay them to have sex. For a woman to pay a man for sex would be contrary to the principle that sex is a female resource. The one-sided nature of prostitution thus fits the social exchange theory.

Rape and Sexual Coercion

Whereas prostitution involves following an explicit set of rules about exchanging for sex, rape involves violating those rules. From this perspective, rape and sexual coercion occur when men try to obtain sex by force, without giving the woman anything in exchange. Rape thus resembles theft or looting of property: Using force to take something from someone else without giving the appropriate value in return.

Several features of rape augment this view. For one, sexually coercive men tend to view gender interactions as based on rules and scripts that are somewhat exploitative and sometimes ignored. In particular, they sometimes endorse the view that men are justified in using force to obtain sex if the woman has encouraged the man or led him on (Kanin, 1985).

Courtship rape patterns also suggest that the sexually coercive males have an implicit concept of exchange. On the face of it, it seems surprising that many rapes occur between people who have been dating for a substantial period of time and have become emotionally intimate. Yet a national survey found that the most commonly reported category of men who had forced women into sex against their will was "someone you were in love with at the time," a category that in fact accounted for nearly half the total (Laumann et al., 1994). It seems reasonable to assume that a man and woman who are in love are not strangers or first dates and that some ongoing relationship exists between them. If rape or sexual coercion occurs, it is presumably because the woman refuses to have sex despite this intimate relationship (which is of course her right). Why then would a man force her at this point? He may well feel that he has invested a substantial amount of time, energy, and expense into wooing her and that her refusal of sexual intercourse is an unfair refusal to give him what he has earned.

The asymmetry of rape is also consistent with the exchange analysis. Recent work suggests that women engage in sexual coercion against male victims less often than men coerce women, although the difference is not as large as has often been thought (Anderson & Struckman-Johnson, 1998). Yet the degree of trauma in male versus female victims is far from equal, and in fact most men who are victims of female sexual coercion recover well and look back on the incident as a relatively minor, unimportant event, even if distasteful. Social exchange theory explains why male victims might suffer less anguish than female ones. Because sex is not a male resource, the male victims have not lost anything of value, as it were. The women do lose, and therefore, are more upset.

If we emphasized social exchange as the only reason for sex, then women would seemingly never coerce men, but this is clearly false. Sometimes women do desire sex and are willing to use pressure and force to gain cooperation from reluctant men. A milder version of the social exchange analysis would allow such incidents to occur but would insist that they lack one dimension of trauma that is central to male rapes of women, namely forcible theft of the female resource. When a woman forces a man to have sex against his will, she does not take a resource from him in the same way that a male rapist takes something from a woman, according to social exchange. Hence the greater trauma of the female victim.

Sex Partners and Social Status

Research on mating and sex partners has long observed that couples are not usually equals in all respects. Typically the man has higher income, status, education, or other resources than the woman (e.g., Bernard, 1982). The difference is usually fairly slight, because people generally mate with people from their own network. Still, it is common for the husband to outrank his wife slightly on various measures of status. Men are typically a little better educated, have more money, come from a higher ranking family, and so forth, than their wives.

Social exchange analysis can explain this inequality. This returns to the point made earlier that a man and woman are not quite equal partners in bed. People must offer each other various rewards in order to attract each other. But since sex is a female resource, it is one of the rewards a woman offers a man, rather than vice versa. Therefore the man has to offer her more in return.

Put another way, sex is not an act of equal contribution by men and women. The woman contributes something more than the man, namely the female resource of sex itself. If everything else is completely equal, then the man has benefited more than the woman by the act of sex. In contrast, if he has more to offer, such as being a slightly higher ranking person according to the values prevailing in society, then that superiority may make up for the difference.

Yet another way to express this point is that people want to mate with the most desirable partners they can attract. Because sex is a female resource, a woman can attract someone better than she could if she were a man with exactly the same social status. She can offer him her education, socioeconomic status, and everything else about who she is—plus sex. Sex is not part of what he gives her, and so the other parts of what he offers (again, education, socioeconomic status, and so forth) have to be that much better, in order to make the deal equitable.

Meanwhile, having sex has consequences for status as well. Insofar as the exchange principle holds and women give sex to men, then having many sex partners will add to men's status but detract from women's. Because men gain by sex whereas women give up something of value, men will look better if they have a high number whereas women look better if they have a low number of partners. This has certainly been the traditional stereotype, according to which a man with many lovers is regarded as having been especially successful, whereas a woman with many partners is derogated as a slut. There is some evidence that these attitudes persist today. Regan and Dreyer (1999) investigated the reasons people gave for engaging in casual sex. Men were significantly more likely than women to say that they would seek such sexual escapades in order to increase their status in the eyes of their friends. In fact, women hardly ever said that engaging in casual sex improved their status.

It also seems likely that the differential implications for status explain the persistent finding that men report having more sex partners than women, even though that is logically impossible: In a population that is half male and half female, men must on average have exactly the same number of heterosexual partners as women. Recent evidence has concluded that the gender discrepancy in reported tallies of partners reflects different cognitive strategies, such as the fact that men count more borderline actions (e.g., oral sex) as qualifying as sex, and that men estimate and round upwards whereas women try to count and selectively forget some experiences (Brown & Sinclair, 1999; Sanders & Reinisch, 1999; Wiederman, 1997). Thus, men count their sex partners in ways that furnish higher tallies whereas women do it in ways that yield lower tallies, which suggests that men are motivated to claim high numbers while women desire to report low tallies (Baumeister & Tice, 2000).

The fact that men report more sex partners than women is also relevant to the notion that the value of having sex with a particular woman is gradually debased as she accumulates many partners. As I explained in the introductory exposition of exchange theory, any commodity is seen as more valuable when it is rare, and this applies to each woman's sexual favors. As she grants them more widely, the scarcity is lost, and so the value of her sexual favors is diminished. Each woman is therefore motivated to have (or at least claim to have had) a low number of sex partners, so that going to bed with her will continue to be a rare and special event for the fortunate man. Furnishing a low tally of prior sex partners would support this strategy. (At the extreme, for example, a prostitute or slut cannot confer much of value by having sex with someone.) No such concerns apply to the man, of course, because there is no sense in which he confers value by having sex with someone. Hence there is no corresponding motivation for the man to claim a low number of partners. If anything, the opposite contingency applies, according to which he gains prestige by having sex with the most valuable women. Having had intercourse with dozens of prostitutes, for example, would not confer much credit to him, whereas having had sex with a series of virgins or other highly selective women will.

Courtship

Processes of courtship conform to the social exchange analysis. To be sure, courtship is not a monolithic or unidimensional process, and many factors are at work. Courtship may involve seeking a desirable parenting partner or reliving one's personal neuroses, among many other goals.

Still, sexual negotiations are one important aspect of sex. A social exchange analysis offers a perspective that can help predict and explain how they proceed. The central point is this: In courtship, the male is typically trying to induce the female to have sex with him.

The basic asymmetry in sexual persuasion is well documented. Men want to have sex earlier in the relationship than women. McCabe's (1987) large study of Australian couples found that at all stages of relationships, men wanted more sexual intimacy than they were getting, whereas women did not. For example, a typical couple would spend some time at a stage in which they both enjoyed heavy petting, and the man wanted to move along to oral or genital intercourse but the woman said no.

Given this asymmetry, it generally falls to the man to try to persuade the woman to have sex, rather than vice versa. For the man, courtship is in substantial part a prolonged campaign to persuade the woman to have sex with him.

In order for the social exchange to result in sex, the man has to invest more resources than the woman does, because sex would constitute an important contribution by her. That is why it falls to the man to pay for dinner, bring flowers, buy the movie tickets, and so forth. Sex is something that she gives him, and so he must first give her some other things in exchange.

What men and women dislike in each other during courtship is often a matter of violating the terms of fair exchange. Buss (1989) studied anger between men and women and drew revealing conclusions. Men object to women who extract resources from them but then fail to come through with sexual favors. The infamous "cockteaser" was disliked not simply for being sexually desirable but for getting the man to spend money (as well as time and other resources) in the hope that she will consent to sex, only to refuse him in the end. Meanwhile, women object most strongly to men who fail to fulfill their part of the bargain too. In particular, some men will falsely say they love the woman or pretend to want to marry her in order to obtain sex, but after bedding her they reveal that they did not really want a lasting relationship or commitment.

Thus, social exchange theory says there is some validity to the stereotypical complaints. Men might say "I paid for her dinner but she didn't give me anything," upset that the woman let him spend his money on her but failed to give sex in return. His indignation seems based on the assumption that they had already made a contractual agreement that he would buy her food in exchange for her letting him have sex.

Women, meanwhile, might worry that "After we had sex, he never called me." Most adult women are very competent at operating a telephone, and so one might ask why she does not call him if she wants to talk, but that misses the point. She consented to sex on the assumption that he wanted a lasting relationship and would continue paying attention to her, and in her view if he fails to call her, he has not fulfilled his part of the bargain. The broader threat is that he simply obtained sex from her and then skedaddled. She wanted to give sex only in exchange for lasting intimacy. In a sense, by failing to call her, he has cheated her out of sex.

Sex, at least the heterosexual kind, is typically understood as something that happens between a man and a woman. Social exchange theory, however, links the couple's actions to what other people are doing as well. In a sense, each small community has a standard going rate that specifies how much a man should invest in exchange for obtaining sex. Clearly the going rate varies widely. In some times and places, a man had to make a lifetime commitment to share all his wealth and earnings with the woman and to forego having sex with anyone else (at least in principle), in order to be permitted to have sex with the woman. At other times and places a much smaller investment of his resources has been considered sufficient. Still, the crucial point is that each couple's sexual negotiations take place with some reference to what everyone else is doing and what the standard going rate is.

As a result, each couple's sexual activity constitutes a relatively good "deal" for one person and a bad "deal" for the other. If the man gets to have sex with the woman without investing the resources or making the commitment that is typical, then he has gained a significant benefit, while the woman has been "cheap" and may regard herself as having been taken advantage of. In contrast, if he has to invest more than usual in order to have sex, then she has done well. It is a fair deal for both only insofar as it conforms roughly to the going rate in that community—in other words, the woman yielded the appropriate amount of sexual favors in return for the man's investment of an appropriate amount of other resources including money, attention, and commitment.

To be sure, these market calculations may be disguised and even subsumed by other factors. If the man is in love with the woman, he may be perfectly willing to marry her before they have sex, even though most other couples in their community have sex after a few dates. Likewise, the woman may give sex more readily than the norm because she loves the man or simply because she has high sexual desire and does not want to hold back in order to get the full measure of what most women in her community can expect. Nonetheless, each couple's activity is probably affected to some degree by the norms and standards, to the extent that they are accurately understood.

It is interesting to note, however, that these may not be accurately understood in many cases. Cohen and Shotland (1996) found that most men and women misperceived the sexual norms on their own campus, specifically overestimating the sexual activity of others. More precisely, most men and women assumed that they themselves would wait longer to have sex than the average man or woman would. It may therefore be that most couples carry out their negotiations under the assumption that sex has a cheaper average "price" than it actually does. In other times and places, this may have been the other way around. For example, in the late 19th and early 20th centuries, virginity until marriage was the norm and the public expectation, whereas in fact many couples started having intercourse prior to marriage (although mainly when they were engaged). The secrecy surrounding premarital sex may therefore have created a false impression of a sexual price that was higher than the reality.

Most theories about sex make some reference to local norms and standards. There is after all little dispute that couples regulate their sexual behavior according to what their peers and fellows consider appropriate. The social exchange theory differs from the others in explaining why people should care about what the norms and standards are, however, and indeed why young people may be so curious about what other couples are doing. The concern arises from the need to negotiate a fair or advantageous exchange: Fairness depends on what the going rate in the local mating marketplace is. For other theories, the interest in conforming to others has to be understood as simply a helpful way of dealing with uncertainty or as an instance of the more general pattern of conformity among young people.

Possibly the two theories can be distinguished by examining the relative importance of norms for heterosexual negotiations, as opposed to other kinds of sexual activity. Masturbation, for example, does not involve social exchange, so the social exchange theory would predict that people would not determine their masturbatory behavior based on what other people are doing. Homosexual couples may also lie outside the normal processes of social exchange (possibly except for cases in which butch-femme roles recreate the exchange), and so they too may be less likely to conform their sexual behavior to what other couples are doing.

Gender Differences in Sex Drive

We return to the central point in the social exchange theory of sex, which is that sex is a female resource. Why? Why do men give women resources in exchange for sex, instead of vice versa? Women like sex too, so why don't they pay men for sex, or at least buy dinner and try to coax their pants off?

The principle of least interest provides a likely answer. Whoever wants the relationship less has more power in it. It applies perfectly well to sex: Whoever wants it more has to do the persuading.

Thus, the whole structure of social exchange seems based on the premise that women want sex less than men. If women wanted sex more than men, sex would essentially be a favor that men do for women. Women would owe the men gratitude for sex and probably would have to be giving them things in return. Women would be spurred on to take chances and perform heroic feats so as to have something to offer men, in exchange for sex.

But they don't. The men do all those things. According to social exchange theory, female sexual desire is weaker and/or less frequent than male sexual desire. The greater desire of males makes them willing to offer women resources in exchange for it.

Is this tenable? Baumeister and Catanese (2000) reviewed a great deal of published research findings to ascertain whether men desire sex more than women. The basis for the approach was to imagine two women (or two men), one of whom had a stronger sex drive than the other. How would a social scientist expect the two women's behavior to differ, given their difference in sex drive? Logically, one would likely expect that the woman with the stronger drive, as compared with the other woman, would think about sex more, have more sexual fantasies, desire more frequent sex, desire more sex partners, masturbate more, be less willing or able to live without sex, and show other, similar signs of high motivation. Given those seemingly straightforward predictions about how to recognize a difference in sex drive, the next step was to compare men versus women on each dimension. We searched the literature for any and all studies that reported data on both men and women.

The picture painted by many dozens of published studies was clear and consistent: Men desire sex more than women. On every dimension we investigated, men showed signs of higher sexual desire. Men think about sex more than women. Men have more frequent sexual fantasies than women. Men report being sexually aroused more often than women. Men desire sex more often than women in nearly all phases of relationships, from first dates to twenty-year marriages. Men like a greater variety of sexual practices than women. Men have more favorable attitudes toward most sexual activities than women, and men also like both their own and their partners' genitals more than women like them (Ard, 1977; Beck, Bozman, & Qualtrough, 1991; Eysenck, 1971; Laumann et al., 1994; Leitenberg & Henning, 1995; McCabe, 1987; Oliver & Hyde, 1993; Reinholtz & Muehlenhard, 1995).

Men desire more partners than women, and men actually report more partners than women. Although the last finding is logically implausible (because most sex acts involve one man and one woman), it probably reflects distorted counting based on the greater desire among men for multiple partners. When different numbers of sex partners are logically possible, such as in homosexual activity, in extramarital activity, or in fantasy, the gender differences are often quite large (Bell & Weinberg, 1978; Blumstein & Schwartz, 1983; Buss & Schmitt, 1993; Laumann et al., 1994; Lawson, 1988).

Masturbation is a fairly straightforward indication of strength of sex drive, and men masturbate considerably more than women (Arafat & Cotton, 1974; Asayama, 1975; Laumann et al., 1994; Sigusch & Schmidt, 1973). Moreover, among people who do not masturbate, women are more likely than men to say the reason is lack of interest or desire (Arafat & Cotton, 1974). Living without sex is much more difficult for men than for women, even when the individual is firmly committed to celibacy (such as among Catholic priests and nuns, for whom celibacy is a sacred obligation; see Murphy, 1992). Girls reach puberty before boys, but boys commence sexual activity at a younger age than girls, and so the interval between being sexually capable and becoming sexually active is shorter at both ends for boys (Asayama, 1975; Knoth, Boyd, & Singer, 1988; Laumann et al., 1994; Lewis, 1973; Wilson, 1975). In adulthood, men seek and initiate sex more than women, whereas women decline and refuse sex more than men (Brown & Auerback, 1981; Byers & Heinlein, 1989; Clark & Hatfield, 1989; LaPlante, McCormick, & Brannigan; 1980; O'Sullivan & Byers, 1992). Men sacrifice more resources to get sex, whether this involves spending money for sexual stimulation or putting one's career or marriage at risk in order to have a brief sexual fling. Last, men rate their sex drives as stronger than women rate theirs (Mercer & Kohn, 1979).

Taken together, these findings make it safe to say that men desire sex more than women. Certainly women desire sex too. Also, these are only averages, and there is plenty of variability within each gender, so undoubtedly there are many women who desire sex more than many men. For the purposes of social exchange theory, however, the crucial fact is simply that one person desires it more—because that person is therefore at a disadvantage. Because men want sex more than women, men will find themselves in the position of having to persuade or induce women to take part, generally by offering women something else in return.

Is this difference the product of socialization and cultural roles, or of biologically innate differences? Our tentative answer is that it is probably a combination of both. It seems undeniable that culture has suppressed female sexuality more strongly than men's, such as in the way that girls are socialized to resist sex and preserve their "virtue." (The different pressures are evident even in the simple fact that sexual restraint is more widely associated with virtue for women than men.) On the other hand, even when society encourages women to enjoy sex (such as in marital intercourse), when high standards of sexual restraint are the same for both men and women (such as among Catholic clergy), or when pressures and warnings have been primarily directed at men (such as with masturbation), the evidence still indicates that women desire sex less than men. At present, therefore, it seems most plausible to suggest that socialization tends to capitalize on and exaggerate differences that are already innately there.

Sex as Benefit

If sex is a female resource, then obtaining sex is a desirable outcome for men but not for women. Sedikides, Oliver, and Campbell (1994) surveyed a sample of students about the costs and benefits they perceived for romantic relationships. Consistent with exchange theory, they found that men said that sex was an important benefit of romantic relationships, and women did not. Thus, although romantic relationships increase sexual experience for both men and women, only the men see this as a benefit that they gain.

If sex is not a benefit for women, is it a cost? Sedikides et al. (1994) did not find that either gender rated having sex as a cost. To be sure, this finding may reflect the relative youth of their sample, and older people may be more likely to rate it as a cost. For example, Beck, Bozman, and Qualtrough (1991) found that most women past the age of 25 reported having engaged in sex when they did not feel any desire, and they did this usually in order to please a relationship partner, which indicates that sex is indeed sometimes an activity that women perform out of duty rather than desire.

Still, the fact that women did not describe sexual activity as one of the costs of romantic relationships fits well with the gender difference in sex drive and with the social exchange theory's principle of least interest. Women desire and enjoy sex too — their desire is merely less insistent than men's desire. Because sex is more widely available to women than to men, sex is not perceived by women as a benefit of romantic relationships, but because it is a positive outcome, it is not a cost either.

A darker side of this exchange was suggested by research on unrequited love. In unrequited love, one person wants a love relationship but the other does not. If the woman desires the relationship, the man may exploit her feelings in order to obtain sex from her. In contrast, if it is the man who desires the relationship, the woman would be less likely to see this as an opportunity to get sex, according to social exchange theory. Some evidence consistent with this was reported by Baumeister and Wotman (1992), who found that only women reported sexual exploitation as one of the costs of unrequited love.

Suppression of Female Sexuality

Although the social exchange theory is partly based on the idea that women's sexual desires are not as strong or frequent as men's, so that the men want sex more than the women (which is why the men have to give something in exchange), this does not mean that all differences in sexual patterns are natural or innate. In fact, we think the relatively weak female sex drive is a product of both nature and culture. Nature may have created some difference to start with, but culture increases it.

This view of gender differences is explicitly based on a mixture of nature and culture. Nature makes the genders somewhat different to start with, and culture either exaggerates or downplays the differences. Our modern society is clearly now in a stage of downplaying them and minimizing them, and our culture seems increasingly annoyed that the differences (e.g., in salary and achievement and time spent with children) refuse to disappear. In contrast, at many times in history culture sought to exaggerate the differences between men and women, assigning them to very separate spheres and life paths.

So how does this suppression come about? There are actually a couple main theories. One is that men suppress women's sexuality. Several reasons have been suggested why men might do this (e.g., Buss, 1994; Sherfey, 1966). One is that men want to possess women and ensure sexual fidelity, so that men can be sure that the children their wives bear are not those of another man. Another is that progress in civilization requires the suppression of female sexuality, because if human women carried on like female chimpanzees—copulating dozens of times per day and exhausting every male in sight—there would be chaos rather than peace and order. A third explanation is that men envy women's greater capacity for sex and feel insecure about having to satisfy them, so they stifle women to make themselves feel good. A fourth explanation is that suppressing female sexuality is part of the broader male project of keeping women in an inferior, subjugated position in society.

A very different explanation could be put forward on the basis of social exchange theory, however. By this approach, women might seek to suppress each other's sexuality. The basis for this is rooted in the idea of sex as a female resource and in simple supply-and-demand principles. Men must give women resources in exchange for sex, and each community has its marketplace according to which there are standards for how much each man must give. As with any resource, scarcity increases the price. Women are in a position comparable to a monopoly: They have control over something that others want, and like other monopolies, they will be tempted to restrict the supply so as to fetch a higher price. This pattern, after all, is the main reason that most countries try to prevent a company from getting a monopoly.

Thus, the two main theoretical approaches differ as to whether women or men are the main agents responsible for the suppression of female sexuality. Baumeister and Twenge (2000) reviewed a broad variety of evidence in the attempt to ascertain whether men or women play the main role in putting pressure on girls and women to restrict their sexual activities. Our findings pointed consistently toward the social exchange (female resource) theory. They can be briefly summarized here.

One important source of evidence concerns the direct influences on adolescent girls to restrain their sexuality. These influences are almost exclusively female. Mothers communicate a significant amount with their teenage daughters about sexual morality, pregnancy, and related topics, whereas fathers communicate very little about such topics (DeLamater, 1989; Du Bois-Reymond & Ravesloot, 1996; Libby, Gray, & White, 1978; Nolin & Petersen, 1992), and closeness and communication with the mother appeared to keep the daughter from becoming promiscuous, whereas a comparable relationship with the father was irrelevant (Kahn, Smith, & Roberts, 1984; Lewis, 1973). A girl's female peers and friends have a significant influence on her sexual activity (and one that restrains her from going too far), whereas her male peers and friends have little or no influence (Billy & Udry, 1985; Du Bois-Reymond & Ravesloot, 1996; Rodgers & Rowe, 1990). The boyfriend is the only male who has been shown to have significant influence on the young woman's sexuality, but his influence is generally in the opposite direction (i.e., he tends to encourage more sexual activity; Du Bois-Reymond & Ravesloot, 1996). In short, the data on adolescent females find no evidence of male influences contributing significantly to suppress sexuality, whereas the female influences are important and significant.

Likewise, studies of adult women suggest that the main restraining influences on sex are female. Women consistently express stronger disapproval than men of premarital sexual activity among women (King, Balswick, & Robinson, 1977; Robinson & Jedlicka, 1982).

Women anticipate that their female friends will disapprove of their sexual adventures and are sometimes inclined to conceal them from their female friends as a result (Carns, 1973).

The "double standard" of sexual morality is particularly relevant to the suppression of female sexuality. The essence of the double standard is that certain sexual activities are acceptable for men but not for women, and so in effect women's sexuality is constrained in ways that men's is not. A meta-analysis by Oliver and Hyde (1993) found that in all studies that investigated this question, women supported the double standard more than men. Although recent data have had difficulty confirming that people continue to endorse a double standard, people still believe that unnamed other people still hold it. Millhausen and Herold (1999) asked young women who they thought would judge a woman more harshly than a man for sexual experiences, and far more respondents said women (than men) were the harsher judges of sexually active women.

In some cultures, female sexuality is suppressed by stronger measures than gossip and a bad reputation. Surgical procedures are used, including subincision (cutting off the clitoris) and infibulation (sewing the vagina shut). Although Western feminists have taken the lead in denouncing these practices, it is mainly women who support, enforce, and administer them. Thus, the mother or grandmother decides whether the daughter will have the operation; the operation is performed by a woman, with no men present; the female peer group mocks and derogates girls who have not yet had the surgery; and the practices are defended and supported by women more than men (Boddy, 1989; Greer, 1999; Hicks, 1996; Lighfoot-Klein, 1989; Williams & Sobieszczyk, 1997). There is some evidence that men oppose the practice and prefer women who can enjoy sex more (Shandall, 1967, 1979; also Greer, 1999; Hicks, 1996).

These and other findings suggest that the suppression of female sexuality has been shaped by social exchange. Women are better off when sex is scarce and men have few outlets for sexual satisfaction, because men will offer women more under those circumstances than they will offer when sexual gratification is widely and freely available. It is rational for women to try to restrict men's sexual opportunities, and one effective way to do this is to enforce norms and informal pressures that hold women in general back from sexual indulgence.

This analysis of the cultural suppression of female sexuality puts the individual woman in a position of conflict. Each individual woman can gain an advantage by going farther than other women in sex, but the cause of all women collectively is best served by sexual restraint. Thus, a woman can gain more attention from men by being willing to offer more sex than other women will offer, and in this way she may be able to get her pick of the most desirable men (including possibly stealing another woman's man). Her own sexual desires may also contribute to pushing her to take part in sexual activities. Yet she is also better off if women in general exhibit sexual restraint, and so her loyalty to the female cause (along with pressure from other women) may induce her to hold back. This dilemma is similar to the "Commons dilemma," in which the best interests of the group are opposed to the best interests of the individual. The term "commons dilemma" comes from common grazing grounds shared by all shepherds. Each individual shepherd may benefit by making maximum use of this common grazing area, but collectively everyone is better off if everyone exercises restraint, because if too many sheep graze on the common grounds, the grass will be unable to replenish itself and the resource will be destroyed. Individual shepherds thus face an ongoing conflict between their private, immediate self-interest and doing what is best for the group in the long run.

The Sexual Revolution

One of the great events of the 20th century was the liberalizing of sexual attitudes and behaviors. This change is commonly called the "Sexual Revolution." Most treatments consider it to have begun soon after the middle of the century and to have wrought its major changes in the late 1960s and early 1970s, with some retreat occurring in the 1980s and 1990s. To be sure, more careful treatments have argued that there were perhaps multiple sexual revolutions, beginning perhaps early in the 20th century when the automobile and urban life enabled young people to spend time together in couples away from chaperones (e.g., Petersen, 1999).

Why did the Sexual Revolution happen? A major social event is likely to have had multiple causes. Undoubtedly one important factor was the invention of the birth control pill, which gave women unprecedented advantages in convenience and reliability of contraception. Yet this alone seems insufficient to explain the full set of changes. For one thing, some forms of reasonably effective contraception had been available for decades if not centuries. For another, some forms of sexual activity (such as oral sex) do not require contraception.

The social exchange theory of sex can make some contribution to understanding the sexual revolution by viewing it as essentially a market correction. In very simple terms, the market price for sex was reduced, and women became willing to offer sex to men at a much more widely affordable price. Whereas previously the majority of women had expected a man to make a lifetime commitment of financial support and sexual fidelity before they went to bed with him, after the sexual revolution many women began to offer sexual favors for a much briefer and more transient commitment, such as a couple of dates, gifts or meals, or a nonbinding declaration of feeling affection for her.

The Sexual Revolution was hardly forced upon women. Instead, most evidence indicates that women changed more than men (Arafat & Yorburg, 1973; Bauman & Wilson; 1974; Birenbaum, 1970; Croake & James, 1973; DeLamater & MacCorquodale, 1979; Sherwin & Corbett, 1985; Schmidt & Sigusch, 1972). Women's attitudes became more positive toward sex, toward their own bodies, and toward greater permissiveness. Many women embraced their new freedom to engage in sex as a form of liberation.

Yet women also appear to have suffered more than men from the new sexual freedom. An early sign was an issue of *Cosmopolitan* magazine in 1980 reporting on a readers' poll that elicited a surprising (to the editors, at least) outpouring of women's negative feelings about the Sexual Revolution and the negative effects it had on women's lives (Petersen, 1999). More systematic data followed, such as careful and systematic national polls that asked people about the greater sexual freedom (Smith, 1994). Although both women and men expressed doubts about whether the new permissiveness was a good thing, women were consistently and significantly more negative about it.

Thus, women changed more than men, but they also came to express doubts and regrets about those changes. The female resource theory helps explain the negative attitudes: The Sexual Revolution greatly reduced what women could expect from men in exchange for sex.

Moreover, the previous section suggested that the suppression of female sexuality is largely enforced by and for women. The Sexual Revolution was clearly a defeat for whoever was trying to suppress female sexuality, because female sexuality became much more liberal and active after that Revolution. If women were suppressing each other's sexuality, then the cause of women suffered a setback.

Why would women have permitted the Sexual Revolution to take place, if it resulted in a weaker bargaining position for them? One answer is that the substantial changes in women's position in society made it far less urgent to go on suppressing each other's sexuality. Nancy Cott (1979), who offered an early form of the social exchange analysis of sex, noted that women during Victorian times had relatively few rights and opportunities, and so effectively sex was the main resource they had with which to make a good life for themselves. Under those circumstances, it was imperative for each woman to get as much as possible in exchange for her sexual favors.

By 1960, however, things had changed dramatically. Women had acquired a broad range of rights and opportunities—political, financial, legal, educational, occupational, and more. Women therefore had opportunities to make decent lives for themselves without having to rely exclusively on using sex to induce a man to make a lifetime commitment. Maintaining sexual scarcity so as to keep the price of sex high was therefore far less necessary for modern women than it had been for previous generations of women, and it became possible to relax the pressures and restraints.

In short, women have spent most of history in a vulnerable, relatively weak position. They had few rights and opportunities, and sex was the main asset they controlled. Under those circumstances, it made rational sense for women to maintain pressure on each other to restrict the availability of sexual gratification to men. As society changed and women gained greater rights and opportunities, however, sex ceased to be their only meal ticket, and eventually the point was reached where women could afford to make sex more readily available outside of marriage. The Sexual Revolution constituted that "market correction" in the price of sex. Yes, the change toward greater sexual permissiveness did weaken women's position in one respect, but women could afford to accept a lower price for sex because they had gained other resources.

Mate Shortages

Most sex acts in human history have involved one man and one woman who were having a lasting relationship with each other. That pattern of mating has important implications for the operation of principles of supply and demand with regard to sex. As it happens, our species tends to produce about equal numbers of males and females, and so one-to-one mating works fairly well on the whole.

In some circumstances, however, an imbalance may develop, resulting in an oversupply of one gender vis-à-vis the other. If decisions were made based on a democratic vote, then the majority gender would have more power. But the mating market is not democratic, and it operates by supply and demand rather than majority rule. Hence, whatever gender is in the minority gains greater power. These processes have been studied in an important work by Guttentag and Secord (1983), who compared many instances of unequal sex ratios across different cultures and historical periods.

Let us start with the obvious fact: If one gender is in the majority, then many of its members will be unable to secure a monogamous mate. For example, if a given college campus has twice as many men as women, then it will be far easier for the women than for the men to get a regular dating partner (or a date at all!). Many more men than women will be alone on Saturday night, or at least will be reduced to spending the time with members of their own gender. Under those circumstances, the men must compete with each other aggressively to attract female attention, and to keep a girlfriend a man must do what she wants. In contrast, if a different campus has twice as many women as men, the competitive pressures will fall more heavily on the women than the men, and each man will have much less trouble or exertion keeping his girlfriend. It is she who will have to do what he wants, in order to keep him from moving on to another woman. (Certainly there are other factors at work, but on average there will be a big difference between the dating environment on those two campuses, and anyone who moves from one to the other will be likely to recognize the contrast.)

According to the social exchange analysis, women control the "supply" of sex while men furnish the "demand." When men outnumber women, the demand will greatly exceed the supply. As with any economic resource, this will make the price high. Guttentag and Secord (1983) found ample evidence of such patterns. When men were in the majority, such as in the American Wild West (where there were dozens of men for every woman), the price of sex was high. Opportunities for premarital and extramarital sex were rare, and a man had to make a serious, long-term commitment to a woman (typically marriage) before he could have sex with her. Community standards were quite prudish. Similar patterns have been found in societies that practiced female infanticide, because that produces a shortage of women. Even today, places such as China have a shortage of women because many couples have abortions when they discover their fetus is female, and sexual morality in China is quite prudish and restrictive.

In contrast, when women are in the majority, the supply of sex is greater relative to the demand. In such cases, the price goes down. Men can get sex outside of marriage, and women have little power to demand commitment or even respectful treatment from men in exchange for sex. In simple terms, sex is free and easy when there are more women than men. Such permissive patterns have been observed after major wars, for example, when large numbers of young men have been killed and there are not enough men to go around. To some extent they arise even during a major foreign war, because the men are away in the military forces and too few remain at home to date the women. The relative shortage of men in modern African-American communities may contribute to similar patterns.

Even the financial aspects of mating change with the sex ratio. Petersen (1999) reported that during World War Two, the shortage of men on American college campuses drove women to advertise for prom dates, sometimes offering to furnish the car and pay all the expenses—a sharp reversal of the usual sex roles. More generally, Guttentag and Secord (1983) concluded that whether a marriage is settled by a dowry (money contributed by the bride's family) or the bride-price (money contributed by the groom's family) depends on the culture's traditional sex ratio. If there is usually a surplus of women, then the dowry becomes large and important, and penniless women will have a hard time finding a husband. If there is usually a shortage of women, however, the bride-price pattern prevails, and the man's family must contribute money.

There is one interesting difference between the dowry and the bride-price, however, as Guttentag and Secord (1983) noted. The bride-price is essentially a sum of money paid by the groom's family to the bride's family, much as if they are purchasing a wife for their son. In contrast, the dowry does not go to the groom's family but rather to the young couple, as a kind of financial endowment to help them get started in life. Guttentag and Secord said they found almost no evidence of any customs that suggest that a woman's family will purchase a husband for her from the man's family. This asymmetry fits neatly into the social exchange analysis. One does not "purchase" a man because he has no inherent value in the sexual sense. Women are the suppliers of sex, and so only women have inherent value. One may augment a woman's value by offering a dowry, as a way of encouraging the man to select her rather than another woman. The dowry resembles a bribe or kickback (to the young man) more than a purchase price (paid to his family). To put this another way, a family cannot make any money selling its sons, even when husbands are in short supply, but when wives are scarce a family can profit by "selling" its daughters.

Pornography

Pornography may also merit consideration in terms of social exchange. Indeed, the frequently repeated charge that pornography "exploits" women seems to suggest an economic analysis, just as natural resources are "exploited" for profit by entrepreneurs.

The basic pattern of pornography resembles that of prostitution: Men are the main consumers and furnish the money that makes the industry profitable. To be sure, most pornography features both men and women, which may seem like an exception to the principle that sex is essentially a female resource. Still, it seems fair to argue that the male consumers of pornography regard the female stars as the crucial ones. For example, if one examines the box packages for pornographic video cassettes, it is immediately apparent that the women are the main attraction: Nearly all videos feature the female stars, and only occasionally is a male star even included. Gay male films are an exception, of course, but those lie outside the heterosexual transaction dynamics, and indeed very few heterosexual men like to watch male homosexual pornography. They do, however, often love to watch female homosexual pornography, to the extent that most feature-length videos include at least one lesbian scene.

Thus, the pornography industry essentially relies on the same fundamental transaction that we have found throughout: Men exchange resources to get sexual stimulation from women. The only major difference is that many purveyors of pornography are men, and so the men may end up taking the profits, but this is not relevant, and it is doubtful that pornography consumers care whether the profits go into male or female hands (just as with prostitution): Their goal is simply to get sexual stimulation, for which a woman is the central and essential ingredient.

A more complex aspect to pornography was suggested by Nancy Cott's (1979) early articulation of a social exchange model of sex. As she put it, pornography (like prostitution) is essentially a low-cost substitute for genuine sexual gratification, and in that sense it threatens women's monopoly over sex—which is why women are likely to oppose pornography as if it were a threat to women in general. This is, after all, a common problem encountered by monopolies of any resource when they try to drive up the price by restricting the supply: Cheap substitutes become available and undercut their monopoly. Thus, if the oil-producing nations were to restrict the world supply of oil to the point where it became extremely expensive, it is likely that many places would turn to other sources of power. This is OPEC's worst nightmare, that the high cost of oil will spur the development of other energy sources and render oil obsolete, so that the oil producers would find themselves out of business. With sex, it hardly seems likely that pornography will actually replace desire for women in general, but there is still legitimate reason to worry that as men can find some degree of sexual gratification from pornography, they will become less dependent on women, and women's ability to get the best possible exchange value for their own sexual favors will be reduced.

Infidelity

Both men and women generally desire their partners to be faithful to them, and sexual jealousy appears to be an almost universal aspect of human relationships (Reiss, 1986). Efforts to decide whether men or women are "more jealous" or "more possessive" have been inconsistent and inconclusive, and possibly the question does not have a meaningful answer when phrased in that way. For example, Blumstein and Schwartz (1983) found that women seemed to be more sexually possessive than men, but this was largely due to the greater vulnerability and dependency that attended the role of a housewife who does not work outside the home. A housewife who lost her husband would not be able to support herself, and so she had good reason to fear her husband's interest in other women, but this fear seems rooted in rational economic circumstances rather than in some innate gender difference in possessiveness.

Although both men and women are sexually possessive to similar degrees, there are some interesting differences in the way these feelings are experienced and expressed. These may be relevant to the social exchange analysis of sex.

First, it appears that men place greater emphasis on the physical aspects of infidelity, namely the sex act itself. Buss, Larsen, Westen, and Semmelroth (1992) asked people whether they would be more upset if their partner had sexual intercourse with another person without emotional intimacy—or formed an intimate emotional attachment without ever having sexual intercourse. Women objected more to the emotional attachment, whereas men objected more strongly to the sex act itself. That finding fits the basic pattern that sex is a female resource: The man seems to feel he loses something when his female partner has sex with someone else, regardless of the emotional attachment to the other person.

When a man is unfaithful, his female partner does not lose as much, unless there is an emotional attachment.

Consistent with that analysis, there has been a clear asymmetry to the penalties for infidelity throughout much of history. Specifically, sexual infidelity by women has been punished much more stringently than comparable actions by men (e.g., Bullough & Brundage, 1982). To some extent, this may simply follow from the difference in power. Men have held greater political power than women, and so men could make the laws, and perhaps men made laws to excuse their own behavior while punishing women. This does not seem to be a fully satisfactory explanation, however, for a variety of reasons—including that fact that today, even though men still make most of the laws, it is irrefutably clear that these man-made laws target men more than women for sexual offenses. Men are arrested for sexual crimes far more often than women (Federal Bureau of Investigation, 1998).

The social exchange analysis is therefore useful as an additional way of understanding the tendency to punish women more severely than men for sexual infidelity. If sex is a female resource, then a wife's infidelity gives away something that belongs to the family and deprives the marriage of that value—in a way that a husband's infidelity does not. The husband does not deprive his wife of anything especially valuable when he has sex with a lover, whereas the unfaithful wife is regarded as depriving her husband of something valuable.

Converging support for this analysis comes from evidence about the gender of the interloper. Many men say that they would not mind their female partner having sex with another woman, even though they would not tolerate her having sex with another man. From the perspective of social exchange, the male lover takes something from the wife that a female lover does not take, and so the cuckolded husband only loses something of value if the wife has sex with another man.

To be sure, there are other possible explanations for the husband's objecting to male rather than female lovers. A man might say, "I don't care if she has sex with another woman, because that would be no threat: I can give her something that no woman can give her." That analysis breaks down, however, when one looks at the data about women's preferences. Wiederman and LaMar (1998) found that women objected more strongly to their male partner having sex with another man than with another woman.

In other words, both men and women preferred to have their partners to have sex with another woman than with a man. Why is the male interloper more threatening to both? The social exchange answer is that, in sex, men take and women give. A male lover thus takes something from your partner, regardless of whether your partner is male or female.

Sex in Abusive Relationships

Domestic violence has gained recognition as a significant social problem. This takes many forms, the most common perhaps consisting of battering between siblings (e.g., Wiehe, 1991), but the present focus is on violence between husbands and wives. Both husbands and wives have been found to engage in spousal aggression, and indeed domestic violence is perhaps the only form of aggression in which women are as frequently aggressive as men (Archer, 2000; Arias, Samios, & O'Leary, 1987; Baumeister & Sommer, 1997; Breslin, Riggs, O'Leary, & Arias, 1990; O'Leary, Barling, Arias, Rosenbaum, Malone, & Tyree, 1989; Straus, 1980). Although women may initiate aggression as often as men, women suffer far more severe injuries (and deaths) at the hands of their spouses than men do (Archer, 2000).

A sample of violent, abusive relationships was studied by DeMaris (1997) with an eye to understanding how sexual relations were affected. One might assume that violence and abuse are signs of a bad relationship and that "making love" would be correspondingly uncommon in these cases, but DeMaris did not find this. Although conflict itself is apparently detrimental to sex, in that couples do not have sex during times of argument, the overall rate of sex in violent marriages appears to be above that in nonviolent marriages. Nor does this high rate of sex appear to be a matter of making up after fights. Rather, Demaris concluded that sex in violent relationships appears to be a matter of "extortion," in which the victim feels pressure to give sex to the the violent partner as a way of appeasing that person.

The notion of giving sex is of course central to the social exchange analysis of sex. Still, social exchange emphasizes that women give sex to men. Is there a corresponding asymmetry in sexual appeasement in violent relationships? Yes. DeMaris found that rates of sexual intercourse were higher than average in relationships containing a violent husband. No such effect for wifely violence was found, however.

Apparently, then, female victims can placate their male abusers by offering sex, whereas male victims cannot placate their female abusers with sex. Sexual bribery is thus unidirectional, consistent with the social exchange analysis.

Conclusion

It is clear that many patterns of sexual behavior can be understood in terms of social exchange. Specifically, it is useful to understand sex as a female resource in the sense of a commodity that women control and men desire, so that men must offer women some other resource or commodity in return for sex.

There are many meanings of sex, and social exchange is only one of them. Undoubtedly many sexual decisions and negotiations have little to do with sex as a form of social exchange, and it would be foolish to propose social exchange as offering a comprehensive explanation of all sexual behavior. Still, social exchange fits a substantial part of sexual activity across a broad range of situations and relationships.

The social exchange analysis is not, strictly speaking, a rival theory that competes with other approaches to sexuality, because it is compatible with many of them. The two main theoretical frameworks in the sexuality area are constructionist (usually feminist) theory and evolutionary theory, and social exchange is compatible with both of them. This compatibility is probably a good thing, because in the long run the goal of advancing sexuality theory may be best served by linking together a composite of contributions from multiple theoretical perspectives, instead of seeking to establish a single theory as the victor by discrediting and disproving all other theories. Social exchange can thus offer a useful addition to the way psychology and other fields understand sex.

REFERENCES

Anderson, P. B., & Struckman-Johnson, C. (Eds.) (1998). *Sexually aggressive women: Current perspectives and controversies*. New York: Guilford.

Arafat, I. S., & Cotton, W. L. (1974). Masturbation practices of males and females. *Journal of Sex Research, 10*, 293–307.

Arafat, I. S., & Yorburg, B. (1973). On living together without marriage. *Journal of Sex Research, 9*, 97–106.

Archer, J. (2000). Sex differences in aggression between heterosexual partners: A meta-analytic review. *Psychological Bulletin, 126*, 651–680.

Ard, B. N. (1977). Sex in lasting marriages: A longitudinal study. *Journal of Sex Research, 13*, 274–285.

Arias, I., Samios, M., & O'Leary, K. D. (1987). Prevalence and correlates of physical aggression during courtship. *Journal of Interpersonal Violence, 2*, 82–90.

Asayama, S. (1975). Adolescent sex development and adult sex behavior in Japan. *Journal of Sex Research, 11*, 91–112.

Bauman, K. E., & Wilson, R. R. (1974). Sexual behavior of unmarried university students in 1968 and 1972. *Journal of Sex Research, 10*, 327–333.

Baumeister, R. F., Catanese, K. R., & Vohs, K. D. (2000). Are there gender differences in strength of sex drive? Theoretical views, conceptual distinctions, and a review of relevant evidence. Manuscript submitted for publication.

Baumeister, R. F., & Sommer, K. L. (1997). What do men want? Gender differences and two spheres of belongingness: Comment on Cross and Madson (1997). *Psychological Bulletin, 122*, 38–44.

Baumeister, R. F., & Tice, D. M. (2000). *The social dimension of sex*. New York: Allyn & Bacon.

Baumeister, R. F., & Twenge, J. M. (2000). Two theories about the cultural suppression of female sexuality. Manuscript submitted for publication, Case Western Reserve University.

Baumeister, R. F., & Wotman, S. R. (1992). *Breaking hearts: The two sides of unrequited love*. New York: Guilford Press.

Beck, J. G., Bozman, A. W., & Qualtrough, T. (1991). The experience of sexual desire: Psychological correlates in a college sample. *Journal of Sex Research, 28*, 443–456.

Bell, A. P., & Weinberg, M. S. (1978). *Homosexualities: A study of diversity among men and women*. New York: Simon & Schuster.

Berger, P., & Luckmann, T. (1967). *The social construction of reality: A treatise in the sociology of knowledge*. Garden City, NY: Doubleday.

Bernard, J. (1982). *The future of marriage*. New Haven, CT: Yale University Press.

Billy, J. O. G., & Udry, J. R. (1985). Patterns of adolescent friendship and effects on sexual behavior. *Social Psychology Quarterly, 48*, 27-41.

Birenbaum, A. (1970). Revolution without the revolution: Sex in contemporary America. *Journal of Sex Research, 6*, 257–267.

Blau, P. N. (1964). *Exchange and power in social life*. New York: Wiley.

Blumstein, P., & Schwartz, P. (1983). *American couples*. New York: Simon & Schuster (Pocket).

Boddy, J. (1989). *Wombs and alien spirits: Women, men and the Zar cult in northern Sudan*. Madison: The University of Wisconsin Press.

Breslin, F. C., Riggs, D. S., O'Leary, K. D., & Arias, I. (1990). Family precursors expected and actual consequences of dating aggression. *Journal of Interpersonal Violence, 5*, 247–258.

Brown, M., & Auerback, A. (1981). Communication patterns in initiation of marital sex. *Medical Aspects of Human Sexuality, 15*, 105–117.

Brown, N. R., & Sinclair, R. C. (1999). Estimating number of lifetime sexual partners: Men and women do it differently. *Journal of Sex Research, 36*, 292–297.

Bullough, V. L., & Brundage, J. (1982). *Sexual practices and the medieval church*. New York: Simon & Schuster.

Buss, D. M. (1989). Conflict between the sexes: Strategic interference and the evocation of anger and upset. *Journal of Personality and Social Psychology, 56*, 735–747.

Buss, D. M. (1994). *The evolution of desire*. New York: Basic Books.

Buss, D. M., Larsen, R. S., Westen, D., & Semmelroth, J. (1992). Sex differences in jealousy: Evolution, physiology, and psychology. *Psychological Science, 3*, 251–255.

Buss, D. M., & Schmitt, D. P. (1993). Sexual strategies theory: An evolutionary perspective on human mating. *Psychological Review, 100*, 204–232.

Byers, E. S., & Heinlein, L. (1989). Predicting initiations and refusals of sexual activities in married and cohabiting heterosexual couples. *Journal of Sex Research, 26*, 210–231.

Carns, D. E. (1973). Talking about sex: Notes on first coitus and the double sexual standard. *Journal of Marriage and the Family, 35*, 677–688.

Clark, R. D., & Hatfield, E. (1989). Gender differences in receptivity to sexual offers. *Journal of Psychology and Human Sexuality, 2*, 39–55.

Cohen, L. L., & Shotland, R. L. (1996). Timing of first sexual intercourse in a relationship: Expectations, experiences, and perceptions of others. *Journal of Sex Research, 33*, 291–299.

Cott, N. F. (1979). Passionlessness: An interpretation of Victorian sexual ideology, 1790–1850. In N. Cott & E. Pleck (Eds.), *A heritage of her own* (pp. 162–181). New York: Simon & Schuster.

Croake, J. W., & James, B. (1973). A four year comparison of premarital sexual attitudes. *Journal of Sex Research, 9*, 91–96.

DeLamater, J. (1989). The social control of human sexuality. In K. McKinney & S. Sprecher (Eds.), *Human sexuality: The societal and interpersonal context* (pp. 30–62). Norwood, NJ: Ablex.

DeLamater, J. D., & Hyde, J. S. (1998). Essentialism vs. social constructionism in the study of human sexuality. *Journal of Sex Research, 35*, 10–18.

DeLamater, J., & MacCorquodale, P. (1979). *Premarital sexuality: Attitudes, relationships, behavior*. Madison: University of Wisconsin Press.

DeMaris, A. (1997). Elevated sexual activity in violent marriages: Hypersexuality or sexual extortion? *Journal of Sex Research, 34*, 367–373.

Downey, L., Ryan, R., Roffman, R., & Kulich, M. (1995). How could I forget? Inaccurrate memories of sexually intimate moments. *Journal of Sex Research, 32*, 177–191.

du Bois-Reymond, M., & Ravesloot, J. (1996). The roles of parents and peers in the sexual and relational socialization of adolescents. In K. Hurrelmann & S. Hamilton (Eds.), *Social problems and social contexts in adolescence* (pp. 175–197). New York: Aldine de Gruyter.

Eysenck, H. J. (1971). Masculinity-femininity, personality and sexual attitudes. *Journal of Sex Research, 7*, 83–88.

Federal Bureau of Investigation (1998). *Crime in the United States*. Washington, DC: U.S. Government Printing Office.

Greer, G. (1999). *The whole woman*. New York: Knopf.

Guttentag, M., & Secord, P. F. (1983). *Too many women? The sex ratio question*. Beverly Hills, CA: Sage.

Hicks, E. K. (1996). *Infibulation: Female mutilation in Islamic Northeastern Africa*. New Brunswick: Transaction Publishers.

Homans, G. C. (1950). *The human group*. New York: Harcourt, Brace, & World.

Homans, G. C. (1961). *Social behavior: Its elementary forms*. New York: Harcourt, Brace, & World.

Kahn, J., Smith, K., & Roberts, E. (1984). *Familial communication and adolescent sexual behavior* (Final report to the Office of Adolescent Pregnancy Programs). Cambridge, MA: American Institute for Research.

Kanin, E. J. (1985). Date rapists: Differential sexual socialization and relative deprivation. *Archives of Sexual Behavior, 14*, 219–231.

King, K., Balswick, J. O., & Robinson, I. E. (1977). The continuing premarital sexual revolution among college females. *Journal of Marriage and the Family, 39*, 455–459.

Kinsey, A. C., Pomeroy, W. B., & Martin, C. E. (1948). *Sexual behavior in the human male*. Philadelphia: Saunders.

Kinsey, A. C., Pomeroy, W. B., Martin, C. E., & Gebhard, P. H. (1953). *Sexual behavior in the human female*. Philadelphia: Saunders.

Knoth, R., Boyd, K., & Singer, B. (1988). Empirical tests of sexual selection theory: Predictions of sex differences in onset, intensity, and time course of sexual arousal. *Journal of Sex Research, 24*, 73–89.

LaPlante, M. N., McCormick, N., & Brannigan, G. G. (1980). Living the sexual script: College students' views of influence in sexual encounters. *Journal of Sex Research, 16*, 338–355.

Laumann, E. O., Gagnon, J. H., Michael, R. T., & Michaels, S. (1994). *The social organization of sexuality: Sexual practices in the United States*. Chicago, IL: University of Chicago Press.

Lawson, A. (1988). *Adultery: An analysis of love and betrayal*. New York: Basic Books.

Leitenberg, H., & Henning, K. (1995). Sexual fantasy. *Psychological Bulletin, 117*, 469–496.

Lewis, R. A. (1973). Parents and peers: Socialization agents in the coital behavior of young adults. *Journal of Sex Research, 9*, 156–170.

Libby, R. W., Gray, L., & White, M. (1978). A test and reformulation of reference group and role correlates of premarital sexual permissiveness theory. *Journal of Marriage and the Family, 40*, 79–92.

Lightfoot-Klein, H. (1989). *Prisoners of ritual: An odyssey into female genital circumcision in Africa*. New York: Haworth Press.

McCabe, P. (1987). Desired and experienced levels of premarital affection and sexual intercourse during dating. *Journal of Sex Research, 23*, 23–33.

Mercer, G. W., & Kohn, P. M. (1979). Gender difference in the integration of conservatism, sex urge, and sexual behaviors among college students. *Journal of Sex Research, 15*, 129–142.

Milgram, S. (1963). Behavioral study of obedience. *Journal of Abnormal and Social Psychology, 67*, 371–378.

Milhausen, R. R., & Herold, E. S. (1999). Does the sexual double standard still exist? Perceptions of university women. *Journal of Sex Research, 36*, 361–368.

Murphy, S. (1992). *A delicate dance: Sexuality, celibacy, and relationships among Catholic clergy and religious*. New York: Crossroad.

Nolin, M. J., & Petersen, K. K. (1992). Gender differences in parent-child communication about sexuality. *Journal of Adolescent Research, 7*, 59–79.

O'Leary, K. D., Barling, J., Arias, I., Rosenbaum, A., Malone, J., & Tyree, A. (1989). *Journal of Consulting and Clincial Psychology, 57*, 263–268.

Oliver, M. B., & Hyde, J. S. (1993). Gender differences in sexuality: A meta-analysis. *Psychological Bulletin, 114*, 29–51.

O'Sullivan, L., & Byers, E. S. (1992). College students' incorporation of initiator and restrictor roles in sexual dating interactions. *Journal of Sex Research, 29*, 435–446.

Petersen, J. R. (1999). *The century of sex*. New York: Grove Press.

Regan, P. C. & Dreyer, C. S. (1999). Lust? Love? Status? Young adults' motives for engaging in casual sex. *Journal of Psychology and Human Sexuality, 11*, 1–24.

Reinholtz, R. K., & Muehlenhard, C. L. (1995). Genital perceptions and sexual activity in a college population. *Journal of Sex Research, 32*, 155–165.

Reiss, I. L. (1986). A sociological journey into sexuality. *Journal of Marriage and the Family, 48*, 233–242.

Robinson, I. E., & Jedlicka, D. (1982). Change in sexual attitudes and behavior of college students from 1965 to 1980: A research note. *Journal of Marriage and the Family, 44*, 237–240.

Rodgers, V. L., & Rowe, D. C. (1990). Adolescent sexual activity and mildly deviant behavior: Sibling and friendship effects. *Journal of Family Issues, 11*, 274–293.

Sanders, S. A., & Reinisch, J. M. (1999). Would you say you "had sex" if . . . ? *Journal of the American Medical Association, 281*, 275–277.

Schmidt, G., & Sigusch, V. (1972). Changes in sexual behavior among young males and females between 1960–1970. *Archives of Sexual Behavior, 2*, 27–45.

Sedikides, C., Oliver, M. B., & Campbell, W. K. (1994). Perceived benefits and costs of romantic relationships for women and men: Implications for exchange theory. *Personal Relationships, 1*, 5–21.

Shandall, A. A. (1967). Circumcision and infibulation of females. *Sudan Medical Journal, 5*, 178–212.

Shandall, A. A. (1979). *Circumcision and infibulation of females*. Switzerland: Terre des Hommes.

Sherfey, M. J. (1966). The evolution and nature of female sexuality in relation to psychoanalytic theory. *Journal of the American Psychoanalytic Asssociation, 14*, 28–128.

Sherwin, R., & Corbett, S. (1985). Campus sexual norms and dating relationships: A trend analysis. *Journal of Sex Research, 21*, 258–274.

Sigusch, V., & Schmidt, G. (1973). Teenage boys and girls in West Germany. *Journal of Sex Research, 9*, 107–123.

Smith, T. (1994). Attitudes toward sexual permissiveness: Trends, correlates, and behavioral connections. In A. S. Rossi (Ed.), *Sexuality across the life course* (pp. 63–97). Chicago, IL: University of Chicago Press.

Straus, M. (1980). Victims and aggressors in marital violence. *American Behavioral Scientist, 23*, 681–704.

Symons, D. (1979). *The evolution of human sexuality*. New York: Oxford.

Waller, W., & Hill, R. (1951). *The family: A dynamic interpretation*. New York: Dryden. Original work published in 1938.

Weis, D. L. (1998). The use of theory in sexuality research. *Journal of Sex Research, 35*, 1–9.

West, S. G., & Brown, T. J. (1975). Physical attractiveness, the severity of the emergency and helping: A field experiment and interpersonal simulation. *Journal of Experimental Social Psychology, 11*, 531–538.

Wiederman, M. W. (1997). The truth must be in here somewhere: Examining the gender discrepancy in self-reported lifetime number of sex partners. *Journal of Sex Research, 34*, 375–386.

Wiederman, M. W., & LaMar, L. (1998). "Not with *him* you don't!": Gender and emotional reaction to sexual infidelity during courtship. *Journal of Sex Research, 35*, 288–297.

Williams, L., & Sobieszczyk, T. (1997). Attitudes surrounding the continuation of female circumcision in the Sudan: Passing the tradition to the next generation. *Journal of Marriage and the Family, 59*, 966–981.

Wilson, W. C. (1975). The distribution of selected sexual attitudes and behaviors among the adult population of the United States. *Journal of Sex Research, 11*, 46–64.

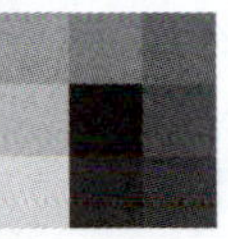

INTRODUCTION TO PART 1

Gender and Sexual Behavior

Do men and women experience sex differently? Do they desire sex in different ways or for different reasons? Do their attitudes about sex differ?

In recent years, debates about gender have shifted repeatedly as to whether to emphasize the differences or similarities. At one extreme, a popular book has depicted men and women as so fundamentally different that they seem to come from different planets (Gray, 1993), and a great many studies have found significant differences. On the other hand, a "significant" difference means only that the difference is not likely to be due to chance, and it does not indicate that the difference is large enough to be meaningful. Systematic statistical examinations of gender differences have concluded that most differences between men and women are "typically less than 5%" of the variance that can be explained (Aries, 1996, p. 7). Thus, men and women are genuinely different, but only slightly, and the range of differences within either gender is larger than the difference between the genders.

Sexuality is at the core of the difference between men and women. In fact, sexuality is probably the reason that there are two genders, and so if men and women differ anywhere, they ought presumably to differ with regard to sex. One might even expect gender differences in sexuality to be especially large.

The first reading in this collection is the important and influential meta-analysis by Oliver and Hyde (1993). Meta-analysis is a statistical method for combining the results of many different studies. Because many research projects on sexuality have studied the same variables and asked the same questions, it is quite possible to combine all their findings, and this process of combination furnishes results that are almost inevitably much more reliable than the conclusions of any single study. Although Oliver and Hyde's survey of the field is now about a decade old, it remains one of the most important and thorough works on sexuality and gender.

The conclusions of Oliver and Hyde confirm that men and women do differ in their sexual attitudes and behaviors, but the size of this difference varies widely from one topic to another. A couple of differences, such as masturbation and the desire for casual sex, are large effects. There are many medium and small effects, and on some variables (such as attitudes toward civil liberties for homosexuals) the aggregation of data across multiple studies yields no significant difference at all. These data suggest that there are both similarities and differences between the two genders.

Oliver and Hyde's (1993) findings have also been used in the ongoing debate about whether gender differences in sexuality indicate natural, innate patterns or cultural, socialized influences. By comparing how findings changed over time, they were able to establish that men and women seemed to become more similar in their sexual attitudes over recent decades. These changes point to the importance of cultural and historical factors, because they suggest that the sexual revolution and other changes have had a significant impact. Then again, the differences have not disappeared, and many of them seem consistent with evolutionary theory, so it would be excessive to take them as disproving hypotheses that men and women have biologically innate differences with regard to sex.

The second reading in this section reports a dramatically large difference between men and women. Clark and Hatfield (1989) conducted a field study of how people would respond to an offer of sex by a stranger. The researchers arranged to have an assistant approach someone of the opposite gender in a public location on campus, pay the person a compliment, and then issue one of three (randomly assigned) invitations: to go out on a date, to come to the person's apartment, or to have sexual intercourse. Men and women were not very different in how they responded to the request for a date, but they were drastically different in how they responded to the offer of sex. In fact, not one woman accepted the sexual invitation, whereas a majority of the men in both studies said yes.

Clark and Hatfield's findings have been discussed by many different writers dealing with sexuality. This high rate of discussion probably reflects two things. First, the findings are undoubtedly important, especially since they show such a large difference. Second, there are different ways of interpreting them. They can be taken to indicate that men and women differ in the strength of sexual desire. They might mean that men and women play different roles in sex (and women are not supposed to make invitations). They may indicate that attitudes toward casual sex are an area of important difference, even if men and women may feel much more similarly to each other in the context of close relationships. Indeed, Oliver and Hyde's (1993) meta-analysis suggested that casual sex with new acquaintainces is an area where men and women are most different. Some suggest that women are more afraid of criminal victimization and hence are more leery of strangers. Other possible interpretations could point to gender differences in willingness to do favors for a stranger, fear of the unknown, desire for adventure, sexual deprivation, or yet, other factors. Read the study and draw your own conclusions about what, exactly, it tells us about the differences between men and women! Whatever the underlying factors, however, it does indicate beyond doubt that sex is far more easily available to women than to men.

REFERENCES

Aries, E. (1996). *Men and women in interaction: Reconsidering the differences*. New York: Oxford University Press.

Clark, R. D., & Hatfield, E. (1989). Gender differences in receptivity to sexual offers. *Journal of Psychology and Human Sexuality, 2*, 39–55.

Gray, J. (1993). *Men are from Mars, women are from Venus*. New York: HarperCollins.

Oliver, M. B., & Hyde, J. S. (1993). Gender differences in sexuality: A meta-analysis. *Psychological Bulletin, 114*, 29–51.

Discussion Questions

1. Do you think the conclusions by Oliver and Hyde (1993) depict men and women as basically similar—or fundamentally different?
2. Why do you think that masturbation emerged as the largest gender difference?
3. Why did women support the double standard more than men?
4. What does it mean that men's and women's attitudes have converged more with respect to sex in committed relationships than toward sex outside such relationships?
5. What do you think caused the women in Clark and Hatfield's study to be so uniformly unwilling to have sex with the men who approached them?
6. Why were the men in Clark and Hatfield's study so agreeable to sexual invitations?
7. Do you think Clark and Hatfield would find different results if they repeated their study today? What about if they had done the study in 1950?
8. Under what circumstances do you think women would agree to have sex with a stranger who approached them in a public place?

Suggested Readings

Aries, E. (1996). *Men and women in interaction: Reconsidering the differences*. New York: Oxford University Press. This work revisits the study of gender differences, looking not only at whether males differ from females but also how big those differences are. There are in fact many differences, but most of them are relatively small, and so in many respects the two genders are more similar than different.

Colapinto, J. (2000). *As nature made him: The boy who was raised as a girl*. New York: HarperCollins. In this fascinating case study, a baby boy's penis was ruined during a circumcision operation, and the family tried to raise him as a girl. The outcome shows the power and the limits of what gender socialization can accomplish.

Guttentag, M., & Secord, P. F. (1983). *Too many women? The sex ratio question*. Beverly Hills, CA: Sage.This important work looks across cultures and histories to examine the consequences of variations in the sex ratio. If your own gender is in the majority, then your chances for finding a mate are limited.

Kinsey, A. C., Pomeroy, W. B., & Martin, C. E. (1948). *Sexual behavior in the human male*. Philadelphia: Saunders, AND Kinsey, A. C., Pomeroy, W. B., Martin, C. E., & Gebhard, P. H. (1953). *Sexual behavior in the human female*. Philadelphia: Saunders. These classic, influential works shaped the way sex was studied and how generations understood men, women, and sexuality.

Laumann, E. O., Gagnon, J. H., Michael, R. T., & Michaels, S. (1994). *The social organization of sexuality: Sexual practices in the United States*. Chicago, IL: University of Chicago Press, OR Michael, R. T., Gagnon, J. H., Laumann, E. O., & Kolata, G. (1994). *Sex in America: A definitive survey*. New York: Warner Books. These two books report on the most important and methodologically rigorous modern survey of sexuality in the United States. The first book contains the full scholarly treatment, with all the information you could want; the second is the simplified version for the general public, made for easy reading and broad conclusions.

Leitenberg, H., & Henning, K. (1995). Sexual fantasy. *Psychological Bulletin, 117*, 469–496. This review brings together the vast area of research on sexual fantasies.

READING 1

Gender Differences in Sexuality: A Meta-Analysis

Mary Beth Oliver • Virginia Polytechnic Institute and State University
Janet Shibley Hyde • University of Wisconsin

This meta-analysis surveyed 177 usable sources that reported data on gender differences on 21 different measures of sexual attitudes and behaviors. The largest gender difference was in incidence of masturbation: Men had the greater incidence (d = .96). There was also a large gender difference in attitudes toward casual sex: Males had considerably more permissive attitudes (d = .81). There were no gender differences in attitudes toward homosexuality or in sexual satisfaction. Most other gender differences were in the small-to-moderate range. Gender differences narrowed from the 1960s to the 1980s for many variables. Chodorow's neoanalytic theory, sociobiology, social learning theory, social role theory, and script theory are discussed in relation to these findings.

It is a widespread belief in American culture that there are gender differences in sexuality, that is, in sexual behaviors and attitudes. For example, in a classic study of gender role stereotypes, one of the male-valued stereotypic traits that emerged was "talks freely about sex with men," reflecting the stereotype that being open and active about sexuality is part of the male role (Rosenkrantz, Vogel, Bee, Broverman, & Broverman, 1968). Reports of empirical findings of gender differences in sexual behaviors have also surfaced periodically and have then been widely cited. For example, Kinsey found a large gender difference in the lifetime incidence of masturbation: 92% for males compared with 58% for females (Kinsey, Pomeroy, Martin, & Gebhard, 1953). Kinsey also found that about half of the men in his sample reported having been aroused at some time by erotic stories; almost all of the women in the sample had heard such stories, but only 14% had been aroused by them (Kinsey et al., 1953).

Meta-analysis is a technique designed to permit the researcher to systematically evaluate the empirical evidence on a particular question by statistically cumulating the data from numerous studies. Recent meta-analyses have challenged many prevailing assumptions about gender differences. For example, although psychologists have believed for decades that the existence of gender differences in verbal ability and in mathematical ability are "well established" (Maccoby & Jacklin, 1974, p. 351), recent meta-analyses indicate that these differences are small or nonexistent (Hyde, Fennema, & Lamon, 1990; Hyde & Linn, 1988). The purpose of the present study was to evaluate the extensive research literature on gender and sexuality to determine the direction and magnitude of gender differences in eight aspects of attitudes about sexuality (attitudes towards premarital intercourse, attitudes about homosexuality, attitudes about extramarital sex, sexual permissiveness, anxiety about sex, sexual satisfaction, double-standard attitudes, attitudes about masturbation) and nine aspects of sexual behavior (incidence of kissing, incidence of petting, incidence of heterosexual intercourse, age of first intercourse, number of sexual partners, frequency of intercourse, incidence of masturbation, incidence of homosexual behavior, and incidence of oral–genital sexual behavior).

Theoretical Perspectives on Gender Differences in Sexuality

A number of theories in psychology either address themselves directly to the issue of gender differences in sexuality or postulate a set of processes that readily lend themselves to predictions of the areas in which gender differences should and should not appear. Here we review the perspectives of the neoanalytic theorists Chodorow and Gilligan, sociobiology, social learning theory, social role theory, and script theory.

Neoanalytic Theories

The neoanalytic theorist Chodorow (1978) understood the causes of psychological gender differences as being rooted in the early family experiences of boys and girls.

Chodorow's (1978) theory begins with the observation that the major responsibility for child care is taken by mothers rather than fathers in virtually all families and all cultures. Therefore, both male infants and female infants form their earliest, most intense emotional attachment to a woman, their mother. The girl's sense of self is profoundly determined by this early relationship, which is never entirely broken. Girls never completely separate themselves from their mother and therefore define themselves throughout life in relational terms. Boys, on the other hand, begin with the same intense attachment but must smash it to form a distinct, masculine identity. Masculinity, according to Chodorow, involves denying feminine maternal attachment. Men's identity, then, is defined not in relational terms, but rather in terms of individuation and independence. It is also defined by rejection and devaluation of the feminine.

Gilligan's (1982) theorizing on moral development derives from Chodorow's thinking. The care perspective in moral reasoning, which is taken more often by women according to the theory, emphasizes the relatedness among people. The justice perspective, taken more often by men, views people as differentiated and emphasizes the rights of the individual.

What do these neoanalytic theories predict about gender differences in sexuality? A superficial consideration of the theories might lead one to say that they predict a stereotyped outcome: Women would be far more oriented to the quality of the relationship and emotional intimacy, whereas men would be more oriented toward body-centered sexuality (Reiss, 1960) that denies attachment and intimacy. However, a careful reading suggests more complex predictions from these theories. As Chodorow commented,

> the nature of the heterosexual relationship differs for boys and girls. Most women emerge from their Oedipus complex oriented to their father and men as primary *erotic* objects, but it is clear that men tend to remain *emotionally* secondary, or at most emotionally equal, compared to the primacy and exclusivity of an oedipal boy's emotional ties to his mother and women. . . . Men defend themselves against the threat posed by love, but needs for love do not disappear through repression. Their training for masculinity and repression of affective relational needs, and their primarily nonemotional and impersonal relationships in the public world make deep primary relationships with other men hard to come by. Given this, it is not surprising that men tend to find themselves in heterosexual relationships. (Chodorow, 1978, pp. 192, 196)

Chodorow's theory focused not only on the consequences of the child's early attachment to their mother but also on male dominance in society. Noting social psychologists' research showing that men fall in love romantically, women sensibly and rationally, she concluded that this was a result of women's economic dependence on men. Women's displays of romanticism, then, may simply be a way of making sure that they and their future children are provided for.

What does Chodorow's theory predict about outcomes of empirical measures of sexual attitudes and behaviors? Two parts of the theory lead to an apparent contradiction that needs to be reconciled. The analytic portion of the theory led Chodorow to conclude that women were oriented toward men as erotic objects but that women could find sufficient emotional satisfaction from men. This would lead to the prediction that women would not require emotional commitment to legitimize heterosexual sexual relationships, that is, that they would approve of casual premarital sex. However, the feminist part of the theory, which stresses male dominance and women's economic dependence, predicts that women will approve of sex only in committed relationships such as marriage, hoping to maximize economic security. On balance, the latter part of the theory must take precedence when making predictions. Therefore, the theory seems to predict that women will be more approving of, and likely to engage in, sex in the context of emotionally committed relationships and relatively disapproving of, and less likely to engage in, sex in casual relationships.

Sociobiology

Sociobiologists attempt to apply evolutionary biology in understanding the distal causes of human social behaviors. The sociobiological approach to human sexuality has been articulated particularly by Donald Symons (1979, 1987; see also Barash, 1977; for a critique, see Travis & Yeager, 1991). The bottom line, according to sociobiologists, is reproductive success, that is, maximizing the number of genes one passes on to the next generations. Therefore, patterns of human sexual behavior should be powerfully shaped by considerations of reproductive success.

Sociobiologists have addressed the existence of the double standard—society's permissive attitudes towards male promiscuity and intolerance for female promiscuity—in two ways. First, they point out that sperm are plentiful (the male body manufactures millions per day) whereas the egg is comparatively rare (only one is produced per month) and therefore precious. Thus, it makes evolutionary sense for the male to inseminate many females but for the female to be careful about which genes are paired with hers in the rare egg. Second, they point out that the woman commits nine months of her body's energy to gestation. Already then, at birth, her parental investment exceeds the man's considerably (Trivers, 1972), leading her to want to continue to ensure the viability of the offspring by caring for them but also leading her to be highly selective in her choice of a mate. She may be particularly likely to prefer a mate who is willing and able to provide resources (Buss, 1989).

The predictions from sociobiology regarding gender differences in behavior, then, are clear: Men should be more approving of casual sex and should have a larger number of different sexual partners, whereas women should be less approving of casual sex and should have a smaller number of different partners.

When the relationship is a long-term, committed one such as marriage, male and female attitudes should be more similar and more approving. In a species that may well require two parents to successfully rear offspring, both men and women maximize their reproductive success by maintaining the relationship. Sociobiologists argue that although men may be somewhat more permissive than women on the issue of extramarital sex, men are especially disapproving of women engaging in extramarital sex. Because paternity certainty is less than 100%, a pregnancy from a woman's extramarital relationship may mean that her husband is spending his resources rearing another man's child and not effectively passing on his own genes to the next generation. These are origins, then, of male sexual jealousy and men's efforts to control the sexuality of women (e.g., Buss, Larsen, Westen, & Semmelroth, 1992; Smuts, 1992).

In fairness to sociobiology, natural selection for patterns of sexual behavior occurred in societies much different from U.S. society today. It may be that the predictions of sociobiology cannot be fairly tested in our present society—which is so different from those traditional, ancestral ones in which natural selection presumably occurred.

Buss and Schmitt (1993) articulated a more nuanced theory of the evolution of human mating patterns in their sexual strategies theory. Theirs is an evolutionary psychology theory, which takes patterns established both by evolution and by current cultural context into account. They argued that men and women have different sexual strategies and, moreover, that the strategies differ for each, depending on whether the context is short-term mating (i.e., casual sex) or long-term mating (i.e., marriage). Buss and Schmitt went on to reach predictions that were similar to sociobiologists (although Buss and Schmitt arrived there by a more complex route): Short-term mating will constitute a larger component of men's sexual strategy than of women's (i.e., men are more interested in and approving of casual sex than women are), and women generally will require reliable signs that a man is committed to them for the long term as a prerequisite for sexual intercourse (i.e., in general women are not terribly interested in casual sex because in that context they cannot be certain of the man's resources to them).

According to many accounts, sociobiology, by arguing that gender differences are controlled by genetic endowment resulting from generations of natural selection, cannot deal well with developmental change over the life span. However, some more recent attempts to apply evolutionary principles argued that natural selection for successful reproductive strategies might have different effects at different stages of development and in different social contexts (e.g., Belsky, Steinberg, & Draper, 1991). Therefore, although sociobiology presently is limited in its ability to deal with developmental change, future theorizing may be able to address these issues.

Social Learning Theory

Although Bandura's original writings on social learning theory did not address the issue of sexuality (e.g., Bandura, 1977; Bandura & Walters, 1963), Mischel (1966) applied principles of social learning theory to understanding gender roles and gender differences in behavior.

According to Mischel's articulation, gender differences are shaped by positive reinforcements for gender-role-consistent behavior, whereas role-inconsistent behavior is ignored or perhaps even punished, thereby becoming less frequent. At the same time, according to the theory, children differentially imitate same-gender adults, so that the gender role behavior of the previous generation perpetuates itself in the next generation.

On the other hand, parents are not the only adults to whom developing children are exposed. The media and other sources present many other models for imitation and observational learning. Thus, social learning theory can readily account for change over time in patterns of gender differences in sexuality. A generation or two ago, young women had chaste Doris Day as their model; today, they have openly sexual Madonna.

Therefore, social learning theory makes two predictions regarding patterns of gender differences in sexual behavior. First, it argues that there can be change over time in gender differences as a function of changing norms for sexual behavior and changing images in the media, which provide models for imitation. Second, to the extent that the double standard is in force (Sprecher, McKinney, & Orbuch, 1987), substantial gender differences in attitudes and behaviors can be expected. In social learning terms, the *double standard* means that women are punished for sexual activities such as having numerous partners or engaging in casual sex, whereas men are not likely to be punished, or perhaps are even rewarded (through admiration or increased social status) for such behaviors. Therefore, social learning theory predicts a lower average number of sexual partners for women than for men. It also predicts that women will hold more negative attitudes about casual sex than men will. Finally, there will be a gender difference in sexual permissiveness: Women will be less permissive than will men.

Social Role Theory and Script Theory

Eagly has articulated social role theory and its application to gender roles and gender differences (e.g., Eagly, 1987; Eagly & Crowley, 1986).

There is no doubt that sexual behaviors are governed by roles and scripts. Sexual behaviors have been described as being scripted (Gagnon & Simon, 1973) or as involving sexual scenarios (DeLamater, 1987). At the same time, sexuality is an important component of gender roles. Heterosexuality is assumed to be part of both the male role and the female role (Bem, 1981), and persons who are described as male but having feminine qualities are assessed as having a higher probability of being gay (.40) than are men described as having masculine qualities (.20; Deaux & Lewis, 1984). However, a person described as female but having masculine qualities is given a lower probability (.27) of being lesbian than a man with nonstereotyped qualities. This suggests that role violations, including homosexuality, are more serious for the male role than for the female role. Social role theory, then, predicts that homosexuality will be viewed as a more serious violation of roles by males than by females, resulting in gender differences in attitudes toward homosexuality, with males holding the more negative attitudes.

The sexual double standard, discussed earlier (e.g., Sprecher et al., 1987), is critical in defining male and female roles in the realm of sexuality. Evidence indicates that the old double standard of several decades ago, in which sexual intercourse outside marriage was acceptable for men but not for women (Reiss, 1960), has largely been replaced by a new, conditional double standard, in which sex outside of marriage is tolerated for both men and women, but under more restrictive circumstances–such as love or engagement—for women (Sprecher et al., 1987).

How far-reaching is the impact of the double standard on role behaviors and attitudes? Certainly, social role theory should predict that women should have fewer premarital sexual partners than men and that women should hold more negative attitudes about casual premarital sex. The theory should predict that currently there should be no gender differences in attitudes about premarital sex in the context of a relationship such as engagement, although there may have been gender differences several decades ago, when a different version of the double standard was in force. Therefore, social role theory, like social learning theory, can account for and predict change over time in patterns of gender differences as gender role change.

Content analyses of marriage and sex manuals give some indications of the content of gender roles in marital sexuality (e.g., Gordon & Shankweiler, 1971; Weinberg, Swensson, & Hammersmith, 1983). These manuals in the 1950s and 1960s espoused a different-equals-less view of the female role in marital sexuality. The man was expected to be experienced and skillful, so that he could awaken the Sleeping Beauty sexuality of his wife. By the 1970s, this model was replaced by a humanistic sexuality model, in which women were viewed as equal partners in the sexual interaction. These widely read manuals doubtlessly had an impact on gender roles in marital sexuality. They led to a prediction of gender differences in sexual satisfaction before approximately 1970 but then no differences or a decline in gender differences in sexual satisfaction in the last two decades.

The classic articulation of script theory applied to sexuality is found in Gagnon and Simon's (1973) *Sexual Conduct*. Gagnon and Simon used the term *script* in two ways. One dealt with the interpersonal, in which the script organized the mutually shared conventions that allowed two people to participate in a complex sexual act involving mutual interaction. The other dealt with internal states and motivations in which the individual has certain scripts that produced arousal and predisposed to sexual activity. Gagnon and Simon directly addressed the issue of gender differences in sexuality. They traced much of the origin of these differences to the period of early adolescence, just after puberty. During this period, they argued, the boy's sexuality is focused on masturbation. He is likely to have a great deal of sexual activity during this period, but because it is masturbation centered, it is typically done alone and secretly. Girls, in contrast, are less likely to engage in masturbation during this period, which is relatively asexual for them. Instead, they spend the period focusing, traditionally, on beginning preparations for the adult female role, or at least on attracting male interest. The girl's earliest experiences with sexuality occur somewhat later than the boy's and are typically heterosexual, that is, in a relational context. Indeed, many females see the existence of a committed relationship as the prerequisite for sexual expression.

Script theory emphasizes the symbolic meaning of behaviors. Gagnon and Simon concluded, following the arguments above, that the meaning of sexuality was tied far more to individual pleasure for males and to the quality of relationship for females.

Mosher and Tomkins (1988) have extended script theory in their writing about the Macho Man and the macho personality constellation in men—which consists of callous sexual attitudes, a belief that violence is manly, and a belief that danger is exciting. Not all men, of course, become macho men, but the existence of the script in the culture means that it influences all men, some to a lesser extent and some to a greater extent. The Macho Man's sense of entitlement to callous sex means that he will have a large number of different sexual partners and that he will hold approving attitudes toward casual sex.

Summary

The five theories reviewed—neoanalytic theories, sociobiology, social learning theory, social role theory, and script theory—are all in agreement in predicting that females will have a smaller number of sexual partners than will males and that females will have more negative attitudes toward casual, premarital sex. Each theory also addresses somewhat different issues in regard to gender and sexuality. The present study was not designed as a critical test of the theories; rather, the theories help illuminate the mechanisms that many be behind the observable differences addressed in this meta-analysis.

The Present Study

The present study used the technique of meta-analysis to synthesize research presenting data on gender differences in sexual attitudes and sexual behaviors. Two variables that might moderate the gender differences in sexuality were also examined: subjects' age and date of data collection (to examine change over time).

Method

Sample of studies. Two primary sources were used to generate the sample of studies: (a) a computerized database search of PsycLIT for the years 1974 (the earliest year available on this database) through 1990, using the key terms *sexual attitudes* and *psychosexual behavior*, and (b) a computerized database search of the Educational Resources Information Center (ERIC) for the years 1966 (the earliest year available on this database) through 1990, using the key term *sexuality*. In addition, data from several well-known and large-scale surveys were included: those of (a) Blumstein and Schwartz (1983), (b) DeLamater and MacCorquodale (1979), (c) Klassen, Williams, and Levitt (1989), and (d) Sorensen (1972) and (e) data from surveys conducted by the National Opinion Research Center (Wood, 1990).[1]

In the case of computerized searches, abstracts were printed for each citation and were examined for relevancy to the topic of study. Studies that had any of the following characteristics were excluded from the sample: (a) a sample of respondents who were not from the United States or Canada, (b) data that were not original, (c) a sample of respondents who were clinical (e.g., seeking help for marital or sexual dysfunctions), or (d) a sample of respondents who were being treated for a medical illness (e.g., burn victims or cancer patients). Subsequently, all remaining articles were photocopied from journals or from microfiche (in the case of ERIC documents) for complete inspection.

It is possible for a single article to report data for several samples such as different age groups or ethnic groups. These groups can be regarded as separate samples (Hedges, 1987, personal communication). Furthermore, it is possible for an article to report data on several variables of interest (e.g., attitudes toward premarital intercourse and attitude toward homosexuality). Therefore, several effect sizes can be computed for a single sample. In this study, all effect sizes were computed for each sample and were analyzed separately.

The result was 177 usable sources yielding 239 independent samples and 490 effect sizes. This represented the testing of 128,363 respondents (58,553 males and 69,810 females).

Coding the studies. For each study, the following information was recorded: (a) all statistics on gender differences in the sexual attitude or behavior measure(s), including means, standard deviations, *t* tests, *F* ratios, and degrees of freedom; (b) the number of male and female respondents; (c) the mean age of the respondents (if the article reported no ages but reported "high school students," the age was set to 16; if the article reported "undergraduates," the age was set to 20; if the article reported "college seniors" or "undergraduate and graduate students," the age was set to 22; if the article reported grade level, five years were added to compute age, e.g., ninth graders were recorded as age 14); (d) the year the data were collected (if the year was not reported, the data year was computed by subtracting two from the year of publication, e.g., an article published in 1978 with no data year reported was recorded as having collected data in 1976).[2] The type of sexual attitude or behavior measure(s) used in a given study was also coded, as explained below.

Sexual attitudes and behavior measures. Twenty-one sexual attitude and behavior measures were included in the analyses. The measures were labeled and defined as follows:

1. *Premarital attitudes.* Attitudes concerning the acceptability of premarital intercourse. If the question was worded so that respondents were asked to indicate the circumstances under

[1]The survey conducted by Hunt (1974) was not included in this study because of insufficient information to compute effect sizes.

[2]Note that the estimates of the year of data collection that were used when such information was not provided are not exact. In some instances, the estimation procedure of subtracting two years from the year of publication would have overestimated the recency of data collection (e.g., two cases in which year data collection was know, Hendrick & Hendrick, 1987; Miller & Simon, 1974). In other instances, however, this procedure would have underestimated the recency of data collection (e.g., Frevert et al., 1981; Zuckerman, 1973).

which premarital intercourse was acceptable, abstinence was coded as nonacceptance of premarital intercourse, and all other categories were coded as acceptance of premarital intercourse.

2. *Intercourse—casual.* Attitudes concerning the acceptability of premarital intercourse in a casual dating relationship or without emotional commitment.
3. *Intercourse—committed.* Attitudes concerning the acceptability of premarital intercourse given love or emotional commitment.
4. *Intercourse—engaged.* Attitudes concerning the acceptability of premarital intercourse given that the couple is engaged.
5. *Homosexuality attitudes.* Attitudes toward homosexuality.
6. *Homosexual civil liberties.* Attitudes towards homosexuals' civil liberties, for example, career opportunities and free speech.
7. *Extramarital attitudes.* Attitudes concerning the acceptability of extramarital intercourse.
8. *Sexual permissiveness.* Attitudes about sexuality per se, such as acceptance of many sexual partners, beliefs that extensive sexual experience is acceptable, for example, Hendrick and Hendrick's (1987) Sexual Permissiveness Scale.
9. *Anxiety/fear/guilt.* Expressed anxiety, shame, disgust, fear, or guilt about sexuality, for example, Mosher's Sex Guilt Inventory (Mosher, 1979). Measures of anxiety, fear, or guilt were excluded if different scales were used for males and females.
10. *Sexual satisfaction.* Satisfaction or contentment with one's sexual activity, either within the current relationship or in general.
11. *Double standard.* Beliefs that female premarital sexual activity is less acceptable than male sexual activity. Because of the calculations involved in the computations of the statistics used in this study, it was not possible to include measures of the double standard that were obtained by asking respondents to indicate separately the acceptability of male premarital intercourse and female premarital intercourse.
12. *Masturbation attitudes.* Attitudes toward masturbation.
13. *Kissing incidence.* Any experience with romantic kissing at any level of sexual intimacy, for example, French or passionate.
14. *Petting incidence.* Any experience with petting at any level of sexual intimacy, for example, clothed, partially clothed, or lying down. This measure was excluded if respondents were asked only to indicate if they had experienced petting to orgasm.
15. *Intercourse incidence.* Any experience with heterosexual, vaginal intercourse.
16. *Age at first intercourse.* The age at which the respondent first experienced sexual intercourse. This measure was excluded unless all of the respondents in the sample had experienced intercourse.
17. *Number of sexual partners.* The number of partners with whom the respondent had experienced sexual intercourse. This measure was excluded unless (a) all of the respondents in the sample had experienced intercourse or (b) nonvirgins were included as having zero partners.
18. *Frequency of intercourse.* The frequency with which the respondent engaged in sexual intercourse. This measure was excluded unless all of the respondents in the sample had experienced intercourse or unless nonvirgins were included as having zero frequency.
19. *Masturbation incidence.* Any experience with masturbation.
20. *Homosexual incidence.* Any sexual experience with a same-sex partner, for example, intercourse or oral sex.
21. *Oral sex incidence.* Any experience with giving or receiving heterosexual oral sex. Because many studies did not differentiate between giving and receiving oral sex in the questions posed to respondents, a distinction between the two could not be made in the present study.

Statistical analysis. The effect size computed for each of the sexual attitude and behavior measures was *d*. This measure was defined as the mean score for males minus the mean score for females, divided by the pooled within-sex standard deviation. In this analysis, positive values of *d* reflected male respondents having more permission or positive attitudes toward premarital intercourse, homosexuality, extramarital intercourse, and masturbation; greater endorsement of the double standard; higher levels of anxiety, fear, or guilt; higher levels of sexual satisfaction; younger age at first intercourse; greater number of sexual partners; and higher incidence of sexual experiences (kissing, petting, intercourse, frequency of intercourse, masturbation, oral sex, and homosexual experience). Negative values of *d* reflected female respondents having more permissive or positive attitudes toward premarital intercourse, homosexuality, extramarital intercourse, and masturbation; greater endorsement of the double standard; higher levels of anxiety, fear, or guilt; higher levels of sexual satisfaction; younger age at first intercourse; greater number of sexual partners; and higher incidence of sexual experiences (kissing, petting, intercourse, frequency of intercourse, masturbation, oral sex, and homosexual experience).

Formulas provided by Hedges and Becker (1986) were used for the computations of *d*, depending on the statistics reported in a given study. In addition, *d* values were first corrected for bias in estimation of the population effect size, using the formula provided by Hedges (1981). Table 1.1 contains the complete listing of studies and effect sizes.

To establish interrupter reliability for coding the 21 categories of sexual attitude and behavior measures, we each independently rated 20 articles. Thirty-seven measures were coded for the type of sexual attitude or behavior, and effect sizes were computed. Interrater reliability was 95%.

Results

Magnitude of gender differences in sexual attitudes and sexual behaviors. Table 1.1 contains the mean effect sizes averaged over the independent samples. This table shows that males reported more permissive attitudes and greater incidence of behaviors on most measures. In terms of attitudes, males reported greater acceptance of premarital intercourse than did females, with a particularly large gender difference revealed for attitudes toward premarital intercourse under casual circumstances. A large gender difference was also revealed for measures of sexual permissiveness: Males reported more permissive attitudes than did females. Moderately large *d* values were obtained for extramarital attitudes and anxiety, fear, or guilt: Males reported greater acceptance of extramarital intercourse and lower levels of anxiety, fear, or guilt than did females. The gender difference for masturbation attitudes also showed that males reported slightly more favorable attitudes than did females, although this difference was trivial.

Surprisingly, a negative *d* value was obtained for attitudes toward the double standard. This negative value reflects a higher level of acceptance among females than among males. We expected that males would be more likely than females to endorse a double standard in sexuality. Perhaps this finding was partially due to the years in which the studies were conducted (the most recent being 1977) and the age of the sample (the oldest being 20 years). Finally, gender differences were essentially nonexistent for both attitudes toward homosexuality and for attitudes toward civil liberties for lesbians and gay men.

In regard to the gender differences for the sexual behavior measures, eight of the nine measures reflected greater experience for males than females. Not surprisingly, the measures of two behaviors that normally precede intercourse, kissing and petting, showed trivially small gender differences. Moderately large gender differences were revealed for incidence of intercourse, age of first intercourse, number of sexual partners, and frequency of intercourse. Males reported a higher incidence of intercourse, a younger age at which they first experienced intercourse, more frequent intercourse, and a larger number of sexual partners than did females. A moderate *d* value was also revealed for homosexual incidence: Males reported a greater incidence than did females.

The largest gender difference revealed among the sexual behavior measures was for masturbation incidence. This difference far overshadowed all other measures examined in this study, with the possible exception of attitudes toward casual premarital intercourse. That females reported a significantly lower incidence of masturbation than did males was especially interesting given the small gender difference revealed for attitudes toward masturbation.

Regression analysis. Homogeneity analyses using procedures specified by Hedges and Becker (1986) indicated that effect sizes were nonhomogeneous for all of the sexual attitudes and behavior measures except for homosexual civil liberties (see Table 1.1) Therefore, we concluded that the effect sizes were heterogeneous, and we conducted multiple regression analyses for each of the attitude and behavior measures (excluding homosexual civil liberties) to examine sources of variation in effect sizes (Hedges & Becker, 1986). Average age of the respondents and year of data collection were used as predictor variables in all of the analyses except for the analysis of the atti-

TABLE 1.1. Magnitude of Gender Differences as a Function of Measure

Measures	*k*	*d*	95% confidence interval for *d*	*H*
Premarital attitudes	46	0.37	0.35 to 0.40	321*
Intercourse—casual	10	0.81	0.75 to 0.87	131*
Intercourse—committed	10	0.49	0.44 to 0.53	44*
Intercourse—engaged	5	0.43	0.32 to 0.54	36*
Attitudes toward homosexuality	28	−0.01	−0.04 to 0.02	187*
Homosexual civil liberties	14	−0.00	−0.03 to 0.02	15
Extramarital attitudes	17	0.29	0.26 to 0.32	87*
Sexual permissiveness	39	0.57	0.55 to 0.60	474*
Anxiety, fear, or guilt	11	−0.35	−0.44 to −0.26	99*
Sexual satisfaction	15	−0.06	−0.09 to −0.03	65*
Double standard	7	−0.29	−0.37 to −0.21	29*
Masturbation attitudes	12	0.09	0.04 to 0.14	86*
Kissing incidence	15	−0.05	−0.10 to 0.01	69*
Petting incidence	28	0.11	0.07 to 0.15	207*
Intercourse incidence	135	0.33	0.32 to 0.35	1087*
Age at first intercourse	8	0.38	0.30 to 0.45	22*
Number of sexual partners	12	0.25	0.19 to 0.32	22*
Frequency of intercourse	11	0.31	0.27 to 0.36	98*
Masturbation incidence	26	0.96	0.92 to 1.00	380*
Homosexual incidence	19	0.33	0.30 to 0.37	175*
Oral sex incidence	21	0.10	0.05 to 0.15	124*

Note. k represents the number of effect sizes; *H* is the within-group homogeneity statistic (Hedges & Becker, 1986).
*Significant nonhomogeneity at $p<.05$, according to the chi-square test.

tude variable labeled *intercourse—engaged.* In this instance, only data year could be used as a predictor variable because all participants had a mean age of 20. Table 1.2 contains the partial correlations of the *d* values with data year and with mean age that were revealed in the regression analyses. Partial correlations are reported to eliminate confoundings between age of subjects, year of data collection, and birth cohort. The partial correlation with age, for example, controls for year of data collection.

Changes in gender differences as a function of year. Eleven of the 21 sexual attitude and behavior measures were significantly correlated with year of data collection. Many of these correlations reflected trends toward smaller differences between males and females over time. For example, gender differences in attitudes toward premarital intercourse in general and attitudes toward premarital intercourse in committed and engaged relationships were significantly negatively associated with year of data collection. These negative correlations reflected a change from large gender differences reported during the 1960s (premarital attitudes, $d = .79$; intercourse—committed, $d = .91$; intercourse—engaged, $d = .80$) to smaller gender differences reported during the 1980s (premarital attitudes, $d = .32$; intercourse—committed, $d = .48$; intercourse—engaged, $d = .17$). A similar, though less pronounced, pattern was revealed for attitudes toward extramarital intercourse (1970s, $d = .33$; 1980s, $d = .25$). These results suggest that although gender differences in these sexual attitudes are becoming smaller over the years, males continue to hold more permissive attitudes toward premarital and extramarital intercourse than do females. However, sexual permissiveness and attitudes toward casual intercourse, both of which showed substantial gender differences (see Table 1.1), were not significantly associated with year, suggesting that they have remained fairly constant over time.

In terms of sexual behaviors, significant negative correlations were revealed for petting incidence, intercourse incidence, number of sexual partners, frequency of intercourse, and masturbation incidence. Again, these correlations reflect moderate-to-large gender differences in data collected during the 1960s (petting, $d = .66$; intercourse incidence, $d = .41$; number of sexual partners, $d = .33$; frequency of intercourse, $d = .34$; and masturbation incidence, $d = 1.07$) and smaller gender differences in data collected during the 1980s (petting, $d = .02$; intercourse incidence, $d = .33$; number of sexual partners, $d = .17$; frequency of intercourse, $d = .14$; and masturbation incidence, $d = .60$). Although the correlation between age at first intercourse and data year did not achieve significance (perhaps because of the small number of studies), it too showed a negative correlation, suggesting that gender differences on this measure have decreased over time as well. Note that although gender differences in these sexual behaviors have decreased over the years, a sizable gender difference remained for masturbation incidence in the most recent studies.

Although most of the significant correlations revealed in the regression analyses reflected reductions in gender differences, two of the measures were significantly associated with data year for alternate reasons. A significant negative correlation was obtained between data year and the double standard. However, because the *d* value for attitudes toward the double standard was negative across all studies (reflecting greater female than male endorsement), the significant negative correlation obtained in the regression analysis reflected an increase in gender differences across the years. Although this finding was unexpected, as mentioned previously, this might reflect the particular range of years in which the data were collected. The most recent year of data collection was 1977; in essence, none of the studies were very recent. In addition, because these statistics represented changes in the magnitude of gender differences, it was unclear whether this significant correlation with data year reflected trends toward greater female acceptance of the double standard, lesser male acceptance of the double standard, or both.

A significant negative correlation was obtained also for attitudes toward homosexuality. However, because gender differences on this measure were almost nonexistent across studies (see Table 1.1), this negative correlation reflected a change from a trivially small difference favoring males in the studies conducted before and during 1975 ($d = .04$) to a trivially small difference favoring females after 1975 ($d = -.05$).

Changes in gender differences as a function of age. Significant correlations between *d* values and the mean age of sample were revealed for 11 of the 21 measures (see Table 1.2). Many of the measures associated with attitudes toward intercourse and intercourse behaviors showed decreases in gender differences with increasing age. For example, sexual permissiveness, attitudes toward extramarital intercourse, and attitudes toward premarital intercourse under casual and committed circumstances were significantly negatively associated with the age of the sample. Given the age ranges covered by most of the studies, this generally reflected trends from adolescence to young adulthood. However, moderate gender differences remained even among respondents greater than 25 years of age (sexual permissiveness, $d = .42$; extramarital attitudes, $d = .28$; intercourse—casual, $d = .46$; intercourse—committed, $d = .46$). Because gender differences associated with attitudes toward intercourse showed significant decreases with age, it is not surprising that incidence of intercourse was also negatively associated with age of the sample. However, as with attitudes associated with intercourse, the gender differences in incidence of intercourse among the older samples (those greater than 20 years) showed that men continued to have a greater incidence than did women ($d = .20$).

Two surprising correlations were revealed in these analyses, considering the negative correlations between age and many of the intercourse-related measures. First, a negative correlation was revealed between age and the double standard. Samples under 18 years of age showed a small negative *d* value ($d = -.06$), value ($d = -.06$), and samples over 18 years of age showed a moderate, negative *d* value ($d = -.33$). This negative correlation should be interpreted with care, however, given the small number of studies involved ($k = 7$) and the young age of the samples overall, the oldest having a mean age of 20. The second surprising correlation was a positive association between age and the magnitude of gender differences in frequency of intercourse. An examination of the *d* values for different categories of age groups showed that the increases in gender differences on this measure reflected almost nonexistent gender differences for college-age samples (19–25 years; $d = .01$) but considerably larger gender differences among samples greater than 25 years ($d = .45$).

Significant positive correlations were obtained also between age and attitudes toward masturbation and between age and masturbation behaviors. The age trend in attitudes toward masturbation occurred because females in the youngest samples (18 years and younger) reported more positive attitudes toward masturbation than did males ($d = -.20$), whereas the reverse was true for the oldest

TABLE 1.2. Partial Correlations Between Magnitude of Gender Differences and Data Year and Age of Respondent

Measure	*pr* for data year[a]	Year Range	*pr* for age[b]	Age range	Q_E	*k*
Premarital attitudes	−.19**	1965–1989	−.11	14–44	292.44*	46
Intercourse—casual	−.05	1966–1983	−.77**	14–43	41.89*	10
Intercourse—committed	−.45**	1966–1987	−.47**	15–43	33.95*	10
Intercourse—engaged[c]	−.82**	1966–1983	—	20	11.77*	5
Attitudes towards homosexuality	−.47**	1970–1989	.69**	14–44	92.13*	28
Homosexual civil liberties	.03	1970–1989	.16	19–44	14.74	14
Extramarital attitudes	−.36**	1970–1989	−.31**	14–44	67.02*	17
Sexual permissiveness	.09	1967–1987	−.40**	13–43	338.45*	39
Anxiety/fear/guilt	.10	1971–1987	−.10	13–43	97.26*	11
Sexual satisfaction[d]	.07	1974–1987	.26	20–47	21.36*	14
Double standard	−.42*	1966–1977	−.41*	14–20	21.73*	7
Masturbation attitudes	−.12	1970–1983	.45**	18-43	62.91*	12
Kissing incidence	−.17	1968–1987	.03	10–22	66.49*	15
Petting incidence	−.25**	1965–1987	−.11	10–22	190.15*	28
Intercourse incidence	−.26**	1963–1990	−.33**	10–27	956.51*	135
Age at first intercourse	−.30	1974–1986	.01	19–25	19.77*	8
Number of sexual partners	−.45*	1973–1985	−.17	16–25	16.91	12
Frequency of intercourse	−.56**	1969–1989	.65**	19–86	46.61*	11
Masturbation incidence	−.57**	1969–1986	.54**	14–43	136.18*	26
Homosexual incidence	.08	1970–1987	.17*	14–43	170.52*	19
Oral sex incidence	−.11	1972–1987	−.09	16–27	121.79*	21

Note. Partial correlations were obtained from entering both data year and age of sample into a regression equation simultaneously; Q_E represents the error sum of squares from the regression equation (Hedges & Olkin, 1985); *k* represents the number of effect sizes.

[a]Partial correlations are between year of data collection and magnitude of the gender difference, *d*, controlling for age. For positive values of *d*, positive correlations generally indicate larger gender differences over time, and negative correlations indicate smaller gender differences over time. For negative values of *d*, negative correlations generally indicate larger gender differences over time, and positive correlations indicate smaller gender differences over time. [b]Partial correlations are between age and magnitude of the gender difference, *d*, controlling for year of data collection. For positive values of *d*, positive correlations generally indicate larger gender differences with age. For negative values of *d*, negative correlations generally indicate larger gender differences with age, and positive correlations indicate smaller gender differences with age. [c]Data year was the only variable entered in the regression equation for intercourse—engaged because all samples had a mean age of 20. [d]One effect size was excluded from the regression analysis because the mean age of the sample was 86 (almost 40 years older than the next oldest sample), which created an undue influence on the correlation coefficient.

*Significant nonhomogeneity at $p < .05$, according to the chi-square test.

samples ($d = .15$). Despite the significant correlation with age, gender differences in attitudes toward masturbation were small overall. However, gender differences in incidence of masturbation were also significantly associated with age, with this correlation reflecting a trend from moderately large differences among the youngest samples (18 years and younger, $d = .44$) to very large differences among the oldest samples (greater than 25 years, $d = 1.33$). It is interesting to contrast the associations of age with intercourse-related variables and with masturbation-related variables. It appears that with age, males and females become more alike in terms of intercourse but more divergent in terms of masturbation.

Finally, the regression analyses showed significant positive correlations between the age of the sample and gender differences in attitudes toward homosexuality and gender differences in homosexual incidence. The findings for attitude toward homosexuality occurred because in the youngest sample (18 years and younger), females expressed more positive attitudes toward homosexuality than did males ($d = -.26$), whereas in the oldest samples (25 years and older), gender differences were close to zero ($d = .04$). The findings for homosexual incidence occurred because the gap between the incidence for males and the incidence for females increased slightly from the youngest samples ($d = .29$) to the oldest samples ($d = .38$).

Discussion

This meta-analysis documented two large gender differences in sexuality: the incidence of masturbation (d = .96) and attitudes toward casual premarital sex (d = .81). As we discuss below, these differences are large whether judged by Cohen's (1969) guidelines or by comparison with the magnitude of gender differences in other areas such as mathematics performance or verbal ability.

At the same time, we found a great range in the magnitude of gender differences in other aspects of sexual attitudes and behaviors. At the other end of the spectrum, there were no gender differences in the following: attitudes about homosexuality, attitudes about civil liberties for gay men and lesbians, sexual satisfaction, attitudes toward masturbation, incidence of kissing, and incidence of oral sex. In the middle, there were small-to-moderate gender differences in attitudes toward premarital intercourse when the couple was engaged or in a committed relationship (males were more permissive, d = .43 and .49 respectively); attitudes toward extramarital sex (males were more permissive, d = .29); sexual permissiveness (males were more permissive, d = .57); anxiety or guilt about sex (females were more anxious, d = –.35); endorsement of the double standard (more endorsement by females, d = –.29); incidence of sexual intercourse (higher incidence with males, d = .33); age of first intercourse (males were younger, d = .38); number of sexual partners (males reported more partners, d = .25); frequency of intercourse (greater reported frequency for males, d = .31); and incidence of homosexual behavior (greater incidence for males, d = .33).

Assessing trends over time, there were significant correlations between the magnitude of gender differences and the year of data collection. Almost all the significant effects showed gender differences becoming smaller over time, especially in regard to attitudes toward premarital sex when the couple was engaged, attitudes toward homosexuality, number of sexual partners, frequency of intercourse, and masturbation.

Examination of age trends was limited in general by the data to shifts from adolescence to early adulthood. Over this age range, gender differences narrowed with age, especially for attitudes toward casual premarital sex, attitudes toward extramarital intercourse, and sexual permissiveness. Gender differences grew larger with age for frequency of intercourse and incidence of masturbation.

One virtue of meta-analysis is that it can identify gaps in the data in a particular field. The analysis of age trends reveal that studies of gender differences in sexual behavior rely far too heavily on data derived from 18- to-20-year-olds (with the exception of Wood, 1990, data, which is from a national opinion survey on attitude). If the developmental processes underlying gender differences in sexuality are to be understood, younger age groups and older age groups must be studied.

One methodological issue must be noted. In all of the studies reviewed, data were collected by self-report method rather than by direct observations of behavior. What we gathered, then, was evidence of gender differences in *reported* sexual attitudes and behaviors. It is possible, therefore, that there are no actual gender differences in sexual attitudes and behaviors. Rather, the gender difference is in reporting tendencies. Males may have a tendency to exaggerate their sexual experiences (at least the socially approved ones). Females may underreport their sexual experiences. Either or both trends could create gender differences in self-reports where no actual differences in behaviors and attitudes exist or could magnify a small gender difference. It is beyond the scope of this review to address this problem, because it is generally unresolved in the methods used by sex researchers. Nonetheless, readers should be aware of this possible limitation in the data.

Note also that this study examines patterns of attitudes and behaviors within a particular cultural context, namely, the United States during the 1960s through the 1980s. We make no claim that these patterns would be found in other cultures or that they would have characterized American culture earlier in its history. The introduction of the birth control pill in 1960 and the availability of other highly effective methods of contraception had a profound effect. These developments are usually credited as being major factors in the liberation of female sexuality, by allowing women to engage in sexual intercourse (marital or nonmarital) with little fear of pregnancy. The effect should be to narrow the gender gap. The cultural context for the studies reviewed here also includes a rapidly rising divorce rate; the legalization of abortion; and, in the 1980s, an epidemic of sexually transmitted diseases, particularly AIDS and herpes, all of which affect the health of the infected person as well as being potentially lethal to offspring.

Theoretical Views

All five theories that were considered in this review agree in their predictions that males will have a greater number of sexual partners and more permissive attitudes toward casual sex than will females. The results of the meta-analysis are consistent with these predictions for attitudes and, to some extent, for behaviors. Gender differences in attitudes toward casual sex were large ($d = .81$). Gender differences in number of partners were in the direction predicted but were surprisingly small ($d = .25$).

There are two possible explanations for the small gender difference in number of sexual partners. The advent of highly effective contraceptives, dating from the introduction of the birth control pill in 1960, many well have changed the nature of reproductive strategies for females. When sexual activity does not involve reproduction, then, in the framework of sociobiology, females can have as many partners as males without squandering precious eggs or making unwise parental investments. This, of course, assumes a cognitive approach to decisions about sexual behavior that is missing in sociobiology. A second explanation comes from the work of DeLamater and MacCorquodale (1979), who found, in a large survey on premarital sexuality, that gender role definitions were not good predictors of patterns of premarital sexuality; the patterns were predicted far better by the nature of the couple's relationship. If this is the case, gender differences in the incidence of premarital sex might well not be large. DeLamater and MacCorquodale's findings and interpretations are consistent with social-psychological models such as Deaux and Major's (1987) that stress the proximal (i.e., situational) determinants of gender differences in behavior over the distal determinants (e.g., early childhood experiences, gender role socialization, evolutionary selection).

Gender Difference in Masturbation

It is striking that the largest gender difference was in the incidence of masturbation, yet only one of the theories, script theory, addressed this point. It will be important for future theories to account for this well-established phenomenon. A number of questions will need to be addressed in the process, all revolving around the issue of the meaning of masturbation, both from a functional or biological point of view and from a psychological point of view. Masturbation is not a behavior that leads to reproduction, so theories such as sociobiology that account for sexual phenomena in terms of reproductive strategy may not account well for patterns of masturbation. On the other hand, masturbation may be a manifestation of generalized sex drive or libido, which influences both reproductive sexual behaviors and nonreproductive sexual behaviors. In any event, a gender difference of this magnitude is worthy of far more theoretical consideration.

Magnitude of Gender Differences

We have offered our own interpretation of the magnitude of gender differences obtained in this meta-analysis. In keeping with Cohen (1969), we interpreted effect sizes, d, of .80 or greater as large effects, those around .50 as moderate, and those around .20 as small. We also interpreted effect sizes less than .10 to be trivial or no difference. The Cohen scheme for interpretation is controversial, and readers may want to form their own interpretations.

An alternative framework for interpretation involves comparing the magnitude of the gender differences found in this meta-analysis with the magnitude of gender differences found in other meta-analyses or with the magnitude of effects in meta-analyses outside the realm of gender issues. For example, for gender differences in verbal ability, $d = -.11$, with the difference favoring females (Hyde & Linn, 1988). For gender differences in mathematical performance, $d = .15$, favoring males (Hyde et al., 1990). For gender differences in spatial ability, d ranges between .13 and .73, depending on the type of spatial ability being measured (Linn & Petersen, 1985). Gender differences in aggressive behavior yielded $d = .50$ in one meta-analysis (Hyde, 1984) and .29 in another (Eagly & Steffen, 1986). In the realm of nonverbal behaviors, Hall (1984) found $d = .42$ for gender differences in decoding nonverbal cues.

By comparison with these other studies, the magnitude of the largest gender differences in sexuality (incidence of masturbation, $d = .96$, and attitudes toward casual sex, $d = .81$) were clearly large, indeed larger than any of the gender differences found in these other studies. On the other hand, there was a broad range of magnitudes of gender differences in the present meta-analysis, and other gender differences were small or nonexistent.

Conclusion

In an era in which gender differences in sexuality are highlighted and male–female conflicts over these issues are exacerbated by events such as the Anita Hill and Clarence Thomas hearings on sexual harassment, psychologists should recognize these gender differences as an important topic of inquiry. The results of this meta-analysis are useful in sorting out the larger differences from the smaller ones. The gender difference in attitudes toward casual sex is large and was predicted well by all of the theories reviewed in this article. Future research could profitably examine the consequences of this large gender difference; it may help to explain, for example, why the same behavior is interpreted as harassment by a woman and reasonable or even flattering behavior by a man.

Gender differences in masturbation need further empirical and theoretical investigation, and their clinical applications are already being explored. Gagnon and Simon (1973) may have been correct when they argued, from their script perspective, that this gender difference was the origin of most other gender differences in sexuality. On the other hand, other mechanisms might be involved, which need to be understood. The gender difference in masturbation has applications in the clinical realm. Orgasmic dysfunction, which is common in women and rare in men, is often treated by sex therapists with a program of directed masturbation (Andersen, 1983; LoPiccolo & Lobitz, 1972; LoPiccolo & Stock, 1986). Essentially, the therapy provides women with masturbation experience that they have missed.

Many gender differences that are moderate in magnitude, such as those in sex guilt and in sexual permissiveness, will benefit from further research. Theoretical models that focus on proximal (situational) causes of gender differences (e.g., Deaux & Major, 1987) have received little application in the area of sexuality but hold promise for future work.

REFERENCES

Andersen, B. L. (1983). Primary orgasmic dysfunction: Diagnostic considerations and review of treatment. *Psychological Bulletin, 93*, 105–136.

Bandura, A. J. (1977). *Social learning theory.* Engelwood Cliffs, NJ: Prentice Hall.

Bandura, A., & Walters, R. H. (1963). *Social learning and personality development.* New York: Holt, Rinehart & Winston.

Barash, D. P. (1977). *Sociobiology and behavior.* New York: Elsevier Science.

Belsky, J., Steinberg, L., & Draper, P. (1991). Childhood experience, interpersonal development, and reproductive strategy: An evolutionary theory of socialization. *Child Development, 62,* 647–670.

Bem, S. (1981). Gender schema theory: A cognitive account of sex-typing. *Psychology Review, 88,* 354–364.

Blumstein, P., & Schwartz, P. (1983). *American couples.* New York: Morrow.

Buss, D. M. (1989). Sex difference in human mate preferences: Evolutionary hypotheses tested in 37 cultures. *Behavioral and Brain Sciences, 12,* 1–49.

Buss, D. M., Larsen, R. J., Westen, D., & Semmelroth, J. (1992). Sex differences in jealousy: Evolution, physiology, and psychology. *Psychological Science, 3,* 251–255.

Buss, D. M., & Schmitt, D. P. (1993). Sexual strategies theory: A contextual evolutionary analysis of human mating. *Psychological Review, 100*, 204–232.

Chodorow, N. (1978). *The reproduction of mothering.* Berkeley: University of California Press.

Cohen, J. (1969). *Statistical power analysis for the behavioral sciences.* San Diego, CA: Academic Press.

Deaux, K. & Lewis, L. L. (1984) Structure of gender stereotypes: Interrelationships among components and gender label. *Journal of Personality and Social Psychology, 46,* 991–1004.

DeLamater, J. (1987). A sociological perspective. In J. H. Geer & W. T. O'Donohue (Eds.), *Theories of human sexuality* (pp. 237–255). New York: Plenum Press.

DeLamater, J., & MacCorquodale, P. (1979). *Premarital sexuality: Attitudes, relationships, behavior.* Madison: University of Wisconsin Press.

Eagly, A. H. (1987). *Sex differences in social behavior: A social role interpretation.* Hillside, NJ: Erlbaum.

Eagly, A. H., & Crowley, M. (1986). Gender and helping behavior: A meta-analytic review of the social psychological literature. *Psychological Bulletin, 100,* 283–308.

Eagly, A. H., & Steffen, V. J. (1968). Gender and aggressive behavior: A meta-analytic review of the social psychological literature. *Psychological Bulletin, 100,* 309–330.

Frevent, R. et al. (1981). *The relationship of sex education to sexual behavior, attitudes, and knowledge.* Paper presented at the annual meeting of the American Education Research Association, Los Angeles. (ERIC Document Reproduction Service No. ED 579).

Gagnon, J. H., & Simon, W. (1973). *Sexual conduct: The social origins of human sexuality.* Chicago: Aldine.

Gilligan, C. (1982). *In a different voice: Psychological theory and women's development.* Cambridge, MA: Harvard University Press.

Gordon, M., & Shankweiler, P. (1971). Different equals less: Female sexuality in recent marriage manuals. *Journal of Marriage and the Family, 33,* 459–466.

Hall, J. A. (1984). *Nonverbal sex differences.* Baltimore: John Hopkins University Press.

Hedges, L. V. (1981). Distribution theory for Glass' estimator of effect size and related estimators. *Journal of Education Statistics, 6,* 108–128.

Hedges, L. V., & Becker, B. J. (1986). Statistical method in the meta-analysis of research on gender differences. In J. S. Hyde & M. C. Linn (Eds.), *The psychology of gender: Advances through meta-analysis* (pp. 14–50). Baltimore: John Hopkins Press.

Hedges, L. V., & Olkin, I. (1985). *Statistical methods for meta-analysis.* San Diego, CA: Academic Press.

Hendrick, S., & Hendrick, C. (1987). Multidimensionality of sexual attitudes. *Journal of Sex Research, 23,* 502–526.

Hunt, M. (1974). *Sexual behavior in the 1970s.* Chicago: Playboy Press.

Hyde, J. S. (1984). How large are gender differences in aggression? A developmental meta-analysis. *Developmental Psychology, 20,* 722–736.

Hyde, J. S., Fennema, E., & Lamon, S. J. (1990). Gender differences in mathematics performance: A meta-analysis. *Psychological Bulletin, 107,* 139–155.

Hyde, J. S., & Linn, M. C. (1988). Gender differences in verbal ability: A meta-analysis. *Psychological Bulletin, 104,* 53–69.

Kinsey, A. C., Pomeroy, W. B., Martin, C. E., & Gebhard, P. H. (1953). *Sexual behavior in the human female.* Philadelphia: W. B. Saunders.

Klassen, A. D., Williams, C. J., & Levitt, E. E. (1989). *Sex and morality in the U.S.: An empirical enquiry under the auspices of the Kinsey Institute.* Middletown, CT: Wesleyan University Press.

Linn, M. C., & Petersen, A. C. (1985). Emergence and characterization of sex differences in spatial ability: A meta-analysis. *Child Development, 56,* 1479–1498.

LoPiccolo, J., & Lobitz, C. (1972). The role of masturbation in the treatment of sexual dysfunction. *Archives of Sexual Behavior, 2,* 163–171.

LoPiccolo, J., & Stock, W. E. (1986). Treatment of sexual dysfunction. *Journal of Consulting and Clinical Psychology, 54,* 158–167.

Maccoby, E. E., & Jacklin, C. N. (1974). *The psychology of sex differences.* Stanford, CA: Stanford University Press.

Miller, P. Y., & Simon, W. (1974). Adolescent sexual behavior: Context and change. *Social Problems, 22,* 58–76.

Mischel, W. (1966). A social-learning view of sex differences in behavior. In E. E. Maccoby (Ed.), *The development of sex differences* (pp.56–81). Stanford, CA: Stanford University Press.

Mosher, D. L. (1979). Sex guilt and sex myths in college men and women. *Journal of Sex Research, 15,* 224–234.

Mosher, D. L., & Tomkins, S. S. (1988). Scripting the Macho Man: Hypermasculine socialization and enculturation. *Journal of Ses Research, 25,* 60–84.

Reiss, I. L. (1960). *Premarital sexual standards in America.* New York: Free Press.

Rosenkrantz, P., Vogel, S., Bee, H., Broverman, I., & Boverman, D. M. (1968). Sex-role stereotypes and self-concepts in college students. *Journal of Consulting and Clinical Psychology, 32*, 287–295.

Smuts, B. (1992). Male aggression against women: An evolutionary perspective. *Human Nature, 3,* 1–44.

Sorensen, R. C. (1972). *Adolescent sexuality in contemporary America: Personal values and sexual behavior ages thirteen to nineteen.* New York: Harcourt Brace Jovanovich.

Sprecher, S., McKinney, K., & Orbuch, T. L. (1987). Has the double standard disappeared? An experimental test. *Social Psychology Quarterly, 50,* 24–31.

Symons, D. (1979). *The evolution of human sexuality.* New York: Oxford University Press.

Symons, D. (1987). An evolutionary approach: Can Darwin's view of life shed light on human sexuality? In J. H. Geer & W. T. O'Donohue (Eds.), *Theories of human sexuality* (pp. 91–126). New York: Plenum Press.

Travis, C. B., & Yeager, C. P. (1991). Sexual selection, parental investment, and sexism. *Journal of Social Issues, 47*(3), 117–130.

Trivers, R. L. (1972). Parental investment and sexual selection. In B. Campbell (Ed.), *Sexual selection and the descent of man* (pp. 136–179). Chicago: Aldine.

Weinberg, M. S., Swensson, R. G., & Hammersmith, S. K. (1983). Sexual autonomy and the status of women: Models of female sexuality in U.S. sex manuals from 1950 to 1980. *Social Problems, 30,* 312–324.

Wood, F. W. (1990). *An American profile–Opinions and behavior, 1972–1979.* Detroit, MI: Gale Research.

Zuckerman, M. (1973). Scales for sex experience for males and female. *Journal of Consulting and Clinical Psychology, 41,* 27–29.

READING 2

Gender Differences in Receptivity to Sexual Offers

Russell D. Clark III • Florida State University
Elaine Hatfield • University of Hawaii at Manoa

According to cultural stereotypes, men are more eager for sex than are women; women are more likely to set limits on such activity. In this paper, we review the work of theorists who have argued in favor of this proposition and review the interview and correlational data which support this contention. Finally, we report two experimental tests of this hypothesis.

In these experiments, conducted in 1978 and 1982, male and female confederates of average attractiveness approached potential partners with one of three requests: "Would you go out tonight?" or "Will you come over to my apartment? or "Would you go to bed with me?" The great majority of men were willing to have a sexual liaison with the women who approached them. Women were not. Not one woman agreed to a sexual liaison. Many possible reasons for this marked gender difference were discussed.

These studies were run in 1978 and 1982. It has since become important to track how the threat of AIDS is affecting men and women's willingness to date, come to an apartment, or to engage in casual sexual relations.

General Background

According to cultural stereotypes, men are eager for sexual intercourse; it is women who set limits on such activity (see McCormick, 1979; Hatfield, 1983; and Peplau, 1983). Theorists from a variety of perspectives have agreed with this observation. What they disagree about is *why* such gender differences exist. Researchers have collected an abundance of interview and correlational data which provide some support for this contention. No experimental support for this hypothesis exists, however. In this research, we report an experimental test of this proposition.

Let us begin by reviewing existing theory and data.

The Sociobiological Perspective

Traditionally, biological determinists such as Sigmund Freud argued that biology is destiny and that interest in sexual activities is determined primarily by genes, anatomy, and hormones. Early sociobiologists assumed that men and women are genetically programmed to be differentially interested in sexual experience/restraint (see Hagen, 1979; Kendrick, 1987; Symons, 1979; or Wilson, 1975). Symons (1979) stated "the comparison of males and females is perhaps the most powerful available means of ordering the diversity of data on human sexuality" (p. 4). His sociobiological argument proceeded as follows: according to evolutionary biology, animals inherit those characteristics which insure that they will transmit as many of their genes to the next generation as possible. It is to both men's and women's advantage to produce as many surviving children as possible. But men and women differ in one critical respect—in order to produce a child, men need only to invest a trivial amount of energy; a single man can conceivably father an almost unlimited number of children. Conversely, a woman can give birth to and raise only a limited number of children; it is to her advantage to insure those few children she does conceive survive. Symons observed: "The enormous sex differences in minimum parental investment and in reproductive opportunities and constraints explain why *Homo Sapiens*, a species with only moderate sex differences in structure, exhibit profound sex differences in psyche" (p.27).

Among the differences Symons cited are: (1) men desire a variety of sex partners; women do not; (2) for men, "sexual attractiveness" equals "youth." For women, "sexual attractiveness" equals "political and economic power"; (3) men have every reason to actively pursue women (they are genetically programmed to impregnate as many women as possible. Women have every reason to be "coy.") It takes time to decide if a man is a good genetic risk—is likely to be nurturant, protective and productive. In all societies, women copulate as a service to men, not vice versa.

Recently, socio-biologists and social psychologists have discovered that the process is a bit more complicated than was initially thought. Kurt Freund and his colleagues (1983 and 1986) observe that courtship normally consists of four phases: (a) initial appraisal and location of a potential partner, (b) pretactile interaction (for example, smiling at someone, laughing, flirting, talking), (c) tactile interaction (touching, embracing), and (d) bringing about genital union. A number of authors have found that women have a far more active role in the first three stages of courtship than the early socio-biologists thought. They do far more than serve as "gatekeepers" who stop action (see Gaulier, Travis, & Allgeier, 1986; Moore, 1985; and Perper, 1985). For example, Moore (1985) found that in a singles bar, it is women who initiate interaction. They signal their interest in a variety of ways—by smiling, laughing, tossing their heads, or hiking up their skirts. Sometimes they "parade" (they walk across the room with an exaggerated swing of their hips, stomach held in, head held high, back arched, so their breasts are pushed out). They then "approach"—they go up to men and position themselves within two feet of them. The next move is up to the men. If the men are interested, the two begin to talk. Eventually, however, it is the men who must "formally" initiate sexual relations, especially the first time sexual intercourse occurs. After that, although men generally initiate sexual relations, women are freer to share initiation.

The Cultural-Contingency Perspective

At the other end of the spectrum are those who argue that sexual behavior is learned (see Bernard, 1973; Byrne & Byrne, 1977; Firestone, 1970; Foucault, 1978; Griffitt & Hatfield, 1984; Rubin, 1973; Tavris & Offir, 1977; Safilios-Rothschild, 1977; or Hatfield & Walster, 1978). According to this model, men and women simply learn the "scripts" that are appropriate for initiating sexual encounters and responding to sexual offers. They simply learn to be as sexually adventuresome or cautious as their culture expects them to be. Cultural rewards and punishments shape behavior. Thus, if men are more adventuresome than women, it is simply because the culture encourages them to be so.

In the late 1970s, when this study was planned, a number of feminist and Marxist scholars were speculating that the socio-political context might shape societal rewards and punishments. Socio-political pressures might have at least some impact on who is supposed to be sexual/who is forbidden to be, who is punished/who is not for violating sexual rules, and even what kinds of foreplay and sexual positions are considered to be "normal." Since this is a male-dominated society, they continued, perhaps existing sexual norms tend to meet the needs of men. Perhaps it is men who are encouraged to express themselves sexually, women who are punished for doing so. It is the style of intercourse men prefer (e.g., the "missionary" position) that is considered normal; the activities that women prefer (e.g., "cuddling," cunnilingus) that are neglected. No wonder then that men find sex in its common forms more appealing than do women (see Firestone, 1970 and Allgeier & McCormick, 1983). (In the 1980s, of course, the power of "socio-political pressures" pales before the threat of AIDS, which makes sexual behavior equally risky for both men and women. One might predict, then, that from the late 1980s into the 1990s, men and women will become far more conservative about engaging in sexual activity. Thus, gender differences in receptivity to sexual offers may soon disappear.)

Regardless of theorists' debate as to *why* men and women may differ in their enthusiasm for sex versus their tendencies to set limits on sexual activity, there is some evidence suggesting that their observations may be correct—even at the present moment, men and women still seem to be differentially interested in sexual activities. Let us review some of these data.

Gender Differences in Interest in Erotic Literature and Tapes

Traditionally, erotica has been written for men. The assumption has been that women are not interested in such things. Kinsey (1948 and 1953) found that the women in his sample were considerably less likely than men to have ever been exposed to erotica, and even when both sexes were familiar with such literature, men reported being more aroused by it then did women. For example, 47% of the men reported having been aroused by erotic stories. Only 14% of the women reported similar levels of arousal. Izard and Caplan (1974), too, found that more men than women reported interest in and arousal in response to erotic passages.

Recently, however, researchers have begun to ask both men and women about their feelings *and* to get objective measures of their psychological arousal in response to erotica. (To do this they generally use two instruments: a penile strain-gauge and a photo-plethysmograph.) In such studies, researchers generally find that although men and women often *report* differential interest in erotica, the objective evidence suggests that both are equally aroused. For example, Veitch and Griffitt (1980) found no gender differences in response to literary erotica. In fact, some data suggest that explicit portrayals of sexual activity may evoke equal or greater erotic responsiveness in women than in men. Jakobovits (1965) found that women consistently rated "hard core" erotic stories as more interesting and sexually stimulating than did men. Heiman (1977) found that both men and women judged audiotapes of exclusively "romantic" encounters less arousing than audiotapes describing either romantic *and* erotic or exclusively erotic sexual encounters. Women actually rated the explicit erotic audiotapes as more arousing than did men. Heiman found no sex differences on the physiological measures of sexual arousal.

Gender Differences in Responsiveness to Erotic Films

Men seem to be more interested in erotica than are women. Kenrick and his colleagues (1980) gave men and women the chance to sign up for an experiment involving erotica. Men were more likely to sign up for such an experiment than were women. Sex-typed women were especially reluctant to participate in such experiments.

Several studies have documented that men may well be more responsive to erotic films than are women, as well (see, for example, Abelson, 1970; Berger, Gagnon, & Simon, 1970; Byrne & Lamberth, 1970; Griffitt, 1975; Heiman, 1977; Izard & Caplan, 1974; Jakobovits, 1965; Kinsey et al., 1953; Mosher, 1973; Schmidt & Segush, 1970; Steele & Walker, 1974). Typical of these findings are those of Abelson et al. (1970) who found that only 7% of women but 20% of men reported that they become aroused when viewing explicit pictures and stag films.

Hatfield et al. (1978) showed 614 men and women sexually explicit films of males and females masturbating or engaged in homosexual or heterosexual acts. They asked two questions: First, do men and women differ in how easily they become aroused by sexually explicit films? The answer to this first question was "No." The authors measured sexual arousal in two ways: via the Byrne-Sheffield (1965) Feeling Scale and via Griffitt's (1975) Physiological Arousal Scale. On both these measures, men's and women's level of arousal was virtually identical. Secondly, they asked whether men and women differ in their perceptions of how arousing the male versus female actors were. Here the answer is "Yes." Both men and women were most sexually aroused by seeing a person of the opposite sex masturbating or having intercourse. They were least aroused by seeing someone of their own sex engaged in these same activities.

Gender Differences in Sexual Activity

Traditionally, theorists have assumed that sex is far more important for men than for women.

Kinsey and his colleagues (1948 and 1953) tried to assess the sexual activity of men compared with women throughout their lives. They asked men and women how often they had an orgasm during a typical week—regardless of whether they achieved it by way of sex dreams, petting, masturbation, sexual intercourse, homosexual encounters, or contacts with animals.

They found that: (1) indeed, men did seem to engage in more sexual activity than women; and (2) men and women had strikingly different sexual histories. At 18, it was usually the men who pushed to have sex. Most men were as sexually expressive at 15 as they would ever be. In fact, according to Masters and Johnson (1966 and 1970) 25% of men are impotent by age sixty-five and 50% are impotent by age seventy-five. Women's experience was markedly different. Most women are slow to begin sexual activity. At 15, most women are quite inactive. Sometime between the ages of 16 and 20, they begin to be more sexually active. Their sexual interest seems to remain high until their late 40s. In commenting on women's sexual histories, Kinsey (1953) observed:

> One of the tragedies which appears in a number of the marriages originates in the fact that the male may be most desirous of sexual contact in his early years, while the responses of the females are still underdeveloped and while she is still struggling to free herself from the acquired inhibitions which prevent her from participating freely in the marital activity. But over the years most females become less inhibited and develop an interest in sexual relations, which they may maintain until they are in their fifties or even sixties. But by then the responses of the average male may have dropped so considerably that his interest in coitus, and especially in coitus with a wife who had previously objected to the frequencies of his requests, may have sharply declined. (pp. 353–354)

In Kinsey's day, a double standard existed. Men were allowed, if not encouraged, to get sex whenever and wherever they could. Women were supposed to save themselves for marriage (see Baker, 1974; Ehrmann, 1959; Kaats & Davis, 1970; Reiss, 1967; Schofield, 1965; or Sorenson, 1973). In light of the double standard, it was not surprising that Ehrmann (1959) found that both men and women college students reported that it was the man who was more likely to initiate sex and it was the woman who was more likely to resist sexual advances.

More recent evidence suggests that traditional standards, although changing, are not dead. For example, the most recent data indicate that it is almost always men who initiate a sexual relationship. While research indicates that contemporary college students reject a sexual double standard (Hopkins, 1977; Komarovsky, 1976; Peplau, Rubin, & Hill, 1976), this new single standard does not seem to have changed the cultural stereotype of males as sexual initiator and female as limit setter (McCormick, 1979). In a recent study, Peplau et al. (1977) found that, among unmarried students, the woman serves as the "gatekeeper"; she has the power to veto sexual activity. Once the couple begins to have sexual relations, however, the man has more to say about the type and frequency of sexual activity.

There is some compelling evidence that a single standard is emerging with regard to sexual *experience*, however. Following Kinsey, researchers (Ehrmann, 1959; Schofield, 1965; Reiss, 1967; Sorenson, 1972; and DeLamater & MacCorquodale, 1980) interviewed samples of young people about their sexual behavior: Had they ever necked? At what age did they begin? Have they french kissed? fondled their lover's breasts or genitals? had their own genitals fondled? had intercourse? engaged in oral-genital sex? When we compare the data from these studies, we find that, indeed, a sexual revolution *is* occurring. In the early study, men were, in general, far more experienced that were women. By the 1980s, these differences have virtually disappeared. As DeLameter and MacCorquodale (1980) observe:

> . . . there are virtually no differences in the incidence of each of the behaviors. Unlike most earlier studies which generally reported lower frequencies of more intimate activities among females, we find that women are as likely as men to have ever engaged in these behaviors. The only exception occurs with coitus, which women...are less likely to have experienced. (*Among students,* 75% of the men and 60% of women had had intercourse. *Among non-students,* 79% of men and 72% of women had had intercourse.)

DeLameter and MacCorquodale continue:

> Thus, the gender differences in lifetime behavior which were consistently found in studies conducted in the 1950's and 1960's have narrowed considerably. This is also an important finding; it suggests that those models which have emphasized gender as an explanatory variable are no longer valid. (p. 58)

Background of this Research

In most areas of social psychology, the experimental paradigm has been *the* paradigm. It is only recently that a "crisis in social psychology" occurred, and social psychologists have begun to urge one another to supplement laboratory findings with naturalistic observations of people engaged in complex social interactions. Only in the area of human sexuality has the social-psychological tradition been reversed. Until recently, studies of love and sex were taboo (see Berscheid & Hatfield [Walster], 1978). Until recently, scientists have had to rely almost exclusively on interviews and naturalistic studies for their information. Only recently have researchers begun to conduct laboratory experiments (see Byrne & Byrne, 1977).

This laboratory research has paid off. It has had a dramatic impact on our thinking about human sexuality. For example, in 1953 Kensey et al. (1953) took it for granted that males and females were very different in their potential to respond to erotic literature, tapes, and films. "So different . . . that they might be considered different species." By 1978, the experimental research, although far from conclusive, had convinced most investigators that men and women were very similar if not identical in their ability to become aroused by erotica (see Hyde, 1979; Byrne & Byrne, 1977).

To date, there have been few, if any *experimental* studies of men and women caught up in the sexual initiation/rejection process. In real life, the intimacy process is obviously a complex ballet. Officially, the man is supposed to initiate sexual encounters. But how overt can he be? Can he be fairly blunt? Or must he be indirect to be effective (see McCormick, 1979)? Surely, before most men extend a proposition to a woman, they look for some kind of evidence of interest on her part. If, in real life interactions, the man waits until the woman is receptive before issuing an invitation, who is inviting whom? How blunt can the woman be in accepting an invitation? Are most men upset by too much enthusiasm? Would such norm violations lead them to say "No"? Would most men be delighted? Such are the questions that can only be answered by careful experimentation.

We begin simply in the following experiment. We asked a straightforward question: *How receptive are men versus women to sexual invitations?* If a reasonably attractive man or woman approached members of the opposite sex and asked them for a date or a sexual encounter, how would men and women respond? We could envision two very different possibilities:

1. *The traditional hypothesis*: Men and women will respond as the sociobiologists, cultural contingency theorists, and social stereotypes predict they should—women wanting love, men wanting sex from a relationship. Men will readily agree to sexual encounters; women will not. Much of the research we have cited in Section 1 provides support for such a hypothesis.
2. *The androgyny hypothesis*: It may be, however, that men and women are not so different as social stereotypes suggest. Again and again, researchers have found that while men and women *expect* the sexes to respond in very different ways, when real men and real women find themselves caught up in naturalistic settings they respond in much the same way (see Maccoby & Jacklin, 1974; Griffitt & Hatfield, 1984). It may be that *both* men and women turn out to be more receptive to sexual invitations than one might expect. (Data such as DeLameter & MacCorquodale's, 1979, might suggest such an outcome.)

Or, both men and women might be far less receptive that one might expect. Traditionally, men are expected to jump at sexual offers. Women are supposed to turn them down. But some investigators have suggested that both men and women might be afraid of casual sex. For example, Hatfield (Walster) et al. (1973), in a study of men's reactions to "easy to get women," found that men are very uneasy about dating an "easy" woman. They saw such encounters as very risky. Such a woman might be easy to get, but hard to get rid of. She might get serious. Perhaps she would be so oversexed or over-affectionate or "hard-up" in public that she would embarrass you. Your buddies might snicker when they saw you together. After all, they would know perfectly well why you were dating her. And, you might get a disease. (The recent epidemics of herpes and AIDS make these concerns especially salient now and into the future. See Baum, 1987.) These were all reservations that men voiced.

In order to secure an answer to our question, we conducted the following experiments.

Method

Confederates. Study #1 was conducted in 1978 and Study #2 was conducted in 1982. In both studies five college women and four college men from an experimental social psychology class served as experimenters. All had volunteered to approach subjects who were alone at five different locations on campus. The confederates were approximately 22 years of age and were neatly dressed in casual attire. The physical attractiveness of *both* the female and male confederates varied from slightly unattractive to moderately attractive. Ratings of the confederate' attractiveness were found to have no effect on the results and thus we will not discuss this variable further.

Subjects. In both Study #1 and Study #2, subjects were 48 men and 48 women who were on the campus of Florida State University. Sixteen subjects were randomly assigned to each of the six conditions.

Procedure. The confederate stood on one of five college quadrangles, and approached members of the opposite sex, who were total strangers. Only one requester made a request in each area at any one time. The requestors were instructed to approach only subjects who were attractive enough that they would be willing to actually sleep with them, if given the opportunity (assuming, of course, that they were appropriate on other grounds as well). On a scale of 1 to 9 (1 = "Very unattractive"; 9 = "Very attractive"), female confederates rated the male subjects $\bar{M} = 7.30$. Male confederates rated female subjects $\bar{M} = 7.70$. (These ratings were not significantly different; $t < 1.00$.) The confederates' ratings make it clear that they only selected "moderately" to "very attractive" male and female subjects.

Once a subject was selected, the requestor approached him/her and said: "I have been noticing you around campus. I find you to be very attractive." The confederate then asked subjects one of three questions: "Would you go out with me tonight?" "would you come over to my apartment tonight?" or "Would you go to bed with me tonight?" Thus, this procedure resulted in a 2 × 3 factorial design [Sex of requestor (2 levels) × Type of request (3 levels)].

The requestor carried a notebook which had one of the three requests written on a separate page. The type of request was randomly determined for each requestor. After the selection of a subject, each requestor flipped a page in the notebook to see what type of request was to be made.

The requests were made during weekdays to decrease the probability of the subjects refusing because they had dates or other social obligations. Subjects were not approached between class periods or during rainy weather.

Subjects were debriefed and thanked for their participation.

Table 2.1. Study #1, 1978 Percentage of Compliance With Each Request

	Type of request		
Sex of Requestor	Date	Apartment	Bed
Male	56%	6%	0%
Female	50%	69%	75%

Results and Discussion

A 2 × 3 × 2 multidimensional chi-square analysis was used to analyze the data (Winer, 1971). In Study #1, conducted in 1978, the results indicated that men were more likely to say yes to each type of invitation than were women (65% versus 21%, χ^2 (1) = 18.78, $p < .001$). However, as can be clearly seen in Table 2.1, Sex of requestor/Sex of subject interacted with Type of invitation, χ^2 (2) = 29.33, $p < .001$. Whereas, both males and females were willing to go out on a date, it was only the males who agreed to go to the female's apartment and go to bed with her, χ^2 (1) = 9.30, $p < .01$ and χ^2 12.52, $p < .001$, respectively.

In Study #2, conducted in 1982, we secured results that were almost identical with those described above. Once again, men were more likely to respond positively to each type of request than were women (63% versus 17%, χ^2 (1) = 21.08, $p < .001$). However, once again, as can be seen in Table 2.2, Sex of requestor/Sex of subject inter-

Table 2.2. Study #2, 1982 Percentage of Compliance With Each Request

	Type of request		
Sex of Requestor	Date	Apartment	Bed
Male	50%	0%	0%
Female	50%	69%	69%

acted with the Type of request, χ^2 (2) = 23.65, p < .001. Whereas, both males and females were equally willing to accept a date, χ^2 (1) = 0, n.s., it was only males who agreed to go to the female's apartment (χ^2 (1) = 16.76, p < .001) or go to bed with her (χ^2 (1) = 16.76, p<.001).

In both studies, we found then that men and women responded as *traditionalists* would expect them to. Men readily accepted a sexual invitation. Women were extremely reluctant to do so.

We now know that this is so. We are not quite sure *why* this is so. It may be that, as sociobiologists suggest, women are eager for love and commitment. Men are eager for sexual activity. Such theorizing is consistent with the data. Both men and women were willing to date a total stranger. (When one goes out on a date, one has the opportunity to assess the probability that a loving relationship could occur.) Women were unwilling to go to a man's apartment or to have sexual relations. Men, on the other hand, were surprisingly willing to go to a strange women's apartment or to bed. (In fact, they were less willing to accept an invitation to date than to have sexual relations!)

Consistent with this interpretation were the subjects' reactions to the requests. In general, the female experimenters reported that men were at ease with the request. They would say "Why do we have to wait until tonight?" or "I cannot tonight, but tomorrow would be fine." The men that said "No" even gave apologies, i.e., "I'm married" or "I'm going with someone." In contrast, the women's response to the intimate requests from males was "You've got to be kidding," or "What is wrong with you? Leave me alone."

Of course, the sociological interpretation—that women are interested in love while men are interested in sex—is not the only possible interpretation of these data. It may be, of course, that *both* men and women were equally interested in sex, but that men associated fewer risks with accepting a sexual invitation than did women. Men may be more confident of their ability to fight back physical assault than are women. Also, the remnants of the double standard may make women afraid to accept the man's invitation.

Regardless of *why* we secured these data, however, the existence of these pronounced gender differences is interesting.

Researchers may well choose to replicate this study sometime in the next five years to ascertain what impact the AIDS epidemic has on the presiding patterns of results. There is some anecdotal evidence that in such major cities as New York, Chicago, Los Angeles, etc. both men and women have become extremely wary of casual sex (see Baum, 1987). This should, of course, markedly alter the preceding pattern of results. On the other hand, some researchers (Weinstein, 1980 and 1984) have found that young people still underestimate the riskiness of their "unsafe" sexual practices and that most young people tend to see themselves as invulnerable to negative events. In that case, the preceding pattern of results might be expected to continue into the future.

REFERENCES

Abelson, H., Cohen, R., Heaton, E., & Slider, C. (1970). *Public attitudes toward and experience with erotic materials.* Technical reports of the Commission on Obscenity and Pornography (Vol. 6). Washington, DC: U. S. Government Printing Office.

Allgeier, E. R., & McCormick, N. B. (Eds.) (1983). *Changing boundaries: Gender roles and sexual behavior.* Palo Alto, CA: Mayfield Publishing.

Baker, J. J. (1974). *The effects of inequity on heterosexual behavior: A test for compensation in unequitable dating relationship.* Unpublished manuscript, University of Wisconsin, Madison, WI.

Baum, A. (Ed.) (March 1987). Special issue on acquired immune deficiency syndrome (AIDS). *Journal of Applied Social Psychology, 17*(3), 189–350.

Berger, A., Gagnon, J., & Simon W. (1970). *Pornography: High school and college years.* Technical reports of the Commission on Obscenity and Pornography (Vol. 7). Washington, DC: U.S. Government Printing Office.

Bernard, J. (1973). *The future of marriage.* New York: Bantam.

Berscheid, E., & Hatfield (Walster), E. (1978). *Interpersonal attraction (Second edition).* Reading, MA: Addison-Wesley.

Brady, J., & Levitt, E. (1965). The relation of sexual preferences to sexual experiences, *The Psychological Record, 15,* 377–384.

Byrne, D., & Lamberth, J. (1970). *The effect of erotic stimuli on sex arousal, evaluative responses, and subsequent behavior.* Technical reports of the Commission on Obscenity and Pornography (Vol. 8). Washington, DC: U.S. Government Printing Office.

Byrne, D., & Byrne, A. (1977). *Exploring human sexuality.* New York: Crowell.

DeLameter, J., & MacCorquodale, P. (1980). *Premarital sexuality: Attitudes, relationships, behavior.* Madison: University of Wisconsin Press.

Ehrmann, W. (1959). *Premarital dating behavior.* New York: Holt, Reinhart & Winston.

Firestone, S. (1970). *The dialectic of sex.* New York: Morrow Paperbacks.

Foucault, M. (1978). *The history of sexuality. Vol. 1: An introduction.* New York: Pantheon Books.

Freund, K., & Blanchard, R. (1968). The concept of courtship disorder. *Journal of Sex and Marital Therapy, 12,* 79–92.

Freund, K., Scher, H., & Hucher, S. (1983). The courtship disorders. *Archives of Sexual Behaviors, 5,* 415–423.

Gaulier, B., Travis, S. K., & Allgeier, E. R. (June 1986). Perceptive behavior and the use of behavioral cues in heterosexual courtship. In the symposium (C. Muehlenhard, Chair), *Miscommunication between male and female students.* Presented at the Annual Meetings of the Mid-continent Region of the Society for the Scientific Study of Sex, Madison, WI.

Griffitt, W. (1975). Sexual experience and sexual responsiveness: Sex differences. *Archives of Sexual Behavior, 4,* 529–540.

Griffitt, W., & Hatfield, E. (9184). Gender identities and gender roles: Psychological considerations. *Human sexual behavior* (pp. 192–212). Glenview, IL: Scott, Foresman.

Hagen, R. (1979). *The bio-sexual factor.* New York: Doubleday.

Hatfield, E. (1983). What do women want from love and sex? In E. R . Allgeier & N. B. McCormick (Eds.), *Changing boundaries* (pp. 106–134). Palo Alto, CA: Mayfield Publishing.

Hatfield, E., Sprecher, S., & Traupmann, J. (1978). Men's and women's reactions to sexually explicit films: A serendipitous finding. *Archives of Sexual Behavior, 7,* 583–592.

Hatfield (Walster), E., Walster, G. W., Piliavin, J., & Schmidt, L. (1973). Playing hard-to-get: Understanding an elusive phenomenon. *Journal of Personality and Social Psychology, 26,* 113–121.

Hatfield, E., & Walster, G. W. (1978). *A new look at love.* Lantham, MA. University Press of America.

Heiman, J. (1977). A psychophsiological exploration of sexual arousal patterns in females and males. *Psychophysiology, 14,* 266–274.

Hopkins, J. R. (1977). Sexual behavior in adolescence. *Journal of Social Issues, 33,* 67–85.

Hyde, J. S. (1986). *Understanding human sexuality. (Third edition).* New York: McGraw-Hill.

Izard, C., & Caplan, S. (1974). Sex differences in emotional responses to erotic literature. *Journal of Consulting and Clinical Psychology, 42,* 468.

Jakobovits, L. (1965). Evaluational reactions to erotic literature. *Psychological Reports, 16,* 985–994.

Kaats, G., & Davis, K. E. (1970). The dynamics of sexual behavior of college students, *Journal of Marriage and the Family, 32,* 390–399.

Kenrick, D. J. (1987). Gender, genes, and the social environment: A biosocial interactionist perspective. In P. Shaver & C. Hendrick (Eds.), *Sex and gender* (pp. 14–43). Newbury Park, CA: Sage Publications.

Kenrick, D. T., Stringfield, D. O., Wagenhals, W. L., Dahl, R. H., & Ransdall, H. J. (1980). Sex differences, androgyny, and approach responses to erotica: A new variation on old volunteer problems. *Journal of Personality and Social Psychology, 38,* 517–524.

Kinsey, A., Pomeroy, W. B., & Martin, C. (1948). *Sexual behavior in the human male.* Philadelphia: W. B. Saunders.

Kinsey, A., Pomeroy, W. B., & Martin, C. (1953). *Sexual behavior in the human female.* Philadelphia: W. B. Saunders.

Komarovsky, M. (1976). *Dilemmas of masculinity.* New York: Norton.

Maccoby, E. E., & Jacklin, C. N. (1974). *The psychology of sex differences.* Stanford, CA: Stanford University Press.

Masters, W. H., & Johnson, V. E. (1966). *Human sexual response.* Boston: Little, Brown.

Masters, W. H., & Johnson, V. E. (1970). *Human sexual inadequacy.* Boston: Little, Brown.

McCormick, N. B. (1979). Come-ons and put-offs: Unmarried students' strategies for having and avoiding sexual intercourse. *Psychology of Women Quarterly, 4,* 194–211.

Moore, M. M. (1985). Nonverbal courtship patterns in women: Context and consequences. *Ethology and Sociobiology, 6,* 201–212.

Mosher, D. (1973). Sex differences, sex experience, sex guilt, and explicitly sexual films. *Journal of Social Issues, 29,* 95–112.

Peplau, L. A. (1983). Roles and gender. In H. H. Kelley, E. Berscheid, A. Christensen, J. H. Harvey, T. L. Huston, G. Levinger, E. McClintock, L. A. Peplau, & D. R. Peterson (Eds.), *Close relationships.* San Francisco: W. H. Freeman.

Peplau, L., Rubin, Z., & Hill, C. (Nov. 1976). The sexual balance of power. *Psychology Today, 10, (6),* 142–151.

Peplau, L., Rubin, Z., & Hill, C. (1977). Sexual intimacy in dating relationships. *Journal of Social Issues, 33,* 86–109.

Perper, T. (1985). *Sex signals: The biology of love.* Philadelphia, PA: ISI Press.

Reiss, I. L. (1967) *The social context of premarital sexual permissiveness.* New York: Holt, Rinehart & Winston.

Rubin, Z. (1973). *Liking and loving.* New York: Holt, Rinehart & Winston.

Safilios-Rothschild, C. (1976). A macro-and-micro-examination of family power and love: An exchange model. *Journal of Marriage and the Family, 38,* 355–362.

Schmidt, G., & Sigush, V. (1970). Sex differences in response to psycho-sexual stimulation by films and slides. *The Journal of Sex Research, 6,* 268–283.

Schofield, M. (1965). *The sexual behavior of young people.* Boston: Little, Brown.

Sorenson, R. C. (1973). *Adolescent sexuality in contemporary America.* New York: World Publishing.

Steele, D., & Walker, E. (1974). Male and female differences in reaction to erotic stimuli as related to sexual adjustment. *Archives of Sexual Behavior, 3,* 459–470.

Symons, D. (1979). *The evolution of human sexuality.* New York: Oxford Press.

Tavris, C., & Offir, C. (1977). *The longest war: Sex differences in perspective.* New York: Harcourt Brace Jovanovich.

Veitch, R., & Griffit, W. (1980). The perception of erotic arousal in men and women by same- and-opposite-sex peers. *Sex Roles, 6,* 723–733.

Weinstein, N. D. (1980). Unrealistic optimism about future life events. *Journal of Personality and Social Psychology, 39,* 806–820.

Weinstein, N. D. (1984). Why it won't happen to me: Perceptions of risk factors and susceptibility. *Health Psychology, 3,* 431–457.

Wilson, E. O. (1975). *Sociobiology.* Cambridge, MA: The Belknap Press.

Winer, B. J. (1971). *Statistical principles in experimental designs.* New York: McGraw-Hill.

INTRODUCTION TO PART 2

Nature and Culture

We turn now to one of the oldest and thorniest questions about sexuality, namely the nature-nurture debate. DeLamater and Hyde (1998) concluded that theories in sexuality can be divided into two main camps. One, the "essentialist" camp, emphasizes innate dispositions. In essence, you are born a certain way and with certain sexual appetites, and culture plays only a small role. The other, the "social constructionist" camp, regards biological foundations as merely a vague and general basis and emphasizes social, cultural, and situational influences. Who desires to do what to whom is seen as depending on what people have learned and how they have been trained, rather than stemming from biologically innate patterns, according to the latter view.

The social constructionist approach dominated sexuality research in the 1970s, and probably for a very good reason. That decade represented the high-water mark of the sexual revolution, and the dramatic changes in sexual behavior that had occurred in a very short time seemed to prove that sexuality was a matter of culture rather than nature. For example, gender differences in sexual attitudes and behaviors had diminished substantially in the preceding decades, and many people thought that they would continue to drop until they had all but disappeared.

During the 1970s, however, some thinkers began to apply evolutionary theory to human behavior, and these approaches tended to emphasize sexuality because of its central importance in evolution. Indeed, the old Darwinian emphasis on "survival of the fittest" in natural selection had been to some extent supplanted by a new emphasis on reproduction, because what counts in evolution is whether you pass along your genes, not how long you live. An organism might live for five hundred years, but if it fails to reproduce it will be gone from the gene pool.

The article by Buss and Schmitt (1993) represents one of the most powerful and comprehensive statements of the evolutionary approach to human sexuality. Building on the ground-breaking work by Symons (1979) and Trivers (1985), as well as on Buss's own program of research, Buss and Schmitt propose a sweeping theory about sexual behavior based on evolutionary theory. The differences are rooted in the different reproductive goals that men and women have. Although both men and women have been selected by evolution to favor modes of action that will pass along their genes effectively, men and women differ in how they go about this. In particular, reproduction is inevitably costly and burdensome for women. In order to have a child, a woman must contend with nine months of pregnancy and the considerable physical discomfort and incapacity that this requires. Then she must give birth, which throughout history has been fraught with risk of complications and even death. After giving birth, the woman tends to remain tied to the child by its needs and demands. In contrast, it is possible for a man to have sex and create a pregnancy without having any further involvement in the process after he ejaculates. A single man can potentially father dozens of children in a single year, whereas each pregnancy takes almost an entire year of a woman's life.

Buss and Schmitt take these and a few other basic, biological facts and elaborate them into a comprehensive theory about how men and women will differ in their approach to sex. They elaborate them by distinguishing between short-term and long-term mating goals. Even within the same gender, people may use different criteria for selecting a partner for a brief sexual fling than for choosing a partner for a potentially lifelong relationship.

The other article in this group proposes a novel answer to the nature-nurture question. Baumeister (2000) proposed that the relative influence of nature and culture differs by gender, with female sexuality being relatively more cultural whereas male sexuality is more natural. The term *erotic plasticity* is used to describe the degree to which a person's sexual desires are shaped by social, cultural, and situational factors, and Baumeister concludes that women have higher erotic plasticity than men.

Why should men and women differ in their degree of erotic plasticity? Baumeister's review was much more thorough and conclusive in concluding that the difference exists than in explaining why it may have arisen. His article was published along with two commentaries that tackled this problem in different ways. One, by Anderson et al. (2000), argued that the difference may well be rooted in innate, biological differences and indeed criticized Baumeister's article for not giving sufficient prominence to evolutionary factors in his theorizing. The other, by Hyde and Durik (2000), took the opposite tack and proposed that social, cultural factors could be responsible for the difference in plasticity. In fact, Hyde and Durik emphasized one particular factor, namely the gender difference in social power, as a potential explanation for everything Baumeister described. Hyde and Durik suggested that women have had less political power and have therefore been generally at the mercy of men, which explains their greater willingness to change in response to external influences. Responding to these, Baumeister, Campbell, Catanese, and Tice (2000) argued that the available evidence was not sufficient to support either approach and reiterated that the difference in plasticity is far better established than the reasons for it.

REFERENCES

Andersen, B. L., Cyranowski, J. M., & Aarestad, S. (2000). Beyond artificial, sex-linked distinctions to conceptualize female sexuality: Comment on Baumeister (2000). *Psychological Bulletin, 126,* 380–384.

Baumeister, R. F. (2000). Gender differences in erotic plasticity: The female sex drive as socially flexible and responsive. *Psychological Bulletin, 126,* 347–374.

Baumeister, R. F., Catanese, K. R., Campbell, W. K., & Tice, D. M. (2000). Nature, culture, and explanations for erotic plasticity: Reply to Andersen, Cyranowski, and Aarestad and to Hyde and Durik. *Psychological Bulletin, 126,* 385–389.

Buss, D. M., & Schmitt, D. P. (1993). Sexual strategies theory: An evolutionary perspective on human mating. *Psychological Review, 100,* 204–232.

DeLamater, J. D., & Hyde, J. S. (1998). Essentialism vs. social constructionism in the study of human sexuality. *Journal of Sex Research, 35,* 10–18.

Hyde, J. S., & Durik, A. M. (2000). Gender differences in erotic plasticity—evolutionary or social forces? Comment on Baumeister (2000). *Psychological Bulletin, 126,* 375–399.

Symons, D. (1978). *The evolution of human sexuality.* New York: Oxford.

Trivers, R. (1985). *Social evolution.* Menlo Park, CA: Benjamin/Cummings.

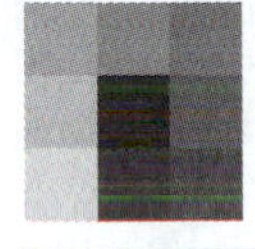

Discussion Questions

1. What factors do you regard as most important for choosing someone to marry?
2. What factors would you emphasize most if you were able to choose anyone you wanted for a one-week sexual affair?
3. Explain the differences in the criteria you listed in answering the previous two questions — that is, what factors are more important in a spouse than in a temporary lover, and vice versa?
4. Could the differences that Buss and Schmitt describe have been created by socialization and social roles?
5. What advantages might there be to having greater erotic plasticity? What disadvantages?
6. Can we generalize from the difference in erotic plasticity to other, nonsexual behaviors? That is, are women more responsive than men to social and cultural influences in other spheres of action?
7. Suggest ways of integrating natural and cultural explanations for sexual behavior. Is there a reason why women might have evolved to be more responsive than men to cultural influences?

Suggested Readings

Abramson, P., & Pinkerton, S. (Eds.) (1995). *Sexual nature sexual culture*. Chicago, IL: University of Chicago Press. This volume contains chapters written by different experts and offering an excellent assortment of perspectives on the nature-nurture debate.

Andersen, B. L., Cyranowski, J. M., & Aarestad, S. (2000). Beyond artificial, sex-linked distinctions to conceptualize female sexuality: Comment on Baumeister (2000). *Psychological Bulletin, 126,* 380–384, AND Hyde, J. S., & Durik, A. M. (2000). Gender differences in erotic plasticity— evolutionary or social forces? Comment on Baumeister (2000). *Psychological Bulletin, 126,* 375–399, AND Baumeister, R. F., Catanese, K. R., Campbell, W. K., & Tice, D. M. (2000). Nature, culture, and explanations for erotic plasticity: Reply to Andersen, Cyranowski, and Aarestad and to Hyde and Durik. *Psychological Bulletin, 126,* 385–389. The article by Baumeister reprinted in this section was originally published in *Psychological Bulletin* together with critical commentaries by Andersen et al. and by Hyde et al., and Baumeister and his colleagues wrote a rejoinder. This lively exchange may prove entertaining to readers interested in disagreements among social scientists and how they present their divergent views. The editors of *Psychological Bulletin* hoped that publishing these commentaries along with the original article would help advance the field and highlight issues for debate.

Buss, D. M. (1994). *The evolution of desire*. New York: Basic Books. The author is one of the most influential figures in evolutionary psychology. In this popular book, he gives an overview of his research program and his main ideas.

DeLamater, J. D., & Hyde, J. S. (1998). Essentialism vs. social constructionism in the study of human sexuality. *Journal of Sex Research, 35,* 10–18. This article is part of a special issue on the state of theory in the field of sexuality. The authors offer an authoritative view of the field as polarized between the two major theoretical approaches.

Eagly, A. H., & Wood, W. (1999). The origins of sex differences in human behavior: Evolved dispositions versus social roles. *American Psychologist, 54,* 408–423. These authors take issue with the recent rush to interpret gender differences in evolutionary, biological terms. In their view, the social roles that men and women play are the decisive determinants of gender differences.

Ridley, M. (1993). *The red queen: Sex and evolution in human nature*. New York: Penguin. An entertaining and very readable introduction to evolutionary, biological approaches to the study of human behavior.

Symons, D. (1978). *The evolution of human sexuality*. New York: Oxford. This influential work was one of the pioneers in applying evolutionary theory to a broad spectrum of human sexual behavior.

READING 3

Sexual Strategies Theory: An Evolutionary Perspective on Human Mating

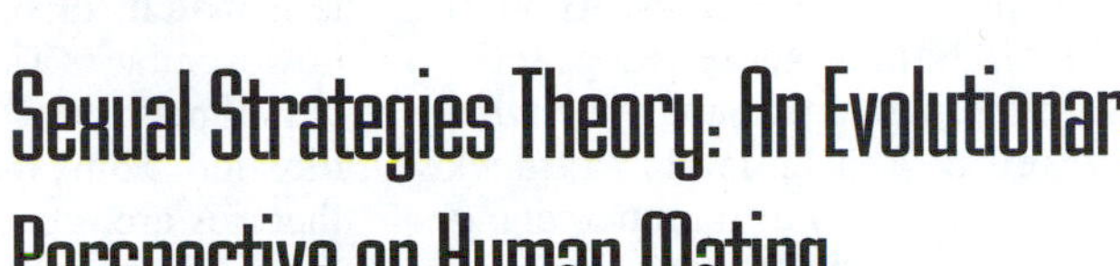

David M. Buss and David P. Schmitt • University of Michigan

This article proposes a contextual-evolutionary theory of human mating strategies. Both men and women are hypothesized to have evolved distrinct psychological mechanisms that underlie short-term and long-term strategies. Men and women confront different adaptive problems in short-term as opposed to long-term mating contexts. Consequently, different mate preferences become activated from their strategic repertoires. Nine key hypotheses and 22 predictions from Sexual Strategies Theory are outlined and tested empirically. Adaptive problems sensitive to context include sexual accessibility, fertility assessment, commitment seeking avoidance, immediate and enduring resource procurement, paternity certainty, assessment of mate value, and parental investment. Discussion summarizes 6 additional sources of behavioral data, outlines adaptive problems common to both sexes, and suggests additional contexts likely to cause shifts in mating strategy.

Mating is a human universal. All known societies have formal marriage alliances between men and women. More than 90% of all people in all societies marry at some point in their lives (Buss, 1985; Epstein & Guttman, 1984; Vandenberg, 1972). In a cross-cultural perspective, marriages are usually regarded as formal reproductive alliances that contain the features of (a) mutual obligation between husband and wife, (b) rights of sexual access, (c) an expectation that the marriage will persist through pregnancy, lactation, and child rearing, and (d) recognition of the legitimate status of the couple's children (Daly & Wilson, 1988, p. 187).

Long temporal durations, however, do not characterize all mating relationships. Mating relationships can last for a few months, a few days, a few hours, or even a few minutes. Matings of short duration have been given many names—brief affairs, one-night stands, or temporary liaisons. In this article, we anchor the ends of this temporal dimension using the descriptively neutral terms *short-term mating* and *long-term mating*. Matings of intermediate-length (e.g., dating, going steady, brief marriages, or intermediate-length affairs) occur between these end points.

Nearly all theories of human mating deal exclusively with long-term mating or marriage (cf. Murstein, 1970; Vandenberg, 1972). This may be due in part to the sheer difficulty of studying short-term mating, which by definition is a more transient phenomenon and one that is sometimes cloaked in greater secrecy. In the classic Kinsey, Pomeroy, and Martin (1953) study on sexual behavior, for example, the question about extramarital sex was the single, largest cause of refusal to be interviewed. Among those who did consent to be interviewed, this question received the highest refusal-to-answer rate, suggesting simultaneously the importance and prevalence of short-term mating outside the marital context.

No comprehensive theory of human mating, however, can ignore short-term mating. Stated simply, lifetime marital monogamy is not characteristic of most people in most societies. Approximately 80% of all human societies practice polygyny, permitting men to take multiple wives or mistresses (Ford & Beach, 1951; Murdock, 1967). In these societies, only a small percentage of men actually acquire multiple mates, but those that do render other men mateless. Even in presumptively monogamous societies such as the United States, divorce rates hover near 50% (H. Fisher, 1987). Serial marriages are common in most cultures (H. Fisher, 1987; Lockard & Adams, 1991). In addition, estimates of adultery among American married couples range from 26% to 70% for women and from 33% to 75% for men (Daly & Wilson, 1983; H. Fisher, 1987; Hite, 1987; Kinsey, Pomeroy, & Martin, 1948, 1953; Symons, 1979). These data do not include the numerous short-term sexual liaisons that occur among single men and women, either before marriage or as an alternative to marriage. In summary, lifelong mating with a single person does not appear to be the norm for humans. Both sexes engage in both short-term and long-term mating. The theory of human sexual stategies proposed here views the temporal context to be pivotal to the adaptive problems men and women have confronted and the adaptive stategies they have subsequently adopted.

Roles of Strategy in Human Mating

Previous theories of human mating differ in whether mating decisions are seen as goal directed and strategic or whether they are merely the product of forces beyond the individual's choice. Freud and Jung, for example, proposed that people seek in mates characteristics that resemble images or archetypes of their opposite-sex parent (Eckland, 1968). Winch (1958) proposed that people seek in mates characteristics they themselves lack: a search for complementarity. Cattell and Nesselroade (1967), Thiessen and Gregg (1980), Rushton (1989), and many others have proposed that people seek similarity in mates: that likes attract likes. Exchange and equity theories posit that people search for those with whom exchange of valuable resources will be in approximate equilibrium (e.g., Berscheid & Walster, 1974; M. S. Clark & Reis, 1988).

All these theories share the notion that human mating is strategic and choices are made, consciously or unconsiously, to maximize some entity, match, or balance. Each of these theories, however, lacks a specification of the paticular content domains toward which strategic effort will be directed. Thus, the strategic components of these theories are broad—to seek equity, to seek similarity, and to seek complementarity—and do not identify equity in which domains or similarity in which domains. These theories, therefore, offer no differential predictions about the content domains in which they will be most and least applicable nor do they offer sex-linked predictions about which strategic goals will be more salient to women or men. In summary, few specific predictions can be derived from any of these theories.

Theories of mating that do not posit a goal-directed or strategic component include various sociological and propinquity theories. These theories propose that people mate with others with whom they come into contact. Support comes from the findings that distance is a powerful predictor of who marries whom. As Eckland (1968) pointed out, "cherished notions about romantic love notwithstanding, the chances are about 50–50 that the 'one and only' lives within walking distance" (p.16). Some theories combine propinquity explanations with class-endogamy explanations, arguing that one's social class determines the pool of potential mates to which one will be exposed by selectively placing similar individuals into close proximity. For example, educational institutions sometimes selectively admit individuals possessing similar characteristics such as socioeconomic status, achievement scores, intelligence test scores, and even social skills in those private colleges that require personal interviews. Assortment, therefore, might in part be attributable to institutional mechanisms placing similar individuals into close proximity.

There is empirical support for some of these theories. Similarity overwhelmingly is the rule in human mating, and this applies to characteristics as diverse as height, weight, personality attributes, intelligence, values, nose breadth, and earlobe length (Buss, 1985). Freud's and Winch's theories of mating, however, have been least supported (Eckland, 1968). The only characteristic on which complementarity is the norm, for example, is on biological sex: men tend to marry women and vice versa (Buss, 1985). For all other characteristics, people tend to mate those who are similar. There is some evidence that people marry those who resemble their parents, but it has never been demonstrated that this occurs above and beyond the resemblance that would be expected solely on the basis of mating with someone who is similar to oneself (Eckland, 1968).

Each of these theories contains key conceptual limitations. The most important limitation is that all fail to provide an account of why humans would be motivated in the directions posited. Why should humans prefer similarity, equity, or proximity? What are the origins of these goals? What functions could they serve? The second limitation is that each of the theories of mating is extraodinarily simplistic, positing typically a single process that determines who mates with whom (although see Murstein, 1970, for a more complex, sequential model). The third limitation is that the generality of the theories precludes the generation of specific predictions in particular domains. The fourth limitation is that each theory assumes that the processes that govern male and female mating are identical, and thus no sex-differentiated predictions can be derived from these theories. The fifth limitation is that previous theories of human mating are context blind, positing the same mating tendencies regardless of circumstances.

The current theory attempts to rectify these omissions by articulating a selective rationale for the origins of the particular strategies that human men and women exhibit. A core premise of the theory is that human mating is inherently strategic: Humans seek particular mates to solve specific adaptive problems that their ancestors confronted during the course of human evolution; humans' mate preferences and mating decisions are hypothesized to be strategic products of selection pressures operating during ancestral conditions. The use of the term *strategies* is meant to connote the goal-directed and problem-solving nature of human mating behavior and carries no implication that the stategies are consciously planned or articulated. The theory is complex in the sense that the number of problem domains that require strategic solutions is proposed to be large. This complexity and numerousity yields a large number of precise predictions about what will be found in each domain. A key ingredient of Sexual Strategies Theory is that mating strategies are context dependent and, in particular, highly sensitive to the temporal context of short-term versus long-term mateships. Finally, a key ingredient of the theory is that men and women have faced different mating problems over human evolutionary history, at least in some delimited domains, and therefore the principles that govern the mating of women and men are predicted to be different in these domains.

This article articulates the key premises of Sexual Strategies Theory. We present the core strategic elements of the theory, hypotheses derived from the theory, and data from a series of empirical studies, many published and some new, to test 22 specific predictions derived from the hypotheses. The core of the theory is summarized in the next section.

Précis of Sexual Stategies Theory

1. In human evolutionary history, both men and women have pursued short-term and long-term matings under certain conditions where the reproductive benefits have outweighed the costs.
2. Different adaptive problems must be solved when pursuing a short-term sexual strategy as opposed to pursuing a long-term sexual strategy.
3. Because of a fundamental asymmetry between the sexes in minimum levels of parental investment, men devote a larger proportion of their total mating effort to short-term mating than do women.
4. Because the reproductive opportunities and reproductive constraints differ for men and women in these two contexts, the adaptive problems that women must solve when pursuing each strategy are different from those that men must solve, although some problems are common to both sexes.
5. Men historically have been constrained in their reproductive success primarily by the number of fertile women they can inseminate. This reproductive constraint on men can be separated into four relatively distinct problems that men historically had to solve to effectively pursue a short-term mating strategy: (a) the problem of partner number, (b) the problem of identifying which women are sexually ac-

cessible, (c) the problem of identifying which women are fertile, and (d) the problem of minimizing commitment and investment.

6. Reproductive constraints on men can be separated into four relatively distinct problems that men historically had to solve to effectively pursue a long-term mating strategy: (a) the problem of identifying reproductively valuable women, (b) the problem of ensuring certainty in paternity, (c) the problem of identifying women with good parenting skills, and (d) the problem of identifying women who are willing and able to commit to a long-term mating relationship.
7. Women historically have been constrained in their reproductive success not by the number of men they can gain sexual access to but rather primarily by the quantity and quality of the external resources that they can secure for themselves and their children and perhaps secondarily by the quality of the man's genes.
8. These reproductive contraints can be separated into two distinct problems that women historically had to solve to effectively pursue a short-term mating strategy: (a) the problem of immediate resource extraction and (b) the problem of assessing prospective long-term mates.
9. These reproductive constraints can be separated into distinct adaptive problems women historically had to solve to effectively pursue a long-term mating strategy: (a) the problem of identifying men who have the ability to invest resources in her and her children on a long-term basis, (b) the problem of identifying men who show a willingness to invest resources in her and her children on a long-term basis, (c) the problem of identifying men with good parenting skills, (d) the problem of identifying men who are willing and able to commit to a long-term relationship, and (e) the problem of identifying men who are able and willing to protect them from aggressive conspecifics (see Table 3.1).
10. Men and women have evolved distinct psychological mechanisms that function to solve the adaptive problems confronted to effectively pursue short-term and long-term matings.
11. These psychological mechanisms and their behavioral manifestations, combined with the temporal contexts in which each set is activated, constitute the evolved sexual strategies of men and women. *Strategies* are defined as evolved solutions to adaptive problems, with no consciousness or awareness on the part of the strategist implied.

Parental Investment and Sexual Selection

Our theory takes as a starting point Trivers's (1972) seminal theory of parental investment and sexual selection. Sexual selection, as originally proposed by Darwin (1871), refers to the evolution of characteristics that give organisms reproductive advantage, as contrasted with survival advantage. Survival is important only insofar as it affects reproduction. Two paths to reproductive advantage are (a) success at intrasexual competition (e.g., one male stag defeating another, with the winner obtaining access to the doe) and (b) success at intersexual attraction (e.g., the male peacock displaying brilliant plumage that is attractive to peahens). Characteristics that lead either to successful competition or to success at being preferentially chosen by the opposite sex will evolve simply because they give organisms reproductive advantage.

Trivers (1972) proposed that a central driving force behind sexual selection is the degree of parental investment each sex devotes to their offspring. *Parental investment* is defined as "any investment by the parent in an individual offspring that increases the offspring's chances of surviving (and hence reproducing) at the cost of the parent's ability to invest in other offspring" (Trivers, 1972, p. 139). Current conceptions of parental investment involve investment that increases an offspring's chances of survival and reproduction at the expense of alternative forms of reproductive investment (e.g., competition for mates), whether or not they involve one's own offspring (Clutton-Brock, 1991). Trivers proposed two related links between parental investment and sexual selection: (a) The sex that invests more in offspring should be more choosy or discriminating about who they mate with (intersexual attraction), and (b) the sex that invests less in offspring should compete more vigorously for access to the valuable high-investing members of the opposite sex (intrasexual competition).

There has been widespread empirical support for Trivers's (1972) theory of parental investment and sexual selection across dozens of species. Among mammals, for example, females typically invest more heavily than do males in offspring, and in hundreds of mammalian species, it has been documented that females are more selective, whereas males compete more vigorously in intrasexual competition (Trivers, 1985).

An even more compelling empirical test came with the discovery of several sex-role-reversed species (e.g., Mormon cricket, Panamanian poison-arrow frog, and several species in the pipefish seahorse family) in which males were observed to invest more in offspring than did females. In these species, females are often larger than males, and they compete more aggressively with each other for access to the more choosy, heavily investing males (Trivers, 1985). In addition to providing powerful support for Trivers's theory, these results highlight the fact that relative parental investment, not biological sex per se, drives the process of sexual selection.

Humans are like most mammals in that women tend to be the more heavily investing sex. This occurs in part because fertilization, gestation, and placentation are internal within women. Women carry the additional parental investment associated with lactation for as many as several years after the birth of a child: often for up to 4 years in tribal societies (e.g., Shostak, 1981). These forms of investment constrain the number of children a women can successfully produce; typically the upper bound is about a dozen under optimal conditions, and that upper bound is rarely reached. Men, in contrast, do not bear these forms of heavy parental investment, although they can and do invest heavily in other ways. The minimum investment by the man is the contribution of his sperm, and men, as a consequence, have a higher ceiling on their potential production of offspring. These sex differences in minimum parental investment, according to Trivers's (1972) theory, suggest that women should be the more selective or discriminating sex with respect to mating partners, whereas men should be less discriminating and be more vigorous in intrasexual competition for mates.

It is important to note that these are generalizations for which there are many exceptions. Human males have many opportunities to invest in their offspring following birth (e.g., through provisioning, protecting, and promoting), and indeed humans arguably show greater parental investment than do any other mammals (Alexander & Noonan, 1979). Where men do invest heavily in their offspring, Trivers's (1972) theory predicts that they will exert greater selectivity in their choice of mates relative to when they invest less in offspring. Thus, although humans are like most mammals in that women tend to be the more heavily investing sex, human males stand out among mammals as often investing substantially in their children, and there exists considerable individual variation within each sex in the amount of investment: a point to be taken up later.

TABLE 3.1. Mate Selection Problems Men and Women Confront in Short-Term and Long-Term Mating Contexts

Type of mating	Men	Women
Short term	1. Problem of partner number 2. Problem of identifying which women are sexually accessible 3. Problem of minimizing cost, risk, and commitment 4. Problem of fertility	1. Problem of immediate resource extraction 2. Problem of evaluating short-term mates as possible long-term mates 3. Problem of gene quality 4. Problem of mate switching, mate expulsion, or mate backup
Long term	1. Problem of paternity confidence 2. Problem of female reproduction value 3. Problem of commitment 4. Problem of good parenting skills 5. Problem of gene quality	1. Problem of identifying men who are able to invest 2. Problem of identifying men who are willing to invest 3. Problem of physical protection 4. Problem of commitment 5. Problem of good parenting skills 6. Problem of gene quality

Adaptive Logic of Men Pursuing a Short-term Sexual Strategy

The reproductive benefits that historically would have accrued to men who successfully pursued a short-term sexual strategy were direct: an increase in the number of offspring produced. A married man with two children, for example, could increase his reproductive success by a full 50% by one short-term copulation that resulted in insemination and birth. This benefit assumes, of course, that the child produced by such a brief union would have survived, which would have depended in ancestral times on a woman's ability to secure relevent resources through other means (e.g., by herself, through kin, or through other men). Historically, men appear to have achieved increases in reproductive success primarily through increases in the number of offspring per partner (Betzig, 1976; Dawkins, 1986).

All sexual strategies carry costs, and short-term mating is no exception. Men can incur major reproductive costs: (a) They risk contracting a sexually transmitted disease, and this increases with the number of women with whom sexual contact is achieved; (b) they risk acquiring a social reputation as a womanizer that could impair their mate value when seeking a long-term mate: Women of high mate value may be reluctant to mate with a man who shows promiscuous proclivities that signal poor prospects for enduring parental investment; and (c) they risk violence at the hands of jealous husbands if the women with whom they are pursuing this strategy are married or mated (Daly & Wilson, 1988).

Problems Men Confront When Pursuing a Short-term Sexual Strategy

Men face a complex and multifaceted problem when they pursue a short-term sexual strategy: Men are constrained in their reproductive success by the number of fertile women they can inseminate. This problem can be separated into four highly specialized adaptive problems or facets: (a) the problem of partner number, or variety (Symons, 1979); (b) the problem of identifying which women are sexually accessible; (c) the problem of identifying which women are fecund; and (d) the problem of minimizing commitment and investment to effectively pursue short-term matings.

Problem of Partner Number

What specific adaptations should be expected in the evolved sexual psychology of men to solve the problem of gaining sexual access to a number of women? One first-line solution to the problem of number can be expected in desire: Men may have evolved over human evolutionary history a powerful desire for sexual access to a large number of women (cf. Symons, 1979). A second specialized adaptation expected on theoretical grounds would be a relaxation of standards imposed for acceptable short-term partners. Elevated standards, by definition, preclude a large number of women from exceeding them. The relaxation of standards should apply to a wide range of mate characteristics, including standards for age, intelligence, personality traits, and personal circumstances such as whether a woman is already involved with someone else. A third specialized feature of men's evolved sexual strategy should be to impose minimum time constraints in knowing a prospective mate before seeking sexual intercourse. The less time that is permitted to elapse before obtaining sexual intercourse, the larger the number of women a man can gain access to. Prolonged time delays, by absorbing more of a man's mating effort, interfere with solving the problem of number.

Problem of Sexual Accessibility

Men, being the less investing sex, are predicted to be less discriminating than are women when seeking short-term mates. Nonetheless, reproductive advantages would accrue to those men who directed their mating effort most intensely toward those women who are sexually accessible. Time, energy, and resources devoted to women for whom sexual accessibility is unlikely would interfere with the successful enactment of a short-term sexual strategy.

Specialized adaptations for solving the problem of sexual access should be embodied in the psychological preferences that men express for short-term mates. Women who are prudish, sexually inexperienced, conservative, or who appear to have a low sex drive, for example, should be disfavored. Signs of sexual accessibility, such as looseness or promiscuity, which would be undesirable in long-term mates, might be desired by men in short-term mates because they signal accessibility.

Problem of Identifying Which Women Are Fertile

Biologists distinguish two facets of the ability to bear offspring: fertility and reproductive value. *Fertility* refers to the probability of present reproduction. Among humans, female fertility typically peaks in the early to mid 20s. A copulation with a woman of this age would be most likely to result in reproduction. *Reproductive value,* in contrast, is in units of expected future generations (R. A. Fisher, 1930). In human females, reproductive value peaks earlier than fertility: in the mid teens.

The difference between fertility and reproductive value can be illustrated by contrasting two women, one age 14 years and one age 24 years. The younger woman would have higher reproductive value than the older one because, actuarially, her future reproduction is expected to be higher. On average, 14-year-old women can expect more future children than can a 24-year-old woman. In contrast, the 24-year-old woman is more fertile than the 14-year-old woman because the current probability of reproduction is higher for the 24-year-old woman. After menarche (onset of menstruation), women generally experience a period of approximately two years in which they cannot conceive (Frayser, 1985). Women in their early teens typically have low fertility, even though their reproductive value is high.

Given these considerations, it may be predicted that men who seek long-term mates would prefer women of high reproductive value rather than women of high fertility. A man who mates with a woman of high reproductive value will have access to a greater reproductive asset than will a man who mates with a woman of lower reproductive value. The same logic dictates that men seeking short-term mating partners would prefer to mate with women of high fertility. The future reproductive potential of a woman is largely irrelevant to men seeking opportunistic copulations.

Although this adaptive problem for men seeking short-term matings is clear, namely to find a woman of high fertility, the solution to this problem is more difficult than it first appears. How can men "figure out" (again, no conscious interest is implied) which women possess the highest fertility or reproductive value? The capacity of a woman to bear children is not stamped on their forhead. It is not part of her social reputation, so no one is in a position to know. Even the woman herself lacks direct knowledge of her fertility and reproductive value. So how could a preference evolve for something that cannot be directly discerned?

The answer lies with those features of women that provide cues that are correlated with fertility or reproductive value. Two obvious cues to these values are age and health. Old unhealthy women have a lower reproductive value capacity than do young and healthy women. Thus, men could solve the problem of desiring reproductively capable women simply by preferring those who are young and healthy. However, age and health, like reproductive capacity, are not qualities that can be observed directly. Counting systems are relatively recent human inventions. In humans' evolutionary past before counting systems, age could not be evaluated directly. Indeed, even in modern times with close monitoring of age, deception about age is not unknown. The same applies to health. Short of securing access to a doctor's report, men have no direct way of evaluating the health of a woman.

Nevertheless, our ancestral humans did have access to three classes of cues that provide probabilistic evidence of a woman's age and health status: (a) features of physical appearence (e.g., full lips, clear skin, smooth skin, clear eyes, lustrous hair, symmetry, good muscle tone, and absence of lesions), (b) observable behavior (e.g., sprightly, youthful gait, and high activity level), and (c) social reputation (e.g., knowledge gleaned from others about a person's age and prior health history).

Because physical and behavioral cues provide the most powerful observable evidence of a woman's reproductive capacity, the evolutionary logic of mating suggests that men may have evolved a preference for, and attraction to, women who display these cues. Men who fail to prefer qualities that signal high reproductive capacity would, on average, leave fewer offspring than would men who prefer to mate with women possessing these qualities.

The reproductive success of women, in contrast to that of men, is not as closely linked with obtaining reproductively valuable mates. A man's reproductive capacity, to the degree that it is valued by women, is less steeply age graded from puberty on than is a woman's. Therefore, it cannot be assessed accurately from physical appearance. Physical appearance should be less central to a woman's mate preferences than to a man's mate preferences. This evolutionary logic leads to a clear prediction: Men, more than women, should value relative youth and physical attractiveness in potential mates because of their powerful links with fertility and reproductive value.[1]

If men in humans' evolutionary past have adopted short-term matings as part of their repertoire of strategies, then one would expect specialized adaptations to solve the problem of fertility. Men's mate preferences should be context dependent: They should seek a reproductively valuable woman for the long term but a fertile one for the short term. This prediction must be qualified, however, by the solution to the problem of number, namely, the relaxation of standards. Although men seeking short-term mates, other things being equal, might prefer fertile women in their early to mid 20s, a wide range of ages should be acceptable in short-term mates because of the relaxation of standards.

Problem of Avoiding Commitment and Investment

Men seeking short-term mates are predicted to avoid those women who will extract commitment or large investment before consenting to sex. The larger the investment in a particular mating, the fewer the number of sexual partners a given man can access. Women who require heavy investment effectively force men into a long-term strategy, which conflicts with the pursuit of opportunistic copulations. The most direct way to instantiate these mate preferneces is to shun women who appear to desire long-term commitments or heavy investment of resources as requirements for mating.

To summarize, men are predicted by Sexual Strategies Theory to pursue, at least in part, short-term sexual strategies. Thousands of generations of human evolution should have produced specialized adaptations for solving the highly specialized problems that constrained men's reproductive success. Evolved solutions are predicted in the form of preferences for mates who possess or exhibit certain short-term characteristics such as fertility, sexual accessibility, and low investment requirements.

Preferences as Psychological Mechanisms

Preferences are evolved psychological mechanisms that solve survival and reproductive problems. Consider a survival problem: What foods should one eat? One is faced with a bewildering array of potential objects to ingest—berries, fruits, nuts, and meat but also dirt, leaves, gravel, poisonous plants, rotting carrion, twigs, and feces. What would happen if one had no taste preferences and instead ingested objects from the environment randomly? Some organisms, by chance variation alone, would ingest objects that provided caloric and nutritive sustenance; others, also by chance alone, would ingest toxins or other objects detrimental to survival. Given a random distribution of preferences, if such variation had even a slight basis in genetic variation, then over time, preferences for nutritive objects would evolve. These preferences in humans turned out to be for objects rich in fat and sugar; aversions evolved for bitterness and sourness (Rozin & Vollmecke, 1986). All existing humans have ancestors who possessed food preferences. These food preferences solved a basic problem of survival.

Mate preferences are in some ways analogous to food preferences. However, rather than solving survival problems, mate preferences solve reproductive problems. Consider one reproductive problem that men in human evolutionary history had to face: selecting a fertile woman. Those men in humans' evolutionary past who chose to mate with infertile women failed to reproduce; those who preferred to mate with fertile women were more successful at reproducing. It is reasonable to suppose that, over thousands of generations, there would evolve in men a preference for those women who were most fertile, or more accurately, a preference for and attraction to female cues that reli-

[1]The evolutionary psychology of physical attractiveness is even more complex than this discussion implies. Whereas it is clear that youth is given greater weight in judgments of women's than of men's attractiveness, cues to health might be important for both sexes. Needed are psychophysical studies that systematically vary cues to youth and health and that identify the weightings given to these components by both sexes. An additional complexity comes from theories that predict that physical attractiveness may be used by women in short-term mating contexts as a cue to health, low parasite load, symmetry, and perhaps benefits of producing children who are attractive to the opposite sex (Gangestad & Simpson, 1990; Gangestad & Thornhill, in press; Hamilton & Zuk, 1982; Trivers, 1985). These theories predict that where women do not secure continuous access to a man's resources, as might be the case in long-term mating, they may secure better genes that are passed on to their children by mating short-term with physically attractive men. Although thorough tests of these controversial theories remain for the future, circumstantial evidence may come from examining whether women value physical attractiveness more in short-term mates than in long-term mates.

ably correlated with fertility. This preference solves a reproductive problem much like food preferences solve survival problems.

When we speak of preferences as solutions to reproductive problems, there is no implication that these preferences, or the reproductive problems they solve, are consciously articulated, although the preferences themselves may be accessible to awareness. Instead, they operate as desires, attractions, and gut-level emotions that characteristically impel a person toward some mates and repel a person from others. Humans like certain foods and are repulsed by others without necessary awareness of the adaptive logic of nutritive content. Similarly, humans are attracted by some potential mates and repulsed by others without any awareness of the adaptive logic behind the preference.

However, the psychological solutions to adaptive problems proposed here are not blind instincts, carried out regardless of circumstances or context. Rather, Sexual Strategies Theory specifies that evolved psychological mechanisms are exquisitely sensitive to context and, in particular, to the temporal dimension of context: whether a short-term or long-term mating relationship is sought or anticipated. The context dependency of the strategic activation of these psychological mechanisms makes this theory unique among all theories of human mating.

In summary, evolved psychological mechanisms are proposed to be the solutions to the specific adaptive problems that each sex has faced when confronted with different types of mating problems. Because this first set of predictions, involving various aspects of men's solutions to the problems of short-term mating, is so central to Sexual Strategies Theory, it is perhaps expedient to examine the empirical results of the studies testing these predictions before shifting to the other three quadrants of the theory. Empirical failure of this first set of predictions would jeopardize the entire theory, and thus it would not be worth proceeding without substantial evidence of their support. The predictions, and the hypotheses on which they are based, are presented in the next section, followed by summaries of the empirical studies conducted to test them.

A Note on the Empirical Tests

This section summarizes the specific hypotheses and predictions that follow from Sexual Strategies Theory and summarizes the relevent empirical tests of each. For those empirical tests that have been published already, readers are referred to the original articles for futher methodological and statistical details. For those tests specifically designed for this article, sufficient methodological and statistical details are presented to allow readers to evaluate the findings and their bearing on the hypotheses and predictions. In all cases, we report sample composition, sample size, the methods used, statistical tests such as *t* tests and associated *p* values, and magnitudes of effect. Although some studies are based on self-report methodology, we note that self-report is a reasonable method of choice for gauging mate preferences (Buss, 1989b), albeit a method with some obvious limitations, and that numerous other studies using alternative methods such as psychophysiological techniques, observational recording, and behavioral decision making are reported to provide convergent evidence for the key hypotheses and predictions. Discussions of the limitations of these studies may be found in the General Discussion section and in the originally published articles.

Hypothesis 1: Because of the Lower Levels of Minimum Parental Investment Incurred by Men, Short-Term Mating Will Represent a Larger Component of Men's Sexual Strategy Than of Womens' Sexual Strategy

Prediction 1: *Men will express greater desire for, or interest in, short-term mates than will women.* To test this prediction, a sample of 148 college students, 75 men and 73 women, rated on 7-point scales (1 = *not at all currently seeking* and 7 = *strongly currently seeking*) the degree to which they were currently seeking a short-term mate (defined as a 1-night stand, brief affair, etc.), and, independently, the degree to which they were currently seeking a long-term mate (defined as a marriage partner). The results are shown in Figure 3.1. Although men and women did not differ in their stated proclivities for seeking a long-term mate ($t = 0.48$, *ns*), men more than women in this study reported that they were currently seeking short-term sexual partners ($t = 5.37$, $p < .001$, $\gamma = 0.87$).[2] These findings, although obviously limited

[2] The effect sizes (γ) reported throughout the article are gammas (Howell, 1987). They signify the difference between means in standard deviation units. Cohen (1977) defines effect

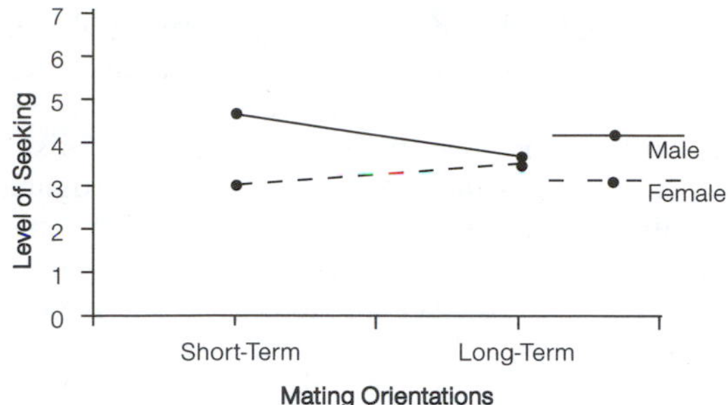

FIGURE 3.1 ■ Mating orientations. (Short-term and long-term mates are rated on a scale from 1 [*not at all currently seeking*] to 7 [*strongly currently seeking*].)

by sample and age restrictions, support the hypothesis that short-term mating strategies represent a larger component of men's mating effort.[3]

Prediction 2: For any given period of time (e.g., a month, a year, a decade, or a lifetime), men will desire a larger number of mates than will women (solution to the problem of number). To test this prediction, 75 men and 73 women estimated how many sexual partners they would ideally like to have over a series of time intervals: during the next month, six months, one year, two years, three years, four years, five years, 10 years, 20 years, 30 years, and a lifetime. The results of this study are shown in Figure 3.2. At each time interval, men reported that they desire a larger number of sex partners than women reported. During the next two years, for example, men reported desiring approximately eight sex partners, whereas women reported desiring approximately one. Over the course of a lifetime, men reported, on average, desiring more than 18 sex partners, whereas women reported desiring four or five. At each time interval men expressed a desire for a greater number of partners ($p < .001$ for t tests conducted for each interval, γ range = 0.49 to 0.87, mean $\gamma = 0.63$). Whether these preferred partners involve premarital-sex partners, extramarital affairs, or serial marriages cannot be evaluated from these data. Nonetheless, these results, although limited in scope, support the hypothesis that short-term mating represents a larger component of men's mating strategies than of women's mating strategies. They also support the prediction that men possess solutions to the problem of partner number, in this case in the form of consciously articulated desires.

Prediction 3: Men will be willing to engage in intercourse after less time has elapsed in knowing a potential partner than will women (solution to the problem of number). To test this prediction, a sample of 75 men and 73 women were posed with the following question: "If the conditions were right, would you consider having sexual intercourse with someone you viewed as desirable . . . if you had known that person for 5 years . . . if you had known that person for 2 years . . . if you had known that person for 1 year. . .if you had known that person for 6 months . . . if you had known that person for 3 months . . . 1 month . . . 1 week . . . 1 day . . . 1 evening . . . 1 hour?" Each time interval was rated on a scale ranging from –3 (*definitely not*) to 3 (*definitely yes*).

The results are summarized in Figure 3.3. When they have known a desirable potential mate for five years, both men and women stated that they would probably have sexual intercourse with that person. At every time interval briefer than five years, however, men stated that they would be more likely to have sexual intercourse with the potential partner. If he has known a woman for six months, for example, a man is just as likely to consent to sex as if he had known her for five years. In contrast, women dropped from 2 (*probably yes*) to close to 0 (*neutral*) when the interval shifted from five years to six months. Having known a potential mate for only 1 week, men were still on average positive about the possibility of consenting to sex. Women, in sharp contrast, stated that they are highly unlikely to have sex after knowing someone for just 1 week. After knowing a potential mate for just 1 hour, men are slightly disinclined to consider having sex, but the disinclination is not strong. For most women, sex after just 1 hour is a virtual impossibility. The sex differences are highly significant ($p < .001$) at each time period less than five years ($\gamma = 0.46$ to 1.21, mean $\gamma = 1.00$).

In an innovative study by different investigators (R. D. Clark & Hatfield, 1989), an attractive man or woman confederate approached strangers of the opposite sex on a college campus and posed one of three randomly selected questions: "I have been noticing you around campus. I find you very attractive. (a) Would you go out with me tonight? (b) Would you come over to my apartment tonight?

sizes as *small* if they are 0.20, *medium* if they are 0.50, and *large* if they are 0.80 or greater.

[3] This and subsequent sections present only those tests that directly bear on the specific predictions derived from the theory. Readers interested in the complete set of analyses may write to us.

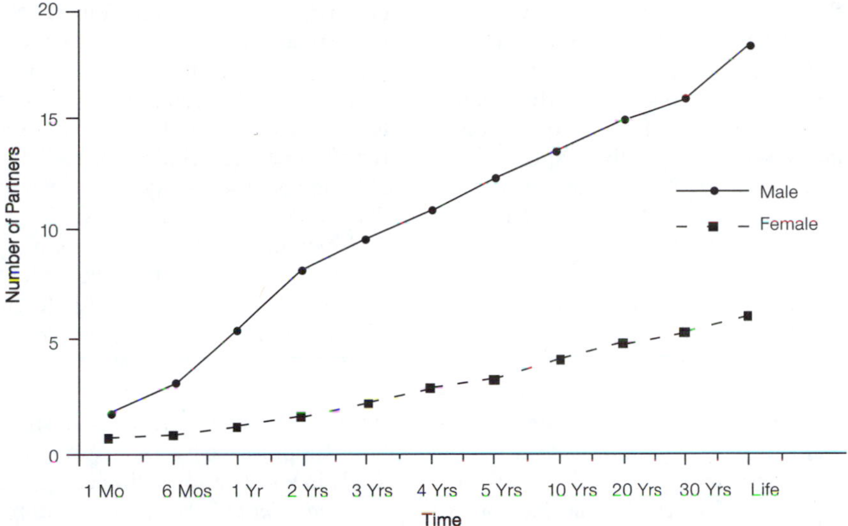

FIGURE 3.2 ■ Number of sexual partners desired. (Subjects recorded in blank spaces provided how many sexual partners they would ideally like to have for each specified time interval.)

(c) Would you go to bed with me tonight?" Of the women approached for a date, roughly 50% consented; of the women approached with an invitation to go back to the man's apartment, only 6% consented; and of the women approached with a request for sex, none consented. Of the men approached, roughly 50% agreed to go out on a date (same percentage as women), 69% agreed to go back to the woman's apartment, and fully 75% agreed to go to bed with her that evening. These findings have been replicated (R. D. Clark & Hatfield, 1989) and appear to be robust.

These behavioral data indicate that men are even more willing to engage in casual sex with a virtual stranger than the self-reported estimates in the aforementioned study. The discrepancy may be due

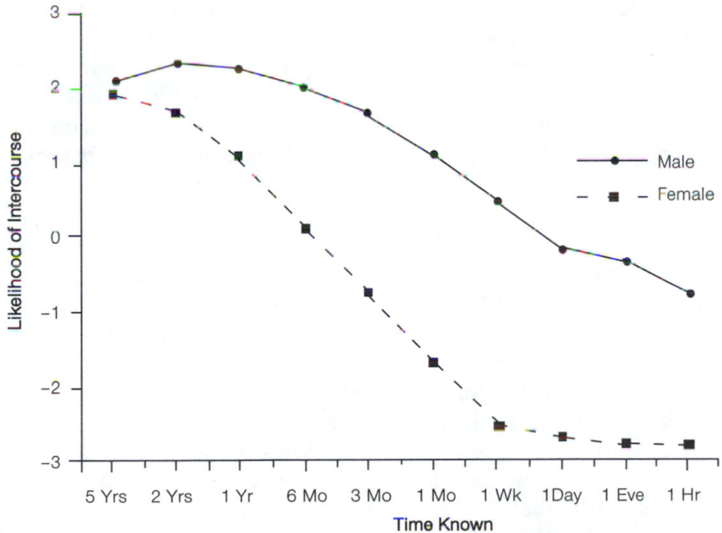

FIGURE 3.3 ■ Probability of consenting to sexual intercourse. (Subjects rated the probability that they would consent to sexual intercourse after having known an attractive member of the opposite sex for each of a specified set of time intervals.)

to two key differences in the studies. First, a living physically attractive woman presented herself in the R. D. Clark and Hatfield (1989) study, whereas it was merely an imagined partner in the self-report study. Second, the female confederates indicated that they found the subjects to be very attractive, which also might have made men even more inclined to casual sex. Taken together, however, both studies support the hypothesis that men are more oriented toward short-term mating opportunites and solve the problem of number in part by allowing little time to elapse before seeking or consenting to sex.

Prediction 4: Across all desired attributes in potential short-term mates, men will impose less stringent standards than women impose (solution to the problem of number). To test this prediction, we assembled 67 characteristics that had previously been nominated as potentially desirable in a mate (see Buss & Barnes, 1986). These spanned a gamut of attributes ranging from adventurous, artistic, and athletic to stylish in appearance, understanding, and well liked by others. A sample of 57 men and 51 women rated each characteristic on a 7-point scale ranging from 3 (*extremely desirable*) through 0 (*inconsequential or uncertain*) to –3 (*extremely undesirable*) in a short-term mate, defined as previously described.

On 41 of the 67 characteristics, approximately two thirds, men's standards for a short-term mate were significantly lower than those of women ($p < .05$, two-tailed, for each t test). For example, men required in a short-term mate lower levels of charm, athleticism, education, devotion, social skills, generosity, honesty, independence, kindness, intellectuality, loyalty, sense of humor, sociability, wealth, responsibility, open-mindedness, spontaneity, courteousness, cooperativeness, and emotional stability. For no characteristics were men more exacting than women in the short-term mating context. A summary score, representing a composite across all 67 characteristics, showed men to be substantially less exacting than women in their standards for a short-term mate ($p < .001$, $\gamma = 0.79$) and less exacting is short-term than in long-term contexts ($p < .001$, $\gamma = 1.90$). These findings support the prediction that men relax their standards in short-term mating contexts, providing a partial solution to the problem of number.

The hypothesis of relaxed male standards in short-term contexts also has received independent empirical support from Kenrick, Sadalla, Groth, and Trost (1990). Using a unique methodology, they asked subjects to report on what their minimum levels of acceptability would be for characteristics such as intelligence and kindness in different types of relationships. They found that, although both sexes expressed high minimum standards in a marriage partner for these traits (at least 60th percentile), the standards men imposed for someone with whom they would have only sexual relations dropped dramatically (e.g., 40th percentile on intelligence), whereas women's standards remained uniformly high for such relationships (e.g., at least 55th percentile on intelligence). In summary, evidence from independent investigations supports the hypothesis of relaxed male standards in short-term mating contexts.

Prediction 5: In short-term mating contexts, men will impose less stringent exclusionary criteria than do women (i.e., they will have fewer characteristics that they find undesirable or abhorrent). To test this prediction, we assembled a list of characteristics that were previously nominated as undesirable in a potential mate. Examples are unaffectionate, bigoted, boring, cheap, dishonest, dumb, lacks ambitions, has bad breath, and so on. A sample of 44 men and 42 women judged each characteristic on a 7-point scale, ranging from 3 (*extremely desirable*) to –3 (*extremely undesirable*) in a short-term mate.

Out of the 61 characteristics, roughly one third were judged to be more undesirable by women than by men. These included mentally abusive, physically abusive, bisexual, disliked by others, drinks a lot of alcohol, dumb, uneducated, a gambler, old, possessive, promiscuous, self-centered, selfish, lacking a sense of humor, not sensual, short, sleeps around alot, submissive, violent, and wimpy. In contrast, only five of the 61 negative characteristics were judged by women. A summary score, based on a composite of all 61 characteristics, showed that women expressed significantly stronger exclusionary standards than did men when evaluating a short-term mate ($p < .001$, $\gamma = 0.57$), and men expressed significantly less stringent exclusionary standards in the short-term context compared with the long-term context ($p < .001$, $\gamma = 1.52$). These results provide further support for the hypothesis that men's standards when seeking a short-term mate become relaxed, thus solving in part the problem of number.

Hypothesis 2: Men have Evolved a Distinct Sexual Psychology of Short-term Mating Such That Preferences for Short-term Mates Will Solve the Problem of Identifying Which Women Are Sexually Accessible

Prediction 6: Cues to immediate available sex (e.g., promiscuity or apparent sexual experience) will be valued by men in short-term mates more than in long-term mates because they provide cues to sexual accessibility. To test this prediction, we examined the men's preferences for short-term mates as opposed to long-term mates for the characteristics of promiscuity, sex appeal, and sexual experience (see the sample and the procedure description for Prediction 5). The results are shown in Table 3.2. All three are significantly more valued by men in a short-term mate, as predicted. It is noteworthy that men find promiscuity mildly desirable in a short-term mate but clearly undesirable in a long-term mate. Also of note is the finding that women find promiscuity extremely undesirable in either context ($M = -1.28$ in short-term mates and $M = -2.15$ in long-term mates). These findings support the hypothesis that men have specific preferences that attend short-term mating, preferences that in part solve the problem of sexual accessibility.

Prediction 7: Cues that signal a disinclination on the part of a woman to engage in short-term sexual intercourse, such as prudishness, sexual inexperience, or apparent low sex drive, will be disliked by men seeking short-term mates. To test this prediction, we selected three key attributes from among the list of 61 undesirable mate characteristics. The results from this study, involving 44 men, are shown in the bottom half of Table 3.2. In short-term mating contexts more than long-term mating contexts, men expressed a particular dislike for women who have a low sex drive, are prudish, and who lack sexual experience, although low sex drive and prudishness are also disliked by men in long-term mates. In contrast, lack of sexual experience is mildly valued by men in a long-term mate. These findings support the hypothesis that men's short-term mate preferences function to solve, at least in part, the problem of identifying women who are sexually accessible.

Hypothesis 3: Men Have Evolved a Distinct Sexual Psychology of Short-Term Mating Such That Preferences for Short-Term Mates Will Solve, in Part, the Problem of Minimizing Commitment and Investment When Pursuing This Strategy

Prediction 8: Because the successful enactment of a short-term sexual strategy for men requires minimizing commitment and investment, men will find undesirable in potential short-term mates any cues

TABLE 3.2. What Men Value and Dislike More in Short-Term Mating Then in Long-term Mating

Characteristic	Short-term mean	Long-term mean	t	p	γ[a]
		Value			
Good-looking	2.67	2.21	5.30	.000	0.61
Physically attractive	2.71	2.31	4.30	.000	0.50
Promiscuous	0.36	−0.99	6.71	.000	0.80
Sex appeal	2.67	2.33	4.10	.000	0.47
Sexually experienced	1.09	0.19	6.55	.000	0.76
		Dislike			
Wants a commitment	−1.40	2.17	−10.08	.000	1.56
Low sex drive	−2.38	−2.02	−3.19	.003	0.49
Prudish	−1.64	−1.14	−2.13	.039	0.33
Not sexually experienced	−0.43	0.52	−4.66	.000	0.72
Physically unattractive	−2.24	−1.88	−2.93	.006	0.45

[a] The effect sizes (γ) are gammas (Howell, 1987). They signify the difference between means in standard deviation units. Cohen (1977) defined effect sizes as *small* if they are 0.20, *medium* if they are 0.50, and *large* if they are 0.80 or greater.

that signal that the woman wants to extract a commitment. To test this prediction, we conducted a *t* test for the variable *wants a commitment* for short-term versus long-term mate preference (see Prediction 5 for the description of the sample and the procedure). Of all the variables, this one showed the most striking context difference for men (see Table 3.2). Specifically, the attribute of wanting a commitment was seen by men as strongly desirable in a long-term mate but strongly undesirable in a short-term mate. For women, this context difference was also found but was not nearly as strong: *Wants a commitment* was seen as highly desirable in a marriage partner but only as mildly undesirable in a short-term sex partner. These findings support the hypothesis that men especially seek to avoid commitment when seeking a short-term mate, a partial solution to the problem of maximizing copulatory opportunities.

Hypothesis 4: Men Have Evolved a Distinct Sexual Psychology of Short-Term Matings Such That Preferences for Short-Term Mates Will Solve, in Part, the Problems of Identifying Which Women Are Fertile

Prediction 9: Because the most important class of cues that are linked with fertility and reproductive value are physical (Buss, 1987, 1989b; Symons, 1979; Williams, 1975), men will place great importance on physical attractiveness in both short-term and long-term mating context. To test this prediction, we examined how desirable men found the characteristics *good looking* and *physically attractive.* The results are shown in Table 3.2 (see the sample and the method description from Prediction 5). Men's preference for physical attractiveness in short-term mates approached the ceiling of the ratings scale. Indeed, this preference was stronger for men seeking short-term mates than for men seeking long-term mates and was stronger for men than for women in both contexts.

For the women, $M = 2.41$ and $M = 1.92$ for good looking and $M = 2.43$ and $M = 2.10$ for the physically attractive, and short-term and long-term context, respectively. Women thus place greater value on physical appearance and short-term debt and long-term mating contexts. Although circumstantial, these findings are consistent with the theories advanced by Gangestad and Simpson (1990), Hamilton and Zuk (1982), and Trivers (1985) about the potential role of better genes in short-term mating contexts.

The finding that men express a stronger desire for physical attractiveness in short-term than in long-term contexts was not predicted in advance and deserves further theoretical and empirical scrutiny. One speculation is that there are a larger number of adaptive problems that men must solve to successfully pursue a long-term strategy, problems involving assessing the degree of commitment, loyalty, signs of good parenting skills, signs of being a good long-term cooperator, signs of fidelity, and so on. In contrast, the adaptive problems that must be solved to pursue a short-term strategy are smaller in number, and the complexity of the relationship is commensurately reduced. Perhaps preferences for cues to the many attributes sought in a long-term mate render physical attractiveness relatively less important in that context, a speculation that must be examined with future empirical work.

Prediction 10: Men will find physically unattractive women to be undesirable in both short-, and long-term mating contexts. The great value men place on physical attractiveness in a short-term mate is mirrored in their dislike of physical unattractiveness in a short-term mate (Table 3.2; see the sample and the method description under Prediction 5). Although unattractive women are not desired by men in either context, men's dislike for absence of beauty is especially strong in the short-term context. Furthermore, physical unattractiveness is seen as more undesirable by men than by women in both mating contexts (for women, $M = -1.77$ and $M = -1.39$ in short-term and long-term contexts, respectively). These results mirror those found for the desire for physical attractiveness. Men express stronger preferences on this attribute in the short-term than in the long-term context, suggesting that this finding is robust across desirable and undesirable modes of preference presentation.

Interim Summary

Four hypotheses and 10 corresponding predictions about the psychology of men's short-term sexual strategies were tested in a series of empirical studies and by independent investigators. The findings support the hypothesis that short-term sexual strategies loom larger in men's strategic repertoire than in women's, at least for the samples. Men reported desiring a larger number of short-term mates, allowing less time to elapse before expressing willingness to have intercourse, expressing less stringent standards for short-term mates, and imposing fewer exclusionary criteria with the exception of physical attractiveness.

Furthermore, the studies support the hypotheses that men's mate preferences solve the distinct adaptive problems that must be solved when pursuing a short-term sexual strategy. Specifically, men value cues to immediately available sex, dislike signs of sexual disinclination, seek to minimize commitment, and value cues that are reliably linked with fertility when evaluating a short-term mate. Many of these preferences are sharply differentiated from what men seek in a long-term mate, supporting the theoretical importance of temporal context in men's mating strategies. Further research, particularly on more diverse samples, is needed to verify these findings. Taken together, however, these findings provide encouraging support for a major set of premises of Sexual Strategies Theory. We now turn to the next quadrant, the psychology of men's long-term mating strategy.

Adaptive Logic of Men Pursuing a Long-Term Mating Strategy

Given the powerful reproductive advantages that accrue to men who pursue short-term sexual strategies, why should men pursue a long-term mate? The primary reproductive advantage to men of long-term mating is that it offers the possibility of monopolizing a woman's lifetime reproductive resources. Additionally, it may offer benefits of prolonged economic cooperation with the woman and the development of long-term alliances with her kin (Barb Smuts, 1991, personal communication).

There are several potentially powerful reproductive reasons why men would seek long-term rather than short-term matings. These include (a) when long-term mating becomes necessary to obtain women of high mate value,[4] (b) to avoid the cost of not pursuing a long-term mate, (c) to increase the genetic quality of children, (d) to solve the problem of concealed ovulation in women, and (e) to reap the benefits of mutual cooperation and division of labor.

Fulfilling Standards Imposed by Women

There is an asymmetrical relationship between the two components of sexual selection. The mate preferences of one sex should influence the competitive tactics used by the opposite sex, either over evolutionary time or over the course of individual development (Buss, 1988a). If women require reliable signs that a man is committed to them for a long-term relationship as a prerequisite for consenting to sexual intercourse, then men will have to display signals of long-term commitment if they are to succeed in acquiring a mate (barring attempts to circumvent female choice).

These signals, of course, can be, and sometimes are, deceptive. Men may feign long-term interest as a tactic for obtaining a short-term mate. However, women should envolve over time to combat deception in three ways: (a) evolving psychological mechanisms that detect when deception is occurring, (b) focusing on cues that reliably predict actual long-term commitment, and (c) requiring increased levels of commitment that are costly to feign before intercourse. Thus, men may be forced de facto into long-term matings to fulfill standards imposed by women.

Costs of Not Pursuing a Long-Term Mate

The costs and benefits of one strategy must be evaluated by contrasting them with the costs and benefits of alternative strategies. The primary alternative to long-term mating a short-term mating. Repeatedly seeking short-term mates, however, can be costly in time, energy, and resources. These costs become especially pronounced in contexts where women show reluctance to mate quickly, requiring instead prolonged courtship, investment, and signs of commitment. Female delay and discrimination in permitting sexual access increase the costs to men pursuing an exclusive strategy of short-term mating. If a man does not form a long-term mateship, he may also lose the opportunity to develop a well-tuned cooperative

---

[4] The concept of mate value was first introduced by Symons (1987b), although similar concepts such as market value (Buss & Barnes, 1986; Frank, 1988) have been used throughout certain literatures. It refers to an overall summary, given a set of weights (Frank, 1985, p. 186), to various component attributes. The obvious implication of Sexual Strategy Theory is that the weights given to the components differ for men and women.

relationship and efficient task specialization or division of labor. Cooperation occurs because of "strategic confluence" (Buss, 1989c), whereby children provide gene vehicles for both parents. For all these reasons, in the economics of reproductive effort, the cost of not pursuing a long-term mate may be prohibitively high.

Potential Increase in Mate Quality

In addition to the cost of short-term mating, the economics of the mating marketplace typically produce an asymmetry between the sexes in the attractiveness or desirability of a mate they can obtain in long-term as opposed to short-term relationships (Symons, 1979, p. 271). Most men can obtain a much more desirable mate if they are willing to invest and commit to a long-term relationship. Most women, in contrast, can obtain a much more desirable short-term mate with whom nothing but sex is exchanged. Thus, men may gain reproductively by obtaining a high quality long-term mate (as opposed to lower quality short-term mates) in the currency of either (a) better phenotypic mate attributes or (b) better genes that are passed on to his sons and daughters (cf. Gangestad, 1989; Gangestad and Simpson, 1990). The potential genetic benefit remains theoretically controversial in evolutionary biology, appears difficult to test at the present (e.g., Trivers, 1985; Williams, 1975), but represents a viable theoretical possibility.

Combating the Problem of Concealed Female Ovulation

Most sexually reproducing species do not form long-term pair-bonds (some bird species provide exceptions). Among most mammals, females enter estrus only at intervals, and mating occurs primarily during those periods. Human females, however, have lost estrus. Women do not have large, red, genital swellings when they ovulate nor is there evidence that emit noticeable pheromonal cues, as some other primates species do. Indeed, women are at least somewhat unique among primates in that ovulation is cryptic, or concealed (although a few other primate species have somewhat cryptic ovulation; Hrdy, 1981). There is no evidence that men can detect when women are ovulating (Symons, 1992).

With the concealment of ovulation came changes in the ground rules of human mating. Concealment of ovulation created a special reproductive problem for men: the problem of decreased probability of their paternity. A nonhuman primate male who is the only one to copulate with a female for the brief period that she is in estrus can be fairly "confident" in his paternity (again, no conscious articulation is implied). The period for which he must guard or sequester a mate to acheive paternity is sharply time constrained. After estrus, he can go about his other business without running the risk that another male will inseminate his mate.

Human males confront a qualitatively different adaptive problem. A man in human ancestral conditions never knew when a woman was ovulating. Because mating is not the only activity that humans must engage in to survive and reproduce, women cannot be guarded around the clock. Even if they could be continuously guarded, the costs in time and energy would seriously impair solving other adaptive problems. Men, therefore, are faced with a unique paternity problem that is not faced by other primate males: How can paternity be ensured under conditions of ovulatory uncertainty?

Concealed ovulation is likely to have been one force in human evolutionary history that selected for men to form long-term mating relationships with women (Alexander & Noonan, 1979). Men who monopolized a woman over long periods of time would carry a selective advantage over men who did not, if by so doing they substantially increased the probability of paternity, and this increase sufficiently outweighed the costs, such as opportunity costs (e.g., the alternative copulations they could achieve if they spent less time mate guarding). This line of reasoning leads to a specific prediction: In the context of long-term mating, men should prefer women who provide evidence that paternity will be likely and after mate selection occurs should have mechanisms that continue to ensure paternity (e.g., sexual jealousy).

Mutual Cooperation and Division of Labor

A final benefit that ancestral men would have received from long-term mating concerned establishing a coordinated mutual relationship such that the couple could function more efficiently in various ways together than either could alone. Division of labor may have been one facet of mutual cooperation, enabling each person to specialize in functions, yielding greater efficiency. Furthermore, mutual cooperation may have allowed more efficient care and provisioning, with less likelihood that a man's investment would be misdirected. The mutual interest in the same children makes it easier for such cooperative relationships to develop (Alexander, 1987). Finally, long-term relationships offer the possibility of fine-tuned efficiency and intermeshing of efforts that may yield greater economy and ultimate payoff compared with a strategy that does not entail forming long-term bonds.

Costs of Long-Term Mating

Long-term mating, like all sexual strategies, carries costs when contrasted with alternative strategies. The primary cost to men is the opportunity cost: the copulations that the man could have obtained if he were not committed to a long-term mating. Over human evolutionary history, we expect that selection would operate on men to reduce these costs where possible. Some men seek extramarital affairs that are concealed from their long-term mate, for example, and in evolutionary history this would have helped to reduce the opportunity cost of long-term mating (Symons, 1979). Nonetheless, the reproductive cost of foreclosed copulations is real.

In summary, there are compelling reproductive reasons for men to seek long-term mating. It is a method of tying up a woman's reproductive effort for years, it is a method of obtaining more attractive and desirable mates, it may take less effort per viable offspring than an exclusive pursuit of short-term mating, it may increase the certainty of paternity, and it may be required to fulfill standards imposed by women. The major cost to men of mating long-term is the foreclosed opportunity to inseminate other women. Natural selection would be unlikely to produce long-term mating strategies in men blindly. Men should have evolved powerful preferences about whom they are willing to mate with long-term. These preferences should serve to ensure that the reproductive benefits men can accrue from long-term matings are delivered. To the extent that men do invest in long-term mating, their preferences should become increasingly exacting for those characteristics that facilitate solving the adaptive problems they face.

Problems Men Must Solve When Pursuing a Long-Term Mating Strategy

Problem of Certainty in Paternity

Humans stand out among the primates as a species in which men provide substantial parental investment to their children (Alexander & Noonan, 1979), including tangible resources such as food, opportunities for learning, and protection against traditionally hostile forces of nature such as predators and conspecific aggressors. Given the tremendous effort that men sometimes expend for their children, we expect that natural selection would not produce men who dispensed it casually or indiscriminately.

Wherever men invest parentally, selection should favor men who act to ensure that their investment is directed toward their own children and not to the children of another man. Sexual jealousy is one adaptation to the problem of paternity uncertainty (Buss, 1988b; Daly, Wilson, & Weghorst, 1982). Male sexual jealousy apparently functions to guard a mate and to dissuade intrasexual competitors, thus lowering the likelihood of alien insemination. Initial mate preferences provide another possible solution to the paternity certainty problem.

The sexes are asymmetrical in probability of parenthood. Because women, like all other mammals, conceive internally, there is never any doubt about their parenthood. Maternity is 100% certain. Men can never be entirely sure. Because ovulation is concealed, or cryptic, in women, a man would have to sequester his mate for a period of months to be entirely sure. Even then, he has to sleep sometimes, and this opens the window of possibility for alien insemination. Two sets of studies will test the paternity certainty hypothesis: studies of sexual jealousy and studies of mate preferences for cues to paternity. Evidence for three mate preferences will be examined to test the hypothesis of men's evolved solutions to the problem of paternity uncertainty: desire for chastity, desire for sexual fidelity, and abhorrence of promiscuity in a long-term mate.

Problem of Female Reproductive Value

The primary reproductive advantage to men of adopting a long-term mating strategy is the possibility of monopolizing a woman's entire reproductive capacity for her lifetime. Given this potential benefit, men have evolved preferences to mate long term with those women who have high reproductive capacity.

Predicting that men will value physical attractiveness in women because of its association with reproductive value does not negate or deny the existence of cultural and other determinants of standards of attractiveness. Ford and Beach (1951) have documented cultural variation in standards for female attractiveness along the dimensions of plump versus slim body build, light versus dark skin, and emphasis for particular physical features such as eyes, ears, or genitals. Symons (1979) has suggested that regularity of features, proximity to the population average, and association with status might also influence attractiveness standards.

The predicted sex differences in mate preferences for youth and physical attractiveness, however, are expected to transcend cultural variations and other determinants of beauty standards. The physical and behavioral cues that signal youth and health, and are regarded as attractive, should be linked with female reproductive value in all cultures. The sex differences are predicted to be species typical among *Homo sapiens*, despite cross-cultural variations in absolute age preferences, the presence or absence of counting systems, or culture-specific criteria for female attractiveness that are not linked with reproductive value.

Hypothesis 5: When Men Pursue a Long-Term Mate, They Will Activate Psychological Mechanisms That Solve the Problem of Paternity Confidence (e.g., Sexual Jealousy and Specific Mate Preferences)

Prediction 11: Men's jealousy will be activated strongly by cues to sexual infidelity because that is the act that would have been reproductively damaging to ancestral men; women's jealousy, in contrast, will focus more on emotional infidelity as a cue to loss of investment and commitment of a man over time (Daly et al., 1982; Symons, 1979). Buss, Lasen, Westen, and Semmelroth (1992) tested this prediction using both self-report methods and psychological methods. They asked subjects the following question: "Imagine that you discover that the person with whom you've been seriously involved became interested in someone else. What would distress or upset you more (please circle one only): (A) Imagining your partner forming a deep emotional attachment to that person. (B) Imagining your partner enjoying passionate sexual intercourse with that other person" (p. 252).

The majority of men (60%) picked sexual infidelity as more distressing, whereas 85% of the women said they would be more upset by their partners emotional infidelity. In a second study, Buss et al. (1992) recorded heart rate, electrodermal activity, corrugator contraction (frown muscle) of men and women while they imagined (separately) their partner having sexual intercourse and their partner becoming deeply emotionally involved. Men showed greater heart-rate acceleration, greater skin conductance, and more facial frowning to imagining their mate having sex with someone else. Women showed the opposite pattern. This evidence supports the hypothesis that, psychologically and physiologically, the weighting given to cues that trigger jealousy differs for the sexes in accordance with the paternity uncertainty hypothesis.

Prediction 12: Compared with the short-term context, in the long-term mating context men should place greater value on characteristics such as faithfulness, sexual loyalty, and chastity that historically solved, in part, the problem of paternity certainty. To test this prediction, two studies were carried out. A sample of 75 men rated the desirability of 67 characteristics in a long-term mate and in a short-term mate. The results for the relevant variables are shown in Table 3.3.

The characteristics of faithfulness and sexual loyalty, although seen as neither particularly desirable nor undesirable in a short-term mate, are near the ceiling of the scale in desirability to long-term mate. Indeed, *faithful* was the single most valued characteristic by men in the context of a long-term mate. Chastity was also valued by men more in long-term than in short term mates, although it was not highly evaluated by this sample in either context.

A cross-cultural examination of preference for chastity was carried out by Buss (1989b), who examined this characteristic in a study of preferences for marital partners in a sample of 37 societies with a sample size of 10,047. Although the temporal context was restricted to long-term mating, and thus we cannot contrast men's short-term preferences with their long-term ones, we can ex-

TABLE 3.3. Preferences Hypothesized to Solve the Problem of Paternity Certainty for Men

Characteristic	Long term *M*	Long term *SD*	Short term *M*	Short term *SD*	*t* tests	γ[a]
			Study 1 (*N* = 75)			
Faithful	2.88	0.37	0.32	0.93	−21.81*	2.52
Sexually loyal	2.85	0.49	0.72	1.05	−17.07*	1.97
Chastity	0.91	1.20	0.19	1.65	−3.73*	0.43
			Study 2 (*N* = 42)			
Unfaithful	−2.93	0.26	−1.21	1.46	7.32*	1.13
Promiscuous	−2.07	1.30	−0.40	1.88	5.82*	0.90
Sleeps around a lot	−2.79	0.65	−1.95	1.23	4.14*	0.64

[a] The effect sizes (γ) are gammas (Howell, 1987). They signify the difference between means in standard deviation units. Cohen (1977) defines effect sizes as *small* if they are 0.20, *medium* if they are 0.50, and *large* if they are 0.80 or greater.
*$p < .001$.

amine sex differences in the value placed on chastity, on the basis of the hypothesis that certainty in parenthood is an adaptive problem that ancestral men, but not ancestral women, had to solve. A sample of the results are shown in Figure 3.4.

Over all 37 samples, 23 samples showed a significant sex difference in the predicted direction. The remaining 14 samples showed no significant sex difference. In no sample did women value chastity more than did men. In addition, there is tremendous variability across cultures in the absolute value placed on chastity: indeed, greater variability than any of the other 30 mate preferences examined across cultures (Buss, 1989b). Most of the Chinese sample, for example, said that chastity was indispensable in a long-term mate, whereas most of the Swedish and Dutch samples judged it to be largely irrelevant or unimportant. These results provide only modest support for the hypothesis that chastity will be valued by men as

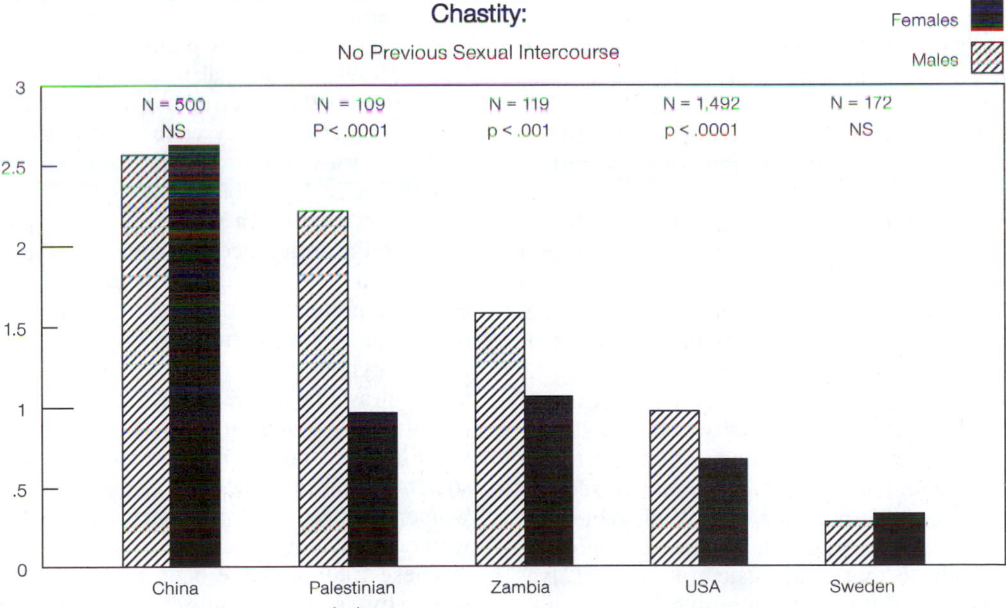

FIGURE 3.4 ■ Chastity: No previous sexual intercourse. (Subjects rated this variable, in the context of 18 other variables, on how desirable it would be in a potential long-term mate or marriage partner using a 4-point scale, ranging from 0 [*irrelevant or unimportant*] to 3 [*indispensable*].)

a cue to increased paternity certainty and suggest that the presence or absence of sex differences in the value placed on chastity are highly variable across cultures. These data do not suggest, however, that men's and women's values are unconstrained and arbitrary: a conclusion that would be supported if there were as many (or even some) cultures in which women valued chastity more than did men.

Combined with the study on the importance men place on faithfulness, we may conclude tentatively that certainty of paternity is more ensured by (a) seeking cues to future sexual conduct—signs of fidelity—rather than signs of prior total abstinence before mate selection and (b) enacting sexual jealousy and various forms of mate guarding after mate selection (Buss, 1988b; Buss et al., 1992; Wilson & Daly, 1992).

Prediction 13: Characteristics such as promiscuity and sexual experience will be shunned by men in long-term mates because they signal lower confidence in paternity, failure to monopolize a woman's reproductive value, and an increased risk of investing in children that are not genetically related (see Buss, 1988b; Daly et al., 1982). The tests of this prediction are shown in Table 3.2, which was described earlier under short-term mate preferences. Although men have a slight preference for promiscuity in a short-term mate, it is seen as undesirable in a long-term mate (women, in contrast, rate it as undesirable in both contexts). Sexual experience, also viewed as desirable in a short-term mate, is seen as neutral in a long-term mate (women, in contrast, judge it to be mildly desirable in both contexts).

Another study asked men to rate 61 characteristics, previously nominated as undesirable in a potential mate, on the degree to which they were undesirable in a short-term and long-term mate. Among the characteristics were the variables *promiscuous, sleeps around a lot,* and *unfaithful.* As shown in Table 3.3, all three characteristics were judged by men to be especially undesirable in a long-term mate, as contrasted with a short-term mate. Indeed, the variable *unfaithful* was seen by men as the single most undesirable characteristic in a long-term mate, providing strong support for the hypothesis that men's mate preferences solve, at least in part, the adaptive problem of paternity uncertainty. Women judge these characteristics also to be highly undesirable in long-term mates but rate them as significantly more undesirable than men do in short-term contexts, suggesting the possibility that women use short-term mating as an assessment device for long-term mating.

Hypothesis 6: When Men Pursue a Long-Term Mate, Men Will Express Preferences That Solve the Problem of Identifying Reproductively Valuable Women

Prediction 14: Men should value physical attractiveness in long-term mates because it provides a powerful cue to age and health, which historically have been powerful cues to reproductive value (Buss, 1989b). Many studies have documented the value that men place on physical appearance and attractiveness in potential mates (Buss, 1987; Buss & Barnes, 1986; Hill, 1945; Hudson & Henze, 1969; McGinnis, 1958). This finding has been documented across 37 societies as well (Buss, 1989b). Figure 3.5 shows a sample of these findings from five diverse cultures. Although the absolute value placed on physical attractiveness varies, men consistently grant it greater importance than do women in the context of seeking a long-term mate.

Prediction 15: Men will value relative youth in long-term mates because it provides a powerful cue to reproductive value. Two recent large-scale studies have tested this prediction. The first by Buss (1989b) found that in each of 37 cultures, men consistently preferred marriage partners who were younger than they were. A sample of these findings for five cultures is shown in Figure 3.6.

The precise degree of relative youth differs from country to country. In Zambia, for example, men expressed a preference for wives who are more than seven years younger, whereas in Italy, men express a preference for wives who are just under three years younger: findings that may be due to the polygynous nature of the Zambian mating system contrasted with the legally legislated monogamous mating system in Italy (Buss, 1989b). The sex difference, however, is consistent across all 37 societies, and in no society do men prefer older women on average nor do they mate with older women on average.

These findings have been replicated and extended by a series of studies by Kenrick and Keefe (1992). They tested a more refined version of this hypothesis: As men get older, they will prefer mates who are progressively younger than they are.

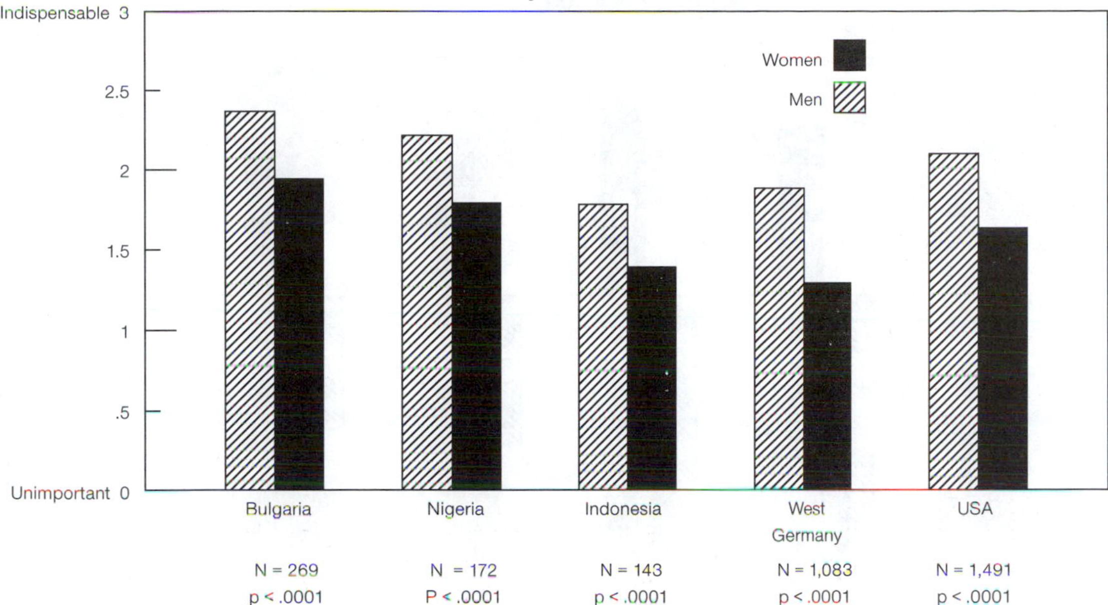

FIGURE 3.5 ■ Physical attractiveness. (Subjects rated this variable, in the context of 18 other variables, on how desirable it would be in a potential long-term mate or marriage partner using a 4-point scale, ranging from 0 [*irrelevant or unimportant*] to 3 [*indispensable*].)

This prediction was confirmed in samples drawn from personals columns across generations within the United States and also across cultures such as India currently. Taken together, these studies support the hypothesis that men seek reproductively valuable women as long-term mates.

Adaptive Logic of Women Pursuing Short-Term Sexual Strategies

The costs incurred by women are likely to be more severe than those incurred by men when pursuing a short-term sexual strategy. Like men, women risk contracting sexually transmitted diseases with increased sexual contact. Also like men, they risk impairing their long-term mate value by acquiring a social reputation as promiscuous. The reputational damage to long-term mate value, however, is likely to be more severe for women than for men. This is ultimately because of the asymmetry between men and women in confidence in parenthood. Because of paternity uncertainty, cues that a woman has had multiple mates should be disfavored by men seeking long-term mates; hence, such women are predicted to experience a decrease in social status.

There is yet another reason why the damage to mate value is expected to be more severe for women than for men. Historically, most human societies have been polygynous, with men being permitted to acquire multiple mates. It is only powerful men who are high in status and resource control, however, who can obtain multiple mates (Beztig, 1986). Because of this association, men who are able to gain sexual access to many women may be credited with being high in status and resource control (cf. Bar-Tal & Saxe, 1976).

Precisely the opposite social inference may operate when people interpret a woman's sexual contact with many men. Because women of high mate value are generally more discriminating than women of low mate value (Buss, 1988a), sexual promiscuity may be interpreted as a sign that a woman cannot obtain a long-term mate of high quality who is willing to commit resources and parental investment. Because lower mate value in women is linked with greater accessibility, a woman may suffer reputational damage that is due to a short-term sexual strategy because people in-

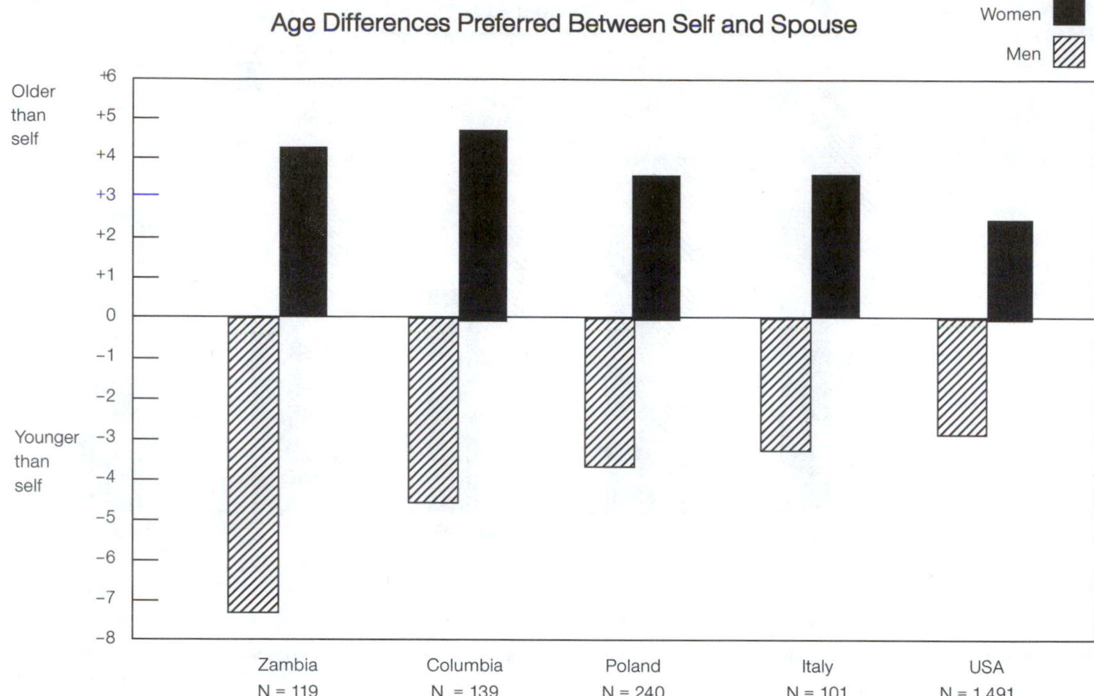

FIGURE 3.6 ■ Age difference preferred between self and spouse. (Subjects recorded their preferred age difference, if any, between self and spouse. The scale shown is in years, with positive values signifying preference for older spouses and negative values signifying preference for younger spouses.)

terpret that strategy as a sign of low mate value: a trend that may occur in relatively promiscuous cultures such as the Ache (Kim Hill, 1991, personal communication).

In addition to sexually transmitted diseases and impairment of long-term mate value, women risk something else that is linked with contact with multiple men: physical abuse and sexual abuse. Because men are physically larger and stronger, they can and sometimes do abuse women physically and sexually, often in an attempt to control them reproductively (Daly & Wilson, 1988). Lacking a long-term mate who could offer physical protection, women who adopt a short-term sexual strategy may be at greater risk (Smuts, 1991). The risk is not only one of physical injury but also one of circumventing a woman's sexual choice through sexual harassment (Studd & Gattiker, 1991) and forced copulation (R. Thornhill & Thornhill, 1983, 1987). Smuts (in press) has made a compelling case for the importance of male protection of females from conspecific aggressors among nonhuman primates species as well.

In spite of the potential cost to women of short-term mating, there are potential reproductive benefits that can accrue to women who pursue a short-term sexual strategy. One hypothesized benefit that has been proposed is the possibility of obtaining better genes that can be passed on to offspring. This possible benefit remains currently controversial and does not appear to be testable given current methodologies. Other key benefits include (a) immediate extraction of resources, (b) using short-term mating to evaluate long-term prospects, and (c) gaining increased protection. These are considered in detail in the next section.

Problems Women Confront When Pursuing a Short-Term Sexual Strategy

According to our temporal theory of sexual strategies, women should typically pursue short-term sexual strategies less often and less intensely than do men. However, this generalization masks a fundamental fact: Women sometimes do seek short-term matings, and there are reproductively beneficial conditions for doing so (see Gangestad,1989; Gangestad &Simpson, 1990). Short-term strategies differ from long-term strategies in that women generally cannot sequester a man's resources or his willingness to provide such resources reliably. Unlike men, obtaining copulatory opportunities per se is unlikely to be a powerful goal of short-term mating for women, who do not face the reproductive constraint of sexual access to mates that men do. Minimal access is all that is needed; there is rarely a shortage of men willing to provide the minimum sperm contribution; additional sperm beyond that are superfluous.

Problem of Immediate Resource Extraction

Are there clear reproductively relevant environmental benefits that a woman could derive from short-term meetings? There are several. First, women can (and frequently do) obtain resources in exchange for short-term copulations. In many societies, men are expected to bring gifts such as food or jewelry to their mistresses, and women may decline to engage in sex if these gifts are not presented (Malinowski, 1929; Shostak, 1981). An obvious form of short-term mating is prostitution. Prostitution involves the direct exchange of money or other resources for temporary sexual access: a phenomenon found cross-culturally in a great many societies from the Aleut to the Zuni in North America, from the Araucanians to the Yaruro in South America and the Caribbean, from Czechoslovakia to Yugoslavia in Europe, from the Amhara to the Yemen in the Middle East, from the Ainu to the Vietnamese Tonkin in Asia, and from the Alor to the Yap in Oceania (Burley & Symanski, 1981). In the most extensive cross-cultural analysis of prostitution yet conducted, Burley and Symanski (1981) concluded that "the motives expressed by many sorts of women in numerous societies are, at their core, clearly economic: men create a demand and women find an economic advantage meeting it" (p. 260).

If immediate extraction of resources is one potential benefit of short-term mating for women, then women who pursue a short-term mating strategy should prefer in mates characteristics that signal immediate resource provisioning. They should dislike characteristics such as frugality that imply that such resources will not be forthcoming.

Problem of Assessing Prospective Long-Term Mates

There is another possible benefit: the use of short-term mating as an assessment device to evaluate potential long-term mating partners. Given the tremendous reproductive importance of the choice of a long-term mate, great effort should be devoted to the assessment of long-term prospects. Short-term mating is often necessary to gauge these long-term prospects. Engaging in several short-term matings allows one to (a) evaluate one's own mate value (How many members of the opposite sex and of what quality are interested in mating with you and for what duration?), (b) assess the intentions of the prospective mate (Is he seeking a brief encounter or marriage partner?), (c) evaluate the enduring characteristics of the potential mate (e.g., How does he hold up under stress? How reliable is he over time?), (d) discern any deception that might have occurred (e.g., Is he truly "free," or is he already involved in a serious relationship?), and (e) evaluate his mate value (How attractive is he to women?). These forms of assessment typically cannot be made with precision without becoming involved in a short-term mating relationship.

The same logic should apply to men who seek long-term mates. Men, no less than women, need to gauge a prospect's mate value, assess enduring characteristics, and penetrate any deception that has occurred (e.g., lies about age). However, as noted in the previous section, men have been selected to seek short-term matings as ends in themselves: The reproductive benefits historically have been large and direct in the currency of number of offspring. For women, however, the reproductive benefits of short-term mating as an end in itself are less direct and the potential costs more steep. The costs to a woman of making a poor choice of a long-term mate are potentially more severe than they are for a man. These considerations suggest that women will place greater emphasis on the assessment process and that short-term mates will be tested and evaluated as long-term prospects rather than being end goals in and of themselves.

If this reasoning is correct, then important empirical predictions follow. The most important prediction is that compared with men, what women seek in a short-term mate should be far more similar to what they seek in a long-term mate. Because men often seek opportunistic sex in short-term mating, they need not impose stringent standards for such low-cost ventures. However, if women seek short-term matings as a means to assess long-term prospects, then they should impose standards that closely approximate those of a long-term mate.

How might this assessment function be revealed in women's short-term mate preferences? Consider two attributes of the prospective mate: (a) The person is already in a relationship and (b) the person is promiscuous. If women were seeking short-term mates for opportunistic sex, as men do, then these qualities should not be particularly bothersome to women. If women are using short-term mates to evaluate long-term prospects, however, the fact that a perspective mate is already in a relationship or is promiscuous would be seen as highly undesirable because it decreases her odds of acquiring a long-term relationship with that person.

Problem of Protection

Among humans and other primates that show substantial sex differences in size and strength, females sometimes face the problem of being physically dominated by larger, stronger males. Females can be susceptible to injury and sexual domination: having males forcing themselves on females, thus circumventing female choice. Under these conditions, females should seek potential mates who have the ability to protect them. These considerations suggest that physical strength should be part of a woman's mate selection preferences. Although gaining protection should be important to women in both short-term and long-term mates, Barkow (1989) advanced compelling arguments that suggest it may be even more important in the short-term context.

A number of complex forces may be operating here. A key distinction is between the abuse women face by mates versus nonmates. Because men in long-term mateships are heavily invested, they should go to greater effort than short-term mates in ensuring protection from abuse by other men. Therefore, women who are in short-term mateships may be more at risk for abuse from nonmated men than are women who are in long-term mateships. Physically strong men in short-term mateship may effectively deter abuse from other men, and the cost to the defender is smaller if he is stronger. Because a woman in a long-term mateship can generally count on the commitment of her mate to protect her, his physical strength may be a bit less important to women compared with that of a less investing short-term mate. Thus, all these forces lead to the prediction that, although women will value physical strength in both mating contexts, it will be more valued in short-term than in long-term mating contexts.

Hypothesis 7: In Short-Term Matings, Women Will Seek Men Who Are Willing to Impart Immediate Resources

Prediction 16: In short-term contexts, women will especially value signs that a man will immediately expend resources on her. To test this prediction, we conducted a study that requested 20 female subjects to evaluate the desirability of the following characteristics in a short-term and long-term mate: *spends a lot of money early on, gives gifts early on,* and *has an extravagant lifestyle.* The results are shown in Table 3.4. For all of the targeted characteristics indicating immediate resource extraction, women placed greater value on them in a short-term mate rather than in a long-term mate, in spite of the fact that women are generally less extracting in short-term than long-term mating contexts.

Prediction 17: In short-term contexts, women will see as undesirable cues that a man is reluctant to expend resources on her immediately. The test of this prediction is also shown in Table 3.4. Women seeking short-term mates especially dislike men who are stingy early on, thus showing reluctance to impart immediate resources. This attribute is seen by women as undesirable in a long-term mate as well, but significantly more so in a short-term mate. This finding occurs in spite of the fact that women generally see more characteristics as strongly undesirable in long-term, rather than in short-term, contexts.

Hypothesis 8: Because Women More Than Men Use Short-term Matings to Evaluate Long-term Perspective Mates, They Will Dislike Characteristics in a Potential Mate That Would Be Detrimental to Long-term Prospects

Prediction 18: Women more than men will dislike in a short-term mate the attribute of that person already being in a relationship. To test this prediction, we examined the relative undesirability

TABLE 3.4. Immediate Extraction of Resources: Women's Preferences

	Short term		Long term			
Characteristic	*M*	*SD*	*M*	*SD*	*t* tests	γ[a]
Spends a lot of money on me early on	1.80	1.28	1.20	1.20	2.85*	0.64
Gives me gifts early on	1.80	1.28	1.20	1.11	3.94**	0.88
Has an extravagant lifestyle	1.10	1.33	0.30	1.46	3.56**	0.64
Stingy early on	−1.90	0.72	−1.60	0.68	−2.85*	0.80

[a] The effect sizes (γ) are gammas (Howell, 1987). They signify the difference between means in standard deviation units. Cohen (1977) defines effect sizes as *small* if they are 0.20, *medium* if they are 0.50, and *large* if they are 0.80 or greater.
$^*p < .01$ $^{**}p < .001$.

to men ($N = 42$) and women ($N = 44$) of a prospective mate who was already in relationship for short-term mating, using a scale from –3 (*extremely undesirable*) to 3 (*extremely desirable*). Whereas men were bothered slightly in a short-term mating by the women already being in another relationship ($M = -1.04$), women saw that characteristic as moderately undesirable ($M = -1.70$) in this mating context ($t = 2.10$, $p < .09$, $\gamma = 0.45$).

Prediction 19: Women more than men will dislike in a short-term mate the attribute of promiscuity because it signals to a woman that the man is pursuing short-term mating relationships and is less likely to commit to long-term mateship. The same sample of 42 men and 44 women evaluated promiscuity in short-term mates using a rating scale from –3 (*extremely undesirable*) to 3 (*extremely desirable*). Whereas men found this attribute to be close to neutral (neither desirable nor undesirable), with $M = -0.41$, women rated promiscuity to be moderately undesirable ($M = -2.00$) in a short-term mate ($t = 4.55$, $p < .0001$, $\gamma = 0.89$).

Prediction 20: Because one hypothesized function for women of short-term mating is protection from aggressive men, women will value attributes such as physical size and strength in short-term mates more than in long-term mates. To test this prediction, the characteristic of *physically strong* was evaluated on its desirability in long-term and short-term mates by women ($N = 73$) and men ($N = 75$). Women placed greater value on physical strength in a short-term mate ($t = 6.49$, $p < .001$, $\gamma = 0.94$) and in a long-term mate ($t = 4.25$, $p < .001$, $\gamma = 0.66$) than did men. Furthermore, women placed greater value on physical strength in a short-term mate than in a long-term mate ($t = 2.19$, $p < .05$, $\gamma = 0.20$), despite women's generally higher standards overall for a long-term mate.

Adaptive Logic of Women Pursuing a Long-Term Sexual Strategy

Benefits of Long-Term Mating for Women

From a reproductive standpoint, why would a woman want a long-term mate, especially if she can obtain a more desirable man for a brief encounter? The key lies in the male parental investment that women garner through long-term mating. Men may provide women with food, find or defend territories, and feed and protect the children. They may also provide opportunities for learning; they may transfer status, power, or resources; and they may aid offspring in forming reciprocal alliances later in life (Buss, 1989b).

In addition to these direct benefits to the children, women are especially vulnerable when pregnant and lactating. A lone woman in ancestral environments may have been susceptible to food deprivation (Shostak, 1981). She also may become a target for aggressive men (Smuts, 1991). Thus, a long-term mate can provide protection for and sustenance to the woman, in addition to the parental investment he devotes to her offspring.

These reproductive resources all garnered by women through long-term matings can be summarized by three categories: (a) immediate material advantage to the woman and her children, (b) enhanced production advantage for her children through acquired social and economic benefits, and (c) genetic reproductive advantage for her children and variations in the qualities that lead to resource acquisition are partly heritable. Women should seek long-term mates who can provide these reproductive benefits, and their mate preferences should embody solutions to these adaptive problems. Exclusive pursuit of short-term mating, while

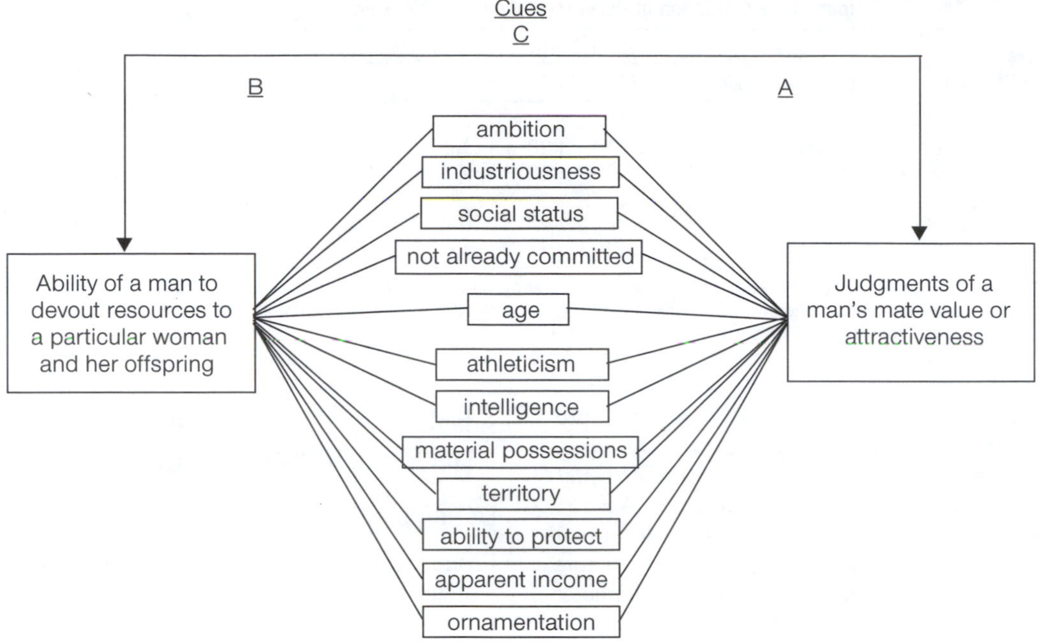

FIGURE 3.7 ■ Lens diagram of hypothesized links between cues, judgment of a man's mate value, and ability to devote resources. (Cues down the center are the potentially observable characteristics. These are hypothesized to be correlated with judgments of a man's attractiveness as a mate because of their links with resource accrual potential. A = Hypothesized links between observable cues and a man's mate value, or attractiveness as a potential mate; B = hypothesized links between a man's mate value, or attractiveness as a potential mate, and his ability to devote resources to a particular woman and her offspring.)

carrying some benefits, does not provide the benefits of long-term mating.

Figure 3.7 graphically depicts the hypothesized links between observable cues, judgments of a man's attractiveness as a long-term mate, and his ability to devote resources to a particular woman. Women are proposed to judge a man's attractiveness or mate value in part on the basis of her observations of his ambition, industriousness, status, lack of existing commitments, intelligence, material possessions, and apparent income (A). These observable cues, in turn, are known to be closely linked with a man's overall ability to devote resources to her (B), at least in North America (Willerman, 1979) and probably among contemporary tribal societies (Chagnon, 1983; Hart & Philling, 1960; Shostak, 1981). Finally, judgments of a man's attractiveness as a long-term mate should be linked with his overall ability to provide resources.

Reproductive Costs of Long-term Mating for Women

The opportunity costs to women of long-term mating are generally less severe than those incurred by men. Foreclosed mating opportunities typically do not restrict the number of children that a woman can bear as in the case of men. Nonetheless, there are benefits of short-term mating for women, benefits in immediate extraction of resources, for example, and these may be lost when pursuing a long-term mating strategy.

Problems Women Confront When Pursuing a Long-Term Mating Strategy

Problem of Male Parental Investment

Sexual Strategies Theory predicts that women will select men on the basis of the parental investment they are willing and able to provide mainly under particular conditions: (a) where resources can be accrued, defended, and monopolized; (b) where men tend to control these resources; (c) where male variance in resource holdings and willingness to invest those resources is sufficiently high; (d) where some men are in fact willing to invest these resources in a woman and her children; and (e) where women have sufficient mate value to attract an investing mate.

Among humans, these conditions are often met. Territory, money, and goods, to name just three resources, are certainly accrued, defended, monopolized, and controlled by men worldwide. Men vary tremendously in the quantity of these resources they command: from poverty and destitution to the billionaires of the jet set. In addition and perhaps most important, men differ from each other in how willing they are to invest their time and resources in long-term mateships. The range is from copulation followed by desertion (minimum parental investment) to lifelong devotion and commitment. Women should have evolved preferences for mates who show an ability and willingness to invest resources in offspring.

Hypothesis 9: Women Seeking a Long-term Mate Will Value the Ability of a Man to Provide Economic and Other Resources That Can Be Used to Invest in Her Offspring

Prediction 21: Women in long-term mating contexts, more than men, will desire cues to a potential mate's ability to acquire resources, including ambition, good earning capacity, professional degrees, and wealth. This prediction has been confirmed extensively across cultures (Buss, 1989b). A representative sample of findings from five countries located on five separate continents is shown in Figure 3.8. Women vary in how much they value good financial prospects in a long-term mate: more in the Zambian sample, for example, than in the Australian sample. Nonetheless, women more than men consistently value the economic resources of the men in prospective long-term mates, regardless of how the question is worded. Similar results occur for *social status* and *ambition–industriousness*, two characteristics known to be linked with resource accrual (Buss, 1989b).

To further test this prediction, we conducted

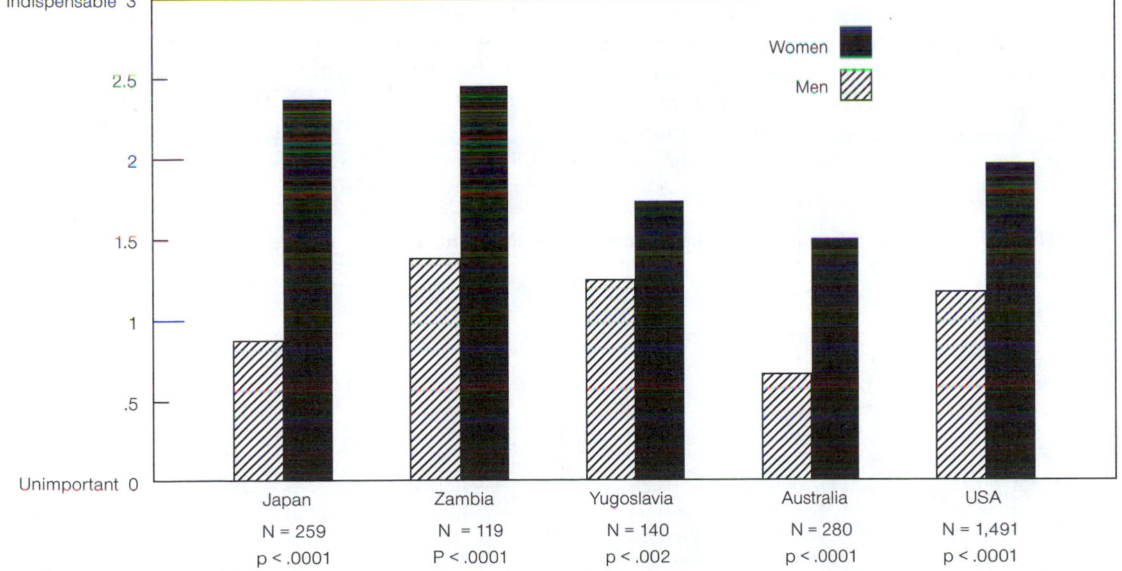

FIGURE 3.8 ■ Good financial prospect. (Subjects rated this variable, in the context of 18 other variables, on how desirable it would be in a potential long-term mate or marriage partner using a 4-point scale, ranging from 0 [*irrelevant or unimportant*] to 3 [*indispensable*].)

another study in which men ($N = 28$) and women ($N = 20$) rated how desirable the "average male" or "average female" would find each attribute in short-term and long-term mating contexts (see the method description under Prediction 16). We focused on future resource acquisition potential with characteristics such as *has a promising career, has good financial prospects, is likely to succeed in profession, is likely to earn a lot of money,* and *has a reliable future career.* The results are shown in Table 3.5. For each attribute indicating future resource potential, women found it more desirable in a long-term mate than in a short-term mate. Furthermore, *t* tests for sex differences showed that women valued each of these characteristics in a long-term mate more than men did. Combined, these studies support the hypothesis that women place a special premium on resource accrual capacities in a long-term mate.

Structural Powerlessness: An Alternative Hypothesis for Female Valuation of Male Resources

Buss (1989b) tested predictions on the basis of an alternative hypothesis, the structural powerlessness hypothesis. This hypothesis, in brief, is that because men across all cultures have greater economic power than women, women value such resources in a mate because it is the only or major route through which they can gain access to such resources (Buss & Barnes, 1986). The structural powerlessness hypothesis assumes that men and women have exactly the same information-processing mechanisms governing mate choice but that their preferences differ because the same mechanisms are getting different informational input. It assumes that a person's mate preference mechanisms assess the level of economic resources available to that person and cause one to prefer mates with a lot of resources when one has few resources oneself. In contrast, Sexual Strategy Theory predicts that the evolved preference mechanisms are, in some cases, sexually dimorphic, and that as women and men get more resources they are in a better bargaining position and hence may expect even more from a prospective mate.

The structural powerlessness hypothesis, stripped of its evolutionary anchor, predicts that (a) in countries were the sexes are more equal in economic power, the preference differences between men and women on the key characteristics should be attentuated; (b) within cultures, those women who are financially successful should value such resources less than women who are less financially successful (i.e., successful women should show preferences more similar to those of men); (c) within cultures, men who are financially less successful should value such resources more than do men who are more financially successful (i.e., they should show preferences more similar to those of women).

All three predictions have been examined. Across cultures, there is no relationship between the economic parity of men and women and the magnitude of the sex differences on the resource variables (Buss, 1989b). In an independent investigation, Townsend (1989) found that occupationally successful women medical students showed the same preferences as other women for mates

TABLE 3.5. Long-Term Resource Potential: Women's Mate Preferences

	Short term		Long term			
Characteristics	M	SD	M	SD	*t* tests	γ[a]
Has a promising career	1.20	1.20	2.30	0.80	−3.49*	0.78
Has good financial prospects	1.20	1.11	2.60	0.50	−5.09**	1.14
Likely to succeed in profession	1.10	0.97	2.60	0.50	−6.38**	1.42
Likely to earn a lot of money	0.90	0.97	2.10	0.85	−4.86**	1.09
Has a reliable future career	0.40	0.50	2.70	0.47	−15.66**	3.50
Unable to support you financially	−0.70	0.92	−1.30	1.38	3.27*	0.78
Financially poor	−0.64	0.87	−1.36	1.14	4.63**	0.70
Lacks ambition	−0.86	1.05	−2.36	0.81	9.14**	1.38
Uneducated	−1.25	1.06	−2.39	0.81	7.05**	1.06

[a] The effect sizes (γ) are gammas (Howell, 1987). They signify the difference between means in standard deviation units. Cohen (1977) defines effect sizes as *small* if they are 0.20, *medium* if they are 0.50, and *large* if they are 0.80 or greater.
*$p < .01$. **$p < .001$.

with financial resources. He concluded that "increasing socioeconomic status (SES) of women does not eliminate and may not even reduce traditional sex differences in mate selection criteria and marital goals" (p. 241). Buss (1989b) found that women with resources value them in mates more than women with less resources, contradicting the structural powerlessness hypothesis and that men who had fewer resources showed preferences indistinguishable from men with a lot of resources. Similar results have been found in two independent investigations by Weiderman and Allgeier (1992). Although additional research is needed, available evidence provides no support for the structural powerlessness hypothesis as an alternative to the evolution-based hypothesis that is based on parental investment theory. Women's sexual psychology, and more specifically their mate preference mechanisms, apparently persevered even across the different contexts of personal access to resources, suggesting the existence of sexual dimorphic, rather than monomorphic, mate preferences.

Prediction 22: In long-term contexts, women find a man's inability to accrue resources particularly undesirable, including signs that a man is poor, lacks ambition, or is uneducated. To test this prediction, 42 women judged the relative desirability–undesirability of the characteristics of *financially poor, lacking in ambition,* and *uneducated* (see Table 3.5; see the description of the procedure under Prediction 5). Women judged all three characteristics to be especially undesirable in long-term mates but only mildly undesirable in short-term mates. Furthermore, women saw these attributes as significantly more undesirable then did men in both contexts. A second study in which women evaluated their perceptions of what the average woman would seek in a mate, the characteristic *unable to support you financially* was seen as especially undesirable in a long-term mate (see Table 3.5; see the description of the procedure under Prediction 16).

General Discussion

Men and women have faced different adaptive problems and different constraints on their reproductive success throughout human evolutionary history. For men, one major reproductive constraint has been the number of reproductively valuable or fertile women they can successfully inseminate. For women, one major reproductive constraint has been obtaining as mates men who showed an ability and willingness to invest resources in themselves and their offspring. These constraints follow from the adaptive logic of Sexual Strategies Theory. They can be separated conceptually into distinct mating problems that ancestral men and women had to solve. A central thesis of this article is that men and women have evolved to pursue both long-term and short-term mating strategies and that the problems they face differ when they pursue these temporally distinct strategies. Sexual Strategies Theory predicts that psychological mechanisms such as mate preferences have evolved in response to selection pressures generated by the adaptive problems confronted in these contexts. Empirical tests of the 22 predictions from nine hypotheses derived from Sexual Strategies Theory suggests that it has heuristic value in guiding research to important domains of inquiry in the study of mating strategies. Furthermore, the theory has the virtue of organizing under one temporally contextual framework a host of findings that would otherwise remain scattered, isolated, and inexplicable. This discussion summarizes the status of the theory and then draws out implications for viewing humans from a psychological strategic perspective.

Evolutionary Psychology of Men's Mating Strategies

The potential reproductive benefit of long-term mating for men is that it offers the possibility of monopolizing a woman's entire lifetime reproductive capacity. At least four mate selection problems must be solved to succeed in this long-term strategy: the problem of identifying which women are reproductively valuable, the problem of ensuring certainty in their paternity in children (a problem exacerbated in humans by concealed ovulation in women), the problem of identifying women likely to strongly commit to a long-term mateship, and the problem of identifying women with good parenting skills.

The reproductive logic of short-term mating strategies of men differs substantially from that of long-term mating strategies. Rather than monopolizing a woman's lifelong reproductive capacity, the short-term strategy entails inseminating a number of fertile women. To succeed in the short-term strategy, men must solve different mating problems: the problem of number, the problem of fertility, the problem of identifying which women are sexually accessible, and the problem of minimizing commitment.

A central thesis of this article is that mate preferences, representing one class of psychological mechanisms, have evolved in men to solve the distinct reproductive problems associated with these strategies. Because for men the problems differ substantially according to the strategy pursued, their mate preferences were hypothsized to be highly contingent on the temporal context of matings of short-term versus long-term duration.

The preferences men express for long-term mates appear to solve the problems of reproductive value and paternity certainty. Men prefer as long-term mates women who are young and physically attractive as indicators of reproductive value (see Buss, 1989b) and who are sexually loyal and likely to be faithful as indicators of paternity certainty. Men in some cultures value chastity in a long-term mate, but this preference is highly variable across cultures, suggesting that if it is an evolved preference, it is one that is highly open to cultural input. One tentative conclusion from these data sets is that the paternity certainty problem is more typically solved by valuing cues to future behavior such as sexual loyalty, rather than cues to prior virginity per se. Furthermore, the psychological and physiological sex differences in the weighting given to events that activate jealousy (Buss et al., 1992) support the hypothesis that there are evolved mechanisms for solving the problem of paternity uncertainity after mate selection has occured.

The mate preferences that men express for short-term mates differ sharply from those expressed for long-term mates. The problem of number of partners looms large for men when pursuing a short-term mating strategy: a strategy that we hypothesized to be a larger component of men's repertoire than of women's repertoire. In human evolutionary history, large and direct increments in a man's reproductive success through the number of offspring presumably accrued from obtaining sexual access to a larger number of partners. Women, in contrast, because they are sharply contrained in the number of offspring they can produce and because sperm are usually readily available, cannot increase the number of offspring (hence, their reproductive success) by increasing the sheer number of sexual partners. The evidence supports the hypothesis that men have evolved specific psychological mechanisms for solving the problem of number. These include being more oriented toward short-term mating, greatly relaxing the standards that the short-term mate must meet, requiring less time to elapse before seeking sexual intercourse, and desiring a large number of sexual partners.

A second problem that faces men who pursue short-term sexual strategies is identifying women who are sexually accessible without a prolonged courtship. This problem appears to be solved by the preferences that men express for short-term partners who are sexually experienced: an attribute that men do not find particularly desirable in a long-term mate. Disliked in short-term mates by men are those who have a slow sex drive, are sexually inexperienced, and who are prudish: qualities that likely signal lack of sexual accessibility in the short term. Promiscuity, sexual experience, high sex drive, and lack of prudishness probably provide strong cues to a woman's relative level of sexual accessibility for short-term mating.

Sexual Strategies Theory suggests that the more resources and commitment a man must devote to a given mate, the fewer mates he can have. Men pursuing a short-term strategy are predicted to avoid women who seek a commitment or who consume large shares of their resources. The preferences that men express for short-term mates appear to reflect these concerns. Men express a strong dislike for potential short-term partners who want a commitment. Also disliked are short-term mates who are prone to spend a lot of their money.

In summary, the psychological preferences of men for mates differ sharply according to temporal context. Three general conclusions can be reached from these data: (a) short-term mating represents a larger proportion of men's mating effort than of most women's mating effort, (b) men have evolved distinct preferences that solve in part the reproductive problems associated with gaining sexual access to a number of short-term partners, and (c) men have evolved distinct preferences that solve the long-term reproductive problems associated with monopolizing a particular woman's lifetime reproductive capacity. The temporal context of mating heavily affects the mate preferences expressed by men and hence the sexual strategies they adopt.

Evolutionary Psychology of Women's Mating Strategies

Temporal context was also hypothesized to effect the mate preferences expressed by women. In principle, there are adaptive benefits that could accrue to women who pursue long-term as well as short-term mating strategies. Therefore, although short-term mating is expected to represent a smaller proportion of women's than of men's mating effort, women were hypothesized to have both strategies in their mating repertoire.

The primary benefit that can accrue to women who pursue long-term matings is gaining continuous access to a man's resources and parental investment. This benefit can be separated into two distinct mating problems: identifying men who are able to invest resources and identifying men who are willing to invest resources in her and her children. Women should value observable cues, such as ambition, industry, income, status, and generosity that are correlated with a man's ability and willingness to invest as shown in Figure 3.7. The data strongly support predictions from the first two hypotheses. Women in long-term contexts do place great value on a man's ambition, earning capacity, and professional degrees. Furthermore, women dislike prospective long-term mates who are poor, who lack ambition, and who are uneducated.

Women seeking short-term mates cannot generally gain continuous access to a mate's resources. In principle, however, there are several distinct benefits that could have accrued to ancestral women who pursued a short-term mating strategy: immediate extraction of resources, using short-term matings as an assessment device to evaluate long-term prospects, securing protection from abuse by nonmated males, and possibly better genes. Do women's short-term mate preferences reflect solutions to these problems? The data support several of these hypotheses about benefits of women's short-term mating. Women seeking short-term mates rather than long-term mates were judged by other women to desire men who spend a lot of money on them early on and give them gifts early on. Especially disliked in a short-term mate by women is the attribute of being stingy early on. These results support the hypothesis that women use short-term mating in part as a strategy for an immediate extraction of resources. Furthermore, although women value physical strength in both temporal contexts, they value it significantly more in short-term than in long-term contexts.

Is there any evidence that women, more than men, use short-term matings to evaluate long-term prospects? The evidence is indirect on this hypothesis. First, there is a significantly stronger correlation between women's short-term and long-term preferences ($r = .81$) than is the case for men ($r = .63$). Second, women see *promiscuity* and *already in a relationship* as highly undesirable qualities in a short-term mate. Men, in contrast, are not particularly bothered by these qualities in short-term mates. If women did not see short-term mates as long-term prospects, why would they be so bothered by the fact that a man is already in a relationship? The somewhat circumstantial data must be regarded as tentative, pending more direct research on the assessment functions of short-term mating for both sexes.

These potential short-term benefits to women clearly do not exhaust the possibilities. Recent evidence on sperm competition in humans suggest that women may have physiological mechanisms that preferentially favor sperm from extra-pair men over sperm from the regular long-term mates (Baker & Bellis, 1993). Recent explorations of female sexuality by female researchers (e.g., Small, 1992; N. Thornhill, 1992) suggest additional potential benefits to women of short-term mating. Future research could explore the hypotheses that women can gain the following potential benefits from short-term mating: (a) getting rid of an unwanted mate, (b) mate switching, (c) clarifying one's mate preferences, (d) deterring a long-term mate from further sexual infidelities, (e) increasing the commitment of a long-term mate, and (f) gaining access to social circles that are otherwise inaccessible.

The evidence also shows clearly that women are far less oriented toward short-term mating that are men. They maintain more exacting standards for potential mates, impose more stringent age criteria, require a longer period of time to elapse before consenting to sexual intercourse, and desire a smaller number of future mating partners. In general, we can conclude that women in the studies are less inclined to short-term mating than are men, but their short-term mate preferences nonetheless correspond to hypothesized adaptive benefits that could accrue from short-term mating.

Links between Preferences and Actual Mating Behavior

Psychological preferences could not have evolved unless they have consequences for actual behavior. Taste preferences for sugary and fatty foods, for example, could not have evolved unless they actually caused people to consume foods containing these substances, and those who did survived and reproduced in greater numbers than those lacking the preferences. Thus, an important source of empirical evidence for Sexual Strategies Theory comes from studies of actual mating behavior.

Before examining this source of evidence, it is important to outline the conceptual relations that are expected between preferences and mating behavior. Preferences are clearly only one cause of mating behavior, and, on conceptual grounds, a one-to-one correspondence between preferences and behavior is not expected. First, people cannot always get what they want. Preferences may not be able to be actualized because the relevant mates possessing all the desired qualities are not available or because one's mate value may not be significantly high to attract such mates. Second, parents and other kin often exert an influence over mating decisions, even in contemporary western societies, although this is likely to be more true where there are arranged marriages such as in India. Third, members of one's own sex often compete for the same mates, thus creating a bottleneck that precludes everyone's preferences from being realized. Finally, members of the opposite sex exert preferences, and these constrain actual mating behavior. If men desire to mate after only a brief time interval has elapsed, for example, and women require more time and investment before consenting, then this constrains the degree to which men and women can translate their preferences into mating behavior.

With these conceptual issues in mind, let us turn to six sources of empirical data bearing on actual mating behavior. First, it has been documented that men in fact marry women who were younger than they are, on average, in every country worldwide for which data exists (Buss, 1989b). Brides are three years younger than grooms on average worldwide, and this age disparity increases with divorce and remarriage. Men marry women five years younger on second marriage and 8 years younger on third marriage, at least within the United States (Secord, 1983). Men's preferences for younger women seem to be translated into actual marriages to younger women (see also Kenrick & Keefe, 1992).

A second source of behavioral data comes from large-scale sociological studies of marriage decisions. Three independent investigations have found evidence that a powerful predictor of the occupational status of the man that a woman marries is her physical attractiveness (Elder, 1969; Taylor & Glenn, 1976; Urdy & Eckland, 1984). Indeed, a woman's attractiveness seems to be a stronger predictor of actual marriage decisions than the variables of a woman's education, her socioeconomic status, or her IQ. These data support the hypothesis that women possessing qualities that are valuable to men are in a position to actualize their mate preferences.

A third source of behavioral data comes from studies that show men's far greater proclivity to seek short-term sexual encounters. R. D. Clark and Hatfield (1989), for example, demonstrated that 75% of the men did consent to having sex with an unknown woman who approached them on campus; in contrast, not a single woman consented to having sex with an unknown man who approached them in the same manner. This study was replicated 4 years later with nearly identical results (R. D. Clark & Hatfield, 1989). Men seem more prone to short-term sexual encounters in preferences, in fantasy, and in actual behavior (Ellis & Symons, 1990).

The fourth source of behavioral data comes from studies of conflict between the sexes. Buss (1989a), for example, predicted from Sexual Strategies Theory that the sources of conflict would be predictable from interference with the respective sexual strategies preferred by each sex. Thus, women were found to complain more about men's sexual aggressiveness and to become more upset when men were sexually aggressive (e.g., men trying to force sex acts on women). Men, in contrast, were found to complain more about women being sexually withholding and were more likely to become upset by sexual withholding than were women. Conflict between the sexes seems to be caused in part by one sex enacting a sexual strategy that interferes with the preferred strategy of the other sex.

A fifth source of behavioral data comes in studies on the causes of conjugal dissolution. In the most extensive cross-cultural study yet conducted on divorce, Betzig (1989) found that the causes were predictable and highly sex linked. The most frequently cited cause of divorce worldwide was sexual infidelity, and infidelity by the wife was far more likely to lead to divorce than vice versa. Other sex-linked causes of divorce across cultures included failure of a man to provide resources to the woman and their children, old age (and hence low reproductive value) on the part of the woman, infertility on the part of the woman, and sexual refusal by the woman (Betzig, 1989). Thus, the causes of divorce all appear to be caused by a failure to provide sex-linked reproductive resources that are central to male and female mate preferences.

The sixth source of behavioral data comes from studies of the tactics that men and women use in the intrasexual mate competition. This represents a more subtle set of predictions from Sexual Strategies Theory: The behavioral tactics used by one sex should be designed to embody or fulfill the mate preferences expressed by the other sex. In a series of six studies, Buss (1988a, 1988b) confirmed this link between the preferences of one sex in the tactics of intrasexual competition used by the other sex. Men were more likely to display resources as a tactic of intrasexual competition, whereas women were more likely to enhance their appearance. Analogous behavioral findings have been discovered in the domains of intersexual and intrasexual deception (Tooke & Camire, 1991).

In summary, all six sources of actual mating behavior confirm basic tenets of Sexual Strategies Theory. Marriage decisions, events leading to actual divorce, behavioral sources of conflict between the sexes, thresholds before seeking or consenting to sexual intercourse, and tactics of intrasexual competition are all predictable from the adaptive problems that each sex confronts in the contexts of short-term and long-term mating strategies. Although more research on mating behavior must be conducted to test additional predictions, the available behavioral evidence suggests that mate preferences are translated to some extent into actual mating behavior.

Unresolved Issues: Mating Problems Faced by Both Sexes and Individual Differences within Sex

Sexual Strategies Theory provides a precise set of predictions about when men and women will differ in their mating psychology and when they will be the same. It predicts that the sexes will differ only in those circumscribed domains where they have faced recurrently different adaptive problems over the course of human evolutionary history. It predicts that the sexes will be the same in all domains where they have faced the same adaptive problems. In this article, we have focused heavily on the differences because it is in these areas where the predictions are often the clearest and most easily subjected to empirical tests. However, it is important to note that there are several domains where the sexes are predicted to be more or less the same in their sexual strategies: (a) the problem of identifying a good reciprocal ally, (b) the problem of commitment, and (c) the problem of identifying mates with good parenting skills. We address these three crucial, and largely unexplored, domains in turn.

Problem of identifying a good reciprocal ally. Long-term mating relationships pose special problems from a reproductive vantage point in that they require the intense and repeated cooperation of two individuals who are genetically unrelated and who may have many competing demands that conflict with the interests of one or another of the parties. Indeed, the reproductive interests of a genetically unrelated man and woman coincide only under conditions where they have mutually produced offspring; where neither will mate with anyone else (i.e., lifetime monogamy); and where there are no genetic relatives, including children from former mates, to whom resources could be differentially diverted (Alexander, 1987; Buss, 1989a).

One crucial problem that both sexes face, therefore, is identifying a potential mate who will be a good cooperator and a good ally (and whose kin will be good cooperators and allies) so that the confluence of interest can be maximized. At the current state of knowledge, we do not know precisely what these cues are. One speculation is that the tremendous value that both sexes place on *kind and understanding* in potential mates across cultures is a possible solution to the problem of identifying a good cooperator (Buss, 1989c). The tendency of both sexes to seek mates who are similar may represent another solution to the problem of strategic confluence (Buss, 1989c). More research is needed, however, to discover empirically what cues men and women use to solve this problem linked exclusively with long-term mating.

Problem of commitment. In selecting a long-term

mate, men and women both face the problem of commitment: the problem of evaluating whether their mate will deliver consistently and over a long time period the relevant reproductive resources. Although the resources lost through commitment failures are different for men and women, they may be as reproductively severe. A woman who mates with a man who is likely to desert, defect, or redirect his mating effort risks the loss of his tangible resources as well as direct parental investment in her children. Although women do not experience lowered maternity probability if their mate is unfaithful, they do risk the diversion of his parental effort away from their children.

Men who choose women who are likely to defect risk the loss of their reproductive value and parental effort. Such women are more likely to conceive by another man and devote parental effort toward another man's children. For both sexes, the tremendous costs of a long courtship suggest that there is likely to have been commensurate reproductive benefit. This benefit cannot typically be reaped without commitment. Both men and women should value signs of commitment when they pursue a long-term mating strategy.

One important domain of future research, therefore, is the study of cues to commitment and the degree to which they are valued in long-term as contrasted with short-term mates. Using the current data sets, we found that both sexes judged the mate attribute *wants a commitment* to be considerably more desirable in a long-term mate than short-term mate. However, this finding is almost definitional and begs the question of what cues reliably forecast commitment. One possibility is provided by Johnson and Rusbult (1989), who found that people started to derogate alternative potential mates as they became more deeply committed to one mate. Thus, signs that a person is derogating other potential mates might be one cue to commitment. There are undoubtedly many more such cues, however, and future research could profitably turn to them directly (see Rusbult, 1983; Shaver, Hazen, and Bradshaw, 1988; Sternberg & Barnes, 1988).

Problem of good parenting skills. A third adaptive problem that both sexes face when pursuing a long-term mating strategy is selecting a partner who will exhibit good parenting skills. Presumably either sex would benefit by selecting a mate who parented mutually produced children in a skillful manner. Unfortunately, it is unclear conceptually how to identify the criteria by which good parenting skill could be evaluated. Some candidate criteria include intelligence, kindness, and nurturance. Barkow (1989), for example, hypothesizes that intelligence is key to good parenting skills: providing good judgment in protecting children in times of danger, good socialization practices to prepare the child for the adult world he or she will enter, and perhaps wisdom to forecast environmental changes and trends that might be impending. Furthermore, Simpson and Gangestad (1992) found through a factor analysis of mate preferences a factor they labeled *personal/parenting qualities,* which included the attributes of *responsibility, kind and understanding,* and *stability of personality*. These results may be used to guide future research that examines skillful parenting and cues that indicate it directly.

Individual Differences in Mating Strategies Within Each Sex

Sexual Strategies Theory, as developed in this article, has focused primarily on the sex-typical adaptive problems that men and women have confronted over evolutionary history when pursuing short-term and long-term strategies. It is clear, however, that individuals vary within each sex in their mating strategies (see Buss, 1991). Snyder, Simpson, and Gangestad (1986), for example, have shown that individuals vary within each sex in what they call *sociosexual orientation,* which refers to the degree to which individuals prefer long-lasting mateships versus brief sexual encounters: a dimension that bears a close resemblance to our temporal contextual dimension of short-term versus long-term mating. These individual differences show interesting links to personality variables such as extraversion and self-monitoring and have implications for a host of attitudinal and sexual variables (e.g., Gangestad & Simpson, 1990; Snyder et al., 1986).

Simpson and Gangestad (1992) offered evidence of a coherent constellation of characteristics that covary with sociosexual orientation. They find, for example, that those with restricted sociosexual orientation (long term, in the language of Sexual Strategies Theory) tend to prefer mates who are kinder, more affectionate, more responsible, and more loyal. Those with an unrestricted sociosexual orientation (short term) tend to seek mates who are physically and sexually attractive. Simpson and

Gangestad offered compelling evolutionary arguments that these alternative strategies could either be maintained by frequency-dependent selection or could be the result of ecologically contingent shifts in mating strategies.

The intriguing theoretical issue, from the vantage point of Sexual Strategies Theory, is why do some individuals favor one component of their sex-typical array of sexual strategies over another and under what conditions do they do so? One theoretical speculation centers on the mate value of the individual. Individuals of high mate value should be more able to carry out their sex-typical preferred strategy, whereas those whose mate value is low may be forced to settle for a less preferred strategy: "Those males most sought after for their adaptive attributes could have afforded to invest less in any one female's offspring. Hence, males could have been selected to invest less exclusively when they possessed adaptive attributes or resources" (Simpson & Gangestad, 1992, p. 45). In historical and cross-cultural perspective, there is some evidence for this proposition for men. Men of high status and wealth have often acquired numerous mates, whether in the form of multiple wives, concubines, mistresses, or brief sexual encounters (e.g., Betzig, 1986; Chagnon, 1983; Hart & Pilling, 1960). Thus, men whose attributes closely embody female mate preferences may more frequently carry out short-term sexual strategies, in addition to whatever long-term strategies they carry out. Alternatively, some men may simply have the power to impose their preferences on others.

Another predictor of individual differences in sexual strategy might be age, especially if short-term mating is used as a means for assessing one's mate value and for evaluating potential mates. Short-term sexual strategies might be more frequently adopted by young people to perform these assessment functions. With increasing age, the information value gleaned from short-term mating may reach diminishing returns. Thus, individuals may shift from a short-term to a long-term mating strategy with increasing age.

A third speculation about situational causes of within-sex variation centers on sudden changes in life circumstances. There is considerable evidence that serial marriage is a common mating pattern among humans across nearly all cultures (e.g., H. Fisher, 1987). Thus, a divorce may produce a period of time in which the assessment (or reassessment) functions of short-term mating again become necessary. Pursuing a short-term strategy, therefore, might be predicted to occur in between bouts of long-term mating. Another shift that could prompt the pursuit of a short-term sexual strategy would be a sudden increase in status or wealth. Any change that renders assessment functions more important would be expected to trigger the pursuit of short-term mating, at least for a period of time.

Other contextual predictors of temporal shifts in mating strategies include operational sex ratio (Petersen, 1991), cultural factors such as food sharing, anticipated future mate value, legal and social sanctions, and the strategies pursued by others (Buss, 1994). These potential predictors of individual differences in sexual strategy remain important avenues for futher development of Sexual Strategies Theory.

Conclusions and Implications

Evidence of adaption is most clearly seen in complex design: Do the design features of a mechanism function to solve special reproductive problems in particular ways that are unlikely to have arisen by chance alone (Williams, 1966)? The evidence from these empirical studies supports the general hypothesis that mate preferences, as one class of psychological mechanisms, differ in predictable ways according to temporal context and according to biological sex in ways that are unlikely to have arisen by chance alone. These preferences, manifesting themselves uniquely in each of the four context-by-sex quadrants, seem tailored to solving particular adaptive problems that are faced by men and women in short-term and long-term contexts: problems predicted by Sexual Strategies Theory.

One misunderstanding of evolutionary predictions in psychology is that postulated adaptions are presumed to be highly intractable, impervious to environmental context. Early sociobiologists may have fostered this misunderstanding by writing as if adaptations were intractable. We have shown precisely the opposite, that it is the context that powerfully determines the nature of the mate preferences observed. However, rather than invoking general, and hence imprecise and typically ill-specified contexts such as culture or socialization, we have identified a specific and theoretically driven contextual variable: Mate preferences, far from being impervious to varying conditions, are highly sensitive to temporal contextual conditions.

The temporal contextual variable, important as it appears to be, is clearly just the start of an examination of important conditions on which mate preferences depend. One excellent candidate for future research involves assessment of one's own mate value. Previous research has shown that men with low self-esteem are reluctant to approach women who are physically attractive (Berscheid & Walster, 1974). Tooby and Cosmides (1990) speculate that "a man's self-esteem may be, in part, a function of his desirability in the marriage market" (p. 53). Another study of personals ads found that men with abundant resources more often advertised for physically attractive women, and women mentioning their physical attractiveness more often advertise for men with resources (see Kenrick & Keefe, 1992). If self-esteem, resources, and attractiveness are reflections of the value, then expressed mate preferences may be calibrated up or down depending on one's mate value (Buss, 1988a). Other important contextual variables probably include age, one's network of family and alliances, the sex ratio in the available mating pool, the degree to which parents and other kin influence the mating decisions, and individual successes or failures in the pursuit of each strategy.

The empirical studies presented here represent just the start of the study of the effects of context on psychological mate preferences. At the current stage, this theory is limited in several important respects: It does not identify all of the conditions affecting when men and women will pursue short-term versus long-term sexual strategies, it does not currently account for individual differences within sex, and it has not accrued empirical support for predictions about the adaptive problems confronted by both sexes such as identifying cues to commitment and cues to good parenting skills. Even with these current limitations, however, Sexual Strategies Theory generates more detailed, more precise, and more numerous predictions than any previous theory of human mating about the adaptive problems that men and women have confronted in different mating contexts. Combined with the supporting empirical tests, we now have the outlines of sexual strategies that men and women have evolved as solutions to these mating problems and a theoretical understanding of why they have done so.

REFERENCES

Alexander, R. D. (1987).*The biology of moral systems.* New York: Aldine de Gruyter.

Alexander, R. D., & Noonan K. M. (1979). Concealment of ovulation, parental care, and human social evolution. In N. A. Chagnon & W. Irons (Eds.), *Evolutionary biology and human social behavior: An anthropological perspective* (pp. 402–435). North Scituate, MA: Duxbury Press.

Baker, R. R., & Bellis, M. A. (1993). Human sperm competition: Ejaculate manipulation by females and a function for the female orgasm. *Animal Behavior,* p. 887–909.

Barkow, J. (1989). *Darwin, sex and status.* Toronto, Ontario, Canada: University of Toronto Press.

Bar-Tal, D., & Saxe, L. (1976). Perceptions of similarly and dissimilarly attractive couples and individuals. *Journal of Personality and Social Psychology, 33,* 772–781.

Berscheid, E., & Walster, E. (1974). Physical attractiveness. In L. Berkowitz (Ed.), *Advances in experimental social psychology* (pp. 157–215). San Diego, CA: Academic Press.

Betzig, L. (1989). Causes of conjugal disillusion: A cross-cultural study.*Current Anthropology, 30,* 654–676.

Burley, N., & Symanski, R. (1981). Women without: An evolutionary and cross-cultural perspective on prostitution. In R. Symanski (Ed.),*The immoral landscape: Female prostitution in western societies* (pp. 239–274). Toronto, Ontario, Canada: Butterworths.

Buss, D. M. (1985). Human mate selection. *American Scientist, 73,* 47–51.

Buss, D. M. (1987). Sex differences in human mate selection criteria: An evolutionary perspective. In C. Crawford, D. Krebs, & M. Smith (Eds.), *Sociobiology and psychology: Ideas, issues, and applications* (pp. 335–352). Hillsdale, NJ: Erlbaum.

Buss, D. M. (1988a). The evolution of human intrasexual competition. *Journal of Personality and Social Psychology, 54,* 616–628.

Buss, D. M. (1988b). From vigilance to violence: Mate guarding tactics. *Ethology and Sociobiology, 9,* 291–317.

Buss, D. M. (1989a). Conflict between the sexes: Strategic interference and the evocation of anger and upset. *Journal of Personality and Social Psychology, 56,* 735–747.

Buss, D. M. (1989b). Sex differences in human mate preferences: Evolutionary hypotheses tested in 37 cultures. *Behavioral and Brain Sciences, 12,* 1–49.

Buss, D. M. (1989c, June). *A strategic theory of trait usage: Personality and the adaptive landscape.* Paper presented at the Invited Workshop of Personality Language, Universities of Groningen, Groningen, The Netherlands.

Buss, D. M. (1991). Evolutionary personality psychology. *Annual Review of Psychology, 42,* 459–491.

Buss, D. M. (1994). *The evolution of desire: Strategies of human mating.* New York: Basic Books.

Buss, D. M., & Barnes, M. F. (1986). Preference is in human mate selection. *Journal of Personality and Social Psychology, 50,* 559–570.

Buss, D. M., Larsen, R. J., Westen, D., & Semmelroth, J. (1992). Sex differences in jealousy: Evolution, physiology, and psychology. *Psychological Science, 3,* 251–255.

Cattell, R. B., & Nesselroade, J. R. (1967). *"Likeness" and "completeness" theories examined by 16 personality factor measures on stably and unstably married couples* (Advanced Publication No. 7). Urbana University of Illinois, The Laboratory of Personality and Group Analysis.

Chagnon, N. (1983). *Yanomamo: The fierce people* (3rd ed.). New York: Holt, Rinehart & Winston.

Clark,M. S. & Reis, H. T. (1988). Interpersonal processes in close relationships. *Annual Review of Psychology and Human Sexuality, 2,* 39–55.

Clutton-Brock, T. H. (1991). *The evolution of parental care.* Princeton, NJ: Princeton University Press.

Cohen, J. (1977). *Statistical power analysis for the behavioral sciences* (rev. ed.). San Diego, CA: Academic Press.

Daly, M., & Wilson, M. (1983). *Sex, evolution, and behavior.* Boston: Willard Grant Press.

Daly, M. & Wilson, M. (1988). *Homicide.* Hawthorne, NY: Aldine de Gruyter.

Daly, M., Wilson, M., & Weghorst, S. J. (1982). Male sexual jealousy. *Ethology and Sociobiology, 3,* 11–27.

Darwin, C. (1871). *The descent of man and selection in relation to sex.* London: Murray.

Dawkins, R. (1986). Wealth, polygyny, and reproductive success. *Behavioral and Brain Sciences, 9,* 190–191.

Eckland, B. (1968). Theories of mate selection. *Social Biology, 15,* 71–84.

Elder, G. H., Jr. (1969). Appearance and education in marriage mobility. *American Sociological Review, 34,* 519–533.

Ellis, B. J., & Symons, D. (1990). Sex differences and sexual fantasy: An evolutionary psychological approach. *Journal of Sex Research, 27,* 527–556.

Epstein, E., & Guttman, R. (1984). Mate selection in man: Evidence, theory, and outcome. *Social Biology, 31,* 243–278.

Fisher, H. (1987). The four year itch. *Natural History, 10,* 22–29.

Fisher, R. A. (1930). *The genetical theory of natural selection.* Oxford, England: Clarendon Press.

Ford, C. S., & Beach, F. A. (1951). *Patterns of sexual behavior.* New York: Harper & Row.

Frank, R. (1988). *Passions within reason: The strategic role of the emotions.* New York: Norton.

Frayser, S. G. (1985). *Varieties of sexual experience.* New Haven, CT: HRAF Press.

Gangestad, S. W. (1989). The evolutionary history of genetic variation: An emerging issue in the behavioral genetic study of personality. In D. M. Buss & N. Cantor (Eds.), *Personality: Recent trends and emerging directions* (pp. 320–332). Berlin, Federal Republic of Germany: Springer-Verlag.

Gangestad, S. W., & Simpson, J. A. (1990). Toward an evolutionary history of female sociosexual variation. *Journal of Personality, 58,* 69–96.

Gangestad, S. W., & Thornhill, R. (1994). Facial attractiveness, developmental stability, and fluctuating asymmetry. *Ethology and Sociobiology, 15,* 73–85.

Hamilton, W. D., & Zuk, M. (1982). Heritable true fitness and bright birds: A role for parasites? *Science, 218* , 384–387.

Hart, C. W., & Pilling, A. R. (1960). *The Tiwi of North Australia.* New York: Holt, Rinehart & Winston.

Hill, R. (1945). Campus values in mate selection. *Journal of Home Economics, 37,* 554–558.

Hite, S. (1987). *Women and love: A cultural revolution in progress.* New York: Knopf.

Howell, D. C. (1987). *Statistical methods for psychology* (2nd ed.). Boston: PWS-Kent.

Hrdy, S. B. (1981). *The woman that never evolved.* Cambridge, MA: Harvard University Press.

Hudson, J. W., & Henze, L. F. (1969). Campus values in mate selection: A replication. *Journal of Marriage and the Family, 31,* 772–775.

Johnson, D. J., & Rusbult, C. E. (1989). Resisting temptation: Devaluation of alternative partners as a means of maintaining commitment in close relationships. *Journal of Personality and Social Psychology, 57,* 967–980.

Kenrick, D. T., & Keefe, R. C. (1989). Time to integrate sociobiology and social psychology. *Behavioral and Brain Sciences, 12,* 24–26.

Kenrick, D. T., & Keefe, R. C. (1992). Age preferences in mates reflect sex differences in reproductive strategies. *Behavioral and Brain Sciences, 15,* 75–133.

Kenrick, D. T., Sadalla, E. K., Groth, G., & Trost, M. R. (1990). Evolution, traits, and the stages of human courtship: Qualifying the parental investment model. *Journal of Personality, 58,* 97–116.

Kinsey, A. C., Pomeroy, W. B., & Martin, C. E. (1948). *Sexual behavior in the human male.* Philadelphia: W. B. Saunders.

Kinsey, A. C., Pomeroy, W. B., & Martin, C. E. (1953). *Sexual behavior in the human female.* Philadelphia: W. B. Saunders.

Lockard, J. S., & Adams, R. M. (1991). Human serial polygyny: Demographic, reproductive, marital, and divorce data. *Ethology and Sociobiology, 2,* 177–186.

Malinowski, B. (1929). *The sexual life of savages in North-Western Malanesia.* London:Kegan Paul, Trench, & Trubner.

McGinnis, R. (1958). Campus values in mate selection. *Social Forces, 35,* 368–373.

Murdock, G. P. (1967). *Ethnographic atlas.* Pittsburgh, PA: University of Pittsburgh Press.

Murstein, B. (1967). Stimulus-value: A theory of marital choice. *Journal of Marriage and the Family, 32,* 465–481.

Petersen, F. A. (1991). Secular trends in human sex ratios: Their influence on individual and family behavior. *Human Nature, 2,* 271–291.

Rozin, P., & Vollmecke, T. A. (1986). Food likes and dislikes. *Annual Review of Nutrition, 6,* 433–456.

Rusbult, C. E. (1983). A longitudinal test of the investment model: The development (and deterioration) of satisfaction and commitment in heterosexual involvements. *Journal of Personality and Social Psychology, 45,* 101–117.

Rushton, J. P. (1989). Genetic similarity, human altruism, and group selection. *Behavioral and Brain Sciences, 12,* 503–559.

Secord, P. F. (1983). Imbalanced sex ratios: The social consequences. *Personality and Social Psychology Bulletin, 9,* 925–542.

Shaver, P., Hazen, C., & Bradshaw, D. (1988). Love as attachment: the integration of three behavioral systems. In R. Sternberg & M. Barnes (Eds.), *The psychology of love* (pp. 66–99). New Haven, CT: Yale University Press.

Shostak, M. (1981). *Nisa: The life and words of a !Kung woman.* Cambridge, MA: Harvard University Press.

Simpson, J. A., & Gangestad, S. W. (1992). Sociosexuality and romantic partner choice. *Journal of Personality, 60,* 31–52.

Small, M. (1992). The evolution of female sexuality and mate selection in humans. *Human Nature, 3,* 133–156.

Smuts, B. B. (1991). Male aggression against women: An evolutionary perspective. *Human Nature ,3,* 1–44.

Smuts, B. B. (in press). Male aggression against female primates: Evidence and theoretical implications. *Advances in the Study of Behavior.*

Snyder, M., Simpson, J. A., & Gangestad, S. (1986). Personality and sexual relations. *Journal of Personality and Social Psychology, 51,* 181–190.

Sternberg, R. J. (1988). *The triangle of love.* New York: Basic Books.

Sternberg, R. J., & Barnes, M. (1988). *The psychology of love.* New Haven, CT: Yale University Press.

Studd, M., & Gattiker, U. E. (1991). The evolutionary psychology of sexual harassment in organizations. *Ethology and Sociobiology, 12,* 249–290.

Symons, D. (1979). *The evolution of human sexuality.* New York: Oxford University Press.

Symons, D. (1987). An evolutionary approach: Can Darwin's view of life shed light on human sexuality? In J. H. Grer & W. O'Donohue (Eds.) *Theories of human sexuality* (pp. 91–122). New York: Plenum Press.

Symons, D. (1992). On the use and misuse of Darwinism in the study of human behavior. In J. Barkow, L. Cosmides, & J. Tooby (Eds.) *The adapted mind: Evolutionary psychology and the generation of culture* (pp. 137–159). New York: Oxford University Press.

Taylor, P. A., & Glenn, N. D. (1976). The utility of education and attractiveness for females' status attainment through marriage. *American Sociological Review, 41,* 484–498.

Thiessen, D., & Gregg, B. (1980). Human assortative mating and genetic equilibrium: An evolutionary perspective. *Ethology and Sociobiology, 1,* 111–140.

Thornhill, N. (1992, August). *Female short-term mating strategies: The self-esteem hypothesis.* Paper presented at the Annual Meeting of the Human Behavior and Evolution Society, Albuquerque, NM.

Thornhill, R., & Thornhill, N. (1983). Human rape: An evolutionary analysis. *Ethology and Sociobiology, 4,* 63–99.

Thornhill, R., & Thornhill, N. (1987). Human rape: The strengths of the evolutionary perspective. In C. Crawford, D. Krebs, & M. Smith (Eds.), *Sociobiology and psychology: Ideas, issues, and applications* (pp. 373–400). Hillsdale, NJ: Erlbaum.

Tooby, J., & Cosmides, L. (1990). On the universality of human nature and the uniqueness of the individual: The role of genetics and adaptation. *Journal of Personality, 58,* 17–68.

Tooke, J., & Camire, L. (1991). Patterns of deception in intersexual and intrasexual mating strategies. *Ethology and sociobiology, 12,* 345–364.

Townsend, J. M. (1989). Mate selection criteria: A pilot study. *Ethology and sociobiology, 10,* 241–253.

Trivers, R. (1972). Parental investment and sexual selection. In B. Campbell (Eds.), *Sexual selection and the descent of man* (pp. 136–179). Chicago: Aldine-Atherton.

Trivers, R. (1985) *Social evolution.* Menlo Park, CA: Benjamin/Cummings.

Urdy, J. R., & Eckland, B. K. (1984). Benefits of being attractive. *Psychological Reports, 54,* 47–56.

Vandenberg, S. (1972). Assortative mating, or who married whom? *Behavior Genetics, 2,* 127–158.

Weiderman, M. W., & Allegier, E. R. (1992). Gender differences in mate selection criteria: Sociobiological or socioeconomic explanation? *Ethology and Sociobiology, 13,* 115–124.

Willerman, L. (1979). *The psychology of individual and group differences.* New York: Freeman.

Williams, G. C. (1966). *Adaptation and natural selection: A critique of some current evolutionary thought.* Princeton: Princeton University Press.

Williams, G. C. (1975). *Sex and evolution.* Princeton, NJ: Princeton University Press.

Wilson, M., & Daly, M. (1992). The man who mistook his wife for a chattel. In J. Barkow, L. Cosmides, & J. Tooby (Eds.), *The adapted mind: Evolutionary psychology and the generation of culture* (pp. 289–322). New York: Oxford University Press.

Winch, R. (1958). *Mate selection.* New York: Harper & Row.

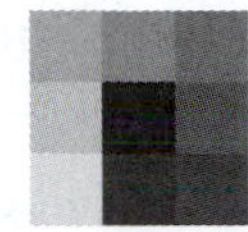

READING 4

Gender Differences in Erotic Plasticity: The Female Sex Drive as Socially Flexible and Responsive

Roy F. Baumeister • Case Western Reserve University

Responding to controversies about the balance between nature in culture in determining human sexuality, the author proposes that the female sex drive is more malleable than the male in response to socioculture and situational factors. A large assortment of evidence supports 3 predictions based on the hypothesis of female erotic plasticity: (a) Individual women will exhibit more variation across time than men in sexual behavior, (b) female sexuality will exhibit larger effects than male in response to most specific socioculture variables, and (c) sexual attitude-behavior consistency will be lower for women than men. Several possible explanations for female erotic plasticity are reviewed, including adaptation to superior male political and physical power, the centrality of female change (from no to yes) as a prerequisite for intercourse, and the idea that women have a milder sex drive than men.

Sex and mating seem to be accomplished in a fairly straightforward, predictable, even routine manner in many species of animals. Human sexuality, in contrast, has long been recognized as a rich, confusing tangle, in which biological drives, sociocultural meanings, formative individual experiences, and additional unknown factors play powerful roles. Among the most basic unresolved questions about human sexuality is that of the relative contributions of nature and culture: Does sexual response depend primarily on socioculture factors such as meanings, context, relationship status, communication, norms, and rules—or is it mainly determined by hormones, genes, and other biological processes? Even in recent decades, theories about human sexual desire have differed radically in their relative emphasis on nature and culture. To be sure, hardly any theorist goes to the extreme of insisting that either nature or culture is totally responsible for determining the human sex drive, but the compromise formulations differ widely in their relative emphasis.

The two most influential theories about sexuality have been the social constructionist and the essentialist (DeLamater & Hyde, 1998). Social constructionist theories have regarded human sexual desire as shaped extensively by culture and socialization, often mediated by language as an ordering principle that is shared in common with other people. These theorists emphasize cross-cultural variation to argue for the cultural relativity of sexual desire (see, e.g., Staples, 1973). Who does what to whom sexually is regarded as a product of cultural rules and individual, linguistically mediated decisions rather than as a biological imperative. Social constructionist theories have also been invoked by feminists to depict human sexual desire as shaped by patriarchal society as part of its efforts to exploit and subjugate women (see, e.g., Kitzinger, 1987). Although social constructionists do not deny that there may be certain biological foundations to sexuality, they emphasize culture and social influence as the decisive factors in explaining human sexuality.

Essentialist theories, in contrast, propose that there are true and definite forms of sexuality that remain constant, even though situational factors may occasionally interfere with or shape their expression. As DeLamater and Hyde (1998) emphasized, evolutionary and sociobiological analyses of sexuality fall in this category, for they explain sexuality in terms of innate motivational patterns that have evolved to suit the reproductive contingencies of males and females so as to maximize the passing on of each person's genes (see, e.g., Buss & Schmitt, 1993). Some of these theories treat culture as a system adapted to accomodate the innate biological patterns (see, e.g., Symons, 1995). In any case, biology, not culture, is featured as the main source of casual explanations.

The present article offers yet another conceptualization of the relative contributions of nature and culture to human sexual desire. The point of departure is that there is no single correct answer that holds true for all human beings. Instead, I suggest that female sexuality, as compared with male, is more subject to the influence of cultural, social factors. Although male sexuality must frequently make concessions to opportunity and other external constraints, male desire is depicted here as relatively rigid, innate determinants. Female sexuality, in contrast, is depicted as fairly malleable and mutable: It is responsive to culture, learning, and social circumstances. The plasticity of the female sex drive offers greater capacity to adapt to changing external circumstances as well as an opportunity for culture to exert a controlling influence. From the global perspective of the broader society, if controlling people's behavior is the goal, women's sexual patterns are more easily changed than men's.

Definitions

I use the term *gender* to refer to maleness and femaleness, whether biological or social, in order to reserve the term *sex* for activities leading to orgasm or genital arousal. The term *erotic plasticity* is used to refer to the degree to which a person's sex drive can be shaped and altered by cultural and social factors, from formal socialization to situational pressures. Thus, high erotic plasticity entails being subject to situational, social, or cultural influence regarding what types of partners and what types of sexual activities one would desire and enjoy. Desiring to perform the same act with a new partner does not necessarily constitute plasticity, for it is quite possible to have a stable, consistent desire to perform certain acts with many different partners.

The "sex drive" is a hypothetical construct, and research studies actually measure attitudes, behavior, and desire. The term *attitude* is used here to refer to general opinions and abstract rules that encompass broad categories and multiple situations. *Desire* refers to situation-specific feelings of sexual arousal and wanting to engage in particular acts with particular partners. *Behavior* refers to what the person actually does, such as physically engaging in particular sex acts. Desire may contradict attitudes, such as when a person feels an urge to have sex with a partner who is regarded as off-limits. Behavior can contradict either desire or attitude, such as when a person refrains from much-wanted sex or has intercourse with a forbidden partner.

Theory: Differential Plasticity

The central idea of this article is that the female sex drive is more malleable than the male, indicating higher average erotic plasticity. More precisely, female sexual responses and sexual behaviors are shaped by cultural, social, and situational factors to a greater extent than male. Plasticity could be manifested through changes in what is desired (e.g., preferred frequency of sex, degree of variety), or in expression of desire (e.g., patterns of activity). Changes in attitudes may contribute to those behavioral changes.

Because debates about female sexuality are often perturbed by bitter conflicts based on implicit value judgments, it is important to address the value question explicitly. Frankly, I see almost no reason to think that it is better or worse to have high erotic plasticity, and so the present hypothesis does not entail that one gender is better (or better off) than the other in this regard. The difference may be important for predicting a variety of behavior patterns, attitudes, misunderstandings, and conflicts, but there is no inherent moral or practical superiority on either side.

There are two small exceptions to the value-free tone of my hypothesis. That is, two small value judgments could be made, and they point to opposite directions. The first is that it is generally better to be flexible because one can adapt more readily to changing circumstances. The capacity to change is inherently adaptive, and being adaptive is good. In this respect, women may be better off than men if the present hypothesis is correct because their sexuality can adjust more easily and readily. Thus, if changes in social circumstances place equal demands for adjustment on males and females, the females will be more successful than the males at making these adjustments, or they will be able to achieve that success with less difficulty.

The other exception is that higher erotic plasticity may render a person more vulnerable to external influences, with the resulting possibility that one could end up being influenced to do things that are not in one's best long-term interests. In simple terms, it may be easier to talk a woman into doing something sexual that she does not really wanted to or something that is not good for her, as compared with talking a man into doing something that is comparably contrary to his wishes and needs. The present hypothesis has to do with receptivity to influence, and being receptive to influence can under some circumstances take on a negative tone (e.g., gullibility).

Neither of these value-linked effects is likely to be widespread or powerful. Hence, erotic plasticity should not be invoked to argue for the superiority of either gender.

Empirical Predictions

The hypothesis of differential erotic plasticity permits empirical predictions. A first, basic prediction is that intraindividual variation (i.e., within-person variance) in sexual behavior will be greater among women than men. If women are malleable in response to situational and social factors, then as a woman moves from one situation to another, her sexual desires and behaviors may be subject to change. The lesser (hypothesized) flexibility of men would mean that male sexual patterns will remain more stable and constant across time and across different situations. (Lack of opportunity may be an exception: A man's sexual behavior may depend on whether he can find a willing partner). Physical changes, such as ill health or major hormonal changes, might well have a strong effect. But as regards changing social situations and different life circumstances, the average man's desires should remain more stable and constant than the average woman's.

This theory does not extend to making predictions about interindividual variations, because these could well depend on innately or genetically prepared patterns. The men in a given culture may collectively have more variations in their individual sexual appetites than do the women without violating the hypothesis of female plasticity. A familiar example of gender differences in interindividual variance in genetically influenced traits is found in research on metal retardation and intelligence: The two genders have nearly identical mean IQ scores, but the males have higher variance, therefore being proportionally overrepresented at both extremes (Jensen, 1998; Lehrke, 1997; J. A. Roberts, 1945). Such patterns are plausible with sexuality, too, and I am not making predictions about interindividual variance (although evidence about paraphilias are considered briefly among the possible limitations and counterexamples). The present hypothesis concerns only intraindividual variance: Once a man's sexual tastes emerge, they are less susceptible to change or adaptation than a woman's.

A second prediction is that specific sociocultural factors will have greater impact on women's sexuality than on men's. To put this prediction in more precise, statistical terms, the sociocultural variables will have bigger effect sizes in predicting responses of women than of men. Thus, women will vary more than men from one culture to another and from one historical period to another. Socializing institutions, such as schools and churches, should produce bigger changes in women than in men with regard to sexual behavior.

A final prediction is that attitude–behavior consistency (with regard to sex) will be lower among women than men. If female sexual response is malleable by situational and social factors, then a woman's behavior cannot be easily predicted by her attitudes (especially general, abstract attitudes). In simple terms, her sexual responses depend more on external context than on internal factors, relative to those of males and so her attitudes are less likely to determine her behavior. She may, for example, hold an attitude in favor of using condoms or against anal intercourse, but situational factors may intrude to cause her to act contrary to those attitudes under some circumstances (and even to desire such attitude-contrary acts). The prediction is methodologically a useful complement to the first one because it avoids the confound that data on women are somehow simply more conclusive or reliable than data on men. The erotic plasticity hypothesis predicts that cultural and social factors will show higher correlations with sexual responses of women than men—whereas attitude–behavior correlations will be lower for women than for men.

Reasons for Plasticity

Why should women have more erotic plasticity than men? I have three different hypotheses, each of which could offer some potential insight into the gender differences in erotic plasticity.

The first is based on difference in power. On average, men are physically stronger and more aggressive than women, and they also tend to hold greater sociopolitical and economic power. If two partners' sexual wishes were to differ, the man would have several advantages over the woman for getting his way. Greater flexibility on the part of women would be one adaptive response to the standard problem of bonding with someone who would be able to impose his desires by means of physical coercion or social power, should that ever become necessary (as he saw it). Biologists and evolutionary psychologists believe that the relative superiority of male physical power is strongly linked in male reproductive patterns and goals (such as male competition under circumstances of extreme polygyny; Gould & Gould, 1997; Ridley, 1993), and feminists emphasize that male political power shapes the sexual interactions between the sexes and results in the cultural suppression of female sexuality. The present suggestion could be seen as another such process, in which women became socially malleable as an adaptation to male power.

The second is that flexibility may be an inherent requirement of the female role in sex. The simplest version of this would emphasize that most societies (including other species similar to humans) limit sexual activity by having the female refuse sexual offers and advances from most males. Of course, if females refused all male advances, the species would fail to reproduce. Women are negative toward most potential sex partners (i.e., most men) but occasionally switch to positive. A negative response is the woman's default option, as it were. In practice, this entails that sex generally commences when the woman switches her initially negative stance to a positive one. That is, when a couple begins having sex, it is mainly because the woman has changed her decision: The woman initially rejects the man's advances but later changes her vote from no to yes. The centrality of this change (from no to yes) in female sexuality requires each woman to have a certain degree of flexibility, and the broader patterns of erotic plasticity would follow from this foundation. Change requires changeability and hence begets further change.

The third possible explanation is based on differential drive strength. This would invoke the politically unpopular but theoretically plausible view that women have a weaker sex drive than men. A relatively weak motivation is presumably easier to redirect, channel, or transform from a powerful one. Women could thus more easily be persuaded to accept substitutes or alternate forms of satisfaction, as compared with men, if women's overall sexual desires are milder.

Proximal Sources of Plasticity

These root causes may be translated into the actual degree of behavioral plasticity of living individuals either through innate, genetic patterns or by social learning processes and personal experiences (even conscious adaptations). The nature of the mediating, proximal causes is not easily resolved, but a few speculative suggestions may be offered. How, then, is erotic plasticity actually instilled?

The possibility that it is biologically based must be considered. Many sexuality-based traits are supposedly genetically prepared by the X chromosome, of which women have two and men only have one. Having two different sets of relevant genes could allow for greater flexibility than having only one. Specifically, the two X chromosomes could carry different prescriptions for behavior, and hence it would be up to the environment to determine which one would prevail. Males also, in contrast, would receive a single and unambiguous genetic program, leaving less opportunity for the environmental influence.

Hormone levels provide another plausible basis for differential plasticity. Research has generally found that testosterone is the single hormone that has the greatest effects on sexual behavior in both males and females. Because males have substantially more testosterone than females, male behavior may be more subject to its casual influence than female behavior. (On the other hand, females receptors may be more sensitive to testosterone than are those of males, which could offset the difference in quantity of the hormone.)

In another relevant line of argument, T. Roberts and Pennebaker (1995; also Pennebaker & Roberts, 1992) have concluded that men are generally better than women at perceiving and detecting their inner bodily states. They noted that in socially impoverished environments such as laboratories and hospitals, males consistently outperform females at estimating their own bodily reactions such as blood pressure, heartbeat, stomach contractions, respiratory resistance, finger temperature, and blood glucose levels. This gender difference disappears when measures are taken in naturalistic and meaning-rich settings, in which multiple cues about sources of feelings are available. Roberts and Pennebaker proposed that men judge their emotional and arousal responses based on direct detection of psychological cues, whereas women rely more on social and situational cues to know how they respond. If this is true generally for all emotions, it would presumably be even stronger for sexual responses, because the signs of arousal are much more salient and unambiguous in the male than in the female. This argument could also explain why testosterone and other inner, biochemical realities have stronger effects on male than female sexuality: If men are more attuned to their inner bodily states, than their level of testosterone would exert a stronger effect on their behavior.

Yet another possibility is that males have evolved to be more strongly driven by natural and genetic factors. Some authors have speculated that there may be a higher rate of mutations among males and females. One such speculation is that the Y chromosome (unique to males) might be a popular target of mutations. Nature may have targeted males and the Y chromosome for trying out new mutations because the greater reproductive variance among males would give more opportunity for natural selection to operate (discussed by Kacelinik, 1999). The difference in reproductive variance is well established. In human beings, for example, most females produce at least one child, and hardly any woman has more than 10 babies. In contrast, many men have zero offspring, and others exceed 10 by substantial amounts (Gould & Gould, 1997; Ridley, 1993). Thus, men exceed women at both extremes of reproductive outcomes (i.e., more at zero and more over 10). These differences help determine how long natural selection takes to sort out whether a particular mutation increases or decreases reproductive success. The relatively small variation in female reproductive outcomes entails that many generations would be required for a given mutant to prove itself better or worse than the original. In contrast, a mutation in males might yield bigger effects within fewer generations: An adaptive mutation might help a male produce dozens of offspring, and a maladaptive one would quickly be eliminated from the gene pool. Because males thus make more efficient vehicles with which to select and evolve, therefore, male sexual behavior may have gradually become more encumbered with such biological influences.

Evolutionary arguments often invoke differential reproductive goals for men and women (see, e.g., Buss & Schmidt, 1993; Gould & Gould, 1997; Ridley, 1993). Because women cannot have as many offspring as men, they are presumably more selective about sex partners. Although one could argue a priori that the greater selectivity could lead to lower plasticity (because the woman can ill afford to compromise or take chances), one might also suggest that selectivity mandates a complex, careful decision process that attends to subtle cues and contextual factors and that this very complexity provides the basis for greater plasticity.

The biological and evolutionary arguments suggest searching for erotic plasticity in other species, which is beyond the expertise of the author and the scope of this review. Still, an important recent study by Kendrick, Hinton, Atkins, Haupt, and Skinner (1998) is relevant. In an experimental design, newborn sheep and goats were exchanged, so that the sheep were raised by goats and vice versa. After they reached adulthood, they were reunited with their biological species, and their mating preferences were observed. Consistent with the hypothesis of female erotic plasticity, the adult females were willing to mate with either species. The males, in contrast, preferred only their adoptive species and refused to mate with their biological conspecifics, even after living exclusively with their own kind for three years. These results suggest that male sexual inclinations are based on a process of sexual imprinting that occurs early in life and remains inflexible, whereas female sexual inclinations can continue to change in adulthood.

The hypothesis that male sexuality is subject to an early imprinting process that is irreversible (as opposed to reversible influences on female sexuality) suggests that both genetic preparation and early experiences are relevant. It qualifies the broad hypothesis about greater female plasticity: Perhaps there is a stage early in life during which male sexuality is highly receptive to social, environmental influences. After this imprinting, however, male sexuality remains relatively rigid and inflexible, whereas female sexuality retains plasticity throughout adolescence and adulthood.

This dovetails well with a recent theory of sexual orientation put forward by Bem (1996, 1998). Bem rejected direct genetic influences on sexual orientation but suggested that genes may affect temperament, which may in turn lead a young person to prefer either males or females as friends and playmates. Later, the less familiar gender creates arousal and thereby becomes the focus of sexual attraction. Bem (1996, 1998) has specifically suggested that his theory predicts that female sexual orientation will be more fluid and changeable than male, because little girls are more likely than little boys to have opposite-sex friends and playmates. Because "women actually grow up in a phenomenologically less gender-polarized culture than do men" (Bem, 1998, p. 398), men tend to be polarized into finding only males or only females sexually appealing, whereas women's greater familiarity with both genders enables them to be attracted to either or both. One can expand Bem's argument to propose that this greater bisexual orientation of women will provide the foundation for other forms of plasticity and change. This extension is similar to the argument I made regarding change and the female sexual script, except that the cause of plasticity depends entirely on social factors and early experiences, and any contribution by genetic factors is indirect.

Other, more purely cultural arguments could be proposed to account for differential plasticity. These would suggest that culture teaches men to obey their biological promptings but teaches women to ignore theirs and obey social prescriptions instead. These arguments seem relatively implausible in light of evidence that, throughout history, the prevailing stereotypes have regarded women as closer to nature than men and that in fact when society does try to change women's behavior it usually does so by telling women what is allegedly in their biological nature, as opposed to teaching them to ignore their biological factuality (see, e.g., Margolis, 1984). Still, it is conceivable that new, more plausible versions of these explanations may be forthcoming.

Casual Processes

Last, it is helpful to consider the possible casual processes, even though these extend the theoretical argument beyond what can be tested against the currently available research literature. If the balance of nature versus cultural determinants of sexuality differs by gender, then the casual processes that direct sexual behavior are also likely to differ.

Natural processes are typically mediated by biochemical processes. Hormones such as testosterone are likely to exert strong and direct effects. Despite the fact that the exact processes leading from genes to behavior are not fully understood (although this field is one in which substantial advances are anticipated in the next decade), one assumes biochemical factors play a crucial role in mediating such processes.

In contrast, cultural processes are mediated by meanings, which is to say informational, symbolic concepts that can be expressed in language and communicated between group members. Norms, attitudes, rules, expectations, and relationship concepts provide contexts from which specific sexual acts and decisions can draw meaning. Behavior depends of these meanings.

The hypothesized gender difference thus predicts that male sexuality will be shaped more than female sexuality by biochemical factors, including genetics and hormones. In contrast, female sexuality will be more meaning-driven than male sexuality, so that contexts and interpretation shape women's sexual decision-making (and other sexual responses) more than men's.

Hypothesis Formation: The Sexual Revolution

The present investigation was initially stimulated by a conclusion drawn by Ehrenreich, Hess, and Jacobs (1986) in their history of the sexual revolution in the United States, namely, that that revolution was mainly a change in women not men. Men's sexual desires and attitudes were pretty much the same after the sexual revolution as before it, although men had more opportunities for finding satisfaction afterward. It was women who changed fundamentally. Indeed, according to Rubin (1990), women changed several times, at first embracing a promiscuous enjoyment of casual sex like men, then shifting toward a more limited permissiveness that accepted sex in affectionate relationships but did not eagerly seek out sex with strangers (see also Robinson, Ziss, Ganza, Katz, & Robinson, 1991).

The conclusion that the sexual revolution was primarily a change in female sexual attitudes and behaviors, rather than male, was made by other researchers beyond Ehrenreich et al., (1986). Arafat and Yorburg (1973) and Birenbaum (1970) had already made similar observations. Empirical studies, particularly those that surveyed the same type of sample (e.g., the same college campus) at repeated intervals, consistently found that women's attitudes and behaviors changed more than men's during the 1960s and early 1970s (Bauman & Wilson; 1974; Croake & James, 1973; DeLamater & MacCorquodale, 1979; Schmidt & Sigusch, 1972; Sherwin & Corbett, 1985; Staples, 1973), continuing even into the 1980s (Robinson et al., 1991). Well-constructed national surveys corroborated these conclusions by comparing older people, who had come of age before the sexual revolution, with younger people, whose sexual prime had occurred after the revolution, and these too found bigger differences in women than men (Laumann, Gagnon, Michael, & Michaels, 1994; Wilson, 1975).

As one good example, Laumann et al. (1994) provided data on the proportion of respondents who had had five or more sex partners by the age of 30 (an age when most people have married and ceased accumulating new sex partners). For the oldest cohort, who came of age prior to the sexual revolution, 38% of men had had five or more sex partners by age 30, whereas for the younger cohort, the proportion increased slightly, to 49%. For women, the corresponding numbers are 2.6% and 22.4%. The sexual revolution thus increased men's likelihood of having many partners by 11 percentage points, or by about a fourth, whereas it multiplied women's likelihood by a factor of more than eight and by 20 points. Put another way, the sexual revolution produced a modest increase in the number of men having five or more sex partners, reflecting perhaps nothing more than increased opportunity, but it radically transformed many women's lives and created a large category of multipartnered women that had been almost nonexistent prior to that revolution (Laumann et al., 1994).

The implication that women were changed more than men by the sexual revolution suggested the broader possibility that female sexuality is more historically malleable than male. The present investigation was spurred by this hypothesis. Given the difficulty of drawing firm conclusions about psychological principles from single historical events, especially highly complex ones influenced by multiple factors, I found it necessary to look elsewhere for evidence.

Evidence of Female Plasticity

The method of reviewing the literature was as follows. I began with the most recently available volume of the *Journal of Sex Research* (1996 at the time) and worked backward to the first volume, reading all abstracts and all relevant articles. By covering the major journal in its entirety, I hoped to minimize the dangers of selective review and confirmation bias. The *Archives of Sexual Behavior* then received a similar treatment by a research assistant. These articles offered a useful starting point, and their reference lists were used to find further sources in other publications. The National Health and Social Life Survey (NHSLS; Laumann et al., 1994) was carefully scrutinized, inasmuch as it offers the most comprehensive and scientifically valid survey data (and indeed it is covered in a separate section). Additional sources were suggested by colleagues and by helpful reviewers of a previous draft, and more recently published work was added during revisions.

Data on sexuality are often less than perfect, partly because of the ethical and practical difficulties of studying sex. A summarizing discussion of limitations in the data and general critique is provided after the evidence itself is presented. Alternative explanations are discussed at that point, but two of them deserve to be acknowledged at the outset.

First, it is conceivable that there are more efforts to control female than male sexuality. This is not actually an alternative explanation in the usual sense, because it is fully compatible with the view of greater female plasticity. If female sexual behavior can be regulated more effectively than male sexuality, then it would make sense for society to focus its efforts on controlling females. Still, it is plausible that some findings regarding greater variation or casual impact among females could reflect variation in sociocultural controls rather than differential plasticity. The so-called double standard may be one example, if indeed it means that society permits or has permitted men to do things forbidden to women.

Second, the findings regarding the power of specific sociocultural variables to change sexual behavior have to contend with different baselines in some cases. For example, if education increases the proportion of men who engage in some sexual practice from 70% to 80% while increasing the corresponding proportion of women from 30% to 80%, some readers might refuse to regard this as evidence of greater impact on women: It might be that the effect of education on men was limited by a ceiling effect.

Intraindividual Variability

The first major prediction is concerned with intraindividual variability. If erotic plasticity is greater among females, then women should show more variation across their individual sexual histories than men. The focus is on whether particular persons exhibit changes in their sexuality across time.

One gender difference in intraindividual variability was noted by Kinsey, Pomeroy, Martin, and Gebhard (1953). Although their sampling has been criticized as not up to the best modern standards, that criticism is irrelevant to this finding, and their data on individual sexual histories are among the most detailed ever collected. They found that some women, but hardly any men, showed patterns of substantial swings in degree of sexual activity. A woman might go through a phase of having a great deal of sex, then have no sexual activity of any sort for months, and then enter into another phase of having a great deal of sex. If a male were to experience a romantic break-up or a physical separation from his sex partner, he would tend to keep his orgasm rate constant by resorting to masturbation or other activities, but women did not necessarily do this. "Discontinuities in total outlet are practically unknown in the histories of males," unlike females (Kinsey et al., 1953, pp. 681–682). These discontinuities are thus an important confirmation of the hypothesis of female erotic plasticity.

Intraindividual change was the focus of an investigation by Adams and Turner (1985), who compared the reports of current sexual activity among an elderly sample (age 60–85) with the same people's retrospective reports of what they did in young adulthood (age 20–30). Adams and Turner pointed out that most studies of the effects of aging on sexuality simply emphasize reductions in drive and energy and hence decreased sexual activity, and so they looked especially for any signs of increasing activity. Only a small minority of their sample showed increases on any of the measures, but this minority was predominantly female. Thus, one pattern of intraindividual change over several decades (increasing sexual activity) was found mainly among females, and this pattern is of particular interest because it is not confounded by loss of vigor or declining health, which would make evidence of reduced sexual activity less relevant to the present theory.

Some of Adams and Turner's (1985) most interesting data concern masturbation. They found that in comparisons of young adulthood with old age, women showed remarkable, significant increases in masturbation (10% to 26%), whereas men showed a nonsignificant decrease over the same age span (32% to 26%). Adams and Turner noted that their sample overrepresented married women, so the change does not simply reflect a shift into masturbation as the women lost their partners. Even more important, Adams and Turner reported that the old men who masturbated were typically continuing a pattern of masturbation that was present in young adulthood, whereas the women who masturbated in their 20s had typically discontinued that activity late in life. (Also, given the increase in overall numbers, the strong majority of the women who masturbated in old age had not done so in their 20s.) The authors concluded that the masturbation data showed that "women displayed more plasticity and behavior than men" (p. 134).

Undoubtedly, some degree of flexibility would be useful in adapting to marriage because the requirement of coordinating one's sexual activities with a particular partner over a long period of time presumably requires some compromises unless the couple is perfectly matched and their desires wax and wane in complete synchrony, which seems unlikely. Data on sexual changes in the adaptation to long-term marriages were provided by Ard (1977), who, in a 20-year follow-up of a longitudinal study, asked the individuals who had remained married for over two decades how much they had changed from their early ideas, habits, and expectations regarding sex. Wives were somewhat more likely than husbands (13% to 9%) to claim that they had changed "a great deal," although this difference fell short of significance. Because some people might inflate their self-reported change in order to look good, Ard also asked people how much their partners had changed along the same lines, and these partner reports confirmed—significantly, this time—that the women had changed more than the men: 12% of the husband, but only 6% of the wives, reported that their spouse had changed a great deal.

The greater change by women than men in adapting to marriage is especially remarkable given some other features of Ard's (1977) data. When asked about their current frequency of sexual activity and their current preferences for frequency of sexual activity, the wives' answers indicated that their marital practices corresponded almost precisely to the amount of sex they wanted, whereas the men reported a significant gap between what they wanted and what they were able to have. Thus, men were not getting what they wanted on this important measure, whereas women were—yet still the evidence showed that women had adapted more than men. Possibly, women succeeded better than the men at adjusting their expectations into line with what they were getting, which could be another manifestation of plasticity and would presumably be a very beneficial adaptation.

Marriage is certainly not the only type of relationship that can produce change in sexual attitudes. Harrison, Bennett, Globetti, and Alsikafi (1974) found that women changed their sexual standards toward being more permissive as they accumulated the dating experience. Men did not seem to change as a function of dating experience. One might have predicted that the necessity of compromise would produce change in attitudes in both genders, but Harrison et al. found change only in the females. Reiss (1967) likewise found that women increased their sexual permissiveness after having steady dates or love relationships, whereas the effects of such experiences on men were small and nonlinear. Reiss reported that 87% of the females, as opposed to 58% of the males, had come to accept sexual behavior that initially made them feel guilty. Of these, far more females than males cited the relationship with the opposite-sex partner as the key factor in bringing about this change. Thus, again, the data suggest greater sexual adaptation in relationship contexts by women.

In the 1960s and 1970s, consensual extramarital sex increased, and researchers were able to examine how people adapted to this unusual behavior (often called swinging). J. R. Smith and Smith (1970) studied this phenomenon and concluded that "women are better able to make the necessary adjustments to sexual freedom after the initial phases of involvement than are men" (p. 136). They noted that this greater adaptability of women was especially remarkable in light of the fact that it had generally been the men who initiated the involvement in swinging. Although Smith and Smith failed to provide quantitative evidence to back their claim of the superior adaptation of women, their observation is noteworthy because it confirms one of the presumptive advantages of plasticity, namely, greater capacity to adapt to new circumstances.

Some of the best and most useful data on intraindividual variability concern sexual orientation and same-sex activity. Operationally, this can be studied by investigating whether homosexual individuals have had heterosexual experience, which would suggest a higher degree of plasticity in their sexual orientation. Beginning with Kinsey's research (Kinsey, Pomeroy, & Martin, 1948; Kinsey et al., 1953), many studies have found that lesbians are more likely to have had heterosexual intercourse than gay males. This effect is especially remarkable given the greater promiscuity of males, although it might have something to do with the greater sexual initiative exhibited by males (which would mean that heterosexuals would likely approach lesbians more than gay males). Savin-Williams (1990) found that four fifths of gay women, but only about half (54%) the gay men, had had heterosexual intercourse. In a quite different sample consisting of gay youth in New York City, Rosario et al. (1996) found nearly identical numbers: 80% of the lesbians had had sex with men, but only 56% of the gay men had had intercourse with women. Bell and Weinberg (1978) found that lesbians exceeded gay men in all categories of heterosexual experience, including coitus, oral sex, interpersonal masturbation, sex dreams, and marriage. In Whisman's (1996) sample, 82% of the lesbians, but only 64% of the gay males, had ever had sex with a member of the opposite gender. Whisman also asked whether the respondent had had a meaningful heterosexual relationship, and again, the rate of affirmative responses was significantly higher among lesbians (72%) than gay men (45%).

The high rates of heterosexual experience among gay females were confirmed by McCauley and Ehrhardt (1980), who found that over half their sample of lesbians had had sex with men. Kitzinger and Wilkinson (1995) described a sample of women who had become lesbian after a period of adult heterosexuality, often including marriage. Rust (1992) described a sample of lesbian women, 43% of whom had had heterosexual relationships after they had identified as lesbians, even many years after adopting the lesbian identity. Bart (1993) also found a small sample of lesbians who entered into relationships with men, a pattern that led Bart to attribute high plasticity to female sexuality. In a survey of female college dormitory residents, Goode and Haber (1977) found that all but one of the women who had had female sex partners had also had male ones (and that one listed having sex with a man as something she wanted to try). Schäfer (1976) reported that lesbians in Germany were more likely than gay males to have heterosexual experience.

Similar findings were reported by the NHSLS (Laumann et al., 1994, pp. 310–313). Multiple tallies over different time spans (e.g., last year, last 5 years, since age 18) repeatedly showed that women were more likely to have both male and female partners, at least if one adjusts for the higher base rate of male homosexuality. Thus, among people who had any same-gender partners in the past five years, half the men, but two thirds of the women, also had sex with opposite-gender partners. "The women are more likely than the men to have had sex with both men and women than only same-gender partners" (p. 311). Likewise, the ratio of bisexual self-identification was higher for women (.56) than for men (.40; p. 311). Similar ratios (.50 and .32, respectively) were found by Whisman (1996, p. 134), and in particular, she found the highest ratio (of 2.00, indicating a majority of bisexuals) among lesbians who indicated that their sexual orientation was a result of personal choice. This last finding is especially relevant to the plasticity hypothesis because it explicitly links self-perceived erotic plasticity to intraindividual variability.

Another way of expressing this finding is that bisexuality requires greater plasticity that homosexuality. Studies of the gay and bisexual community show a different balance between bisexuality and homosexuality depending on gender: Of the people who take part in same-gender sex, more women than men identify themselves as bisexual. In fact, the relatively large bisexual community is regarded by the exclusively lesbian contingent as a threat, and the gay–bi conflict is thus greater among women than men (see, e.g., Rust, 1993). Many lesbians view bisexual women as being in transition and as denying their true sexuality, and they regard them with distrust (Clausen, 1990; Rust, 1993).

Female plasticity is particularly apparent in the findings that some women who enjoy sex with men start having sex with women also and that they do so even after their sexual patterns and habits are well established. Dixon (1984) reported on a sample of married, heterosexual women who had never felt any attraction to women prior to the age of 30 but who, at a mean age 37, had begun having sex with women as well as men. This occurred in the context of swinging (i.e., consensual extramarital sex) and was often encouraged by the husbands. It does not appear to be late conversion upon awakening of latent lesbianism because the women continued to enjoy having sex with men.

Men do not appear to exhibit that form of plasticity. Several studies of swinging and group sex found that women, but not men, commenced same-sex intercourse under those circumstances. In a study of mainly unmarried people who took part in group sex, O'Neill and O'Neill (1970) found over half (60%) of the women, but only 12% of the men, engaged in homosexual activity. A much larger investigation by Bartell (1970) of a predominantly married sample involved in swinging yielded parallel findings. Looking at the great many episodes in which two married couples would exchange partners for sex, Bartell found that wives would have oral intercourse with each other about 75% of the time, whereas the husbands had oral intercourse with each other less than 1% of the time.

Fang (1976) concluded that among swingers, same-gender sexual activity "is rare for males yet is common for females" (p. 223). She noted that many women swingers begin having sex with other women "in order to please their husbands or to be sociable" (p. 223) but then come to enjoy it.

One additional place to test the hypothesis of intraindividual variability is erotic activity in places where heterosexuality is impossible, such as prison. This test may however be strongly biased against the female plasticity hypothesis, if women have less sexual desire than men or if they are simply more willing than men to forgo sex altogether for a period of time, as the Kinsey et al. findings suggested. Despite this possible bias, the evidence is largely supportive. Gagnon and Simon (1968) examined homosexuality activity in prisons and concluded that half the women in prison, but less than half the men (estimates range from 30% to 45%), engaged in homosexual physical acts, most of which were consensual. When one considers that (a) base rates of homosexuality are higher among men than women, (b) men force other men more than women force other women (Propper, 1981; Scacco, 1975), and (c) women can live without any sexual contact more easily than men, these results point toward a substantially greater willingness among women than men to indulge in same-sex activity during prison.

One should recognize that data on sexual activity in prison are subject to question on grounds of self-report biases, lying, skepticism about research, environmental and organizational-culture differences between male and female prisons, and possibly other problems. A solution to some of these methodological problems is to ask prison inmates to estimate the degree of homosexuality among other inmates. With this method, people do not have to report on their own activities but merely give their estimates of what others are doing. Ward and Kassebaum (1965) used this method in both male and female prisons. Their data suggested that far more female than male inmates engage in homosexual activity. Collapsing the multiple-choice format to look at how many respondents thought that over half of the inmates at their prison engaged in such activities, Ward and Kassebaum found that a great many female respondents (51%) but relatively few male ones (21%) offered such a high estimate of the prevalence of prison homosexuality. Consistent with the plasticity interpretation, the researchers also found that the vast majority of inmates and staff thought that homosexuality in prison was merely a temporary adaptation to prison life and would not be continued outside of prison. (In fact, Giallombardo, 1966, concluded that most female inmates maintained a strong distinction between true lesbians who would prefer women outside prison and were therefore regarded as sick and women who merely turned temporarily gay while in prison.) Ward and Kassebaum also found converging evidence by examining the prison records of inmates, in which mention of homosexual activity was more frequent for women than male inmates.

Sociocultural Factors

The second major prediction derived from the female plasticity hypothesis is that sociocultural factors will have a greater impact on female than on male sexuality. As already noted, the impetus for this investigation was the contention that the sexual revolution had a larger effect on women than on men and that this was part of a broader pattern in which historical changes altered female sexuality more than male. The present section examines evidence as to whether socializing influences, cultural institutions, ideology, and other causes produce larger effects on females. It must be acknowledged that although the plasticity hypothesis predicts greater casual effects by these factors, the majority of available findings are only correlational. These can falsify the casual hypothesis but cannot prove it.

Culture and acculturation. If women are more socioculturally malleable, they ought to vary more than men from one culture to another. A variety of evidence supports this view, although considerably more work in this area is desirable. As one example, Christensen and Carpenter (1962) compared rates of premarital sex across three Western cultures and found much greater variation in the females than in the males.

An unusually broad investigation was conducted by Barry and Schlegel (1984), who used the compiled ethnographic data on 186 cultures to compare sexual behavior patterns in adolescents. On all measures of sexual behavior, they found greater cross-cultural variation among females than males, leading them to conclude that "variations among the societies in sexual customs are apparently greater for girls than for boys" (p. 325).

The greater impact of culture on females than males was demonstrated in a different way by Ford and Norris (1993). These researchers studied a sample of Hispanic immigrants to the United States and included a (nonsexual) measure of acculturation that revealed how much the immigrant had adopted American culture. The acculturation measure correlated significantly (and positively) with several sexual practices for women but not men, including genital intercourse in the past year, anal sex, and use of condoms. The acculturation measure also correlated significantly with engaging in oral sex and having had sex with a non-Hispanic partner for both men and women, but the correlations were stronger for women: .51 versus .26 for oral sex and .64 versus .55 for non-Hispanic partners. These data suggest that when a woman moves from one country to a different one that has different sexual attitudes, her behavior is likely to change—especially to the extent that she adopts the values and outlook of the new culture. In contrast, men tend to remain the same when they change countries, regardless of the degree to which they adopt the values and outlook of the new culture.

Education. The effects of education on age of first intercourse were studied by Wilson (1975), using a national sample in a 1970 survey. On this survey, higher levels of education were associated with delays in starting sexual behavior, and these delays appear to have affected women more than men. The portions of men who were virgins on their 21st birthday varied only slightly from the least educated (19%) to the most educated (25%), but for women, the difference between the least educated (18%) and most educated (43%) was substantial.[1]

On that same survey, an intriguing item asked people whether they believed that there was a substantial difference between what most people did sexually and what they wanted to. Responses to this may reflect personal experience, observations about others, and projection of own feelings on to others (e.g., see Finger, 1975, on projection of sexual material). Once again, women varied more than men as a function of education. In fact, men's agreement with this item was the same for the most educated (69%) to the least (69%), whereas the highly educated women agreed less (51%) then the least educated women (65%). Thus, the perception of a gap between desire and reality in sex depended significantly on a woman's level of education, but the man's level of education was irrelevant. Highly educated women were also twice as likely as uneducated women to hold liberal, permissive attitudes toward sex, whereas the corresponding difference for men was much smaller.

Education is not of course aimed mainly at altering sexual attitudes, so the effects of educational level should be considered by-products. It is useful to consider separately the question of sex education. This was done by Weis, Rabinowitz, and Ruckstuhl (1992). They sampled three college courses on human sexuality and obtained measures of sexual attitudes and behaviors both before and after the classes. Perhaps surprisingly, they did not find that the courses produced any significant changes in behavior, and many attitudes (e.g., on abortion) likewise remained impervious to the course. However, they did find some changes in attitudes, generally toward greater sexual permissiveness—but only among females. These changes were found regardless of whether the initial baseline (precourse) attitudes showed greater permissiveness among males (e.g., on oral sex) or female (e.g., on homosexuality). Males did not change, but females did, and the differences are not attributable to baseline differences.

Religion. Church attendance and religious belief seem to have a stronger (negative) effect on female than male sexuality. Reiss (1967) found notably bigger differences in sexual permissiveness for females than males as a function of frequency of church attendance. The result holds up independent of the higher base rate of church attendance by women.

The stronger link between religion and female sexuality (than male) was confirmed by Adams and Turner (1985). Among elderly women, they found that church attendance strongly predicted not masturbating (19% vs. 83% for nonattenders), whereas no significant effect was found among men. Harrison et al. (1974) found that religious participation significantly predicted the permissiveness and sexual standards of rural females but not males. They also found that females who had more experience with steady dating were more permissive,

[1] In Wilson's (1975) data, education had a negative effect on sexual activity, whereas most later findings show a positive effect, and so this seems to be a contradiction. Wilson's sample included substantial proportions of people who came of age before the sexual revolution, which may help explain the difference. Prior to the sexual revolution, college was associated with delayed mating and marriage. It may however still be true that intelligent, college-bound individuals begin sex later than others but do in the long run become more liberal and experienced sexually.

whereas dating experience was irrelevant to males' permissiveness.

Among students at a small religious college, Earle and Perricone (1986) found that religion correlated negatively with sexually permissive attitudes for both men and women, but socioeconomic status correlated with those attitudes for women only. Moreover, when they compared freshmen's vs. seniors' attitudes, they found that "the attitudes of women seem to change more during college years than those of the male peers" (p. 308).

Murphy (1992) found that female Catholic clergy were more successful at fulfilling their vows of celibacy than were male Catholic clergy. This held up across a variety of measures (ever had sex, how many partners, how often) and appeared to be broadly true. Thus, female sexuality is better able than male sexuality to conform to highly nonpermissive standards in a religious context, which again suggests greater plasticity.

Peers and parents. The peer group is not as formal an institution as the school or church, but it too has effects in socializing sexual behavior. Effects of peer group attitudes and behavior on loss of virginity were studied by Sack, Keller, and Hinkle (1984). The behavior of the peer group affected both genders: Whether the respondents' friends were having sex correlated with whether the respondents themselves were having sex for both males (r = .47) and females (r = .49). The peer group's approval was more strongly linked to the sexual behavior of females than males, however. When asked how their friends would feel about them having sex, females' responses significantly predicted whether they had had sex (r = .53), but the effect for males was not significant (r = .26). The authors also reported direct effects that were corrected for effects of other variables. The direct effect of the peer group's approval for males was negligible, .00, but it remained significant for females, .25. It is also worth noting that the proportions of virgins versus people who had sex were nearly identical in the two genders, so the results of this study cannot be ascribed to any restrictions of range or floor/ceiling effects. (There is however the possibility that choice of peers was a result, rather than a cause, of sexual intentions and practices. On the other hand, Billy and Urdy, 1985, found such selection effects to be bigger among males, which would bias the results against the plasticity hypothesis.)

Similar results were obtained by Mirande (1968), who found a significant link between peer group approval and sexual activity for females but not for males. Of women who had had sexual experience, 62% associated with reference groups who approved of premarital intercourse, whereas only 17% of the sexually inexperienced women associated with such groups; for men, the corresponding figures were 100% and 64%. Group encouragement made a big difference, too. Over half (55%) the women with coital experience had peer groups who encouraged sexual activity, whereas almost none (3%) of the virgin women associated with such groups. For men, the effect approached significance but was still smaller (88% to 50%). The correlation between having friends with sexual experience and having sexual experience oneself was significant for females but not for males. Thus, Mirande's data suggest that the approval, encouragement, expectations, and behaviors of friends had a bigger influence on women than on men, although again self-selection of friends may contribute to these findings.

Further evidence was provided by Billy and Udry (1985). They were alert to the methodological problem that females might be more likely to associate with similar others than males, which would create an illusion of peer influence, but they were able to rule out this confound by demonstrating that there was no gender difference in sexual homogeneity of friendships. By collecting data from the same sample on two occasions separated by 2 years, they were able to ascertain whether friendship patterns at Time 1 predicted changes in sexual status, which makes casual inferences more plausible than purely cross-sectional data permit. These effects were consistently stronger for White females than for males. Specifically, a White female virgin at Time 1 who had a nonvirgin best female friend was six times more likely to lose her virginity by Time 2 than a White female virgin with a virgin best friend. If the data was restricted to stable friendship pairs (i.e., people who cited the same person as best friend on both occasions), the relationship was even stronger. Males showed no such effect.

Parents can also be considered agents of socialization, and they are relatively immune to the self-selection bias problem insofar as children cannot choose their parents. On the other hand, it does not seem safe to assume that they socialize boys and girls the same (see, e.g., Libby & Nass, 1971).

Still, one literature review suggested that the weight of evidence indicates that the parental and family environment has a stronger effect on daughters than on sons (B. C. Miller & Moore, 1990). Longitudinal research found that living with a single parent increased the likelihood of early loss of virginity for girls but not boys (Newcomer & Urdy, 1987). (Parental divorce during the study was associated with increased sexual activity by both sons and daughters.) A broader study of multiple family (especially maternal) influence repeatedly found that daughters' sexual attitudes and sexual behaviors were more closely related than sons to most social variables, including parents' age at their wedding, parental divorce, mother's premarital pregnancy, and mother's attitude about sex (Thornton & Camburn, 1987). (Specifically, daughters' permissive sexuality was increased by having older parents, earlier parental marriage, parental divorce, mother's premarital pregnancy, and mothers with permissive attitudes.)

A study of sex education by Lewis (1973) counted the number of topics that children learned about from their parents as an index of parental information transmission. This index correlated significantly with likelihood of having intercourse and with number of sex partners for young women (such that more parental education predicted less sex and less promiscuity), but the correlations were not significant for young men. Lewis also found that marital conflict in the parental home had a stronger effect on daughter's sexual development (leading to more sexual experience and more promiscuity) than on the son's, although both effects were weak.

Both parental and peer influences were studied by Reiss (1967). He found that female permissiveness was more influenced than male permissiveness by a broad spectrum of social forces. Both peer and parental standards had a stronger correlation with the permissiveness of females.

Genetic versus environmental factors. A different way of looking at sociocultural effects is to consider the opposite, namely genetic predictions. Research on behavior genetics has occasionally examined sexual factors by looking at correlations between twins. By comparing monozygotic and dizygotic twins, the degree of genetic contribution can be estimated, and the remainder of the variance can be tentatively chalked up to erotic plasticity. This technique was employed by Dunne et al. (1997) with a large sample of Australian twins in the effort to predict age at first intercourse. Among the people born after the sexual revolution (i.e., those under age 40), the authors concluded that the genetic contribution accounted for 72% of the variance for males but only 40% of the variance for females. This discrepancy suggests that male sexuality is more determined by genetic factors, which in turn implies a greater role for sociocultural factors for females.[2]

The behavior genetics approach has also been applied to homosexuality, and indeed, the question of whether sexual orientation is a matter of nature or nurture (i.e., socially influenced choice over genetically/biologically ingrained pattern) remains the focus of considerable political, social, intellectual, and emotional controversy. Some studies do suggest a greater effect of genetic factors on men. Using a twin registry, Bailey and Martin (1993; see Bem, 1996) found that heritability of sexual orientation was significant for men but not women. Hu et al. (1995) likewise found a significant linkage between chromosome and homosexuality patterns for men but not women. On the other hand, Hershberger (1997) found effects for both genders, and the female effects were stronger. A pair of studies using the less optimal method of starting with self-defined gay people (which may conceal gender differences if women are slower to make firm, definite self-identification as gay) and examining siblings found stronger effects among the men, but the differences were slight (Bailey & Pillard, 1991; Bailey, Pillard, Neale, & Agyei, 1993). Genetic explanations were also favored by Bailey and Zucker (1995) in their review of findings that sought to predict adult sexual orientation from retrospective studies that effects are strong for both genders but significantly stronger for males than females. Prospective studies have thus far found strong, significant predictions only for males.

A recent review by Bailey and Pillard (1995) is one of the few to sort the evidence by gender. They concluded that the evidence for genetic contribu-

[2] The older sample, which came of age prior to the sexual revolution, showed quite different patterns, and indeed, the genetic contribution for males over age 41 was 0%, which was lower than that for females (32%). A likely guess at explanation would be that age of first intercourse prior to the sexual revolution was a matter of highly restricted activity for males, and Dunne et al. (1997) make the same point. Hence, these findings are not relevant to the plasticity hypothesis, but I acknowledge that this finding contradicts the general pattern.

tion to homosexuality was far stronger for males than for females. To be sure, this difference in strenght of evidence does not necessarily mean the true effect size is larger for males because there have been more male-only studies and larger samples. Bailey and Pillard said that some experts have begun to conclude "that female sexual orientation is less heritable than male sexual orientation" (p. 136), but they themselves regard that conclusion as premature and prefer to wait for further confirming evidence. If further work continues to have greater success establishing genetic contributions to male than female homosexuality, that will strengthen the view that female sexual orientation is more socioculturally malleable.

Personal choice. Another way to approach the question of plasticity is to examine whether people receive their sexuality as a matter of choice and something that is as least partly under their control, as opposed to regarding it as something inborn and unchangeable. In an important sense, this approach takes the question of essentialism versus social constructionism in sexuality (see DeLamater & Hyde, 1998) and asks individuals which view seems to fit their sense of their own sexuality. Do they feel they can socially construct their sexuality, or does it seem to be an innate part of their essence?

Several studies have explicitly examined whether people perceive their orientation to be a matter of choice. Whisman (1996) interviewed self-identified homosexuals and found that a higher percentage of lesbians (31%) than gay men (18%) described their sexual orientation as having been a matter of conscious, deliberate choice. Using a more nuanced measure Rosenbluth (1997) found that over half a sample of lesbians perceived their homosexuality to be the result of a conscious, deliberate choice. Savin-Williams (1990) found that lesbians felt they had more control than gay men over their sexual orientation. In addition, lesbians were more likely to think that they could renounce their gay orientation and less likely to regard their sexual orientation as beyond their personal control. Thus, subjective perceptions of one's own homosexuality suggest that erotic plasticity is higher in females.

These data dovetail well with the trend in the genetics research. Although in neither case is the mass of evidence fully rigorous and overwhelmingly solid, the currently available data offer the best guess that male homosexuality is more strongly linked to innate or genetic determinants whereas female homosexuality remains more subject to personal choice and social influence.

Political ideology. Consistent with the view that lesbianism can reflect personal choice and social construction, there are reports that some females became gay for political reasons associated with the women's movement. Blumstein and Schwartz (1977) reported that some women became lesbian under the influence of political ideology that defined heterosexuality as a form of sleeping with the enemy whereas lesbianism was the only politically correct form of sexuality. They noted in their conclusions that such changes raise theoretical questions about the plasticity of sexual desire, and thus they anticipated the present argument to some degree. Kitzinger (1987) summarized the radical feminist view that "patriarchy (not capitalism or sex roles or socialization or individual sexist men) is the root of all forms of oppression [and] that all men benefit from and maintain it and are, therefore, [women's] political enemies" (p. 64). In consequence, the politically optimal choice of women should be to reject heterosexuality. Kitzinger quoted a woman who asserted "I take the label 'lesbian' as part of the strategy of the feminist struggle" (p. 113). Johnston's (1973) formulation was blunter: "Feminists who still sleep with the man are delivering their most vital energies to the oppressor" (p. 167).

Similar reports of politically motivated lesbianism are found in other sources. Pearlman (1987), for example, in discussing the rise of political lesbianism in the 1970s, wrote, "Many of the new, previously heterosexual, radical lesbians had based their choice as much on politics as on sexual interest in other women" (p. 318). Rosenbluth (1997) found that 12% of a sample of lesbians (and a similar proportion of heterosexual women) cited political reasons as the basis for their sexual orientation and relationship style choice. Charbonneau and Lander (1991) found that a third of their sample of women who converted to lesbianism during mid-life cited reading feminist texts as a reason, and they spoke of the feminist path to homosexuality in which lesbianism was an outgrowth of the commitment to feminism. In that sample, moreover, some women described the change as one of self-discovery, whereas others regarded it as an active choice, and the latter found the adjustment more difficult (not surprisingly). Whisman (1996) likewise found that women, but not men, cited political reasons as a reason for choosing homosexuality. Echols' (1984) history of feminist sexual politics recorded the lesbian separatists' phase of "establishing lesbianism as a true measure of one's commitment to feminism" (p. 56), and other leading feminist denounced heterosexuality as a choice that was in fact coerced by the patriarchal political system.

Although further evidence would be desirable, the finding that some women have seemingly exchanged male for female sex partners under the influence of political ideology constitutes compelling evidence for erotic plasticity. No such claims have been made regarding men, and it does seem intuitively doubtful that political writings and speeches would persuade some men to give up women and heterosexuality and begin having intercourse with other men instead. If some women have indeed made such a switch under similar influences, that would confirm the greater sociopolitical plasticity of the female sex drive.

The reports of women with a history of exclusively heterosexual desires changing to have homosexual relations because of political reasons resemble a finding that was presented as evidence of intraindividual variability: When married couples start congregating for mate swapping, after a while the women begin having sex with other women, often under the encouragement of the men, who like to watch this (Dixon, 1984). The reverse pattern is almost unheard of (i.e., heterosexual men taking up homosexual acts in group settings, especially if the ostensible purpose is to entertain their wives). Such adaptations in women provide a salient and vivid illustration of erotic plasticity.

There is not much evidence on gender differences in degree of political influence on other aspects of sexuality beyond sexual orientation. DeLamater and MacCorquodale (1979) reported that general political stance, measured either in terms of self-reported liberal versus conservative classification or in terms of reported political participation, predicted sexual permissiveness more strongly for females than for males (p. 127). This again suggests greater political influence on female than male sexuality, but more evidence is desirable.

Education and Religion in the NHSLS

The other sections of this article present evidence from many different investigations, but this section considers only one, although it is a very large and thorough one. The best data available on modern American sexual practices are provided in the NHSLS (Laumann et al., 1994; Michael, Gagnon, Laumann, & Kolata, 1994). These data represent a carefully, proper constructed national sample, with lengthy individual interviews plus written questionnaires, which had unusual success at securing high response rates and thus avoiding the volunteer bias that seriously compromises the value of many sex surveys (e.g., see Morokoff, 1986; Weiderman, 1993). The NHSLS therefore deserves special attention.

Although the NHSLS researchers did not have any apparent interest in the question of differential plasticity (and did not even bring up the issue), the extensive tables reported in the fuller version of their work (Laumann et al., 1994) permit comparison of males and females in terms of sociocultural predictors. They present extensive data on the effects (correlates) of two main sociocultural institutions, namely, school and church. More precisely, they break their data on many sexual practices and attitudes down by educational levels and by religious affiliation. These data enable one to compare whether males or females show greater variation in response to these two institutional forces. If female plasticity is greater, the variation across categories should be greater among females than males. Because the effects are typically linear, the present coverage can be simplified by considering merely the uppermost and lowermost categories (exceptions are noted below). For education, these are the people with the least education (less than high school) versus those with the most (graduate or advanced degrees). For religion, the extreme cases were what the researchers called Type II Protestants, representing conservative, evangelical, fundamentalist Christian denominations, and at the opposite, the people listing "none" as their religion. The latter were typically more active in whatever sexual category was being considered.

The information presented here is based on Laumann et al.'s (1994) tables, not (in most cases) their statistical analyses, and so it is not possible to report statistical significance. One can however meta-analyze the directions of effects, and I report such a summary analysis at the end of this section.

It was necessary to make a priori decisions about what dependent variables to consider. The main sexual practices that any researcher would presumably expect to include are oral sex (performing and receiving), anal sex, masturbation, homosexual activity, and contraceptive use. (Vaginal intercourse is too standard to be useful; that is, nearly all heterosexual adults who have sex have vaginal intercourse.) Additionally, I report evidence about sexual satisfaction, frequency of sex, sexual dysfunction, duration of sex, and fertility; these are more peripheral, and some researchers might prefer not to include them. I present these to avoid charges of selective reporting and to permit readers who judge centrality differently to draw their own conclusions.

Oral sex. Beginning with the main sexual practices, it is clear that the differences associated with education and religion are consistently greater for women than men. On the item of whether the person had ever performed oral sex on a partner, having a high level of education raised men's affirmative answers from 59% to 80.5% (roughly a one-third increase), whereas women's increased from 41% to 79% (nearly double; note, though, that there could be a ceiling effect, given the similarity among highly educated men and women). On the complimentary question about whether the person had ever received oral sex, the most and the least educated men differed by less (81% and 61%) than the most and least educated women (82% and 50%). Thus, on both giving and receiving oral sex, education level predicted bigger differences in women's sexual behavior.

With religion, the differences between the most liberal and most conservative categories were again larger for females. The differences on performing[3] and receiving oral sex, respectively, were 12 and 13 percentage points for men, whereas for women, they were 22 and 19 percentage points. The effects of religion are thus opposite to education, and indeed, religiosity appeared to make women more different from men even as education made them more similar.

Anal sex. Anal sex provides a useful counterpoint because the base rates on the NHSLS were quite low, in contrast to oral sex, which had high base rates, and so the findings are less vulnerable to explanations based on ceiling effects. The difference between high school dropouts and people with master's degrees (or more) was only 8 percentage points for males but 16 points for females. Moreover, the proportional change makes the difference even more dramatic: Education produced only about a one-third increase in males' likelihood of engaging in anal sex (from 21% to 29%), whereas it more than doubled the women's likelihood (from 13% to 29%). Similar patterns were found for religion: Women showed much greater variation than men, and the difference between categories represented more than doubling women's likelihood (from 17% to 36%, or 19 points), whereas men increased by only about half (from 21% to 34%, or 13 points). The difference is even more dramatic if one looks only at incidence of anal sex within the past year, which is probably a more accurate measure and more closely linked to current religiosity: The most and least religious men scarcely differed (7% vs. 9%), whereas the most (6%) and the least (17%) religious women showed very different incidence rates of anal intercourse.

Masturbation. With masturbation, comparisons are difficult because the base rates differed substantially among males versus females and because the activity is arguably different in the different genders. There seemed to be no clear gender difference in the correlations between level of education and frequency of masturbation. Success at masturbation (measured by likelihood of reporting that one always or usually has an orgasm during masturbation) did vary more as function of both education and religion in women than men, consistent with the hypothesis of erotic plasticity. The education effect was not large, however. To be conservative, I count the masturbation data as inconclusive.

Sexual variety. Next consider sexual interest and arousal in response to novel, assorted sexual practices. The NHSLS researchers offered a list of sexual practices and asked people to indicate how many appealed to them. The least educated men expressed interest in 2.3 practices (out of 15), whereas the most educated men expressed interest in only 2.6, so the difference was negligible. For women, however, the difference was from 1.3 to 2.1 out of 14. (The item about active anal sex was deleted for women.) Results for religion were not reported in their work, presumably because differences were generally not significant. It is also

[3] On this item, the most and least religious men did not have the largest differences, contrary to the general pattern. Catholic males engaged in slightly more cunnilingus than the artheists and agnostics. If one looks at variance across all categories, however, it remains true that women differed more than men.

possible to compare responses item by item, but these simply confirm the pattern reflected in the summary means: Level of education predicted bigger differences in the breadth of women's sexual interests than men's.

Homosexual activity. Education and religion were also linked to same-gender activity. Several items were used. Three asked whether the person had ever had any same-sex partners in the past year, in the past 5 years, or since age 18. These did not show linear effects of education, nor was there any consistency as to whether men or women differed more across categories, so they do not furnish useful information relevant to the plasticity hypothesis (Laumann et al., 1994, p. 302).

Clearer results were obtained by asking whether the individual self-identified as gay or bisexual. College education doubled men's likelihood of becoming gay, whereas for women, the likelihood increased by a factor of nine. Likewise, a composite of items asking for same-gender desire, attraction, or appeal found that with increasing education, the likelihood of men's positive answers increased by about half (5.8% to 9.4%), whereas for women, the increase was nearly quadruple (3.3% to 12.8%). In determining same-gender sexual interest and activity, the authors themselves articulated the differential effect of education by saying that "education . . . does seem to stand out for women in a way that it does not for men" (Laumann et al., 1994, p. 309) and that the increase in same-gender sexuality as a function of education was "more pronounced and more monotonic for women" than men (p. 309).

For religion, too, the predictive effects on gay/bisexual identification and on the composite interest were larger for women than for men. Women's gay/bisexual identification differed by a factor of 15 (from .3 to 4.6) in comparing conservative Protestants to people with no religion, whereas men's identification differed by a factor of only nine (from .7 to 6.2; note, though, that given the higher base rate, the men increased by an extra percentage point). On the composite item, women increased from 5.5 to 15.8, whereas men increased from 5.6 to 12.9.

Contraception. The last of the major sexual practices I consider is contraceptive use. Contraception in marriage is too complex and multidetermined an issue to use for present purposes, insofar as people may or may not be having sex in order to have children. Contraception in extramarital or extradyadic activity is far more straightforward, however, because it is reasonable to assume that if one is married or partnered, one does not want to create pregnancy with someone else. For this item, the researchers restricted their data to people who were having extradyadic sexual partners, which meant that many categories had too few data points to be reported. Still, there were sufficient data to permit comparisons based on education (Laumann et al., 1994, p. 451). The category of people who reported always using contraception with the secondary partner showed a significant rise among women as a function of increasing education, from 55% to 79%. For men, ironically, the same two educational categories showed a small trend in the opposite direction, dropping from 65% to 54%, suggesting that the more educated men were actually more careless about contraception.[4] In any case, the correlation with education was greater for women than men.

Other dependent variables. As noted above, it is also possible to consider some less central aspects of sex. On reporting that one was extremely satisfied with one's partnered sex (in a physical sense), the difference between the least and most educated women was greater than the corresponding difference for men, although the difference was not large and the progress across educational categories was not linear, so this result may not be conclusive. The difference between conservative Protestants and nonreligous people was also larger for women than men on this item.

Frequency of partnered sex is of potential interest, but Laumann et al. (1994, p. 90) reported that neither religion nor education had any relation to frequency of partnered sex. The differences between the most and least educated in the number of people reporting highly frequent sex were greater for women than for men, consistent with the hypothesis, but given the lack of significance overall, this finding probably should not be accorded much weight. The authors noted that there was a slight tendency for men with no religious affiliation to be more likely to report highly fre-

---

[4] There was also a category of more highly educated men whose rate of contraceptive use in secondary relationships was about the same as the low-education category. The data for women did not include this category because too few women with that level of education reported secondary sexual relationships. If one uses this category for the men, then there is no change as a function of educational level, confirming the conclusion of greater change among women.

quent sex than the conservative Protestants, whereas there was no difference among women in these categories, so this effect would be in the direction contrary to the plasticity hypothesis. Oddly, though, the other religious categories showed greater variation among women than men, so this item departed from the typical pattern in which conservative Protestants and people with no religion constituted the extremes. The variance across the four religion categories was greater for women than for men, consistent with the hypothesis of female erotic plasticity. Probably, these numbers just reflect nonsignificant, random variations, and so they too should be discounted.

In terms of duration of most recent sexual event, there was a suggestive trend. Education produced a greater variation in the percentage of women than men saying that their most recent sexual encounter lasted under fifteen minutes.[5]

A subsequent work with the same data set examined influences on sexual dysfunction (Laumann, Paik, & Rosen, 1999). It found that more education was associated with less sexual dysfunctions for women, whereas there was no significant effect for men. Thus, again, sociocultural variables were linked to bigger differences in females than males.

Last, one may consider fertility, which may or may not be relevant insofar as one considers sex to be aimed at reproduction. Educational level predicted a bigger difference in women's reproductive patterns than those of men, measured in terms of number of children. Religion did too. Unlike other variables, fertility showed directionally similar effects to religion and education: Highly educated women and highly religious women had fewer children than other women.

Summary. On the main aspects of sex covered in the NHSLS, it was possible to construct eight comparisons as a function of education. One (masturbation) was inconclusive, and the other seven showed greater effects of education on women than men. There were five comparisons as a function of religion, and all five showed bigger effects on women than men. Combining these thus yielded 12 comparisons showing greater sociocultural effect sizes on women and none showing greater effects on men. This may be considered a statistically significant pattern, insofar as meta-analytic combination yields a very small likelihood ($p<.001$) of such a result occurring by chance (Darlington, 1975).

Among the less central practices, results were somewhat more mixed. Still, even among these, the preponderance of comparisons showed greater effects of education and religion on women than on men.

Thus, the findings from the best database available clearly and consistently fit the hypothesis of female erotic plasticity. The two major cultural factors studied in that investigation, namely, education and religion, were associated with bigger changes in women's than men's sexual behavior. This was true regardless of whether base rates were high (as in oral sex) or low (as in anal sex or same-gender activity). It was also true regardless of whether the effect of the institution was generally to constrain sexual activity (as with religion) or to promote liberal attitudes and broad interests (as, apparently, with education). Ceiling effects and baseline differences could contribute to some findings, but other findings are immune to these problems, and they all point to the same conclusion of greater female plasticity.

Attitude–Behavior Consistency

The third prediction derived from the plasticity hypothesis is that women will show lower attitude–behavior consistency with regard to sex. If women's behavior is more malleable by situational forces than men's, then women will be more likely than men to do things contrary to their general attitudes.

With regard to sex, the discrepancy between women's attitudes and behavior has been noted by several authors. Commenting on their study of Black high school girls, Roebuck and McGee (1977) said that "of interest are incongruities in expressed attitudes and behavior" (p. 104). Social class correlated with sexual attitudes, for example, but not with behavior. Antonovsky, Shoham, Kavenocki, Modan, and Lancet (1978) devoted

[5] There was also a category of people making the doubtful claim that their most recent sex act had lasted more than an hour; the effects of education were not linear, reflecting perhaps some mixture of altered time perceptions and boastfulness. If one ignores these problems and simply compares the most and least educated categories, the difference for males (16.7 vs. 19.9) is slightly larger than for females (13.3 vs. 14.2), which is contrary to the female plasticity hypothesis. I acknowledge it for the sake of completeness, but the discrepancy of two percentage points seems too small to be meaningful.

special study to the inconsistency between attitudes and behavior in their study of Israeli adolescent girls, in which they found that a third of the nonvirgins endorsed as important the value of a female remaining a virgin until she married. These researchers found that such apparent self-disapproval was partly maintained by making external attributions for their past sexual experiences—yet the girls continued to engage in sex even when they disapproved of their doing so. In considering the gap between attitudes and behavior, Antonovsky et al. pointed out that "overt behavior is much more influenced by situational factors than are attitudes" (p. 270), which confirms the present rationale for using attitude–behavior consistency to test the erotic plasticity hypothesis.

The attitude–behavior gap was noted by Croake and James (1973). Their research involved multiple surveys of college students of both genders. Comparing their findings regarding sexual attitudes with concurrent findings from other work on coital experience, they noted "a much higher percentage [of women] experiencing sexual intercourse than those in the same age group who approve of such behavior" (p. 96) as evidence of inconsistency among females.

A similar conclusion was found in a cross-cultural investigation by Christensen and Carpenter (1962). They computed an approval–experience ratio that permitted them to investigate participation in premarital sex even when it went against one's own values. In all three cultures they studied, these ratios were lower for women than men, and in their sample of Americans in the sexually conservative Utah region, the women's ratio was only .33, indicating that two thirds of the women who engaged in premarital sex had done so against their personal values. (The men in that sample had a ratio of .59.) Because base rates of participation in premarital sex differed substantially by gender, these authors did find that numerically more men than women acted against their values. Still, the ratio seems the more meaningful and relevant indicator because it is not confounded by base rate, and it suggests that premarital sex involves a higher rate of attitude violation for women than men.

Because the base rates of adultery are quite low and attitudes of both genders are fairly negative, it is difficult to get good data on attitude–behavior consistency in that sphere. One creative solution, developed by Hansen (1987), involved looking at dating couples' involvement in any extraneous erotic activity, such as kissing or petting. Sure enough, Hansen found that majorities of both men and women in his sample had experienced extradyadic contacts (by self or partner). Despite the high frequency, tolerance was low, and both men and women expressed some degree of opposition to such activity. For present purposes, however, the crucial comparisons involved whether the attitudes (and other predictor variables) correlated with having engaged in extradyadic activity.

The most directly relevant variable was extradyadic permissiveness, that is, the attitude toward such activity. The correlation between tolerating such activity and having participated in it was stronger for men ($r = .48$) than for women ($r = .31$). Other variables, including religiosity, sexual attitudes in general, and identification with gender roles, also showed stronger correlations for men than for women. Combining the effects of all these attitudinal predictor variables enabled Hansen (1987) to account for a third (33%) of the variance in whether men had strayed, but the same predictors accounted for only a ninth (11.4%) of the variance in women's behavior.

Another area in which attitude–behavior consistency can be examined is use of condoms. Herold and Mewhinney (1993) conducted a survey of people in a singles bar. The authors remarked on the "obvious discrepancy between the reported favorable attitudes toward condoms and the findings that most respondents did not consistently use condoms during their last experience with casual sex" (p. 42). The inconsistency was apparently greater among women: Women reported a higher intention than men to use condoms, as well as reporting greater fear of sexually transmitted diseases, but actual condom use was the same for both genders. Because people use condoms less than they say they should, the behaviors of the women were more inconsistent with their attitudes than were the men's behaviors. Moreover, the temptation factor should have produced the opposite effect: Condoms are generally regarded as detracting more from male than female pleasure, and so males should be more willing to betray their pro-condom attitudes.

The singles bar sample studied by Herold and Mewhinney (1993) also showed inconsistency between women's attitudes and behaviors regarding casual sex itself, which was defined as having erotic contact beyond hugging and kissing with someone the respondent had just met that same day. Only 28% of the women said they anticipated sometimes having sex with someone they had just met, but the majority (59%) had done it. The high rate of having had sex with a new acquaintance was especially remarkable in view of the findings that the women reported high rates of guilt over such activities (72%) and low rates (2%) of saying they consistently enjoyed them. The authors pointed out that this inconsistency was peculiar to women, although they had not predicted it and had no explanation: "The apparent contradiction between the negative attitudes expressed by many of the women regarding casual sex and the fact that most of them had engaged in casual sex provides more questions than answers" (p. 41).

Below, I consider the possibility that one reason for female erotic plasticity is that women's role requires them to participate in sex even when they do not particularly wish to do so. Having sex without desire is one form of inconsistency (although it may involve specific desires rather than general attitudes that are inconsistent with behavior). Beck, Bozman, and Qualtrough (1991) surveyed people as to whether they had participated in sex without desiring it. Although a majority of both genders reported having done this, the proportion was higher for women (82%) than for men (60%), and the authors noted further nearly all (97%) of the women past the age of 25 reported having engaged in sex when they lacked desire for it. High rates of unwanted sex also emerged from a study of people in committed relationships: During a 2-week period, 50% of the women, but only 26% of the men, engaged in unwanted sexual activity at least once (O'Sullivan & Allgeier, 1998)

Homosexuality provides another sphere in which attitude–behavior consistency can be studied. Laumann et al. (1994) approached this question by calculating the overlap between three categories of same-gender sexuality, namely, desire, behavior, and identity. Desire consisted of a positive response to questions about sexual attraction to a same-gender person and about finding the idea of same-gender sex appealing. Behavior consisted of having had sex (past age 18) with someone of one's own gender. Identity referred to self-identification as gay or bisexual. Attitude–behavior inconsistency is perhaps best known by people who fail to implement their behavior or identity . . . [characterized] 59 percent of the women and 44 percent of the men" (p. 298). Maximal consistency, in contrast, would be exhibited by people who registered positive on all three indicators. Consistency was greater among men (24% of those who scored positive on any same-gender item) than women (15%).

The purist attitude measure regarding homosexuality in the NHSLS was whether the person rated same-gender sex as appealing. This item did not depend on actual experiences of desire or behavior but was a simple rating of attitude in the abstract. This item also has the advantage that men and women had approximately equal rates of positive responses to it. Hence the attitude–behavior consistency question can be formulated by examining whether these attitudinal responses correlated with current behavior. Laumann et al. (1994, p. 159) found that less than half the women who liked the idea of same-gender sex had actually had sex with another woman in the past year. In contrast, nearly 85% of the men who found same-gender sex appealing had had sex with a man in the past year. Although it is possible that gender differences in opportunity and initiative contributed to this difference, it is clear that attitude–behavior consistency was substantially lower among females.

Attitude–behavior discrepancies regarding homosexuality were also documented by Bell and Weinberg (1978). They found that gaps between homosexual feelings (or desires) and homosexual behavior was much larger for the lesbians (22 percentage points) than for gay males (3 percentage points). Moreover, lesbians were more likely than males to have tried to relinquish their homosexuality and "go straight"—which is ironic because lesbians expressed fewer regrets about their homosexuality and were less likely to wish for a "magic pill" that would instantly transform them into heterosexuals. Golden (1987) too was struck by inconsistencies between women's thoughts and feelings regarding sexual orientation. Her sample exhibited remarkable incongruences, including women who identified as lesbians (often for political reasons) but whose sexual behavior had been exclusively heterosexual, as well as the reverse pattern of women who identified themselves as heterosexuals but had only had sex with women. Consistent with the present hypothesis that females have higher erotic plasticity, Golden contended that gay men would have fewer such inconsistencies, would be less likely than the lesbians to regard their homosexuality as elective, and would in general be less likely to exhibit the "fluid and dynamic as opposed to fixed and invariant" (p. 19) patterns of sexual behavior that she characterized women as having.

To get evidence converging with the homosexuality findings, one can consider research findings on sexual masochism. Males are somewhat more likely than females to engage in this form of sexual activity (see Baumeister, 1989), and indeed, some researchers have focused on male masochism simply out of convenience: It is easier to get a sample of participants who have engaged in this activity if one uses males rather than females (see, e.g., Moser & Levitt, 1987; Scott, 1983; Spengler, 1977). Studies that have compared the two generally find more male masochists than female ones (Moser & Levitt, 1987), although the differences are not large.

Yet data on fantasy and desire do not fit the usual pattern of males showing more. If anything, women have more fantasies and desires for submission. This was confirmed in a recent review by Leitenberg and Henning (1995), although their analytic approach combined being forced into sexual activities with being tied up, humiliated, made into a sex slave, and other hallmarks of masochism (cf. Baumeister, 1989). Still, across many studies and different kinds of measures, women are more likely than men to have submissive and masochistic fantasies. Thus, the masochism data resemble the homosexuality data: Women are more likely than men to report having such desires and interests, but they are less likely than men to report taking part in such activities. Hence, for women, there is a larger gap between attitude (or desire) and behavior.

The masochism data are especially useful because they rule out one further alternative explanation that could apply to the homosexuality data. I have said that men mainly show discrepancies between desire and behavior because of lack of opportunity: Many men want to engage in sex but cannot find a willing female partner. The generally more conservative and selective attitude of women toward sex entails that women are less likely than men to comply with requests for sex (Clark & Hatfield, 1989). The difficulty of finding a female sex partner could conceivably help explain why women are less successful than men in enacting their same-sex desires. In masochism, however, it is usually opposite-sex partners who are sought, and so women would be seeking men to dominate them. Women ought therefore to enjoy an advantage over men when both are trying to act out their submissive fantasies, and so this alternative explanation would predict that women would have higher attitude–behavior consistency in this sphere. Instead, women again show more inconsistency, which fits the broad pattern I have hypothesized, namely that women's attitudes and behaviors are less consistent than men's when it comes to sex.

Assessing the Evidence and Possible Problems

Contrary Evidence

A few studies have yielded findings that seem to contradict the general pattern of lower attitude–behavior consistency among women than among men. In a survey of students at a small, private, southern, church-related university, Earle and Perricone (1986) found that women's attitudes toward premarital sex more strongly predicted whether they had had premarital sex than did men's attitudes. One possible explanation is that the lower prediction rates for males reflected lack of opportunity: Many men may have wanted sex but been unable to find a willing partner, particularly at a religious institution. The finding that women's attitudes toward sex were far more conservative than the men's attitudes supports this view, and so the finding may not be a meaningful exception to the female plasticity pattern.

McCabe (1987) surveyed an Australian sample of people involved in serious relationships as to whether they were having sex and whether they were pleased with having (or not having) it. She found "a greater congruence between desire and experience for women than for men" (p. 31). This discrepancy was mainly due to the imbalance in the category of people who were not having sex but wished they were having it. This category of "reluctant virgins" was almost entirely male. Again, this seems to reflect a lack of opportunity for males to act on their wishes.

DeLamater and MacCorquodale (1979) found higher correlations for women than men between personal sexual ideology (i.e., attitudes of approving particular activities) and recent sexual activity within a relationship. This too could reflect lack of opportunity for males. The nature of the measures seems especially conducive to such consistency, insofar as the measures assessed sexuality within a relationship and approval of such activity. The bulk of the evidence for inconsistency did not refer to relationship contexts (and much of it was even explicitly outside of relationships).

A different sort of contrary evidence was found in the NHSLS. Laumann et al. (1994) reported that urban (instead of rural) residence was more strongly correlated with male than with female homosexuality, and this runs contrary to the general pattern of greater sociocultural influences on females. To some extent, this finding could be explained on the basis of homosexuality inclined men moving to big cities in order to find others, but Laumann et al. found that some difference remained even if they considered only whether the person was born in an urban versus rural environment. Thus, growing up in a big city apparently had a bigger chance of influencing men to become gay than women.

The urban–rural difference was not predicted by Laumann et al. (1994), nor did they have any clear idea of what it meant or why it occurred. Considering the large number of analyses they conducted and the preponderance of evidence for greater influence on females, this finding might conceivably be a statistical fluke. Then again, it seems necessary to consider the possibility that it reflects a genuine difference and hence a legitimate contradiction to the broad pattern of greater plasticity among females. Crucially, however, it refers to childhood experiences: Where the person grows up affects the male more than the female. Cities undoubtedly offer a substantially higher likelihood of encountering gay people, as compared with rural life; and if males are subject to sexual imprinting early in life, the childhood environment could have a stronger effect on the male.

One reviewer of a previous draft of this article proposed that men have higher erotic plasticity based on two facts: First, men are more willing to have sex with many different partners (see, e.g., Buss & Schmitt, 1993; Clark & Hatfield, 1989), and second, women have a longer decision process about whether to have sex with a particular man. The greater willingness of men to have sex with different partners is probably not a result of idiosyncratic personal choice or flexible change, however; more likely, it reflects a fairly stable aspect of male sexual desire (see, e.g., Buss & Schmitt, 1993; Ridley, 1993). L. C. Miller and Fishkin (1997) asked a sample of college students how many lifetime sexual partners they would like to have, and the mean male response was over five dozen (as compared with 2.7 for women), which suggests that interest in multiple partners is a stable aspect of sexuality for many men.

As for the decision process, it seems likely that a longer, more complex process is more flexible and more subject to situational and social factors, rather than less. It is well established that quick, automatic responses tend to be simple and efficient but inflexible, whereas controlled, deliberate processes tend to be slow, complex, and highly flexible (see, e.g., Bargh, 1982, 1994, 1997). The longer decision process should therefore be construed as supporting the hypothesis that female erotic plasticity is higher than male.

What About Paraphilias?

One important and potentially contrary pattern is found in gender differences in paraphilias (also known as sexual variations or perversions). Nearly all sources report that males engage in these more than females, although there are some ambiguities in the evidence (e.g., certain patterns such as exhibitionism and bestiality may be more tolerated among females and hence not regarded as paraphilias; see Amsterdam Sex Museum, 1999). If males engage in more varied sexual practices, does this constitute a form of sexual plasticity in which males surpass females?

As already noted, my predictions regarding variance are limited to intraindividual variance. Interindividual variance can well have a strong genetic basis. It is possible that the greater variation in male sexual tastes reflects genetic or biological variation rather than sociocultural plasticity.

Then again, some paraphilias seem incontrovertibly learned. Latex, for example, has not existed on the planet long enough to influence evolutionary processes and genetic markers, and so a latex fetish seems most plausibly interpreted as something learned rather than innate (although it is difficult to rule out the possibility that this fetish is a byproduct of some other genetic, innate tendency; moreover, latex fetishes may be popular with both genders). If males are more likely than females to adopt such paraphilias, then certain social and situational variables apparently have stronger effects on males than females.

Research has not yet provided a clear understanding of the causes of paraphilias. For present purposes, it is merely necessary to suggest some plausible way that males could show greater and more varied paraphilias without contradicting this article's main hypothesis about female plasticity. The most plausible suggestion, in my view, is that males actually do have a brief period of plasticity during childhood, after which the sexual patterns are reasonably rigid. Such a difference in childhood would not run against the substantial body of evidence reviewed in this article, which has depicted female sexuality as more socioculturally malleable during adulthood.

The experimental evidence on sexual imprinting in sheep and goats (Kendrick et al., 1998) is consistent with the view that males are sexually malleable during childhood and inflexible during adulthood. Early imprinting effects were strong and irreversible for males but weak and reversible for females, indicating that female sexuality remained subject to environmental influence during adulthood to a much greater degree than male sexuality, even though males were more strongly affected by the childhood learning environment. The environmental influence during childhood was unmistakable because male sheep who had been raised by goats would not mate with their own species but only with their adoptive species.

Current evidence is consistent with such a characterization of human sexuality, too. Recent Kinsey Institute work (Reinisch, 1990) reported that paraphilias are now believed to originate in childhood (see also Money, 1990). Moreover, they appear to be quite difficult to change during adulthood. Professional therapeutic treatment relies heavily on hormone treatments or castration, both of which are strong biological interventions and therefore suggest that purely meaning-based interventions are not effective—a conclusion that would be very consistent with the belief that male sexuality is relatively unresponsive to social and cultural influences during adulthood.

Sexual imprinting on male children might well also be used to explain the homosexuality patterns that were presented earlier. The view that homosexuality is purely innate and genetic suffers from the implausibility that natural selection would produce genes for a pattern of behavior that precludes reproduction. As noted in the previous section, however, some data suggest that childhood experiences have a stronger effect on males than females in dictating whether one becomes a homosexual (Laumann et al., 1994), and these fit a sexual imprinting explanation. Converging evidence was provided by Bailey and Zucker (1995), who reviewed studies that sought to predict adult homosexuality from cross-sex behavior during childhood. They noted that the effects were larger and stronger for males than for females. Although there may well be genetic factors responsible for both the childhood behavior and the adult sexual orientation (cf. Bem, 1998), as well as possible methodological factors to consider, these findings are consistent with the view that male adult sexuality is more firmly and irrevocably shaped during childhood than female sexuality.

The greater power of childhood imprinting on males is also suggested by recent findings on sexual dysfunction. Using the NHSLS data set, Laumann, Paik, and Rosen (1999) found that childhood sexual experience (i.e., being touched sexually before puberty) was much more likely to lead to adult sexual dysfunctions in males than females and that it also predicted more different types of dysfunction. Women are not immune to effects of trauma, and indeed, adult victimization such as rape has strongly adverse effects on women's sexuality, but the childhood experiences have a greater effect on men.

These findings raise the possibility that there is a brief developmental window of opportunity during which the male sex drive is malleable. A sexual imprinting stage may be biologically mandated for males, during which environmental (and thus sociocultural) influences can exert a strong effect. The hypothesis of greater female plasticity thus may have to recognize childhood experiences as an exception. Still, from adolescence onward, it appears to be the females who are more flexible.

Selective Control and the Double Standard

Although the preceding sections have offered ample evidence consistent with the hypothesis of greater female erotic plasticity, it is necessary to consider one major alternative explanation: male control over female sexuality as reflected in the double standard. The essence of this view is that cultural and social factors selectively target their efforts to control sexuality at women. That is, culture permits male sexual desire and activity to follow their own course, whereas it tries to control and stifle women's sexuality, and that is why many of the present effects were found. In this view, culture is essentially patriarchal, which is to say that it seeks to control and exploit women for the benefit of men. It therefore selectively tries to control women, not because women are easier to control, but because women have less power and because the male-dominated culture seeks to shape female sexuality so women can best serve men's wishes.

As already noted, the argument about superior male power can be advanced as either an explanation for plasticity or an alternative explanation for the findings. The former is covered in the next section, along with other possible explanations for plasticity. The issue here is whether it is possible to explain all the findings as a direct result of patriarchal exploitation of women and its various consequences (including emancipation through education and the sexual revolution)—and hence to reject the hypothesis of greater erotic plasticity among females.

Some findings might be explained on the basis of direct patriarchal control, but others do not fit well. The fact that women report more choice than men regarding sexual orientation (Savin Williams, 1990; Whisman, 1996; see also Rosenbluth, 1997, on voluntary heterosexuality) runs directly counter to the view that men have all the choices and women are imprisoned by rigid social factors. Likewise, the evidence about women who in midlife start having sex with other women while still enjoying sex with men suggests plasticity rather than coercion (Dixon, 1984). If the behavior genetic data continue to indicate greater genetic influence on male than female sexuality, they too will be a powerful argument that the female sex drive is indeed more socioculturally malleable.

The patriarchal oppression theory particularly invokes the so-called double standard, under which certain acts are more permissible for men than for women. This view has difficulty explaining many of the modern findings, however, because the double standard has been difficult to document in modern research and many researchers have concluded that it has disappeared or is disappearing, especially among women (DeLamater & MacCorquodale, 1979; Sprecher, 1989; Sprecher & Hatfield, 1996; cf. Robinson et al., 1991). If American college students do not endorse a double standard, then the many findings based on them cannot easily be explained by reference to that standard. A double standard might help explain some of the older data, but even such arguments are questionable: For example, T. Smith (1994) reports that national (Roper) polls found only a small minority endorsing a double standard in 1959 (8%) and even 1937 (7%). In any case, the double standard cannot account for a large part of the evidence covered here, even if it may have influenced an occasional finding.

The greater consensual lesbianism in prison (as compared with consensual homosexuality among imprisoned males) would be interpreted by the selective control explanation as a sign that prison frees women from the compulsive heterosexuality enforced by society. This alternative explanation thus rests on the doubtful assumption that women are more free in prison than out of it. It also suggests that when a woman reverts to heterosexuality after prison, she is simply coming back under the control of patriarchy. These views stretch the bounds of plausibility. Most situational analyses would conclude that people are less free in prison than out of it—especially with regard to sexual choices.

As already reported, female sexual behavior varies far more than male as a function of education. The selective control hypothesis holds that women are no different than men but have been sexually stifled by patriarchal society and so education creates only the illusion of change insofar as it frees women from their exploited status, enabling them to become like men. Sure enough, in many cases education produces a convergence between men and women, so that highly educated women resemble men. In some cases, though, the effect is not in this direction, and women become unlike men when highly educated. Wilson (1975) found that agreement with the view that sexual desires and sexual realities diverge was similar between educated men, uneducated men, and uneducated women, whereas educated women held a quite different view. Weis et al. (1992) found that sex education produced bigger increases in tolerant, permissive attitudes in females than males, regardless of which gender started off more tolerant—thus, in some cases, females were initially more tolerant and became even more so after education. The NHSLS found that across increasing levels of education, women varied from less to substantially more interested than men in homosexual experiences (Laumann et al., 1994) and that education also made women more different than men in contraceptive use.

Religion was also shown to have greater effects on female than male sexuality. Someone might argue that religion is a tool of male oppression (which entails suppressing female sexuality) whereas education liberates women and allows them to discover and pursue their own desires. This explanation has difficulty explaining the powerful historical facts that Christianity has long appealed to women more than to men, both during its rise to power in the Roman empire (see Stark, 1996) and during the transition into the modern era (Cott, 1977), and that even today female church attendance and membership rates are higher than male. The selective control explanation seemingly must propose that women wanted to be exploited and sexually stifled by Christian doctrines (and still do), a stance that seems sufficiently questionable as to call for strong supporting evidence before it can be accepted.

Moreover, if religion is a tool of patriarchy that shapes women to serve men, then the highly religious should show the greatest convergence between the genders in practices that serve men, such as fellatio. The evidence indicates the opposite, however: The fellatio gap between men and women is greatest among the most religious people (Laumann et al.,1994). Religious women are least likely to serve their husbands in this and similar ways and fall most short of their husbands' preferences.

Similar findings emerge from studies of the influence of peer groups. Evidence indicates that female sexuality is more influenced than male sexuality by the peer group (Billy & Udry, 1985; Mirande, 1968; Sack et al., 1984). If socializing influences reflect the patriarchal male culture, it is necessary to assume that female peer groups are instruments of patriarchy, at least sometimes, and this too seems dubious.

Most societies encourage heterosexuality for the sake of reproduction, and certainly the Judeo-Christian tradition is strongly opposed to homosexuality in both genders. These Christian-influenced societies have apparently been more successful at stifling female than male homosexuality, insofar as there are more gay males than females (Laumann et al., 1994), and this greater success comes despite generally greater condemnation of male homosexuality (see, e.g., Herek, 1988). Moreover, among homosexuals, more females than males engage in heterosexual activity, as already reported. Women thus appear more socially flexible than males on both scores.

To conclude: Evidence clearly supports the historical reality that males have generally enjoyed superior sociopolitical power. It also seems plausible, although the evidence is weaker, that males have used this power to constrain female sexuality. To incorporate this insight into the analysis of erotic plasticity, it seems far more plausible to suggest that female plasticity is a result of or response to superior male power than to suggest that male power directly caused all the behavioral and attitudinal effects reviewed here without any need to invoke differential plasticity. In other words, male political power and the double standard may offer an explanation for erotic plasticity, but they are not fully viable as an alternative explanation.

Other Alternative Explanations

The extent and variety of evidence make alternative explanations rather difficult to propose for the entire body of evidence, although specific findings can be subject to such explanations. The large mass of evidence that sociocultural factors predict women's behavior more strongly than men's might be questioned by suggesting that data for women are more reliable than for men, possibly because women furnish more accurate self-reports or are subject to fewer sources of error variance than men. Such an explanation however would also propose that attitude–behavior consistency ought to be higher among women than men, whereas in fact it was lower.

With self-report data, one often worries about the possibility of experimenter bias and demand characteristics, especially if the researcher is not blind to condition. With regard to erotic plasticity, however, the possibility of researcher bias can be almost entirely ruled out, because none of the researchers appear to have been actively looking for greater malleability among females. Most researchers covered in this review paid no attention at all to the gender difference in effect sizes. The suggestion that dozens of different researchers systematically biased their data to provide confirmation of a hypothesis that they did not even acknowledge seems implausible.

A final alternative explanation would be that the effects reviewed here merely show changes in overt behavior rather than inner, psychological changes in women. This view suggests that erotic plasticity may be greater for females than males but that the difference is chiefly in terms of behavioral choices rather than inner states. Against this view, it is easy to cite evidence that women's sexual attitudes change substantially and significantly as a function of education, peer influence, and other factors. Whether specific feelings of sexual desire change, however, is far more difficult to assess. The NHSLS found that education had a bigger effect on women's rating of the appeal of various sexual practices, including homosexual activity and various heterosexual activities (Laumann et al., 1994), but it is not entirely clear whether those findings should be considered as manifestations of specific desires or general attitudes.

The measurement of sexual desire (e.g., situation-specific sexual arousal) is undoubtedly more difficult than the measurement of behavior or attitudes, and so it has received less study. One recent investigation by Regan and Berscheid (1995) handled the problem by surveying people about their beliefs about the causes of sexual desire, which is at least a valuable first step. Consistent with the plasticity hypothesis, both men and women agreed in perceiving men's sexual desires (far more than women's) as arising from intraindividual forces, which would therefore be relatively independent of the situation and presumably consistent across broadly similar circumstances (assuming the men were healthy). Both genders also agreed in characterizing female sexual desire (as compared with male) as far more dependent on person by situation interaction effects, and these would certainly be much more variable than the intraindividual causes. This study thus provides preliminary evidence that desire conforms to the same patterns of male consistency and female malleability, but much further work is needed. Given the present state of evidence, the gender difference in erotic plasticity is far better supported with respect to attitudes and behavior than desire itself.

General Critique of Evidence

In general, data on sexual behavior fall short of the highest standards of methodological rigor. It is often impossible to conduct laboratory experiments to test causal hypotheses about sexual activity. Most findings are therefore correlational. Surveys and interviews rely on self-report data, and with sexuality, there are multiple factors that can distort such data, including social desirability biases, wishful thinking, memory biases, and self-deception. In general, however, these sources of bias do not provide clear alternative explanations for findings of greater malleability of female sexual behavior than male.

Direction of causality. Several limitations are relevant and pervasive. Most of the findings regarding the sociocultural factors are correlational, partly because both ethical and pragmatic difficulties preclude full experimental study of sexual behavior. Alternative explanations could therefore be raised. For example, instead of concluding that educational and religious institutions have stronger effects on female than on male sexual behavior, perhaps women's sexual inclinations dictate (more than men's) how much education they pursue and how religious they become. Although such explanations do not seem highly plausible a priori (e.g., why would engaging in anal sex increase a person's likelihood of earning a master's degree?), they cannot be ruled out with available data. One study that attempted to disentangle these competing causal pathways concluded that adolescent sexuality and religiosity are marked by reciprocal causal influences: Religious adolescents are less likely to have sex, and adolescents who do have sex tend to become less religious (Thornton & Camburn, 1989). Why sexually permissive women would seek and achieve higher levels of education is however a mystery, and it seems more plausible to propose that education affects sexuality.

On some variables, reverse causal explanations are fairly plausible. The correlations of sexual behavior with peer attitudes and behavior, for example, could well reflect a tendency for a person to self-select similar peers instead of simple direct influence of peers on the person's sexual behavior. Some studies have been alert to this methodological problem and have had some success ruling it out, however. Billy and Udry (1985) found no difference in peer group homogeneity between males and females nor any tendency (in either gender) to deselect friends based on discrepant sexual status. As for acquiring new friends based on similarity in sexual status, males were more selective in this regard, which would operate against the pattern of higher self–peer correlations among females. Thus, the greater predictive impact of peers on females than on males cannot be dismissed as an artifact of peer selection patterns. The convergence between peer influence and family influence is also reassuring on this score because children cannot select their families.

One may also consider the possibility that third variables account for some of the correlations. For example, the link between education and permissive sexuality could conceivably derive from parental openness to new ideas, insofar as parental openness encourages both pursuit of advanced degrees and of sexual adventure. Still, this analysis does not truly constitute an alternative explanation because, to account for the greater link between education and sex among women than men, one would have to postulate that parental openness has a stronger effect on daughters than sons—which again would indicate greater female plasticity.

The causal question is most relevant to sociocultural factors (i.e., the second prediction). The evidence about intraindividual variability is far less compromised by that issue. Likewise, the evidence about attitude–behavior consistency is not greatly diminished by the limitations of correlational data. Thus, there is a substantial amount of evidence that is not affected by issues of causal direction.

Baseline differences and ceiling effects. With some findings, baseline rates are substantially higher among males than among females, which raises the possibility that ceiling effects concealed male plasticity. This possibility seems contradicted by many findings in which greater female plasticity was found despite low base rates overall (e.g., anal sex) and by findings in women that ended up above the putative male ceiling (e.g., contraception during infidelity, desire for same-gender sex). In such cases, clearly, the effects cannot be attributed to a ceiling effect for males.

Given that males tend to be more sexually permissive than females overall, it is not surprising that many variables that increase sexual behavior encounter the baseline problem. It is therefore instructive to examine factors that restrict or decrease sexual behavior because, with these, it is the males who have more room to change. If the evidence for plasticity consisted of artifactual findings based on ceiling effects and baseline differences, then one would expect sex-restricting causes to have stronger effects on males than on females. Repeatedly, however, the opposite has been found to be correct. I summarize some of that evidence here.

The most salient sociocultural factor that causes restriction in sexual behavior is religion, insofar as religious people tended to report lower levels of most sexual activities than nonreligious people. If men start off more sexually permissive than women, then they ought to have more room to be affected by religion, and so religiosity should produce bigger changes among men than women. The opposite has been consistently found, which supports the hypothesis of female erotic plasticity and contradicts the artifact explanation.

A determined advocate of the ceiling artifact might dismiss the findings about religion by suggesting that religion mainly tries to control female behavior and is relatively indifferent to male sexual behavior. This view is implausible on several counts. As Tannahill (1980) pointed out in her history of sex, early Christianity was more hostile and restrictive toward sex than any of its contemporary religions, and its restrictiveness applied to both genders. The basic Christian view was that "physical pleasure of all kinds is sinful" (DeLamater, 1981, p. 264). This doctrine appears to have had strong appeal to women, and in fact, the early rise in Christian church membership involved a more rapid expansion of female than male members (Stark, 1996). Celibacy was in fact sought and cultivated as a lifestyle by many early Christian women (McNamara, 1985). It seems most plausible that Christianity sought to control sexuality of both males and females but succeeded better with females—which again would point toward greater plasticity among females. This conclusion is also well supported by the evidence about religious celibacy: When identical standards of sexual purity are held up to both men and women, the women are far more successful at meeting them (Murphy, 1992; sec also Sipe, 1995).

Another important point is that the baseline and ceiling arguments apply mainly to the evidence about specific sociocultural variables. They do not seem relevant to the intraindividual variance or attitude–behavior consistency evidence. Thus, even if the baseline problem were serious, it would only undermine one of the three predictions of the plasticity hypothesis.

Thus, baseline differences and ceiling effect problems are relevant to only a small part of the evidence for plasticity. In all fairness, it is quite possible that some individual findings of greater variation among women do indicate a ceiling effect for males. It does not seem plausible that such artifacts constitute a substantial amount of the evidence for plasticity, given that some findings directly contradict this explanation and others are immune to it.

Strengths of evidence. Several strong features of the literature reviewed here are encouraging with respect to the validity of the conclusions. First, a wide range of methods and populations has been used. Consistency of evidence across multiple methods can help substantially in overcoming concerns about methodological weaknesses because a bias or artifact in one method would likely be absent from some others, so if conclusions are similar, confidence in them increases. It is unlikely that multiple methods and approaches would all share the same biases or artifacts.

Second, the consistency of findings is itself persuasive. Across three major predictions and a wide assortment of methods, the evidence pointed consistently to greater erotic plasticity in the female than in the male. The main exception (which was also consistent) is that male sexual behavior is often constrained by lack of opportunity, and so many men would like to have more sex (or more partners or different varieties of sex) than they are able to have. Apart from opportunity constraints, however, female sexuality shows greater responsiveness and flexibility than male sexuality.

A last encouraging feature is that the evidence for female plasticity remains robust and is perhaps even strongest in the methodologically most rigorous work. If the pattern of female plasticity were an artifact of sloppy methods, then its evidence should diminish in proportion to the rigor of the methods, but the opposite has been found. Thus, in the NHSLS (which used some of the most rigorous, thorough, and careful methods), a substantial number of pointed comparisons repeatedly confirmed greater plasticity in females than in males.

Differential critique. To criticize the evidence for the three predictions separately: The evidence about intraindividual variability (the first prediction) is sufficiently strong, diverse, and consistent to be satisfactory for now, although further evidence would be desirable, particularly in regard to issues such as change in prison environments and the like. Second, the evidence for greater responsiveness to sociocultural factors is fairly extensive and convincing, although it would be desirable to have more direct studies of cross-cultural variation and more longitudinal designs or other methods that can overcome the ambiguity about direction of causation. The evidence regarding attitude–behavior consistency is encouraging as far as it goes, but there are many gaps in the range of possible evidence, and conceivably major exceptions or even a large contrary pattern could yet be found. The attitude–behavior prediction is therefore the most weakly supported of the three, although even on that prediction, the evidence is generally supportive. Still, the attitude–behavior prediction is the least central of the three, insofar as many factors other than basic erotic plasticity could affect such data, and so the relative weakness of the literature on that question is least worrisome with respect to the present theory.

Assessment of Possible Explanations

Three possible explanations for the gender difference in erotic plasticity are now considered. Although these explanations can be considered as competing, they are not mutually exclusive, and it is possible from an a priori standpoint that more than one could be correct.

Male Strength and Power

The first explanation is that men are generally stronger and more physically aggressive than women, as well as generally holding superior political, social, and economic power, and so women have to accommodate themselves to men. In this view, men can coerce women to do what they want, and so as men pursue their sexual desires, women must go along with what men want to some extent. Even if the man rarely or never uses his physical or political advantage to get his way, the fact that he could do so remains implicit and could affect relationships.

It is common knowledge that men are physically stronger than women on average and that men have generally had superior political and economic power. Men also exceed women in aggressiveness (Eagly, 1987; National Research Council, 1993). In romantic and sexual relationships, men do sometimes inflict harm on women in connection with various disputes, and in some cases men use physical force to obtain sex from their romantic partners (Laumann et al., 1994). Men's superior socioeconomic power also seems to give them some leverage toward eliciting sex from their wives and partners (Blumstein & Schwartz, 1983).

Thus, gender differences in physical strength and political power have been long-standing and have had some effect on sexual relations. Whether these differences could be responsible for the gender difference in sexual plasticity is far more difficult to say. There are at least two ways that this could be true. In one, evolution may have made female sexuality more plastic (socially malleable) because of millennia of having to adapt to stronger, politically dominant males. In the other, women continue to be conscious of the greater power held by males and hence learn to be more malleable and flexible as a result.

One relevant aspect of this explanation that is different than the other two is that it is not confined to sexuality. If men's greater physical strength causes women to be more malleable and flexible as a submissive adaptation, this should presumably be true across multiple spheres. Women should therefore show greater flexibility and malleability on multiple measures apart from the sexual sphere. In other words, sociocultural factors should have stronger effects on women than men, intraindividual variability across time should be greater in women, and attitude–behavior consistency should be generally lower. The question of whether women are more malleable than men as a general principle across the majority of spheres of behavior is far beyond the scope of this article. Note, however, that experts on gender differences have not thus far recorded any widespread pattern of greater malleability in females, which casts doubt on this as an explanation. Although both gender differences and attitude–behavior consistency have been studied extensively, I have been unable to find any evidence of a general pattern of lesser attitude-behavior consistency among women, even after contacting authoritative experts in the field (A. H. Eagly, personal communication, 1998; R. E. Petty, personal communication, 1998). There is some evidence that women are more easily persuaded than men under a variety of conditions, although numerous exceptions and boundary conditions exist (see, e.g., Eagly, 1987; Petty & Wegener, 1998). Meanwhile, recent work has found that females show more genetic and less sociocultural influence on aggression than males (Eley, Lichtenstein, & Stevenson, 1999; see also Christiansen, 1977), which likewise depicts the difference in erotic plasticity as specific rather than part of a general pattern. If future research continues to suggest that women are not more socioculturally malleable than men across the board, then the explanations based on differential strength and power will be less plausible than the following two.

Change and the Female Sexual Script

A second possibility is that change is an inherent part of the female role in sex, and so women are required to have some degree of flexibility in their patterns of erotic response. In this view, the standard script for sex between first-time human partners depends vitally on the woman changing her mind. In nearly all known societies (and in many other primate species as well), females constitute the restraining force on sex. That is, they refuse many offers or chances for sexual activity. When sex happens, it is because the woman has changed her vote from no to yes. This crucial change might be the basis for greater erotic plasticity in women, because it instills a capacity for change at the center of the female sex drive.

There is evidence that the decisive determinant of whether a couple has sex involves the women changing her position from no to yes. It is well documented that in heterosexual attraction, the man is typically ready for sex long before the woman (Buss & Schmitt, 1993). Men are more willing than women to have sex with someone they have just met (see, e.g., Herold & Mewhinney, 1993; see also Oliver & Hyde, 1993). The precise prediction that women will change more than men toward a more sexually permissive attitude as a function of increasing duration of dating was confirmed by Harrison et al. (1974).

Also relevant is the fact that men fall in love faster than women and hence are likely to feel loving affection and the accompanying sexual desire at an earlier point in the relationship (Baumeister, Wotman, & Stillwell, 1993; Hill, Rubin, & Peplau, 1976; Huston, Surra, Fitzgerald, & Cate, 1981; Kanin, Davidson, & Scheck, 1970). Studies of adult virginity have found that many more men than women report that they have remained virgins because their romantic partner refuses sex (McCabe, 1987; Sprecher & Regan, 1996). Even apart from virginity, far more men than women cite a partner's unwillingness as a major reason that they are not having sex (Mercer & Kohn, 1979). Both genders agree that men want and expect sex earlier in a relationship than women (Cohen & Shotland, 1996).

Direct evidence about refusing sex was provided by Clark and Hatfield (1989). In one condition of their study, participants were approached by an opposite-sex research confederate who invited the participant to have sex that same evening. All the women in both studies refused this invitation, whereas most of the men accepted (see also Jesser, 1978). By the same token, Mercer and Kohn (1979) found that both male and female participants rated all different strategies of avoiding sex as more typical of women than of men, whereas all the strategies for initiating and obtaining sex were rated as more typical of men than women. Clearly, these participants associated seeking sex with maleness and refusing sex with femaleness. If that is correct, then sex would depend on the woman changing from refusal to acceptance.

Further evidence about the female script and the transition from no to yes comes from research on erotica and pornography. Cowan and Dunn (1994) exposed both male and female participants to pornographic films that were classified into nine different story themes, and participants were asked to rate their arousal levels. One of these themes, labeled "submission" by the researchers, involved a woman who was initially reluctant to have sex but changed her mind during the scene and became an active, willing participant in sexual activity. Women rated this theme by far the most sexually arousing of the nine (see also Fisher & Byrne, 1978). These studies thus suggest that the woman's transition from no to yes, as an idea, increases sexual excitement.

A review of the literature on sexual fantasies found that fantasies of being overpowered and forced to have sex were far more common among women than men (Leitenberg & Henning, 1995). In some studies (e.g., Pelletier & Herold, 1988), over half the female sample reported fantasies of being overpowered, and other research found a third of women endorsing such specific fantasies as being a slave who must obey a man's every wish (Arndt, Foehl, & Good, 1985). When women are given lists of sexual fantasies to choose among, that of being forced sexually is sometimes the first or second most frequently chosen one (Hariton & Singer, 1974; Knafo & Jaffe, 1984). In a study of the content of fantasies people have during intercourse with a partner, Sue (1979) found that women were significantly more likely than men to fantasize about being overpowered and forced to have sex. Leitenberg and Henning cautioned further, as other researchers have, that such fantasies do not reflect any genuine desire to be raped, and indeed, the fantasies often involve the man overcoming the woman's token resistance so as to bring about mutual pleasure and satisfaction. Thus, these fantasies likewise suggest that a particular sexual charge is associated with the woman's changing from no to yes, under strong male influence.

In sum, the transition from no to yes appears to characterize the female role in sex. It also appears to be marked by a special emotional charge and high sexual excitement. It is therefore conceivable that this transition, requiring as it does a diametrical reversal in women's attitude toward having sex with a particular man, may have some role in the broader phenomenon of erotic plasticity.

A variation on this explanation is based on the observation that there is a chronic pattern of mismatch between when a woman wants sex and when she has it, so she has to be flexible enough to participate positively and competently in sex when she does not particularly want it. This view is well expressed in Wallen's (1995) point that it is essential to distinguish between receptivity (willingness) versus desire when talking about female sexuality, a distinction that is far less important with male sexuality and hence with traditional male-centered theories of sex in general. To explain when and whether a female has sex, according to Wallen, it is more useful to understand receptivity than actual, proactive desire.

Evidence for this theory is based on temporal patterns in sex. Palmer, Udry, and Morris (1982) found that intercourse patterns for couples had clear daily and weekly patterns but not monthly patterns. That is, couples tend to have sex at a particular time of day (usually in the evening) and on some weekdays more than others (Sundays especially). Other research on female sexual desire suggests however that monthly variations are significant and important (Stanislaw & Rice, 1988). In other words, women feel most sexually desirous at a particular point in the menstrual cycle, usually one associated with ovulation (Stanislaw & Rice, 1988; also Luschen & Pierce, 1972; see Wallen, 1995).

Putting these findings together indicates that women's sexual behavior does not correlate most strongly with their desires. The monthly rhythm of rising and falling sexual desire does not predict their likelihood of intercourse. The implication is that women in general are flexible enough to have sex when they do not most want it. This flexibility points to the importance of receptivity rather than desire and could also provide a basis for a more general pattern of erotic plasticity.

Do Women Have a Milder Sex Drive?

The third explanation is that women have a milder, weaker sex drive than men and that this difference allows the female sex drive to be more easily molded. It is common knowledge that in taming animals, which is to say bringing their behavior under meaningful rules determined by somebody else, that the weaker their urges are, the easier they are to tame. If women's desire for sex were less powerful, less relentless, and less urgent than men's, then as a result, their sex drive could well be more malleable.

Although a full review is beyond the scope of this article, that evidence does suggest that women have a milder sex drive. Women report spontaneous sexual desire less often than men and think about sex less often than men (Beck, Bozman, & Qualtrough, 1991; Eysenck, 1971; Knoth, Boyd, & Singer, 1988; Laumann et al., 1994). They have fewer sexual fantasies involving fewer partners and less variety of activity (Ellis & Symons, 1990; Leitenberg & Henning, 1995). Women report less enjoyment of erotica and pornography (see, e.g., Reed & Reed, 1972; Schmidt & Sigusch, 1970; Sigusch, Schmidt, Reinfeld, & Wiedemann-Sutor, 1970). They desire less frequent sex and fewer sexual practices than men (Ard, 1977; Bergström-Walan & Nielsen, 1990; Julien, Bouchard, Gagnon, & Pomerleau, 1992; Laumann et al., 1994). Women initiate sex less often and refuse it more often (Byers & Heinlein, 1989; Clark & Hatfield, 1989; LaPlante, McCormick, & Brannigan, 1980; O'Sullivan & Byers, 1992). Women desire fewer partners than men (Buss & Schmitt, 1993; Miller & Fishkin, 1997) and seek out fewer extramarital partners (Cotton, 1975; Lawson, 1988; Spanier & Margolis, 1983; Thompson, 1983). Women and girls masturbate less often than men and boys (Arafat & Cotton, 1974; Asayama, 1975; Laumann et al., 1994; Oliver & Hyde, 1993; Sigusch & Schmidt, 1973). Women rate their sexual urges as less strong than men rate men's (Mercer & Kohn, 1979). Women are more likely to cite lack of interest and enjoyment as a reason for not having sex (Leigh, 1989).

Can the relative mildness of female sexual desire explain plasticity? Once again, it is far easier to establish that something is correct than to establish its link to erotic plasticity. On an a priori basis, it would seem easier to transform a desire for A into a desire for B if the desire for A is not as strong. Still, direct evidence of the link is lacking. The most relevant research agenda would be to examine possible links between strength of sex drive and plasticity within gender. For example, in an all-male sample, would the men with weaker sex drives be more affected by education, religion, or situational influences than men with strong sex drives? This question remains for future research.

General Discussion

The central question addressed in this article has been whether the female sex drive is more plastic and malleable than that of the male, in response to social, cultural, and situational causes. The evidence reviewed here supports the three basic predictions derived from that hypothesis. First, intraindividual variation (personal change) is higher among females than among males. The average woman is more likely to change her sexual patterns over the course of adult life than the average man is, in such areas as discontinuity in total orgasmic outlet, adaptation within marriage, adoption of new activities over the adult years, and changes in sexual preference. Second, sociocultural factors such as education, religion, political ideology, acculturation, and peer influence generally have stronger effects on female sexuality than on male. Third, females exhibit less consistency between sexual attitudes and behavior on a variety of measures, including attitudes about virginity, approval of extramarital or extradyadic sexual activity, intended condom usage, having sex despite not wanting it, and interest in or desire for same-gender sex. The low attitude–behavior consistency among women presumably occurs because sex depends on many specific contexts, circumstances, and other meanings, and so the broad attitudes are poor predictors.

Two main exceptions have been found. The first is relatively trivial: Men sometimes exhibit low attitude–behavior consistency because of lack of opportunity. Many men are unable to find a willing partner, and so they cannot act consistently with their preferences.

The second exception, however, suggests a theoretically important qualification to the female plasticity view. Evidence about sexual dysfunction, paraphilias, cross-gender behavior, and locale of upbringing suggests that childhood experiences have stronger and more lasting effects on male than female sexuality. In adolescence and adulthood, erotic plasticity is higher among females, but male sexuality may undergo a childhood phase (akin to imprinting in animals) during which social and environmental influences can have a major influence. Ironically, the relative inflexibility of adult male sexuality may entail that these childhood influences have strong and durable effects. In contrast, the plasticity of adult female sexuality may permit the effects of childhood experiences to be overridden. With regard to sexual abuse and dysfunction, such plasticity would constitute an important adaptive benefit of female plasticity.

The general conclusion from the adolescent and adult evidence is that the balance between nature and culture is different for the two genders, at least in terms of their sexuality. Men's sexuality revolves around physical factors, in which nature is predominant and the social and cultural dimension is secondary. For women, social and cultural factors play a much greater role, and the role of physical processes and biological nature is relatively smaller. These findings reverse one cultural stereotype, which is that civilization is male whereas women are closer to nature. In sexuality, at least, women are the creatures of meaning (which invokes the sociocultural contexts), whereas men are the creatures of nature. (Of course, these differences are relative, not absolute.)

The large preponderance of supporting evidence thus supports the firm conclusion that the female sex drive is in fact more malleable than that of the male. It must be acknowledged that essentially none of the studies reviewed was intended to provide a direct test of the hypothesis of female plasticity, and so some prospective tests may be warranted. Still, the fact that researchers were not specifically looking to establish differential plasticity tends further confidence to the conclusion because it rules out any concern that their results are due to experimenter bias, demand characteristics, or selective testing of the hypothesis. To put it simply, researchers have repeatedly confirmed that women's sex drives are more malleable even though they did not intend to show this and, indeed, generally failed to suspect that this feature of their data may have fit a more general pattern.

It would however be useful for further research to search for boundary conditions, counterexamples, and mediating or moderating factors regarding differential plasticity. Any exceptions to the general pattern of erotic plasticity would add valuable insight into gender differences in sexuality. Attitude–behavior inconsistency is the least thoroughly supported of the three major predictions, and so this may be an area for further work that might either provide useful confirmation of the broad plasticity hypothesis or, indeed, reveal exceptions and boundary conditions that would be theoretically enlightening.

Three possible explanations for gender differences in erotic plasticity have been suggested: differences in power and strength, the requirement of change as part of the female sexual script, and a relative mildness in female sexual desire. On the basis of currently available evidence, I conclude that each of these three possible explanations has a valid basis, but at present, there is little conclusive evidence to suggest which of them is actually linked to erotic plasticity.

Proximal causes also remain to be explicated. These may include direct genetic influence, such as the notion that having two X chromosomes gives women alternative blueprints for sexual responses, whereas males have only the one. Sexual imprinting may be more influential and irreversible with males than females, so that women continue to have sexually formative experiences throughout life whereas men have them only at one early point. Hormones may affect men more than women, either because men have more of the most influential hormone (testosterone) or because men are more directly attuned to their inner states without any mediation through social cues and information (T. Roberts & Pennebaker, 1995).

Another intriguing possibility is suggested by Bem's (1996, 1998) theory proposing that sexual orientation is shaped by childhood social patterns, such that the less familiar gender becomes the more arousing and sexually appealing one (i.e., exotic becomes erotic). Bem's theory could be reconciled with several of the explanations I have suggested. The notion that females have more mixed-gender social groups in childhood than males do leads, in Bem's analysis, to suggesting that female sexual arousal would distinguish less between males and females than would male sexual arousal. This plasticity of sexual orientation could contribute to more general patterns of plasticity (i.e., change begets change), as with the second explanation I proposed. Alternatively, one could use Bem's line of reasoning to suggest that, because both genders are familiar to females, neither is exotic, and hence neither is likely to become erotic—and this could contribute to my third explanation, namely, the weaker female sex drive.

In terms of the daily lives and actual experiences of individual men and women, the difference in plasticity may be felt in terms of the relative importance of physical factors versus social meanings. The importance of social, situational, and cultural influences on women suggests that sex depends very prominently on the meanings and interpretations that a given sex act may have. The relative inflexibility of males with regard to sociocultural factors suggests that meanings matter less than simpler, physical aspects of sex.

The current status of knowledge may therefore be described as follows. The female sex drive is more plastic and malleable than that of the male; several well-founded explanations for this differential plasticity can be articulated, but there is no adequate basis at present for preferring any of these explanations over the others. It is also possible that all three explanations are correct and that the difference in plasticity is multidetermined.

Implications

If women are indeed more responsive to sociocultural changes, then forecasting the future shape of sexuality will be less reliable when it comes to women than men. Had someone at the close of the 19th century sought to predict what would happen in the 20th century, he or she might have been fairly accurate at predicting men (because they have not changed much), but predicting the fluctuations and vicissitudes of female sexuality would have been considerably more difficult. It is, in other words, far more difficult to predict what women will want and expect sexually a century hence than it is to predict men's wants and expectations.

From the point of view of society, the gender difference in erotic plasticity suggests that it will be more productive and effective to try to control female than male sexuality. It is possible that a society's survival would be jeopardized by historical events that might require more reproduction (e.g., due to war or famine) or less (e.g., overpopulation) or that the desirability of promiscuity would increase (e.g., if the sex ratio departs far from equality) or decrease (e.g., if AIDS or another venereal disease raises health risks). A society that needs a change in sexual behavior in order to survive or flourish would do better to target its messages and other pressures at women rather than men because of the greater difficulty in changing the sexual desires and habits of men.

From the point of view of the individuals, women will be better able than men to adapt to new social conditions and demands. If social conditions do change in a meaningful fashion, resulting in a need for serious changes in sexual attitudes and behavior, women are likely to make the adjustment better. True, one might argue on the basis of the relative mildness of the female sex drive that sex matters less to women than men and so women might be more willing to accept different circumstances and contingencies. However, even if changes in active desires and behaviors are needed, women should make these more easily. This may be particularly important if the pace of social change continues to accelerate, as is generally assumed to be the trend in modernity. In sex, at least, women should be able to keep up with changing times better than men.

Some misunderstandings and potential conflicts between the genders could be affected by the difference in plasticity. Modern norms of egalitarianism and equitable relationships suggest that people should compromise and seek joint, mutually satisfying decisions, but the calculation of compromise is rendered more difficult by differential plasticity. In simple terms, sexual compromise will be easier for women than men. I cited several findings indicating that women find their sexual relationships more satisfying than men, which could reflect the women's greater plasticity. For example, in response to Ard's (1977) survey, women indicated that their actual frequency of intercourse was nearly identical to their desired frequency, whereas for the men a substantial gap existed. One interpretation of this finding is that women have greater power and can dictate the sexual terms of the relationship. Another, however, is that women are better able to adjust their preferences and expectations to what is actually available to them, and so a compromise gradually ceases to seem like a compromise.

Conflict and misunderstanding can exist between members of the same gender, too, and again differential plasticity could play a role. Homosexual communities, for example, are in a sense oppressed minority groups and ones from which members may be tempted to defect. If people leave such communities and join the heterosexual mainstream, the survival of the communities could be jeopardized. Given the data reviewed here, such defections are likely to be a bigger problem and threat for female than male homosexual groups. Sure enough, lesbian communities have ongoing and sometimes bitter struggles over defectors to heterosexuality, which may be less of a problem for gay male groups (see Clausen, 1990; Rust, 1993).

There are clear and important implications for clinical practice. The greater plasticity of female sexuality suggests that sex therapists should be more effective at treating women than men. In particular, cognitive–behavioral treatments and other social interventions should be much more effective with female than male clients. The relative inflexibility of males suggests that sexual problems may require more physiologically and biochemically oriented interventions. Some recent evidence fits this view, although further research is needed. Laumann et al. (1999) found that male sexual dysfunction was more linked to physical factors such as poor overall health than was female sexual dysfunction. Meanwhile, female dysfunction was more strongly linked than male to sociocultural factors such as education and change in socioeconomic status (loss of income). The link to broadly meaningful context was also evident in the fact that female sexual dysfunction correlated more strongly than male dysfunction with broad measures of happiness and quality of life. The main exception to these patterns was that childhood sexual experiences predicted male sexual dysfunction more strongly than they did female dysfunction, which fits the hypothesis that sexual imprinting produces relatively strong and irreversible effects on males but not on females.

Sexual self-knowledge, meanwhile, should be far easier for males than females to achieve. The male's understanding of his own sex drive is essentially a matter of gathering information about a stable, fixed entity. In contrast, the female's self-exploration is to some extent pursuing a moving, shape-changing target. The evidence for sociocultural influence and intraindividual change could itself persuade some women that they require a long period of inner exploration, experimentation, and soul-searching in order to ascertain what they truly desire in sex, whereas men would have difficulty appreciating how so much introspective exertion could be required for the sake of understanding one's own sexuality. The sexual consciousness-raising of the women's movement during and after the sexual revolution, which never evoked much of an echo among males, could reflect the greater difficulty of understanding female sexuality due to its greater plasticity. Consistent with this view, some recent findings suggest that women are less certain than men of what they want in sex and how to get it (Vanwesenbeeck, Bekker, & van Lenning, 1998).

Sexual decision-making is also likely to be a far more complex and subtle matter for women than for men. If women's sexual desires and actions are strongly influenced by sociocultural factors, then the social context and situation would potentially be able to alter the desirability of performing a particular sex act with a particular partner. For men, in contrast, performing a particular sex act with a particular person may be a straightforward decision depending on salient, unchanging cues, whereas for women, the answers might fluctuate as a function of a host of intangible social and contextual factors.

Last, the ongoing debate as to the degree of influence by nature or culture could well end up being somewhat artificially prolonged by the gender difference in plasticity. Feminist analysis has favored the social construction of sexuality, whereas the subsequent rise of evolutionary theories has been dominated by male theorists. If women are indeed more socioculturally malleable than men, then the social constructionist theories would resonate intuitively with women more than men, whereas the reverse would hold for biological and evolutionary theories.

Concluding Remarks

Human progress is generally regarded as a matter of either reforming society so as to improve its capacity to guide people toward more fulfilling lives or, at least, allowing people freedom to make their own conscious choices and pursue their individual goals. Moreover, it seems highly likely that sex, love, and mating will continue to play a central part in human happiness and fulfillment. The question of how much human sexuality can be transformed based either on utopian social arrangements or individual choice is therefore one that has more than abstract theoretical implications. If the sex drive is socioculturally malleable, then there exist many possible directions in which to pursue social progress and individual fulfillment. In contrast, if the sex drive is fixed and static, then society must ultimately accommodate and confront those patterns, and individual choice will be a matter of pursuing those innate, inflexible desires.

The gender difference in erotic plasticity suggests that women present a better prospect for achieving cultural progress than men, at least with regard to sexuality. To be sure, the differences are relative rather than absolute, but, on both individual and collective measures, there was consistent evidence that women's sexuality can adapt and change more effectively than men's. To the extent that the road to utopia runs through the bedroom, social engineers may find that male inflexibility presents the greater problem whereas female plasticity represents the more promising opportunity.

Meanwhile, the sexual responses of individuals are likely to continue to take shape in different ways, particularly with respect to the relative importance of physical versus sociocultural dimensions. The relatively low plasticity of the male sex drive suggests that biochemical factors such as hormones, age, general health, and genetic predispositions may often be the driving forces, and men's sexual wishes may be relatively indifferent to the social context. For women, in contrast, sex is driven by sociocultural factors, interpretations, context, expectations, and the like. The question of "What does it mean?"—in other words, what does a particular sex act signify and communicate—is centrally important to the female sexual experience, before, during, and after. For men, in contrast, the different possible meanings matter less, and sex might often be a perfectly fine experience even if it hardly means anything at all. These differences could make mutual intuitive understanding between men and women elusive.

REFERENCES

Adams, C. G., & Turner, B. F. (1985). Reported change in sexuality from young adulthood to old age. *Journal of Sex Research, 21,* 126–141.

Amsterdam Sex Museum. (1999). [Exhibit notes]. Amsterdam: Author.

Antonovsky, H. F., Shoham, I., Kavenocki, S., Modan, B., & Lancet, M. (1978). Sexual attitude–behavior discrepancy among Israeli adolescent girls. *Journal of Sex Research, 14,* 260–272.

Arafat, I. S., & Cotton, W. L. (1974). Masturbation practices of males and females. *Journal of Sex Research, 10,* 293–307.

Arafat, I. S., & Yorburg, B. (1973). On living together without marriage. *Journal of Sex Research, 9,* 97–106.

Ard, B. N. (1977): Sex in lasting marriages: A longitudinal study. *Journal of Sex Research, 13,* 274–285.

Arndt, W. B., Foehl, J. C., & Good, F. E. (1985). Specific sexual fantasy themes: A multidimensional study. *Journal of Personality and Social Psychology, 48,* 472–480.

Asayama, S. (1975). Adolescent sex development and adult sex behavior in Japan. *Journal of Sex Research, 11,* 91–112.

Bailey, J. M., & Martin, N. G. (1993, September). *A twin registry study of sexual orientation.* Paper presented at the annual meeting of the International Academy of Sex Research, Provincetown, MA.

Bailey, J. M., & Pillard, R. C. (1991). A genetic study of male sexual orientation. *Archives of General Psychiatry, 48,* 1089–1096.

Bailey, J. M., & Pillard, R. C. (1995). Genetics of human sexual orientation. *Annual Review of Sex Research, 6,* 126–150.

Bailey, J. M., Pillard, R. C., Neale, M. C., & Agyei, Y. (1993). Heritable factors influence sexual orientation in women. *Archives of General Psychiatry, 50,* 217–223.

Bailey, J. M., & Zucker, K. J. (1995). Childhood sex-typed behavior and sexual orientation: A conceptual analysis and quantitative review. *Developmental Psychology, 31,* 43–55.

Bargh, J. A. (1982). Attention and automaticity in the processing of self-relevant information. *Journal of Personality and Social Psychology, 43,* 425–436.

Bargh, J. A. (1994). The four horsemen of automaticity: Awareness, intention, efficiency, and control in social cognition. In R. S. Wyer, Jr., & T. K. Srull (Eds.), *Handbook of social cognition* (pp. 1–40). Hillsdale, NJ: Erlbaum.

Bargh, J. A. (1997). The automaticity of everyday life. In R. S. Wyer (Ed.), *The automaticity of everyday life: Advances in social cognition* (Vol. 10, pp. 1–61). Mahwah, NJ: Erlbaum.

Barry, H., & Schlegel, A. (1984). Measurements of adolescent sexual behavior in the standard sample of societies. *Ethnology, 23,* 315–329.

Bart, P. B. (1993). Protean women: The liquidity of female sexuality and the tenaciousness of lesbian identity. In S. Wilkinson & C. Kitzinger (Eds.), *Heterosexuality: Feminism and psychology reader* (pp. 246–252). London: Sage.

Bartell, G. D. (1970). Group sex among the mid-Americans. *Journal of Sex Research, 6,* 113–130.

Bauman, K. E., & Wilson, R. R. (1974). Sexual behavior of unmarried university students in 1968 and 1972. *Journal of Sex Research, 10,* 327–333.

Baumeister, R. F. (1989). *Masochism and the self.* Hillsdale, NJ: Erlbaum.

Baumeister, R. F., Wotman, S. R., & Stillwell, A. M. (1993). Unrequited love: On heartbreak, anger, guilt, scriptlessness, and humiliation. *Journal of Personality and Social Psychology, 64,* 377–394.

Beck, J. G., Bozman, A. W., & Qualtrough, T. (1991). The experience of sexual desire: Psychological correlates in a college sample. *Journal of Sex Research, 28,* 443–456.

Bell, A. P., & Weinberg, M. S. (1978). *Homosexualities: A study of diversity among men and women.* New York: Simon & Schuster.

Bem, D. J. (1996). Exotic becomes erotic: A developmental theory of sexual orientation. *Psychological Review, 103,* 320–335.

Bem, D. J. (1998). Is EBE theory supported by evidence? Is it androcentric? A reply to Peplau et al. (1998). *Psychological Review, 105,* 395–398.

Bergström-Walan, M.-B., & Nielsen, H. H. (1990). Sexual expression among 60–80-year-old men and women: A sample from Stockholm, Sweden. *Journal of Sex Research, 27,* 289–295.

Billy, J. O. G., & Udry, J. R. (1985). Patterns of adolescent friendship and effects on sexual behavior. *Social Psychology Quarterly, 48,* 27–41.

Birenbaum, A. (1970). Revolution without the revolution: Sex in contemporary America. *Journal of Sex Research, 6,* 257–267.

Blumstein, P. W., & Schwartz, P. (1977). Bisexuality: Some social psychological issues. *Journal of Social Issues, 33*(2), 30–45.

Blumstein, P., & Schwartz, P. (1983). *American couples.* New York: Simon & Schuster.

Buss, D. M., & Schmitt, D. P. (1993). Sexual strategies theory: An evolutionary perspective on human mating. *Psychological Review, 100,* 204–232.

Byers, E. S., & Heinlein, L. (1989). Predicting initiations and refusals of sexual activities in married and cohabiting heterosexual couples. *Journal of Sex Research, 26,* 210–231.

Charbonneau, C., & Lander, P. S. (1991). Redefining sexuality: Women becoming lesbian in midlife. In B. Sang, J. Warshow, & A. J. Smith (Eds.), *Lesbians at midlife: The creative transition* (pp. 35–43). San Francisco: Spinsters Books.

Christensen, H. T., & Carpenter, G. R. (1962). Value–behavior discrepancies regarding premarital coitus in three Western cultures. *American Sociological Review, 27,* 66–74.

Christiansen, K. O. (1977). A preliminary study of criminality among twins. In S. Mednick & K. Christiansen (Eds.), *Biosocial bases of criminal behavior* (pp. 89–108). New York: Gardner Press.

Clark, R. D., & Hatfield, E. (1989). Gender differences in receptivity to sexual offers. *Journal of Psychology and Human Sexuality, 2,* 39–55.

Clausen, J. (1990). My interesting condition. *Journal of Sex Research, 27,* 445–459.

Cohen, L. L., & Shotland R. L. (1996). Timing of first sexual intercourse in a relationship: Expectations, experiences, and perceptions of others. *Journal of Sex Research, 33,* 291–299.

Cott, N. F. (1977). *The bonds of womanhood.* New Haven, CT: Yale University Press.

Cotton, W. L. (1975). Social and sexual relationships of lesbians. *Journal of Sex Research, 11,* 139–148.

Cowan, G., & Dunn, K. F. (1994). What themes in pornography lead to perceptions of the degradation of women? *Journal of Sex Research, 31,* 11–21.

Croake, J. W., & James, B. (1973). A four-year comparison of premarital sexual attitudes. *Journal of Sex Research, 9,* 91–96.

Darlington, R. B. (1975). *Radicals and squares: Statistical methods for the behavioral sciences.* Ithaca, NY: Logan Hill Press.

DeLamater, J. (1981). The social control of sexuality. In R. Turner & J. Short (Eds.), *Annual review of sociology* (Vol. 7, pp. 263–290). Palo Alto, CA: Annual Reviews.

DeLamater, J. D., & Hyde, J. S. (1998). Essentialism vs. social constructionism in the study of human sexuality. *Journal of Sex Research, 35,* 10–18.

DeLamater, J., & MacCorquodalc, P. (1979). *Premarital sexuality: Attitudes, relationships, behavior.* Madison: University of Wisconsin Press.

Dixon, J. K. (1984). The commencement of bisexual activity in swinging married women over age thirty. *Journal of Sex Research, 20,* 71–90.

Dunne, M. P., Martin, N. G., Statham, D. J., Slutske, W. S., Dinwiddie, S. H., Bucholz, K. K., Madden, P. A. F., & Heath, A. C. (1997). Genetic and environmental contributions to variance in age at first sexual intercourse. *Psychological Science, 8,* 211–216.

Eagly, A. H. (1987). *Sex differences in social behavior: A social-role interpretation.* Hillsdale, NJ: Erlbaum.

Earle, J. R., & Perricone, P. J. (1986). Premarital sexuality: A ten-year study of attitudes and behavior on a small university campus. *Journal of Sex Research, 22,* 304–310.

Echols, Al. (1984). The taming of the id: Feminist sexual politics, 1968–83. In C. Vance (Ed.), *Pleasure and danger: Exploring female sexuality* (pp. 60–72). Boston: Routledge & Kegan Paul.

Ehrenreich, B., Hess, E., & Jacobs, G. (1986). *Re-making love: The feminization of sex.* Garden City, NY: Doubleday Anchor.

Eley, T. C., Lichtenstein, P., & Stevenson, J. (1999). Sex differences in the etiology of aggressive and nonaggressive antisocial behavior: Results from two twin studies. *Child Development, 70,* 155–168.

Ellis, B. J., & Symons, D. (1990). Sex differences in sexual fantasy: An evolutionary psychological approach. *Journal of Sex Research, 27,* 527–555.

Eysenck, H. J. (1971). Masculinity-femininity, personality and sexual attitudes. *Journal of Sex Research, 7,* 83–88.

Fang, B. (1976). Swinging: In retrospect. *Journal of Sex Research, 12,* 220–237.

Finger, F. W. (1975). Changes in sex practices and beliefs of male college students: Over 30 years. *Journal of Sex Research, 11,* 304–317.

Fisher, W. A., & Byrne, D. (1978). Sex differences in response to erotica: Love versus lust. *Journal of Personality and Social Psychology, 36,* 117–125.

Ford, K., & Norris, A. E. (1993). Urban Hispanic adolescents and young adults: Relationship of acculturation to sexual behavior. *Journal of Sex Research, 30,* 316–323.

Gagnon, J. H., & Simon, W. (1968). The social meaning of prison homosexuality. *Federal Probation, 32,* 28–29.

Giallombardo, R. (1966). *Society of women: A study of a women's prison.* New York: Wiley.

Golden, C. (1987). Diversity and variability in women's sexual identities. In Boston Lesbian Psychologies Collective (Eds.), *Lesbian psychologies: Explorations and challenges* (pp. 19–34). Urbana: University of Illinois Press.

Goode, E., & Haber, L. (1977). Sexual correlates of homosexual experience: An exploratory study of college women. *Journal of Sex Research, 13,* 12–21.

Gould, J. L., & Gould, C. G. (1997). *Sexual selection: Mate choice and courtship in nature.* New York: Freeman/Scientific American.

Hansen, G. L. (1987). Extradyadic relations during courtship. *Journal of Sex Research, 23,* 382–390.

Hariton, E. B., & Singer, J. L. (1974). Women's fantasies during sexual intercourse. *Journal of Consulting and Clinical Psychology, 42,* 313–322.

Harrison, D. A., Bennett, W. H., Globetti, G., & Alsikafi, M. (1974). Premarital sexual standards of rural youth. *Journal of Sex Research, 10,* 266–277.

Herek, G. M. (1988). Heterosexuals' attitudes toward lesbians and gay men: Correlates and gender differences. *Journal of Sex Research, 25,* 451–477.

Herold, E. S., & Mewhinney, D.-M. K. (1993). Gender differences in casual sex and AIDS prevention: A survey of dating bars. *Journal of Sex Research, 30,* 36–42.

Hershberger, S. L. (1997). A twin registry study of male and female sexual orientation. *Journal of Sex Research, 34,* 212–222.

Hill, C. T., Rubin, Z., & Peplau, L. A. (1976). Breakups before marriage: The end of 103 affairs. *Journal of Social Issues, 32,* 147–168.

Hu, S., Pattatucci, A., Patternson, C., Li, L., Folker, D., Cherny, S., Kruglyak, L., & Hamer, D. (1995). Linkage between sexual orientation and chromosome Xq28 in males but not in females. *Nature Genetics, 11,* 248–256.

Huston, T. L., Surra, C. A., Fitzgerald, N. M., & Cate, R. M. (1981). From courtship to marriage: Mate selection as an interpersonal process. In S. Duck & R. Gilmour (Eds.), *Personal Relationships: 2. Developing personal relationships* (pp. 53–88). New York: Academic Press.

Jensen, A. R. (1998). *The g factor.* Westwood, CT: Praeger.

Jesser, C. J. (1978). Male responses to direct verbal sexual initiatives of females. *Journal of Sex Research, 14,* 118–128.

Johnston, J. (1973). *Lesbian nation: The feminist solution.* New York: Simon & Schuster.

Julien, D., Bouchard, C., Gagnon, M., & Pomerleau, A. (1992). Insiders' views of marital sex: A dyadic analysis. *Journal of Sex Research, 29,* 343–360.

Kacelnik, A. (1999, March). *Sex, mind behaviour, and evolution.* Paper presented at the annual meeting of Eastern Psychological Association, Providence, RI.

Kanin, E. J., Davidson, K. D., & Scheck, S. R. (1970). A research note on male-female differentials in the experience of heterosexual love. *Journal of Sex Research, 6,* 64–72.

Kendrick, K. M., Hinton, M. R., Atkins, K., Haupt, M. A., & Skinner, J. D. (1998, September 17). Mothers determine sexual preferences. *Nature, 395,* 229–230.

Kinsey, A. C., Pomeroy, W. B., & Martin, C. E. (1948). *Sexual behavior in the human male.* Philadelphia: Saunders.

Kinsey, A. C., Pomeroy, W. B., Martin, C. E., & Gebhard, P. H. (1953). *Sexual behavior in the human female.* Philadelphia: Saunders.

Kitzinger, C. (1987). *The social construction of lesbianism.* London: Sage.

Kitzinger, C., & Wilkinson, S. (1995). Transitions from heterosexuality to lesbianism: The discursive production of lesbian identities. *Developmental Psychology, 31,* 95–104.

Knafo, D., & Jaffe, Y. (1984). Sexual fantasizing in males and females. *Journal of Research in Personality, 18,* 451–467.

Knoth, R, Boyd, K., & Singer, B. (1988). Empirical tests of sexual selection theory: Predictions of sex differences in onset intensity, and time course of sexual arousal. *Journal of Sex Research, 24,* 73–89.

LaPlante, M. N., McCormick, N., & Brannigan, G. G. (1980). Living the sexual script: College students' views of influence in sexual encounters. *Journal of Sex Research, 16,* 338–355.

Laumann, E. O., Gagnon, J. H., Michael, R. T., & Michaels, S. (1994). *The social organization of sexuality: Sexual practices in the United States.* Chicago: University of Chicago Press.

Laumann, E. O., Paik, A., & Rosen, R. C. (1999). Sexual dysfunction in the United States: Prevalence and predictors. *Journal of the American Medical Association, 281,* 537–544.

Lawson, A. (1988). *Adultery: An analysis of love and betrayal.* New York: Basic Books.

Lehrke, R. (1997). *Sex linkage of intelligence: The X -factor.* Westport, CT: Praeger.

Leigh, B. C. (1989). Reasons for having and avoiding sex: Gender, sexual orientation, and relationship to sexual behavior. *Journal of Sex Research, 26,* 199–209.

Leitenberg, H., & Henning, K. (1995). Sexual fantasy. *Psychological Bulletin, 117,* 469–496.

Lewis, R. A. (1973). Parents and peers: Socialization agents in the coital behavior of young adults. *Journal of Sex Research, 9,* 156–170.

Libby, R. W., & Nass, G. D. (1971). Parental views on teenage sexual behavior. *Journal of Sex Research, 7,* 226–236.

Luschen, M. E., & Pierce, D. M. (1972). Effect of the menstrual cycle on mood and sexual arousability. *Journal of Sex Research, 8,* 41–47.

Margolis, M. L. (1984). *Mothers and such: Views of American women and why they changed.* Berkeley: University of California Press.

McCabe, P. (1987). Desired and experienced levels of premarital affection and sexual intercourse during dating. *Journal of Sex Research, 23,* 23–33.

McCauley, E. A., & Ehrhardt, A. A. (1980). Sexual behavior in female transsexuals and lesbians. *Journal of Sex Research, 16,* 202–211.

McNamara, J. A. (1985). *A new song: Celibate women in the first three Christian centuries.* New York: Harrington Park Press.

Mercer, G. W., & Kohn, P. M. (1979). Gender difference in the integration of conservatism, sex urge, and sexual behaviors among college students. *Journal of Sex Research, 15,* 129–142.

Michael, R. T., Gagnon, J. H., Laumann, E. O., & Kolata, G. (1994). *Sex in America: A definitive survey.* New York: Warner Books.

Miller, B. C., & Moore, K. A. (1990). Adolescent sexual behavior, pregnancy, and parenting: Research through the 1980s. *Journal of Marriage and the Family, 52,* 1025–1044.

Miller, L. C., & Fishkin, S. A. (1997). On the dynamics of human bonding and reproductive success: Seeking windows on the adapted-for human-environmental interface. In J. Simpson & D. Kenrick (Eds.), *Evolutionary social psychology* (pp. 197–235). Mahwah, NJ: Erlbaurn.

Mirande, A. M. (1968). Reference group theory and adolescent sexual behavior. *Journal of Marriage and the Family, 30,* 572–577.

Money, J. (1990). *Vandalized lovemaps.* Buffalo, NY: Prometheus.

Morokoff, P. J. (1986). Volunteer bias in the psychophysiological study of female sexuality. *Journal of Sex Research, 22,* 35–51.

Moser, C., & Levitt, E. E. (1987). An exploratory-descriptive study of a sadomasochistically oriented sample. *Journal of Sex Research, 23,* 322–337.

Murphy, S. (1992). *A delicate dance: Sexuality, celibacy, and relationships among Catholic clergy and religious.* New York: Crossroad.

National Research Council. (1993). *Understanding and preventing violence.* Washington, DC: National Academy Press.

Newcomer, S., & Udry, J. R. (1987). Parental marital status effects on adolescent sexual behavior. *Journal of Marriage and the Family, 49,* 235–240.

Oliver, M. B., & Hyde, J. S. (1993). Gender differences in sexuality: A meta-analysis. *Psychological Bulletin, 114,* 29–51.

O'Neill, G. C., & O'Neill, N. (1970). Patterns in group sexual activity. *Journal of Sex Research, 6,* 101–112.

O'Sullivan, L. F., & Allgeier, E. R. (1998). Feigning sexual desire: Consenting to unwanted sexual activity in heterosexual dating relationships. *Journal of Sex Research, 35,* 234–243.

O'Sullivan, L. F., & Byers, E. S. (1992). College students' incorporation of initiator and restrictor roles in sexual dating interactions. *Journal of Sex Research, 29,* 435–446.

Palmer, J. D., Udry, J. R., & Morris, N. M. (1982). Diurnal and weekly, but no lunar rhythms in human copulation. *Human Biology, 54,* 111–121.

Pearlman, S. F. (1987). The saga of continuing clash in lesbian community, or will an army of ex-lovers fail? In Boston Lesbian Psychologies Collective (Ed.), *Lesbian psychologies: Explorations and challenges* (pp. 313–326). Urbana: University of Illinois Press.

Pelletier, L. A., & Herold, E. S. (1988). The relationship of age, sex guilt, and sexual experience with female sexual fantasies. *Journal of Sex Research, 24,* 250–256.

Pennebaker, J. W., & Roberts, T. (1992). Toward a his and hers theory of emotion: Gender differences in visceral perception. *Journal of Social and Clinical Psychology, 11,* 199–212.

Petty, R. E., & Wegener, D. T. (1998). Attitude change: Multiple roles for persuasion variables. In D. Gilbert, S. Fiske, & G. Lindzey (Eds.), *Handbook of social psychology* (4th ed., Vol. 1, pp. 323–390). Boston: McGraw-Hill.

Propper, A. M. (1981). *Prison homosexuality: Myth and reality.* Lexington, MA: Heath.

Reed, J. P., & Reed, R. S. (1972). Pornography research using direct erotic stimuli. *Journal of Sex Research, 8,* 237–246.

Regan, P. C., & Berscheid, E. (1995). Gender differences in beliefs about the causes of male and female sexual desire. *Personal Relationships, 2,* 345–358.

Reinisch, J. M. (1990). *The Kinsey Institute new report on sex.* New York: St. Martin's Press.

Reiss, I. L. (1967). *The social context of premarital sexual permissiveness.* New York: Holt, Rinehart, & Winston.

Ridley, M. (1993). *The red queen: Sex and evolution in human nature.* New York: Penguin.

Roberts, J. A. F. (1945). On the difference between the sexes in dispersion of intelligence. *British Medical Journal, 1,* 727–730.

Roberts, T., & Pennebaker, J. W. (1995). Gender differences in perceiving internal state: Toward a his-and-hers model of perceptual cue use. In M. Zanna (Ed.), *Advances in experimental social psychology* (Vol. 27, pp. 143–175). San Diego, CA: Academic Press.

Robinson, R., Ziss, K., Ganza, B., Katz, S., & Robinson, E. (1991). Twenty years of the sexual revolution, 1965–1985: An update. *Journal of Marriage and the Family, 53,* 216–220.

Roebuck, J., & McGee, M. G. (1977). Attitudes toward premarital sex and sexual behavior among Black high school girls. *Journal of Sex Research, 13,* 104–114.

Rosario, M., Meyer-Bahlburg, H. F. L., Hunter, J., Exner, T. M., Gwadz, M., & Keller, A. M. (1996). The psychosexual development of urban lesbian, gay, and bisexual youths. *Journal of Sex Research, 33,* 113–126.

Rosenbluth, S. (1997). Is sexual orientation a matter of choice? *Psychology of Women Quarterly, 21,* 595–610.

Rubin, L. (1990). *Erotic wars: What happened to the sexual revolution?* New York: Farrar, Straus, & Giroux.

Rust, P. C. (1992). The politics of sexual identity: Sexual attraction and behavior among lesbian and bisexual women. *Social Problems, 39,* 366–386.

Rust, P. C. (1993). Neutralizing the political threat of the marginal woman: Lesbians' beliefs about bisexual women. *Journal of Sex Research, 30,* 214–228.

Sack, A. R., Keller, J. F., & Hinkle, D. E. (1984). Premarital sexual intercourse: A test of the effects of peer group, religiosity, and sexual guilt. *Journal of Sex Research, 20,* 168–185.

Savin-Williams, R. C. (1990). *Gay and lesbian youth: Expressions of identity.* New York: Hemisphere.

Scacco, A. M. (1975). *Rape in prison.* Springfield, IL: Charles C Thomas.

Schafer, S. (1976). Sexual and social problems of lesbians. *Journal of Sex Research, 12,* 50–69.

Schmidt, G., & Sigusch, V. (1970). Sex differences in response to psychosexual stimulation by films and slides. *Journal of Sex Research, 6,* 268–283.

Schmidt, G., & Sigusch, V. (1972). Changes in sexual behavior among young males and females between 1960–1970. *Archives of Sexual Behavior, 2,* 27–45.

Scott, G. G. (1983). *Erotic power: An exploration of dominance and submission.* Secaucus, NJ: Citadel Press.

Sherwin, R., & Corbett, S. (1985). Campus sexual norms and dating relationships: A trend analysis. *Journal of Sex Research, 21,* 258–274.

Sigusch, V., & Schmidt, G. (1973). Teenage boys and girls in West Germany. *Journal of Sex Research, 9,* 107–123.

Sigusch, V., Schmidt, G., Reinfeld, A., & Wiedemann-Sutor, I. (1970). Psychosexual stimulation: Sex differences. *Journal of Sex Research, 6,* 10–24.

Sipe, A. W. R. (1995). *Sex, priests, and power: Anatomy of a crisis.* New York: Brunner/Mazel.

Smith, J. R., & Smith, L. G. (1970). Co-marital sex and the sexual freedom movement. *Journal of Sex Research, 6,* 131–142.

Smith, T. (1994). Attitudes toward sexual permissiveness: Trends, correlates, and behavioral connections. In A. S. Rossi (Ed.), *Sexuality across the life course* (pp. 63–97). Chicago: University of Chicago Press.

Spanier, G. P., & Margolis, R. L. (1983). Marital separation and extramarital sexual behavior. *Journal of Sex Research, 19,* 23–48.

Spengler, A. (1977). Manifest sadomasochism of males: Results of an empirical study. *Archives of Sexual Behavior, 6,* 441–456.

Sprecher, S. (1989). Premarital sexual standards for different categories of individuals. *Journal of Sex Research, 26,* 232–248.

Sprecher, S., & Hatfield, E. (1996). Premarital sexual standards among U.S. college students: Comparison with Russian and Japanese students. *Archives of Sexual Behavior, 25,* 261–288.

Sprecher, S., & Regan, P. C. (1996). College virgins: How men and women perceive their sexual status. *Journal of Sex Research, 33,* 3–15.

Stanislaw, H., & Rice, F. J. (1988). Correlation between sexual desire and menstrual cycle characteristics. *Archives of Sexual Behavior, 17,* 499–508.

Staples, R. (1973). Male-female sexual variations: Functions of biology or culture. *Journal of Sex Research, 9,* 11–20.

Stark, R. (1996). *The rise of Christianity.* Princeton, NJ: Princeton University Press.

Sue, D. (1979). Erotic fantasies of college students during coitus. *Journal of Sex Research, 15,* 299–305.

Symons, D. (1995). Beauty is in the adaptations of the beholder: The evolutionary psychology of human female sexual attractiveness. In P. Abramson & S. Pinkerton (Eds.), *Sexual nature, sexual culture* (pp. 80–118). Chicago: University of Chicago Press.

Tannahill, R. (1980). *Sex in history.* New York: Stein & Day/Scarborough.

Thompson, A. P. (1983). Extramarital sex: A review of the research literature. *Journal of Sex Research, 19,* 1–22.

Thornton, A., & Camburn, D. (1987). The influence of the family on premarital attitudes and behavior. *Demography, 24,* 323–340.

Thornton, A. D., & Camburn, D. (1989). Religious participation and adolescent sexual behavior. *Journal of Marriage and the Family, 51,* 641–653.

Vanwesenbeeck, I., Bekker, M., & van Lenning, A. (1998). Gender attitudes, sexual meanings, and interactional patterns in heterosexual encounters among college students in the Netherlands. *Journal of Sex Research,* 35, 317–327.

Wallen, K. (1995). The evolution of female sexual desire. In P. Abramson & S. Pinkerton (Eds.), *Sexual nature, sexual culture* (pp. 57–79). Chicago: University of Chicago Press.

Ward, D. A., & Kassebaum, G. G. (1965). *Women's prison: Sex and social structure.* Chicago: Aldine.

Weis, D., Rabinowitz, B., & Ruckstuhl, M. F. (1992). Individual changes in sexual attitudes and behavior within college-level human sexuality courses. *Journal of Sex Research, 29,* 43–59.

Whisman, V. (1996). *Queer by choice.* New York: Routledge.

Wiederman, M. W. (1993). Demographic and sexual characteristics of nonresponders to sexual experience items in a national survey. *Journal of Sex Research, 30,* 27–35.

Wilson, W. C. (1975). The distribution of selected sexual attitudes and behaviors among the adult population of the United States. *Journal of Sex Research, 11,* 46–64.

INTRODUCTION TO PART 3

Virginity

Most people retain lifelong memories of the first time they had sex, and in at least some cases these first experiences have a lasting impact on their sexual attitudes, feelings, and behaviors. In this section, an article by Sprecher, Barbee, and Schwartz (1995) reports an investigation of these experiences of losing one's virginity. Sprecher et al. found a broad range of feelings and reactions in connection with the loss of virginity.

Many factors seem to influence the quality and pleasantness of the first sexual experience. One was gender: Men seemed to have more positive attitudes than women about the first experience, although plenty of men and women reported negative feelings, anxieties, and other problems. Beyond that, however, there were several things that people can exert control over and might well want to heed in order to improve their first sexual experiences. Consuming alcohol seemed to make for a less pleasant first time, whereas having sex with a loving partner in a close relationship seemed to make for a better experience. The practical message is that people should rely more on love than on alcohol to make the first experience go smoothly!

This article is part of Sprecher's research program on virginity. An important companion article appeared in the same journal the following year. Sprecher and Regan (1996) surveyed college students who had remained virgins. They found that the general feelings about virginity had become more positive over the years during the 1990s, partly because AIDS and other sexually transmitted diseases had made a dark side of sexual activity more familiar to everyone. Apart from that, they found that women felt more pressure than men to remain virgins but also reported more positive feelings about virginity. In particular, female virgins were more proud and happy about being virgins than were males, whereas the men felt more guilty and embarrassed about it. When all the feelings were combined into a composite emotional index, the men were roughly neutral about being virgins (equally positive and negative), whereas the women were overwhelmingly positive about it.

Neither men nor women said they abstained from sex because they lacked sexual desire—on the contrary, most said they did feel sexual desire but actively refrained from taking the steps to lose their virginity (Sprecher & Regan, 1996). On the contrary, the primary reasons for having remained virgins typically focused on not having found the right person, as well as some degree of parental influence. These applied to both men and women. There were some differences, however, such as the fact that more men than women reported having remained virgins because their dating partners refused to have sex, and because they feared that they would respond inadequately or improperly under the pressure of having sex.

REFERENCES

Sprecher, S., Barbee, A., & Schwartz, P. (1995). "Was it good for you, too?": Gender differences in first sexual experiences. *Journal of Sex Research, 32,* 3–15.

Sprecher, S., & Regan, P. C. (1996). College virgins: How men and women perceive their sexual status. *Journal of Sex Research, 33,* 3–15.

Discussion Questions

1. Virginity is unusual among adults these days. Do you think that adult virgins would have reported different feelings several generations ago, when adult virginity was more common?
2. Will the AIDS epidemic eventually lead to a resurgence in adult virginity? Has it changed people's feelings about the experience of losing their virginity?
3. The research by Sprecher, Barbee, and Schwartz (1995) focused on heterosexuals. How might the loss of virginity be different for homosexuals?
4. The most common occasion for losing one's virginity was once the wedding night; then it shifted to the period of being engaged to be married; then to early adulthood; and now it occurs earlier and earlier in one's teen years. How do you think these changes have altered the experience of losing virginity?
5. What do you think is the ideal way to lose one's virginity?
6. Are people's sexual responses affected in any lasting way by their first experiences? If so, how?

Suggested Readings

Murphy, S. (1992). *A delicate dance: Sexuality, celibacy, and relationships among Catholic clergy and religious.* New York: Crossroad. This is an intriguing exploration of people who refrain from sex for religious reasons.

Sprecher, S., & Regan, P. C. (1996). College virgins: How men and women perceive their sexual status. *Journal of Sex Research, 33,* 3–15. This fascinating study of adult virgins found some people proud, some ashamed to have refrained from sexual intercourse. Important gender differences were found.

Diamond, L. M., Savin-Williams, R. C., & Dube, E. M. (1999). Sex, dating, passionate friendships, and romance: Intimate peer relations among lesbian, gay, and bisexual adolescents. In W. Furman, B. Brown, & C. Feiring (Eds.), *The development of romantic relationships in adolescence* (pp. 175–210). New York: Cambridge. This chapter provides a good introduction and overview for the special problems that face gay, lesbian, and bisexual youth as they begin to become sexually active.

READING 5

"Was it Good For You, Too?": Gender Differences in First Sexual Intercourse Experiences

Susan Sprecher • Illinois State University
Anita Barbee • University of Louisville
Pepper Schwartz • University of Washington

First sexual intercourse is considered to be a major life transition, but it is not always a pleasurable experience, especially for females. The major purposes of this research were to examine gender differences in emotional reactions (pleasure, anxiety, and guilt) to first intercourse and to test possible explanations for these gender differences. Based on data collected from 1,659 college students who had had sexual intercourse, we found that men reported experiencing more pleasure and anxiety than did women, whereas men reported experiencing less guilt than did women. Men's greater subjective pleasure in response to first intercourse was explained, in part, by their greater likelihood of having an orgasm. Similar gender differences in emotional reactions were found regardless of the stage and length of the relationship in which first intercourse occurred; both genders reported more pleasure, more anxiety, and less guilt when sex occurred in a close relationship than in a casual one. However, continuing involvement in the relationship was associated with a pleasurable reaction for women. Other ways in which gender was related to the first intercourse experience are also presented.

The experience of sexual intercourse is considered to be a major life transition, one that people recall as memorable throughout their lives (Harvey, Flanary, & Morgan, 1986). In the modern U.S., first intercourse is most likely to occur in adolescence (Laumann, Gagnon, Michael, & Michaels, 1994; Miller & Moore, 1990). Because of the widespread increase in adolescent sexual intercourse in the past few decades, there has been a surge of research interest on the diverse experiences associated with the initiation to sexual intercourse. Many researchers have focused on predictors of its occurrence during teenage years. For example, researchers have examined how sociodemographic variables (e.g., race, socioeconomic status), family structure, personality characteristics, and attitudes predict whether sexual activity has already begun and/or the age at first intercourse (for a review, see Miller & Moore, 1990). In addition, the "first time" from the perspective of the teenager or young adult has also been studied. For example, teenagers and young adults have been asked what motivated them to have sex when they did (e.g., Christopher & Cate, 1984) and what the experience was like (e.g., Weis, 1983). Popular books have also been written on this important rite of passage, including, most recently, Bouris's (1993) *The First Time*, which contains women's accounts of their first intercourse experiences.

In this study, we investigated college students'

recollections of their first sexual intercourse experiences. With data collected from a large sample of students ($N = 1{,}659$), we examined several ways in which men and women may differ in their experiences.

Sexual Script for the First Time

A person's first sexual intercourse experience often follows a sexual script that dictates social and sexual conduct (e.g., DeLamater, 1987; Gagnon, 1990; Gagnon & Simon, 1973). Most people in a society have the experience under somewhat similar conditions. Recent research indicates that first intercourse in the U.S. most often occurs within a dating relationship, is a spontaneous and an unplanned event, occurs at the home of one partner, does not include good contraceptive practices, and may involve some but not excessive alcohol consumption (e.g., DeLamater, 1987; Zelnik & Shah, 1983). Gender differences have also been found in some aspects of the sexual script for first intercourse. For example, females describe the relationship to be closer or more intimate than do males (DeLamater, 1987). However, the largest gender differences seem to be found in emotional reactions.

Gender Differences in Emotional Reactions to First Intercourse

A number of researchers have documented that males have a more positive emotional reaction to first intercourse than do females. DeLamater (1987) reviewed three early studies on gender differences in reactions to first intercourse (Bell, Weinberg, & Hammersmith, 1981; Simon & Gagnon, 1968; Sorensen, 1972). These researchers found that males experienced more satisfaction and pleasure than did females in response to first intercourse. Furthermore, females were more likely to feel guilty. In summarizing these studies, DeLamater (1987) wrote: "Of the men, 75 to more than 90 percent characterized it as enjoyable and satisfying. Females were less positive: 50 to 75 percent reported a favorable reaction" (p. 132). Other early studies on teenage sexuality, many of them based on qualitative data, also showed that females experienced more negative or less pleasant reactions to first sexual intercourse than did young males (e.g., Eastman, 1972; Hass, 1979; Schofield, 1973).

In only a few recent studies have males and females been compared on emotional reactions to their first intercourse. With a sample of 114 female and 94 male college students, Darling, Davidson, and Passarello (1992) found that men reported feeling more pleasure and less guilt than did women. Rubin (1990) interviewed more than 1,000 teenagers and adults throughout the U.S. and reported that both men and women described feelings of fear and anxiety surrounding their first sexual intercourse. Rubin reported that only about one tenth of the men and women used words of pleasure to describe their first intercourse.

Some researchers have focused only on women's reactions to first intercourse. In the first systematic investigation of emotional responses to first intercourse, Weis (1983) asked 130 women to rate their affective reactions to their first sexual intercourse on a series of 12 affect terms. Factor analyses of these items produced three factors, which Weis labeled as pleasure, anxiety, and guilt. Weis (1983) found that fewer than 40% of these women described their first intercourse as pleasurable, anxiety was experienced by more than 50% of the women, and 38% reported feeling guilt. In a second study, Weis (1985) found that about one third of these women reported that their first sexual intercourse was extremely painful. Thompson (1990) interviewed females about their first intercourse and found that one half of the sample described their first time in negative terms, such as painful, disappointing, and/or boring. In a cross-cultural comparison of women's reactions to first intercourse, Schwartz (1993) found that U.S. women reported more negative affective reactions than did Swedish women, but the two groups reported similar levels of positive emotions. The studies that have included only female respondents further document that first intercourse is often not a pleasurable experience for females.

Explanations for Gender Differences in Emotional Reactions to First Intercourse

Explanations have been offered for these gender differences in emotional reactions to first intercourse. For example, DeLamater (1987) proposed two reasons why men have more favorable reactions. The first reason is based on the "assumption that males are more likely to experience an orgasm the first time they have intercourse" and "thus have more positive reactions because they are more likely than women to experience physical gratification" (p. 132). Researchers have documented that males are more likely than females to experience an orgasm the first time (e.g., Simon & Gagnon, 1968). Physiological differences in male and female anatomy contribute to the greater likelihood of male orgasm. Other factors may also contribute to this, including males' previous noncoital sexual experience in the form of masturbation and petting and lower guilt about sex.

The second explanation DeLamater (1987) offered is that females need more closeness with their partners to enjoy fully the first intercourse. He wrote that "[w]omen might evaluate the first experience in terms of whether it occurred in a romantic setting and had the appropriate emotional tone. Such expectations are less likely to be met, and women are therefore more likely to be dissatisfied" (p. 132). Researchers have found that love is a more important self-reported sexual motivation for women than for men (e.g., Carroll, Volk, & Hyde, 1985; Christopher & Cate, 1984, 1985). There may be several reasons why females are more likely than males to need or desire commitment and romance from their partners to find the first intercourse experience enjoyable (Haas, 1979). Evolutionary theorists hypothesize that, because females get pregnant and have more investment in fewer offspring, they are more concerned that partners either exhibit commitment or demonstrate traits that show a capacity for taking responsibility for their partners (Buss & Schmitt, 1993). Thus, evolutionary theorists predict that females will enjoy intercourse more if the relationship is long lasting, stable, exclusive, and close. This predisposition for females to look for a trustworthy partner has been expanded by cultural mandates for a proper mate-selection criterion. Females are encouraged to wait until the male agrees to a commitment, whereas males are taught that sexual experience is a part of being masculine. Sexually experienced peers are admired and envied by males.

Although there is research to show both that males are more likely than females to experience orgasm during first intercourse and that females are more likely than males to link love and sex, no one has examined whether these differences between males and females account for the specific gender difference found in subjective pleasure experienced after first intercourse.

Other Predictors of Emotional Reactions to First Intercourse

Gender is a strong predictor of emotional reactions to first intercourse, but many other factors are also likely to affect or be related to how people respond to their first time. For example, circumstances surrounding first intercourse (e.g., condom use, alcohol consumption) may be related to emotional reactions.

Very few researchers have examined other correlates or predictors of emotional reactions to first intercourse. In one exception, Weis (1983) examined several possible correlates of emotional reactions for women. In support of DeLamater's (1987) argument, Weis found evidence that both the occurrence of an orgasm and relationship factors are related to emotional reactions to first intercourse. More specifically, he found that experiencing an orgasm was a positive predictor of subjective pleasure and that commitment to the relationship and the perception that the partner was gentle, loving, and considerate were also associated with positive emotional reactions to first intercourse. He also examined several other possible correlates of reactions to first intercourse. Demographic or social background variables (e.g., race, religious denomination) were generally unrelated to emotional reactions. Age at first intercourse was positively related to pleasure and negatively related to guilt. Previous sexual experience and liberal sexual attitudes were associated with more pleasure and/or less anxiety and guilt. Although the Weis (1983) study is informative about correlates of emotional reactions for females, Weis did not sample males and therefore was unable to examine how the correlates of reactions to first intercourse might differ for males and females.

Purposes of This Investigation

The current investigation was conducted to understand more fully how males and females differ in their first sexual intercourse experiences. Specifically, there were four goals for this study.

The first goal was to provide descriptive information about the circumstances surrounding the first intercourse experience for males vs. females. For example, we examined gender differences in own age and partner's age, relationship involvement with the partner, contraceptive use, and alcohol and drug use. Although men and women are likely to have similar conditions under which they had first intercourse, some differences were expected. For example, males would be more likely to be younger at first coitus than females, and females would be more likely to describe their relationship involving first coitus as committed.

The second goal was to examine gender differences in affective reactions to first intercourse. We hypothesized that males would experience more pleasure and that females would experience more guilt. Because no previous researcher has examined gender differences in anxiety experienced after first intercourse, we were less sure what to predict for this specific emotion. However, there is suggestive evidence that males experience more of at least one type of anxiety, performance anxiety, than do females (Hass, 1979).

The third goal was to go beyond documenting *whether* there are gender differences in emotional reactions to first intercourse and consider why these gender differences exist. We tested two explanations of *why* males report more subjective pleasure than do females after first intercourse. Based on DeLamater's (1987) arguments, we expected that the occurrence of an orgasm *mediates* the effect of gender on subjective pleasure, and relationship factors (e.g., relationship stage) *moderate* the effect of gender. In the examination of how gender is related to affective reactions to first intercourse, mediating and moderating variables are both "third variables," but they have different functions. As explained by Baron and Kenny (1986), a variable is a mediator "to the extent that it accounts for the relation between the predictor and the criterion" (p. 1176). We hypothesized that the experience of an orgasm may account, at least in part, for the relationship between gender and subjective pleasure. A moderator variable is a "variable that affects the direction and/or strength of the relationship between an independent or predictor and a dependent or criterion variable" (p. 1174). We hypothesized that the closeness of the relationship would moderate the strength of gender differences in subjective pleasure. More specifically, we hypothesized that gender differences would be more pronounced if first sexual intercourse occurred in a casual (short-term) relationship than if it occurred in a more committed (long-term) relationship. We also examined the degree to which the current status of the relationship moderated the degree of gender differences in pleasure. In fact, current status of the relationship may be the moderator variable that best tests DeLamater's (1987) second explanation for gender differences in subjective pleasure. If the relationship in which first sexual intercourse occurred is still continuing it is more likely that a female will give a positive report on the emotional tenor of the first sexual intercourse experience and therefore report more pleasure.

Our final goal for this investigation was to examine how other aspects or conditions of the first intercourse (e.g., age, condom use) are related to emotional reaction to first intercourse for males vs. females. We examined how gender moderated the associations the other variables had with emotional reactions. This was important to investigate because few researchers have examined other predictors or correlates of emotional reactions to first intercourse, and almost no one has examined how correlates or predictors of emotional reactions might differ for males and females. In sum, the focus of this research was on the ways gender is related, either directly or indirectly, to first intercourse experiences, particularly emotional reactions.

Method

Overview of the Data

The data were obtained from a survey study conducted with undergraduate students at a large Midwestern university over eight semesters, from Fall 1990 to Spring 1994. A questionnaire was administered each semester in an introductory human sexuality course taught in the Sociology Department. The questionnaire was designed both for instructional and research purposes and assessed many sexual attitudes and behaviors. Only the data on first sexual intercourse from the nonvirgin students are presented in this article.

Participants

From a larger sample of 2,066 students who completed the questionnaire over four years, we selected a subsample of respondents who met the following criteria: (a) they had usable data (e.g., had completed most of the questionnaire); (b) they responded yes to the question, "Have you ever had sexual intercourse?" and then completed a set of questions on their first intercourse experience; (c) they identified their sexual orientation as heterosexual; and (d) their gender was identified. We selected only the heterosexual respondents from the larger sample because we had no way of knowing whether the homosexual and bisexual respondents had responded to the set of questions on first intercourse for a same-gender or an other-gender partner.

Of the 1,659 respondents who qualified for analyses, 638 (39%) were men, and 1,021 (62%) were women. The demographic information, which is presented later in the Results, indicated that this Midwestern university sample may have overrepresented some groups (such as Catholics) and underrepresented other groups (such as people from large cities). Although the data were obtained from students enrolled in a human sexuality course, this course fulfills a general education requirement and attracts a cross-section of students. The nonprobability sample of young adults should not be considered problematic in our focus on gender differences in reactions to first sexual intercourse. However, if there is any bias in the results, it would be in the direction of more positive and fewer negative experiences related to first intercourse for both genders, relative to other college students.

Measures

In one section of the questionnaire, the students who reported that they had had sexual intercourse were directed to respond to several questions about their first sexual intercourse experience. The questions about first intercourse are described next.

Age. Students were asked how old they were the first time they had sexual intercourse. Ten options were presented, ranging from "under 14" to "over 21." The options in between these endpoint ranges were discrete, specific ages (15, 16, etc.). The students were also asked the age of their partner, and the same response options were listed.

Relationship with the partner. Students were asked to indicate the type of relationship they had with their first intercourse partner at the time of the first intercourse. The eight options were *prostitute, just met that day, casual acquaintance, friend, casual dating partner, serious dating partner, engaged,* and *married* (e.g., wedding night). Another question asked how long students had been in a relationship with the person. The options were *less than a week, 1 week to 1 month, 1–3 months, 4–8 months, 9-12 months,* and *over 1 year.* Students were also asked whether they were still dating or romantically involved with the person (1 = yes; 2 = no) and whether this was the partner's first sexual intercourse experience (1 = no; 2 = yes; 3 = I don't know).

Contraceptive use. One question asked the respondents if they had used condoms during first intercourse. The options were *yes, no,* and *I can't remember*. Another question asked if they had used any other form of contraception. The options were *nothing* (didn't use condoms either), *nothing other than condoms, Pill, diaphragm, IUD, foam or jelly, withdrawal,* and *other*.

Alcohol or drug use. Students were asked three questions about their alcohol and drug use during their first intercourse: (a) Had either of you had any alcohol to drink before you had sex for the first time?, (b) Were either of you drunk at the time?, and (c) Had either of you taken any other drugs before you had sex for the first time? Five options were presented for each of these questions: *yes, we both had (or were); my partner had (was) but I had (was) not; I had (was) but my partner had (was) not; neither of us had (were):* and *I can't remember*.

Emotional reactions to first intercourse. Students were asked the degree to which they experienced each of the three emotions that Weis (1983) identified as being the primary emotional reactions to first sexual intercourse—pleasure, anxiety, and guilt. The three questions were (a) At the time, how pleasurable was this first sexual intercourse experience for you?, (b) At the time, how anxious were you about this first sexual intercourse experience?, and (c) At the time, how guilty did you feel about this first sexual intercourse experience? The response scale provided for each emotion ranged from 1 (not at all) to 7 (a great deal).

Physical reaction (orgasm). Students were asked, Did you have an orgasm? Four possible responses were presented: *yes, no, I can't remember,* and *I'm not sure*.

Procedure

The questionnaire was administered in a large lecture course during class time. It was administered very early in the semester (typically the second week), in part to avoid contamination from course information. It was stated in the questionnaire and in the oral instructions presented by the instructor that the completion of the questionnaire was anonymous and voluntary. Almost all students present on the day the questionnaire was administered completed the questionnaire. We estimated that fewer than 2% of the students did not complete the questionnaire (this was based on an informal count of the number of students each semester who attended class the day the questionnaire was distributed but chose not to complete it).

Students placed their responses to the questionnaire items on opscan sheets. This procedure was used for two reasons: (a) to reduce the likelihood that students would be able to see how others next to them were responding to sensitive items and (b) to make it possible for the data to be presented to the class within a week or two.

Results

In the following section, we present descriptive information about the respondents' first sexual intercourse experience and highlight ways that the experience was different for men and women. In the second section, we present data on gender differences in emotional reactions to first intercourse. In the third section, we present tests of the two explanations offered in the literature (e.g., DeLamater, 1987) for men's greater subjective pleasure. Finally, we look at the associations other predictors have with emotional reactions for men vs. women. Demographic information on the sample is presented in Table 5.1.

A Description of the First Intercourse Experience

Age. No significant difference was found between men and women in their age at first intercourse, $t = -.17$, $p =$ n.s. For both men and women, the average age at first intercourse was around 16.5. On the other hand, there was a significant difference between men and women in the age of the partner, $t = -11.38$, $p < .001$. Women had sex with someone approximately 1.5 years older on the average, whereas men had sex with someone only a couple of months older on the average.

Relationship with the partner. A majority of the women described the relationship with their first intercourse partner as serious dating (60%). Men were more likely to have first intercourse in a less than serious dating relationship than in a serious relationship. The differences between men and women in the type of relationship was significant, $\chi^2 = 115.02$, $p < .001$.

Responses to the question asking about the length of the relationship paralleled the findings on relationship stage. Women knew their first sexual intercourse partner for a significantly longer

TABLE 5.1. Demographic Information on the Sample (*N* = 1,659)

Background Variable	
Gender	
Men	*n* = 638 (39%)
Women	*n* = 1021 (62%)
Age	
17–19	*n* = 720 (43%)
20–21	*n* = 707 (42%)
22 or older	*n* = 235 (14%)
Year in school	
First-year student	*n* = 220(13%)
Sophomore	*n* = 616 (37%)
Junior	*n* = 545 (33%)
Senior	*n* = 268(16%)
Other	*n* = 10 (1%)
Race/ethnicity	
White	*n* = 1467 (88%)
Black	*n* = 131 (8%)
Hispanic	*n* = 21 (1%)
American Indian	*n* = 2 (< 1%)
Asian	*n* = 19 (1%)
Other	*n* = 19 (1%)
Religion	
None	*n* = 281(17%)
Protestant	*n* = 318 (19%)
Catholic	*n* = 674 (41%)
Jewish	*n* = 51 (3%)
Other	*n* = 335 (20%)
Setting in which raised	
Rural community	*n* = 152 (9%)
Small town	*n* = 263 (16%)
Large town or small city	*n* = 386 (23%)
Suburb or large city	*n* = 714 (43%)
Large city	*n* = 143 (9%)
Social class of family	
Upper class	*n* = 37 (2%)
Upper middle class	*n* = 460 (28%)
Middle class	*n* = 903 (55%)
Lower middle class	*n* = 173 (10%)
Working	*n* = 70 (4%)
Lower	*n* = 14(1%)

period of time than did men, $t = -9.95$, $p < .001$. For example, only about 19% of women knew their partner less than a month, whereas 40% of the men knew their partner less than a month.

Most respondents were no longer dating or romantically involved with their first partner. Only 23% of the women and 16% of the men were still dating their first co-partner, $\chi^2 = 11.05$, $p < .01$. A minority of the respondents reported that this was also the first intercourse experience for the partner, but a smaller proportion of women than men reported that it was the first experience for partner, $\chi^2 = 28.09$, $p < .001$.

Contraceptive use. Forty-seven percent of the men but 58% of women reported that condoms were used during their first intercourse $\chi^2 = 36.32$, $p < .001$. To a separate question that asked about all posible forms of contraception approximately 40% of both men and women reported either that they used nothing or used withdrawal during first intercourse. The most common contraceptive form respondents reported using during first sexual intercourse was the condom. For the description of contraceptive methods used during first coitus, see Table 5.2.

Alcohol or drug use. Almost 40% of first sexual intercourse experiences involved alcohol, but only a small minority of students reported that they, their partner, or both were drunk at the time. Very few students (< 10%) reported any drug use before the first sexual intercourse experience (see Table 5.2).

TABLE 5.2. Characteristics and Conditions of First Intercourse for Men vs. Women

Variable	Men (n = 638)	Women (n = 1021)
Own age		
under age 14	6%	2%
14–15	22%	23%
16–17	44%	47%
18–19	22%	25%
20–21	4%	3%
over 21	2%	4%
mean age	16.5	16.5
Age of partner		
under 14	4%	.4%
14–15	24%	8%
16–17	38%	35%
18–19	25%	35%
20–21	5%	14%
over 21	4%	7%
mean age	16.75	18.00
Relationship to the partner		
a prostitute*	.2%	.1%
just met that day	9%	3%
casual acquaintances	12%	6%
friends	18%	9%
casual dating	25%	21%
serious dating	36%	60%
engaged	.3%	.7%
married	.2%	0%
Length of relationship		
less than a week	23%	8%
1 week to 1 month	17%	11%
1–3 months	23%	28%
4–8 months	17%	27%
9–12 months	6%	10%
over 1 year	14%	17%
Current status of relationship		
still dating	16%	23%
no longer dating	84%	77%
First intercourse for partner		
yes	37%	30%
no	54%	66%
don't know	9%	4%
Contraception used		
nothing	33%	24%
condoms only	42%	52%
Pill	15%	7%
diaphram	.2%	.1%
IUD	0%	.2%
foam & jelly	1%	1%
withdrawal	9%	14%
other	1%	1%
Alcohol consumption		
both had	32%	27%
partner had	2%	3%
I had	2%	2%
neither had	61%	64%
can't remember	3%	4%
Drunk at the time?		
both were	15%	10%
I was	3%	5%
partner was	3%	3%
neither was	76%	80%
can't remember	4%	2%
Drugs used?		
both used	3%	2%
partner had	2%	2%
I had	3%	.2%
neither had	90%	94%
can't remember	3%	1%

*One man and one woman said they had first intercourse with a prostitute. Some readers may question whether a woman really went to a prostitute. In fact, this could have been an error on the op-scan sheet or be her post-event interpretation of the relationship.

Gender Differences in Emotional Reactions to First Sexual Intercourse

Next, we examined gender differences in pleasure, anxiety, and guilt experienced after the first intercourse experience. The mean response to each emotion for men and women separately are presented in Table 5.3.

Our hypotheses about gender differences in emotional reactions to first coitus were supported. The largest gender difference was for pleasure. As hypothesized, men reported experiencing more subjective pleasure than did women, $t = 22.97$, $p < .001$. Men reported more anxiety than did women, $t = 13.17$, $p < .001$, and men experienced less guilt than did women, $t = -12.59$, $p < .001$.

For both genders, anxiety was experienced to a significantly greater degree than either guilt or pleasure (pairwise comparisons were significant at $p < .001$). Furthermore, pleasure was experienced to a significantly greater degree than was guilt among men, whereas the reverse was found among women (both significant at $p < .001$).

We also examined the intercorrelations among the emotional reactions for men and women. These results are presented in Table 5.4. Although pleasure and anxiety are emotions with opposite valences, they were positively correlated in the context of first intercourse. The greater the anxiety, the more that pleasure was experienced, for both men and women. Furthermore, for both men and women, pleasure and guilt were negatively associated—the greater the guilt, the less the pleasure. The association between anxiety and guilt was negative and significant for women (greater anxiety was associated with less guilt) but at zero for men.

Tests of Explanations for Gender Differences in Emotional Reactions

In this section, we describe our tests of two explanations for men's greater subjective pleasure. First, we examine the mediating role of having an orgasm. Second, we examine the moderating role of relationship factors.

TABLE 5.3. Gender Differences in Affective Reactions to First Intercourse

Emotion	Mean for men	Mean for women
Pleasure	5.00	2.95
Anxiety	5.93	4.85
Guilt	2.60	3.88

Note: The response scale for each emotion ranged from 1 (not at all) to 7 (a great deal). All of the differences between men and women significant at $p < .001$.

TABLE 5.4. Intercorrelations Among Affective Reactions to the First Time for Men vs. Women

	Pleasure	Anxiety	Guilt
Pleasure		.19*	–.25*
Anxiety	.23*		.00
Guilt	–.29*	–.20*	

Note: Correlations above the diagonal are for men; correlations below are from women.
*$p < .01$

The mediating role of having an orgasm. First, we looked at whether males' greater likelihood of having an orgasm the first time explains why there are gender differences in subjective pleasure. To do this, we first needed to establish that there were gender differences in the likelihood of experiencing an orgasm during first intercourse. Not surprisingly, men were much more likely than women to report that they experienced an orgasm, $\chi^2 = 716.54$, $p < .001$. Whereas 79% of the men reported that they were certain they had one the first time (6% were either not sure or could not remember, and 15% said no), only 7% of the women reported having an orgasm (10% were not sure or could not remember, and 83% said no).

Next, we examined whether the 7% of the women who had an orgasm reported as much subjective pleasure as did the men. In Table 5.5 we present the mean subjective pleasure for the four groups represented by the cross-classification of gender and the occurrence of orgasm during first intercourse. Within each gender, the group who experienced an orgasm reported significantly more subjective pleasure than the group who did not or were not sure ($p < .001$). However, the 2 (gender) × 2 (orgasm) interaction from ANOVA was significant, $F = 14.74$, $p < .001$. The association between having an orgasm and subjective pleasure differed for men and women. More specifically, the difference in subjective pleasure between orgasmic first-timers and non-orgasmic first-timers was larger for women, $t = 10.51$, $p < .001$, than for men, $t = 7.39$, $p < .001$. On the other hand, there was *no* significant difference in subjective pleasure between the women who had an orgasm and the men who had an orgasm, as indicated by a simple comparison between these two groups, $t = .85$, n.s.

TABLE 5.5. Men Subjective Pleasure Ratings by Gender and Occurrences of an Orgasm

	Had an orgasm	Did not have an orgasm Not sure
Men	5.27 (*n* = 491)	4.00 (*n* = 133)
Women	5.09 (*n* = 70)	2.79 (*n* = 944)

Note: The response scale for the pleasure item ranged from 1 (not at all) to 7 (a great deal).

To test more formally the mediating role of orgasms, however, we conducted a series of regression models (Baron & Kenny, 1986). First, we regressed the occurrence of orgasms (the mediator) on gender (the independent variable). Gender was strongly related to the occurrence of an orgasm; it explained 54% of the variance. Second, we regressed subjective pleasure (the dependent variable) on gender. Gender also was strongly related to subjective pleasure, explaining 24% of the variance. Third, we regressed subjective pleasure on both gender and the experience of orgasm. Together, gender and the occurrence of orgasms explained 31% of the variance in subjective pleasure. To establish the mediating role of an orgasm, the following conditions would have to be met:

> First, the independent variable must affect the mediator in the first equation; second, the independent variable must be shown to affect the dependent variable in the second equation; and third, the mediator must affect the dependent variable in the third equation. If these conditions all hold in the predicted direction, then the effect of the independent variable on the dependent variable must be less in the third equation than in the second. Perfect mediation holds if the independent variable has no effect when the mediator is controlled. (Baron & Kenny, 1986, p. 1177)

As shown in Table 5.6, results indicate that the relationship of gender to subjective pleasure was partially mediated by the occurrence of an orgasm. The relationship between gender and subjective pleasure was weaker in Equation 3 (which included the orgasm variable) than in Equation 2.

The moderating role of relationship factors. Next, we tested the second explanation that has been offered for women's lower level of subjective pleasure relative to men in response to first intercourse. DeLamater (1987) suggested that the emotional tone of the relationship is more important for women's subjective pleasure than for men's. This would suggest that the degree to which the relationship with a first intercourse partner was not (or is no longer) close should reduce the self-reported pleasure for women to a greater degree than for men. Following from this logic, we argued that the effect of gender on subjective pleasure should be moderated by aspects of the closeness of the relationship with the first intercourse partner. Although we did not have a measure of perceived closeness of the relationship, we did have the following measures of relationship involvement: the stage of the relationship, the length of the relationship, and whether the relationship was still intact (at the time the questionnaire was completed). In the analyses that follow, each of these relationship variables was represented by a dichotomy. When both the independent variable and the moderator variable are dichotomies, the appropriate test for moderation is a "2 × 2 ANOVA, and moderation is indicated by an interaction" (Baron & Kenny, 1986, p. 1175).

First, we tested the moderating influence of *relationship stage* represented by the dichotomy (a) casually dating or less committed vs. (b) serious dating or more committed. The interaction from the 2 (gender) × 2 (relationship stage) ANOVA, with subjective pleasure as the dependent variable, was not significant, $F = 1.75$, n.s. However, the main effect of relationship stage was significant, $F = 29.46$, $p < .001$. As the means in the top left panel of Table 5.7 show, for both men and women, more subjective pleasure was experienced in response to first intercourse if the relationship in which it occurred was serious rather than casual.

TABLE 5.6. Summary of Regression Analyses Assessing the Mediational Effect of Orgasm on the Association Between Gender and Subjective Pleasure in Response to First Intercourse

Predictor (s)	Dependent Variable
Equation 1:	Orgasm
Gender	*Beta* = .73**
	$R^2 = .54$
	$F = 1921.91$***
Equation 2:	Subjective pleasure
Gender	*Beta* = −.49**
	$R^2 = .24$
	$F = 519.26$***
Equation 3:	Subjective Pleasure
Gender	*Beta* = −.20***
Orgasms	*Beta* = −.39***
	$R^2 = .31$
	$F = 368.12$***

*$p \le .05$ **$p \le .01$ ***$p \le .001$

TABLE 5.7. Mean Subjective Pleasure, Anxiety, and Guilt Ratings for Different Types of Relationships for Men vs. Women

	Pleasure		Anxiety		Guilt	
	Men	Women	Men	Women	Men	Women
Stage of Relationship						
Casual (393 M. 396 W.)	4.87	2.60	5.81	4.63	2.72	4.27
Serious (228 M. 615 W.)	5.21	3.17	6.13	4.99	2.37	3.62
Length of the Relationship						
Brief (251 M. 183 W.)	4.83	2.54	5.88	4.69	2.65	4.37
>1 month (369 M. 829 W.)	5.12	3.04	5.97	4.89	2.55	3.77
Current Status of Relationship						
Not still together (514 M. 776 W.)	4.96	2.71	5.96	4.70	2.60	4.10
Still together (97 M. 230 W.)	5.27	3.69	5.95	5.43	2.70	3.16

Next, we examined the moderating influence of the *length of the relationship.* We dichotomized the length of relationship into (a) one month or less vs. (b) more than one month. In a 2 (gender) × 2 (length of relationship) ANOVA, with subjective pleasure as the dependent variable, the interaction was not significant, $F = 1.05$, n.s. However, the main effect of length of the relationship was significant, $F = 14.80$, $p < .001$. For both men and women, those who had first intercourse in a relationship that had existed for a month or more reported more pleasure than those who had sex for the first time in a brief or just beginning relationship (see the means in the second left panel of Table 5.7).

Finally, we looked at the moderating influence of the *current status* of the relationship (still together vs. no longer together). The main effect of current status was significant, $F = 50.74$, $p < .001$. Students who remained with their first intercourse partner reported that they experienced more pleasure the first time than those who were no longer with their partner (see the means in the bottom left panel of Table 5.7). This time, however, the relationship variable also moderated the effect of gender. The 2 (gender) × 2 (current status of the relationship) interaction was significant, $F = 8.20$, $p < .01$. Although men reported experiencing more pleasure than women regardless of whether the relationship was still intact, the gender difference in pleasure was larger for those who were no longer in the relationship, $t = 22.76$, $p < .001$, than for those who were, $t = 7.70$, $p < .001$ (see means in the bottom left panel of Table 5.7). Continued involvement with the first intercourse partner increased the likelihood of reports of subjective pleasure to a greater degree for women than for men.

Relationship factors as moderators of the effects of gender on anxiety and guilt. Although DeLamater's (1987) explanations for differential emotional reactions between men and women apply to why men have a more *favorable* reaction (e.g., pleasure, satisfaction) than women, we also examined whether these relationship factors moderate the association gender has with the other two emotional reactions—anxiety and guilt.

Anxiety. A significant main effect was found for stage of relationship, $F = 15.27$, $p < .01$. For both men and women, anxiety was experienced to a greater degree when first intercourse occurred in a serious relationship than when it occurred in a casual relationship (see means in the top middle panel of Table 5.7). The effect of gender on anxiety (men experiencing greater anxiety) was not moderated by relationship stage. The 2 (gender) × 2 (relationship stage) ANOVA interaction was not significant, $F = .03$, n.s.

The length of the relationship was not a significant predictor of anxiety, either as a main effect variable, $F = 2.23$, n.s., or as a moderator variable, $F = .28$, n.s. The level of anxiety was reported to be approximately the same regardless of how long the relationship had lasted, and this was true for both men and women.

On the other hand, the current status of the relationship was associated with how much anxiety was reported. A significant main effect was found for current relationship status, $F = 22.30$, $p < .001$. However, this main effect was qualified by a significant 2 (gender) × 2 (current status) interaction, $F = 10.62$, $p < .001$. Men's reported level of anxiety was the same regardless of whether the relationship was still intact. However, women who were still involved with their first intercourse partner recalled more anxiety than women who were no longer involved with their partner, $t = 5.77$, $p < .001$ (see means in bottom middle panel of Table 5.7).

Guilt. The results showing the association between relationship factors and guilt for men vs. women are presented in the right panel of Table 5.7. Stage of relationship had a significant main effect on reported guilt, $F = 25.74$, $p < .001$. As the means in the top right panel of Table 5.7 show, both men and women experienced more guilt if they had sexual intercourse for the first time in a casual relationship than in a serious relationship. The 2 (gender) × 2 (relationship stage) ANOVA interaction was not significant, $F = 1.92$, n.s., which indicates that women's greater experience of guilt relative to men was found, regardless of the relationship stage.

Length of relationship was also associated with how much guilt was reported. Students who had first sexual intercourse in a brief relationship felt more guilt than did students who had first intercourse in a long-term relationship. $F = 8.51$, $p < .01$. In addition, the 2 (gender) × 2 (relationship length) interaction was significant, $F = 4.58$, $p < .05$, which means that relationship length moderated the association between gender and guilt. The difference in guilt between short-term relationships and long-term relationships was greater for women, $t = 3.32$, $p < .001$, than for men, $t = .65$, n.s.

Finally, current relationship status was related to the level of guilt experienced. The main effect was significant, $F = 22.62$, $p < .001$, but this was qualified by a significant 2 (gender) × 2 (current status) ANOVA interaction, $F = 14.33$, $p < .001$. As the results in Table 5.7 show, there was no difference in guilt between men who were still with their first partner and men who were not, $t = .39$, n.s. However, women recalled less guilt if they were still with their first intercourse partner than if they were not, $t = -6.14$, $p < .001$.

Other Predictors of Emotional Reactions to the First Time and the Moderating Role of Gender

Our final purpose in this study was to examine how other aspects of the first intercourse experience are related to emotional reactions for men vs. women. To test how gender moderated the associations between these other variables and emotional reactions, we conducted a series of ANOVAs. Our focus in this section is on the main effect of each of the other variables and the interaction between each other variable and gender. We conducted the regression version of ANOVA to examine the effect of the other variable while controlling for gender. In Table 5.8, from each ANOVA, we present the *F*-value for the main effect of the *other* (independent) variable and the *F*-value for the interaction between the other variable and gender. The means for men and women under different levels of each of the other variables are also presented in Table 5.8.

Respondent's age was significantly associated with the degree to which subjective pleasure was experienced. Among both men and women, those who waited until they were 17 or older to have sex for the first time reported more pleasure than those who had sex at age 16 or younger. Partner's age relative to own age had a significant association with the degree to which subjective pleasure was experienced. Students who were the same age or younger than their partner reported more pleasure than did students who were older than their partner (although the differences were greater for women). Whether it was partner's first time was not related to the emotional reactions.

Whether condoms or another form of contraception was used was associated with affective reactions. First, those who used any form of contraception (as opposed to nothing or withdrawal) during first intercourse experienced more pleasure, more anxiety, and less guilt. Second, those students who reported, to a separate question, that condoms were used the first time experienced more anxiety and less guilt.

Consumption of alcohol was also related to emotional reactions. Students who reported that alcohol was consumed by at least one partner ex-

TABLE 5.8. Other Predictors of Affective Reactions to the First Time for Men vs. Women: Mean Ratings and Results from ANOVAs

	Pleasure		Anxiety		Guilt	
	Men	Women	Men	Women	Men	Women
Own age						
16 or under	4.84	2.70	5.95	4.72	2.50	4.00
17 or older	5.15	3.18	5.91	4.98	2.67	3.75
Main effect *F*	19.14***		1.54		.17	
x gender *F*	1.12		2.97		4.06*	
Partner's age relative to own						
Younger or same	5.01	3.19	5.92	5.05	2.67	3.74
older	4.97	2.83	5.96	4.75	2.45	3.93
Main effect *F*	4.35*		1.92		.01	
x gender *F*	2.95		3.58		3.53	
Partner's first time						
yes	4.99	3.13	5.93	5.05	2.51	3.72
no or don't know	5.00	2.87	5.94	4.77	2.65	3.94
Main effect *F*	1.75		2.08		2.65	
x gender *F*	2.05		2.40		.11	
Use of condoms						
yes	5.00	3.05	6.03	4.96	2.59	3.69
no or can't remember	4.99	2.80	5.84	4.69	2.61	4.12
Main effect *F*	2.25		6.74**		4.61	
x gender *F*	1.78		.22		3.69	
Contraception used						
an effective method	5.04	3.07	6.00	5.02	2.50	3.66
nothing or withdrawal	4.93	2.76	5.86	4.57	2.73	4.22
Main effect *F*	5.46*		11.25***		13.09***	
x gender *F*	1.22		3.15		2.38	
Alcohol consumed						
one or both did	4.89	2.71	5.82	4.78	2.74	4.24
neither did	5.07	3.09	5.99	4.90	2.53	3.69
Main effect *F*	8.35***		2.46		11.41***	
x gender *F*	1.09		.08		2.20	

*$p < .05$ **$p \leq .01$ ***$p \leq .001$

perienced less pleasure and more guilt than those who reported that no alcohol was consumed.

These results indicate that many factors are associated with affective reactions to first intercourse. Furthermore, how these factors are associated with emotional reactions is quite similar for men and women. In fact, there was only one significant interaction between one of the other factors and gender, and this was for guilt. Women reported more guilt when they had first sexual intercourse at a younger age than at an older age; the reverse difference was found for men. However, these differences within each gender were not significant, as indicated by simple *t*-test comparisons.

Discussion

The major purposes of this investigation were to examine gender differences in emotional reactions (pleasure, anxiety, and guilt) to first intercourse and to test possible explanations for these differences. We also explored other ways that men and women differed in their first intercourse.

The Sexual Script for the First Time

Men and women were similar in many aspects of the first intercourse. The "typical" respondent (regardless of gender) had sex for the first time between the ages of 16 and 17 years, was more likely to have used a contraceptive method than not, and was unlikely to be drunk or on drugs at the time. Some gender differences were found: women's first partner was older than men's; women were more likely than men to have first intercourse in a serious dating relationship; more women than men were still with the first intercourse partner (although it was a minority for both genders); and more women than men said they used condoms the first time. These results are similar to results found in earlier studies (e.g., DeLamater, 1987), although greater similarity between men and women in age at first intercourse was found in this study than in other research.

Gender Differences in Emotional Reactions to First Intercourse

We found fairly large differences between men and women in how they emotionally responded to first intercourse, with differences in pleasure showing the strongest distinction. The emotion men and women shared the most was anxiety. Both genders experienced anxiety to a greater degree than the other emotions. Apparently, both genders are scared about personal performance, acceptability, or possible negative outcomes of having intercourse. However, men experienced more anxiety than women, perhaps because they were more likely to be the planner and/or initiator. Men reported much stronger pleasure than guilt and felt significantly less guilt than did women. Women felt less pleasure than men and had stronger feelings of guilt than pleasure. These gender differences suggest that women may still feel there is something wrong about losing their virginity. Women could also have such high standards about the conditions of first intercourse that they are rarely met, leading to feelings of failure to meet their or other people's expectations. Men may find sex more confirming and therefore may feel that their first sexual act implies ignoble conduct. Of course, one major reason men may experience more pleasure is because they received more physical gratification from first intercourse, an explanation we were able to test with our data.

Explanations for Men's Greater Subjective Pleasure

After we documented gender differences in emotional reactions, we tested some possible explanations for these differences, focusing first on explaining the large gender differences for subjective pleasure. DeLamater's (1987) hypothesis, that having an orgasm explains gender differences in sexual pleasure, was supported by our research. Many more men (79%) than women (7%) had an orgasm the first time. The women who had an orgasm reported a level of pleasure similar to the men's level. Furthermore, our formal tests (hierarchical regression analyses) of the mediating role of the orgasm found support that having an orgasm partially mediates the association between gender and subjective pleasure.

There may be explanations why, men are more likely to have an orgasm the first time than are women that are also associated with men's greater subjective pleasure. For example, different socialization experiences may account for men's greater freedom to enjoy sex. Or perhaps the difference in early masturbation habits and prior petting experiences allow more men than women to be orgasmic and therefore more pleased with first intercourse. Research shows that more young men than women masturbate (Oliver & Hyde, 1993). In any case, when young women are orgasmic during first intercourse, whether because they have a talented lover, atypical personal history, or other reasons, they, like their male counterparts, have greater subjective pleasure.

We also found some support for DeLamater's (1987) second explanation for men's greater pleasure. Examining the issue of "relationship context," we found what we call a "love effect." People recalled more sexual pleasure when they reported having first intercourse in a relationship that continued to the point at which they answered the questionnaire. Although only 23% of the women and 16% of the men were still dating their first partner at the time of the survey, this group's reactions were significantly more positive than the majority who no longer had a relationship with their first sexual partner. Furthermore, the differences were greater for women than for men, as hypothesized.

This "love effect" may be explained in several competing ways. It may be that the continuing partners were truly so sexually talented that they were retained as partners, and therefore objective pleasure played a role in relationship longevity. However, the fact that more women than men reported increased pleasure with a continuing partner more easily leads to hypothesizing that the fact that the relationship still exists has, retrospectively, increased the recollection of how good the initial sexual experience really was. In other words, love, at least durable love, or perhaps the sexual achievements of the present state of the relationship, cast a sunny light on the initial intimacies of the couple. The actual commitment level of the relationship (e.g., casual vs. serious) and the length of the relationship were also related to how much subjective pleasure was reported. Both men and women reported more subjective pleasure if they had sexual intercourse for the first time in a more serious or long-term relationship than in a casual or brief one. These results suggest that love and sexual pleasure do go together—that sex is more pleasurable when there is love or commitment.

Relationship Factors Moderating Anxiety and Guilt

We also explored how the relationship context of the first intercourse was related to how much anxiety and guilt were experienced. Somewhat surprisingly, both men and women experienced more anxiety if they had sex in a serious relationship than in a casual one. This was probably because men and women who were seriously involved with their partner had more at stake as a result of how the first experience played out. It could also be that the type of individual who waits for a level of commitment before having sex is also the type of individual who gets more anxious about sex. Stage of the relationship, as well as length, were also related to the level of guilt experienced. As would be expected, more guilt was experienced when first intercourse occurred the first time in a casual or brief relationship than in a serious or long-term relationship. Women's level of guilt was more highly associated with the length of the relationship than was men's guilt, which suggests that even the subsample of women who depart from traditional standards in their behaviors by having sex without much relationship depth are still affected emotionally by these traditional standards.

For women only, reported anxiety and guilt were related to the current status of the relationship in which first intercourse had occurred. Women reported more anxiety and less guilt if the relationship was still continuing than if it was not. It may be that women who are still with their first partner remember everything more intensely, and remembering anxiety or nervousness is seen as a complimentary emotion showing that the relationship was special, consequential, and worthy of feeling nervous and worried about. Women's greater guilt if they were no longer with their first partner affirms the hypothesis that relationship context does matter.

The Relationship of Age and Other Factors with Emotional Reactions and the Moderating Influence of Gender

We also looked at how other factors might be related to the emotional reactions experienced after first intercourse. In general, the results were similar for men and women. The factor that had the strongest association with emotional reactions was age at first intercourse. Having sex for the first time at age 16 or younger was associated with less pleasure, for both genders. Several reasons may account for this finding. Young teenagers may be unable to understand or cope with their feelings about love and intercourse. Sex this early may be motivated in part by the pressure from the peer group or from the partner. These results are consistent with a study of adolescents by Zabin, Hirsch, Smith, and Hardy (1984), who found that many sexually active teens believe that the best age for first intercourse is older than the age they began having sex.

Partner's age also was associated with reported pleasure. Those who had sex with someone who was younger or the same age experienced more pleasure than those who had sex with someone older. This was found especially for the women, which may indicate that some women who had sex with a older partner had sex that was unwanted, an issue that needs to be examined in future research.

The degree to which the participants engaged in responsible behaviors (e.g., used condoms and other effective contraceptive methods, did not drink alcohol) during first intercourse was also related to emotional reactions to the first time, and in the same way for men and women (i.e., gender did not moderate these associations). Somewhat surprising, use of condoms or another form of contraception was associated with more anxiety. One might assume that those who use condoms or another contraceptive would experience less anxiety because they are reducing the chances that pregnancy and/or the infection with a sexually transmitted disease will be the outcome of this first intercourse experience. However, because the type of person who prepares for sexual precautions may need to plan ahead, he or she may have had a buildup of anxiety.

Alcohol is commonly thought to have an aphrodisiac effect because of the reduction of inhibitions. However, the results of this study provide evidence that the first experience was more pleasurable and less guilt free for both men and women if there was no alcohol consumed.

Limitations and Future Research Directions

Although we believe this study furthers our understanding of gender differences in emotional reactions to first sexual intercourse, particularly by elucidating and explaining some reasons for gender differences in reactions to first intercourse, we realize that limitations of the study caution against overgeneralization of the findings. First and foremost, these are recollections, which could be colored by subsequent outcomes of the relationship. What was actually experienced at the moment or next day may be quite different and either more or less pleasant, worrisome, or guilt producing than what participants recorded on a questionnaire months or years after the event. Second, the participants were primarily White, middle class, Midwestern college students, responding to personal questions in an efficient manner in a college classroom. Furthermore, these were students enrolled in a human sexuality class. How much their experience and feelings mirror other types of samples remains to be seen. These limitations suggest a need to study more varied populations in more proximal studies, perhaps a long-term commitment to diverse samples of young people in their earliest dating years who are tracked before and after their first sexual experience. Another limitation of the study is that psychological closeness and attachment to the partner were not assessed in this study.

The question of the impact of first intercourse deserves continued attention. First intercourse is a momentous occasion for both young men and women. Later sexual experience and evolution of present and future relationships may be seriously influenced by first sexual experience (e.g., Cate, Long, Angora, & Draper, 1993), and we need to find how much and in what ways. This is also a good laboratory for further insight into how differences between men and women are created or how differences in men and women may inhibit their sexual satisfaction, interpersonal happiness, and mental health. Additionally, the study of relationships increasingly relies on understanding the production of emotion. Men's and women's adult relationships will profit from researchers' continuing focus on how experiences are related to positive or negative feelings that support or undermine happy lives and close personal ties.

REFERENCES

Baron, R. M., & Kenny, D. A. (1986). The moderator–mediator variable distinction in social psychological research: Conceptual, strategic, and statistical considerations. *Journal of Personality and Social Psychology, 51,* 1173–1182.

Bell, A., Weinberg, M., & Hammersmith, S. (1981). *Sexual preference: Statistical appendix.* Bloomington: Indiana University Press.

Bouris, K. (1993). *The first time.* Berkeley CA: Conari Press.

Buss, D. M., & Schmitt, D. P. (1993). Sexual strategies theory: An evolutionary perspective on human mating. *Psychological Review, 100,* 204–232.

Carroll, J. L., Volk, K. D., & Hyde, J. S. (1985). Differences between males and females in motives for engaging in sexual intercourse. *Archives of Sexual Behavior, 14,* 131–139.

Cafe, R., Long, E., Angera, J., & Draper, K. K. (1993). Sexual intercourse and relationship development. *Family Relations, 42,* 158–164.

Christopher, F. S., & Cate, R. M. (1984). Factors involved in premarital sexual decision-making. *The Journal of Sex Research, 20,* 363–376.

Christopher, F. S., & Cate, R. M. (1985). Anticipated influences on sexual decision-making for first intercourse. *Family Relations, 34,* 265–270.

Darling, C. A., Davidson, K., & Passarello, L. C. (1992). The mystique of first intercourse among college youth: The role of partners, contraceptive practices, and psychological reactions. *Journal of Youth and Adolescence, 21,* 97–117.

DeLamater, J. (1987). Gender differences in sexual scenarios. In K. Kelley (Ed.), *Females, males, and sexuality* (pp. 127–140). Albany: State University of New York Press.

Eastman, W. F. (1972). First intercourse. *Sexual Behavior, 2,* 22–27.

Gagnon, J. H. (1990). The explicit and implicit use of scripting perspective in sex research. In J. Bancroft, C. M. Davis, & D. Weinstein (Eds.), *Annual review of sex research* (Vol. 1, pp. 1–43). Mt. Vernon, IA: Society for the Scientific Study of Sex.

Gagnon, J. H., & W. Simon (1973). *Sexual conduct: The social sources of human sexuality.* Chicago: Aldine.

Harvey, J. H., Flanary, R., & Morgan, M. (1986). Vivid memories of vivid loves gone by. *Journal of Social and Personal Relationships, 3,* 359–373.

Hass, A. (1979). *Teenage sexuality: A survey of teenage sexual behavior.* New York: Macmillan.

Laumann, E. O., Gagnon, J. H., Michael, R. T., & Michaels, S. (1994). *The social organization of sexuality.* Chicago: University Chicago Press.

Miller, B. C., & Moore, K. A. (1990). Adolescent sexual behavior, pregnancy, and parenting: Research through the 1980s. *Journal of Marriage and the Family, 5,* 1025–1044.

Oliver, M. B., & Hyde, J. S. (1993). Gender differences in sexuality: A meta-analysis. *Psychological Bulletin, 114,* 29–51.

Rubin, L. B. (1990). *Erotic wars: What happened to the sexual revolution?* New York: Harper Collins.

Schofield, M. (1973). *The sexual behavior in young adults.* Boston: Little, Brown.

Schwartz, I. (1993). Affective reactions of American and Swedish women to their first premarital coitus: A cross-cultural comparison. *The Journal of Sex Research, 30,* 18–26.

Simon, W., & Gagnon, L. (1968). *Youth cultures and aspects of the socialization process: College study marginal book.* Bloomington, IN: Institute for Sex Research.

Sorensen, R. C. (1972). *Adolescent sexuality in contemporary America.* New York: World.

Thompson, S. (1990). Putting a big thing into a little hole: Teenage girls' accounts of sexual initiation. *The Journal of Sex Research, 27,* 341–361.

Weis, D. L. (1983). Affective reactions of women to their initial experience of coitus. *The Journal of Sex Research, 19,* 209–237.

Weis, D. L. (1985). The experience of pain during women's first sexual intercourse: Cultural mythology about female sexual initiation. *Archives of Sexual Behavior, 14,* 421–438.

Zabin, L. S., Hirsch, M. B., Smith E. A., & Hardy, J. B. (1984). Adolescent sexual attitudes and behavior: Are they consistent? *Family Planning Perspectives, 11,* 181–185.

Zelnik, M., & Shah, F. K. (1983). First intercourse among young Americans. *Family Planning Perspectives, 15,* 64–72.

INTRODUCTION TO PART 4

Sex and the Peer Group

One of the most controversial works in recent years was Jean Harris's conclusion that the process of growing from an infant into an adult is shaped more powerfully by the peer group than by the parents. Although this debate rages unresolved, most people are probably willing to accord it some degree of validity when it comes to sex. Young people's forays into sexual activity occur under the influence and guidance of peers, whereas people often deliberately try to keep their interests and activities in the sexual realm secret from their parents and typically regard their parents' views as irrelevant and archaic.

This section presents two articles dealing with peer influence on sex. The first one is by Billy and Udry (1985). Like other works (e.g., Mirande, 1968; Sack, Keller, & Hinkle, 1984), they found that peer groups are often composed of people who are similar to each other in their sexual attitudes and behaviors. Unlike many previous studies, Billy and Udry's investigation used methodological and statistical techniques to help confirm that this resemblance indicates that peer groups do have an influence on sex. The question that dogged much research in the area was determining what was cause and what was effect. That is, best friends might be similar to each other in their sexuality, but is this because the friends influence each other's sex lives—or because people's sexual values dictate whom they choose as best friends? Or, in even simpler terms, do nonvirgins end up in the same peer group because the group influences everyone to lose virginity around the same time, or because when people lose their virginity they dump their virgin friends and start associating with other nonvirgins? By revisiting groups of friends at different times, Billy and Udry were able to see which came first, and their main answer was that the friendship came first and therefore influenced the sexual behavior.

A more recent study by Maticka-Tyndale, Herold, and Mewhinney (1998) examined the sexual behaviors of college students on spring break trips to Florida. This article is included in the peer group section because it showed important effects of peer groups during these trips. Indeed, half the men and two thirds of the women said they currently had a relationship partner but did not bring that person along on spring break, going instead with a group of peers. Of particular interest was the fact that the male peer groups agreed to support each other in their efforts to obtain sexual experiences during the vacation, whereas the female peer groups were more likely to agree to support each other in refraining from sex.

The Maticka-Tyndale et al. (1998) study had other findings that went beyond peer influence, of course. They noted some remarkable gaps between intentions and actual experiences. In particular, most of the men intended (or at least hoped) to engage in casual sex during the spring break trip, whereas relatively few of the women reported such an intention–however, in the event, roughly the same (low) percentage of men and women actually did engage in such sexual activity on the trip.

REFERENCES

Billy, J. O. G., & Udry, J. R. (1985). Patterns of adolescent friendship and effects on sexual behavior. *Social Psychology Quarterly, 48,* 27–41.

Maticka-Tyndale, E., Herold, E. S., & Mewhinney, D. (1998). Casual sex on spring break: Intentions and behaviors of Canadian students. *Journal of Sex Research, 35,* 254–264.

Mirande, A. M. (1968). Reference group theory and adolescent sexual behavior. *Journal of Marriage and the Family, 30,* 572–577.

Sack, A. R., Keller, J. F., & Hinkle, D. E. (1984). Premarital sexual intercourse: A test of the effects of peer group, religiosity, and sexual guilt. *Journal of Sex Research, 20,* 168–185.

Discussion Questions

1. Do you think peer pressure operates to increase or to decrease sexual activity, or both?
2. What factors might enable people to resist peer pressure in sexual behavior?
3. Do people engage in sex (or refrain from it) in order to make a good impression on their peers? How important a factor is that?
4. According to the Maticka-Tyndale study, most young men hope to engage in casual sex during spring break, but relatively few actually do. Does this mean that spring break trips to Florida are mostly disappointing for the young men?
5. Would people be more likely to engage in casual sex on spring break than at other times? If so, what factors would contribute to that difference?

Suggested Readings

Coleman, J.S. (1961). *The adolescent society.* New York: Free Press. This offers an intriguing look at teenage life and society on the eve of the Sexual Revolution.

Du Bois-Reymond, M., & Ravesloot, J. (1996). The roles of parents and peers in the sexual and relational socialization of adolescents. In K. Hurrelmann & S. Hamilton (Eds.), *Social problems and social contexts in adolescence* (pp. 175–197). New York: Aldine de Gruyter. This work describes the results of studies of adolescent peer groups today in the Netherlands, which is one of the most modern and successful societies in the world.

READING 6

Patterns of Adolescent Friendship and Effects on Sexual Behavior

John O. G. Billy • Battelle Memorial Institute, Seattle, Washington
J. Richard Udry • Carolina Population Center, University of North Carolina at Chapel Hill

Using panel data from a junior high school system in an urban area of Florida we investigate adolescent friendship structure along the dimension of sexual behavior. White females and white males tend to name same-sex friends whose sexual intercourse behavior is like their own. Sexual intercourse is not a significant factor in accounting for adolescent friendship structure among blacks, males or females. We then specify models which permit us to answer whether observed homogeneity bias in sexual behavior is due to a process of influence, deselection, and/or acquisition. The sexual behavior of white females is influenced by their same-sex friends' sexual behavior. There is no evidence that adolescents deselect friends on the basis of dissimilarity in sexual behavior. Both white males and white females acquire friends whose sexual behavior is like their own. We suggest that race-sex differences with respect to degree of adolescent-friend similarity in sexual behavior and the sources of this similarity may center around differences in group relevance or salience of the sexual act and race-sex differences in the nature of friendships.

Introduction

In an earlier analysis using data from a junior high school in an urban area of North Carolina we found that there is homogeneity bias in adolescent same-sex friendship choice along the dimension of sexual behavior (Billy et al., 1984). Adolescents who have had sexual intercourse are more likely to name as friends adolescents who have had sexual intercourse even when in grade school, other more visible deviant behaviors, and a composite index of deviance proneness are taken into account.

Having demonstrated that there is structure in adolescent same-sex friendships along the dimension of sexual behavior, a second problem involves the question of *why* similarity between respondents and their peers with respect to sexual behavior occurs. Three mechanisms might operate: influence, deselection and/or acquisition. Regardless of their prior similarity in sexual behavior, adolescents and the individuals named as friends may be alike due to the influence of friends upon adolescents. Alternatively, homogeneity bias might obtain among a group of adolescents because of an individual's elimination or deselection of a friend whose sexual behavior is unlike the adolescent's own. Finally, two individuals may be the same in their sexual behavior and one may acquire or name the other as a friend on the basis of that likeness (Cohen, 1977, p. 227).

We should note that while deselection and acquisition are parts of an overall selection process, the two are conceptually and empirically distinct. Any one or a combination of influence, deselection and acquisition may be responsible for observed homogeneity bias among a group of adolescents. Our task in this paper is to separate the three sources empirically and to assess which factors are important in accounting for friendship similarity with respect to sexual intercourse.

Background

In our earlier paper we provide a detailed discussion of the influence and selection processes to explain why similarity in sexual behavior between adolescents and their same-sex friends is likely to obtain. With regard to influence, a basic assumption is that during adolescence close friends become increasingly important as reference points in guiding various behaviors, including sexual behavior (Reiss, 1967, 1970). The influence of the peer group may occur either through the modeling of peer behavior, whereby the adolescent imitates the behavior of valued others, or through peer expression of normative standards for adolescent conduct such that the adolescent responds to the advice given by significant others. Peer advice regarding appropriate sexual behavior is presumably an outcome of their own sexual experiences or the lack of such experiences. Both mechanisms of peer influence may indirectly affect the adolescent's sexual behavior through the formation of the adolescent's own values and preferences for sexual conduct (Herold, 1980; Teevan, 1972).

With regard to the selection process, social psychologists account for interpersonal attraction in terms of similarity in attitudes, values and behaviors. Hallinan and Tuma (1978) summarize the many social-psychological arguments that have been used to explain the importance of similarity for friendship formation, maintenance or dissolution. First, similarity makes interaction between two persons more rewarding because it increases each member's approval of the other. Second, similarity minimizes hostility between two persons by reducing the number of potential points of conflict. Third, it reduces psychological discomfort caused by cognitive inconsistency. Finally, similarity is a means for two persons to validate their respective identities. Assuming that having or not having sex is a salient aspect in adolescents' lives, all of these arguments may be used to explain why friends who are similar in terms of sexual behavior are likely to maintain the friendship, and conversely, why friends who are dissimilar with respect to sexual behavior are likely to dissolve the friendship (deselection).

The same arguments can be used to explain the process of friendship formation (acquisition); two adolescents who have similar sexual behaviors should be more likely to name each other as friends. Of course, since sexual acts are low in physical and normative visibility, it may be difficult for adolescents to discover other adolescents like themselves. However, a number of conditions under which adolescent friendships are formed may increase the probability of discovery. First, adolescents in the same public school or college are in close physical proximity to one another. Proximity encourages interaction and interaction, in turn, permits recognition of similarity in attitudes and behavior (Newcomb, 1956). Second, sexual behavior may determine in what type of social setting adolescents most often find themselves, a "fast crowd" or a "slow crowd." The proximity of the members of each of these two subgroups and the consequent interaction that such proximity permits may further increase the likelihood of finding other adolescents who have similar sexual behavior. Finally, Reiss (1970) suggests that today's adolescents talk more openly about their sexual attitudes and behaviors. If so, not only may adolescents be sufficiently proximate but their behavior may be sufficiently visible to allow for the acquisition of friends on the basis of sexual behavior.

The adolescent-sexuality literature contains numerous studies that have examined the relationship between adolescents and their peers' sexual behavior.[1] Despite differences in study design and method of analysis, these studies generally find a strong, positive relationship between peers' sexual attitudes and behaviors and the respondent's sexual attitudes and behaviors. This positive relationship has been interpreted almost exclusively in terms of the influence process. Almost all of these stud-

---

[1]Examples of such studies include Carns, 1973; Clayton, 1972; Davis, 1971; Davis, 1974; DeLamater and MacCorquodale, 1979; Finkel and Finkel, 1975, 1976; Herold, 1980; Jackson and Potkay, 1973; Jessor and Jessor, 1975; Jessor et al., 1983; Kaats and Davis, 1970; Miller and Simon, 1974; Mirande, 1968; Reiss, 1967; Shah and Zelnik, 1981; Spanier, 1975; Teevan, 1972; Walsh et al., 1976.

ies, however, have used cross-sectional data, and cross-sectional data prohibits the separation of the influence, deselection, and acquisition processes.[2] To analyze these processes separately, longitudinal data that provide information on friendship choices at two or more points in time and delineate changes in sexual behavior over time are needed. Hence, previous researchers' emphasis on the influence process and disregard for the deselection or acquisition processes are unwarranted.

While to date no study of the peer–adolescent sexual behavior relationship has been able to delineate the process(es) that lead to observed similarity in sexual behavior between adolescents and their friends, our view of the three processes leads us to expect that in addition to the contribution of influence toward observed homogeneity bias, both deselection and acquisition may play an important role. Moreover, two prior studies of the relationship between student friendships and adolescent attitudes and behavior unrelated to sex provide indirect support for our overall hypothesis.

In a study of adolescent drug use, Kandel (1978) conducted a longitudinal analysis of friendship pairs among New York State high school students. She concludes that

> adolescents coordinate their choices of friends and their behaviors, in particular the use of marijuana, so as to maximize congruency within the friendship pair. If there is a state of unbalance such that the friend's attitude or behavior is incongruent with the adolescent's, the adolescent will either break off the friendship and seek another friend or will keep the friend and modify his own drug behavior. (Kandel, 1978, pp. 433–435)

Kandel finds that the effects of selection and socialization (influence) in contributing to adolescent–friend similarity in drug use are approximately 50–50. As such, cross-sectional analyses which attribute the similarity of marijuana use between friends to the mutual influence of friends on each other overestimate the influence of friends by approximately 100 percent by failing to take into account the process of friendship selection.

Similarly, Cohen (1977) concludes that the status attainment literature, by virtue of its reliance on cross-sectional data, overestimates the magnitude of peer influence on adolescent aspirations and behaviors. He studies homogeneity along a variety of attitudinal and behavioral dimensions in 49 student friendship groups in an all-white high school. Using a longitudinal survey design, Cohen finds that "homophilic selection" (acquisition) accounts for much of the cliques' homogeneity, "conformity pressures" (influence) make a small contribution, and "group leaving" (deselection) contributes nothing to clique homogeneity.

Race–Sex Differences in Homogeneity Bias and its Sources

We analyze homogeneity bias and its sources separately by race-sex subgroup for two reasons. First, as will be seen, there are large differences in the reported incidence of sexual activity among these groups. Second, there are a number of reasons to expect that males and females, blacks and whites, will differ both with respect to the degree of adolescent–friend similarity in sexual behavior and with respect to the processes that account for this similarity. These reasons center around race-sex differences in group relevance or salience of sexual behavior and race-sex differences in the nature of friendships.

It is well documented that black adolescents are more likely than white adolescents to have permissive sexual standards (Reiss, 1964, 1967; Staples, 1978) and to have had premarital intercourse (Finkel and Finkel, 1975; Gebhard et al., 1958; Sorensen, 1973; Udry et al., 1975; Zelnik and Kantner, 1980). Similarly, males have been found to have more permissive sexual attitudes than females (Reiss, 1967; Staples, 1978) and more likely to have had premarital intercourse (Sorensen, 1973; Vener and Stewart, 1974; Zelnik and Kantner, 1980).

To the extent that such permissive attitudes and behaviors reflect a "norm against sexual norms" this greater approval of premarital coitus may precipitate more of a nonjudgmental stance among blacks and among males with respect to the sexual behavior of others. If so, then we might expect less similarity in sexual behavior between black adolescents and their friends compared to white adolescent friendships, and less similarity between male adolescents and their friends compared to

[2]Jessor and Jessor (1975), Jessor et al. (1983) and Walsh et al. (1976) use longitudinal survey designs in their analyses of the relationship between adolescents and their peers' sexual behavior. None of these studies, however, has the data needed to distinguish between the influence, deselection, and acquisition processes.

female adolescent friendships. Males, for whom sexual activity represents less of a departure from sex-appropriate norms, may be less influenced by their same-sex friend's sexual behavior than females because they may regard sexual behavior more casually and assume that at some point almost all adolescent males will engage in premarital sex. The same may be true of blacks as compared to whites. Also, the greater nonjudgmental stance of males and blacks with respect to the sexual activity of others may limit the extent to which the members of these two groups acquire or deselect friends on the basis of similarity in sexual behavior. In contrast, females and whites, for whom sexual behavior represents a greater departure from sex-appropriate or race-appropriate norms, may be very critical of and sensitive to the behavior of their friends. A nonexperienced female or white should therefore be more prone to end a friendship with an adolescent who is sexually experienced and to acquire a nonexperienced friend. Conversely, nonvirgin females or whites may, through the process of deselection or acquisition, align themselves with a nonvirgin friend with whom they can discuss a common salient experience that is frowned upon by other societal members.

We should further note that in groups in which almost no members or almost all members are sexually active, the group relevance or salience of sexual behavior as a basis for friendship deselection or acquisition may be greatly diminished. In such cases similarity in sexual behavior as a friendship criterion may not be expected to arise. Members of these groups have no choice but to choose friends like themselves.

With regard to race-sex differences in the nature of friendships, there is evidence from the psychological literature that emotional intimacy and exchange of personal information is more characteristic of female than male same-sex friendships (Kon, 1981; Lewis, 1978; Sattel, 1976; Wheeler and Nezlek, 1977). The greater affective content of female friends' conversations may make it more likely that a female will be influenced by her female friend than a male is influenced by his male friend. Moreover, females compared to males, and whites compared to blacks, typically score higher on measures of self-disclosure to their same-sex or same-race peers (Cozby, 1973; Dimond and Hellkamp, 1969; Jourard, 1971; Jourard and Lasakow, 1958; Mulcahy, 1973; Pearce et al., 1974; Rivenbark, 1971). There is also evidence that there are race-sex differences with respect to conformity behavior. Under a number of experimental testing conditions, females have been found to conform to the attitudes and behavior of their same-sex friends more than males, and whites tend to conform to their same-race peers more so than blacks (Costanzo and Shaw, 1966; Douvan and Adelson, 1966; Iscoe et al., 1964; Schneider, 1970), White females typically display the greatest amount of conformity to their same-sex peers.

In sum, there are a number of reasons to expect race–sex differences in the amount of similarity in sexual behavior observed between adolescents and their same-sex friends. Previous research of the peer–adolescent sexual behavior relationship lends support for this notion. Investigators who have defined peers as "friends" or "close associates" find a stronger positive relationship for females than males between the respondents' sexual behavior and their *perception* of their close friends' sexual behavior (DeLamater and MacCorquodale, 1979; Jessor and Jessor 1975; and Mirande, 1968). In our earlier analysis of junior high school students in an urban area of North Carolina we found that similarity in sexual intercourse behavior between respondents and their same-sex friends was greatest for white females. Much weaker but significant homogeneity bias along the dimension of intercourse behavior was observed for black females. No significant homogeneity bias was found for either white males or black males.

Data and Measurement

Data used in this analysis are part of a larger panel study of biological and social factors affecting adolescent sexuality. Two study sites were chosen, one in an urban area of North Carolina and the other in an urban area of Florida. Selection of the study sites was dictated by the availability of public lists of students and their addresses.

As mentioned earlier, our original analysis of homogeneity bias along the dimension of sexual behavior used data from the North Carolina sample of adolescents. This earlier analysis used only one round of the North Carolina data. Because of the limited size of the initial sample and attrition of respondents from round to round, we were unable to take advantage of the study's panel design to assess the contributions of the influence, deselection, and acquisition processes toward homogeneity bias. Instead, we had to be content to observe that there is structure in adolescent friendship choice in terms of sexual behavior. The size of the Florida sample and its panel design now afford us the opportunity to remedy this research gap. Hence, our present analysis uses data collected in the two rounds of the Florida study.

Data collection in Florida began in February, 1980. Self-administered questionnaires were completed by 1405 adolescents in their homes. This sample represents 73 percent of the eligible population of 7th, 8th and 9th graders at four selected public schools in Florida. The adolescents ranged from 11 to 17 years of age, with a mean age of 13.6. Within the study site, the schools were purposively selected to assure a sufficient sample size and to be generally representative of other schools in Florida cities.

Two years after the base interview, a follow-up questionnaire was administered to the original sample of adolescents. Of the 1405 respondents from the first round, 1153 completed questionnaires in Round 2, an 82 percent follow-up rate. At the time of the second interview, adolescents were in grades 9, 10, and 11. They ranged from 13 to 19 years of age, with a mean age of 15.4.

For respondents in the Florida study to be included in the present analysis, two initial restrictions are imposed. The adolescent must have participated in both rounds of the study and must have indicated at each round whether he or she had had sexual intercourse. Further restrictions on the sample will be made when we consider separate models of the influence, deselection, and acquisition processes. The number of subjects meeting the initial restrictions varies by race and sex: 390 white males; 163 black males; 426 white females; and 169 black females.

The basic data needed for our analysis include the respondent's sexual behavior at Rounds 1 and 2, the respondent's friends at Rounds 1 and 2, and the respondent's friends' sexual behavior at Rounds 1 and 2. Sexual behavior is measured by the adolescent's "yes" or "no" reply to the question, "Have you ever had sexual intercourse?"[3] In each of the two rounds the percentage of respondents answering "yes" to this question differs sharply by race-sex subgroup. For Round 1 the percentages are 24.9 for white males, 77.3 for black males, 10.3 for white females, and 39.1 for black females. For Round 2 the percentages are 46.9 for white males, 91.4 for black males, 31.2 for white females, and 63.3 for black females.[4] There is also considerable difference among the race-sex subgroups in the percentage of virgin respondents at Round 1 who made the transition to intercourse by Round 2: 29.4 percent for white males, 62.2 percent for black males, 23.3 percent for white females, and 39.8 percent for black females.

A major problem in past studies of the peer–adolescent sexual behavior relationship deals with the measurement of peers' sexual behavior. A friend's sexual behavior has consistently been measured by the respondent's perception of that behavior. The positive association observed by previous investigators between peers' sexual behavior and the adolescent's sexual behavior has been based on an analysis of the relationship between the respondent's *perception* of the friend's sexual activity and the respondent's sexual activity. For example, researchers have used a questionnaire that asks the respondents whether they have had sexual intercourse and whether the respondents *think* their friends have had intercourse.

As argued by Kerckhoff and Huff (1974) and Davies and Kandel (1981), this reliance on perception data can both overestimate and underestimate the strength of the relationship between respondents' attitudes and behavior and their friends' (or parents') attitudes and behavior. Adolescents may have a propensity to overestimate the similarity of their attitudes and behavior with their friends by attributing their *own* attitudes and behavior to the friends. In other words, adolescents may report more similarity in sexual behavior than actually exists because they are rationalizing their own behavior. Moreover, the perceived sexual behavior may come from some exogenous source totally unrelated to the friend's actual sexual behavior; there may be some variable that affects the respondent's perception of the friend's behavior and the respondent's own sexual behavior which therefore causes the relationship to be spurious. The point is that the sources of the perception are unknown, and the perception may or may not accurately reflect the "true" relationship between a

---

[3]To avoid any confusion in the meaning of "sexual intercourse" this question was prefaced with the statement: "To *have sex* (sexual intercourse) is to put the male penis into the female vagina. This is sometimes called 'screwing' or 'getting laid.'"

[4] Both sets of percentages pertain to respondents who participated in both rounds of the study.

friend's sexual behavior and the respondent's sexual behavior.

With regard to how perception data may underestimate the effect, it is not necessarily the case that in order for adolescents to be affected by their friends' behavior they must perceive what the friends' behavior is. A sexually experienced friend may establish some type of opportunity structure that makes it more likely that the adolescent will also become sexually experienced. The friend may create or place the adolescent in settings that provide the adolescent with more opportunities to have sex. In sum, there is good reason to question the usefulness of perception data for evaluating the peer–adolescent sexual behavior relationship. Our survey design permits us to match the respondents' sexual behavior with their friends' sexual behavior as *actually* reported by those friends, eliminating the problems inherent in the use of perception data.

To elicit friendship information in Round 1 of the study each respondent was asked to select (name) a best same-sex and a best opposite-sex friend from the same school. A list of the names of eligible respondents from the same school was searched by the interviewer with the respondent, and a code number was assigned for that friend. If the named friend was not on that list, the respondent was asked to name another person as best friend. Two other male friends and two other female friends were also named in a similar manner and coded into the respondent's questionnaire.[5] No individuals involved in the present analysis had information needed to link identification numbers with names; hence the confidentiality of both respondents and their friends was maintained.

In the present analysis only same-sex best friends are used. Our primary purpose is to assess homogeneity bias and its sources along the dimension of sexual intercourse. Analysis of opposite-sex choices risks finding homogeneity not because two adolescents are simply friends but because they have been sex partners. Our questionnaire does not permit us to assess whether an opposite-sex friend is one with whom the respondent has had intercourse. Not all same-sex best friends named by the respondents participated in the study; hence, it is not possible to match an adolescent's sexual behavior with the same-sex best friend's sexual behavior for all respondents. In constructing respondent–best-friend matches, if we had no questionnaire for the same-sex best friend listed, we substituted one of the other friends named by the respondent. This procedure enabled us to identify another respondent in the survey for whom we had intercourse data as same-sex "best" friend for most of our sample. Specifically, we have a same-sex "best" friend for 94.9 percent of the white males originally included in the analysis, 90.8 percent of the black males, 94.8 percent of the white females, and 95.9 percent of the black females.[6]

To elicit friendship information in Round 2 of the study each respondent was again asked to select (name) three same-sex and three opposite-sex friends and to indicate a best-friend choice. However, the list of names from which respondents were asked to make their selections differed somewhat from the list used in Round 1. The second-round list contained only the names of adolescents who participated in the first round. Since only adolescents who participated in Round 1 were allowed to participate in Round 2, we would not have Round 2 information on the sexual behavior of a named friend who had not participated in the first round. Hence, including names of adolescents who had not participated in Round 1 on the friendship list would have been superfluous.

As in Round 1, not all same-sex best friends named by respondents in Round 2 participated in the second round. Therefore, in constructing Round 2 respondent–best-friend matches we followed the same procedure as used in Round 1. That is, if we had no second-round questionnaire for the same-sex best friend listed, we substituted one of the other friends named by the respondent. This enabled us to identify another adolescent in Round 2 for whom we had intercourse data as same-sex "best" friend for 90.5 percent of the white males originally included in the analysis, 82.8 percent of the black males, 94.1 percent of the white females, and 87.6 percent of the black females. Like the Round 1 same-sex "best" friends, the majority

---

[5]Holland and Leinhardt (1973) discuss the limitations in using a fixed-choice sociometric procedure. The limitations seem to be most severe when the task is to re-create the underlying network or clique structure of a group rather than when the task is to assess homogeneity bias and its sources. We note, however, that because of the use of the fixed-choice sociometric technique some measurement error may be introduced into our study. This error is most likely to occur in cases where the respondent was forced to name three adolescents but in fact had no friends.

[6]Of these same-sex "best" friends, 65.9 percent are truly best friends named by white males, 68.9 percent named by black males, 72.5 percent named by white females, and 77.2 percent named by black females.

TABLE 6.1. Homogeneity Bias (Log-Odds) in Same-Sex Best-Friendship Choice for Intercourse, by Race-Sex Subgroup[a]

	White Males	Black Males	White Females	Black Females
Round 1	1.26**	.39[ns]	1.91**	1.08**
	[3.53]	[1.48]	[6.75]	[2.94]
	(336)	(122)	(382)	(142)
Round 2	1.12**	.73[ns]	1.64**	.42[ns]
	[3.06]	[2.08]	[5.16]	[1.52]
	(336)	(122)	(382)	(142)

[a] Table sizes are in parentheses; odds ratios are in brackets; log-odds ratios are not.
[ns] Nonsignificant.
** $p < .01$.

of the Round 2 same-sex "best" friends are truly best friends.

We should note that the difference between the Round 1 and Round 2 pools of eligible adolescents from which respondents could make their friendship selections should not harm our evaluation of the deselection or acquisition processes. The Round 2 friendship list is a subset of the Round 1 list; it contains the names of the adolescents who participated in the first round. While the Round 1 friendship list contains many more names, only those adolescents on the list who participated in the first round of the study are used in the respondent–best-friend matches because they are the only ones for whom we have intercourse data. Hence, given the criterion that the friend used in the respondent–best-friend match must have intercourse data, the two pools are essentially comparable.

Results: Homogeneity Bias

Before presenting the results for the models that delineate the three possible sources of homogeneity bias, we first demonstrate that there is similarity between respondents and their friends with respect to intercourse behavior for at least some race-sex subgroups. Table 6.1 presents homogeneity bias in same-sex best-friend choices for intercourse by race-sex subgroup for Round 1 and Round 2. The sample is restricted to respondents who have no missing intercourse data at both rounds and who have best friends with no missing intercourse data at both rounds.

To examine homogeneity bias we use a contingency table approach and calculate log-odds ratios. For each round the respondent's intercourse behavior is crosstabulated by the adolescent's same-sex best friend's sexual behavior. The log-odds ratios in Table 6.1 express the log of the odds that a virgin names a virgin as a friend compared to the odds that a nonvirgin names a virgin as a friend. Log-odds ratios can range from minus to plus infinity; a value of "0" indicates no relationship. A log-odds ratio is a symmetric measure of association; it is invariant under interchanges of rows and columns. It is also unaffected by the absolute or relative sizes of the row and column marginals. This property is advantageous since it permits comparison among different samples or groups (Goodman, 1969). For convenience and ease of interpretation of Table 6.1 and all subsequent tables, we have converted the log-odds ratios into simple odds ratios. The odds ratios, where a value of "1" indicates no relationship, appear in brackets in the tables.

Table 6.1 reveals that there is significant homogeneity bias along the dimension of sexual behavior for white males and white females at both rounds. In neither round are black males more likely to have friends with the same intercourse status than if they named friends at random. Black females have significant homogeneity bias at Round 1 but not at Round 2. In our earlier analysis of the North Carolina data we argued that other individual characteristics may affect adolescent friendship choice and that it is important to take these factors into account when investigating homogeneity bias by sexual behavior. Table 6.1 portrays only zero-order homogeneity bias for intercourse, uncontrolled for any other possible sources of friendship alignment. We have subjected the Florida data used in this analysis to the same type of rigid control procedure used for the North Carolina study. We do not present the results of that analysis in detail here. Controlling for grade in school, other more visible deviant behaviors, and a composite index of deviance proneness does not affect the magnitude of the log-odds ratios in Table 6.1 for white males or white females. The log-odds ratios for black males remain small and nonsignificant when controls are introduced. However, for black females the significant homogeneity bias for intercourse observed in Round 1 becomes weak and nonsignificant when homogeneity bias by grade in school is taken into account. Hence, there is homogeneity bias for intercourse for whites in both rounds of the Florida study, but no homogeneity bias for blacks in either round. This race difference is significant. There is no significant difference in homogeneity bias between white males and white females but there is a significant difference between whites and blacks.[7, 8]

In Table 6.1 the homogeneity bias does not increase from Round 1 to Round 2; in fact, with the exception of black males a small, nonsignificant decrease is found. An important question is whether adolescent–friend similarity in sexual behavior must necessarily increase over time before the process of influence, deselection, or acquisition can be said to be operating. In her study of adolescent–peer similarity in drug use, Kandel (1978) suggests that this must be the case. For example, among stable friendship pairs, Kandel finds that homogeneity bias in marijuana use increases over time and interprets this as partial evidence that the process of influence is operating. In fact, she implies that in order to maintain such influence is occurring, there must be increasing homogeneity bias among stable friendship pairs. We do not agree with this conclusion.

The key to our objection lies in the distinction between stable friendship pairs and stable, reciprocal friendship pairs. In both Kandel's analysis and our analysis person A's choice of person B as a friend is all that is considered; the fact that B may reciprocate and choose A as a friend is not taken into account. Consider the case in which A chooses B at Time 1 and Time 2; at Time 1 and 2, A and B are virgins, but at Time 2 A remains a virgin and B becomes a nonvirgin. A preponderance of stable friendship pairs such as this will cause the system of stable friendship pairs to be reduced in homogeneity bias over time. But does this mean that the process of influence is not operating? We might suppose that A was influenced by B's Time 1 "no-sex" behavior and, hence, remains a virgin. At any point between Time 1 and Time 2 B may have become a nonvirgin because of the influence of someone else B names as a friend; note that B does not choose A as a friend and therefore should not be expected to be influenced by A's sexual behavior. That A remains a virgin at Time 2 may be due to the lag in A's perception that B became a nonvirgin and, once A learned that B made the change, the amount of time A needs to find a sex partner.

To summarize, we contend that if, in a system of stable friendship pairs, the system does not increase in homogeneity bias this does not necessarily mean that the influence process is not operating. Stable *reciprocal* friendship pairs should be expected to increase in homogeneity bias over time if influence is operating, but stable nonreciprocal friendship pairs need not. We suggest that the reason Kandel finds increased homogeneity bias over time for her stable friendship pairs is due to a preponderance of reciprocal stable friendship pairs in her sample. We further suggest that Kandel's method of determining whether influence is a source of homogeneity bias is not totally appropriate and that our models of influence, deselection and acquisition, which do not presuppose that simi-

---

[7] These significance tests were performed using Goodman's (1970, 1972) procedure of testing the goodness of fit of a model which specifies no difference in the relationship between the respondent's sexual behavior and the friend's sexual behavior by sex of the white adolescents. Similarly, racial differences were tested by comparing white males with black males, white females with black females, and additionally by employing Goodman's ECTA program for detecting race-sex interactions in multiway contingency tables.

[8] Throughout this paper we place emphasis on racial as opposed to class differences in the homogeneity of sexual behavior. While it is possible that the difference between blacks and whites is due to the socioeconomic-status difference of the two groups rather than race per se, our emphasis on race flows from the theoretical orientation adopted here which stresses black-white differences both in the salience of sexual intercourse and in the nature of friendships. We cannot empirically examine racial differences in homogeneity bias apart from class differences because in our sample race and class are synonymous. Seventy-nine percent of the fathers of white adolescents are in white-collar occupations, whereas 83 percent of the fathers of black adolescents are in blue-collar occupations. We can report, however, that *within* each race-sex subgroup socioeconomic status as measured by a race-specific dichotomy of father's occupation does not affect the size of the coefficients reported in Table 6.1. That is to say, for no race-sex subgroup at either round does SES significantly affect both friendship choice and sexual intercourse, the condition that must obtain in order for the sexual behavior–friendship choice relationship to be rendered spurious.

larity in adolescent–peer sexual behavior must necessarily increase over time, are more appropriate.

Model Specifications and Results of the Influence, Deselection, and Acquisition Processes

The models by which we empirically separate the three possible sources of homogeneity bias and assess which sources are important in accounting for friendship similarity with respect to sexual intercourse are discussed below .

Influence

If the influence process is operating then we would expect that among adolescents who are virgins in Round 1, those whose same-sex best friend has had intercourse at Round 1 will be more likely to make the transition to intercourse by Round 2 than those whose best friend is also a virgin at Round 1. Thus, the sample used for the influence model is restricted to virgins at Round 1. The dependent variable is whether the adolescent becomes a nonvirgin by Round 2, and it is predicted by the respondent's best friend's intercourse status at Round 1. This definition/model of influence does not permit us to examine *how* influence takes place. It does not allow us to examine whether influence occurs through the modeling of peer behavior or, alternatively, through peer expression of normative standards for adolescent conduct. Nor does it distinguish between the *indirect* effect of a friend's behavior on the adolescent's sexual behavior via the respondent's perception of the friend's sexual activity and the *direct* effect of the friend's behavior owing to the increased opportunities for having sex that the friend may provide.

To make sure that the influence process is not contaminated by any selection process, we also consider a more stringent influence model in which only adolescents who keep their best friend from Round 1 to Round 2 are considered in the analysis. We should note that examining only stable friendship pairs may be expected to increase the influence effect. Adolescents who dissolved their friendship with the person named in Round 1 shortly after the first round of the survey would have less time to be influenced by that person than adolescents who retained their friend for the entire two-year interval between rounds.

To examine the influence models we use a contingency table approach and calculate log-odds ratios. Whether the respondent makes the transition to intercourse between Rounds 1 and 2 is crosstabulated by the adolescent's best friend's sexual behavior at Round 1. The log-odds ratios express the log of the odds of a respondent with a "No" friend at Round 1 remaining a "No" at Round 2 compared to the odds of a respondent with a "Yes" friend at Round 1 remaining a "No" at Round 2.

Table 6.2 presents the results of our analysis of the influence model.[9] In Table 6.2a, where we consider *all* respondents who are virgins at Round 1, only the log-odds ratio for white females is significant.[10] Taking the antilog of 1.78, we get an odds ratio of 5.93. This indicates that a virgin white female who has a nonvirgin female friend at Round 1 is six times as likely to make the transition to intercourse than a virgin white female who has a virgin female friend at Round l. In Table 6.2b we consider only those adolescents who kept their best friends from Round 1 to Round 2. Again, only the log-odds ratio for white females is significant and it is larger than the corresponding ratio in Table 6.2a. Taking the antilog of 2.51, we get an odds ratio of 12.30. This indicates that among white females who retain their friendship ties between rounds, a virgin who has a nonvirgin friend at Round 1 is over 12 times as likely to make the intercourse transition than a virgin who has a virgin friend at Round 1. As noted earlier, this increase of the influence effect when only stable friendship pairs are considered is to be expected since such adolescents have a full two years to be influenced by these friends.

Deselection

Our definition of deselection and the model by which we assess its operation are described as follows. We would expect that an adolescent's decision to maintain or dissolve a friendship with a person of a given intercourse status at Round 1 will depend on the adolescent's own pattern of

---

[9] Because only a small number of black males were virgins at Round 1 and therefore eligible to make the transition, we cannot compute stable log-odds ratio for this subgroup. To test the influence model for black males a younger sample would be required.

[10] While not shown explicitly in the table, we note that white females differ significantly from all other race-sex subgroups, for which there is no influence effect.

TABLE 6.2. Influence: Transition to Nonvirginity by Round 2 Predicted by Same-Sex Best Friend's Sexual Behavior at Round 1 (Log-Odds Ratios): Sample = Virgins at Round 1[a]

a. All Friendship Pairs

White Males	Black Males	White Females	Black Females
.35[ns]	–	1.78**	.06[ns]
[1.42]		[5.93]	[1.06]
(280)	(28)	(363)	(100)

b. Stable Friendship Pairs

White Males	Black Males	White Females	Black Females
.82[ns]	–	2.51**	−1.46[ns]
[2.27]		[12.30]	[.23]
(121)	(10)	(134)	(34)

[a] Table sizes are in parentheses; odds ratios are in brackets; log-odds ratios are not.
[ns] Nonsignificant.
** $p < .01$.

intercourse behavior between rounds. That is, the odds that an adolescent will deselect a same-sex best friend who is a virgin at Round 1 should differ by the respondent's pattern of intercourse behavior between Rounds 1 and 2. A respondent who is a virgin at Round 1 and remains a virgin at Round 2 (0 → 0) should be less likely by Round 2 to deselect a friend who is a virgin at Round 1 than a respondent who is either a virgin at Round 1 and becomes a nonvirgin by Round 2 (0 → 1) or a nonvirgin at both rounds (1 → 1). A respondent who is a virgin at Round 1 and becomes a nonvirgin at Round 2 (0 → 1) should be less likely by Round 2 to deselect a friend who is a virgin at Round 1 than a respondent who is a nonvirgin at both rounds (1 → 1) *but* more likely to deselect a friend who is a virgin at Round 1 than a respondent who remains a virgin (0 → 0).

For clarification, we can restate our conditions for the operation of the deselection process as follows:

1. A virgin who remains a virgin should be very likely to retain at Round 2 a friend who is a virgin at Round 1.
2. A respondent who makes the transition to intercourse should be slightly less likely to retain at Round 2 a friend who is a virgin at Round 1.
3. A nonvirgin at Round 1 should be very unlikely to retain at Round 2 a friend who is a virgin at Round 1.

To test the deselection model we need the respondent's sexual intercourse behavior at Round 1 and Round 2, the respondent's best friend's sexual behavior at Round 1, and a knowledge of whether the respondent's best friend in Round 1 was retained or eliminated in Round 2. We created a dichotomous "deselected-retained" variable by checking to see if the friend named in Round 1 appeared on the respondent's friendship list in Round 2. If the Round 1 friend appeared on the Round 2 list, the respondent is defined as having retained the Round 1 same-sex best friend. The percentage of respondents who retained their Round 1 friend does not differ greatly by race-sex subgroup: 40.5 for white males; 32.4 for black males; 36.4 for white females; and 35.2 for black females.

The dependent variable in the deselection model is whether the adolescent retained or eliminated the Round 1 friend by Round 2, and it is predicted by the friend's sexual behavior at Round 1 as conditioned by the respondent's pattern of sexual behavior between rounds. To test this model we again use a contingency table approach and log-odds ratios. We crosstabulate the "deselected–retained" variable by the best friend's sexual behavior at Round 1 for each pattern of the respondent's Round 1 to Round 2 sexual behavior and compute three log-odds ratios. We then test the goodness of fit of a model which specifies no difference by pattern of respondent sexual behavior in the relationship between deselecting a friend and the friend's Round 1 intercourse behavior—i.e., a model specifying no interaction effect.

There is no evidence that deselection operates for any of the subgroups. In Table 3a we find that white males who are virgins at both rounds (0 → 0) are significantly less likely to deselect a friend who is a virgin at Round 1 than a friend who is a nonvirgin at Round 1. That is, the –.87 log-odds ratio means that (0 → 0) white males are likely to retain a best Friend who is a virgin at Round 1. However, although the log-odds ratios are not significant, white males who make the intercourse transition between rounds (0 → 1) and those who are nonvirgins at both rounds (1 → 1) are *also* likely to retain a best friend who is a virgin at Round 1. The log-odds ratios for the (0 → 1) group and the (1 → 1) group are both negative. Using a procedure developed by Goodman (1970, 1972), we tested the goodness of fit of a model which specifies no difference in the relationship between deselecting a friend and the friend's Round 1 sexual behavior by pattern of respondent sexual behavior. The results of these tests are presented in Table 6.3b. For white males, the "no-interaction" model fits the data quite well ($p = .55$). We conclude that a white males's decision to dissolve his friendship with a person of a given intercourse status at Round 1 does not depend on that adolescent's pattern of intercourse status between rounds. Given that almost all of the black males are nonvirgins at Round 1, our data do not permit a test of the deselection process for this race-sex subgroup.

The nonsignificant –.13 log-odds ratio for the (0 → 0) group of white females indicates that these adolescents are no more likely to retain a friend who is a virgin in Round 1 than a friend who is a nonvirgin in Round 1. Similarly, the nonsignificant .28 log-odds ratio for the (1 → 1) group of white females indicates that these respondents are no more likely to deselect a friend who is a virgin in Round 1 than a friend who is a nonvirgin in Round 1. However, the significant 1.00 log-odds ratio for the (0 → 1) white females indicates that members of this group are significantly more likely to deselect a friend who is a virgin at Round 1 than a friend who is a nonvirgin at Round 1.

While the finding that respondents who make the transition to intercourse are more likely to dissolve their friendships with virgins than with nonvirgins may have intuitive appeal, it must not be interpreted as evidence that the deselection process is operating. We must still take into account the findings that both respondents who remain virgins at Round 2 and respondents who are nonvirgins at both rounds are no more likely to retain or dissolve their friendships with virgins than with nonvirgins. These latter two findings do not fit our theoretical model of the deselection process. In other words, as we go from white females who are virgins in both rounds to white females who are nonvirgins in both rounds there is no theoretically grounded pattern in the log-odds ratios. Finally, Table 6.3b reveals that the three log-odds ratios are not significantly different from one another. The "no-interaction" model fits the data reasonably well for white females.

Of all of the "no-interaction" models presented in Table 6.3b, the model for black females pro-

TABLE 6.3. Deselection: Likelihood of Deselecting vs. Retaining the Same-Sex Best Friend Given the Friend's Sexual Behavior at Round 1 and the Respondent's Round 1–2 Pattern of Behavior (Log-Odds Ratios): Sample = All Respondents[a]

a. Log-Odds Ratios

Log-Odds of Deselecting a Virgin Best Friend	Respondent Pattern of Behavior (Round 1–2) (0 → 0)	(0 → 1)	(1 → 1)
White Males	$-.87^{**}$	$-.16^{ns}$	$-.66^{ns}$
	[.42]	[.85]	[.52]
	(197)	(83)	(90)
Black Males	—	—	—
	(10)	(18)	(120)
White Females	$-.13^{ns}$	1.00^{*}	$.28^{ns}$
	[.88]	[2.72]	[1.32]
	(277)	(86)	(41)
Black Females	–.18	-2.27^{**}	-1.41^{**}
	[.84]	[.10]	[.24]
	(61)	(39)	(62)

b. Goodness of Fit of No-Interaction Model

	χ^2	D.F.	Probability
White Males (370)	1.20	2	.55
Black Males (148)	—	—	—
White Females (404)	1.88	2	.39
Black Females (162)	3.14	2	.21

[a] Table sizes are in parentheses; odds ratios are in brackets; log-odds ratios are not.
[ns] Nonsignificant.
* $p < .05$.
** $p < .01$.

vides the poorest fit to the data ($p = .21$). This result alone, however, is not sufficient grounds for concluding that the deselection process may be operating for black females. When we examine the three log-odds ratios presented in Table 6.3a, we find that the (0 → 0) black females are no more likely to retain a friend who is a virgin in Round 1 than a friend who is a nonvirgin in Round 1; however, both the (0 → 1) and (1 → 1) black females *are* significantly more likely to retain a friend who is virgin than a friend who is a nonvirgin. While substantively interesting and perhaps worthy of future inquiry, these results are clearly counter to our theoretical model of the deselection process. We conclude that the deselection process does not operate for black females.

Acquisition

According to our definition of acquisition, if the acquisition process is operating then we would expect that newly acquired friends will be similar to the respondents in terms of sexual behavior. That is, the respondent's pattern of sexual behavior between Rounds 1 and 2 should predict the sexual behavior of a best friend newly acquired at Round 2. Among respondents who acquire a new best friend at Round 2, an adolescent who is a virgin at Round 1 and remains a virgin at Round 2 (0 → 0) should be more likely to acquire a new friend who is a virgin at Round 2 than a respondent who is either a virgin at Round 1 and becomes a nonvirgin at Round 2 (0 → 1) or a nonvirgin at both rounds (1 → 1). A respondent who is a virgin at Round 1 and becomes a nonvirgin at Round 2 (0 → 1) should be less likely to acquire a new friend who is a virgin at Round 2 than a respondent who is a virgin at both rounds (0 → 0) *but* more likely to acquire a new friend who is a virgin at Round 2 than a respondent who is a nonvirgin at both rounds (1 → 1).

To test the acquisition model we need the respondent's sexual intercourse behavior at Round 1 and Round 2, the respondent's best friend's sexual behavior at Round 2, and a knowledge of whether the respondent's best friend in Round 2 was newly acquired or retained from Round 1. We created a dichotomous "newly acquired–retained" variable by checking to see if the best friend named in Round 2 appeared on the respondent's friendship list in Round 1. If the Round 2 friend did not appear on the Round 1 list, the respondent is defined as having newly acquired the Round 2 same-sex best friend. The percentage of respondents with newly acquired Round 2 friends differs very little by race-sex subgroup; 62.9 for white males; 65.9 for black males; 69.6 for white females; and 62.8 for black females. The sample used for the acquisition model is restricted to respondents who acquired a new best friend at Round 2.

The dependent variable in the acquisition model is the newly acquired friend's intercourse behavior, and it is predicted by the respondent's pattern of sexual behavior between Rounds 1 and 2. To test this model we compute log-odds ratios that separately compare the odds that a (0 → 0) respondent acquires a virgin friend to both the odds that a (0 → 1) respondent acquires a virgin friend and the odds that a (1 → 1) respondent acquires a virgin friend. We also compute a log-odds ratio that compares the odds that a (0 → 1) respondent acquires a virgin friend to the odds that a (1 → 1) respondent acquires a virgin friend. This is equivalent to a dummy-variable regression in which two patterns of the respondent's Round 1 to Round 2 sexual behavior are each compared to the third pattern.

Table 6.4 presents the results of our test of the acquisition model. For neither black males nor black females does the adolescent's pattern of sexual behavior between Round 1 and Round 2 predict the sexual behavior of a best friend newly acquired at Round 2. However, the acquisition process clearly operates for white males. Among white males who acquire a new best friend at Round 2, an adolescent who remains a virgin at both rounds (0 → 0) is 4 times as likely (antilog of 1.37 = 3.94) to select a new friend who is a virgin at Round 2 as a respondent who is a nonvirgin at both rounds (1 → 1). An adolescent who is a (0 → 0) is almost twice (antilog of .63 = 1.88) as likely as a (0 → 1) to select a new friend who is a virgin at Round 2. Finally, a (0 → 1) adolescent is more than twice (antilog of .74 = 2.10) as likely as a (1 → 1) adolescent to select a new friend who is a virgin at Round 2.

For white females the pattern denoting the operation of the acquisition process is slightly less clear, but we nevertheless conclude that the process operates in this subgroup. Among white females who acquire a new best friend at Round 2, an adolescent who remains a virgin at both rounds (0 → 0) is almost four times (antilog of 1.30 = 3.67) as likely as a nonvirgin (1 → 1) to select a

TABLE 6.4. Acquisition: Round 2 Sexual Behavior of Newly Acquired Same-Sex Friends Predicted by Respondent's Round 1–2 Pattern of Behavior (Log-Odds Ratios): Sample = Respondents with Newly Acquired Friends[a]

	Respondent Pattern of Behavior (Round 1–2)		
Log-Odds of Acquiring a Virgin Best Friend	(0 → 0) compared to (0 → 1)	(0 → 1) compared to (1 → 1)	(0 → 0) compared to (1 → 1)
White Males (222)	.63*	.74*	1.37**
	[1.88]	[2.10]	[3.94]
Black Males (89)	.69[ns]	–.14[ns]	.56[ns]
	[1.99]	[.87]	[1.75]
White Females (279)	1.41**	–.11[ns]	1.30**
	[4.10]	[.90]	[3.67]
Black Females (93)	.42[ns]	.11[ns]	.53[ns]
	[1.52]	[1.52]	[–1.70]

[a] Table sizes are in parentheses; odds ratios are in brackets; log-odds ratios are not.
[ns] Nonsignificant.
* $p < .05$.
** $p < .01$.

new friend who is a virgin at Round 2. An adolescent who is a (0 → 0) is over four times (antilog of 1.41 = 4.10) as likely as a (0 → 1) to select a new friend who is a virgin at Round 2. However, a (0 → 1) adolescent is no more likely than a (1 → 1) to select a friend who is a virgin at Round 2. This result is not too surprising and is not too counter to our conditions for the operation of the acquisition process. White females who made the intercourse transition were virgins for at least some amount of time between Rounds 1 and 2, and we might therefore expect them to be somewhat more likely to name a friend who is a virgin at Round 2 than adolescents who were nonvirgins for the entire two-year interval. However, our results suggest that white females who make the intercourse transition forget their former virgin status and select a friend who is similar to their current nonvirgin status.[11]

Summary

Our task in this paper has been to separate empirically the three sources of homogeneity bias and to assess which factors are important for friendship similarity with respect to sexual intercourse. We can summarize our results from the influence, deselection and acquisition models as follows. White females constitute the only race-sex subgroup in which the influence process is found to operate. The deselection process does not operate in any race-sex subgroup. The acquisition process operates for whites, males and females, but not for blacks. We hasten to add, however, that our data do not permit an appropriate test of the influence and deselection models for black males.

Our results are consistent with the findings reported by Kandel (1978) and Cohen (1977) with regard to adolescent friendship similarity along attitudinal and behavioral dimensions other than sexual attitudes and behavior. Like Kandel and Cohen we find that for groups in which there is significant homogeneity bias, influence is not the sole contributor to this similarity. For white females, similarity in adolescent-friend sexual behavior appears to be due to both the influence and acquisition processes. For white males, only acquisition appears responsible for the observed homogeneity bias. Like Cohen, we fail to find any evidence that the process of deselection contributes to adolescent–friend similarity. Unfortunately, since our models of the three processes use different subsamples of the adolescents,[12] we cannot directly assess the relative magnitude of the three processes. For example, unlike Kandel, we cannot conclude that for white females the effects of influence and acquisition in contributing to homo-

[11]While not shown explicitly in Table 6.4, the difference between blacks and whites with respect to the odds of acquiring virgin best friends is statistically significant.

[12]For example, only virgins in Round 1 are used to evaluate the influence process, and only adolescents with newly acquired friends at Round 2 are used to evaluate the acquisition process.

geneity bias in sexual behavior are approximately 50–50. We can conclude, however, that using cross-sectional data and interpreting a positive relationship between peers' sexual behavior and the respondent's sexual behavior as being totally the result of an influence process is unwarranted. Such a conclusion, which previous researchers have been prone to make, appears in our data set to be an overestimate of the importance of influence in contributing to homogeneity bias along the dimension of sexual behavior.

Discussion and Conclusion

There is no similarity in sexual behavior between adolescents and their friends for black males or black females at either round of our Florida study. For white males and white females, however, there is structure in adolescent same-sex best-friendships along the dimension of intercourse behavior.

Why homogeneity bias obtains for whites but not for blacks is unclear. We earlier suggested that differences with respect to degree of adolescent–similarity in sexual behavior may center around differences in the normative salience of sexual behavior and race-sex differences in the nature of friendships. Black adolescents have been found to have more permissive sexual standards than whites and to have a greater incidence of premarital intercourse. To the extent that permissive sexual attitudes and behavior give rise to a more nonjudgmental stance with respect to the sexual behavior of others (i.e., a norm against sexual norms) we might expect there to be less similarity between adolescents and their friends. Moreover, as previously noted, a number of studies not pertaining to adolescent sexuality have shown that blacks tend to conform to the attitudes and behavior of their same-sex, same-race peers much less than whites conform to the attitudes and behavior of their same-sex, same-race peers. One explanation for this race difference is the greater emphasis placed on autonomy by black parents in childrearing (Schneider, 1970).

We should note that the group differences in homogeneity bias found in our earlier analysis of the North Carolina data are not totally replicated in the Florida study. As in the present analysis, homogeneity bias in the North Carolina sample was strongest for white females and weak and nonsignificant for black males. However, unlike the results for the Florida study, the North Carolina data revealed relatively strong, significant homogeneity bias for black females and weak, nonsignificant adolescent–friend similarity for white males. The North Carolina data therefore give clearer evidence of a sex difference in homogeneity bias, while the present analysis yields a race difference in adolescent-friend similarity in sexual behavior. We cannot evaluate whether the two samples are different with respect to the operation of the influence, deselection, or acquisition processes.

The analysis of homogeneity bias reported in our earlier paper using the North Carolina data differs from the present analysis. The North Carolina study used the adolescents' total same-sex friends (same-sex best friend and other same-sex friends), while this study considers only same-sex best friends. The North Carolina and Florida samples also differ with respect to such characteristics as the age distribution of the adolescents, the number of stable friendship pairs, the number of reciprocal friendship pairs, etc.[13] We spent considerable time making the two samples as comparable as possible on each of these varying dimensions and reanalyzed homogeneity bias for each race-sex subgroup in each study site. We still find that in the North Carolina data there is a sex difference in homogeneity bias while in the Florida data there is a race difference. Although it is gratifying to find that in both study sites white females exhibit the greatest adolescent–friend similarity in sexual behavior and black males the weakest, the differences between samples observed for white males and black females are inexplicable. Clearly, further analyses of homogeneity bias by race-sex subgroups using other data sets is called for.

With regard to the question of *why* similarity in sexual behavior between respondents and their friends occurs for whites, we find that the sources of this homogeneity bias differ somewhat by sex. Both white males and white females *acquire* friends who are similar to themselves in terms of sexual behavior. However, only white females appear to be influenced by their friends' behavior.

If it is reasonable to assume that intercourse is of considerable salience for *both* white males and white females, then finding the acquisition pro-

[13] When the age distributions are made comparable, however, the reported incidences of sexual intercourse are the same for the two samples for each race-sex subgroup.

cess operating for whites is understandable. White males and females may be more sensitive to or critical of the sexual behavior of their potential friends. The lack of any evidence that the deselection process operates among whites, however, suggests that having sex is not so salient or disvalued as to be a criterion for dissolving a friendship. Once a friendship has been formed perhaps behavioral characteristics other than similarity in sexual behavior are more important in the adolescent's decision to retain or dissolve the friendship.

Why are white females influenced by their friends while white males are not? As earlier discussed, it has been argued that for girls conversations with close friends involve "personal" themes whereas boys more often discuss "objective" topics. Female friendship is oriented toward "emotional-expressive" values while male friendship is oriented toward "instrumental-group oriented" values (Kon, 1981). Females may derive more emotional support from their close female friends for having or not having sex than males do from their close male friends. More importantly, the greater affective content of female conversations regarding sex may serve to make the probability that a female will be influenced by her female friend's sexual behavior higher than the probability that a male will be influenced by his male friend's behavior. Of all race-sex subgroups, white females typically display the greatest amount of conformity to their same-sex peers.

The present study contributes to our knowledge of the structure of adolescent friendships. We provide evidence that for whites, both male and female, a subtle, nonpublic behavior like sexual intercourse is a strong and pervasive factor in adolescent friendship structure. Unlike previous researchers, we do so while avoiding problems inherent in the use of perception data to measure peer-adolescent similarity by matching respondents' sexual behavior with their friends' sexual behavior as actually reported by the friends. In addition, we separate the three possible sources of any observed homogeneity bias empirically and assess which processes are important in accounting for friendship similarity with respect to sexual intercourse. By using a longitudinal survey design we have been able to *investigate* whether any observed similarity in sexual behavior is due to influence rather than, as previous researchers have done, to *assume* that adolescent–friend similarity is due to a process of influence. A line of inquiry along which future studies of adolescent friendship structure could and should proceed consists of a more complete explanation of *how* friends influence one another and *how* adolescent friendships are formed, maintained, and dissolved.

REFERENCES

Billy, J. O. G., Rodgers, J. L., & Udry, R. (1984). Adolescent sexual behavior and friendship choice. *Social Forces 62*, 653–678.

Carns, D. (1973). Talking about sex: Notes on first coitus and the double standard. *Journal of Marriage and the Family 35*, 677–688.

Clayton, R. R. (1972). Premarital sexual intercourse: A substantive test of the contingent consistency model. *Journal of Marriage and the Family, 34*, 273–281.

Cohen, J. M. (1977). Sources of peer group homogeneity. *Sociology of Education, 50*, 227–241.

Costanzo, P. R., & Shaw, M. E. (1966). Conformity as a function of age level. *Child Development, 37*, 967–975.

Cozby, P. C. (1973). Self-disclosure: A literature review. *Psychological Bulletin, 79*, 73–91.

Davies, M., & Kandel, D. B. (1981). Parental and peer influences on adolescents' educational plans: Some further evidence. *American Journal of Sociology, 87*, 363–387.

Davis, K. E. (1971). Sex on the campus: Is there a revolution? *Medical Aspects of Human Sexuality, 5*, 128–412.

Davis, P. (1974). Contextual sex-saliency and sexual activity: The relative effects of family and peer group in the sexual socialization process. *Journal of Marriage and the Family, 36*, 196–202.

DeLamater, J., & MacCorquodale, P. (1979). *Premarital Sexuality*. Madison: University of Wisconsin Press.

Dimond, R. E., & Hellkamp, D. T. (1969). Race, sex, ordinal position of birth, and self-disclosure in high school students. *Psychological Bulletin, 25*, 235–238.

Douvan, E., & Adelson, J. (1966). *The Adolescent Experience*. New York: Wiley.

Finkel, M. L., & Finkel, D. J. (1975). Sexual and contraceptive knowledge, attitudes, and behavior of male adolescents. *Family Planning Perspectives, 7*, 256–260.

Finkel, M. L., & Finkel, D. J. (1976). The influence of the peer group on sexual behavior: Implications for educators. *High School Behavioral Science, 4*, 19–23.

Gebhard, P., Pomeroy, W., Martin, C., & Christenson, C. (1958). *Pregnancy, Birth and Abortion*. New York: Harper & Row.

Goodman, L. A. (1969). How to ransack social mobility tables and other kinds of cross-classification tables. *American Journal of Sociology, 75*, 1–40.

Goodman, L. A. (1970). The multivariate analysis of qualitative data. *Journal of the American Statistical Association, 65*, 226–256.

Goodman, L. A. (1972). A general model for the analysis of surveys. *American Journal of Sociology, 77*, 1035–1086.

Hallinan, M. T., & Tuma, N. B. (1978). Classroom effects on change in children's friendships. *Sociology of Education, 51*, 270–282.

Herold, E. S. (1980). *Contraceptive Attitudes and Behavior of Single Adolescent Females*. NICHD Contract No. H01-HD-92809.

Holland, P., & Leinhardt, S. (1973). The structural implications of measurement error in sociometry. *Journal of Mathematical Sociology, 3,* 85–112.

Iscoe, I., Williams, M., & Harvey, J. (1964). Age, intelligence, and sex as variables in the conformity behavior of negro and white children. *Child Development, 35,* 451–460.

Jackson, E., & Potkay, C. (1973). Pre-college influences on sexual experiences of coeds. *Journal of Sex Research, 9,* 143-149.

Jessor, S. L., & Jessor, R. (1975). Transition from virginity to nonvirginity among youth: A social-psychological study over time. *Developmental Psychology, 11,* 473–484.

Jessor, R., Costa, F., Jessor, L., & Donovan, J. E. (1983). Time of first intercourse: A prospective study. *Journal of Personality and Social Psychology, 44,* 608–626.

Jourard, S. M. (1971). *The Transparent Self.* New York: D. Van Nostrand.

Jourard, S. M., & Lasakow, P. (1958). Some factors in self-disclosure. *Journal of Abnormal and Social Psychology, 56,* 91–98.

Kaats, G. R., & Davis, K. E. (1970). The dynamics of sexual behavior of college students. *Journal of Marriage and the Family, 32,* 390–399.

Kandel, D. B. (1978). Homophily, selection, and socialization in adolescent friendships. *American Journal of Sociology, 84,* 427–436.

Kerckhoff, A. C., & Huff, J. L. (1974). Parental influence on educational goals. *Sociometry, 3,* 307–327.

Kon, I. S. (1981). Adolescent friendship: Some unanswered questions for future research. In S. Duck & R. Gilmour (Eds.), *Personal relationships: Developing personal relationships* (pp. 178–204). London: Academic Press.

Lewis, R. (1978). Emotional intimacy among men. *Journal of Social Issues, 34,* 109–121.

Miller, P. Y., & Simon, W. (1974). Adolescent sexual behavior: Context and change. *Social Problems, 22,* 58–76.

Mirande, A. M. (1968). Reference group theory and adolescent sexual behavior. *Journal of Marriage and the Family, 30,* 572–577.

Mulcahy, G. A. (1973). Sex differences in patterns of self-disclosure among adolescents: A developmental perspective. *Journal of Youth and Adolescence, 2,* 343–356.

Newcomb, T. M. (1956). The prediction of interpersonal attraction. *American Psychologist, 11,* 575–586.

Pearce, W., Wright, P., Sharp, S., & Slama, K. (1974). Affection and reciprocity in self-disclosing communication. *Human Communication Research, 1,* 5–14.

Reiss, I. L. (1964). Premarital sexual permissiveness among negroes and whites. *American Sociological Review, 29,* 688–698.

Reiss, I. L. (1967). *The Social Context of Premarital Sexual Permissiveness.* New York: Holt, Rinehart & Winston.

Reiss, I. L. (1970). Premarital sex as deviant behavior: An application of current approaches to deviance. *American Sociological Review, 35,* 78–87.

Rivenbark, W. H. (1971). Self-disclosure patterns among adolescents. *Psychological Reports, 28,* 35–42.

Sattel, J. (1976). The inexpressive male? Tragedy of sexual politics? *Social Problems, 23,* 469–477.

Schneider, F. W. (1970). Conforming behavior of black and white children. *Journal of Personality and Social Psychology, 16,* 466–471.

Shah, F., & Zelnik, M. (1981). Parent and peer influence on sexual behavior, contraceptive use, and pregnancy experience of young women. *Journal of Marriage and the Family, 43,* 339–348.

Sorensen, R. C. (1973). *Adolescent Sexuality in Contemporary America.* New York: World.

Spanier, G. (1975). Sexualization and premarital sexual behavior. *Family Coordinator, 24,* 33–41.

Staples, R. (1978). Race, liberalism-conservatism and premarital sexual permissiveness: A bi-racial comparison. *Journal of Marriage and the Family, 40,* 733–742.

Teevan, J. J., Jr. (1972). Reference groups and premarital sexual behavior. *Journal of Marriage and the Family, 34,* 283–291.

Udry, J. R., Bauman, K. R., & Morris, N. M. (1975). Changes in premarital coital experience of recent decade-of-birth cohorts of urban American women. *Journal of Marriage and the Family, 37,* 783–787.

Vener, A. M., & Stewart, C. S. (1974). Adolescent sexual behavior in middle America revisited: 1970–1973. *Journal of Marriage and the Family, 36,* 728–735.

Walsh, R. H., Ferrell, M. Z., & Tolone, W. L. (1976). Selection of reference group, perceived reference group permissiveness, and personal permissiveness attitudes and behavior: A study of two consecutive panels (1967–1971; 1970–1974). *Journal of Marriage and the Family 38,* 495-507.

Wheeler, L., & Nezlek, J. (1977). Sex differences in social participation. *Journal of Personality and Social Psychology, 35,* 742–754.

Zelnik, M., & Kantner, J. F. (1980). Sexual activity, contraceptive use and pregnancy among metropolitan-area teenagers: 1971–1979. *Family Planning Perspectives, 12,* 230–237.

READING 7

Casual Sex on Spring Break: Intentions and Behaviors of Canadian Students

Eleanor Maticka-Tyndale • University of Windsor
Edward S. Herold and Dawn Mewhinney • University of Guelph

Using Triandis's theory of interpersonal behavior, we analyzed factors related to casual sex among Canadian university students on a spring break vacation. Two samples were obtained: 151 students completed a questionnaire before a spring break trip to Daytona Beach, Florida and 681 completed a questionnaire during or immediately following the vacation. More men than women intended to have casual sex but similar percentages of men (15%) and women (13%) had actually engaged in casual sex. In ordinary least squares regression, expectation of participation in spring break activities, social norms expressed through peer group influences, and personal attitudes explained 74% of the variance in the intentions to engage in casual sex. In logistic regression, intentions and participation in spring break activities correctly classified 80% of the men into those who did and did not engage in casual sex. Agreements formed with friends about casual sex and the proportion of friends who participated in coitus on spring break correctly classified 88% of women.

Although numerous studies have been conducted on the sexual behavior of young people, there is little research on sexual behavior occurring in specific contexts. One context that has been ignored by researchers is the North American spring break holiday, a one-week break in the school calendar in late February or early March. Approximately one million U.S. students participate in some form of spring break vacation (Josiam, Clements, & Hobson, 1995). Spring break vacations are also popular among Canadians, with thousands of students heading to popular vacation spots (S. Cox, Inter-Campus Programs, personal communication, September, 1995).

Mewhinney, Herold, and Maticka-Tyndale (1995), using focus groups and interviews with Canadian students who had traveled to Florida for spring break, found the key elements of a spring break vacation to include a group holiday with friends traveling and rooming together, a perpetual party atmosphere, high alcohol consumption, sexually suggestive contests and displays, and the perception that casual sex is common. Overall, there is the perception that sexual norms are far more permissive on spring break vacation than at home, providing an atmosphere of greater sexual freedom and the opportunity for engaging in new sexual experiences. Smeaton and Josiam (1996) reported similar findings from their survey of U.S. students on spring break vacation in Panama City Beach, Florida.

The behavior patterns found on spring break have also been found among nonstudent samples of holiday travelers. In their review of the tourism and vacation literature, Herold and van Kerkwijk (1992) identified the characteristics of vacations that were conducive to casual sex activity as a sense of freedom from at-home restrictions, a relaxation of inhibitions, a focus on having a good time, and high alcohol consumption.

We examined factors that might influence university students to engage in coitus with a new partner while on spring break. For the purpose of this paper, we refer to this behavior as *casual sex*: This was the term used by students in a preliminary study (Mewhinney et al., 1995) to refer to the type of sex engaged in while on spring break. The students portrayed spring break sexual partnerships as initiated rapidly, often within hours of meeting, and as temporary, not lasting beyond the spring break period. Given our focus on new, casual partnerships, we excluded from our analysis those young adults who were sexually active on spring break with a relationship partner from home or with someone whom they had known before spring break.

Triandis's theory of interpersonal behavior (TIB; 1977, 1980, 1994) was selected to guide data collection and analysis because it includes peer influences and situational characteristics in explaining behavior, both of which were identified in preliminary research (Mewhinney et al., 1995) as important influences, on spring break sexual activity. The TIB belongs to the school of cognitive models that includes the theory of reasoned action (TRA; Ajzen & Fishbein, 1980) and the theory of planned behavior (TPB; Ajzen, 1985). These theories explain the influence of attitudes and norms on intentions, with these intentions, in turn, directly influencing behaviors. Triandis's model goes beyond the others by examining how factors other than intentions influence behavior, and by more fully specifying the factors that influence intentions. The TIB has proven useful in understanding complex behaviors, particularly those that may be influenced by the social and/or physical environment (e.g., in sexuality research, see Boyd & Wandersman, 1991; Godin, et al., 1996).

Using the framework of the TIB, we predicted that whether a young adult on spring break in Daytona Beach would engage in casual sex would be influenced by an expectation or intention to engage in coitus with a new partner on spring break, prior experience with casual sex, and an environment conducive to new coital partnerships. The first factor, intention, has received considerable attention in the social psychological literature (e.g., Fishbein & Jaccard, 1973; Jorgensen & Sonstegard, 1984; White, Terry, & Hogg, 1994). Although factors that might intervene in the intention-behavior link have been discussed (e.g., Randall & Wolff, 1994), only Triandis has explicitly focused on variables such as prior experience and situational conditions that may facilitate, impede, or replace intentions as determinants of behavior.

Previous research supports the inclusion of these additional variables in explanations of sexual behavior. For example, researchers have found that for individuals with a greater number of past coital partners, erotic cues (e.g., arousal and situational cues) have a stronger influence on whether coitus occurs than does the quality of a relationship (Christopher & Cate, 1984; D'Augelli & D'Augelli, 1977). The TIB would make a similar prediction, although prior experience is conceptualized somewhat differently. In the TIB, prior experiences that closely approximate the current sexual situation, such as having coitus with someone within hours of meeting him or her, can replace intentions and independently influence a behavior. The influence of prior experience is strongest when the new event closely parallels the prior experiences (for this study, if the prior experience of casual sex occurred while on a previous spring break vacation in Daytona Beach) and when there are multiple instances of that prior experience.

Situational conditions work with intentions and prior experience to facilitate the likelihood of particular behaviors by providing opportunity and cues that contribute to an individual's erotic expectations (see also D'Augelli & D'Augelli, 1977; Rook & Hammen, 1977). In the TIB, situational conditions that are conducive to actions are specific to the action and situation of interest. Thus, for this study, we must consider conditions associated with being on vacation (Herold & van Kerkwijk, 1992).

Triandis suggests that intentions and prior experiences are the dominant influences on behavior, with situational conditions acting as mediators that facilitate or impede behaviors. Thus, if the situation prohibits or impedes casual sex, prior behavior and/or intentions will not result in the predicted behaviors. If conditions conducive to casual sex are present, then its realization will depend on prior experience with casual sex and/or intentions.

The TIB also provides an explanation of how intentions are formed. As in other cognitive models (e.g., TRA and TPB), personal attitudes and social norms are presented as influencing the formation of intentions or plans. However, the TIB more fully specifies the personal and social dimensions. Personal attitudes include affective and evaluative components. The affective component of attitudes toward casual sex involves the feelings that one anticipates as part of casual sex (e.g., pleasure, elation, fear, disgust). The evaluative component of attitudes is the cognitive evaluation of the probable consequences of casual sex (e.g., desirable, undesirable, good, bad). These two forms of attitudes are specified separately because each has a distinct influence on the formation of intentions. For example, a young adult may anticipate feelings of pleasure and excitement at the thought of casual sex on spring break but may judge the potential results of engaging in casual sex to be undesirable.

Social norms emanating from an individual's reference group are the second component influencing the formation of intentions. Here the TIB's predictions are similar to those of reference group theory (Christopher & Cate, 1984; Winslow, Franzini, & Hwang, 1992). As with personal attitudes, Triandis specifies several dimensions of reference group influence: (a) agreements or promises that are formed between friends (pacts either to engage or not to engage in casual sex); (b) the perceived norms and expectations of one's immediate reference group (subjective social norms); (c) beliefs about what is appropriate for a member in one's position or status (role beliefs); and (d) the internalized personal standards or moral codes (personal normative beliefs). The first two dimensions represent the social group as the point of reference. The second two dimensions represent the individual's transformation of social norms into self-expectations and standards and take the self as the point of reference. As with affective and evaluative components of attitudes, each of these may exert different pressures on the individual. For example, there may be pressure to fulfill the pacts or agreements made with friends or to act in accordance with the norms and expectations set by the reference group. There may also be pressure to act in a way that is considered appropriate to one's age, gender, or relationship status, or that is in accord with one's personal standards or moral code.

The conceptualization of the components of the theory of interpersonal behavior, the relationships among them, and the inclusion of new components have evolved over time (Triandis, 1977, 1980, 1994). Figure 7.1 presents the full structural model for the theory of interpersonal behavior as used in this study. In accordance with Triandis's suggestion that additional factors may be tested for their potential contribution to the explanatory power of the model, we have added situational expectations to the prediction of intentions and two measures of peer influence to the prediction of behavior.

Situational expectations are the expectational predecessors of situational conditions. These are conceptualized as the individual's expectations about whether spring break experiences will be conducive to casual sex. It is similar to the control belief concept in the TPB (Ajzen, 1991), a variable that is indicative of the degree to which a behavior is under the control of an individual. We suggest that when there are situational expectations conducive to casual sex, the individual expects that casual sex will occur. Triandis models participation in activities (situational conditions) as directly influencing the behavior. The addition of the expectation of participation as an influence on intentions permits us to examine more precisely the impact of the spring break environment, both as anticipated and as experienced, on casual sex.

We also added two peer influences to the explanation of casual sex activity: pacts and role modeling. These fit within Triandis's conceptualization of social norms and relate to our specific interest in the spring break environment. In preliminary

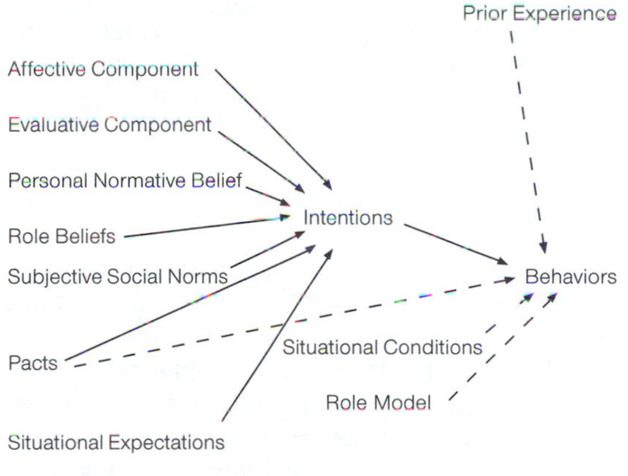

FIGURE 7.1 ■ Structural Model for Triandis Theory of Interpersonal Behavior.

research (Mewhinney et al., 1995), we found that a spring break vacation was a group activity. By including characteristics of peer influence that are part of the spring break experience, we are able to examine the direct effect of these aspects of the environment on engaging in casual sex.

We completed this study in two parts. First, in the prebreak study, we examined expectations and intentions before a spring break trip and tested the portion of the TIB that explains the formation of intention. Second, in the Daytona study, we examined experiences on the trip and tested the portion of the TIB that explains behavior. The methodology, results and discussion specific to each study are presented separately. The discussion following these presentations addresses portions of the results that bridge both studies.

Study 1: Prebreak Study

Methods

RECRUITMENT OF PARTICIPANTS

In February, 1996, students from four universities in southern Ontario who were planning a one-week spring break vacation in Daytona Beach, Florida were recruited before their trip through travel agents, advertisements in campus papers, posters on campus, class announcements, and campus information booths. Self-administered questionnaires were given or mailed to students following telephone or face-to-face contact with a research assistant. In addition, questionnaires were distributed and collected by research assistants at the beginning of chartered bus rides to Daytona Beach. In this prebreak sample, 151 surveys were completed.

QUESTIONNAIRE DEVELOPMENT

Triandis's (1977, 1980) theory includes a measurement model that operationalizes each concept in a manner that is specific to the time, context, and behavior of interest. Triandis provides the structure and form of measurement for each concept (e.g., personal attitudes are measured using semantic differential scales, social norms are measured using Likert scales), but the specific items and indicators must be established based on preliminary elicitation research. Elicitation research was conducted following Triandis's guidelines (Ajzen & Fishbein, 1980; Triandis, 1977, 1980). Students who had traveled to Florida for spring break before 1996 participated in semistructured, open-ended group and individual interviews. Concepts were operationalized based on content analysis of the interviews.

A draft of the prebreak questionnaire was tested and refined in a two-week test-retest procedure with a sample of 10 men and 10 women who anticipated going on a spring break vacation. Items that did not meet criteria set for test-retest reliability (kappa coefficient of at least 0.70) or that were more weakly correlated with other items measuring the same construct (evaluated using Cronbach's alpha) were eliminated from the final questionnaire. The specificity of items used in the scalar measures of constructs was tested using confirmatory factor analysis to ensure that items loaded only on their designated constructs. Construct validity was assessed by examining correlation matrices to verify that scalar measures correlated with criterion factors of gender, age, and prior coital experience in a manner consistent with prior research in the field.

The prebreak surveys included questions about sexual history, spring break plans and expectations, and the constructs used to predict intentions to engage in sexual activity. The final prebreak questionnaire could be completed in an average of 20 minutes.

MEASUREMENT OF CONSTRUCTS

Seven-point semantic differential scales consisting of adjective pairs used by students in the elicitation research to describe the experience and consequences of casual sex on spring break measured affective and evaluative attitude components. Participants were asked to rate their feelings about and evaluation of the consequences of "having sex with someone you meet on spring break." To ensure that this was a measure of attitudes toward coitus and not toward condom use, we asked participants to make this assessment without consideration of whether condoms were used. The adjective pairs measuring feelings when thinking about casual sex (affective component) were fun-loving/serious, exciting/dull, pleasant/unpleasant, adventuresome/ordinary. The adjective pairs measuring cognitive evaluations of the potential consequences of casual sex were good/bad, smart/stupid, responsible/irresponsible. Mean scores of the pairs for each attitude were used to measure the affective attitude and cognitive evaluations toward casual sex on spring break. Cronbach's alpha for the affective and cognitive measures was 0.76 and 0.82. respectively.

The four dimensions of social norms—personal norms, subjective social norms, role beliefs, and pacts—were measured. The strength of personal norms supporting casual sex was measured by the mean score of responses to three questions, each with a 7-point bipolar response: (1) "When on Spring Break . . . you feel you *should* have sex with someone you meet there if you want to"; (2) " . . . you would feel guilty if you have sex with someone you meet there" (reverse-coded); (3) " . . . it would be against your values to have sex with someone you meet there" (reverse-coded). Cronbach's alpha for this measure was 0.83.

Subjective social norms, or the perception of how much one's reference group approves or disapproves of his or her casual sex activity, was measured using the mean score of 7-point bipolar responses to three questions. Respondents indicated how likely or unlikely it was that each of three groups of referent others (male friends, female friends, and friends who went with them to Daytona Beach) would think that they *should* have sex if they met someone who was appealing. Cronbach's alpha for subjective social norms was 0.85.

Role beliefs, or the strength of beliefs about whether casual sex is appropriate for someone given his or her status or position, was measured using the mean score of 7-point bipolar (*strongly agree* [1] to *strongly disagree* [7]) responses to three questions. Respondents were asked whether having sex with someone met on spring break was "OK for someone of my gender . . . of my age . . . of my relationship status," Cronbach's alpha for role beliefs was 0.79.

To measure pacts, we asked participants whether they had made promises, agreements, or pacts with the friends who would accompany them to Daytona either to engage or not to engage in casual sex. The presence and nature of these pacts or agreements was effect coded as –1 for an agreement not to have sex, 0 for no pact or agreement, and 1 for an agreement to have sex.

Because situational expectations closely parallel Ajzen's (1991) control belief, Ajzen's method for operational control beliefs was used to assess situational expectations. During the elicitation phase, students identified specific situations or experiences that had occurred in Daytona Beach that they thought were conducive to or impeded enaging in coitus with a new partner while in Daytona. Ten experiences were identified and used in measuring the influence of anticipated situations on engaging in casual sex: partying, being in a break-loose mood, drinking alcohol, getting drunk, watching contests such as "hot body" and "wet t-shirt," dancing dirty, trying to "pick someone up," someone trying to "pick up" the respondent, the appearance that everyone was having sex, and someone wanting to have sex with the respondent. Participants used a 4-point scale ranging from *never* (1) to *frequently* (4), to rate the frequency with which they expected to be involved in each of the experiences. The perceived degree of influence of each experience on whether they engaged in casual sex was scored on a 7-point bipolar scale (*strongly agree* [1] to *strongly disagree* [7]) in response to the question "How likely is it that you would have sex with someone you meet on Spring Break if. . . ." The score for each experience or situation was constructed from the product of the frequency rating and the degree-of-influence rating. Cronbach's alpha for the total situational expectation score consisting of the mean of the 10 items' scores was 0.96.

To measure the criterion variable, we asked participants how often they expected or intended to engage in casual sex on spring break (defined as sexual intercourse with someone they had met on spring break). Answers ranged from *never* (1) to *frequently* (4).

DATA ANALYSIS

In the TIB, personal and status characteristics, such as gender, are external to the model: Their influence on intentions and behaviors is mediated through their influence on attitudes, norms, and experiences. Research on sexuality, however, has documented interactions between gender and attitudes, norms, experiences, and behaviors, suggesting that gender may also influence intentions and behaviors from within the model. These interactions include the way peer influences affect attitudes and behaviors (e.g., Christopher & Cate, 1984), the way attitudes and behaviors are linked (e.g., Oliver & Hyde, 1993), the way prior experiences influence future behaviors (Christopher & Roosa, 1991), and the characteristics of relationships that are necessary for coital interaction (e.g., Christopher & Roosa, 1991). These findings necessitate a consideration of potential gender interactions when designing an analysis plan. In this study, men's and women's covariance matrices for all variables used in the multivariate procedures were tested for significant differences using LISREL VI (Joreskog & Sorbom, 1986). This procedure permitted us to identify the number and location of interactions. With the exception of the covariance of subjective social norms and intentions, there were no significant differences between the covariance matrices for men and women. The interaction of gender with subjective social norms was accommodated in this analysis by using gender-specific terms for men's and women's subjective social norms. Because there was only one interaction between gender and an independent variable, the remainder of the data for men and women were aggregated.

During exploratory research, students argued that the interpretation of spring break activities was influenced by one's peer group. If friends endorsed casual sex, for example, then a student expected and interpreted the activities on spring break as conducive to casual sex. If friends did not endorse casual sex, the same activities would not necessarily be seen as leading to or facilitating casual sex. The possible mediator role of peers with respect to situational expectations was tested using four regression analyses. In each, intention was regressed on situational expectations along with one measure of social norms and the interaction between expectations and social norms. The interaction between situational expectations and pacts was the only significant interaction. Therefore, it was included in the final analysis.

Including several dimensions of complex constructs such as personal attitudes and social norms in an analysis allows us to identify the contribution and relative strength of each dimension in explaining the dependent variable. However, because dimensions are expected to be closely related to one another, they present the possibility of multicollinearity. The presence of multivariate collinearity was tested using measures of tolerance and variance inflation, comparisons of the eigenvalues of the variables' uncentered cross-products matrix, and examination of the proportion of variance of each independent variable associated with each eigenvalue (Smith & Sasaki, 1979). These supported the conclusion that each predictor variable represented a sufficiently independent portion of variance in intentions to conduct multivariate analyses. Because the inclusion of interaction and gender-specific terms in the proposed analysis further heightened the possibility of multicollinearity, all independent variables measured at the interval level were centered around their mean values as suggested by Smith and Sasaki (1979) and Aiken and West (1991). The measure for agreements with friends (pact) retained its original unweighted effect coding.

The model for intentions was tested using hierarchical ordinary least squares regressions. The predictor variables in the original TIB were entered as a block in the first regression followed by the addition of situational expectations and the interaction between pacts and situational expectations.

Results

PROFILE OF THE SAMPLE

Participants were 66 males and 85 females aged 18–31 (77% were ages 21–23). All participants were White and identified themselves as heterosexual and single. Thirty-five percent of men and 38% of women reported they were in a long-term relationship.

Spring break expectations. As seen in Table 7.1, this was the first spring break trip and the first trip to Daytona Beach for most students. Consistent with descriptions in the elicitation research, spring break in Daytona is a social event, with 82% of men and 88% of women accompanied by friends. However, this is not necessarily a vacation for couples: Forty-eight percent of the men and 68% of the women who were in relationships reported that their partners would not accompany them to Daytona.

Almost all who traveled to Daytona Beach had prior coital experience. The median number of prior coital partners was six for men and three for women. Fewer women than men intended to engage in casual sex on spring break. Women were less likely than men to form pacts or agreements with friends about casual sex; but when they did, women made agreements with friends *not* to engage in sex while in Daytona (15%), whereas men formed agreements to have sex (46%). In the elicitation interview, students described agreements among women to "pull your friend out of a situa-

TABLE 7.1. Percentage of Men and Women With Different Sexual and Spring Break Experiences and Intention

Variable	Male	Females
Prior Sexual Experience		
Previous coital experience	95%	92%
Ever coitus within 24 hrs. of meeting partner	65%++	34%
Spring Break Experience		
1st spring break trip	73%++	48%
1st Daytona Beach trip	73%	87%
Plan to Go With Friends	82%	88%
Plan to Go with Relationship Partner[a]	18%	12%
Pacts or Agreement Formed with Friends:		
Not to engage in casual sex	8%	15%
To engage in casual sex	46%+++	1%
Coital Intention for Spring Break		
Intend Coitus with relationship partner	18%	9%
Intend coitus with acquaintance	62%+++	25%
Intend coitus with someone met on Spring break	76%+++	19%
Do not intend to engage in coitus	8%+++	61%

Note. Sample comprised of 66 males and 85 females.
[a]48% of men and 68% of women are in a relationship and report their partners will not accompany them. [b]Someone the participant knew before coming on spring break but with whom the participant had not engaged in coitus. [c]Casual sex.
++ Difference between percentages significant at $p < .01$ (Chi-square test).
+++ Difference between percentages significant at $p < .001$ (Chi-square test).

tion" if it appeared she might become sexually involved; men described competitive pacts to see who could "get laid" the most. The gender pattern seen in Table 7.1 is replicated in the mean score, on the scalar measures of attitudes, norms, and expectations related to casual sex. Men's scores were higher than women's on each measure, indicating that men's attitudes and beliefs were more supportive of casual sex on spring break than were women's.

Intentions to engage in casual sex. The Pearson produced moment correlations between all variables used in the analysis ranged from .14 to .71. Those between intention and predictor variables were positive and ranged from .18 (attitudes with intentions) to .71 (situational expectation with intentions). Table 7.2 reports the results of the ordinary least squares regression of intention to engage in casual sex on centered predictors. Both the TIB (Model 1) and the enhanced TIB (Model 2) explained sizable portions of the variance in intentions ($R^2 = .70$ and .74 respectively). The enhanced TIB explained a significantly larger portion of the variance than the original TIB, $F(2.134) = 12.51, p < .001$. The strongest influence on men's intentions was their perceptions of the degree of endorsement they would receive from their friends for participation in casual sex while on spring break. Women, however, were not influenced by the perceived endorsement of others. For both men and women, all indicators except personal standards and role beliefs had a significant influence on the formation of intentions. Thus, it was the social norms using the peer group as the point of reference rather than those using the self that influenced intentions. The results of the interaction between pacts and situational expectations coincided with the comments students made during the elicitation phase. The positive effect of situational expectations was enhanced when there was a pact to engage in coitus with a new partner while on spring break. However, when there was a pact *not* to engage in coitus with a new partner, the association disappeared—the pact counteracted the anticipated environmental influence.

Study 2: Daytona Study

Methods

RECRUITMENT

One male and one female graduate student who had experience and training in research methods and who were in the age range of students on the spring break trip collected the data for the Daytona study during the 1996 spring break season. Three methods of recruitment were used: on-site at Daytona Beach, on buses returning home, and through the mail. On-site recruitment procedures were similar to those followed by Smeaton and Josiam (1996) in their study of spring break in Panama City Beach, Florida, and by Eiser and Ford (1995) in their study of a British beach resort. Participants were recruited on beaches and pool decks between 11 a.m. and 4 p.m. from Wednesday to Saturday of each of the two weeks when Canadian students were in Daytona. This timing ensured that participants had been in Daytona for at least 2 days before completing the questionnaire and that they were likely to be sober, as the heavi-

TABLE 7.2. Ordinary Least Squares Regression Coefficients for Intentions to Engage in Casual Sex on Centered Predictors

	Model 1: TIB			Model 2: Enhanced TIB		
Variable	*B*	*S.E.*	β	*B*	*S.E.*	β
Affective Component	0.12**	0.04	0.15	0.12**	0.04	0.15
Evaluative Component	0.18***	0.04	0.27	0.16***	0.04	0.25
Personal Standard	0.05	0.04	0.10	0.01	0.03	0.03
Role Belief	0.04	0.03	0.08	0.03	0.04	0.06
Subjective Social Norm: Women	0.05	0.04	0.06	0.02	0.04	0.02
Subjective Social Norm: Men	0.38***	0.05	0.45	0.27***	0.05	0.32
Pact[a]	0.39***	0.11	0.20	0.26**	0.11	0.14
Situational Expectation				0.13**	0.05	0.20
Pact x Situational Expectation[b]				0.21***	0.06	0.20
Constant	1.55	0.06		1.49	0.06	
R^2		.70		.74		

Notes. *N* = 151. All independent variables except *Pact* are centered around their mean.
[a]Effect coded −1 = pact not to engage in coitus: 0 = no pact: 1 = pact to engage in coitus.
[b]Interaction between pacts and situational expectations.
p* < .50. *p* < .001.

est alcohol consumption began in the late afternoon. Students were approached by the research assistants who explained the survey procedures and ethical guidelines and verified that potential participants were from Canada (all were from eastern Ontario). Those who agreed to participate were provided with a pencil and the questionnaire on a clipboard. Up to five questionnaires were distributed at one time. Research assistants ensured that each participant completed the questionnaire privately and out of the range of vision of others. Of the 494 students approached in this manner, 484 completed questionnaires, for a response rate of 98%. This closely matches Smeaton and Josiam's (1996) response rate of 99%.

In the second recruitment strategy, questionnaires were distributed to students for completion at the beginning of the return bus trip home. Research assistants explained the purpose and procedures of the study, and one person on the bus was delegated to collect and return completed surveys in a pre-addressed envelope. It was not possible to calculate a valid response rate: A number of students declined to complete a survey because they had already done so, but 119 questionnaires were completed in this manner.

In the final recruitment strategy, questionnaires were mailed to the 151 students who had completed prebreak surveys (all had agreed to receive a post-break survey) within one week of returning home. These students were provided with an addressed, stamped return envelope and a separate stamped, addressed postcard. All who did not return a postcard received up to three phone reminders. Seventy-eight participants returned these questionnaires, for a response rate of 52%.

Participants' birthdates and university student numbers were used to match questionnaires and to eliminate duplicates. Three duplicates were found. In each case, the questionnaire completed after the longest time in Daytona was retained.

COMPARISON OF SURVEYS FROM DIFFERENT RECRUITMENT STRATEGIES

Responses on questionnaires using the three recruitment strategies were compared on 60 items, controlling for gender and duration of time in Daytona. Of the 60 comparisons, 3 were significant at $p < .05$. This number of significant comparisons would be expected by chance at this level of significance. Based on these results, the three sampling strategies were judged to produce similar results, and data were combined for the Daytona analyses.

QUESTIONNAIRE DEVELOPMENT AND MEASUREMENT OF CONSTRUCTS

The Daytona survey contained questions on sexual and spring break history and activities and experiences while in Daytona Beach. It could be completed in 10 minutes. Questions for this survey were developed using the same procedures described for the prebreak survey. Where questions addressed the same concepts in both surveys, wording was modified to accommodate the different time frame. Several constructs were unique to the Daytona survey: the spring break experience, prior casual sex experience, role modeling, and engaging in casual sex.

First, the degree of participation in spring break experiences conducive to casual sex was measured using mean scores of participants' ratings (on a 4-point scale ranging from *never* to *frequently*) of how often they participated in each of the ten experiences listed in the prebreak questionnaire as situational expectations. Cronbach's alpha was 0.82.

In the TIB, prior experience is measured as the number of times an individual has already engaged in the behavior of interest. Because few students had ever been to Daytona Beach for spring break vacation before this trip, the use of experiences specific to this environment was judged unfeasible. As an alternate indicator of similar prior experience, we examined whether an individual had ever engaged in coitus with someone they had known for less than 24 hours. This was scored dichotomously (0 = no, 1 = yes).

Participant reports of the proportion of friends who had participated in coitus while on spring break (0 = none: 1 = few: 2 = about half: 3 = most) were used as a measure of perceived role modeling of coital activity.

To measure the criterion variable we asked participants whether they engaged in coitus while on spring break and what their relationship was to the partner. For purposes of this analysis, a *casual sex* variable was created that was coded 0 if the respondent had not engaged in coitus while on spring break ($N = 499$) and 1 if the respondent had engaged in coitus with someone they met while on spring break ($N = 94$).

Data Analysis. The tests for equivalence of men's and women's covariance matrices and the collinearity diagnostics conducted for the prebreak analysis were replicated for the Daytona sample. Although men's and women's covariance matrices were not significantly different for the original TIB constructs, they were significantly different when the two peer influence variables were added. Consequently, separate regression analyses were conducted for each gender. No multicollinearity was identified, and there were no interaction terms in these regression models. Therefore, variables were not centered.

The models for coitus with someone who was met on spring break were tested separately for men and women using hierarchical logistic regressions with forced entry of blocks of variables. The predictor variables in Triandis's original model were included in the first model. Two variables were added in the second: proportion of friends who had engaged in coitus on spring break and the form of agreement or pact struck with friends about casual sex on spring break.

Result

SAMPLE PROFILE

Participants were 306 males and 375 females from six universities in Ontario, Canada. They ranged in age from 18 to 30 years with 69% clustering between ages 21 and 23. All participants were White and identified themselves as heterosexual and single. Twenty-eight percent of men and 35% of women reported that they were in a long-term relationship.

Spring break experiences. Table 7.3 reports responses to questions about sexual history and spring break intentions and experience. The gender differences identified in the prebreak sample were replicated here. Consistent with these differences, men reported participating in significantly more spring break activities condusive to casual

TABLE 7.3. Percentage of Men and Women Reporting Sexual and Spring Break Experience and Intentions

Variable	Male	Females
Prior Sexual Experience		
Previous coital experience	91%	87%
Ever coitus within 24 hrs. of meeting partner	61%+++	34%
Pact or Agreements Formed with Friends		
Not to engage in casual sex	5%+++	21%
To engage in casual sex	30%+++	5%
Intend to Engage in Casual Sex	55%+++	11%
Coital Activity on Spring Break		
Coitus with relationship partner	7%	8%
Coitus with acquaintance[a]	6%	4%
Coitus with someone met on spring break[b]	15%	13%
No coital activity	72%	77%

Note. Sample comprises 306 males and 375 females.
[a]Someone the participant knew before coming on spring break but with whom the participant had not engaged in coitus.
[b]Casual sex.
+++Difference between percentages significant at $p < .001$ (Chi-square test).

sex ($M = 2.96$, $SD = 0.58$) than did women ($M = 2.79$, $SD = 0.57$; $p < .05$), and a significantly larger percentage of men's friends engaged in coitus on spring break ($M = 0.22$, $SD = 0.24$) than did women's friends ($M = 0.12$, $SD = 0.21$; $p < .001$). However, there were no significant differences in the coital activity that men and women reported on spring break. Seventy-four percent of students did not engage in coitus during the spring break trip. Those whose relationship partners accompanied them restricted coital activity to these partners. Most others engaged in casual sex.

Fewer men engaged in coital activity with new partners than intended to (55% of the men in this sample intended to engage in coital activity, but only 15% did). For women, however, there was almost no difference in the percentages who intended and who engaged in coitus with a new partner. For those who engaged in coitus with a new partner, there was no significant gender difference in the number of partners. During spring break, 68% had one partner, 13% two partners, and 19% had more than two partners.

Explaining participation in casual sex. When considered separately (Table 7.4), intentions to engage in casual sex, prior casual sex experience, participation in spring break activities, the proportion of friends who engaged in coitus while on spring break, and the formation of pacts about casual sex with friends were significantly different for those who engaged and did not engage in casual sex while on spring break. Having a relationship partner at home did not necessarily impede engaging in casual sex on spring break.

Table 7.5 reports hierarchical logistic regressions of the dichotomous measure of participation in casual sex first on the variables in the TIB, and then with the addition of two measures of peer influence. Regressions were conducted separately for women and men. In the first regression, using variables from the TIB, results were similar for men and women. Intentions and spring break experience significantly differentiated between those who engaged and did not engage in casual sex, with spring break experiences the stronger of the two predictors. The absence of a significant effect for prior casual sex experience could be related to the measurement of this construct. Because of the novelty of the Daytona Beach experience for the majority of students, prior experience was measured using any casual sex experience rather than the more specific measure of casual sex on spring break recommended by Triandis.

Results of the second regression were different for men and women. For men, the addition of two measures of peer influence did not improve the predictive power of the model, as seen in the absence of a significant increase in the improvement in chi-square or in the percentage of cases that were correctly classified. Intentions and prior casual sex experience remained the significant predictors of engaging in casual sex. For women, however, there was a significant improvement in the predictive power of the model. The two peer influences, perceived role modeling and pacts, were the significant factors in classifying students correctly. Although the frequency of participation in spring break experiences conducive to forming new coital partnerships had the strongest effect in Model 1, it was just below statistical significance ($p = .06$) in Model 2. In Model 2, the proportion of

TABLE 7.4. Percentages and Mean Scores on Selected Predictor Variables, by Casual Sex Activity

	Coital Activitv on Spring Break	
Variable	No Coital Activity	Casual Sex
Women		
Intend to engage in casual sex	8%+++	31%
Prior casual sex experience	23%+++	55%
Spring break activities	2.75***	3.28
Proportion of friends engaged in coitus		
Pacts formed with friends	0.07***	0.38
No casual sex	24%+++	8%
Casual sex	2%+++	19%
Currently in a relationship[a]	31%	26%
Men		
Intend to engage in casual sex	50%+++	88%
Prior casual sex experience	51%+	71%
Spring break activities	2.93***	3.41
Proportion of friends engaged in coitus	0.19***	0.38
Pacts formed with friends		
No casual sex	2%++	7%
Casual Sex	27%++	48%
Currently in a relationship[a]	26%	18%

Notes. This table excludes data for students who engaged in coitus with someone they knew. Sample comprises 268 women and 205 men who did not engage in coital activity, and 48 women and 46 men who engaged in casual sex.

[a]None of these relationship partners were in Daytona Beach. ***p < .001 (t-test). +$p < .05$ (Chi-square test). ++$p < .01$ (Chi-square test). +++$p < .001$ (Chi-square test).

TABLE 7.5. Hierarchical Logistic Regression Coefficients for Casual Sex[a] on Predictors From Two Models, Women and Men Regressed Separately

	Model 1: TIB			Model 2: Enhanced TIB		
Variable	Odds (Antilog)	Log Odds	Partial Correlation	Odds (Antilog)	Log Odds	Partial Correlation
Women						
Prior experience[b]	1.85	0.62	0.03	1.40	0.34	0.00
Intentions[c]	2.94	1.08*	0.11	2.41	0.88	0.00
Spring break experience	5.57	1.72***	0.25	2.81	1.03	0.09
Role model[d]				3.59	1.28***	0.28
Pact[e]				11.92	2.48**	0.16
Constant		-7.30			-5.79	
Men						
Prior experience[b]	0.74	-0.30	0.00	0.806	-.23	0.00
Intentions[c]	3.68	1.30**	0.14	4.83	1.58**	0.15
Spring break experience	6.14	1.82***	0.24	12.27	2.51***	0.28
Role model[d]				1.22	0.20	0.00
Pact[e]				0.51	-0.67	0.00
Constant		-8.04			-10.49	

Notes. N = 306 women; N = 251 men. All coefficients are maximum-likelihood estimates. Models 1 and 2 both correctly classified 80% of the cases. For women, 1 over baseline. Chi-square improvement was 38.236 ($df = 3$; $p < .01$): and for 2 over 1, Chi-square improvement was 35.747 ($df = 2$; $p < .01$). For men, 1 over baseline, Chi-square improvement was 33.300 ($df = 3$; $p < .01$), and for 2 over 1, Chi-square improvement was 5.441 ($df = 2$; $p = 06$).

[a]0 = no coital activity: 1 = coitus with a partner met on spring break. [b]0 = no prior casual sex experience; 1 = prior casual sex experience; [c]0 = no intension to engage in casual sex on spring break; 1 = intend to engage in casual sex on spring break. [d]Measured as proportion of friends who engaged in coitus on spring break. [e]1 = pact to engage in casual sex; 0 = no pact; -1 = pact not to engage in casual sex.

*$p < .05$. **$p < .01$. ***$p < .001$.

friends engaging in sex had the strongest effect on whether women engaged in casual sex.

Discussion

In their review of research on premarital sexual decision-making Christopher and Roosa (1991) noted that the contexts and settings in which coital partnerships are formed have received little research attention. The research reported in this paper focused on the North American spring break vacation and its influence on a young adult to engage in casual sex. It built on the review of characteristics of vacations that contribute to engaging in sex by Herold and van Kerkwijk (1992), and on the research on "vacation sex" conducted by Eiser and Ford (1995) and Smeaton and Josiam (1996). In this study, 21% of men and 17% of women reported engaging in coitus with a new partner, 15% and 13%, respectively, with someone they met on spring break.

Three factors stand out about these percentages. First, there is greater similarity in the percentages of men and women who engaged in casual sex than would be expected considering the degree of dissimilarity between men and women on all other variables examined in this research. On variables used to predict either the formation of intentions or engaging in casual sex, men's scores clustered in the direction of acceptance, endorsement, and expectation of situations conducive to casual sex; women's clustered in the opposite direction. This finding is consistent with previous research (for reviews, see Christopher & Roosa, 1991; Oliver & Hyde, 1993). Despite this clustering, casual sex did not occur for most men. This suggests that women's attitudes, norms, expectations, and intentions, which were less supportive of engaging in casual sex, determined whether coitus occurred, consistent with the traditional image of women as "gatekeepers" (Herold, 1984).

The second factor of interest is that the percentages reporting coital activity with a new partner were similar to the British beach resort vacationers in Eiser and Ford's (1995) study (22% for men and 20% for women). However, the percentages for women in our study and in the British study were considerably higher than that reported by Smeaton and Josiam (1996) in their Panama City Beach spring break study where only 4% of women reported sex with a new partner. In our study and the British study, data were collected by male and female research assistants who were close in age to the vacationers, whereas Smeaton and Josiam's data were collected by two male professors. Our procedure may have produced greater comfort and honesty among the female participants, resulting in greater consistency in women's and men's reports.

The third factor to note is that the percentage of men and women reporting casual sex on spring break was considerably lower than the percentage of students reporting prior casual sex. Thus, although spring break is a vacation conducive to new coital partnerships for some, most students on spring break did not participate in coitus.

Since Reiss's (1967) work on personal standards for sexual behavior, consideration of the relationship between standards and behavior has had a prominent place in sexuality research. In this research it was personal *attitudes* rather than personal *standards* (as differentiated by Triandis) that influenced casual sex, with attitudes influencing intentions to engage in casual sex. Personal standards and role beliefs—that is, the variables that measured social norms as expressed in personal moral codes or standards—did *not* have a significant influence on intentions or expectations about casual sex. These results contrast with those of other studies using the Triandis model in which personal standards or role beliefs were found to have an effect that was stronger than that of attitudes (Boyd & Wandersman, 1991; Godin et al., 1996). This highlights a characteristic of the spring break environment and the behavior under consideration that was more fully described by students in the elicitation phase: Activities on spring break, including coitus, were described as exceptions to the everyday experience—as outside of usual expectations, standards, or norms. Students used phrases such as "what happens in Daytona, stays in Daytona," "nothing that happens there comes home," and "nothing counts." They portrayed an atmosphere in which the usual rules and moral codes did not apply. Students provided detailed descriptions of how some had behaved "totally out of character" or in ways that "they never would at home." These illustrations and the results of the statistical analysis support the picture of spring break as an environment in which personal codes are temporarily suspended.

Although personal codes did not influence spring break coital behaviors, perceptions of peer expectations and promises or pacts made with peers did. This also conformed to the image of spring break described in the elicitation phase of the research: Friends travel and "hang" together in Daytona Beach. In statistical analyses, peers had a significant influence on both the formation of intentions to engage in casual sex and in casual sex activity when in Daytona Beach. However, peer group influence took different forms for men and women. For men, peer influence operated through pacts formed with friends about casual sex and perceptions of friends' approval or disapproval of casual sex. In both cases this influence was the formation of intentions to engage in casual sex. Peer influences did not have a direct effect on engaging in casual sex. For women, peer influence operated through the formation of pacts between friends about casual sex and through role modeling (i.e., the percentage of friends on spring break who participated in coitus). Pacts influenced intensions and, along with the percentage of friends who engaged in coitus on spring break, had a direct effect on engaging in casual sex in the Daytona sample. Thus, men's *intentions* were more strongly influenced by the effect of peers than were women's. However, peers had an additional direct influence on women's coital *activity* on spring break. A common finding in other studies is that peers had a stronger influence on men than on women (for a review, see Christopher and Roosa, 1991), though some have found that the influence is experienced equally by men and women (e.g. Winslow et al., 1992). However, in past research only one form of peer influence is tested, the effect of different forms of peer influence found in this study leads us to concur with Wilcox and Udry's (1986) suggestion that it is important to examine more fully the different types of peer influence in future work.

The activities and experiences that students considered conducive to casual sex paralleled those identified by Herold & van Kerkwijk (1992): a perpetual party atmosphere, high rates of alcohol consumption, sexual contests, dancing dirty, frequent attempts made to "pick up" a sexual partner, and being in a break-loose mood. Along with positive attitudes toward casual sex while on spring break and perceived peer support for casual sex, anticipation of a spring break experience led to the formation of intentions or expectations of engaging in casual sex. Once in Daytona Beach, participation in casual sex depended not only on prior intentions but also on the degree of participation in spring break activities. For women, however, peer influences in Daytona Beach were more important in determining casual sex activity than were intentions or participation in spring break activities. For men, the greater consistency in the importance of the spring break environment on both expectations of casual sex and casual activity suggests that they are more susceptible to influences from the external environment and potentially are more likely to interpret the environment as providing sexual cues.

There are limitations to the generalizability of the results of this research. First, because of the voluntary nature of the samples and the restriction to one research it is difficult to know whether the results can be generalized to other vacations. The high response rate for recruitment at Daytona Beach, the consistency in results across the different sampling designs in the Daytona study, the similarity in the reports of prior sexual activity with reports obtained in Canadian studies using national probability samples (Maticka-Tyndale, 1997), and the similarities of our results to those of other studies of vacation sex in other locations (Eiser & Ford, 1995; Herold & van Kerkwijk, 1992; Smeaton & Josiam, 1996), support confidence in the findings. However, the generalizability of findings of a study of this nature must always be treated with caution until more research, ideally with improved sampling strategies, has been conducted.

A second limitation is the absence of a longitudinal design to test the full Triandis model. Initially, one of our goals was to obtain such a sample. However, because of the last-minute nature of spring break holidays and the intense academic schedule of midterm exams during the weeks just before spring break it was difficult to recruit a sufficient number of participants before spring break. Although the lack of a significant difference between the responses of students recruited in Daytona and those recruited before spring break gave us confidence that results in both studies were reflective of the same population, a full test of the Triandis model awaits a longitudinal sample.

Some researchers may feel that the absence of standardized measures of constructs introduced an additional limitation to the generalizability of our results. Triandis's theory stresses the importance of measurements specific to the time, place, event, and population, and provides a methodology for creating and testing such measures. We followed these recommendations for creating measures and testing their reliability and validity. However, Triandis's rejection of standardized scales for their lack of specificity to the topic of study may be viewed with skepticism by some researchers. Whether one sees the types of measures used in this study as enhancing or limiting the quality of the results depends on whether the measures are considered a strength or a weakness of the design.

These limitations point to two methodological directions for future work. The first is the exploration of more representative sampling designs either for studies of contexts such as vacations or for sampling diverse contexts and comparing them for their influence on different forms of sexual partnering. Second, an empirical comparison of Triandis's measurement model to the use of standardized scales could help resolve some of the questions raised about potential limitations of Triandis's approach.

The areas of gender difference and similarity also suggest areas for future inquiry. The gender differences in all but coital activity on spring break remind us that coitus occurs between partners. A full understanding of how sexual activity and partnerships occur requires future research at the level of the couple. In addition, further inquiry is necessary to understand the variations in peer influence on men and women.

The sexual activity on spring break was described by students as a temporary, rapidly progressing partnership. This raises questions about how different forms of sexual partnerships are formed, what meaning they hold, and how they fit within the overall sexual scripts of young adults. Further investigation of environments conducive to rapid and casual sexual encounters, the specific characteristics of these environments that encourage sexual partnering, and the differences between those who are influenced and those who resist the influence of the environment is another area of inquiry suggested by this research.

Finally, the TIB provided a powerful multivariate model that integrated personal, social, and situational factors in explaining sexual planning and activity. This suggests that this model could be helpful in more fully explaining sexual partnering in other contexts.

REFERENCES

Aiken, L. S., & West, S. G. (1991). *Multiple regression: Testing and interpreting interactions.* Newbury Park, CA: Sage Publications.

Ajzen, I. (1985). From intentions to actions: A theory of planned behavior. In J. Kuhl and J. Beckmann (Eds.), *Action-control: From cognition to behavior* (pp. 11–39). Heidelberg, Germany: Springer.

Ajzen, I. (1991). The theory of planned behavior. *Organizational Behavior and Human Decision Processes, 50,* 179–211.

Ajzen, I., & Fishbein, M. (1980). *Understanding attitudes and predicting social behavior.* Englewood Cliffs, NJ: Prentice-Hall.

Boyd, B., & Wandersman, A. (1991). Predicting undergraduate condom use with the Fishbein and Ajzen and the Triandis attitude-behavior models: Implications for public health interventions. *Journal of Applied Social Psychology, 21,* 1810–1830.

Christopher, F. S., & Cate, R. M. (1984) Factors involved in premarital sexual decision-making. *The Journal of Sex Research, 25,* 255–266.

Christopher, F. S., & Roosa, M. W. (1991). Factors affecting sexual decisions in the premarital relationships of adolescents and young adults. In K. McKinney & S. Sprecher (Eds.), *Sexuality in close relationships* (pp. 111–134). Hillsdale, NJ: Erlbaum.

D'Augelli, J. F., & D'Augelli, A. R. (1977). Moral reasoning and premarital sexual behavior: Toward reasoning about relationships. *Journal of Social Issues, 33,* 46–66.

Eiser, J. R., & Ford, N. (1995). Sexual relationships on holiday: A case of situational disinhibition? *Journal of Social and Personal Relationships, 12,* 323–339.

Fishbein, M., & Jaccard, J. (1973). Theoretical and methodological considerations in the prediction of family planning intentions and behavior. *Representative Research in Social Psychology, 4,* 37–51.

Godin, G., Maticka-Tyndale, E., Adrien, A., Manson-Singer, S., Willms, D., & Cappon, P. (1996). Cross-cultural testing of three social cognitive theories: An application to condom use. *Journal of Applied Social Psychology, 26,* 1556–1586.

Herold, E. S. (1984). *Sexual behavior of Canadian young people.* Toronto: Fitzhenry & Whiteside.

Herold, E. S., & van Kerkwijk, C. (1992). AIDS and sex tourism. *AIDS and Society,* 4, 1–8.

Joreskog, K. G., & Sorbom, D. (1986). *LISREL: Analysis of linear structural relationships by the method of maximum likelihood. Version VI.* Mooresville, IN: Scientific Software.

Jorgensen, S. R., & Sonstegard, J. (1984). Predicting adolescent sexual and contraceptive behavior: An application and test of the Fishbein model. *Journal of Marriage and the Family, 46,* 43–55.

Josiam, B., Clements, J. S., & Hobson, P. (1995). *Spring break student travel: A longitudinal study.* Unpublished manuscript.

Maticka-Tyndale, E. (1997). Reducing the incidence of sexually transmitted disease through behavioral and social change. *The Canadian Journal of Human Sexuality, 6,* 89–104.

Mewhinney, D. M., Herold, E. S., & Maticka-Tyndale, E. (1995). Sexual scripts and risk-taking of Canadian university students on spring break in Daytona Beach, Florida. *The Canadian Journal of Human Sexuality, 4,* 273–288.

Oliver, M. B., & Hyde, J. S. (1993). Gender differences in sexuality: A meta-analysis. *Psychological Bulletin, 114,* 29–51.

Randall, D. M., & Wolff, J. A. (1994). The time interval in the intentionbehavior relationship: Meta-analysis. *British Journal of Social Psychology, 33,* 405–418.

Reiss, I. L. (1967). *The social context of premarital sexual permissiveness.* New York: Holt, Rinehart, & Winston.

Rook, K. S., & Hammen, C. L. (1977). A cognitive perspective on the experience of sexual arousal. *Journal of Social Issues, 33,* 7–29.

Smeaton, G., & Josiam, B. (1996). *Sex, drugs and alcohol on the beach. "Where the boys are in the age of AIDS."* Paper presented at the meeting of the Society for the Scientific Study of Sex, Houston, TX.

Smith, K. W., & Sasaki, M. S. (1979). Decreasing multicollinearitv: A method for models with multiplicative functions. *Sociological Methods and Research, 8,* 35–56.

Triandis, H. C. (1977). *Interpersonal behavior.* Monterey, CA: Brooks/Cole.

Triandis, H. C. (1980). Values, attitudes, and interpersonal behavior: In H. Howe & M. Page (Eds.), *Nebraska Symposium on Motivation 1979* (pp. 195–295). Lincoln, NE: University of Nebraska Press.

Triandis, H. C. (1994). *Culture and social behavior.* New York: McGraw-Hill Inc.

White, K. M., Terry, D. J., & Hogg, M. A. (1994). Safer sex behavior: The role of attitudes, norms, and control factors. *Journal of Applied Social Psychology, 24,* 2164–2192.

Wilcox, S. & Dury, W. (1986). Autism and accuracy in adolescent perceptions of friends' sexual attitudes and behaviors. *Journal of Applied Social Psychology, 16,* 361–374.

Winslow, R. W., Franzini, L. R., & Hwang, J. (1992). Perceived peer norms, casual sex and AIDS risk prevention. *Journal of Applied Social Psychology, 22,* 1809–1827.

INTRODUCTION TO PART 5

Homosexuality and Homophobia

In recent decades there has been a movement to integrate our understanding of homosexuality with the broader understanding of sexuality. In many respects, homosexuals confront the same problems as heterosexuals; finding a partner, deciding whether and when to have sex, infidelity, disease, sustaining passion. On the other hand, homosexuals face certain problems that heterosexuals do not, such as a tendency to feel attracted to someone whose sexual orientation excludes you, broad societal condemnation of one's sexual feelings, and the "double rejection" aspect of infidelity: If your homosexual partner is unfaithful to you, that person might in principle have chosen you instead of your lover, and so in a sense both of them have rejected you.

The very phenomenon of homosexuality raises an important challenge to sexuality theory, however. As already discussed, theory of sexuality tends to fall into two camps, one of which emphasizes innate predispositions and evolutionary processes, and the other pointing to socialization and cultural influences. Neither approach has an easy time explaining homosexuality. Homosexual intercourse does not lead to reproduction, and so it is difficult to explain why homosexuality would have evolved and survived across countless generations. Meanwhile, social and cultural pressures have generally been firmly opposed to homosexual activity (with some notable exceptions), and yet again the practice survives despite steady and sometimes brutal efforts by societies to suppress it.

The data that have gradually come forward with regard to homosexuality have not been helpful at providing a speedy resolution to the issue. Early excitement over a possible "gay gene" that would dictate homosexual orientation has dissipated as follow-up studies have not confirmed the initial findings, although most evidence does point toward some degree of genetic influence (see Bailey & Pillard, 1995, for review). Moreover, there seems ample evidence of some genetic contribution to homosexuality, such as in the finding that when one twin is homosexual, the other twin has a higher-than-average likelihood of being homosexual too. Then again, even though identical twins have identical genes, they are not uniformly identical in sexual orientation too, and if two people with identical genes can develop different sexual preferences, then something other than genes must be at work. The biological data are thus less than conclusive—but so is the evidence for cultural and socialization theories. As Bem's (1996) review makes clear, several large and ambitious projects have offered no support for some of the leading theories about homosexuality, such as that a domineering mother and remote father can cause a son to become gay.

The first article in this section offers a bold new theoretical approach to explaining why people become homosexuals. Bem (1996) accepts the failure of both the simple genetic theories and the complex socialization theories, and he proposes a novel solution. He says that genes do not prescribe sexual orientation, but they do help determine temperament, and because of temperament some children will find the opposite sex to be more appealing as playmates than their own gender. For these children, their own gender will therefore be relatively unfamiliar and "exotic"—and so at puberty, when sexual feelings begin to emerge, these will become focused on one's own gender rather than the other sex. The arousal that comes from interacting with different, "exotic" other people will become sexual interest.

Bem offers an assortment of evidence to back up his theory. Some crucial aspects of it remain largely untested, though, and so at present it is best to regard his theory as a promising, intriguing possibility rather than as a proven fact. His work has been criticized by various sources, including Peplau et al. (1998) who accused him, among other things, of having offered a sex-biased theory that explains male homosexuality better than female, a characterization that Bem himself has rejected and refuted (Bem, 1998). Undoubtedly the coming decades will bring significant further advances in the understanding of homosexuality, and it will be interesting to see whether Bem's theory turns out to be largely correct or shares the dismal fate of so many previous theories about homosexuality.

The second article in this section is concerned with anti-gay prejudice. Researchers who are interested in prejudice have been known to remark informally that anti-gay prejudice is far stronger, more blatant, and more bitter than most other forms of prejudice, even among liberal university students. This prejudice often takes a dark and ugly form, and the many hate crimes that have been perpetrated against homosexuals indicate the depth of hostility with which many people regard this unfortunate class of human beings.

Psychoanalytic theory, whose roots go back to Sigmund Freud's thinking, has proposed an intriguing theory about prejudice (see West, 1977). The central point is that people hate most in others what they loathe and fear most in themselves. According to that view, people who most stridently oppose homosexuality are actually struggling with their own inner feelings that may have a strong component of homosexual desire. The anti-gay prejudice is thus a defense mechanism by which people try to deny their own homosexual feelings.

Although many of Freud's more complex and subtle

ideas have fared badly in laboratory tests, the study by Adams, Wright, and Lohr (1996) does seem consistent with Freud's theory about homosexuality. In the crucial part of their research, they showed homosexual pornography to heterosexual men. The men with the strongest anti-gay feelings said they did not find that form of erotica exciting, but direct measurements of their penises showed that they did become aroused.

REFERENCES

Adams, H. E., Wright, L. W., & Lohr, B. A. (1996). Is homophobia associated with homosexual arousal? *Journal of Abnormal Psychology, 105,* 440–445.

Bailey, J. M., & Pillard, R. C. (1995). Genetics of human sexual orientation. *Annual Review of Sex Research, 6,* 126–150.

Bem, D. J. (1996). Exotic becomes erotic: A developmental theory of sexual orientation. *Psychological Review, 103,* 320–335.

Bem, D. J. (1998). Is EBE theory supported by evidence? Is it androcentric? A reply to Peplau et al. (1998). *Psychological Review, 105,* 395–398.

Peplau, L., Garnets, L., Spalding, L., Conley, T., & Veniegas, R. (1998). A critique of Bem's "exotic becomes erotic" theory of sexual orientation. *Psychological Review, 105,* 387–394.

West, D. J. (1977). *Homosexuality re-examined.* Minneapolis: University of Minnesota Press.

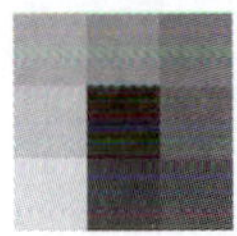

Discussion Questions

1. Do you think that homosexual activity is higher or lower in single-gender boarding schools than at coeducational schools? What would Bem's theory say?
2. In recent decades, men and women have become more similar to each other and the separate spheres that kept the genders apart have broken down their walls. According to Bem's theory, what effects are likely to follow from these changes?
3. If it could be proven that homosexuality were directly caused by a genetic pattern, would this make people more or less likely to tolerate homosexuals?
4. How does anti-gay prejudice make it more difficult for homosexuals to form and maintain long-term loving relationships?
5. The study by Adams et al. was done with males only. Do you think a study of females would yield comparable results? How might the women be different?
6. Both Bem's theory and the Adams et al. paper are based on people becoming aroused in response to people who are different. Why does that arousal lead to love under some circumstances and hate in others?

Suggested Readings

Bailey, J. M., & Pillard, R. C. (1995). Genetics of human sexual orientation. *Annual Review of Sex Research, 6,* 126–150. An authoritative overview of research on genetic contributions to homosexual orientation.

Bell, A. P., & Weinberg, M. S. (1978). *Homosexualities: A study of diversity among men and women.* New York: Simon & Schuster. This was a classic, influential study of homosexual behavior during the 1970s.

Peplau, L., Garnets, L., Spalding, L., Conley, T., & Veniegas, R. (1998). A critique of Bem's "exotic becomes erotic" theory of sexual orientation. *Psychological Review, 105,* 387–394. AND Bem, D. J. (1998), Is EBE theory supported by evidence? Is it androcentric? A reply to Peplau et al. (1998). *Psychological Review, 105,* 395–398. This pair of articles debated the merits of Bem's theory.

Savin-Williams, R. C. (1990). *Gay and lesbian youth: Expressions of identity*. New York: Hemisphere. This is an excellent overview of the field by one of its leading scholars.

READING 8

Exotic Becomes Erotic: A Developmental Theory of Sexual Orientation

Daryl J. Bem • Cornell University

A developmental theory of erotic/romantic attraction is presented that provides the same basic account for opposite-sex and same-sex desire in both men and women. It proposes that biological variables, such as genes, prenatal hormones, and brain neuroanatomy, do not code for sexual orientation per se but for childhood temperaments that influence a child's preferences for sex-typical or sex-atypical activities and peers. These preferences lead children to feel different from opposite or same-sex peers—to perceive them as dissimilar, unfamiliar and exotic. This, in turn, produces heightened nonspecific autonomic arousal that subsequently gets eroticized to that same class of dissimilar peers: Exotic becomes erotic. Specific mechanisms for effecting this transformation are proposed. The theory claims to accommodate both the empirical evidence of the biological essentialists and the cultural relativism of the social constructionists.

The question "What causes homosexuality?" is both politically suspect and scientifically misconceived. Politically suspect because it is so frequently motivated by an agenda of prevention and cure. Scientifically misconceived because it presumes that heterosexuality is so well understood, so obviously the "natural" evolutionary consequence of reproductive advantage, that only deviations from it are theoretically problematic. Freud himself did not so presume: "[Heterosexuality] is also a problem that needs elucidation and is not a self-evident fact based upon an attraction that is ultimately of a chemical nature" (Freud, 1905/1962, pp. 11–12).

Accordingly, this article proposes a developmental theory of erotic/romantic attraction that provides the same basic account for both opposite-sex and same-sex desire—and for both men and women. In addition to finding such parsimony politically, scientifically, and aesthetically satisfying, I believe that it can also be sustained by the evidence.

The academic discourse on sexual orientation is currently dominated by the biological essentialists—who can point to a corpus of evidence linking sexual orientation to genes, prenatal hormones, and brain neuroanatomy—and the social constructionists—who can point to a corpus of historical and anthropological evidence showing that the very concept of sexual orientation is a culture-bound notion (De Cecco & Elia, 1993). The personality, clinical, and developmental theorists who once dominated the discourse on this topic have fallen conspicuously silent. Some have probably become closet converts to biology because they cannot point to a coherent corpus of evidence that supports an experience-based account of sexual orientation. This would be understandable; experience-based theories have not fared well empirically in recent years.

The most telling data come from an intensive, large-scale interview study conducted in the San Francisco Bay area by the Kinsey Institute for Sex Research (Bell, Weinberg, & Hammersmith, 1981a). Using path analysis to test several developmental hypotheses, the investigators compared approximately 1,000 gay men and lesbians with 500 heterosexual men and women. The study (hereinafter, the San Francisco study) yielded virtually no support for current experience-based accounts of sexual orientation. With respect to the classical psychoanalytic account, for example,

> our findings indicate that boys who grow up with dominant mothers and weak fathers have nearly the same chances of becoming homosexual as they would if they grew up in "ideal" family settings. Similarly, the idea that homosexuality reflects a failure to resolve boys' "Oedipal" feelings during childhood receives no support from our study. Our data indicate that the connection between boys' relationships with their mothers and whether they become homosexual or heterosexual is hardly worth mentioning. . . . [Similarly] we found no evidence that prehomosexual girls are "Oedipal victors"—having apparently usurped their mothers' place in the fathers' affections. . . . [Finally] respondents' identification with their opposite-sex parents while they were growing up appears to have had no significant impact on whether they turned out to be homosexual or heterosexual. (pp. 184, 189)

More generally, no family variables were strongly implicated in the development of sexual orientation for either men or women.[1]

The data also failed to support any of several possible accounts based on mechanisms of learning or conditioning, including the popular layperson's "seduction" theory of homosexuality. In particular, the kinds of sexual encounters that would presumably serve as the basis for such learning or conditioning typically occurred after, rather than before, the individual experienced the relevant sexual feelings. Gay men and lesbians, for example had typically not participated in any "advanced" sexual activities with persons of the same sex until about three years after they had become aware of same-sex attractions. Moreover, they neither lacked opposite-sex sexual experiences during their childhood and adolescent years nor found them unpleasant.

And finally, there was no support for "labeling" theory, which suggests that individuals might adopt a homosexual orientation as a consequence of being labeled homosexual or sexually different by others as they were growing up. Although gay men and lesbians were, in fact, more likely to report that they had been so labeled, the path analysis revealed the differential labeling to be the result of an emerging homosexual orientation rather than a cause of or even a secondary contributor to it.

But before we all become geneticists, biopsychologists, or neuroanatomists, I believe it's worth another try. In particular, I believe that the theoretical and empirical building blocks for a coherent, experience-based developmental theory of sexual orientation are already scattered about in the literature. What follows then, is an exercise in synthesis and construction—followed, in turn, by analysis and deconstruction.

Overview of the Theory

The theory proposed here claims to specify the causal antecedents of an individual's erotic or romantic attractions to opposite-sex and same-sex persons. In particular, Figure 8.1 displays the proposed temporal sequence of events that leads to sexual orientation for most men and women in a gender-polarizing culture like ours—a culture that emphasizes the differences between the sexes by pervasively organizing both the perceptions and realities of communal life around the male-female dichotomy (Bem, 1993). The sequence begins at the top of the figure with biological variables (labeled A) and ends at the bottom with erotic/ romantic attraction (F).

A → B. Biological variables such as genes or prenatal hormones do not code for sexual orientation per se but for childhood temperaments, such as aggression or activity level.

B → C. A child's temperaments predispose him or her to enjoy some activities more than others. One child will enjoy rough-and-tumble play and competitive team sports (male-typical activities); another will prefer to socialize quietly or play jacks or hopscotch (female-typical activities). Children

[1]This finding is consistent with accumulating evidence that family variables account for much less of the environmental variance in personality than previously thought. Harris (1995) has proposed that a significant portion of the variance in personality development is accounted for by peer-related variables, which is where the theory proposed in this article locates the source of sexual orientation.

will also prefer to play with peers who share their activity preferences; for example, the child who enjoys baseball or football will selectively seek out boys as playmates. Children who prefer sex-typical activities and same-sex playmates are referred to as gender conforming; children who prefer sex-atypical activities and opposite-sex playmates are referred to as gender nonconforming.

C → D. Gender-conforming children will feel different from opposite-sex peers, perceiving them as dissimilar, unfamiliar, and exotic. Similarly, gender-nonconforming children will feel different—even alienated—from same-sex peers, perceiving them as dissimilar, unfamiliar, and exotic.

D → E. These feelings of dissimilarity and unfamiliarity produce heightened autonomic arousal. For the male-typical child, it may be felt as antipathy or contempt in the presence of girls ("girls are yucky"); for the female-typical child, it may be felt as timidity or apprehension in the presence of boys. A particularly clear example is provided by the "sissy" boy who is taunted by male peers for his gender nonconformity and, as a result, is likely to experience the strong autonomic arousal of fear and anger in their presence. Although girls are punished less than boys for gender nonconformity, a "tomboy" girl who is ostracized by her female peers may feel similar, affectively toned arousal in their presence. The theory claims, however, that every child, conforming or nonconforming, experiences heightened, nonspecific autonomic arousal in the presence of peers from whom he or she feels different. In this modal case, the arousal will not necessarily be affectively toned or consciously felt.

E → F. Regardless of the specific source or affective tone of the childhood autonomic arousal, it is transformed in later years into erotic/romantic attraction. Steps D → E and E → F thus encompass specific psychological mechanisms that transform exotic into erotic (D → F). For brevity, the entire sequence outlined in Figure 8.1 is referred to as the EBE (Exotic Becomes Erotic) theory of sexual orientation.

As noted above, Figure 8.1 does not describe an inevitable, universal path to sexual orientation but the modal path followed by most men and women in a gender-polarizing culture like ours. Individual variations, alternative paths, and cultural influences on sexual orientation are discussed in the final sections of the article.

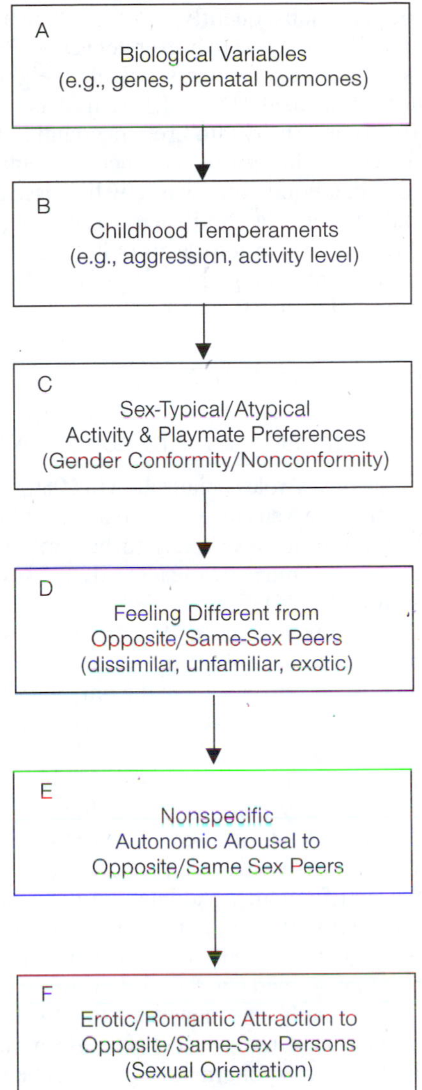

FIGURE 8.1 ■ The temporal sequence of events leading to sexual orientation for most men and women in gender-polarizing culture.

Evidence for the Theory

Evidence for EBE theory is organized into the following narrative sequence: Gender conformity or nonconformity in childhood is a causal antecedent of sexual orientation in adulthood (C → F). This is so because gender conformity or nonconformity causes a child to perceive opposite- or same-sex peers as exotic (C → D), and the exotic class of peers subsequently becomes erotically or romantically attractive to him or her (D → F). This occurs because exotic peers produce heightened autonomic arousal (D → E), which is subsequently transformed into erotic/romantic attraction (E → F). This entire sequence of events can be initiated, among other ways, by biological factors that influence a child's temperaments (A → B), which, in turn, influence his or her preferences for gender-conforming or gender-nonconforming activities and peers (B → C).

Gender Conformity or Nonconformity in Childhood Is a Causal Antecedent of Sexual Orientation in Adulthood (C → F)

In a review of sex-role socialization in 1980, Serbin asserted that "there is no evidence that highly sex-typed children are less likely to become homosexual than children showing less extreme sex-role conformity" (p. 85).

Well, there is now. In the San Francisco study, childhood gender conformity or nonconformity was not only the strongest but the only significant childhood predictor of later sexual orientation for both men and women (Bell et al., 1981a). As Table 8.1 shows, the effects were large and significant. For example, gay men were significantly more likely than heterosexual men to report that as children they had not enjoyed boys' activities (e.g., baseball and football), had enjoyed girls' activities (e.g., hopscotch, playing house, and jacks), and had been nonmasculine. These were the three variables that defined gender nonconformity in the study. Additionally, gay men were more likely than heterosexual men to have had girls as childhood friends. The corresponding comparisons between lesbian and heterosexual women were also large and significant. Moreover, the path analyses implied that gender conformity or nonconformity in childhood was a causal antecedent of later sexual orientation for both men and women—with the usual caveat that even path analysis cannot "prove" causality.

It is also clear from the table that relatively more women than men had enjoyed sex-atypical activities and had opposite-sex friends during childhood. (In fact, more heterosexual women than gay men had enjoyed boys' activities as children—61% vs. 37%, respectively.) As I suggest later, this might account, in part, for differences between men and women in how their sexual orientations are distributed in our society.

The San Francisco study does not stand alone. A meta-analysis of 48 studies with sample sizes ranging from 34 to 8,751 confirmed that gay men and lesbians were more likely to recall gender-nonconforming behaviors and interests in childhood than were heterosexual men and women (Bailey & Zucker, 1995). The differences were large and significant for both men and women, ranging (in units of standard deviation) from 0.5 to 2.1 across studies, with means of 1.31 and 0.96 for men and women, respectively. As the authors noted, "these are among the largest effect sizes ever reported in the realm of sex-dimorphic behaviors" (p. 49).

Prospective studies have come to the same conclusion. The largest of these involved a sample of 66 gender-nonconforming and 56 gender-conforming boys with a mean age of 7.1 years (Green, 1987). The researchers were able to assess about two thirds of each group in late adolescence or early adulthood, finding that about 75% of the previously gender-nonconforming boys were either bisexual or homosexual compared with only

TABLE 8.1. Percentage of Respondents Reporting Gender-Nonconforming Preferences and Behaviors During Childhood

	Men		Women	
Response	Gay (*n* = 686)	Heterosexual (*n* = 337)	Lesbian (*n* = 293)	Heterosexual (*n* = 140)
Had not enjoyed sex-typical activities	63	10	63	15
Had enjoyed sex-atypical activities	48	11	81	61
Atypically sex-typed (masculinity–femininity)	56	8	80	24
Most childhood friends were opposite sex	42	13	60	40

Note. Percentages have been calculated from the data given in Bell, Weinberg, and Hammersmith (1981b, pp. 74–75, 77). All chi-square comparisons between gay and heterosexual subgroups are significant at $p < .0001$.

one (4%) of the gender-conforming boys. In six other prospective studies, 63% of gender-nonconforming boys whose sexual orientations could be ascertained in late adolescence or adulthood had homosexual orientations (Zucker, 1990). Unfortunately, there are no prospective studies of gender-nonconforming girls.

This body of data has led one researcher in the field to assert that the link between childhood gender nonconformity and an adult homosexual orientation "may be the most consistent, well-documented, and significant finding in the entire field of sexual-orientation research and perhaps in all of human psychology" (Hamer & Copeland, 1994, p. 166). That may be a bit hyperbolic—Hamer is a molecular geneticist, not a psychologist—but it is difficult to think of other individual differences (besides IQ or sex itself) that so reliably and so strongly predict socially significant outcomes across the life span, and for both sexes, too. Surely, it must be true.

Gender Conformity and Nonconformity Produce Feelings of Being Different From Opposite and Same-Sex Peers, Respectively (C → D)

EBE theory proposes that gender-conforming children will come to feel different from their opposite-sex peers and gender nonconforming children will come to feel different from their same-sex peers. To my knowledge, no researcher has ever asked children or adults whether they feel different from opposite-sex peers, probably because they expect the universal answer to be yes. The San Francisco researchers, however, did ask respondents whether they felt different from same-sex peers in childhood. They found that 71% of gay men and 70% of lesbian women recalled having felt different from same-sex children during the grade-school years, compared with 38% and 51% of heterosexual men and women, respectively ($p < .0005$ for both gay–heterosexual comparisons).

When asked in what way they felt different, gay men were most likely to say that they did not like sports; lesbians were most likely to say that they were more interested in sports or were more masculine than other girls. In contrast, the heterosexual men and women who had felt different from their same sex peers in childhood typically cited differences unrelated to gender. Heterosexual men tended to cite such reasons as being poorer, more intelligent, or more introverted. Heterosexual women frequently cited differences in physical appearance.

Finally, the data showed that the gender-nonconforming child's sense of being different from same-sex peers is not a fleeting early experience but a protracted and sustained feeling throughout childhood and adolescence. For example, in the path model for men, gender nonconformity in childhood was also a significant predictor of feeling different for gender reasons during adolescence (which was, in turn, a significant predictor of a homosexual orientation). Similarly, the statistically significant difference between the lesbians and heterosexual women in feeling different from same-sex peers during childhood remained significant during adolescence. This is, I believe, why sexual orientation displays such strong temporal stability across the life course for most individuals.

Exotic Becomes Erotic (D → F)

The heart of EBE theory is the proposition that individuals become erotically or romantically attracted to those who were dissimilar or unfamiliar to them in childhood. We have already seen some evidence for this in Table 8.1: Those who played more with girls in childhood, gay men and heterosexual women, preferred men as sexual/romantic partners in later years; those who played more with boys in childhood, lesbian women and heterosexual men, preferred women as sexual or romantic partners in later years. As we shall now see, however, the links between similarity and erotic/romantic attraction are complex.

Similarity and complementarity. One of the most widely accepted conclusions in social psychology, cited in virtually every textbook, is that similarity promotes interpersonal attraction and that complementarity ("opposites attract") does not.

For example, the vast majority of married couples in the United States are of the same race and religion, and most are significantly similar in age, socioeconomic class, educational level, intelligence, height, eye color, and even physical attractiveness (Feingold, 1988; Murstein, 1972; Rubin, 1973; Silverman, 1971). In one study, dating couples who were the most similar were the most likely to be together a year later (Hill, Rubin, & Peplau, 1976). In a longitudinal study of 135 married couples, spouses with similar personalities reported more closeness, friendliness, shared enjoyment in daily activities, marital satisfaction, and less marital conflict than less similar couples (Caspi & Herbener, 1990). In contrast, attempts to identify complementarities that promote or sustain intimate relationships have not been very successful (Levinger, Senn, & Jorgensen, 1970; Strong et al., 1988). Marital adjustment among couples married for up to 5 years was found to depend more on similarity than on complementarity (Meyer & Pepper, 1977).

But there is an obvious exception: sex. Most people choose members of the opposite sex to be their romantic and sexual partners. It is an indication of how unthinkingly heterosexuality is taken for granted that authors of articles and textbooks never seem to notice this quintessential complementarity and its challenge to the conclusion that similarity produces attraction. They certainly don't pause to ponder why we are not all gay or lesbian.

The key to resolving this apparent paradox is also a staple of textbooks: the distinction between liking and loving or between companionate and passionate love (Berscheid & Walster, 1974; Brehm, 1992). The correlation among dating or engaged couples between liking their partners and loving them is only .56 for men and .36 for women (Rubin, 1973). Both fiction and real life provide numerous examples of erotic attraction between two incompatible people who may not even like each other. Collectively, these observations suggest that similarity may promote friendship, compatibility, and companionate love, but it is dissimilarity that sparks erotic/romantic attraction and passionate love.

This is the resolution proposed by both Tripp (1975) and Bell (1982), the senior author of the San Francisco study:

> a necessary ingredient for romantic attachment is one's perception of the loved one as essentially different from oneself in terms of gender-related attributes. According to this view it would be argued that, among homosexuals and heterosexuals alike, persons perceived as essentially *different* from ourselves become the chief candidates for our early romantic and, later, erotic investments. Only a superficial view of the matter would maintain that *heterogamy*, as it has been called, operates only among heterosexuals where anatomical differences make the principle, "opposites attract," most obvious. Among both groups we find romantic and sexual feelings aroused by others perceived to be different from ourselves, unfamiliar in manner, attitude, and interests, and whose differences offer the possibility of a relationship based upon psychological (not necessarily genital) complementarity. On the other side of the coin is the principle of *homogamy* in which perceived similarity and mutual identification and familiarity makes for friendship as opposed to the romantic . . . state. (Bell, 1982, p. 2)[2]

But this account fails to resolve the paradox because it errs in the opposite direction, failing to account for the previously cited evidence that, except for sex itself, it is similarity and not complementarity that sustains the majority of successful heterosexual relationships. Similarly, for every gay or lesbian relationship that conforms to the "butch-femme" stereotype of the popular imagination, there appear to be many more in which the partners are strikingly similar to each other in both psychological and physical attributes—including sex. Bell's account resolves the paradox only if one is willing to accept the implausible implication that all those happy, similar partners must be devoid of erotic enthusiasm for each other.

Like the accounts of Tripp and Bell, EBE theory also proposes that dissimilarity promotes erotic/romantic attraction, but it locates the animating dissimilarity in childhood. Consider, for example, a gender-nonconforming boy whose emerging homoeroticism happens to crystallize around the muscular athlete or leather-jacketed motorcyclist. As he moves into adolescence and adulthood, he may deliberately begin to acquire the attributes and trappings of his eroticized hypermasculine ideal—working out at the gym, buying a leather jacket, getting a body tattoo, and so forth. This acquired "macho" image is not only self-satisfying but is also attractive to other gay men who have eroticized this same idealized image. Two such men will thus be erotically attracted to each other, and their striking similarities, including their shared eroticism, will have been produced by their shared childhood dissimilarities from highly masculine boys.

---

[2]It is puzzling that Bell does not cite Tripp's virtually identical but more elaborate account, especially because both have been associated with the Kinsey Institute. Neither Bell nor Tripp (in his 2nd edition, 1987) cite Stoller's (1979) psychoanalytically based account, which also lists dissimilarity—along with mystery, risk, and (especially) hostility—as a generator and enhancer of sexual arousal.

EBE theory thus proposes that once the dissimilarities of childhood have laid the groundwork for a sustained sexual orientation, the noncriterial attributes of one's preferred partners within the eroticized class can range from extremely similar to extremely dissimilar. More generally, the theory proposes that the protracted period of feeling different from same- or opposite-sex peers during childhood and adolescence produces a stable sexual orientation for most individuals but that within that orientation, there can be wide-ranging—and changing—idiosyncratic preferences for particular partners or kinds of partners.

Familiarity and unfamiliarity. Like similarity, familiarity is a major antecedent of liking. In fact, similarity probably promotes liking precisely because it increases familiarity: Social norms, situational circumstances, and mutual interests conspire to bring people together who are similar to one another, thereby increasing their mutual familiarity. When college roommates were systematically paired for similarity or dissimilarity in Newcomb's (1961) ambitious two-year study of the acquaintance process, familiarity turned out to be a stronger facilitator of liking than similarity.

The "familiarity-breeds-liking" effect has been confirmed in so many contexts that it is now considered to be a general psychological principle. For example, rats repeatedly exposed to compositions by Mozart or Schönberg have shown an enhanced preference for the composer they heard, and humans repeatedly exposed to nonsense syllables, Chinese characters, or real people have come to prefer those they saw most often (Harrison, 1977).

But like childhood similarity, childhood familiarity does not produce erotic or romantic attraction; on the contrary, it appears to be antithetical to it. This was observed over a century ago by Westermarck (1891), who noted that two individuals who spent their childhood years together did not find each other sexually attractive even when there were strong social pressures favoring a bond between them. For example, he reported problematic sexual relations in arranged marriages in which the couple was betrothed in childhood and the girl was taken in by the future husband's family and treated like one of the siblings; similar findings have emerged from more recent studies of arranged marriages in Taiwan (cited in Bateson, 1978a).

A contemporary example is provided by children on Israeli kibbutzim, who are raised communally with age-mates in mixed-sex groups and exposed to one another constantly during their entire childhood. Sex play is not discouraged and is quite intensive during early childhood. After childhood, there is no formal or informal pressure or sanction against heterosexual activity within the peer group from educators, parents, or members of the peer group itself. Yet despite all this, there is a virtual absence of erotic attraction between peer group members in adolescence or adulthood (Bettelheim, 1969; Rabin, 1965; Shepher, 1971; Spiro, 1958; Talmon, 1964). A review of nearly 3,000 marriages contracted by second-generation adults in all Israeli kibbutzim revealed that there was not a single case of an intrapeer group marriage (Shepher, 1971).

These several observations have figured prominently in debates over the existence and psychodynamics of the incest taboo (e.g., R. Fox, 1962; Spiro, 1958). I will not venture into that thicket but rest content with the relatively atheoretical empirical generalization that close childhood familiarity either extinguishes or prevents the development of manifest erotic/ romantic attraction.

The Sambian culture in New Guinea illustrates the phenomenon in a homosexual context. As described by Herdt in several publications (1981, 1984, 1987, 1990), Sambian males believe that boys cannot attain manhood without ingesting semen from older males. At age seven years, Sambian boys are removed from the family household and initiated into secret male rituals, including ritualized homosexuality. For the next several years, they live in the men's clubhouse and regularly fellate older male adolescents. When they reach sexual maturity, they reverse roles and are fellated by younger initiates. During this entire time, they have no sexual contact with girls or women. And yet, when it comes time to marry and father children in their late teens or early twenties, all but a tiny minority of Sambian males become preferentially and exclusively heterosexual. Although Sambian boys enjoy their homosexual activities, the context of close familiarity in which it occurs either extinguishes or prevents the development of strongly charged homoerotic feelings.

During the years that a Sambian boy is participating in homosexual activities with his male peers, he is taught a misogynist ideology that portrays women as dangerous and exotic creatures—almost a different species. According to EBE theory, this should enhance their erotic attractiveness for him.

More generally, EBE theory proposes that heterosexuality is the modal outcome across time and culture because virtually all human societies polarize the sexes to some extent, setting up a sex-based division of labor and power, emphasizing or exaggerating sex differences, and, in general, superimposing the male–female dichotomy on virtually every aspect of communal life. These gender-polarizing practices ensure that most boys and girls will grow up seeing the other sex as dissimilar, unfamiliar, and exotic—and, hence, erotic. Thus, the theory provides a culturally based alternative to the assumption that heterosexuality must necessarily be coded in the genes. I return to this point later.

Finally, the assertion that exotic becomes erotic should be amended to exotic—but not too exotic—becomes erotic (cf. Tripp, 1987). Thus, an erotic or romantic preference for partners of a different sex, race, or ethnicity is relatively common, but a preference for lying with the beasts in the field is not. This phenomenon appears to be a special case of the well-established motivational principle that there is an optimal, nonzero level of stimulus novelty and a correspondingly optimal nonzero level of internal arousal that an organism will seek to attain or maintain (Monk, 1987).

How Does Exotic Become Erotic? (D → E → F)

In Plato's *Symposium*, Aristophanes explained sexual attraction by recounting the early history of human beings. Originally, we were all eight-limbed creatures with two faces and two sets of genitals. Males had two sets of male genitals, females had two sets of female genitals, and androgynes had one set of each kind. As punishment for being overly ambitious, Zeus had all humans cut in half. But because the two halves of each former individual clung to each other in such a desperate attempt to reunite, Zeus took pity on them and invented sexual intercourse so that they might at least reunite temporarily. Sexual attraction thus reflects an attempt to complete one's original self, and heterosexual attraction is what characterizes the dependents of the androgynes.

It is a durable myth. Both Bell (1982) and Tripp (1987) proposed that we are erotically attracted to people who are different from us because we are embarked on a "quest for androgyny" (Bell); we seek to complete ourselves by "importing" gender-related attributes that we perceive ourselves as lacking (Tripp). As noted earlier, I do not believe that this accurately characterizes the data; but even if it did, it would constitute only a description of them, not an explanation. There may not be much evidence for Aristophanes' historical account, but epistemologically at least, it is an explanation.

Because I prefer mechanism to metaphor, EBE theory is unabashedly reductionistic. As already discussed, it proposes that exotic becomes erotic because feelings of dissimilarity and unfamiliarity in childhood produce heightened nonspecific autonomic arousal (D → E), which is subsequently transformed into erotic/romantic attraction (E → F). To my knowledge, there is no direct evidence for the first step in this sequence beyond the well-documented observation that novelty and unfamiliarity produce heightened arousal (Mook, 1987); filling in this empirical gap in EBE theory must await future research. In contrast, there are at least three mechanisms that can potentially effect the second step, transforming generalized arousal into erotic/romantic attraction: the extrinsic arousal effect, the opponent process, and imprinting.

THE EXTRINSIC AROUSAL EFFECT

In his first-century Roman handbook, *The Art of Love*, Ovid advised any man who was interested in sexual seduction to take the woman in whom he was interested to a gladiatorial tournament, where she would more easily be aroused to passion. He did not say why this should be so, however, and it was not until 1887 that an elaboration appeared in the literature:

> Love can only be excited by strong and vivid emotion, and it is almost immaterial whether these emotions are agreeable or disagreeable. The Cid wooed the proud heart of Donna Ximene, whose father he had slain, by shooting one after another of her pet pigeons. (Horwicz, quoted in Finck, 1887, p. 240)

A contemporary explanation of this effect was introduced by Walster (1971; Berscheid & Walster, 1974), who suggested that it constituted a special case of Schachter and Singer's (1962) two-factor theory of emotion. That theory states that the physiological arousal of our autonomic nervous system provides the cues that we feel emotional but that the more subtle judgment of which emotion we are feeling often depends on our cognitive appraisal of the surrounding circumstances. According to Walster, then, the experience of passionate love or erotic/ romantic attraction results from the conjunction of physiological arousal and the cognitive causal attribution (or misattribution) that the arousal has been elicited by the potential lover.

There is now extensive experimental evidence that an individual who has been physiologically aroused will show heightened sexual responsiveness to an appropriate target stimulus. In one set of studies, male participants were physiologically aroused by running in place, by hearing an audiotape of a comedy routine, or by hearing an audiotape of a grisly killing (White, Fishbein, & Rutstein, 1981). They then viewed a taped interview with a woman who was either physically attractive or physically unattractive. Finally, they rated the woman on several dimensions, including her attractiveness, her sexiness, and the degree to which they would be interested in dating her and kissing her. The results showed that no matter how the arousal had been elicited, participants were more erotically responsive to the attractive woman and less erotically responsive to the unattractive women than were control participants who had not been aroused. In other words, the arousal intensified both positive or negative reactions to the woman, depending on which was cognitively appropriate.

This extrinsic arousal effect (my term) is not limited to the individual's cognitive appraisal of his or her emotional state. In two studies, men or women watched a sequence of two videotapes. The first portrayed either an anxiety-inducing or nonanxiety-inducing scene; the second videotape portrayed a nude heterosexual couple engaging in sexual foreplay. Preexposure to the anxiety-inducing scene produced greater penile tumescence in men and greater vaginal blood volume increases in women in response to the erotic scene than did preexposure to the nonanxiety-inducing scene (Moon, Wineze, & lloon, 1977; Wolchik et al., 1980).

In addition to the misattribution explanation, several other explanations for the extrinsic arousal effect have been proposed, but experimental attempts to determine which explanation is the most valid have produced mixed results and the dispute is not yet settled (Allen, Kenrick, Linder, & McCall, 1989; Kenrick & Cialdini, 1977; McClanahan, Gold, Lenney Ryckman, & Kulberg, 1990; White & Kight, 1984; Zillmann, 1983). For present purposes, however, it doesn't matter. It is sufficient to know that autonomic arousal, regardless of its source or affective tone, can subsequently be experienced cognitively, emotionally, and physiologically as erotic/romantic attraction. At that point, it *is* erotic/romantic attraction.

The pertinent question, then, is whether this effect can account for the link between autonomic arousal in childhood and erotic/romantic attraction later in life. In one respect, the experiments may actually underestimate the strength and reliability of the effect in real life. In the experiments, the arousal is deliberately elicited by a source extrinsic to the intended target, and there is disagreement over whether the effect even occurs when participants are aware of that fact (Allen et al., 1989; Cantor, Zillmann, & Bryant, 1975; McClanahan et al., 1990; White & Kight, 1984). But in the real-life scenario envisioned by EBE theory, the autonomic arousal is genuinely elicited by the class of individuals to which the erotic/ romantic attraction develops. The exotic arousal and the erotic arousal are thus likely to be phenomenologically indistinguishable.

But there are at least two apparent difficulties in generalizing the effect to the scenario proposed by EBE theory. First, the effect occurs in the laboratory over time intervals measured in minutes, whereas the proposed developmental process spans several years. The time gap may be more apparent than real, however. As noted earlier, an individual's sense of being different from same- or opposite-sex peers is not a one-time event but a protracted and sustained experience throughout the childhood and adolescent years. This implies that the arousal will also be present throughout that time, ready to be converted into erotic or romantic attraction whenever the maturational, cognitive, and situational factors coalesce to provide the defining attributional moment.

A second apparent difficulty is posed by the experimental finding, described above, that when a participant was exposed to an unattractive woman on the videotape, extrinsic arousal only increased the negativity of the response to her; it did not transform it into a positive erotic response. This might seem to suggest that the extrinsic arousal effect cannot account for those individuals who are erotically or romantically attracted to others whom they dislike. In particular, it suggests that the effect cannot account for the special case of the gender-nonconforming boy who develops an erotic or romantic attraction to precisely that class of persons, males, he fears or dislikes because they have taunted him for his gender nonconformity.

But the videotaped woman in the experiment was not unlikable but physically unattractive, and these are quite different attributes. As noted earlier, both fiction and real life provide numerous examples of erotic attraction between people who may not even like one other; one can dislike a person or class of persons overall but still be attracted to their physical appearance or idealize and eroticize one or more of their attributes. An all too-familiar example is the misogynist heterosexual man who is not only erotically aroused by women's bodies but by narrowly specific attributes of their bodies, such as large breasts. Similarly, even those gay men and heterosexual women who find much to dislike about men in general may be turned on by a muscular male body or a pair of tight "buns:" In short, the extrinsic arousal effect remains a viable explanation of erotic/romantic attraction, even to disliked individuals.[3]

Nevertheless, there is an alternative mechanism that accounts even more elegantly for both the proposed developmental time course of erotic/ romantic attraction and the conversion of negative to positive affect: the opponent process (Solomon, 1980; Solomon & Corbit, 1974).

THE OPPONENT PROCESS

The theory of opponent process is a homeostatic theory of affect. When strong affect occurs, the nervous system responds by initiating an opponent process of opposite affective valence that reduces the intensity of the original affect. Strong negative affect is countered by internally generated positive affect and vice versa. (Only the case of initial negative affect is discussed here.) For example, prolonged stress that activates the sympathetic nervous system can produce a parasympathetic rebound when it is suddenly withdrawn. Intense pain is countered by the internal release of endorphins in the brain, which produce positive affect. The affect that the person experiences is the difference between the two opposing affects and shifts over time. For example, if an initial negative affect triggers a positive opponent process but then diminishes, the individual experiences a euphoric aftereffect as the opponent process overcompensates.

The theory further proposes that if the opponent process is evoked repeatedly, it will begin to respond more strongly over time and will become conditioned to the external situation so that it continues to be evoked even if the initiating negative affect no longer occurs. For example, parachutists experience terror on their first jump (Epstein, 1967). Their hearts race, their breathing is irregular, and their bodies are curled and stiff. After landing, they appear stunned, remaining mute and facially unexpressive. After a few minutes, however, they enter a period of mild euphoria, smiling and talking excitedly. After many more jumps, the fear extinguishes and the opponent process dominates. At this point, parachutists regularly experience a strong euphoric "high" after each jump. Similarly, long distance runners push past the pain barrier to feel a runner's high, and beginning sauna bathers suffer through several sessions of pain and burning before beginning to feel "exhilaration" and "a sense of well-being" after each sauna (Solomon, 1980). It seems likely that "masochistic" sexual pleasure that derives from initially painful stimulation follows a similar developmental course.

We can now return to the case of the gender-nonconforming boy who is taunted by other boys. At first this produces strong negative arousal, but with repeated encounters over time, the fear and anger habituate and the opponent process becomes the conditioned, dominant affect. He thus emerges into late childhood or adolescence experiencing positive affective arousal to males, an arousal ready to be eroticized.

IMPRINTING

The temporal stability of sexual orientation across the life course for most individuals has suggested to some theorists that it may be the result of an early imprinting-like process (e.g., Archer, 1992; Bateson, 1978a). There are at least two distinct imprinting phenomena that might be pertinent. In

[3]For most individuals, cultural norms define which male and female attributes, if any, are to be idealized and eroticized; when a nonnormative attribute is eroticized, it is clinically defined as a paraphilia or a fetish and popularly stigmatized as a perversion. Tripp (1987) makes the intriguing suggestion—without citing evidence—that Hindu cultures have a lower incidence of male homosexuality than Muslim cultures because they do not idealize individualized masculine attributes.

filial imprinting, precocial birds, such as ducks and geese, become attached to and follow the first large moving object they encounter after hatching. The imprinting stimulus is usually the bird's mother but, as every introductory textbook in psychology notes, it can also be an inanimate moving object or even the ethologist. The more relevant phenomenon is probably sexual imprinting, a separate process that occurs during a later sensitive period (roughly equivalent to middle childhood) and is the precursor of both species-specific and within-species mate choice after sexual maturity has been attained (Bateson, 1979; Immelmann, 1972).

There are several specific features of sexual imprinting in birds that appear to be analogous to the development of sexual orientation in humans (Archer, 1992). First, sexual imprinting establishes an attraction to an entire class of individuals well before sexual maturity. Second, after imprinting has been established, the sexual preference is quite stable, even irreversible. In one study, male zebra finches were reared in nests of Bengalese finches for periods as brief as 1 week during the sensitive period. When they reached sexual maturity, they preferred to mate with Bengalese finch females even when presented with more receptive females of their own species. Even after considerable sexual experience with females of their own species, these zebra finches still preferred Bengalese finches when again given a choice several years later (Immelmann, 1972). The preference was sustained over both time and alternative experience.

Third, imprinting appears to follow the principle that exotic—but not too exotic—becomes erotic. For example, both male and female Japanese quail reared with their siblings later preferred their slightly different-appearing cousins both to their own siblings and to unrelated, more different-appearing quail (Bateson, 1978b). This has been interpreted as a mechanism that prevents inbreeding, a biologically promoted incest taboo. In fact, the author of the kibbutz study, cited earlier, has interpreted the exogamy of kibbutz members as the product of "negative imprinting" (Shepher, 1971).

Finally, physiological arousal appears to strengthen imprinting. If ducks or chickens are given electric shocks or are otherwise made anxious during the initial filial imprinting, they acquire a stronger attachment to the imprinting stimulus than they do in the absence of such arousal (e.g., Hess, 1959; Moltz, Rosenblum, & Halikas, 1959; Pitz & Ross, 1961). Analogously, the strong autonomic arousal elicited in the gender-nonconforming boy by his taunting male peers may intensify his later erotic/romantic attraction to males. It is also possible that this phenomenon is just another instance of the opponent process; there is other evidence that the opponent process occurs in imprinting (Solomon, 1980).

PUTTING IT ALL TOGETHER

The general model outlined in Figure 8.1 does not indicate which, if any, of these processes underlie the transformation of nonspecific autonomic arousal to erotic attraction. Here are my best guesses. I believe that the extrinsic arousal effect eroticizes the relatively mild autonomic arousal experienced by virtually all children when they are in the presence of dissimilar peers. In the special case of a gender-nonconforming child who is taunted by same-sex peers, this is augmented by the opponent-process mechanism, which builds up a conditioned positive arousal to that same class of peers over time. Finally I am willing to entertain the possibility that a process akin to imprinting may also contribute to the eroticization of arousal and the temporal stability of sexual orientation across the life course, again with particular force for the gender-nonconforming child who is taunted by same-sex peers.

One testable hypothesis that emerges from this analysis is that children who appear to their peers to be particularly gender nonconforming are likely to identify homoerotic feelings earlier or feel them more intensely than less strongly nonconforming children. This prediction is supported by data from the San Francisco study. About 44% of the gay men rated themselves as having been feminine in childhood and were also rated at the time of the study as "effeminate" in appearance by the interviewers. A separate path analysis for this subsample of gay men revealed that the variable "homosexual feelings in childhood" was the strongest predictor of their homosexual orientation in later years. In contrast, this variable does not even appear in the path analysis for noneffeminate gay men. Using parallel criteria, 54% of the lesbian women were categorized as "masculine." Separate path analyses showed that even the causal link between childhood gender nonconformity and a homosexual orientation in adulthood was significant only for the masculine lesbians. (The path to sexual orientation for nonmasculine lesbians is discussed later.)

The Biological Connection: (A → F) Versus (A → B)

In recent years, researchers, the mass media, and segments of the lesbian/gay/bisexual community have rushed to embrace the thesis that a homosexual orientation is coded in the genes or determined by prenatal hormones and brain neuroanatomy. Even the authors of the San Francisco study, whose findings disconfirm most experience-based theories of sexual orientation, seem ready to concede the ball game to biology. In contrast, EBE theory proposes that biological factors influence sexual orientation only indirectly, by intervening earlier in the chain of events to determine a child's temperaments and subsequent activity preferences. Accordingly, my persuasive task in this section is to argue that any nonartifactual correlation between a biological factor and sexual orientation is more plausibly attributed to its influence in early childhood than to a direct link with sexual orientation.

GENES

Recent studies have provided some evidence for a correlation between an individual's genotype and his or her sexual orientation. For example, in a sample of 115 gay men who had male twins, 52% of monozygotic twin brothers were also gay compared with only 22% of dizygotic twin brothers and 11% of gay men's adoptive brothers (Bailey & Pillard, 1991). In a comparable sample of 115 lesbians, 48% of monozygotic twin sisters were also lesbian compared with only 16% of dizygotic twin sisters and 6% of lesbian women's adoptive sisters (Bailey, Pillard, Neale, & Agyei, 1993). A subsequent study of nearly 5,000 twins who had been systematically drawn from a twin registry confirmed the significant heritability of sexual orientation for men but not for women (Bailey & Martin, 1995). And finally, a pedigree and linkage analysis of 114 families of gay men and a DNA linkage analysis of 40 families in which there were two gay brothers suggested a correlation between a homosexual orientation and the inheritance of genetic markers on the X chromosome (Hamer & Copeland, 1994; Hamer, Hu, Magnuson, Hu, & Pattatucci, 1993).[4]

But these same studies have also provided evidence for the link proposed by EBE theory between an individual's genotype and his or her childhood gender nonconformity, even when sexual orientation is held constant. For example, in the 1991 twin study of gay men, childhood gender nonconformity was assessed by a composite of three scales that have been shown to discriminate between gay and heterosexual men: childhood aggressiveness, interest in sports, and effeminacy. Across twin pairs in which both brothers were gay ("concordant" pairs), the correlation on gender nonconformity for monozygotic twins was as high as the reliability of the scale would permit, .76 ($p < .0001$), compared with a correlation of only .43 for concordant dizygotic twins, implying significant heritability (Bailey & Pillard, 1991). In the family pedigree study of gay men, pairs of gay brothers who were concordant for the genetic markers on the X chromosome were also more similar on gender nonconformity than were genetically discordant pairs of gay brothers (Hamer & Copeland, 1994). Finally, childhood gender nonconformity was significantly heritable for both men and women in the large twin registry study, even though sexual orientation itself was not heritable for the women (Bailey & Martin, 1995).

These studies are thus consistent with the link specified by EBE theory between the genotype and gender nonconformity (A → C). The theory further specifies that this link is composed of two parts, a link between the genotype and childhood temperaments (A → B) and a link between those temperaments and gender nonconformity (B → C). This implies that the mediating temperaments should possess three characteristics: First, they should be plausibly related to those play activities that define gender conformity and nonconformity. Second, because they manifest themselves in sex-typed preferences, they should show sex differences. And third, because they are hypothesized to derive from the genotype, they should have significant heritabilities.

One likely candidate is aggression and its benign cousin, rough-and-tumble play. As noted above, gay men score lower than heterosexual men on a measure of childhood aggression (Blanchard, McConkey, Roper, & Steiner, 1983), and parents

[4] This last finding is currently in dispute, and an independent attempt to replicate it has failed (Rice, Anderson, Risch, & Ebers, 1995).

of gender-nonconforming boys specifically rate them as having less interest in rough-and-tumble play than do parents of gender-conforming boys (Green, 1976). Second, the sex difference in aggression during childhood is about half a standard deviation, one of the largest psychological sex differences known (Hyde, 1984). Rough-and-tumble play in particular is more common in boys than in girls (DiPietro, 1981; Fry, 1990; Moller, Hymel, & Rubin, 1992). And third, individual differences in aggression have a large heritable component (Rushton, Fulker, Neale, Nias, & Eysenck, 1986).

Another likely candidate is activity level, considered to be one of the basic childhood temperaments (Buss & Plomin, 1975, 1984). Like aggression, differences in activity level would also seem to characterize the differences between male-typical and female-typical play activities in childhood, and gender-nonconforming boys and girls are lower and higher on activity level, respectively, than are control children of the same sex (Bates, Bentler, & Thompson, 1973, 1979; Zucker & Green, 1993). Second, the sex difference in activity level is as large as it is for aggression. A meta-analysis of 127 studies found boys to be about half a standard deviation more active than girls. Even before birth, boys in utero are about one third of a standard deviation more active than girls (Eaton & Enns, 1986). And third, individual differences in activity level have a large heritable component (Plomin, 1986).

In sum, existing data are consistent with both a direct path between the genotype and sexual orientation and the EBE path, which channels genetic influence through the child's temperaments and subsequent activity preferences. So why should one prefer the EBE account?

THE MISSING THEORY FOR THE DIRECT PATH

The EBE account may be wrong, but I submit that a competing theoretical rationale for a direct path between the genotype and sexual orientation has not even been clearly articulated, let alone established. At first glance, the theoretical rationale would appear to be nothing less than the powerful and elegant theory of evolution. The belief that sexual orientation is coded in the genes would appear to be just the general case of the implicit assumption, mentioned in the introduction, that heterosexuality is the obvious, "natural" evolutionary consequence of reproductive advantage.

But if that is true, then a homosexual orientation is an evolutionary anomaly that requires further theoretical explication. How do lesbians and gay men manage to pass on their gene pool to successive generations? Several hypothetical scenarios have been offered (for a review, see Savin-Williams, 1987). One is that social institutions such as universal marriage can ensure that lesbians and gay men will have enough children to sustain a "homosexual" gene pool (Weinrich, 1987). Another is that the genes for homosexuality are linked to, or piggyback on, other genes that themselves carry reproductive advantage, such as genes for intelligence or dominance (Kirsch & Rodman, 1982; Weinrich, 1978). A third, based on kin selection, speculates that homosexual individuals may help nurture a sufficient number of their kin (e.g., nieces and nephews) to reproductive maturity to ensure that their genes get passed along to successive generations (Weinrich, 1978; Wilson, 1975, 1978).

Although these speculations have been faulted on theoretical, metatheoretical, and empirical grounds (Futuyma & Risch, 1983/84), a more basic problem with such arguments is their circularity. As Bleier has noted about similar accounts,

> this logic makes a *premise* of the genetic basis of behaviors, then cites a certain animal or human behavior, constructs a speculative story to explain how the behavior (*if* it were genetically based) could have served or could serve to maximize the reproductive success of the individual, and this *conjecture* then becomes evidence for the *premise* that the behavior was genetically determined. 1984, p. 17).

When one does attempt to deconstruct the evolutionary explanation for sexual orientation, homosexual or heterosexual, some problematic assumptions become explicit. For example, the belief that sexual orientation is coded in the genes embodies the unacknowledged assumption that knowledge of the distinction between male and female must also be hardwired into the human species, that sex is a natural category of human perception. After all, we cannot be erotically attracted to a class of persons unless and until we can discriminate exemplars from nonexemplars of that class.

Given what psychology has learned about human language and cognition in recent decades, the notion that humans have innate knowledge of the male–female distinction is not quite so inconceivable as it once was. An explicit version of this notion is embodied in the Jungian belief that an animus-anima archetype is part of our collective unconscious. It could also be argued that functional, if not cognitive, knowledge of the male–female distinction is embodied in innate responses to pheromones or other sensory cues, as it is for several other species.

As it happens, I find all these possibilities implausible, but that is not the point. Rather, it is that those who argue for the direct heritability of sexual orientation should be made cognizant of such assumptions and required to shoulder the burden of proof for them. More generally, any genetic argument, including a sociobiological one, must spell out the developmental pathway by which genotypes are transformed into phenotypes (Bronfenbrenner & Ceci, 1994). This is precisely what EBE theory attempts to do and what the competing claim for a direct path between genes and sexual orientation fails to do. It is not that an argument for a direct path has been made and found wanting, but that it has not yet been made.

I am certainly willing to concede that heterosexual behavior is reproductively advantageous, but it does not follow that it must therefore be sustained through genetic transmission. As noted earlier, EBE theory implies that heterosexuality is the modal outcome across time and culture because virtually every human society ensures that most boys and girls will grow up seeing the other sex as exotic and, hence, erotic.

The more general point is that as long as the environment supports or promotes a reproductively successful behavior sufficiently often, it will not necessarily get programmed into the genes. For example, it is presumably reproductively advantageous for ducks to mate with other ducks, but as long as most baby ducklings encounter other ducks before they encounter an ethologist, evolution can simply implant the imprinting process itself into the species rather than the specific content of what, reproductively speaking, needs to be imprinted.[5] Analogously, because most cultures ensure that the two sexes will see each other as exotic, it would be sufficient for evolution to implant exotic-becomes-erotic processes into our species rather than heterosexuality per se. In fact, as noted earlier, an exotic-becomes-erotic mechanism is actually a component of sexual imprinting. If ducks, who are genetically free to mate with any moving object, have not perished from the earth, then neither shall we.

PRENATAL HORMONES

One of the oldest hypotheses about sexual orientation is that gay men have too little testosterone and lesbians have too much. When the data failed to support this hypothesis (for reviews, see Gartrell, 1982, and Meyer-Bahlburg, 1984), attention turned from adult hormonal status to prenatal hormonal status. Reasoning from research on rats in which the experimental manipulation of prenatal androgen levels can "masculinize" or "feminize" the brain and produce sex-atypical mating postures and mounting responses, some researchers hypothesized that human males who are exposed prenatally to substantially lower than average amounts of testosterone and human females who are exposed to substantially higher than average amounts of testosterone will be predisposed toward a homosexual orientation in adult life (Ellis & Ames, 1987).[6]

One body of data advanced in support of this hypothesis comes from interviews with women who have congenital adrenal hyperplasia (CAH), a chronic endocrine disorder that exposes them to abnormally high levels of androgen during the prenatal period, levels comparable to those received by normal male fetuses during gestation. Most of these women were born with virilized genitalia, which were surgically corrected soon after birth, and placed on cortisol medication to prevent further anatomical virilization. In three studies, CAH women have now reported more bisexual or homosexual responsiveness than control women (Dittmann et al., 1990a; Money, Schwartz, & Lewis, 1984; Zucker et al., 1992).

But a number of factors suggest that this link from prenatal hormones to sexual orientation is better explained by their effects on childhood temperaments and activity preferences. For example, both boys and girls who were exposed to high levels of androgenizing progestins during gestation have shown increased aggression later in childhood (Reinisch, 1981), and girls with CAH have shown stronger preferences for male-typical ac-

[5]Although imprinting birds to other birds is still easier and more stable than imprinting them to ethologists (Immelmann, 1972).

[6] As Adkins-Regan (1988) pointed out, some authors erroneously refer to the sex-atypical mating postures and mounting responses in rats as "homosexual," even though the rats' preferences for same- or opposite-sex mates is not assessed.

tivities and male playmates in childhood than control girls (Berenbaum & Hines, 1992; Berenbaum & Snyder, 1995; Dittmann et al., 1990b; Money & Ehrhardt, 1972).

It is also possible that the correlation itself is artifactual, having nothing to do with prenatal hormonal exposure—let alone "masculinization" of the brain. The contemporaneous hormonal status of CAH girls could be producing some of these childhood effects. It is even conceivable that the cortisol medication could be increasing their activity level, thereby promoting their preference for male-typical activities (Quadagno, Briscoe, & Quadagno, 1977).

But from the perspective of EBE theory, the major reason for expecting CAH girls to be disproportionately homoerotic in adulthood is that they are overwhelmingly likely to feel different from other girls. Not only are they gender nonconforming in their play activities and peer preferences, as most lesbians are during the childhood years, but the salience of their CAH status itself aids and abets their perception of being different from other girls on gender-relevant dimensions. For example, they know about their virilized genitalia and they may be concerned that they will not be able to conceive and bear children when they grow up, one of the frequent complications of the CAH disorder. According to EBE theory, these are not girls who need masculinized brains to make them homoerotic.

A more critical test of the direct link between prenatal hormones and sexual orientation would seem to require a prenatal hormonal condition that is correlated with an adult homosexual orientation but uncorrelated with any of these childhood effects. Meyer-Bahlburg, Ehrhardt, Rosen, and Gruen (1995) hypothesized that abnormally high levels of prenatal estrogens might produce such an outcome in women by masculinizing their brains.

Although the theoretical reasoning behind this hypothesis has been questioned (Byne & Parsons, 1993), Meyer-Bahlburg et al. (1995) cited some supporting evidence from women whose mothers had taken diethylstilbestrol (DES), a synthetic estrogen that was used to maintain high-risk pregnancies until it was banned in 1971. Three samples of such women have now been interviewed and rated on several Kinsey-like scales for heterosexual and homosexual responsiveness. According to the investigators, "more DES-exposed women than controls were rated as bisexual or homosexual . . ." (p. 12). Because DES does not produce any visible anomalies during childhood and evidence for childhood gender nonconformity among DES-exposed women was weak, this outcome would seem to favor the argument for a direct link between prenatal hormones and sexual orientation over the EBE account.

But the evidence for a bisexual or homosexual orientation among the DES-exposed women was also very weak. As Meyer-Bahlburg et al. (1995) noted, "the majority of DES-exposed women in our study were exclusively or nearly exclusively heterosexual, in spite of their prenatal DES exposure" (p. 20). In fact, of 97 DES-exposed women interviewed, only 4 were rated as having a predominantly homosexual orientation, and not a single woman was rated as having an exclusively homosexual orientation. I think the jury is still out on the link between prenatal estrogens and sexual orientation.

A third line of research on the masculinized or feminized brain hypothesis is based on hormonal feedback mechanisms. In adult female rats, the hypothalamic-pituitary-gonadal axis responds to estrogen input with a release of the pituitary hormone LH (luteinizing hormone). This estrogen-evoked LH response can be altered prenatally in both male and female rats by hormonal treatments that do, in fact, masculinize or feminize their brains. These observations led to the prediction that gay men should show a greater LH response to estrogen input than heterosexual men and that lesbians should show a smaller LH response than heterosexual women.

There are many logical flaws in this jump from rats to humans. For example, several lines of evidence imply that primates, including humans, do not even show a sex difference in the potential hypothalamic regulation of the LH feedback response (Byne & Parsons, 1993). There are also theoretical reasons to expect that it is not possible to obtain a genuine LH feedback response in any gonadally intact man, an expectation that has now been confirmed in an experiment with both gay and heterosexual men (Gooren, 1986b). Finally, there is evidence that the LH response is dependent largely on the concurrent hormonal status of the individual, not on any putative sex-dimorphic prenatal influence. (For more extended discussions, see Byne & Parsons, 1993; Gooren, 1990; Zucker & Bradley, 1995.)

But these conceptual difficulties are overshadowed by the poor track record of empirical attempts to confirm the hypotheses. Although two early studies claimed to find support for an enhanced LH response in gay men (Dorner, Rhode, Stahl, Krell, & Masius, 1975; Gladue, Green, & Hellman, 1984), the Dorner et al. study found that bisexual men had a lower LH response than heterosexual men, and unpublished data from the Gladue et al. study showed that lesbian women had a higher LH response than did heterosexual women—directly opposite to prediction (Gladue, 1988). More recent studies have failed even to replicate the predicted effect for gay men (Gooren, 1986a; Gooren, 1986b; Hendricks, Graber, & RodriguezSierra, 1989). In general, this line of research is no longer being pursued, and the conceptual criticisms have led some researchers to conclude that even if sexual orientation effects exist, they are probably unrelated to prenatal psychosexual differentiation (for a summary, see Zucker & Bradley, 1995).

NEUROANATOMICAL CORRELATES OF SEXUAL ORIENTATION

Even the general public now knows that there are neuroanatomical differences between the brains of gay men and those of heterosexual men and that some of these correspond to differences between the brains of women and men (Allen & Gorski, 1992; LeVay, 1991, 1993; Swaab & Hofman, 1990). Gay men also perform less well than heterosexual men on some cognitive, motor, and spatial tasks on which women perform less well than men (e.g., Gladue, Beatty, Larson, & Staton, 1990; McCormick & Witelson, 1991). (There are no comparable studies of lesbian women.)

But such differences are also consistent with the EBE account. Any biological factor that correlates with one or more of the intervening processes proposed by EBE theory could also emerge as a correlate of sexual orientation. For example, any neuroanatomical feature of the brain that correlates with childhood aggression or activity level could also emerge as a difference between gay men and heterosexual men, between women and men, and between heterosexual women and lesbians. Even if EBE theory turns out to be wrong, the more general point, that a mediating personality variable could account for observed correlations between biological variables and sexual orientation, still holds.

Like all well-bred scientists, biologically oriented researchers in the field of sexual orientation dutifully murmur the mandatory mantra that correlation is not cause. But the reductive temptation of biological causation is so seductive that the caveat cannot possibly compete with the excitement of discovering yet another link between the anatomy of our brains and the anatomy of our lovers' genitalia. Unfortunately, the caveat vanishes completely as word of the latest discovery moves from *Science* to *Newsweek*. The public can be forgiven for believing that research is but one government grant away from pinpointing the penis preference gene.

Individual Variations and Alternative Paths

As noted earlier, Figure 8.1 is not intended to describe an inevitable, universal path to sexual orientation but only the modal path followed by most men and women in a gender-polarizing culture like ours. Individual variations can arise in several ways. First, different individuals might enter the EBE path at different points in the sequence. For example, a child might come to feel different from same-sex peers not because of a temperamentally induced preference for gender-nonconforming activities but because of an atypical lack of contact with same-sex peers, a physical disability, or an illness (e.g., the CAH girls). Similarly, I noted earlier that the nonmasculine lesbians in the San Francisco study were not significantly gender nonconforming in childhood. But they were more likely than heterosexual women to have mostly male friends in grade school, and, consistent with the subsequent steps in the EBE path, this was the strongest predictor for these women of homosexual involvements in adolescence and a homosexual orientation in adulthood.

In general, EBE theory predicts that the effect of any childhood variable on an individual's sexual orientation depends on whether it prompts him or her to feel more similar to or more different from same-sex or opposite-sex peers. For example, it has recently been reported that a gay man is likely to have more older brothers than a heterosexual man (Blanchard & Bogaert, 1996). This could come about, in part, if having gender-conforming older brothers especially enhances a gender-nonconforming boy's sense of being different from other boys.

Individual variations can also arise from differences in how individuals interpret the "exotic" arousal emerging from the childhood years, an interpretation that is inevitably guided by social norms and expectations. For example, girls might be more socially primed to interpret the arousal as romantic attraction whereas boys might be more primed to interpret it as sexual arousal. Certainly most individuals in our culture are primed to anticipate, recognize, and interpret opposite-sex arousal as erotic or romantic attraction and to ignore, repress, or differently interpret comparable same-sex arousal. In fact, the heightened visibility of gay men and lesbians in our society is now prompting individuals who experience same-sex arousal to recognize it, label it, and act on it at earlier ages than in previous years (R. C. Fox, 1995).

In some instances, the EBE process itself may be supplemented or even superceded by processes of conditioning or social learning, both positive and negative. Such processes could also produce shifts in an individual's sexual orientation over the life course. For example, the small number of bisexual respondents in the San Francisco study appeared to have added same-sex erotic attraction to an already established heterosexual orientation after adolescence. Similar findings were reported in a more extensive study of bisexual individuals (Weinberg, Williams & Pryor, 1994), with some respondents adding heterosexual attraction to a previously established homosexual orientation This same study also showed that different components of an individual's sexual orientation need not coincide; for example, some of the bisexual respondents were more erotically attracted to one sex but more romantically attracted to the other.

Negative conditioning also appears to be an operative mechanism in some cases of childhood sexual abuse or other upsetting childhood sexual experiences. For example, a reanalysis of the original Kinsey data revealed that a woman was more likely to engage in sexual activity with other women as an adult if she had been pressured or coerced into preadolescent sexual activity with an older male (Van Wyk & Geist, 1984).[7]

Finally, some women who would otherwise be predicted by the EBE model to have a heterosexual orientation might choose for social or political reasons to center their lives around other women. This could lead them to avoid seeking out men for sexual or romantic relationships, to develop affectional and erotic ties to other women, and to self-identify as lesbians or bisexuals. In general, issues of sexual orientation identity are beyond the formal scope of EBE theory.

Deconstructing the Concept of Sexual Orientation

As noted in the introduction, the academic discourse on sexual orientation is currently dominated by the debate between the biological essentialists, who can point to the empirical links between biology and sexual orientation, and the social constructionists, who can point to the historical and anthropological evidence that the concept of sexual orientation is itself a culture-bound notion (De Cecco & Elia, 1993). I suggest that EBE theory can accommodate both kinds of evidence. I have already shown how the theory incorporates the biological evidence. To demonstrate how EBE theory also accommodates the cultural relativism of the social constructionists, it is necessary to deconstruct the theory itself, to explicitly identify its essentialist and culture-specific elements and to see what remains when the latter are stripped away.

There are three essentialist assumptions underlying the scenario outlined in Figure 8.1. First, it is assumed that childhood temperaments are partially coded in the genes and, second, that those temperaments can influence a child's preferences for male-typical or female-typical activities. Third, and most fundamentally, it is assumed that the psychological processes that transform exotic into erotic are universal properties of the human species. That's it. Everything else is cultural overlay, including the concept of sexual orientation itself.

During the last half of the 19th century, there were two kinds of people: normal people and sexual inverts. The latter included feminine men,

---

[7]More generally, these authors advocate a social-learning model of sexual orientation in which early sexual experiences play an important causal role. The San Francisco data, however, imply that most of the other sexual experiences they cite are more likely to be effects rather than causes of an emerging sexual orientation.

masculine women, cross-dressers of both sexes, individuals with same-sex desires—and suffragists. In 1895, the French writer M. A. Raffalovich took one of the first steps toward deconstructing this typology by separating same-sex eroticism from other gender violations: "The inverts are not at all content with the old explanation of the feminine soul in the masculine body. Some of them are more masculine than other men and are attracted to their own sex in proportion to the resemblance" (quoted in Birken, 1988, pp. 105–106). After that, the conceptual space of sexual orientation contained two kinds of people: heterosexuals and homosexuals.

In 1948, Alfred Kinsey took the next major step in the deconstruction of the typology by construing sexual orientation as a bipolar continuum, ranging from exclusive heterosexuality, through bisexuality, to exclusive homosexuality. Placement on the original Kinsey scale was determined jointly by the individual's sexual behaviors and fantasies. Since then, many researchers have criticized this merging of two distinct components of sexual orientation and have variously proposed that separate scales be used to index sexual behaviors, sexual feelings, erotic fantasies, interpersonal affection, social preference, sexual lifestyle, and self-identification (e.g., Klein, Sepekoff, & Wolf, 1985; McWhirter, Sanders, & Reinisch, 1990; Shively & De Cecco, 1977). Thus, Kinsey's single dimension fractionated into as many as seven bipolar dimensions of sexual orientation.

Because many of the studies cited in this article have selected their participants on the basis of Kinsey-like scales, EBE theory has necessarily been couched in that language, but the theory itself is not constrained by such bipolar dimensions. In fact, sexual orientation is actually treated in Figure 8.1 as two conceptually independent dimensions: a heteroerotic dimension and a homoerotic dimension. This approach, first suggested by Shively and De Cecco (1977), parallels contemporary treatments of masculinity and femininity in which independent masculinity and femininity scales are combined into a four-way typology: Those high on one scale and low on the other are defined as either masculine or feminine; those high on both are defined as androgynous; and those low on both are defined as undifferentiated (Bem, 1974; Bem, Martyna, & Watson, 1976; Spence & Helmreich, 1978). Correspondingly, it is possible to identify individuals in shorthand terms as heterosexual, homosexual, bisexual, or asexual, depending on the respective intensities of their heteroerotic and homoerotic responsiveness.

But EBE theory is not about types of persons, but about the processes that determine any individual's location on each of the two dimensions. Thus, Figure 8.1 actually describes two paths for each individual: a heteroerotic path and a homoerotic path. Conceptually, the two paths are independent, thereby allowing for a panoply of individual differences, including several variants of bisexuality (e.g., being erotically attracted to one sex and romantically attracted to the other). Empirically, however, the two dimensions are likely to be negatively correlated in a gender-polarizing culture like ours in which most individuals come to be familiar with one sex while being estranged from the other. EBE theory predicts that this should be especially true for men in our society because, as shown in Table 8.1, boys are less likely than girls to have childhood friends of both sexes. This prediction is supported in a survey of a national probability sample of Americans (Laumann, Gagnon, Michael, & Michaels, 1994). When asked to whom they were sexually attracted, men yielded a bimodal distribution, being more likely to report either exclusively heterosexual or exclusively homosexual attraction than bisexual attraction. In contrast, women were more likely to report bisexual attraction than exclusively homosexual attraction.

Culture thus influences not only the structure and distribution of sexual orientation in a society but also how its natives, including its biological and behavioral scientists, think about sexual orientation. Like the natives of any gender-polarizing culture, we have learned to look at the world through the lenses of gender, to impose the male–female dichotomy on virtually every aspect of life, especially sexuality. Which brings us, finally, to the most deeply embedded cultural assumption of all—that sexual orientation is necessarily based on sex. As Sandra Bem (1993) remarked,

> I am not now and never have been a "heterosexual:" But neither have I ever been a "lesbian" or a "bisexual" . . . The sex-of-partner dimension implicit in the three categories . . . seems irrelevant to my own particular pattern of erotic attractions and sexual experiences. Although some of the (very few) individuals to whom I have been attracted . . . have been men and some have been women, what those individuals have in common

> has nothing to do with either their biological sex or mine—from which I conclude, not that I am attracted to both sexes, but that my sexuality is organized around dimensions other than sex. (p. vii)

This statement also suggests the shape that sexual orientation might assume in a non-gender-polarizing culture, a culture that did not systematically estrange its children from either opposite-sex or same-sex peers. Such children would not grow up to be asexual; rather, their erotic and romantic preferences would simply crystallize around a more diverse and idiosyncratic variety of attributes. Gentlemen might still prefer blonds, but some of those gentlemen (and some ladies) would prefer blonds of any sex. In the final deconstruction, then, EBE theory reduces to but one "essential" principle: Exotic becomes erotic.

REFERENCES

Adkins-Regan, E. (1988). Sex hormones and sexual orientation in animals. *Psychobiology, 16,* 335–347.

Allen, J. B., Kenrick, D. T., Linder, D. E., & McCall, M. A. (1989). Arousal and attraction: A response-facilitation alternative to misattribution and negative-reinforcement models. *Journal of Personality and Social Psychology, 57,* 261–270.

Allen, L. S., & Gorski, R. A. (1992). Sexual orientation and the size of the anterior commissure in the human brain. *Proceedings of the National Academy of Sciences, 89,* 7199–7202.

Archer, J. (1992). *Ethology and human development.* Savage, MD: Barnes & Noble.

Bailey, J. M., & Martin, N. G. (1995, September). *A twin registry study of sexual orientation.* Paper presented at the annual meeting of the International Academy of Sex Research, Provincetown, MA.

Bailey, J. M., & Pillard, R. C. (1991). A genetic study of male sexual orientation. *Archives of General Psychiatry, 48,* 1089–1096.

Bailey, J. M., Pillard, R. C., Neale, M. C., & Agyei, Y. (1993). Heritable factors influence sexual orientation in women. *Archives of General Psychiatry, 50,* 217–223.

Bailey, J. M., & Zucker, K. J. (1995). Childhood sex-typed behavior and sexual orientation: A conceptual analysis and quantitative review. *Developmental Psychology, 31,* 43–55.

Bates, J. E., Bentler, P. M., & Thompson, S. K. (1973). Measurement of deviant gender development in boys. *Child Development, 44,* 591–598.

Bates, J. E., Bentler, P. M., & Thompson, S. K. (1979). Gender-deviant boys compared with normal and clinical controls boys. *Journal of Abnormal Child Psychology, 7,* 243–259.

Bateson, P. P. G. (1978a). Early experience and sexual preferences. In J. B. Hutchison (Ed.), *Biological determinants of sexual behavior* (pp. 29–53). New York: Wiley.

Bateson, P. P. G. (1978b). Sexual imprinting and optimal outbreeding. *Nature, 273,* 659–660.

Bateson, P. P. G. (1979). How do sensitive periods arise and what are they for? *Animal Behaviour, 27,* 470–486.

Bell, A. P. (1982, November). Sexual preference: A postscript. *Siecus Report, 11,* 1–3.

Bell, A. P., Weinberg, M. S., & Hammersmith, S. K. (1981a). *Sexual preference: Its development in men and women.* Bloomington: Indiana University Press.

Bell, A. P., Weinberg, M. S., & Hammersmith, S. K. (1981b). *Sexual preference: Its development in men and women. Statistical appendix.* Bloomington: Indiana University Press.

Bem, S. L. (1974). The measurement of psychological androgyny. *Journal of Consulting and Clinical Psychology, 42,* 155–162.

Bem, S. L. (1993). *The lenses of gender. Transforming the debate on sexual inequality.* New Haven, CT: Yale University Press.

Bem, S. L., Martyna, W., & Watson, C. (1976). Sex typing and androgyny: Further explorations of the expressive domain. *Journal of Personality and Social Psychology, 34,* 1016–1023.

Berenbaum, S. A., & Hines, M. (1992). Early androgens are related to childhood sex-typed toy preferences. *Psychological Science, 3,* 203–206.

Berenbaum, S. A., & Snyder, E. (1995). Early hormonal influences on childhood sex-typed activity and playmate preferences: Implications for the development of sexual orientation. *Developmental Psychology, 31,* 31–42.

Berscheid, E., & Walster, E. (1974). A little bit about love. In T. Huston (Ed.), *Foundations of interpersonal attraction* (pp. 355–381). New York: Academic Press.

Bettelheim, B. (1969). *The children of the dream.* New York: Macmillan,

Birken, L. (1988). *Consuming desire: Sexual science and the emergence of a culture of abundance, 1871–1914.* Ithaca, NY: Cornell University Press.

Blanchard, R., & Bogaert, A. F. (1996). Homosexuality in men and number of older brothers. *American Journal of Psychiatry, 153,* 27–31.

Blanchard, R., McConkey, J. G., Roper, V, & Steiner, B. W. (1983). Measuring physical aggressiveness in heterosexual, homosexual, and transsexual males. *Archives of Sexual Behavior, 12,* 511–524.

Bleier, R. (1984). *Science and gender: A critique of biology and its theories on women.* New York: Pergamon Press.

Brehem, S. S. (1992). *Intimate relationships* (2nd ed.). New York: McGraw-Hill.

Bronfenbrenner, U., & Ceci, S. J. (1994). Nature-nurture reconceptualized in developmental perspective: A bioecological model. *Psychological Review, 101,* 568–586.

Buss, A. H., & Plomin, R. (1975). *A temperament theory of personality development.* New York: Wiley.

Buss, A. H., & Plomin, R. (1984). *Temperament: Early developing personality traits.* Hillsdale, NJ: Erlbaum.

Byne, W., & Parsons, B. (1993). Human sexual orientation: The biologic theories reappraised. *Archives of General Psychiatry, 50,* 228–239.

Cantor, J. R., Zillmann, D., & Bryant, J. (1975). Enhancement of experienced sexual arousal in response to erotic stimuli through misattribution of unrelated residual excitation. *Journal of Personality and Social Psychology, 32,* 69–75.

Caspi, A., & Herbener, E. S. (1990). Continuity and change: Assortative marriage and the consistency of personality in adulthood. *Journal of Personality and Social Psychology, 58,* 250–258.

De Cecco, J. P., & Elia, J. P. (Eds.). (1993). *If you seduce a straight person can you make them gay? Issues in biological essentialism versus social constructionism in gay and lesbian identities.* New York: Harrington Park Press.

DiPietro, J. A. (1981). Rough and tumble play: A function of gender. *Developmental Psychology, 17,* 50–58.

Dittmann, R. W., Kappes, M. H., Kappes, M. E., Borger, D., Meyer-Bahlburg, H. F. L., Stegner, H., Willig, R. H., & Wallis, H. (1990a). Congenital adrenal hyperplasia: II. Gender-related behavior and attitudes in female salt-wasting and simple-virilizing patients. *Psychoneuroendocrinology, 15,* 421–434.

Dittmann, R. W., Kappes, M. H., Kappes, M. E., Borger, D., Stegner, H., Willig, R. H., & Wallis, H. (1990b). Congenital adrenal hyperplasia: I. Gender-related behavior and attitudes in female patients and sisters. *Psychoneuroendocrinology, 15,* 410–420.

Dörner, G., Rhode, W., Stahl, F., Krell, L., & Masius, W. G. (1975). A neuroendocrine predisposition for homosexuality in men. *Archives of Sexual Behavior, 4,* 1–8.

Eaton, W. O., & Enns, L. R. (1986). Sex differences in human motor activity level. *Psychological Bulletin, 100,* 19–28.

Ellis, L., & Ames, M. A. (1987). Neurohormonal functioning and sexual orientation: A theory of homosexuality-heterosexuality. *Psychological Bulletin, 101,* 233–258.

Epstein, S. M. (1967). Toward a unified theory of anxiety. In B. A. Maher (Ed.), *Progress in experimental personality research* (Vol. 4, pp. 1–89). New York: Academic Press.

Feingold, A. (1988). Matching for attractiveness in romantic partners and same-sex friends: A meta-analysis and theoretical critique. *Psychological Bulletin, 104,* 226–235.

Finck, H. T. (1887). *Romantic love and personal beauty: Their development, causal relations, historic and national peculiarities.* London: Macmillan.

Fox, R. (1962). Sibling incest. *British Journal of Sociology, 13,* 128–150.

Fox, R. C. (1995). Bisexual identities. In A. R. D'Augelli & C. J. Patterson (Eds.), *Lesbian, gay and bisexual identities over the lifespan* (pp. 48–86). New York: Oxford University Press.

Freud, S. (1962). *Three essays on the theory of sexuality.* New York: Basic Books. (Original work published 1905)

Fry, D. P. (1990). Play aggression among Zapotec children: Implications for the practice hypothesis. *Aggressive Behavior, 17,* 321–340.

Futuyma, D. J., & Risch, S. J. (1983/84). Sexual orientation, sociobiology, and evolution. *Journal of Homosexuality, 9,* 157–168.

Gartrell, N. K. (1982). Hormones and homosexuality. In W. Paul, J. D. Weinrich, J. C. Gonsiorek, & M. E. Hotvedt (Eds.), *Homosexuality: Social psychological and biological issues* (pp. 169–182). Beverly Hills, CA: Sage.

Gladue, B. A. (1988, August). Neuroendocrine response to estrogen in lesbians compared to heterosexual women. Paper presented at the annual meeting of the International Academy of Sex Research, Minneapolis, MN.

Gladue, B. A., Beatty, W. W., Larson, J., & Staton, R. D. (1990). Sexual orientation and spatial ability in men and women. *Psychobiology, 28,* 101–108.

Gladue, B. A., Green, R., & Heilman, R. E. (1984). Neuroendocrine response to estrogen and sexual orientation. *Science, 225,* 1496–1499.

Gooren, L. (1986a). The neuroendocrine response of luteinizing hormone to estrogen administration in heterosexual, homosexual and transsexual subjects. *Journal of Clinical Endocrinology and Metabolism, 63,* 583–588.

Gooren, L. (1986b). The neuroendocrine response of luteinizing hormone to estrogen administration in the human is not sex specific but dependent on the hormonal environment. *Journal of Clinical Endocrinology and Metabolism, 63,* 589–593.

Gooren, L. (1990). Biomedical theories of sexual orientation: A critical examination. In D. P. McWhirter, S. A. Sanders, & J. M. Reinisch (Eds.), *Homosexuality/heterosexuality: Concepts of sexual orientation* (pp. 71–87). New York: Oxford University Press.

Green, R. (1976). One-hundred ten feminine and masculine boys: Behavioral contrasts and demographic similarities. *Archives of Sexual Behavior, 5,* 425–426.

Green, R. (1987). *The "sissy boy syndrome" and the development of homosexuality.* New Haven, CT: Yale University Press.

Hamer, D., & Copeland, P. (1994). *The science of desire: The search for the gay gene and the biology of behavior.* New York: Simon & Schuster.

Hamer, D. H., Hu, S., Magnuson, V. L., Hu, N., & Pattatucci, A. M. L. (1993). A linkage between DNA markers on the X chromosome and male sexual orientation. *Science, 161,* 321–327.

Harris, J. R. (1995). Where is the child's environment? A group socialization theory of development. *Psychological Review, 101,* 458–489.

Harrison, A. A. (1977). Mere exposure. In L. Berkowitz (Ed.), *Advances in Experimental Social Psychology* (Vol. 10, pp. 39–83). New York: Academic Press.

Hendricks, S. E., Graber, B., & Rodriguez-Sierra, J. F. (1989). Neuroendocrine responses to exogenous estrogen: No differences between heterosexual and homosexual men. *Psychoneuroendocrinology, 14,* 177–185.

Herdt, G. (1981). *Guardians of the flutes: Idioms of masculinity.* New York: McGraw-Hill.

Herdt, G. (Ed.). (1984). *Ritualized homosexuality in Melanesia.* Berkeley: University of California Press.

Herdt, G. (1987). *Sambia: Ritual and gender in New Guinea.* New York: Holt, Rinehart & Winston.

Herdt, G. (1990). Developmental discontinuities and sexual orientation across cultures. In D. P McWhirter, S. A. Sanders, & J. M. Reinisch (Eds.), *Homosexuality/heterosexuality: Concepts of sexual orientation* (pp. 208–236). New York: Oxford University Press.

Hess, E. H. (1959). The relationship between imprinting and motivation. In M. R. Jones (Ed.), *Nebraska Symposium on Motivation: Vol. 7* (pp. 44–77). Lincoln: University of Nebraska Press.

Hill, C., Rubin, Z., & Peplau, L. A. (1976). Breakups before marriage: The end of 103 affairs. *Journal of Social Issues, 31,* 147–168.

Hoon, P. W., Wincze, J. P., & Hoon, E. F. (1977). A test of reciprocal inhibition: Are anxiety and sexual arousal in women mutually inhibitory? *Journal of Abnormal Psychology, 86,* 65–74.

Hyde, J. S. (1984). How large are gender differences in aggression? A developmental meta-analysis. *Developmental Psychology, 10,* 722–736.

Immelmann, K. (1972). Sexual and other long-term aspects of imprinting in birds and other species. In D. S. Lehrman, R. A. Hinde, & E. Shaw (Eds.), *Advances in the study of behavior* (Vol. 4, pp. 147–174). New York: Academic Press.

Kenrick, D. T., & Cialdini, R. B. (1977). Romantic attraction: Misattribution versus reinforcement explanations. *Journal of Personality and Social Psychology, 35,* 381–391.

Kinsey, A. C., Pomeroy, W. B., & Martin, C. E. (1948). *Sexual behavior in the human male.* Philadelphia: W. B. Saunders.

Kirsch, J. A. W., & Rodman, J. E. (1982). Selection and sexuality: The Darwinian view of homosexuality. In W. Paul, J. D. Weinrich, J. C. Gonsiorek, & M. E. Hotvedt (Eds.), *Homosexuality: Social psychological and biological issues* (pp. 183–195). Beverly Hills, CA: Sage.

Klein, F., Sepckoff, B., & Wolf, T. J. (1985). Sexual orientation: A multi-variable, dynamic process. *Journal of Homosexuality, 11,* 35–49.

Laumann, E. O., Gagnon, J. H., Michael, R. T., & Michaels, S. (1994). *The social organization of sexuality: Sexual practices in the United States.* Chicago: University of Chicago Press.

LeVay, S. (1991). A difference in hypothalamic structure between heterosexual and homosexual men. *Science, 153,* 1034–1037.

LeVay, S. (1993). *The sexual brain.* Cambridge, MA: MIT Press.

Levinger, G., Senn, D. J., & Jorgensen, B. W. (1970). Progress toward permanence in courtship: A test of the Kerckhoff-Davis hypotheses. *Sociometry, 33,* 427–443.

McClanahan, K. K., Gold, J. A., Lenney, E., Ryckman, R. M., & Kulberg, G. E. (1990). Infatuation and attraction to a dissimilar other: Why is love blind? *Journal of Social Psychology 130,* 433–445.

McCormick, C. M., & Witelson, S. F. (1991). A cognitive profile of homosexual men compared to heterosexual men and women. *Psychoneuroendocrinology, 16,* 459–473.

McWhirter, D. P., Sanders, S. A., & Reinisch, J. M. (Eds.). (1990). *Homosexuality/heterosexuality: The Kinsey scale and current research.* New York: Oxford University Press.

Meyer, J. P., & Pepper, S. (1977). Need compatibility and marital adjustment in young married couples. *Journal of Personality and Social Psychology, 35,* 331–342.

Meyer-Bahlburg, H. F. L. (1984). Psychoendocrine research on sexual orientation: Current status and future options. *Progress in Brain Research, 61,* 375–398.

Meyer-Bahlburg, H. F. L., Ehrhardt, A. A., Rosen, L. R., Gruen, R. S., Veridiano, N. P., Vann, F H., & Neuwalder, H. F. (1995). Prenatal estrogens and the development of homosexual orientation. *Developmental Psychology, 31,* 12–21.

Moller, L. C., Hymel, S., & Rubin, K. H. (1992). Sex typing in play and popularity in middle childhood. *Sex Roles, 26,* 331–353.

Moltz, H., Rosenblum, L., & Halikas, N. (1959). Imprinting and level of anxiety. *Journal of Comparative and Physiological Psychology, 51,* 240–244.

Money, J., & Ehrhardt, A. A. (1972). *Man and woman, boy and girl: The differentiation and dimorphism of gender identity from conception to maturity.* Baltimore: Johns Hopkins Press.

Money, J., Schwartz, M., & Lewis, V. G. (1984). Adult erotosexual status and fetal hormonal masculinization and demasculinization: 46, XX congenital virilizing adrenal hyperplasia and 46, XY androgen-insensitivity syndrome compared. *Psychoneuroendocrinology, 9,* 405–414.

Mook, D. B. (1987). *Motivation: The organization of action.* New York: Norton.

Murstein, B. I. (1972). Physical attractiveness and marital choice. *Journal of Personality and Social Psychology, 22,* 8–12.

Newcomb, T. M. (1961). *The acquaintance process.* New York: Holt, Rinehart & Winston.

Pitz, G. F., & Ross, R. B. (1961). Imprinting as a function of arousal. *Journal of Comparative and Physiological Psychology, 54,* 602–604.

Plomin, R. (1986). *Development, genetics, and psychology.* Hillsdale, NJ: Erlbaum.

Quadagno, D. M., Briscoe, R., & Quadagno, J. S. (1977). Effects of perinatal gonadal hormones on selected nonsexual behavior patterns: A critical assessment of the nonhuman and human literature. *Psychological Bulletin, 84,* 62–80.

Rabin, I. A. (1965). *Growing up in a kibbutz.* New York: Springer.

Reinisch, J. M. (1981). Prenatal exposure to synthetic progestins increases potential for aggression in humans. *Science, 111,* 1171–1173.

Rice, G., Anderson, C., Risch, N., & Ebers, G. (1995, September). *Male homosexuality: Absence of linkage to micro satellite markers on the X-chromosome in a Canadian study.* Paper presented at the annual meeting of the International Academy of Sex Research, Provincetown, MA.

Rubin, Z. (1973). *Liking and loving.* New York: Holt, Rinehart & Winston.

Rushton, J. P., Fulker, D. W., Neale, M. C., Nias, D. K. B., & Eysenck, H. J. (1986). Altruism and aggression: The heritability of individual differences. *Journal of Personality and Social Psychology, 50,* 1192–1198.

Savin-Williams, R. C. (1987). An ethological perspective on homosexuality during adolescence. *Journal of Adolescent Research, 2,* 283–302.

Schachter, S., & Singer, J. E. (1962). Cognitive, social, and physiological determinants of emotional state. *Psychological Review, 69,* 379–399.

Serbin, L. A. (1980). Sex-role socialization: A field in transition. In B. B, Lahey & A. E. Kazdin (Eds.), *Advances in clinical child psychology* (Vol. 3, pp. 41–96). New York: Plenum.

Shepher, J. (1971). Mate selection among second generation kibbutz adolescents and adults: Incest avoidance and negative imprinting. *Archives of Sexual Behavior, 1,* 293–307.

Shively, M., & De Cecco, J. (1977). Components of sexual identity. *Journal of Homosexuality, 3,* 41–48.

Silverman, I. (1971). Physical attractiveness and courtship. *Archives of Sexual Behavior, 1,* 22–25.

Solomon, R. L. (1980). The opponent-process theory of acquired motivation: The costs of pleasure and the benefits of pain. *American Psychologist, 35,* 691–712.

Solomon, R. L., & Corbit, J. D. (1974). An opponent-process theory of motivation: I. Temporal dynamics of affect. *Psychological Review, 81,* 119–145.

Spence, J. T., & Helmreich, R. (1978). *Masculinity and femininity: Their psychological dimensions, correlates, and antecedents.* Austin: University of Texas Press.

Spiro, M. E. (1958). *Children of the kibbutz.* Cambridge, MA: Harvard University Press.

Stoller, R. J. (1979). Sexual excitement: Dynamics of erotic life. New York: Simon & Schuster.

Strong, S. R., Hills, H. I., Kilmartin, C. T., DeVries, H., Lanier, K., Nelson, B. N., Strickland, D., & Meyer, C. W., III. (1988). The dynamic relations among interpersonal behaviors: A test of complementarity and anticomplementarity. *Journal of Personality and Social Psychology, 54,* 798–810.

Swaab, D. F., & Hofman, M. A. (1990). An enlarged suprachiasmatic nucleus in homosexual men. *Brain Research, 537,* 141–148.

Talmon, Y. (1964). Mate selection in collective settlements. *American Sociological Review, 29,* 481–508.

Tripp, C. A. (1975). *The homosexual matrix.* New York: McGraw-Hill.

Tripp, C. A. (1987). *The homosexual matrix* (2nd ed.). New York: New American Library.

Van Wyk, P. H., & Geist, C. S. (1984). Psychological development of heterosexual, bisexual, and homosexual behavior. *Archives of Sexual Behavior, 13,* 505–544.

Walster, E. (1971). Passionate love. In B. I. Murstein (Ed.), *Theories of attraction and love* (pp. 85–99). New York: Springer.

Weinberg, M. S., Williams, C. J., & Pryor, D. W. (1994). *Dual attraction: Understanding bisexuality.* New York: Oxford University Press.

Weinrich, J. D. (1978). Nonreproduction, homosexuality, transsexualism, and intelligence: I. A systematic literature search. *Journal of Homosexuality, 1,* 275–289.

Weinrich, J. D. (1987). A new sociobiological theory of homosexuality applicable to societies with universal marriage. *Ethology and Sociobiology, 8,* 37–47.

Westermarck, E. (1891). *The history of human marriage.* London: Macmillan.

White, G. L., Fishbein, S., & Rutstein, J. (1981). Passionate love and the misattribution of arousal. *Journal of Personality and Social Psychology, 41,* 56–62.

White, G. L., & Kight, T. D. (1984). Misattribution of arousal and attraction: Effects of salience of explanations for arousal. *Journal of Experimental Social Psychology, 10,* 55–64.

Wilson, E. O. (1975). *Sociobiology: The new synthesis.* Cambridge, MA: Harvard University Press.

Wilson, E. O. (1978). *On human nature.* Cambridge, MA: Harvard University Press.

Wolchik, S. A., Beggs, V. E., Wincze, J. P., Sakheim, D. K., Barlow, D. H., & Mavissakalian, M. (1980). The effect of emotional arousal on subsequent sexual arousal in men. *Journal of Abnormal Psychology, 89,* 595–598.

Zillmann, D. (1983). Transfer of excitation in emotional behavior. In J. T. Cacioppo & R. E. Petty (Eds.), *Social Psychophysiology: A sourcebook.* New York: Guilford Press.

Zucker, K. J. (1990). Gender identity disorders in children: Clinical descriptions and natural history. In R. Blanchard & B. W. Steiner (Eds.), *Clinical management of gender identity disorders in children and adults* (pp. 1–23). Washington, DC: American Psychiatric Press.

Zucker, K. J., & Bradley, S. J. (1995). *Gender identity disorder and psychosexual problems in children and adolescents.* New York: Guilford Press.

Zucker, K. J., Bradley, S. J., Oliver, G., Hood, J. E., Blake, J., & Fleming, S. (1992, July). *Psychosexual assessment of women with congenital adrenal hyperplasia: Preliminary analyses.* Paper presented at the annual meeting of the International Academy of Sex Research, Prague, Czechoslovakia.

Zucker, K. J., & Green, R. (1993). Psychological and familial aspects of gender identity disorder. *Child and Adolescent Psychiatric Clinics of North America, 2,* 513–542.

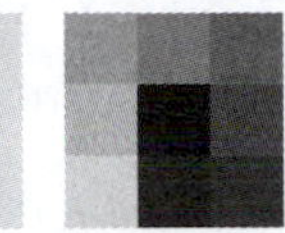

READING 9

Is Homophobia Associated with Homosexual Arousal?

Henry E. Adams, Lester W. Wright, Jr., and Bethany A. Lohr

• University of Georgia

The authors investigated the role of homosexual arousal in exclusively heterosexual men who admitted negative affect toward homosexual individuals. Participants consisted of a group of homophobic men (n = 35) and a group of nonhomophobic men (n = 29); they were assigned to groups on the basis of their scores on the Index of Homophobia (W. W. Hudson & W. A. Ricketts, 1980). The men were exposed to sexually explicit erotic stimuli consisting of heterosexual, male homosexual. and lesbian videotapes, and changes in penile circumference were monitored. They also completed an Aggression Questionnaire (A. H. Buss & M. Perry, 1992). Both groups exhibited increases in penile circumference to the heterosexual and female homosexual videos. Only the homophobic men showed an increase in penile erection to male homosexual stimuli. The groups did not differ in aggression. Homophobia is apparently associated with homosexual arousal that the homophobic individual is either unaware of or denies.

Hostility and discrimination against homosexual individuals are well-established facts (Berrill, 1990). On occasion, these negative attitudes lead to hostile verbal and physical acts against gay individuals with little apparent motivation except a strong dislike (Herek, 1989). In fact, more than 90% of gay men and lesbians report being targets of verbal abuse or threats, and more than one-third report being survivors of violence related to their homosexuality (Fassinger, 1991). Although negative attitudes and behaviors toward gay individuals have been assumed to be associated with rigid moralistic beliefs, sexual ignorance, and fear of homosexuality, the etiology of these attitudes and behaviors remains a puzzle (Marmot, 1980). Weinberg (1972) labeled these attitudes and behaviors *homophobia*, which he defined as the dread of being in close quarters with homosexual men and women as well as irrational fear, hatred, and intolerance by heterosexual individuals of homosexual men and women.

Hudson and Ricketts (1980) have indicated that the meaning of the term *homophobia* has been diluted because of its expansion in the literature to include any negative attitude, belief, or action toward homosexuality. Fyfe (1983) has also argued that the broad definition of homophobia threatens to restrict our understanding of negative reactions to gay individuals. Furthermore, Hudson and Ricketts criticized studies for not making the distinction between intellectual attitudes toward homosexuality (*homonegativism*) and personal, affective responses to gay individuals (*homophobia*). They indicated that many researchers do not state the operational definition of what they term *homophobic*. To clarify this problem, Hudson and Ricketts defined *homonegativism* as a multidimensional construct that includes judgment regarding the morality of homosexuality, decisions concerning personal or social relationships, and any response concerning beliefs, preferences, legality, social desirability, or similar cognitive responses. *Homophobia*, on the other hand, was defined as an emotional or affective response including fear, anxiety, anger, discomfort, and aversion that an individual experiences in interacting with gay individuals, which may or may not involve a cognitive component. For example, ego-dystonic homosexuality or marked distress about one's sexual orientation may be a type of homonegativism but does not necessarily imply homophobia. This clarification is consistent with Weinberg's (1973) definition of homophobia, as well as Haaga's (1992) suggestion that the term be restricted to clearly phobic reactions.

It has also been argued that the term *homophobic* may not be appropriate because there is no evidence that homophobic individuals exhibit avoidance of homosexual persons (Bernstein, 1994; Rowan, 1994). Nevertheless, the only necessary requirement for the label of phobia is that phobic stimuli produce anxiety. Whether the individual exhibits avoidance or endures the anxiety often depends on the nature of the stimuli and the environmental circumstances. MacDonald's (1976) suggestions are consistent with this analysis because he defined *homophobia* as anxiety or anticipatory anxiety elicited by homosexual individuals. O'Donahue and Caselles (1993) noted that McDonald's definition parallels the diagnostic criteria of the *Diagnostic and Statistical Manual of Mental Disorders* (DSM–IV; American Psychiatric Association. 1994) for simple phobia and captures the negative emotional reactions toward homosexuality that seem to have motivated use of the term. In a similar analysis, O'Donahue and Caselles described a tripartite model of homophobia consisting of cognitive, affective, and behavioral components that may interact differently with various situations associated with homosexuality.

Although the causes of homophobia are unclear, several psychoanalytic explanations have emerged from the idea of homophobia as an anxiety-based phenomenon. One psychoanalytic explanation is that anxiety about the possibility of being or becoming a homosexual may be a major factor in homophobia (West, 1977). For example, de Kuyper (1993) has asserted that homophobia is the result of the remnants of homosexuality in the heterosexual resolution of the Oedipal conflict. Whereas these notions are vague. psychoanalytic theories usually postulate that homophobia is a result of repressed homosexual urges or a form of latent homosexuality. *Latent homosexuality* can be defined as homosexual arousal which the individual is either unaware of or denies (West, 1977). Psychoanalysts use the concept of repressed or latent homosexuality to explain the emotional malaise and irrational attitudes displayed by some individuals who feel guilty about their erotic interests and struggle to deny and repress homosexual impulses. In fact, West (1977, p. 202) stated, "when placed in a situation that threatens to excite their own unwanted homosexual thoughts, they overreact with panic or anger." Slaby (1994) contended that anxiety about homosexuality typically does not occur in individuals who are same-sex oriented, but it usually involves individuals who are ostensibly heterosexual and have difficulty integrating their homosexual feelings or activity. The relationship between homophobia and latent homosexuality has not been empirically investigated and is one of the purposes of the present study.

Specifically, the present study was designed to investigate whether homophobic men show more sexual arousal to homosexual cues than nonhomophobic men as suggested by psychoanalytic theory. As O'Donahue and Caselles (1993, p. 193) have noted, and investigation of whether those who "aggress against homosexuals become sexually aroused to homosexual stimuli (as certain psychoanalytic theories might predict)" would contribute to our understanding of homophobia. A secondary goal was to evaluate whether homophobic individuals are persons who are more generally hostile or aggressive than nonhomophobic men. The present investigation was designed to evaluate these two hypotheses.

Method

Participants

Caucasian heterosexual male volunteers ($n = 64$) recruited from the Psychology Department Research Subject Pool at the University of Georgia participated in the study. They were screened during large group testing during which time they completed the modified version of the Kinsey Heterosexual–Homosexual Rating Scale (Kinsey, Pomeroy, & Martin, 1948), the Index of Homophobia (IHP; Hudson & Ricketts. 1980), and the Aggression Questionnaire (Buss & Perry, 1992). They were contacted by telephone at a later date to schedule the laboratory portion of the study. All participants received partial course credit. The mean age of the men was 20.3 years (range = 18 to 31 years).

Screening Measures

Kinsey Heterosexual–Homosexual Rating Scale. A modified version of the Kinsey Heterosexual–Homosexual Rating Scale was used to assess sexual arousal and prior sexual experiences. This version of the Kinsey is a 7-point scale on which individuals separately rated their sexual arousal and experiences from *exclusively homosexual* to *exclusively heterosexual.* Only participants who reported exclusively heterosexual arousal and experiences (i.e., 1 on both sections) were selected for participation.

IHP. The IHP is the most widely used measure of homophobia (O'Donahue & Caselles. 1993). The items of the IHP assess affective components of homophobia. The scale contains 25 items, and scores range from 0 to 100. Respondents were divided into four groups on the basis of their score: 0–25, high-grade nonhomophobic men; 26–50, lowgrade nonhomophobic men; 51–75, low-grade homophobic men; and 76–100, high-grade homophobic men. The score obtained is a measure of "dread," an individual experiences when placed in close quarters with a homosexual: a low score equals low dread, and a high score equals high dread. Because most of the items contain the terms *comfortable* or *uncomfortable* dread can be assumed to mean anticipatory anxiety about interacting with a homosexual person. For example, one item states "I would feel nervous being in a group of homosexuals." Positive and negative statements are used to control for response set biases. The authors reported .90 reliability coefficient on a sample of 300 respondents. O'Donahue and Caselles (1993, p. 187) commented that the authors of the IHP used a "more empirical and psychometrically sophisticated approach than previous researchers who have produced instruments to measure homophobia."

The men were divided into two groups on the basis of their scores on the IHP: 0–50 = nonhomophobic men, n = 29, M = 30.48, SD = 14.70; 51–100 = homophobic men, n = 35, M = 80.40, SD = 13.2. This split was necessary because of an inability to find an adequate number of exclusively heterosexual men who scored in the high-grade nonhomophobic range (0–25).

Response Measures

Penile plethysmography. A mercury-in-rubber (MIR) circumferential strain gauge (Bancroft, Jones, & Pullan, 1966) was used to measure erectile responses to the sexual stimuli. When attached, changes in the circumference of the penis caused changes in the electrical resistance of the mercury column, which were detected by a Parks Model 270 Plethysmograph (pre-amplifier: Parks Electronic Laboratory, Beaverton, OR). The pre-amplifier output was channeled into a Grass polygraph. Tumescence responses were recorded on the chart drive of the polygraph and were channeled to an analog-to-digital (A-to-D) interface connected to an IBM computer. A parallel recording on chart paper was used to identify abrupt changes suggestive of movement artifacts, which were eliminated from the data before analysis. The strain gauge was calibrated prior to each evaluation using a plexiglass calibrating cone, allowing for conversion (approximately 130 time/s) to millimeters (approximately 275 A-to-D units per mm) of penile circumference, which served as the primary dependent variable. The internal consistency and test-retest reliability of the penile plethysmograph is acceptable (O'Donahue & Letourneau, 1992), and penile plethysmographic responses to sexually explicit stimuli have been shown to discriminate between homosexual and heterosexual men (Tollison, Adams, & Tollison, 1979). Zuckerman (1971) described penile plethysmographic reponses as the most specific measure of sexual arousal because significant changes occur only during sexual stimulation and sleep.

Aggression Questionnaire. Buss and Perry's (1992) 29-item scale was used to assess an overall trait of aggression. The men rated each item on a scale of 1 (*extremely uncharacteristic of me*) to 5 (*extremelv characteristic of me*). Items targeted four aspects of aggression: physical aggression, verbal aggression, anger, and hostility. Buss and Perry (1992) provided intercorrelation data suggesting a unitary trait of aggression. Only this overall score of aggression was used as the dependent variable.

Stimulus Materials

The stimuli were 4-min segments of explicit erotic videotapes depicting consensual adult heterosexual activity, consensual male homosexual activity, and consensual female homosexual activity. The sexual activity in the videos included sexual foreplay (e.g., kissing and undressing), oral-genital contact (e.g., fellatio or cunnilingus), and intercourse (i.e., vaginal penetration, anal penetration, or tribadism in the lesbian film). The lesbian videotape was included because it has been shown to be highly sexually arousing to heterosexual men and is a better discriminator between heterosexual and homosexual men than other stimuli (Mavissikalian, Blanchard, Abel, & Barlow, 1975).

Procedure

The procedure was explained to the participant on arrival at the laboratory. He was informed that he could terminate participation at any time, and he signed informed consent. The participant was accompanied to a soundproof chamber, where he was seated in a comfortable reclining chair and was given instructions on the proper placement of the MIR strain gauge. After the experimenter's departure from the experimental chamber into the adjoining equipment room, the participant attached the penile strain gauge. The adjoining equipment room housed the Grass polygraph, the videotape player, an IBM-compatible computer, and the two-way intercom. Once the participant indicated that the apparatus was in place by way of the intercom, a 4-min baseline was recorded in the absence of any stimuli. Next, the three sexually explicit videos were presented to the participant. Following each video-taped presentation, he rated his level of subjective sexual arousal (i.e., how "turned on" he was) and the degree of penile erection (i.e., from no change to 100% erection) on a scale of 0 to 10. The participant's penile circumference was allowed to return to baseline levels before the next stimulus was presented. The sequence of presentation was counterbalanced across participants to avoid order effects. Following the final presentation, the participant was debriefed and dismissed.

Data Reduction

A change score was used to analyze the penile plethysmographic data where the mean penile circumference (in millimeters) in the first second of time was subtracted from subsequent seconds for each video presentation. These scores were divided into six 40-s time blocks. The average change score in penile circumference for each time block was then analyzed.

Results

Penile Plethysmography

The data were analyzed using mixed model analysis of variance (ANOVA) with one between-subjects factor (Groups) and two within-subjects factors (Stimulus Type and Time Blocks). The main effect for stimulus type, $F(2, 124) = 23.67, p < .001$; time blocks, $F(5, 3101) = 137.46, p < .001$; and their interaction, $F\ (10, 620) = 21.73, p < .001$, were all significant, as was the Groups × Stimulus Type × Time Blocks interaction, $F\ (10, 620) = 2.1$ $1, p <$ .OS. No other main effects or interactions were significant. The data for each time block for the two groups are presented separately for each stimulus type to Figure 9.1. Inspection of this figure suggests that the interaction is due to difference between homophobic and nonhomophobic men across time blocks for only the homosexual video.

In order to evaluate this impression, we conducted ANOVAs of Groups × Time Blocks for each stimulus type. For the heterosexual and lesbian videos, only time blocks were significant, indicating increases in penile engorgement over time blocks, $F\ (5, 310) = 115.321, p < .001$, and F $(5, 310) = 64{,}878, p < .001$, respectively. There were no significant main effects of groups or an interaction with these two videos, indicating that both groups showed significant engorgement to these videos. For the male homosexual video, there was a significant main effect of groups, time blocks, and their interaction: $F(1, 62) = 6.14, p <$ $.05$; $F\ (5, 310) = 19.04, p < .001$; and $F\ (5, 310) =$ $5.14, p < .001$, respectively. These results indicate that the homophobic men showed a significant increase in penile circumference to the male homosexual video but that the control men did not. An analysis of the simple effects of this interaction with pairwise Tukey tests indicate that the groups were significantly different at time blocks 4, 5, and 6 ($p < .01$).

Another way of evaluating these data is to calculate the percentage of men who demonstrated

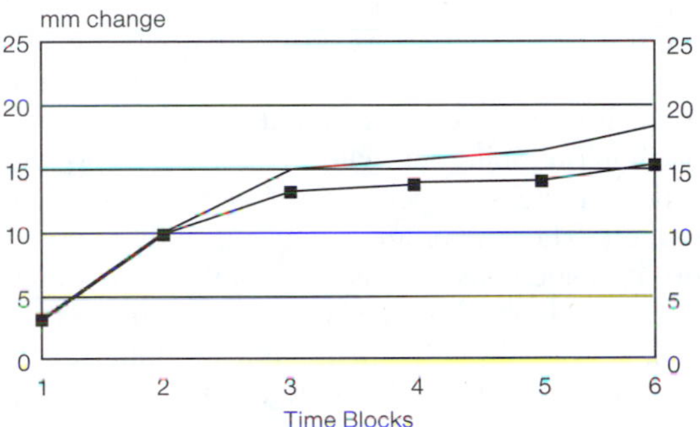

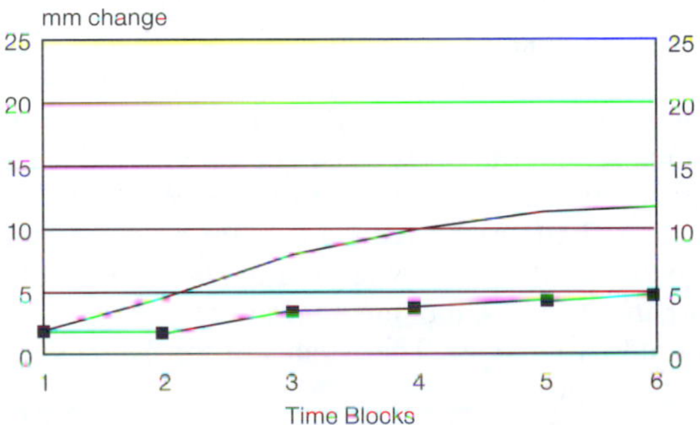

FIGURE 9.1 ■ Stimulus presentations by groups across time blocks. The only significant difference is with the homosexual video. The blocked line represents the nonhomophobic group; the solid line represents the homophobic group. Top: Heterosexual video; middle: lesbian video; bottom: homosexual video.

no significant tumescence (i.e., 0–6 mm), modest tumescence (i.e., > 6–12 mm), and definite tumescence (i.e., > 12 mm) based on their mean tumescence score to the homosexual video. In the homophobic group, 20% showed no significant tumescence, 26% showed moderate tumescence, and 54% showed definite tumescence to the homosexual video; the corresponding percentages in the nonhomophobic group were 66%, 10%, and 24%, respectively.

Subjective Ratings

The data for the subjective estimates of sexual arousal and penile erection were analyzed with a mixed model ANOVA with one fixed factor (groups) and two repeated factors (stimuli and erection vs. arousal ratings). The main effect of stimulus type was significant, $F(2, 124) = 90.93$, $p < .001$, indicating significantly greater arousal and erection ratings to the heterosexual and lesbian videos than to the male homosexual video. The main effect of ratings (arousal vs. erection) was also significant, $F(1, 62) = 8.78$, $p < .01$, indicating the men rated more erection than arousal to the videos. The interaction of stimuli and arousal versus erection ratings was also significant, $F(2, 124) = 9.34$, $p < .001$. This interaction is primarily due to greater ratings of erection and arousal to heterosexual and lesbian videos than to the male homosexual video. Furthermore, the interaction reveals little differences between the types of rating (arousal vs. erection) with the exception of the homosexual video, where there were significantly greater ratings of erection than arousal. These means are shown in Table 9.1. There were no other significant main or interaction effects of subjective ratings.

Pearson correlation coefficients were computed between the penile response measures and subjective ratings of arousal and erection, as shown in Table 9.1. These correlations ranged from .53 to .66 and indicate that participants' ratings were generally in agreement with their penile responses. Pearson correlations coefficients were also computed with subjective ratings of arousal and erection ratings for each group, as shown in Table 9.2. These correlations are quite high and are all significant at the $p < .01$ level of confidence, indicating that these two ratings are essentially measuring the same event. The correlation of erection and arousal to the homosexual video in the nonhomophobic group was significantly smaller (i.e., $p < .05$ or $p < .01$ in all comparisons) when compared to other correlations. The decreased consistency between erection and arousal may have been due to the smaller changes in penile responses in this group, making subjective estimates more difficult.

Because of the above findings, we conducted three analyses of covariance for each video using the mean penile response across time blocks for each group, with subjective arousal as the

Table 9.1. Means and Correlations of Subjective Ratings With Penile Response

	Arousal			Erection		
Video	*M*	*SD*	*r*[a]	*M*	*SD*	*r*[a]
Heterosexual	7.14	1.97	.57*	7.10	1.88	.64*
Lesbian	6.28	2.94	.63*	6.31	2.79	.66*
Male homosexual	2.03	2.74	.53*	2.79	3.06	.64*

[a]Subjective ratings were correlated with mean penile response across time blocks.
*$p < .01$.

covariate. There were no significant group differences for the heterosexual or lesbian videos, indicating that the reports of arousal were consistent with penile responses. However, there remained a significant difference between groups for the male homosexual video, F (1, 60) = 8.10, $p < .01$, to which homophobic men continued to display more penile erection after subjective arousal was statistically controlled. This finding indicates that reports of subjective arousal were not consistent with penile responses with the male homosexual video. These data appear to be due to underestimates of arousal, particularly by homophobic men, to the homosexual stimuli.

Aggression Questionnaire

A t test between groups was conducted on the Aggression Questionnaire. The difference between the scores for the homophobic (M = 58.37, SD = 14.39) and the nonhomophobic men (M = 55.96, SD = 14.75) was not statistically significant, t (62) = .65, $p > .05$. This result indicates that these groups did not differ in aggression as measured by this questionnaire.

Discussion

The results of this study indicate that individuals who score in the homophobic range and admit negative affect toward homosexuality demonstrate significant sexual arousal to male homosexual erotic stimuli. These individuals were selected on the basis of their report of having only heterosexual arousal and experiences. Furthermore, their ratings of erection and arousal to homosexual stimuli were low and not significantly different from nonhomophobic men who demonstrated no significant increase in penile response to homosexual stimuli. These data are consistent with response discordance where verbal judgments are not consistent with physiological reactivity, as in the case of homophobic individuals viewing homosexual stimuli. Lang (1994) has noted that the most dramatic response discordance occurs with reports of feeling and physiologic responses. Another possible explanation is found in various psychoanalytic theories, which have generally explained homophobia as a threat to an individual's own homosexual impulses causing repression, denial, or reaction formation (or all three; West, 1977). Generally, these varied explanations conceive of homophobia as one type of latent homosexuality where persons either are unaware of or deny their homosexual urges. These data are consistent with these notions.

Another explanation of these data is found in Barlow, Sakheim, and Beck's (1983) theory of the role of anxiety and attention in sexual responding. It is possible that viewing homosexual stimuli causes negative emotions such as anxiety in homophobic men but not in nonhomophobic men. Because anxiety has been shown to enhance arousal and erection, this theory would predict increases in erection in homophobic men. Further-

TABLE 9.2. Correlations Between Subjective Arousal and Subjective Erection Ratings

		Video		
Group	*N*	Heterosexual	Lesbian	Male homosexual
Homophobic	35	.91	.95	.90
Nonhomophobic	29	.93	.94	.78

more, it would indicate that a response to homosexual stimuli is a function of the threat condition rather than sexual arousal per se. Whereas difficulties of objectively evaluating psychoanalytic hypotheses are well-documented, these approaches would predict that sexual arousal is an intrinsic response to homosexual stimuli, whereas Barlow's (1986) theory would predict that sexual arousal to homosexual stimuli by homophobic individuals is a function of anxiety. These competing notions can and should be evaluated by future research.

The hypothesis that homophobic men are merely aggressive individuals is not supported by the present data. There were no differences in aggression scores between groups as measured by the Aggression Questionnaire. However, this questionnaire is a general measure of aggression and does not address the possibility of situational aggression or hostility where the situation involves homosexuality or interacting with a homosexual person. It is possible that aggressiveness in homophobic individuals is specific to homosexual cues.

These data also indicate that subjective estimates of arousal and erection are largely consistent with physiological indices of penile erections, with correlation coefficients ranging from .53 to .66. Because the relationships between subjective measures of erection and arousal were quite high, ranging from .78 to .95, it is likely that these two estimates are measures of similar or identical events. Most of these latter correlations were in the .90 range with the exception of nonhomophobic individuals' ratings of arousal and erection to homosexual stimuli, which was .78. As noted before, these results were probably due to the small penile responses to this stimulus, making subjective estimates more difficult and less consistent.

A major difficulty in this area of research is in defining and measuring homophobia. For example. with the scale used in the present study. we found it difficult to find heterosexual men who scored in the high-grade nonhomophobic range (0–25). Similarly, Hudson and Ricketts (1980) found that 56% of their sample scored in the homophobic range (i.e., > 51). This problem may be due not to a high prevalence of homophobia; rather, it may be the result of the nature of this and similar scales. As O'Donahue and Caselles (1993) suggested, scales that assess homophobia measure only cognitive and affective components. The IHP and similar scales would be greatly strengthened by inclusion of a behavioral component that measures "fight or flight" reactions commonly found in phobia scales, such as the Fear Questionnaire (Marks & Mathews, 1978). Modification of these scales is needed and should include items that specifically assess actual or potentially aggressive or avoidant acts toward homosexual individuals or homosexual activities, as suggested by O'Donahue and Caselles (1993). In our opinion, negative attitudes and cognitions toward homosexuality are probably not sufficient to warrant the label of homophobia.

Future research should focus on several issues. First, more reliable scales for measuring homophobia should be devised that incorporate cognitive, affective, and behavioral components. Second, the issue of whether homophobic individuals meet the definitional criteria for simple phobia should be investigated by determining whether these individuals experience anxiety or avoidance when confronted with homosexual cues. Third, the issue of whether homophobia is specific to men or may also occur in women has not been addressed systematically, nor is it clear whether homophobic women may show sexual arousal to erotic lesbian stimuli. Fourth, it has been claimed that homophobic individuals have poor heterosexual adjustment, and this issue should be documented. With answers to these and similar issues, a clearer understanding of the nature of homophobia will be possible.

REFERENCES

American Psychiatric Association. (1994). *Diagnostic and statistical manual of mental disorders* (4th ed.). Washington, DC: Author.

Bancroft, J. H., Jones, H. G., & Pullan, B. R. (1966). A simple transducer for measuring penile erection with comments on its use in the treatment of sexual disorders. *Behaviour Research and Therapy, 4,* 230–241.

Barlow, D. H. (1986). Causes of sexual dysfunction: The role of anxiety and cognitive interference. *Journal of Consulting and Clinical Psychology, 54,* 140–148.

Barlow, D. H., Sakheim, D. K., & Beck, J. G. (1983). Anxiety increases sexual arousal. *Journal of Abnormal Psychology, 92,* 49–54.

Bernstein, G. S. (1994). A reply to Rowan. *Behavior Therapist, 17,* 185–186.

Berrill, K. T. (1990). Anti-gay violence and victimization in the United States: An overview. *Journal of Interpersonal Violence, 5,* 274–294.

Buss, A. H., & Perry, M. (1992). The aggression questionnaire. *Journal of Personality and Social Psychology, 63,* 452–459.

de Kuyper, E. (1993). The Freudian construction of sexuality: The gay foundations of heterosexuality and straight homophobia. *Journal of Homosexuality, 24,* 137–144.

Fassinger, R. (1992). The hidden minority: Issues and challenges in working with lesbian women and gay men. *Counseling Psychologist, 19,* 157–176.

Fyfe, B. (1983). "Homophobia" or homosexual bias reconsidered. *Archives of Sexual Behavior, 12,* 549–554.

Haaga, D. (1992). Homophobia? *Journal of Social Behavior and Psychology, 6,* 171–174.

Herek, G. (1989). Hate crimes against lesbians and gay men: Correlates and gender differences. *American Psychology, 44,* 948–955.

Hudson, W. W., & Ricketts, W. A. (1980). A strategy for the measurement of homophobia. *Journal of Homosexuality, 5,* 356–371.

Kinsey, A. C., Pomeroy, W. B., & Martin, C. E. (1948). *Sexual behavior in the human male.* Philadelphia: W. B. Saunders.

Lang, P. J. (1994). The varieties of emotional experiences: A meditation on James–Lang theory. *Psychological Review, 101,* 211–221.

MacDonald, A. P., Jr. (1976). Homophobia: Its roots and meanings. *Homosexual Counseling Journal, 3,* 23–33.

Marks, I. H., & Mathews, A. M. (1978). Brief standard self-ratings for phobic patients. *Behaviour Research and Therapy, 17,* 253–267.

Marmor, J. (1980). Overview: The multiple roots of homosexual behavior. In J. Marmor (Ed.), *Homosexual behavior—A modern reappraisal* (pp. 3–22). New York: Basic Books.

Mavissikalian, N., Blanchard, E. D., Abel, G. G., & Barlow, D. H. (1975). Responses to complex erotic stimuli in homosexual and heterosexual males. *British Journal of Psychiatry, 126,* 252–257.

O'Donahue, W., & Caselles, C. E. (1993). Homophobia: Conceptual, definitional, and value issues. *Journal of Psychopathology and Behavioral Assessment, 15,* 177–195.

O'Donahue, W., & Letourneau, E. (1992). The psychometric properties of the penile tumescence assessment of child molesters. *Journal Psycholopathology and Behavioral Assesment, 14,* 123–174.

Rowan, A. (1994). Homophobia: A new diagnosis for DSM-V? *Behavioral Therapist, 17,* 183–184.

Slaby, A. E. (1994). *Handbook of psychiatric emergencies* (4th ed.). East Norwalk, CT: Appleton & Lange.

Tollison, C. D., Adams, H. E., & Tollison, J. W. (1979). Cognitive and physiological indices of sexual arousal in homosexual, bisexual, and heterosexual males. *Journal of Behavioral Assessment, 1,* 305–314.

Weinberg, G. (1972). *Society and the healthy homosexual.* New York: St. Martin's Press.

West, D. J. (1977). *Homosexuality re-examined.* Minneapolis: University of Minnesota Press.

Zuckerman, M. (1971). Physiological measures of sexual arousal in the human. *Psychological Bulletin, 75,* 297–329.

INTRODUCTION TO PART 6

Rape and Harassment

At its best, sex is a mutual expression of love between two people who are devoted to each other and who are both trying to help the other achieve the maximum pleasure and satisfaction. However, at its worst, sex is a one-sided activity in which one person exploits, degrades, and harms another person against that person's wishes. Sexual contact without consent is defined as rape, although many people (including researchers) shy away from that term and prefer to speak of "sexual coercion" and the like.

Psychology's attempts to understand rape have evolved through several generations of theory, but even today there is no theory that seems adequate to cover what is known. Early theories proposed that rape was mainly perpetrated by men who could not get sex in any other way (such as because they lacked social skills), but this view has lost favor in view of evidence that rapists have social skills comparable to those of non-rapists and, even more tellingly, rapists tend to have consenting sex partners and even seem to have more frequent sex than nonrapists.

A feminist theory of rape was put forward in the 1970s, most famously articulated in Susan Brownmiller's (1975) bestselling book *Against Our Will*. According to this view, rape is not about sex at all but rather is an act of violence and hatred, scarcely distinguishable from beating someone up. Brownmiller asserted that all men are involved in a deliberate, conscious conspiracy to use rape as a weapon for intimidating all women and keeping them in a subservient position in society. Although seemingly farfetched, this theory enjoyed wide support for years and was even favored by many men, who would presumably have known that they were not participating in any such conspiracy and who most likely opposed rather than supported the rapes perpetrated by other men.

The first article in this section is a widely cited paper by Palmer (1988) in which he expresses his disagreement with the feminist views of Brownmiller and others. He does not even focus on the idea that rape is part of a conspiracy by all men, choosing instead to focus on the assertion that rape is not essentially about sex. In Palmer's analysis, the arguments that have been used to claim that "rape is not sex" have logical and empirical flaws. For example, some have pointed to the fact that rapists often include married men or men with girlfriends, leading them to say that rape cannot be about the quest for sex because these perpetrators already have consenting sex partners. Palmer replies that most customers of prostitutes have wives or girlfriends, but no one claims that prostitution is not about sex.

Although Palmer's article has many good points, one should be careful to consider both sides of an issue. Baumeister and Tice (2000) have proposed a way to salvage at least part of the feminist theory that rape is not sex: In particular, rape is not sex for the victims. Because victims and perpetrators often have radically different ways of perceiving, experiencing, and interpreting the same event (see Baumeister, Stillwell, & Wotman, 1990), certain conclusions and perspectives may be utterly wrong and irrelevant for one but quite accurate for the other. Rape may well be sex for the perpetrators but nonsexual violence for the victims. The feminists who proposed the "not sex" theory were, after all, typically identifying more closely with the victims than with the perpetrators.

The next two papers in this section deal separately with perpetrators and victims, and the differential centrality of sex emerges loud and clear from those pages. Kanin's (1985) paper is an impressive contribution to the area, because Kanin managed to assemble a fairly large sample of men who admitted having committed date rape. Although date rape does not make headlines the way stranger rapes do, date rape appears to be far more common. The sexual aspect of date rape seems unmistakable, particularly in view of the fact that most of the couples had been engaging in some degree of sexual contact by mutual consent just prior to the rape. The woman then wanted to stop whereas the man desired to continue to have intercourse, and instead of respecting her wishes (as most men do in that circumstance) these men pressed forward to force themselves on their dates. Many of the men seemed to not have even acknowledged that they had done anything wrong until much later, when they heard Kanin lecture about date rape and realized that their own past actions fell in that category.

Meanwhile, a paper by Meyer and Taylor (1986) examined how victims cope with the trauma of rape. They were struck by the variability in responses: Some victims of rape suffer severe and lasting problems as a result, whereas others seem to bounce back reasonably well and move on with their lives. Meyer and Taylor sought to test several theories about what causes the difference. One of these was the popular and influential view by Janoff-Bulman (1979, 1992) that there are two kinds of self-blame which have opposite effects on trauma victims. Meyer and Taylor failed to find support for the difference between kinds of self-blame, but they did find other factors that distinguished the good versus poor copers (such as use of meditation and withdrawing from social contact), although it is difficult to know what is cause and what is effect. For example, does withdrawing from social contact and staying at home after being raped cause poor coping and make recovery more difficult—or do women who are coping poorly tend to stay home as a result?

Despite these ambiguities, this paper represented an important step forward in understanding how individuals deal with sexual victimization.

The last paper in this section deals with sexual harassment rather than rape. Harassment is a form of sexual victimization that does not usually extend to forcible intercourse but, being less extreme, may be more common than rape and thus may affect a larger number of lives. What causes men to harass women sexually, such as by making unwanted advances or demanding sexual favors in exchange for occupational rewards? John Pryor has emerged as one of the nation's leading experts on sexual harassment by virtue of a long research program, and in this paper he collaborated with several other well-respected social psychologists to furnish insight into the mind of the harasser. Bargh, Raymond, Pryor, and Strack (1985) used some of the latest technology and research methods for the study of social cognition, and they showed that in the harasser's mind sex and power are closely linked in ways that most people do not connect the two.

REFERENCES

Bargh, J. A., Raymond, P., Pryor, J. B., & Strack, F. (1995). Attractiveness of the underling: An automatic power → sex association and its consequences for sexual harassment and aggression. *Journal of Personality and Social Psychology, 68,* 768–781.

Baumeister, R. F., Stillwell, A., & Wotman, S. R. (1990). Victim and perpetrator accounts of interpersonal conflict: Autobiographical narratives about anger. *Journal of Personality and Social Psychology, 59,* 994–1005.

Baumeister, R. F., & Tice, D. M. (2000). *The social dimension of sex.* New York: Allyn & Bacon.

Brownmiller, S. (1975). *Against our will: Men, women, and rape.* New York: Simon & Schuster.

Janoff-Bulman, R. (1979). Characterological versus behavioral self-blame: Inquiries into depression and rape. *Journal of Personality and Social Psychology, 37,* 1798–1809.

Janoff-Bullman, R. (1992). *Shattered assumptions: Towards a new psychology of trauma.* New York: Free Press.

Kanin, E. J. (1985). Date rapists: Differential sexual socialization and relative deprivation. *Archives of Sexual Behavior, 14,* 219–231.

Meyer, C. B., & Taylor, S. E. (1986). Adjustment to rape. *Journal of Personality and Social Psychology, 50,* 1226–1234.

Palmer, C. T. (1988). Twelve reasons why rape is not sexually motivated: A skeptical examination. *Journal of Sex Research, 25,* 512–530.

Discussion Questions

1. Do you agree that rape may be more sexual in the perpetrator's mind than in the victim's? What other differences in perception would you expect between the perpetrators and victims of rape?
2. In the fight against rape, do you think date rape or stranger rape should get higher priority?
3. Based on Meyer and Taylor's findings, how would you advise a friend who fell victim to rape to deal with the trauma?
4. Kanin's data suggest that many problems arise because a woman consents to limited sexual activity but not "going all the way." Yet juries often regard her consent to some activities as a sign that she must have consented to everything. How might laws or practices be changed so as to strengthen a woman's right to consent to some activities but refuse others, in a legally sustainable fashion?
5. What experiences might create the associative links between power and sex that Bargh and his colleagues demonstrated among harassment-prone men?

6. Do you think that sexual aggressors use sex as a means to gain and enjoy power, or do they use power as a means to gain and enjoy sex?
7. Why do some perpetrators of rape continue to deny having done anything wrong, while others admit their crimes?

Suggested Readings

Anderson, P. B., & Struckman-Johnson, C. (Eds.). (1998). *Sexually aggressive women: Current perspectives and controversies*. New York: Guilford. This fascinating compilation of contributions by multiple experts studies the hitherto neglected phenomenon of sexual aggression by women.

Betzig, L. (1986). *Despotism and differential reproduction: A Darwinian view of history*. New York: Aldine. This work looks at sex and power in history, concluding that power has been a principal means by which men could improve their reproductive success.

Brownmiller, S. (1975). *Against our will: Men, women, and rape*. New York: Simon & Schuster. This book is a classic statement of feminist theory about rape. Brimming with outrage, it galvanized protest and action against this terrible category of crime.

Groth, A. N. (1979). *Men who rape: The psychology of the offender*. New York: Plenum. This is an influential work by a leading researcher on rape. Sympathetic to feminist theories of the time, it presents the results and conclusions from many studies, including those by the author himself.

Thornhill, R., & Palmer, C. T. (2000). *A natural history of rape*. Cambridge, MA: MIT Press. This book sparked controversy immediately, advocating as it does an approach to rape that relies heavily on evolutionary theory. The authors do not shy away from controversy and in fact often present their views in a deliberately inflammatory manner, seemingly going out of their way to derogate rival opinions.

READING 10

Twelve Reasons Why Rape is Not Sexually Motivated: A Skeptical Examination

Craig T. Palmer • Arizona State University

The most popular current explanation of rape holds that rapists are seeking power, control, violence, and/or domination instead of sex. After reviewing the history of this explanation, this chapter examines the evidence that has been used to demonstrate that rapists are not sexually motivated. Twelve specific arguments are examined in light of existing data on rape. All twelve of the arguments are found to be either logically unsound, based on inaccurate definitions, untestable, or inconsistent with the actual behavior of rapists. The implications of these findings are discussed.

The feminist movement has had a tremendous impact on the issue of rape in the last twenty years. Feminists are largely responsible for the fair and humane treatment of rape victims by police, courts, and the general public. Additionally, the feminist movement has significantly changed the misguided view that rape victims are responsible for the attacks against them. Furthermore, feminists have also had success in making women less vulnerable to sexual assault through general education and self-defense classes. Perhaps most importantly, the feminist movement has made it difficult for anyone to treat rape as a "joke," instead of the heinous offense that it is.

In addition to these major accomplishments, the feminist movement has also had a profound impact on explanations of the rapist's motives. Until the early 1970s, most researchers of rape, while acknowledging that many motivations could be involved in any given rape, assumed that sex was a predominant motive (Amir, 1971; Gebhard et al., 1965; LeVine, 1959; Schultz, 1965; Schiff, 1971). This viewpoint was "significantly altered by the feminist movement" (Sanders, 1980, p. 22). In fact, revealing rape "to be a political act that indicated nothing about male sexuality" (Symons, 1979, p. 104) became a "focal point of feminist theory" (Sanders, 1980, p. 22). This paper evaluates twelve specific arguments that have been used to support the claim that rapists are not motivated by sex.

History of the "Not Sex" Explanation of Rape

The view that rape is not a sexually motivated act was first put forth by Millet (1971), Griffin (1971), and Greer (1970; 1973). These authors placed the cause of rape, now seen as a political act of violence and domination, squarely in the patriarchal traditions and sexist socialization patterns of American society. Other writers soon began to incorporate this viewpoint into their writings (Betries, 1972; Burgess & Holmstrom, 1974; Cobb & Schauer, 1974; Cohen et al., 1971; Cohn, 1972; Davis, 1975; Findlay, 1974; LeGrand, 1973; Mehrhof & Kearon, 1972; Russell, 1975; Schwendinger & Schwendinger, 1974). However, it was not until Susan Brownmiller's 1975 book *Against Our Will* that this "not sex" explanation became widely known and accepted.

Following the publication of *Against Our Will*, the view that sex was not a primary part of the motivation of rape was taken up by feminist and nonfeminist researchers alike. In fact, this view became a "central theme," as Thornhill and Thornhill (1983) call it, in nearly every work written on rape and child sexual abuse in the following years (Baron, 1985; Bart, 1975; Beh-Horin, 1975; Bercovitch, Sladky, Roy and Goy, 1987; Brecher, 1978; Burt, 1980; Cager & Schurr, 1976; Dean & de Bruyn-kopps, 1982; Delin, 1978; Denmark & Friedman, 1985; Dusek, 1984; Frude, 1982; Griffin, 1979; Harding, 1985; Hilberman, 1976; Holmstrom & Burgess, 1980; Kaufman et al., 1980; Kemmer, 1977; Klein & Kress, 1976; Linner, 1976; Malamuth, 1981; Metzger, 1976; Rafter & Natalizia, 1981; Robertson, 1981; Rodabaugh & Austin, 1981; Rose, 1977; Salerno, 1975; Sanford & Fetter, 1979; Scarpitti & Scarpitti, 1977; Schwendinger & Schwendinger, 1985; Sgroi, 1982; Shields & Shields, 1983; Straus, 1976).

The most influential endorsement of this "not sex" explanation of rape came from Nicholas Groth (Groth, 1979a, 1979b; Groth & Birmbaum, 1978; Groth & Burgess, 1977a, 1977b; Groth, Burgess, & Holmstrom, 1977; Groth & Hobson, 1983; Groth, Hobson, & Gary, 1982). These works, especially the 1979 book *Men Who Rape*, buttressed the new explanation with data on convicted rapists. Groth's endorsement, and the mere repetition of the claim in so many works, made it possible by 1980 for a researcher to rightfully claim that "It is now generally accepted by criminologists, psychologists, and other professionals working with rapists and rape victims that rape is not primarily a sexual crime, it is a crime of violence" (Warner, 1980, p. 94).

Opposition to the "Not Sex" Explanation

Adherence to the "not sex" explanation of rape was not quite unanimous. Several researchers took a more moderate position that proposed sexual, as well as hostile, motivation as contributing to rape (Clark & Lewis, 1977; Finkelhor, 1984; Medea & Thompson, 1974; Rada, 1978a; Sanders, 1980; Thornhill & Thornhill, 1983). Other works implied sexual motivation without explicitly addressing the issue (Abel, 1978; Abel, Blanchard & Becker, 1978; Marshall & Barbare, 1978). Still other works implied sexual motivation even though they explicitly adhered to the new feminist viewpoint. For example, Dr. Charles Hayman follows his statement that "In our opinion, rape has little to do with sexual desire" with the warning that in order to avoid rape, women and girls "should not behave in a sexually provocative manner, especially with strangers" (Zusspan, 1974, pp. 149–150; see also Dean & de Bruyn-kopps, 1982; Sussman & Bordwell, 1981). A few researchers even directly challenged the newly established explanation. Warnings of the potential dangers involved in ignoring the sexual motivation involved in rape were issued by Geis (1977), Smithyman (1978), and Symons (1979). Hagen made the most vehement denial of the "not sex" argument when he called it "silly" (1979, p. 97).

The vast amount of attention this one issue has received has led some researchers to express a desire to move on to other matters. Geis expresses the hope that the "not sex" argument is a "popular trend that may now have run its course" (1980, p. 11). Finkelhor also states that "The debate about the sexual motivation of sexual abuse is something of an unfortunate red herring" (1984, p. 34), and goes on to suggest that "The goal should be to explain how the sexual component fits in" (1984, pp. 34–35). However, the majority of researchers do not share this goal since they remain committed to the "not sex" explanation.

What the Debate is Over

The first step in evaluating the "not sex" explanation of rape is to establish exactly what the debate is over. Thanks to the feminist movement, no one any longer defends the dangerous claim that rape is a sexually arousing or sought-after experience on the part of the *victim*. Neither does anyone deny that male sex organs are necessarily involved in the act. The debate is over the motivation of the rapist in using his sex organs in a way that constitutes rape. Motivation refers to the purpose or goal of a behavior. Proponents of the "not sex" explanation hold that the occurrence of rape cannot be accounted for by the hypothesis that sexual stimulation is the *goal* of rapists. These authors hold that the occurrence of rape can only be explained by the hypothesis that sex is just a *means* used to attain the goals of power, control, domination, and violence.

Unfortunately, motivation is a covert entity, existing solely in the minds of individuals (either consciously or unconsciously). The problem with viewing motivation as covert is that such an entity is not externally identifiable. Statements about motivation *in this sense* are completely untestable. No data of any kind could falsify a statement about such a "motivation." Therefore, as an alternative, at least one major researcher on rape has stressed the necessity of inferring motives "only from observed concrete behavior" (Amir, 1971, p. 132; see also Snelling, 1975). In this sense, a statement about the motivation for a given behavior is a prediction about the situations in which it occurs, the people involved, and the other behaviors with which it is found. This makes it possible to compare the actual behavior of some one with what would be expected *if* they were motivated in one way or another.

Vague semantics have also clouded the issue of whether sex is a "means" or an "end" for rapists. For example, Bercovitch et al. state that "Human rape seems to be an outcome of status assertion by males which acts as a form of power domination used to copulate with a female who could not be attained with conventional methods" (Bercovitch et al., 1987). This statement appears to imply that sex (i.e., "copulation") is the sought-after goal of rape, since "power" is "used to" accomplish this goal. However, the authors use this statement to support the claim that "Rape is probably not primarily a sexually motivated phenomenon" (ibid.).

While the literature on rape motivation is often clouded by vague semantics and uncheckable claims, the issue "is an important one, and how the verdict is rendered determines whether fundamental matters are obfuscated or come into more useful analytical light" (Geis & Huston, 1980, p. 187). Consequently, the present paper attempts to resolve this controversy by examining 12 arguments given to support the "not sex" explanation.

Supporting Arguments for the "Not Sex" Explanation

Argument 1

> When they say sex or sexual, these social scientists and feminists mean the *motivation*, moods, or drives associated with honest courtship and pair bonding. In such situations, males report feelings of tenderness, affection, joy and so on. . . . It is this sort of pleasurable motivation that the socioculturists (and feminists) denote as sexuality. . . . (Shields & Shields, 1983, p. 122; original emphasis)

The validity of this argument depends on the accuracy of its definition of "sex," and there appears to be considerable evidence that this definition of sex is unduly limiting. First,

> it is abundantly self evident . . . that a large percentage of males have no difficulty in divorcing sex from love. Whistles and wolf-calls, attendance at burlesque shows, patronizing of call girls and prostitutes—all of these are probably manifestations of a sexual urge totally or largely bereft of romantic feelings. (Hagen, 1979, pp. 158–159)

More fundamentally, the word "sexual" (but not "tenderness," "affection," or "joy") is routinely used to refer to the motivation of nonhuman animals involved in reproductive acts.

Argument 2

> Rape is not sexually motivated because of the "fact that most rapists have stable sexual partners." (Sanford & Fetter, 1979, p. 8)

This widely mentioned argument (Brownmiller, 1975; Finkelhor & Yllo, 1985; Groth, 1979a; Groth & Hobson, 1983; Medea & Thompson, 1974; Queen's Bench Foundation, 1978; Rada, 1978a; Rodabaugh & Austin, 1981; Shields & Shields, 1983) hinges on the assumption that a male's sexual desire is exhausted by a single "outlet." Symons points out that this does not appear to be true: "Most patrons of prostitutes, adult bookstores, and adult movie theatres are married-men, but this is not considered evidence for lack of sexual motivation" (Symons, 1979, p. 280).

Argument 3

> Rape is not sexually motivated because rapes are often "premeditated." (See Brownmiller, 1975; Griffin, 1971)

The fact that many rapes are premeditated does not nullify that many rapes are also spontaneous. However, this argument presumes that all sexually motivated behavior is spontaneous. Obviously, this is untrue since there are many kinds of consenting sexual acts (affairs, rendezvous, seductions) which are highly planned and still considered to be sexually motivated (see Symons, 1979, p. 279).

Argument 4

The age distribution of rapists demonstrates that rape is a crime of violence and aggression instead of sex:

> the violence prone years for males extend from their teenage years into their late forties, this is the age range into which most rapists fall. *Unlike sexuality*, aggression does diminish with age and, therefore, a male's likelihood of committing a rape diminishes with the onset of middle age. (Groth & Hobson, 1983, p. 161; my emphasis)

It is unfortunate that the authors of this argument do not cite the basis for their claim that the human male sexual drive does *not* decrease with age. There is abundant evidence that numerous types of male sexual activity peak in the late teens and then slowly diminish (Kinsey, Pomeroy, & Martin, 1948; Goethals, 1971). Not only does the age of most rapists fail to disprove that rape is sexually motivated, the general correlation between the age distribution of rapists and the general level of sexual activity of males is very consistent with the view that rape is sexually motivated.

Argument 5

> The common occurrence of rape in war shows that rape is motivated by hostility instead of sex. (See Brownmiller, 1975, pp. 23–118; Shields & Shields, 1983)

The prevalence of rape during war has indeed been well documented by Brownmiller and others. However, the writers who see this as evidence of a lack of sexual motivation are often the same ones who stress that vulnerability is a critical variable in victim selection (see Shields & Shields, 1983). Females in war situations are vulnerable to an exceptional degree. While hostility may be involved in any rape, the tremendously high degree of female vulnerability is both a sufficient and more parsimonious explanation of the high frequency of rape in war situations. Thus, the high frequency of rape during war is not evidence for the absence, or even unimportance, of sexual motivation. In fact, Brownmiller herself implies the importance of sexual motivation by reporting that: "In some of the camps, pornographic movies were shown to the soldiers, 'in an obvious attempt to work the men up'" (Brownmiller, 1975, p. 83; see also Medea & Thompson, 1974, p. 32).

Argument 6

> Instead of being a sexually motivated act, rape is a form of "social control" because it is used as a form of punishment in some societies. (See Brownmiller, 1975, p. 319)

Symons clearly demonstrates the problem with this argument by pointing out that the use of rape as a punishment "does not prove that sexual feelings are not also involved, any more than the deprivation of property as punishment proves that the property is not valuable to the punisher" (Symons, 1979, p. 280).

Argument 7

> "Men have been asked why they raped and many have said it was not out of sexual desire but for power and control over their victims." (Dean & de Bruyn-kopps, 1982, p. 233; citing evidence from Groth, 1979a; see also Shields & Shields, 1983, p. 121.)

This might appear to be the simplest way to decide the issue—just ask rapists. However, such an approach requires the problematical assumption that one clearly experiences, remembers, and truthfully reports his motives. Such an assumption is especially troublesome when the subjects in question are convicts: "it is difficult to avoid the conclusion that the men's conscious attempts to emphasize their correct attitudes and to minimize their sexual impulsiveness were to some extent calculated to foster the impression that they no longer constituted a threat" (Symons, 1979, p. 283).

Even if the truthfulness of rapists' statements could be assumed, there is still the problem of interpretation. Symons (1979, pp. 282–283) cites several questionable interpretations present in the literature at that time (also see the Queen's Bench Foundation, 1978). This problem became particularly crucial with the subsequent publication of Groth's influential book *Men Who Rape.* Not only did Groth's interpretations go against other findings such as those by Smithyman (1978, p. iv) in which 84% of the rapists cited sexual motivation "solely or in part" as the cause of their acts (see also Ageton, 1983; Geis, 1977; Katz & Mazur, 1979; Rada, 1978a; Russell, 1975; Sussman & Bordwell, 1981), but even the examples Groth selected to support his argument make his interpretations questionable. One rapist explains his behavior by saying, "She stood there in her nightgown, and you could see right through it—you could see her nipples and breasts and, you know they were just waiting for me, and it was just too much of a temptation to pass up" (Groth, 1979a, p. 38). Another rapist reported that "I just wanted to have sex with her and that was all" (Groth, 1979a, p. 42; see also Groth, 1979a, pp. 50, 55, 93, 159, 161, 181, and 183).

Groth's reasons for not considering such statements as evidence for sexual motivation being primary in rape are interesting in light of some of the previously discredited arguments:

> Although the power rapist [by far the most common type in Groth's classification] may report that his offense was prompted by a desire for sexual gratification, careful examination of his behavior typically reveals that efforts to negotiate the sexual encounter or to determine the woman's receptiveness to a sexual approach are noticeably absent, as are any attempts at lovemaking or foreplay. (Groth, 1979a, p. 28)

Here again we see an attempt to redefine "sex." This time it must include concern for the other person's arousal to "really" be sexual. Even if this was true, some of Groth's own examples show evidence of negotiation and foreplay (Groth, 1979a, p. 29). Other studies on victims have found that many rapes, particularly "date rapes," often involve extensive negotiation and foreplay (e.g., Ageton, 1983; Katz & Mazur, 1979; Kirkpatrick & Kanin, 1957; Rada, 1978a). It appears that the data gathered from the statements of convicted rapists are inconclusive at best. Such "evidence" does not demonstrate the absence of sexual motivation in rape.

Argument 8

> "The high incidence (1 out of 3 cases) of sexual dysfunction is further evidence for the relative unimportance of sexual desire in the act of rape." (Groth & Hobson, 1983, p. 171; see also Groth, 1979a; Harding, 1985)

The evidence of dysfunction during rape has been subject to questionable definitions (see Thornhill & Thornhill, 1983) and varies greatly between different studies (see Rada, 1978a). Hence, despite the claims of Harding (1985), sexual dysfunction in rape has not been conclusively shown to be significantly higher in rapes than in consenting acts. Even if a higher rate of actual dysfunction was conclusively demonstrated, it could be easily accounted for by the adverse circumstances under which rape often occurs. Symons (1980) points out that even the most sexually motivated rapist might experience dysfunction due to anxiety over the possibility of severe punishment and the existence of conflicting emotions. There is also the fact that offenders are often under the influence of drugs. Groth reports that 50% of the rapists in his study were drunk or on drugs at the time of the assault (1979a, p. 96). Smithyman reports that 32% of the rapists in his study were intoxicated in some way (1978, p. 60). The Queen's Bench Foundation found that 61.6% of the rapists had consumed alcohol before the rape (1978, p. 773).

Argument 9

> Rape is motivated by aggression instead of sex because "changes in number of rapes and assaults showed similar seasonal patterns, suggesting that rape comprised a subcategory of aggressive behavior" (Michael & Zumpe, 1983, p. 883; cited as evidence of the unimportance of sexual motivation in rape by Bercovitch et al., 1987.)

Rape and non-sexual assault both appear to occur most frequently in the summer months (Michael & Zumpe, 1983). The conclusion that this is evidence for a lack of sexual motivation in rape is seriously flawed in a number of ways. First, it ignores numerous alternative explanations of why rape might occur most frequently in the summer, such as greater social interaction and greater visual cues, which are quite compatible with the assumption that sex is an important motivation in rape (see Chappell et al., 1977). Second, if seasonality of occurrence is an indicator of motivation, then all aggressive behaviors should follow the same pattern. The same study that reports a correlation between assault and rape reports a dramatic difference in the seasonal pattern of rape and murder (Michael & Zumpe, 1983). Finally, this argument ignores the drastic differences in other patterns of assault and rape. Many of these patterns, especially the age and sex of victims, are much more likely to be related to the motivation of the offenders than is seasonality (see Thornhill & Thornhill, 1983).

Argument 10

The real motivation in rape is violence instead of sex because castrated rapists just find other ways of doing violence to women. (See Cohen et al., 1971; Dusek, 1984; Groth, 1979a, p. 10; Katz & Mazur, 1979; LeGrand, 1973: MacDonald, 1971; Rada, 1978a.)

All data on the effects of castration must be viewed skeptically because of the many uncontrolled variables involved (Greene, 1979). Existing data suggest that castrated sex offenders have significantly lower recidivism rates in regard to *sexual* offenses (Bremer, 1959; MacDonald, 1971; Rada, 1978b; Sturup, 1960, 1968). Proponents of the "not sex" argument have refused to see this as evidence of rape being sexually motivated. This is because "Those who view rape as primarily an aggressive offense do not believe that castration will cure the rapist's aggressive impulses" (Rada, 1978b, p. 143). People holding this view would predict that castrated offenders would simply replace their "sexual" assaults with "non-sexual" assaults. It is debatable that such a finding would actually be evidence of the unimportance of sexual motivation in rape. However, the existing evidence shows that castrated sex offenders have lower recidivism rates for sexual *and* nonsexual crimes than do non-castrated offenders:

> From 1933 to 1951, Herstedvester [an institute in Denmark] received over 200 males sentenced for a sex offense. Of the 147 castrated offenders, 18 have recidivated; 5 suffered relapses and committed new sex offenses, and *13 committed other crimes [8.8%]*. Of the 81 noncastrated offenders, 41 recidivated; 24 suffered relapses and committed new sex offenses, and *17 committed other crimes [21.%]*. (Rada, 1978b, p. 144; my emphasis; see also Bremer, 1959; Kopp, 1938; MacDonald, 1971; Sturup, 1960, 1968.)

Argument 11

Rape is clearly an act of aggression. McCahil et al. (1979) in their study of 1,401 rape victims show that: (1) a majority of victims (64%) reported being pushed or held during the incident, (2) victims are often slapped (17%), beaten (22%), and/or choked (20%), and (3) 84% of victims experienced some kind of nonphysical force during the incident (threat of bodily harm, etc.). (Thornhill & Thornhill, 1983, p. 163)

To determine the significance of data on rapist violence and victim injury, it is crucial to make the distinction between instrumental force used to accomplish the rape (and possibly to influence the female not to resist and/or not to report the rape), and excessive violence that appears to be an end in itself. This distinction is necessary because only excessive force is a possible indication of violent motivation on the part of the rapist.

Harding makes the following claim: "In many cases of rape in humans, assault seems to be the important factor, not sex. . . . [because] . . . In most cases the use of force goes beyond that necessary to compel the victim's compliance with the rapist's demands" (Harding, 1985, p. 51). However, existing evidence, including that cited by Harding (1985, p. 51), indicates that excessive force is actually only used in a minority of cases. Consistent with the previously cited figures by McCahil, Meyer and Fischman (1979), Chappell and Singer found only 15 to 20 percent of rape victims required hospital treatment for physical injuries (1977). Katz and Mazur also report the following: "Although most rape victims encountered some form of physical force, few experienced severe lasting [physical] injuries" (1979, p. 171; see also Burgess & Holmstrom, 1974; Schiff, 1971). Amir even found that "In a large number of cases (87%), only temptation and verbal coercion were used to subdue the victim" (Amir, 1975, p. 7).

Other evidence also indicates that it is only in a minority of cases that violence and injury are even one of the goals of a rapist. Smithyman found that 88% of his respondents reported using force, but did so "instrumentally" (Smithyman, 1978, p. 68). This is consistent with the fact that only 18% of the rapists in Smithyman's study reported "hating" the victim. Gebhard et al. (1965) also found that the vast majority of sex offenders used force only when required. Also consistent with the view that force is primarily used only when it is needed is the finding by Geis (1977) that 78% of the rapists in his study wanted the victim to cooperate. Force is also absent in 87% of child sexual abuse cases (Groth, 1979a). Instead of the conclusion reached by Harding (1985), existing evidence appears to be more consistent with the conclusion reached by Hagen: "If violence is what the rapist is after, he's not very good at it. Certainly he has the victim in a position from which he could do all kinds of physical damage" (Hagen, 1979, p. 87).

The importance of the distinction between violence as a means to an end and violence as an end in itself is demonstrated by the Queen's Bench Foundation's dismissal of statements by rapists in which they reported "sex" to be the goal of their behavior: "Others said 'sex' *but when prodded further, indicated they knew it had to be forcible sex*" (Queen's Bench Foundation, 1978, p. 772; my emphasis). The fact that the rapists were aware that they would probably have to "force compliance" to attain sex is taken by the authors as evidence that the rapists were actually after violence instead of sex. This is in spite of the fact that 71.2% of the rapists stated that they were hoping the victim would comply with their expectations (1978, p. 774), 61.7% said they had *not* intended to use violence (1978, p. 774), and only 22.7% had ended up inflicting "very severe injury" (1978, p. 778). These figures are particularly significant because the study was restricted to only "overly violent rapists" (1978, p. 768).

Contrary to the popular claim that rape is "an act of violence, with sex as the weapon" (Burgess & Holmstrom, 1974, p. 1982), the evidence of physical injury suffered by rape victims is actually more consistent with the view that in most cases rape is an act aimed at attaining sex, with violence being the means to that end. A minority of rapes do involve violence far beyond that needed to accomplish the rape. However, this does not imply that sexual motivation is absent in these assaults. Even the existence of excessive violence cannot account for why the rapist committed rape instead of nonsexual assault. Sexual motivation always appears to be a necessary ingredient for a rape to occur instead of a nonsexual assault. As Rada states: "If aggression were the sole motive it might be more simply satisfied by a physical beating" (Rada, 1978a, p. 22).

Of course, it has been suggested that the sexual act itself is aimed at attaining a nonsexual goal for the rapist. It has even been claimed that a sex act is the "best" way to attain a nonsexual goal such as "control" (Rada, 1978a). While such claims may be true, they are inherently uncheckable. They do not refer to the rapist's behavior, which is identifiably sexual, but to his nonidentifiable thoughts and feelings which he may or may not report truthfully (see Argument 7). No conceivable behavior on the part of the rapist could disprove any claim about such a "motivation."

Finally, while instances of excessive violence may indicate hostile motivation, this assumption should not be made automatically. Rape victims may be murdered, not because of hostile motivation on the part of the rapist, but because the killing of the victim greatly increases the rapist's chances of escaping punishment by removing the only witness to the crime (Alexander & Noonan, 1979; Groth, 1979a; Hagen, 1979). This might be particularly likely when there is little or no difference between the punishment for rape and the punishment for murder (Lyle Steadman, personal communication, May 14, 1984).

Argument 12

"IT IS NOT A CRIME OF LUST BUT OF VIOLENCE AND POWER [because] . . . RAPE VICTIMS ARE NOT ONLY THE 'LOVELY YOUNG BLONDS' OF NEWSPAPER HEADLINES—RAPISTS STRIKE CHILDREN, THE AGED, THE HOMELY—ALL WOMEN." (Brownmiller, 1975, back cover; original emphasis)

It is fitting that Brownmiller chose this argument to place in bold type on the cover of her milestone book. Whether rapists prefer sexually attractive victims, or only select victims who are most vulnerable, forms a major argument of those on both sides of the debate (e.g., Alcock, 1983; Brownmiller, 1975; Dean & de Bruyn-kopps, 1982; Denmark & Friedman, 1985; Groth, 1979a; Groth & Hobson, 1983; Rodabaugh & Austin, 1981; Symons, 1979).

The argument that rape is not sexually motivated because rapists allegedly do not prefer attractive victims begins with the accurate observation that "Any female may become a victim of rape" (Brownmiller, 1975, p. 388). This is then taken as evidence that the sexual attractiveness of victims is unimportant: "I already knew that the rapist chooses his victim with a striking disregard for conventional 'sex appeal'—she may be seventy-four and senile or twelve and a half with braces on her teeth" (Brownmiller, 1975, p. 376). This alleged unimportance of attractiveness is then understandably assumed to demonstrate the unimportance of sexual motivation in the act of rape: "Only young attractive women are raped. This myth is another that stems from the belief that rape is a crime of passion and sex rather than what it is: a crime of violence" (Dean & de Bruyn-kopps, 1983, p. 36; see also Brownmiller, 1975, pp. 131–132).

The weak link in this argument is the assumption that the rape of unattractive females implies that rapists lack a preference for attractive victims. This conclusion is unjustified because it ignores the fact that rape victims are not a representative cross-section of all women. It also ignores the possibility that victim selection is based on *both attractiveness and vulnerability*.

Perhaps the most consistent finding of studies on rape, and one not likely to be merely the result of reporting bias (see Hindelang, 1977), is that women in their teens and early twenties are vastly overrepresented among rape victims (Amir, 1971; Hindeland & Davis, 1977; Kramer, 1987; MacDonald, 1971; Miyazawa, 1976; Svalastoga, 1962; Thornhill & Thornhill, 1983). This fact is crucial because age can be used as at least a rough indicator of female attractiveness: "Physical characteristics that vary systematically with age appear to be universal criteria of female physical attractiveness; Williams (1975), in fact, remarks that age probably is the most important determinant of human female attractiveness" (Symons, 1979, p. 188). It also appears reasonably certain that "Judgments of female physical attractiveness will correspond in females closely to the age of maximum reproductive value or fertility, which peaks in the mid-teens and early 20's respectively and drops off sharply in the late 30's" (Buss, 1987, p. 342; see also Shields & Shields, 1983; Symons, 1979, 1987; Thornhill & Thornhill, 1983; Williams, 1975). This means there is a strong correlation between attractiveness and the likelihood of becoming a rape victim.

The existence of such a correlation would appear to be conclusive evidence that rapists prefer attractive victims (see Alcock, 1983; Symons, 1979). However, backers of the "not sex" explanation continue to claim that rapists do not prefer attractive victims. For example, Groth states: ". . . vulnerability and accessibility play a more significant role in determining victim selection than does physical attractiveness or alleged provocativeness. Rape is far more an issue of hostility than of sexual desire" (Groth, 1979a, p. 173). There is, however, a drastic inconsistency in attempts to account for the age distribution of rape victims on the basis of vulnerability. This is the fact that supporters of the "not sex" explanation of rape state that vulnerability to rape "may be a function simply of the age of the victim, *with both the very young and the very old at high risk because of their inability to resist*" (Robabaugh & Austin, 1981, p. 44; my emphasis; see also Abel, 1978; Dean & de Bruyn-kopps, 1982; Groth, 1979a; Groth & Hobson, 1983; Warner, 1980). Groth also points out that "Advanced age and *the related life situation (for example living alone)* make them [the elderly] particularly vulnerable . . . " (Groth, 1979a, p. 173; emphasis added).

The high vulnerability of the elderly is indeed reflected in their high susceptibility to a number of types of violent crimes (Hindelang, 1977). However, contrary to the claims of Katz and Mazur (1979), the age distribution of rape victims is vastly different from the age distributions of victims of nonsexual violent crimes (Lennington, 1985; Thornhill & Thornhill, 1983). In fact, the age distributions are so different that studies, including Groth's own study, consistently find that *less than five percent of rape victims are over the age of fifty*. The fact that elderly women are very rarely raped *despite* being "particularly vulnerable" is strong evidence that rapists have a very definite preference for younger (and therefore more attractive) victims.

This does not mean that vulnerability is irrelevant to victim selection. It only means that vulnerability must be combined with attractiveness in order to account for the age distribution of rape victims. Numerous studies have found evidence that both attractiveness and vulnerability are important aspects of victim selection (Abel, 1978; Ageton, 1983; Queens Bench Foundation, 1978; Smithyman, 1978). A clue to the likely interaction between these two variables in victim selection is provided by Geis (1977) in his summary of a study by Chappell and James (1976).

> Asked to describe the kinds of victims they 'prefer,' the respondents [convicted rapists] portrayed the 'American dream ideal'—a nice, friendly, young, pretty, middle-class, white female. . . . [However], on the basis of inventories of [actual] victim characteristics, it is likely that the offenders actually raped in a more indiscriminate manner than their responses would indicate (Geis, 1977, p. 27).

Therefore, it appears that the vulnerability distinguishes the preferred from actual victims. While attractiveness maximizes the sought-after sexual goal that supplies the motivation for the act, vulnerability maximizes the chances of escaping injury and punishment for the act. This could account for why very old and very young females are raped more often than would be expected on the basis of their attractiveness, *but at a rate far below what would be expected if vulnerability was the only factor involved.*

Conclusion

Public awareness of the violence and horror of the act of rape *as experienced by the victim* has been crucial to facilitating social change. However, at present, the evidence does not justify the denial of sexual motivation on behalf of the *rapist*. This point is significant since adherence to the "not sex" explanation may have the unintended consequence of hindering attempts to prevent rape. For example, the effectiveness of instruction manuals on how to avoid rape (see Crook, 1980), treatment programs for rapists (see Brecher, 1978), and public policy perspectives are potentially compromised by the denial of the sexual aspect of the crime.

Although there may be evidence of the unimportance of sexual motivation in the act of rape, such evidence cannot be unskeptically adopted. Rape is prevented by accurate knowledge about its causes, and accurate knowledge can only be obtained by the objective examination of evidence and the skeptical evaluation of conclusions based on that evidence. The preceding twelve arguments have gone unquestioned for nearly twenty years, suggesting that skepticism has been noticeably absent from recent research on rape.

Perhaps the reason for this lack of skepticism and accurate knowledge about rape is that "rape" the behavior has become obscured by the politics of "rape" the "master symbol of women's oppression" (Schwendinger & Schwendinger, 1985, p. 93). An objective and accurate approach to the prevention of rape requires that the subject of rape be "de-politicized," Unfortunately, many researchers on rape fear such an objective approach: "To use the word *rape* in a de-politicized context functions to undermine ten years of feminist consciousness-raising" (Blackman, 1985, p. 118; original emphasis). Surely such fears are unfounded. "Consciousness-raising" is the act of falsifying unsupported dogma. Adherence to unsupported dogma like the "not sex" explanation of rape not only prohibits true "consciousness-raising" but potentially does so at the expense of an increased number of rape victims.

REFERENCES

Abel, G. (1978). Treatment of sexual aggressives. *Criminal Justice and Behavior, 5*(4), 291–293.

Abel, G., Blanchard, E. B., & Becker, J. V. (1978). An integrated treatment program for rapists. In R. T. Rada (Ed.), *Clinical aspects of the rapist* (pp. 161–214). New York: Grune and Stratton.

Ageton, S. (1983). *Sexual assault among adolescents*. Lexington, MA: Lexington Books.

Alcock, J. (1983). *Animal behavior: An evolutionary approach, third edition.* Sunderland, MA: Sinaur Associates.

Alexander, R. A., & Noonan, K. M. (1979). Concealment of ovulation, parental care, and human social evolution. In N. A. Chagnon & W. G. Irons (Eds.), *Evolutionary biology and human social behavior: An anthropological perspective* (pp. 436–453). North Scituate, MA: Duxbury Press.

Amir, M. (1971). *Patterns in forcible rape*. Chicago: University of Chicago Press.

Amir, M. (1975). Forcible rape. In L. G. Schultz (Ed.), *Rope victimology* (pp. 43–58). Springfield, IL: Charles C. Thomas.

Baron, L. (1985). Does rape contribute to reproductive success: Evaluations of sociobiological views of rape. *International Journal of Women's Studies, 8*(3), 266–277.

Bart, P. B. (1976). Rape doesn't end with a kiss. *Viva, 2,* 39–42, 100–101.

Ben-Horin, D. (1975). Is rape a sex crime? *The Nation, 221,* 112–115.

Bercovitch, F. B., Sladky, K. K., Roy, M. M., & Goy, R. W. (1987). Intersexual aggression and male sexual activity in captive Rhesus Macaques. *Aggressive Behavior, 13,* 347–358.

Betries, J. (1972). Rape: An act of possession. *Sweet Fire, 23,* 12–16.

Brecher, E. M. (1978). *Treatment Programs for Sex Offenders.* Washington, DC: U.S. Government printing Office.

Bremer, J. (1959). Aesexualization. New York: Macmillan.

Brownmiller, S. (1975). *Against our will: Men, women and rape.* New York: Simon and Schuster.

Burgess, A. W., & Holmstrom, L. L. (1974). *Rape: Victims of crisis*. Bowie, MD: Brady.

Burt, M. (1980). Cultural myths and supports for rape. *Journal of Personality and Social Psychology, 38*(2), 217–230.

Buss, D. M. (1987). Sex differences in human mate selection criteria: An evolutionary perspective. In C. Crawford, M. Smith, & D. Krebs (Eds.). *Sociobiology and psychology: Ideas, issues, and applications* (pp. 335–352). Hillsdale, NJ: Erlbaum.

Cager, N., & Shurr, C. (1976). *Sexual assault: Confronting rape in America.* New York: Grosset and Dunlap.

Chappell, D., Geis, G., Schafer, S., & Siegel, L. (1977). A comparative study of forcible rape offenses known to the police in Boston and Los Angeles. In D. Chappell, R. Geis, & G. Geis (Eds.), *Forcible rape, the crime, the victim and the offender* (pp. 169–187). New York: Columbia University

Press.

Chappell, D., & James, J. (1976). *Victim selection and apprehension from the rapist's perspective: A preliminary investigation.* Paper presented to the second International Symposium on Victimology, Boston, September 8.

Chappell, D., & Singer, S. (1977). Rape in New York City: A study of material in the police files and its meaning. In D. Chappell, R. Geis, & G. Geis (Eds.), *Forcible rape, the crime, the victim and the offender* (pp. 245–271). New York: Columbia University Press.

Clark, L. M. G., & Lewis, D. J. (1977). *Rape: The price of coercive sexuality.* Toronto: The Women's Press.

Cobb, K. A., & Schaurer, N. R. (1974). Michigan's criminal sexual assault law. *Journal of Law Reform, 8,* 217–236.

Cohen, M. L., Garofalo, R., Boucher, R., & Seghorn, T. (1971). The psychology of rapists. *Seminars in Psychiatry, 3*(6), 307–327.

Cohn, B. (1972). Succumbing to rape? *The Second Wave: A Magazine for the New Feminism, 2*(2), 24–27.

Crook, D. (1980). *What every woman should know about rape.* South Deerfield, MA: Channing L. Bete.

Davis, A. (1975). JoAnn Little: The dialectics of rape. *Ms., 3,* 74–77, 106–108.

Dean, C., & De Bruyn-Kopps, M. (1982). *The crime and consequences of rape.* Springfield, IL: Charles C. Thomas.

Delin, B. (1978). *The sex offender*. Boston: Beacon Press.

Denmark, F. L., & Friedman, S. B. (1985). Social psychological aspects of rape. In S. R. Sunday & E. Tobach (Eds.), *Violence against women: A critique of the sociobiology of rape* (pp. 59–84). New York: Gordian Press.

Dusek, V. (1984). Sociobiology and rape. *Science for the People, 16,* 10–16.

Findlay, B. (1974). The cultural context of rape. *Women's Law Review, 60,* 198–297.

Finkelhor, D. (1984). *Child sexual abuse.* New York: The Free Press.

Finkelhor, D., & Yllo, K. (1985). *License to rape: Sexual abuse of wives.* New York: Holt, Rinehart and Winston.

Frude, N. (1982). The sexual nature of sexual abuse. *Child Abuse and Neglect, 6,* 211–223.

Gebhard, P. H. Gagnon, J. H., Pomeroy, W. B., & Christenson, C. U. (1965). *Sex offenders: An analysis of types.* New York: Harper & Row.

Geis, G. (1977). Forcible rape: An introduction. In D. Chappell, R. Geis, & G. Geis (Eds.), *Forcible rape, the crime, the victim, and the offender* (pp. 1–37). New York: Columbia University Press.

Geis, G. (1980). Forward. In W. B. Sanders, *Rape and women's identity* (pp.1–7). Beverly Hills, CA: Sage.

Geis, G., & Huston, T. L. (1980). Forcible rape and human sexuality. In multiple book reviews of Donald Symon's The evolution of human sexuality. *The Behavioral and Brain Sciences, 3,* 171–214.

Goethals, G. (1971). Factors affecting permissive and nonpermissive rules regarding premarital sex. In J. M. Henslin (Ed.), *Studies in the sociology of sex* (pp. 9–25). New York: Basic Books.

Greene, R. (1979). Biological influences on sexual identity. In H. A. Katchadouriam (Ed.), *Human sexuality: A comparative and developmental perspective* (pp. 115–133). Berkley, CA: University of California Press.

Greer, G. (1970). *The Female Eunuch.* New York: Bantam.

Greer, G. (1973). Seduction is a four-letter word. *Playboy, 20,* 80–82, 164, 178, 224–228.

Griffin, S. (1971). Rape: The all-American crime. *Ramparts, 10,* 26–36.

Griffin, S. (1979). *Rape: The power of consciousness.* New York: Harper and Row.

Groth, N. A. (1979a). *Men who rape.* New York: Plenum Press.

Groth, N. A. (1979b). Sexual trauma in the life histories of rapists and child molesters. *Victimology: An International Journal, 4*(1), 10–16.

Groth, N. A., & Birmbaum, J. (1978). Adult sexual orientations and attraction to underage persons. *Archives of Sexual Behavior, 7*(3), 175–181.

Groth, N. A., & Burgess, A. W. (1977a). Rape: A sexual deviation. *American Journal of Orthopsychiatry, 47,* 401–406.

Groth, N. A., & Burgess, A. W. (1977b). Motivational intent in the sexual assault of children. *Criminal Justice and Behavior, 4,* 253–264.

Groth, N. A., Burgess, A. W., & Holstrom, L. L. (1977). Rape: Power, anger, and sexuality. *American Journal of Psychiatry, 134*(11), 1239–1243.

Groth, N. A., & Honson, W. (1983). The dynamics of sexual thought. In L. Schlesinger & E. Revitch (Eds.), *Sexual dynamics of anti-social behavior* (pp. 129–144). Springfield, IL: Charles C. Thomas.

Hagen, R. (1979). *The biosexual factor.* New York: Doubleday.

Harding, C. F. (1985). Sociobiological hypotheses about rape: A critical look at the data behind the hypotheses. In S. R. Sunday & E. Tobach (Eds.), *Violence against women: A critique of the sociobiology of rape* (pp. 23–58). New York: Gordian Press.

Huberman, E. (1976). *The rape victim.* New York: Basic Books.

Hinderlang, M. J. (1977). *Criminal victimization in eight American cities: A descriptive analysis of common theft and assault.* Cambridge, MA: Ballinger Publishing.

Hinderlang, M. J., & Davis, B. J. (1977). Forcible rape in the United States: A statistical profile. In D. Campbell, R. Geis, & G. Geis (Eds.), *Forcible rape: The crime, the victim, and the offender* (pp. 87–114). New York: Columbia University Press.

Holmstrom, L. L., & Burgess, A. W. (1980). Sexual behavior of assailants during reported rapes. *Archives of Sexual Behavior, 9*(5), 427–439.

Katz, S., & Mazul, M. A. (1979). *Understanding the rape victim.* New York: Wiley.

Kaufman, A. P., Divasto, P., Jackson, R., Voorhees, D., & Christy, J. (1980). Male rape victims: Noninstitutionalized assault. *American Journal of Psychiatry, 137*(2), 221–223.

Kinsey, A. C., Pomeroy, W. B., & Martin, C. E. (1948). *Sexual behavior in the human male.* Philadelphia: Saunders.

Kirkpatrick, C., & Kanin, E. J. (1957). Male sex aggression on a university campus. *American Sociological Review, XXII,* 52–58.

Klein, D., & Kress, J. (1976). Any women's blues. *Crime and Social Justice, 3,* 34–47.

Kopp, M. E. (1938). Surgical treatment as sex crime prevention measure. *Journal of Criminal Law, Criminology, and Police Science, 28,* 692–706.

Kramer, L. L. (1987). Albuquerque rape crisis center: Annual report. Bernalillo County Mental Health/Mental Retardation Center.

LeGrand, C. E. (1973). Rape and rape laws: Sexism in society and law. *California Law Review, 8,* 263–294.

Lennington, S. (1985). Sociobiological theory and the violent abuse of women. In S. R. Sunday & E. Tobach (Eds.), *Violence against women: A critique of the sociology of rape* (pp. 13–22). New York: Gordian Press.

LeVine, R. A. (1959).????? sex offenses: A study in social control. *American Anthropologist, 61,* 963–990.

Linner, B. (1976). Status of women and law in Sweden. *Columbia Human Rights Law Review, 8,* 263–294.

McCahill, T. W., Meyer, L. C., & Fischman, A. M. (1979). *The aftermath of rape*. Lexington, MA: D. C. Heath and Company.

MacDonald, J. M. (1971). *Rape offenders and their victims.* Springfield, IL: Charles C. Thomas.

Malamuth, N. M. (1981). Rape proclivity among males. *Journal of Social Issues, 37*(4), 138–157.

Marshall, W., & Barbare, H. (1978). The reduction of deviant arousal. *Criminal Justice and Behavior, 5*(4), 294–303.

Medea, A., & Thompson, K. (1974). *Against rape*. New York: Strauss and Giroux.

Mehrof, B., & Kearon, P. (1972). Rape: An act of terror. In Anonymous (Ed.), *Notes from the third year* (pp. 86–99). New York: Women's Liberation Press.

Metzger, D. (1976). It is always the woman who is raped. *American Journal of Psychiatry, 133,* 405–408.

Michael, R. P., & Zumpe, D. (1983). Sexual violence in the United States and the role of the season. *American Journal of Psychiatry, 140,* 883-886.

Millett, K. (1971). *The prostitution papers: A candid dialogue.* New York: Basis Books.

Miyazawa, K. (1976). Victimological studies of sexual crimes in Japan. *Victimology, 1*(Spring), 107–129.

Queen's Bench Foundation. (1978). The rapist and his victim. In L. D. Savitz & N. Johnson (Eds.), *Crime and society* (pp. 767–787). New York: Wiley.

Rada, R. T. (1978a). Psychological factors in rapist behavior. In R. T. Rada (Ed.), *Clinical aspects of the rapist* (pp. 21–58). New York: Grune and Stratton.

Rada, R. T. (1978b). Biological aspects and organic treatment of the rapist. In R. T. Rada (Ed.), *Clinical aspects of the rapist* (pp. 133–160). New York: Grune and Stratton.

Raftner, N. F., & Natalizia, E. M. (1981). Marxist feminism. *Crime and Delinquency, 28,* 81–87.

Robertson, I. (1981). *Sociology (second edition).* New York: Worth.

Rodabraugh, B. J., & Austin, M. (1981). *Sexual assault: A guide for community action.* New York: Garland STPM.

Rose, V. M. (1977). Rape as a social problem: A byproduct of the feminist movement. *Social Problems, 25*(1), 75–89.

Russell, D. E. H. (1975). *The politics of rape: The victim's perspectives.* New York: Stein and Day.

Salerno, M. (1975). Violence, not sex: What rapists really want. *New York Magazine*, June 23, 36–40.

Sanders, W. B. (1980). *Rape and women's identity.* Beverly Hills, CA: Sage.

Sanford, L. T., & Fetter, A. (1979). *In defense of ourselves.* New York: Doubleday.

Scarpitti, F. R., & Scarpitti, E. C. (1977). Victims of rape. *Society, 14*(5), 29–32.

Schiff, A. F. (1971). Rape and other countries. *Medicine, Science, and Law, 11,* 139–143.

Schultz, G. D. (1966). *How many more victims? Society and the sex criminal.* Philadelphia: Lippincott.

Schwendinger, J. R., & Schwendinger, H. (1974). Rape myths: In legal, theoretical and everyday practice. *Crime and Social Justice, 1,* 18–25.

Schwendinger, J. R., & Schwendinger, H. (1985). Homo economicus as the rapist. In S. R. Sunday & E. Tobach (Eds.), *Violence against women: A critique of the sociobiology of rape* (pp. 85–114). New York: Gordian Press.

Sgori, S. (1982). An approach to case management. In *Handbook of clinical intervention in child sexual abuse.* Lexington, MA: Lexington Books.

Shields, W. M., & Shields, L. M. (1983). Forcible rape: An evolutionary perspective. *Ethology and Sociobiology, 4,* 115–136.

Smithyman, S. D. (1978). The undetected rapist. Ph.D. Dissertation. Claremont Graduate School. University Microfilms International: Ann Arbor, MI.

Snelling, H. A. (1975). What is Non-consent (in rape?). In D. G. Schultz (Ed.), *Rape victimology* (pp. 157–163). Springfield, IL: Charles C. Thomas.

Straus, M. A. (1976). Sexual inequality, cultural norms, and wife-beating. In E. C. Viano (Ed.), *Victims and society.* Washington, DC: Visage Press.

Sturup, G. K. (1960). Sex offenses: The Scandinavian experience. *Law and Contemporary Problems, 25,* 361–375.

Sturup, G. K. (1968). Treatment of sexual offenders in Hestodvester, Denmark. *Acta Psychiatric Scandinavia, Supplement, 204.*

Sussman, L. & Bordwell, S. (1981). *The rapist file.* New York: Chelsea House.

Symons, D. (1979). *The evolution of human sexuality.* New York: Oxford University Press.

Symons, D. (1980). The evolution of sexuality revisited, in multiple book reviews of Donald Symons' The Evolution of Human Sexuality. *The Behavioral and Brain Sciences, 9*(2), 171–214.

Symons, D. (1987). If we're all Darwinians, what's the fuss about? In C. Crawford, M. Smith, & D. Krebs (Eds.), *Sociobiology and psychology: Ideas, issues and applications* (pp. 121–146). Hillsdale, NJ: Erlbaum.

Thornhill, R., & Thornhill, N. W. (1983). Human rape: An evolutionary analysis. *Ethology and Sociobiology, 3,* 137–143.

Warner, C. G. (1980). *Rape and sexual assault: Management and intervention.* Germantown, MD: Aspen Publication.

Williams, G. (1975). *Sex and evolution.* Princeton, NJ: Princeton University Press.

Zussman, F. P. (1974). Alleged rape: An invitational symposium. *Journal of Reproductive Medicine, 12,* 133–152.

READING 11

Date Rapists: Differential Sexual Socialization and Relative Deprivation

Eugene J. Kanin • Purdue University

Deviant sexual behavior has often been portrayed as the consequence of the frustration of legitimate sexual outlets. This study of date rapists reveals that these men, as a result of a hypersexual socialization process, are sexually very active, successful, and aspiring. These exaggerated aspiration levels are seen as responsible for instituting a high degree of sexual frustration. This acute relative deprivation, it is hypothesized, is a significant process responsible for precipitating these rape episodes

Introduction

There is a long tradition among a number of academic disciplines of attributing sexual deviance to a paucity of legitimate sexual outlets. The central theme is that deviance is an adaptation to the frustration of the "normal" sex drive. For example, the hoboes' homosexual activities and their association with prostitutes have been seen as the consequence of a nonmarital existence (Anderson, 1923). Cohen (1961) observed that Jamaican girls can turn to homosexuality when deprived of heterosexual intercourse for prolonged periods. Others have depicted deviant sexual adaptations in sex-segregated penal institutions (Fishman, 1934; Clemmer, 1958; Sykes, 1958; Lockwood, 1980) and in areas having distorted sex ratios (Wheeler, 1960). Perhaps the most frequently heard justification for legalized prostitution focuses on its ability to curtail rape. Bonger (1916) long ago viewed unemployment and the resultant inability to marry as conditions precipitating rape. Psychiatrists have also held that sexual frustrations can result in explosive sexual expressions (Cohen, Garofolo, Baucher, & Seghorn, 1971; Guttmacher, 1951; Karpman, 1954). Recently, some criminologists have strongly implied that rape is the consequence of the male's inability to acquire sexual activity legitimately (Clark and Lewis, 1977). And lastly, trying to explain the differential rape rates of Boston and Los Angeles, sociologists have applied the concept of relative frustration (Chappell, Geiss, Schafer, & Siegel, 1977). Essentially, they contend that it is sexually less frustrating to be rejected by a woman in a sexually restrictive society than in a sexually permissive setting, thereby hypothesizing higher rates for the latter.

It seems in order to acknowledge that the most influential perspective today largely opposes the idea that sexual frustration is a cause of rape; this is particularly so when sexual frustration is ascribed a primary role. Thio (1983), for example, has little trouble with this issue, blanketly stating, without supporting empirical evidence, that "the assumption that *sexual* frustration causes rape is hardly tenable because *nonsexual* frustration has much more to do with rape"[1] (p. 156). This issue will certainly not be resolved in this paper, but we will introduce an analysis of a variant rapist population, admittedly biased but probably no more so than any other studied rapist population, and make an effort to demonstrate that intellectual parochialism arising from the study of those who officially become labeled as rapists seems hardly appropriate.

In this paper we will study a group of self-disclosed rapists in order to determine whether these men are encountering difficulties in obtaining heterosexual outlets by more conventional means. Our principal objective, then, is to examine the sexual histories of rapists and nonrapists and attempt to determine if the former are more sexually deprived. It is apparent here that rape is *primarily* being examined from a sexual perspective rather than from one that views it as an expression of power and aggression. The assumption of a sexual perspective has its genesis in the nature of these acts and is not an expression of a polemic to cover all rape. Our study of this particular sample reveals all the offenses to have been date rapes and to have occurred only after intensive consensual sexual encounters between the rapist and their victims. We have argued elsewhere that a sexual framework is more appropriate to the facts regarding these men, acknowledging, of course, that in rape the power-aggression component is, in one form or another, *ipso facto* present (Kanin, 1984) and, in some cases, dominant.

Method

In this paper we will report on 71 self-disclosed rapists. These 71 men are all white, unmarried college undergraduates who came to our attention as solicited volunteers during the past decade from university classes and campus organizations where this writer has lectured. In all instances, these men voluntarily presented themselves as possible rapists who were amenable to study by interview and questionnaire. Anonymity of response and the option to terminate participation at any time were emphatically stressed.

An arresting issue here concerns the validity of these disclosures and the subsequent attachment of the rape label. For these volunteers to be accepted as rapists, it was necessary to conform to the legal criterion that penetration was accomplished on a nonconsenting female by employing or threatening force. In every case, a validity check was exercised by having the respondent give two accounts of the assaultive incident, one at the beginning and one at the end of the interview. All 71 cases reported here satisfied these conditions. Fifteen additional volunteered cases were rejected for inclusion in this study because they either failed to conform to the foregoing criterion (13) or decided to discontinue the interview (2). Not one case was concluded on the basis of mendacity. This should be no surprise, since the events reported here could hardly be considered ego enhancing, particularly since they are not being related to select peers.

A short profile of these men and the nature of their assaults is in order to appreciate the assumption of a sexually dominant perspective rather than the currently more popular power-aggression stance. First, these were all cases of date rape. The majority of the pairs had two to five dates together prior to the rape, and most or these pairs had sexually interacted on a prior date(s) in a fashion comparable to the sexual interaction that immediately preceded the rape. Every case of rape followed a fairly intensive bout of sex play, the most common activity being orogenital. Only six men were reported to the police, and in every case the charges were dropped. Thus, these date rapists are not represented in any official tally of rapists. Also crucial to an understanding of these rapists is that only six volunteered that they were recidivists, and all these admitted to but a single prior rape, all under comparable circumstances.

Since there was a conspicuous absence of the use of weapons and fists, it is virtually impossible, in any objective sense, to evaluate realistically the amount of force necessary to have brought these females to victimization. This is due to the fact that the rape interaction would have to take into account the male's execution of force, which usually includes both a physical and verbal dimension, and his companion's interpretation of that force which would result in the victim's determining if sexual compliance were the most judicious adaptation. It was not unusual for some of these men to report that they had exerted greater efforts on dates with other women but were clearly successfully rebuffed, and for some men to express surprise that their partners were so readily intimi-

[1] Italics are in the original.

dated.[2] There is a strong fortuitous factor contributing to these rapes, namely, the interaction stemming from the unique characteristics and perspectives of both the aggressor and the victim.

The control group consists of 227 white, undergraduate, unmarried college males from 15 assorted university classes. The age composition of this group was comparable to that of the rapists. Every male in class at the time of the administration of the schedule cooperated. Eleven schedules were deemed incomplete, and eight others were eliminated because the respondent identified himself as a homosexual. Thirty-six others were excluded from the control group because they indicated that they had engaged in heterosexual encounters with dates where they either tried to gain coitus by employing force or threats or did, in fact, succeed in "forcing" a female to have intercourse. Considering the chance element involved in date rape, viz., that the degree of force necessary to rape successfully may be less important than the nature of the particular victim involved, it was assumed that a high proportion of these men had probably engaged in behavior comparable to our rapists. Therefore, their inclusion would introduce an undesirable bias in the controls. In other words, what we wanted to avoid in our control sample was including men who had been involved in heterosexual performances that could very well have precipitated a rape of the type with which we are dealing.[3]

Results and Discussion

Sexual Histories

Rape is clearly only one facet of a wide range of erotic activities engaged in by these men. These rapists have had, comparatively speaking, considerably more heterosexual experience, have engaged in a more persistent quest for heterosexual encounters, and have utilized more exploitative techniques in their efforts to gain sexual expression. To be specific, the rapist appears considerably more sexually successful and active. Regarding the incidence of coitus exclusive of the rape experiences, inspection of these data show that the rapists are more experienced than the controls, 100% and 59%, respectively. It is worth noting that this 100% incidence characterized these men at the time of the rape. In addition, the frequency of consensual heterosexual outlets as estimated by the respondents for the past year are overwhelmingly in favor of the rapist. Heterosexual orgasms resulting from coitus, fellatio, and masturbation average 1.5 per week for the rapists, while the mean for the controls is 0.8 per month. It is obvious that these rapists represent a very sexually active group of young men.

Much of this success can probably be attributed to the fact that these men are sexually predatory, that is, they are much more apt to attempt to precipitate new sexual experiences and to employ a variety of surreptitious seductive techniques. For example, when our respondents were asked the frequency with which they attempt to seduce a new date, 62% of the rapists and 19% of the controls responded "most of the time." The rapists' quests for heterosexual engagements largely borders on a no-holds-barred contest. To illustrate, these men were asked about efforts to gain coital access by employing such methods as trying to intoxicate their companions, threatening to terminate the relationship, falsely promising some sort of relationship permanence, i.e., "pinning," engagement, or marriage, falsely professing love, and threatening to abandon their dates, e.g., make them walk home. Table 11.1 rather cogently portrays these rapists as most apt to pursue their sexual goals by employing drugging, extortion, fraud, and lying: 93% of the rapists, compared to 40% of the controls, used at least one of these techniques while in college. Crucial to the central argument of this paper is the finding that 93% of the rapists, but only 37% of the controls, said that their best friends would "definitely approve" of such tactics for *certain* women. Furthermore, 91% of the rapists, in contrast to 32% of the controls, have had such procedures seriously suggested to them by their best friends as functional for sexual success. Sexual exploitation of the female largely permeates their entire male-female approach. The foregoing is compelling testimony to the fact that those who have

[2]None of this is to imply that these women were merely being respectably reluctant. All cases where the female metamorphosed into an active participant were discarded, along with cases where she apparently showed no traumatic consequences.

[3]In view of the nature of the accidental samples of rapists and controls, all percentages were rounded off, and no tests of statistical significance were employed. Instead, we relied exclusively on the pronounced differences between the rapists and the nonrapists.

TABLE 11.1. Incidence of Sexual Exploitation Techniques Employed by Rapists and Controls since College Entrance, by Percentage

	Rapists (N =71)	Controls (N = 227)
Attempt to intoxicate female with alcohol	76[a]	23[b]
Falsely profess love	86	25
Falsely promise "pinning," engagement, or marriage	46	6
Threaten to terminate relationship	31	7
Threaten to leave female stranded	9	0

[a]28% also involved marijuana.
[b]19% also involved marijuana.

been most successful in obtaining heterosexual outlets are also those who resort to deviant means.

Regarding the question of assessing sexual frustration by the criterion of sexual experience, it has usually been assumed on a priori grounds that a comparative lack of sexual encounters can be roughly translated into proportional increases of frustration. However, it is necessary first to aspire to a goal in order to experience frustration. If the controls should demonstrate a comparatively lesser interest in sex for whatever reasons, then it would be questionable simply to attribute frustration to those with less experience and sexual satisfaction to those with greater experience. It is plausible, of course, that a male with few, if any, heterosexual outlets can still assess himself as not sexually frustrated. The sexually more successful male, on the other hand, may be experiencing frustration if his aspirations exceed his achievements. Asking the respondents to indicate the degree of satisfaction with which they view their sexual activities of the past year, the rapists with their more extensive experience are more apt to report dissatisfaction than the controls with their comparative lack of sexual activity, 79% and 32%, respectively. These findings suggest that satisfaction with one's sexual activity might be only casually related to one's sexual activities. It will be argued here that the dissatisfaction manifested by the rapists is due to a differential socialization in a hyperorotic male culture, a culture where sexual success is of paramount importance in the maintenance of self-esteem, and the inability to achieve sexual success can, on a select occasion, result in an expression of violence sufficient to achieve rape.

Differential Sexual Socialization: Peer Groups

In trying to conceptualize a socialization process that would increase the likelihood of date rape, it became very apparent from the study of these data that direct tutelage or example, for all practical purposes, be totally excluded. However, it is feasible to think in terms of a sexual socialization that not only would make sex a highly valued and prestigious activity but also would provide justifications for directing sexual efforts toward specific targets. More specifically, sexual socialization can be thought to comprise influences positive to sexual predation, including providing stereotypes of ideal victims, and of the absence of negative definitions that serve to counteract or insulate against the positive "pulls." Agents that could be considered central to providing such definitions would be an individual's peers and family.

An attempt was made to gauge the degree that one's current peer group would condone aggressive and offensive sexual efforts by obtaining the *imputed* reputational consequences of such behavior. The respondents were asked what they thought would be the reputational consequences in the eyes of their best friends "if they found out that you offended a woman by *trying* to force her to have sexual intercourse, during the course of which you used physical force and/or threats." It is patently implicit here that these are not successful efforts and, therefore, that these acts do not constitute forcible rape. The question was phrased so as to apply to aggressions committed against five hypothetical women, each possessing a significant characteristic that might affect her attractiveness as an aggression target. Table 11.2 shows the percentage of rapists and controls who believe that their reputations would be enhanced by aggressing against a woman playing a role with a stereotyped

TABLE 11.2. Imputed Positive Reputational Consequences of Aggressively Offending Five Select Hypothetical Women, by Percentage

	Rapists (N = 71)	Controls (N = 227)
Bar "pick-up"	54	16
Woman with "loose" reputation	27	10
Known "teaser"	81	40
Economic exploiter	73	39
A more or less regular date	9	7

sexual significance in the male world. Although it is apparent that the "teaser" and economic exploiter are prime targets for both groups, positive reputational consequences are dramatically seen as forthcoming from the friends of the rapists. Their erotic subculture has adequately conferred the label of legitimate sexual targets on certain "deviant" females. In a substantial segment of the male culture, four of these women qualify as social deviants by violating expectations in the dating encounter. Essentially, the "pick-up," the "loose woman," and the "teaser" are viewed as upending sexual expectations after "flaunting," "advertising," and "promising" sexual accessibility. The economic exploiter, although less sexually explicit, earns her deviant label by violating reciprocity norms held by some segments of the male culture. In short, these women are seen as not playing by the rules of the game, and, therefore, the man feels justified in suspending the rules regarding his dating conduct. It should be noted that these men are aware that frequent encounters with "rough sex" would evoke suspicion of derangement, even from their close friends. Only a minority, about 25%, would tell their friends about such encounters. There is, additionally, an anxiety that these aggressions could be status detracting in that they highlight sexual failure and the inability to succeed by more sophisticated means. Essentially, their friends are not seen as rewarding violence; the offensive sexuality that receives acclaim—or at least does not draw opprobrium—is largely due to the "provocative" conduct of the victim.

Not only do these males have associates who they believe would condone aggressive behavior, but they are also subjected to peer influences to be sexually active. Responses to the question, "What degree of pressure do your best friends exert on you to seek sexual encounters?" shows that the rapists are indeed the recipients of such spheres of influence. Table 11.3 clearly portrays the rapists as receiving such peer enticements, whereas the controls are overrepresented as receiving little or no pressure from their friends. The evidence thus far shows that the rapists have a differential association with close friends who encourage and reward sexual experience and who will also support sexual transgressions on select females.

It is crucial to note that these men did not acquire their aggressive sexuality in college. Although they definitely tended to immerse themselves in an erotic culture that served normative reference-group functions for them, this current culture functioned as a reference group primarily by supporting and sustaining values acquired prior to college entrance. Of course the newly acquired collegiate friendship groups did serve reference-group functions in that they embellished old values, provided new vocabularies of adjustment, altered old norms, and introduced new norms. If we look at the behaviors of these men while they were still in high school, we find the same peer group phenomenon operating, only in an exaggerated fashion. For example, 85% of the rapists, in contrast to 26% of the controls, reported high school friendships where pressure for heterosexual expression was "great and considerable."

TABLE 11.3. Degree or Pressure Exerted by Current Friends for Sexual Activity, by Percentage

	Rapists (N = 71)	Controls (N = 227)
Great deal and considerable	40	9
Moderate	45	28
Little and none	15	63
Totals	100	100

It seems appropriate here to raise the question as to the nature of the perceptions of these respondents regarding their peer group influences. Specifically, it may be charged that these perceptions are largely defensive and, therefore, represent distortions. Our evidence, however, does not lend support to such a hypothesis but rather bolsters the position that the sexual socialization of these rapists was substantially influenced by a supportive hypererotic male culture. This is particularly the case when we examine some of the more concrete behavioral aspects involving the rapists and their close associates. For example, it can be pointed out that the rapists are much more apt to have a history of collaborative sex. Fully 41 % of the rapists, but only 7% of the controls, were ever involved in either a "gang-bang" or a sequential sexual sharing of a female with a male friend. Furthermore, over 67% of the rapists had had intercourse with a female whom a friend had recommended as sexually congenial. Only 13% of the controls indicated that they were ever recipients of such a friendship referral network. Lastly, 21% of the rapists reported that their first female-genital contact, whether manual, oral, or coital, was the direct consequence of having been "fixed-up" by a friend(s). This contrasts rather sharply with the 6% of the controls who reported that such third-party arrangements had entered into their premier episode. All these data tend uniformly to confirm these respondents' perceptions that their close associates do indeed represent an active hypererotic influence.

Differential Sexual Socialization: Family Influences

A basic socialization role could also be played by the fathers of these men. Fathers are observed to exhibit a wide spectrum of attitudes toward their sons' sexual activities, ranging from severely proscribing such conduct to virtually condoning and even encouraging "manly" pursuits. Although some fathers were reported to have urged their sons to go out and "get some," this attitude was quite the exception; very few men reported paternal sexual encouragement. In fact, in order to compose a working category of fathers whose attitudes were not unequivocally unfavorable to premarital sex, as checked on a 5-point Likert-type scale, it was necessary to combine the categories "very favorable," "favorable," and "neutral." Even here we find only 21% of our total sample, and the rapists are only represented about 4% more than the controls, a negligible difference.

However, when we inspect the unfavorable attitude categories, a very striking contrast appears only in the "very unfavorable." Approximately equal representation of rapists and controls are found with fathers whose attitudes are "unfavorable," 46% and 54%, respectively. But in the case where the father's attitude toward premarital sex is perceived to be "very unfavorable," we find 72% of the controls and only 28% of the rapists. It may well be that the father's major influence on his son's sexual activities is not to be found in encouragement and support but rather in a very strong posture of disapproval. In other words, the nature of paternal influence on a son's sexual orientation is more the product of a strong proscriptive position than a positive encouraging one.

Differential Sexual Socialization: Justifications

An integral aspect of the variety of differential sexual socialization with which we are dealing should involve the provision for a vocabulary of adjustment, a means of justifying behavior. It has been shown that these rapists see their prestige as being enhanced for sexually exploiting select women. It would seem to follow that their associates, those who encourage them to deviate, would provide them with—or reinforce—appropriate vocabularies of adjustment so that they can continue to maintain their conception of themselves as beings of worth and esteem while continuing to exploit and degrade. Such a process would be an essential prerequisite for the maintenance and perpetuation of group values. Approximately 86% of these rapists believe that rape, in the abstract, and not necessarily in their own behavior, can be justified under certain conditions. This contrasts rather sharply with the 19% of the controls who believe in the justifiability of rape. These justifications, as one would expect, are almost completely made up of women viewed as "teasers," economic exploiters, and "loose." The more extensive information gathered through the interviews with the rapists seems to point to a composite of teaser-exploiter-loose as the quintessential deviant dating companion. She is seen as the one who financially extends the man, who enters into sex play with sufficient enthusiasm to convey a presupposition of having "been around," and who insists on stabilizing the sexual aspect of the relationship short of coitus. It should be pointed out, however, that in reality victims only seldom qualify, even under student standards, as economic exploiters but eminently qualify as "teaser-loose" because of the nature of their role in the sexual encounter, namely, one that is consensual and active.

Considering again peer group influence on the ability to perceive a deviant act as justified, it is found that 93% of the rapists who indicated they were recipients of great, considerable, or moderate peer group pressure for sexual activity indicated that rape can be justified. The rapists who reported that their peers exerted little or no pressure for sexual involvement were considerably less apt to believe in the justification of rape, only 45%.

Relative Deprivation

Now that it has been established that these rapists were the recipients of strong social pressures for sexual achievement, it is time to return to the finding that these more experienced men reported a greater incidence of sexual dissatisfaction than the sexually less experienced controls. As previously stated, more extensive sexual experience could readily be associated with greater dissatisfaction if one's peers highly value sexual accomplishment and confer prestige rewards for success. In effect, an exaggerated level of sexual aspiration is introjected from one's erotically oriented significant others, a level that, at best, will be difficult for the majority of college males to maintain continually. Aspiration levels may be reflected in the subjective estimates held by these men regarding their sexual needs. When asked, "How many orgasms (ejaculations) per week, from any source, do you think you would require in order to give you sexual satisfaction?", the rapists report a mean number of 4.5, in contrast to 2.8 for the controls. It could be inferred that these men are experiencing relative deprivation in that dissatisfaction largely stems from their inability to achieve ambitious goals (see Kanin, 1967).

Evidence supporting this position comes from demonstrating that the degree of the rapists' sexual satisfaction with their sexual accomplishment for the previous year appears strongly related to the degree of pressure their friends exert for sexual experience. The rapists show the most pronounced inclination to report sexual satisfaction when little or no group pressure is applied, 71%, while satisfaction is less frequently indicated by the recipients of great, considerable, and moderate pressures, 40%. Although this finding does not prove a causal nexus exists here, it is compatible with "reference group theory."

Conclusions

The purpose of this paper was to show that these date rapists experienced a differential sexual socialization that resulted in the development of an exaggerated sex impulse and the placing of an inordinately high value on sexual accomplishment. Consequently, a frustration of the aroused impulse led these men to undergo an acute sense of goal deprivation that can best be understood in the context of relative deprivation. Specifically, it is sexually less frustrating to encounter rejection when one's socialization has provided for a lower level of aspiration than when one's socialization has instilled a high expectancy of sexual success (see Kanin, 1967; Chappell et al., 1977). The female's rejection of coital intimacy after rather intensive advanced sexual interaction is primarily the expression of her need to stabilize intimacy for personal reasons, and not to exploit or to be fashionably provocative.[4] The male fails to recognize this. Instead, he focuses on whether her rejection is genuine and/or on the adequacy of his sexual powers, a very likely manifestation of a perceptual defense process. This results in his bewilderment and anxiety. The disregard for her rejection behavior and the subsequent display of aggressive presentations, verbal and physical, intended and/or unintended, readily led to the rape episode on this occasion. The inflicting of punishment or suffering through the rape appears incidental in the vast majority of cases and, at best, serves a secondary function. There is very little evidence here that violence functioned as a sexual stimulant for these men (see Barbaree, Marshall, & Lanthier, 1979). The coital experience, the manifest and anticipated benefit, and the accompanying reaffirmation of self-worth, not entirely lost to consciousness, appear to be prime movers for these rapes.

Although this paper imputes a prime role to reference groups, there exists a possibility that these exaggerated levels of sexual aspiration and the accompanying aggressive behaviors have their genesis in other than positive reference groups. Early familial and other primary group influences might have affected aspects of personality development of (1) a generalized hostility toward the female world, (2) an aggressive component and (3) a hypererotic orientation. The foregoing could have the effect of prompting one to seek out membership groups holding sexually congenial perspectives. However, the reference group interpretation is favored since it is grounded in a substantial body of research that has consistently demonstrated the significance of peer influence on sexually aggressive behavior (Reiss, 1960; Polk et al., 1981; Kanin, 1967; Ageton, 1983).

REFERENCES

Ageton, S. S. (1983). *Sexual assault among adolescents*. Lexington, MA: D. C. Heath.

Anderson, N. (1923). *The Hobo*. Chicago, IL: University of Chicago Press.

Barbaree, H. E. Marshall, W. L., & Lanthier, R. D. (1979). Deviant sexual arousal in rapists. *Behav. Res. Ther., 17,* 215–221.

Bonger, W. A. (1916). *Criminality and economic conditions*. Boston, MA: Little, Brown.

[4]The great majority of our respondents concurred with this interpretation at the time of the interview.

Chappell, D., Geis, G., Schafer, S., & Siegel, L. (1977). A comparative study of forcible rape offenses known to the police in Boston and Los Angeles. In Chappell, D., Geis, R., & Geis, G. (Eds.). *Forcible rape*. New York: Columbia University Press.

Clark, L., & Lewis, D. (1977). *Rape: The price of coercive sexuality.* Toronto: The Woman's Press.

Clemmer, D. (1958). *The prison community.* New York: Rinehart and Co.

Cohen, Y. A. (1961). *Social structure and personality*. New York: Holt, Rinehart, and Winston.

Cohen, M. L., Garofalo, R. B., Boucher, R. B., & Seghorn, T. (1971). The psychology of rapists. *Sem. in Psychiat., 3,* 307–327.

Fishman, J. F. (1934). *Sex in prison.* New York: Podell.

Guttmacher, M. S. (1951). *Sex offenses*. New York: Norton.

Kanin, E. (1967). Reference groups and sex conduct norm violations. *Soc. Quart., 8,* 495–504.

Kanin, E. (1984). Date rape: Unofficial criminals and victims. *Victimology, 9,* 95–108.

Karpman, B. (1954). *The sexual offender and his offenses.* New York: Julian Press.

Lockwood, D. (1980). *Prison sexual violence*. New York: Elsevier.

Polk, K., Adler, C., Bazemore, G., Blake, G., Corday, S., Coventry, G., Galrin, J., & Temple, M. (1981). Becoming adult: An analysis of motivational development from age 16 to 30 of a cohort of young men: *Final report of the Marion County youth survey.* Eugene, OR: University of Oregon.

Reiss, A. J. (1960). Sex offenses: The marginal status of the adolescent. *Law Contemp. Prob.,* 25, 309–333.

Sykes, G. (1958). *The society of captives*. Princeton, NJ: Princeton University Press.

Thio, A. (1983). *Deviant behavior.* Boston: Hougton-Mifflin.

Wheeler, S. (1960). Sex offenses: A sociological critique. *Law Contemp. Prob.,* 25, 258–278.

READING 12

Adjustment to Rape

C. Buf Meyer and Shelley E. Taylor • University of California, Los Angeles

This questionnaire study of rape victims' reactions, causal attributions for the rape, coping behaviors after the rape, and psychological adjustment to the rape were examined. As in previous research, high levels of behavioral and characterological self-blame for rape were found. Contrary to prior hypotheses, behavioral self-blame was not associated with good adjustment. Rather, both behavioral and characterological self-blame were associated with poor adjustment. Societal blame was the only causal attribution for rape that was unassociated with adjustment. Remaining at home and withdrawing from others were both associated with poor adjustment, and the use of stress reduction techniques was associated with good adjustment. The implications of the results for theories of victimization and for clinical interventions with rape victims are discussed.

Being raped has negative and often long-lasting psychological consequences. More than one year after a rape, victims experience more rape-related fear and anxiety (Kilpatrick, Resick, & Veronen, 1981), sexual dissatisfaction (Feldman-Summers, Gordon, & Meagher, 1979), depression (Atkeson, Calhoun, Resick, & Ellis, 1982), and family-related problems (Ellis, Atkeson, & Calhoun, 1981) than do other women. Women's work and social adjustment are also likely to be impaired for as long as eight months after a rape (Resick, Calhoun, Atkeson, & Ellis, 1981). Repeated assessment and participation in research may attenuate adverse psychological reactions to rape (Resick et al., 1981), which suggests that current research findings may underrepresent the severity of the typical psychological reaction to rape.

Despite the clear possibility that a woman will suffer from psychological problems after a rape, some victims are virtually symptom-free within months of their assault (Veronen & Kilpatrick, 1983). Researchers have identified several factors that influence the severity of a woman's response to being raped. Thus far, it has been shown that preexisting factors such as previous victimizations (Frank, Turner, & Stewart, 1980), prior psychiatric history, and physical illnesses (Atkeson et al., 1982) will aggravate a woman's reaction to a sexual assault. Previous life changes have been shown to bear a curvilinear relation to adjustment, such that a moderate amount of life change is associated with better adjustment (Ruch, Chandlers, & Harter, 1980). Characteristics of the assault (e.g., the victim's relationship to the assailant, brutality of the assault) may be associated with the severity of a victim's reaction to the assault (e.g., Ellis et al., 1981; Frank et al., 1980), although the precise nature of these relations has yet to be identified. Overall, then, the factors that have been identified thus far as contributing to an adaptive or maladaptive response to rape have concerned the victim's life situation and characteristics of the assault.

The primary purpose of this study was to examine the coping patterns used by victims of rape and relate them to postrape adjustment. Coping behaviors are defined here as cognitive and motoric activities that a victim uses to master, reduce, or recover from the characteristic symptoms of emotional distress that may develop after rape (cf. Lazarus & Launier, 1978; Lipowski, 1970). Although some coping researchers have maintained that the emotional consequences of stress are themselves coping efforts, most researchers distinguish emotional consequences from active behavioral responses to a crisis; the term *coping efforts* is typically reserved for these latter responses (F. Cohen & Lazarus, 1975; Freedman, Kaplan, & Sadock, 1975; Haan, 1977; Lipowski, 1970; Vaillant, 1971; Worden & Sobel, 1978).

Some researchers have already examined the use of coping behaviors among rape victims. Using unstructured interview data from 149 rape victims, Burgess and Holmstrom (1979) described several different coping patterns observed in women after they had been assaulted. These authors reported that women consciously using coping behaviors recovered more quickly from rape than did rape victims not actively trying to cope. The coping patterns described as successful by Burgess and Holmstrom (1979) are explanation (identifying a reason why the rape occurred), minimization (telling oneself that the rape was not really so terrifying), suppression (making a conscious effort to avoid thinking about the rape), action (keeping busy, changing jobs, or moving), and stress reduction (using specific techniques such as meditation). Maladaptive coping patterns included decreased activity (not going out of the house), withdrawal from people, and substance abuse.

Explanation is the coping strategy described by Burgess and Holmstrom (1979) that has received the most attention in the social psychological literature. Previous researchers have found that causal attributions for a serious event can sometimes have a substantial impact on posttraumatic adjustment. Bulman and Wortman (1977) found that the spinal-cord-injured accident victims who felt responsible for their accidents were better adjusted to their injuries than were those who did not. On the basis of these findings, the authors concluded that self-blame may be an adaptive attribution for victims of severe accidents. However, research on self-blame among other victimized populations has not supported the Bulman and Wortman prediction (Miller & Porter, 1983; Silver, Boon, & Stones, 1977; Taylor, Wood, & Lichtman, 1983).

Janoff-Bulman (1979) surveyed counselors at 40 rape crisis centers in order to document blaming strategies used by victims of sexual assault. On the basis of these findings, she proposed that a distinction be made between behavioral and characterological self-blame. *Behavioral self-blame* occurs when a victim assigns responsibility for her rape to her own modifiable behaviors (e.g., not locking the front door, hitchhiking). Such explanations are expected to facilitate adjustment by enhancing a victim's sense of control, thereby decreasing the fear of being raped again. *Characterological self-blame* involves attributions to stable aspects of a person (e.g., "I am too trusting" "I am a bad person"); it implies inevitability and a feeling that the attack was deserved. These attributions are expected to make the future seem menacing and uncontrollable. Behavioral versus characterological self-blame can be distinguished best, then, on the basis of "the perceived controllability (i.e., modifiability through one's own effort) of the factor(s) blamed" (Janoff-Bulman, 1979, p. 1799).

On the basis of her preliminary research, Janoff-Bulman (1979) estimated that 70% of all rape victims who seek counseling attribute causality for the rape to their behavior, whereas only 20% blame aspects of their character (see also Libow & Doty, 1979). According to Janoff-Bulman, behavioral self-blame should be associated with more effective postrape adjustment than should characterological self-blame. However, this hypothesis has not yet been empirically tested.

In this study, we sought to identify causal attributions for rape and relate them to psychological adjustment. Following Janoff-Bulman (1979), we predicted that behavioral self-blame would be associated with fewer adverse consequences of rape and that characterological self-blame would be correlated with more adverse consequences of rape.

Another coping response investigated in this research is the use of precautionary behaviors after rape (e.g., locking doors carefully, not talking to strangers). Clinical observers often describe rape victims as very cautious and self-protective. We hypothesized that the adoption of precautionary behaviors would be most likely to occur in women who felt that they could somehow prevent another rape (i.e., in women whose explanations included behavioral self-blame). Consequently, we predicted that the use of precautionary behaviors after rape would be associated with better postrape adjustment.

It should be noted that Riger and Gordon's (1981) results lead to a contrary prediction. Their work suggests that individuals who are most frightened of becoming victims of crime are most likely to restrict their behavior so as to avoid potentially dangerous situations. From this standpoint, the adoption of precautionary behaviors among rape victims would suggest a greater fear of being raped again and worse overall adjustment. In light of these contrary hypotheses, we tested whether greater reliance on precautionary behaviors is associated with more fear and anxiety or with behavioral self-blame and less fearfulness.

The general purpose of this research was to determine whether any particular causal attributions for rape and other coping behaviors are associated with the magnitude of symptoms experienced after being raped. We predicted that (a) women who attribute responsibility for their rape to modifiable factors (i.e., behavioral self-blame) would experience fewer adverse effects of rape, and (b) women whose attributions include characterological self-blame would experience more adverse consequences of rape. With regard to other coping strategies, we hypothesized that (c) women who use stress reduction techniques or behavioral precautionary strategies or both would experience fewer adverse consequences of rape. In accordance with previous research, (d) those women who take drugs, withdraw from others, or stay at home after their assault were expected to have more severe consequences of rape (e.g., more sexual dissatisfaction, fear, and depression).

Method

Recruitment of Subjects

Subjects were recruited from six rape crisis centers in Southern California and one in New York. Because of human subjects' restrictions, subjects from all but one center could not be recruited directly by the investigators and instead had to be recruited through their rape counselors. Questionnaires were left with these counselors, who were asked to distribute them to their clients when they saw them for their next session. Because of concern that participation in the research might be upsetting to certain women, counselors did not consistently invite all their clients to participate. On the basis of counselor reports, response rate of completed questionnaires is estimated at 60%. The combination of counselor selection and compliance factors may have resulted in a subsample of rape victims who were somewhat more emotionally stable than average.

Because the first author worked at a rape crisis center, women who attended this facility could be asked to participate during a routine follow-up counseling call. This method of recruiting subjects supplemented the procedures just described. All 56 of the women contacted by phone agreed to fill out the questionnaire. Only 18 of these women actually completed and mailed back the questionnaire, which made the response rate for this group 32%. The discrepancy in the two response rates is most likely due to differences in the two recruitment methods: A personal request from a counselor is clearly more compelling than a request from an unknown person over the telephone.

Subjects

Subjects were 58 women, all of whom had been raped within the past two years; median time since the rape was 16 weeks. All respondents had contacted a rape crisis center for counseling usually shortly after the rape. All but one of the respondents ranged in age from 16 to 42; one woman was 76 years old. Average educational attainment was two years of college; six women were still completing their schooling. The average occupational rating of the 41 working women was a six on the Hollingshead (1975) scale; employment was largely in technical or secretarial jobs. Four women were homemakers and seven more were unemployed, disabled, or retired. At the time of the assault, 77% of the sample was single and dating, 14% was married, and 9% was neither married nor dating. Participants in this study were similar to other samples of urban rape victims in that they were young and single; they differed from other samples in that they were better educated and less economically disadvantaged (cf. Katz & Mazur, 1979).

Forty-three percent of the assaults were initiated in the victim's home, usually while she was asleep; another 43% began in a public place, and the remaining 14% occurred in the home of the assailant or his accomplice. Most of the rapes were not physically brutal, but 16% of the victims were badly beaten. Eighty-three percent of the women were raped by strangers, whereas 17% of them knew their assailants beforehand. All but six of the 58 women had reported their rape to the police.

Questionnaires

Subjects were asked to complete a questionnaire concerning their attributions for the rape, how they had coped with the rape, their current level of rape-related symptoms, characteristics of the assault, and demographic variables.

Attributions. Respondents' attributions for the rape were assessed in four different ways in the questionnaire. First, they were asked to rate 24 specific statements according to their importance in "helping you explain why you were attacked." Responses were made on a 5-point Likert-type scale. Statements were designed to enable us to assess behavioral self-blame (e.g., "I should have been more cautious"), characterological self-blame (e.g., "I am the victim type"), blame placed on uncontrollable factors (e.g., "I have bad luck"), and societal blame (e.g., "It is unsafe for a woman to go anywhere by herself"). Second, subjects were presented with a list of 10 causal agents (chance, society, self, rapist, fate, parents, God, person they were with at the time of the assault, roommate, husband/ lover/boyfriend) and were asked, "To what extent do you blame the following factors for your attack?" They then rated each causal agent on a 5-point Likert-type scale ranging from *completely* (2) to *not at all* (–2). Third, respondents were asked to identify which of the 10 causal agents they blamed most for their assault. Last, subjects were asked to respond to the open-ended question, "Explain the reasons you believe account for why you were raped."

Coping. Women's methods of coping were assessed through their responses to 50 statements about their attitudes and behaviors after their rape. Statements were designed to enable us to assess several of the coping styles that Burgess and Holmstrom (1979) had observed in rape victims. In addition, some coping statements were adapted from Riger and Gordon's (1979) rape prevention items. The coping patterns assessed were suppression (e.g., "There is no reason to think about the rape"), minimization (e.g., "I am very lucky, it could have been much worse"), stress reduction (e.g., "I meditate frequently"), activity (e.g., "I keep myself exceptionally busy"), precautionary behavior (e.g., "I always lock my door"), withdrawal (e.g., "I rarely leave my house anymore"), and substance abuse (e.g., "I have more than two drinks a day").

Outcomes. Adverse consequences of rape were assessed from subjects' responses to 37 statements about sexual satisfaction, physical and emotional symptoms of depression, and rape-related fear and anxiety. Statements that we used to measure sexual satisfaction and rape-related fear were modified from scales developed by Feldman-Summers et al. (1979) and Kilpatrick, Veronen, and Resick (1979), respectively. Questions selected had previously discriminated rape victims from a nonvictim group. Statements used to assess psychological and somatic aspects of depression were derived from Norris and Feldman-Summers's (1981) psychosomatic scale and clinical descriptions by Burgess and Holmstrom (1979). Responses were recorded on 5-point Likert-type scales ranging from *completely true* (2) to *completely false* (–2).

Subjects were also asked to respond to the open-ended question, "What is the biggest change that has occurred in your life since the rape?"

Results

Our findings are presented in two major sections. The first section contains information about the validation, reliability, and construction of the factor scores, women's responses to open-ended questions, and ratings of causal agents blamed for the rape. In the second section, we discuss the interrelations among the measures.

Measures

FACTOR SCORE CONSTRUCTION

Principal-components factor analyses were used to determine (a) whether the a priori hypothesized item groupings corresponded to actual item groupings and (b) which items should be selected for inclusion in each factor. Because of the large number of items in relation to the small size, separate factor analyses were performed on the three subsets of items that represent our major classes of variables: attribution, coping behaviors, and outcomes.

We performed trial rotations, varying the number of factors selected for rotation. Factor solutions were evaluated in terms of the meaningfulness and interpretability of the factors. We also considered whether to alter or divide major factors by rotating additional factors.

Having chosen a particular factor solution, analyses were rerun with only those items that loaded .3 or more on only one factor. Items selected for inclusion on a scale were those that loaded .3 or more on the same scale in both analyses (the first analysis contained all the items; the second contained only the items that had previously loaded .3 or more on only one factor). Many items were not included on any scale as a result of these criteria. These procedures were used to minimize random inclusion of items on scales, which is a problem likely to result from factor analysis with a large number of items in relation to a small number of subjects. Separate factor scores were then calculated for each subject by means of summing responses selected for inclusion on each scale.

Attributions. We predicted that causal attributions for rape would fall into four basic categories: the victim's behaviors, the victim's characteristics, uncontrollable forces, and societal problems. The 24 Likert items with which we measures attributions were entered into a principal-components factor analysis. This procedure yielded seven factors, each of which accounted for more than 5% of the total variance and had an eigenvalue greater than one. Regardless of the number of factors rotated, two self-blame factors emerged, consistently retaining their fundamental character. We ultimately decided to use a three-factor solution because the non-self-blame factor in this solution appeared to be a measure of a broader, more theoretically meaningful construct (attribution of blame to societal factors) than were the numerous non-self-blame factors generated by the extraction of larger numbers of factors.

The three attribution factors were labeled *Poor Judgment*, *Societal Factors*, and *Victim Type*. The items included in each of these factors are shown in Table 12.1. Poor Judgment accounted for 46% of the total variance and had a reliability coefficient of .79 (Cronbach's alpha). The five questions on this scale appeared to be a measure of the extent to which a woman blamed her behaviors, abilities, and attitudes for her rape, and therefore the scale is similar to Janoff-Bulman's (1979) concept of behavioral self-blame. Victim Type accounted for 25% of the total variance and had an alpha coefficient of .64. The four items loading on this scale appeared to be a measure of blame attributed to victim's characteristics and uncontrollable forces—that is, the extent to which a woman blamed her proclivity to attract an assault. Thus this factor is close to Janoff-Bulman's concept of characterological self-blame. Societal Factors was the only non-self-blame factor. It accounted for 29% of the total variance and had an alpha coefficient of .71. The six questions on this scale were measures of the extent to which a woman blamed external, tangible forces for her rape. Intercorrelations among the factor scores and analysis of the factor structure after oblique rotation indicated that these three factors were orthogonal.

TABLE 12.1. Factor Loadings of Items on Attribution Scales

Factor/item	Factors 1	2	3
1. Poor Judgment			
I am too trusting	*.67*	−.14	.03
I made a rash decision	*.74*	.12	−.06
I should have been more cautious	*.66*	.03	.11
I am a poor judge of character	*.56*	−.02	.14
I am too impulsive	*.69*	.11	.05
2. Societal Factors			
There are never people around when you need them	.35	*.40*	.13
There is too much pornography	.07	*.44*	−.05
People are too scared to get involved	.20	*.58*	−.08
Men have too little respect for women	.15	*.42*	.17
There is never a policeman around when you need him	.13	*.66*	.13
There is too much violence on TV.	−.16	*.60*	.03
3. Victim Type			
I got what I deserved	.16	−.40	*.34*
I can't take care of myself	.20	−.02	*.44*
I am a victim type	.06	.15	*.63*
I have bad luck	.03	.27	*.81*

Note. Italics indicate factor loadings for those items included on each scale.

In response to the question that concerned which of 10 causal agents a victim blamed most for her rape, 56% of the women blamed the rapist, 20% blamed themselves, 15% blamed chance, and 11% blamed society. Of the 54 women who responded to this question, 13% listed more than one factor. No more than one person blamed God, their roommate, parents, husband/lover/ boyfriend, or the person they were with at the time of the assault.

Intercorrelation of the three attribution factor scores with women's 5-point ratings of the five causal agents most likely to have been blamed for the rape provided a measure of convergent validity for the meaning of the factor scores. Scores on Poor Judgment were significantly correlated only with ratings of self ($r = .58, p < .001$). Scores on Victim Type were significantly correlated with ratings of self ($r = .29, p = .02$) and fate ($r = .27, p = .03$) and marginally related to ratings of chance ($r = .23, p = .06$), which suggests that this factor has a great deal to do with uncontrollable forces. Scores on Societal Factors were significantly correlated only with society ($r = .35, p = .005$).

A subjective account for women's causal attributions for rape is best gleaned from a report of their responses to the open-ended question of why they believed they were raped. Responses to all open-ended questions were read by independent raters. After applying kappa to correct for chance (J. Cohen, 1960), we determined that interrater agreement on all the open-ended questions had a reliability coefficient between .7 and .9. Twenty-six percent of the women blamed society and its treatment of women, 20% felt they had been too trusting, 17% cited their behavioral carelessness, 17% mentioned the rapist or his family and friends, and 15% referred to fate. Other responses (e.g., God, ignoring one's instincts) were given by less than 8% of the women. Of the 54 women who responded to this question, 30% provided multiple explanations. Nearly half of the respondents mentioned some form of self-blame.

Coping. It was expected that seven different sets of coping behaviors could be identified from women's questionnaire responses: minimization, suppression, keeping active, use of precautionary behaviors, stress reduction, phobic withdrawal, and substance abuse. The 50 Likert items that measured coping behaviors were entered into a principal-components factor analysis. Each of the first seven factors accounted for more than 5% of the variance and had an eigenvalue greater than one. After varimax rotation, these seven factors appeared to correspond reasonably well with the factors that had been initially hypothesized.

The seven resulting factors were labeled *Precaution, Remain Home, Withdrawal, Activity, Suppression, Minimization,* and *Stress Reduction*. The items included on each of these scales are shown in Table 12.2. Precaution accounted for 28% of the total variance; the five items on this scale had an alpha coefficient of .75. Remain Home accounted for 18% of the total variance; the three items on this scale had an alpha coefficient of .67. Withdrawal accounted for 15% of the total variance; the four items on this scale had an alpha coefficient of .58. Activity accounted for 12% of the total variance; the two items on this scale had an alpha coefficient of .67. Minimization accounted for 10% of the total variance; the two items on this scale had an alpha coefficient of .49. Stress Reduction accounted for 9.4% of the variance; the two items on this scale had an alpha coefficient of .54. The final coping factor was Suppression, which accounted for 7% of the variance; the two items on this scale had an alpha coefficient of .47.

Women's responses to the open-ended question "What, if anything, have you done since the rape that has made you feel better?" reflect their ideas about which coping responses were most helpful to them. Of the coping responses described as effective by these women, 73% fell into four categories: counseling (mentioned by 45% of respondents), use of precautionary behaviors (36%), talking to friends and family (27%), and making life changes such as moving or quitting work (18%).

Outcome. The questionnaire was expected to measure four different areas of postrape adjustment: psychological symptoms, physical symptoms, sexual dissatisfaction, and rape-related fear and anxiety. The 37 Likert items measuring outcome were entered into a principal-components factor analysis. This procedure yielded five factors, each of which accounted for more than 5% of the total variance and had an eigenvalue greater than one. After varimax rotation in which we extracted five factors, the decision was made to drop the fifth factor because only one item loaded .3 or more on this factor exclusively. Although the resulting four-factor solution had item loadings similar to what had been expected, a three-factor solution was ultimately chosen. This solution was selected because of the conceptual clarity gained from having psychological and somatic symptoms load on one factor, forming a unitary measure of depression.

The resulting three outcome factors were labeled *Depression, Sexual Dissatisfaction,* and *Fear*. The items included on each of these scales are shown in Table 12.3. The Depression factor accounted for 59% of the total variance; the 12 items on this scale had an alpha coefficient of .89. Sexual Dissatisfaction accounted for 25% of the total variance;

TABLE 12.2. Factors Loadings of Items on Coping Scales

	Factor						
Factor/item	1	2	3	4	5	6	7
1. Precaution							
Always lock car door	*.64*	–.11	.02	–.04	.15	.08	–.05
Check door before opening	*.70*	.15	–.20	–.11	–.05	–.07	–.02
Keep doors locked at home	*.80*	.21	–.08	–.10	–.01	–.07	.24
Walk with keys ready	*.53*	.11	.21	.07	.01	–.06	–.04
No public transportation at night	*.53*	.10	.21	.23	.22	.09	–.51
2. Stay Home							
Rarely leave home	.05	*.76*	–.10	–.01	.42	.07	.14
Dress modestly	–.07	*.57*	.17	–.28	–.25	.02	–.34
Only leave house when necessary	.27	*.67*	.14	.13	.00	.00	–.10
3. Withdraw							
Don't answer doorbell	.05	.11	*.52*	–.01	–.22	–.11	–.02
Don't answer phone	–.11	.01	*.87*	–.07	.03	.24	.05
More than two drinks a day	.17	.03	*.34*	–.02	.17	–.08	–.01
Glad to be alive	.27	–.04	*–.46*	.05	.21	.33	.11
4. Active							
Keep exceptionally busy	–.09	–.10	–.12	*.68*	–.18	–.07	–.01
Keep busy with work	–.01	.10	.05	*.77*	.07	.14	.12
5. Minimization							
Can't imagine worse	.06	.07	–.09	.06	*.74*	–.06	.08
Worst experience ever	.03	.04	.01	–.06	*.46*	.11	–.09
6. Stress Reduction							
Think positive thoughts	–.20	.03	–.24	–.05	–.02	*.57*	.06
Use techniques to reduce stress	–.07	.06	.11	.06	.04	*.68*	–.17
7. Suppression							
Put rape behind me	–.02	–.02	.02	.03	–.01	.02	*.37*
No reason to think about it	.06	–.03	–.08	.32	.06	.07	*.41*

Note. Italics indicate factor loadings for those items included on each scale.

the eight items on this scale had an alpha coefficient of .9. The Fear scale accounted for 15% of the total variance; the six items on this scale had an alpha coefficient of .83.

Interrelations Among the Measures

RELATION ATTRIBUTIONS AND OUTCOMES

Because the factors Poor Judgment and Victim Type corresponded closely to Janoff-Bulman's (1979) behavioral self-blame and characterological self-blame respectively, we predicted that Poor Judgment would be associated with superior postrape adjustment and that Victim Type would be associated with more severe consequences of rape. Pearson product–moment correlations were computed among the three attribution factors and the three outcome factors in order to determine how women's causal attributions for rape were associated with postrape adjustment. These relations are shown in Table 12.4.

Contrary to prior hypotheses, Poor Judgment was not associated with good adjustment. Rather, increasing amounts of Poor Judgment and Victim Type were clearly associated with poorer postrape adjustment. The more a woman attributed blame to her own modifiable behaviors (Poor Judgment), the more likely she was to experience sexual dissatisfaction and symptoms of depression. The more a woman felt that her attack was part of a general pattern of victimization and bad luck (Victim Type) the more likely she was to experience fear and symptoms of depression. These findings were in marked contrast to Societal Factors, which was uncorrelated with any of the measures of adjustment; this indicates that there was no relation between the extent to which a woman blamed society and the severity of her postrape symptoms.

To gain more information about the construct of self-blame and its relation to postrape adjustment, we analyzed women's outcome factor scores in relation to their ratings of the item *self*, one of the 10 causal agents rated for blame on a 5-pont scale. We performed *t* tests to compare the outcome factor scores of women who felt largely or completely to blame for their rape (ratings of 1 or 2 on the item *self*) with those of women who felt a little or not at all to blame (ratings of –1 or –2 on the item *self*). Those women who felt largely or completely to blame for their rape had worse outcomes on all three measures than did women who felt a little or not at all to blame for the rape, although only the measure of sexual dissatisfaction reached significance, $t(41) = 3.27$, $p = .002$. We also calculated *t* tests on the four other causal agents that had received high ratings of blame. These analyses revealed no significant differences in postrape adjustment between women who blamed society, fate, chance, or the rapist to a larger extent than those who did not.

RELATION OF COPING BEHAVIORS AND OUTCOMES

It was initially hypothesized that Stress Reduction and Precaution would be associated with fewer adverse consequences of rape, whereas Remaining Home and Withdrawal would be associated with worse postrape adjustment. Pearson product–moment correlations were computed between subjects' scores on the seven measures of coping and three measures of outcome to test these hypotheses.

The analyses shown in Table 12.5 demonstrate that several coping factor scores were clearly associated with outcome factor scores. As we had expected the more frequently a woman reported using stress reduction techniques, the less likely she was to report experiencing symptoms of depression and fear. The predictions about negative coping patterns were also supported. High scores on Remain Home were associated with more Depression and Fear, and high scores on Withdrawal were associated with more Depression and Sexual Dissatisfaction. It is possible that more significant relations between coping patterns and outcomes were not observed because the coping scales had lower reliability than the other sets of scales.

As noted earlier, one set of predictions maintained that the use of precautionary behaviors would be associated with less fear and better adjustment. A contradictory prediction maintained that the use of precautionary behaviors would be associated with more fear and worse adjustment (Riger & Gordon, 1981). Neither prediction was supported. The use of precaution was associated

TABLE 12.3. Factor Loadings of Items on Outcome Scales

	Factors		
Factor/item	1	2	3
1. Sexual Dissatisfaction			
I enjoy kissing	*.71*	.21	.18
Smelling erotic scents	*.56*	.07	–.01
Undressing my partner	*.58*	.34	.08
No interest in sex	*.71*	.12	.06
Going out with new people	*.43*	.18	–.02
Seeing naked men	*.90*	.05	–.06
Stroking my partner	*.80*	.00	.25
Sexual intercourse	*.69*	.13	.32
2. Depression			
Cry easily	.04	*.40*	–.14
Feel accomplished	.17	*.46*	.24
Feel calm	.20	*.60*	.28
Often nauseous	.08	*.47*	.21
Suicidal	.13	.51	.10
Take tranquilizers	.16	*.55*	.05
Feel lonely	.06	*.71*	.05
Like work	.11	*.30*	.03
Self-pity	–.12	*.68*	.01
Sleeping problems	.07	*.57*	.18
Stuttering	.20	*.58*	–.01
Hard to make decisions	*.10*	.54	.24
3. Fear			
Scared if awakened at night	.22	.19	*.50*
Fear of knives	.15	.11	*.73*
Footsteps scary	–.06	–.06	*.44*
Noises scary	–.05	.11	*.60*
Dislike blind dates	.05	.05	*.30*
Fear of being raped again	.23	.21	*.43*

Note. Italics indicate factor loadings for those items included on each scale.

only with less sexual dissatisfaction. None of the other coping styles (suppression, minimization, activity) were significantly related to any of the measures of postrape adjustment.

Discussion

Results from this study support the idea that particular attributions and coping patterns that follow a sexual assault are predictably associated with the severity of the psychological consequences of that event.

One of the primary aims of this study was to examine empirically Janoff-Bulman's (1979) hypotheses about self-blame among rape victims. Janoff-Bulman ventured three predictions: first, that self-blame is common among rape victims; second, that self-blame is of two sorts, behavioral and characterological; and third, that behavioral

TABLE 12.4. Correlations Among Attribution Factor Scores and Outcome Factor Scores

Attribution factors	Outcome factors		
	Depression	Fear	Sexual dissatisfaction
Poor Judgment	.28*	−.06	.34**
Victim Type	.46***	.34**	.20
Societal Blame	.02	−.06	.03

* $p < .05$. ** $p < .01$. *** $p < .001$.

self-blame is associated with positive adjustment and characterological self-blame is associated with negative adjustment. Our evidence addresses all three hypotheses. First, in accordance with Janoff-Bulman's results, our study revealed a high rate of self-blame among rape victims. Janoff-Bulman's interviews with rape crisis counselors yielded an estimate that 74% of women blame themselves, at least in part, for the rape. In our study, the figure was closer to 50%. It is unclear whether this modest discrepancy is due to differences in the subject population (rape counselors vs. rape victims), differences in the rape victim clientele, or differences in the wording of the questions in the two studies.[1]

Why there should be such a high prevalence of self-blame among rape victims is still unknown. Brownmiller (1975) theorized that women are socialized into a victim role which leads them to accept responsibility for victimizing events that befall them. However, this explanation has never been tested. Moreover, there is, as yet, insufficient evidence to suggest that rape victims, or women more generally, are predisposed to blame themselves more for violent crime or other victimizing events than are men. Thus future researchers might contrast men's and women's causal attributions for such victimizing events as violent crimes, focusing on the prevalence of self-blame for these events and its relation to adjustment.

Janoff-Bulman's (1979) second prediction, that there are two types of self-blame, behavioral and characterological, is also largely supported by our study. Results from our factor analysis provide partial support for this distinction. Behavioral self-blame, as defined by Janoff-Bulman and as measured by our factor score, Poor Judgment, included self-blame that was potentially modifiable in the future, creating the possibility of avoiding future rapes. Characterological self-blame, as defined by Janoff-Bulman, reflects blame attributed to unavoidable past behaviors that rendered the victim deserving of the rape. Our attribution factor score, Victim Type, was comparable to Janoff-Bulman's conception of characterological self-blame, in that victims who scored high on this measure felt that their rapes were unavoidable and were deserved.

The results of this study directly challenge Janoff-Bulman's (1979) third prediction that behavioral self-blame is associated with positive adjustment to rape, whereas characterological self-blame is associated with negative adjustment to rape. In this study, no form of self-blame was an adaptive response to rape by women. Behavioral self-blame was associated with sexual dissatisfaction and symptoms of depression, whereas characterological self-blame was associated with high levels of fear and symptoms of depression. Only societal blame was unassociated with the severity of negative outcomes after a rape.

Because of the correlational nature of these data, there is no way of knowing whether women's attributions for rape actually cause differences in postrape adjustment. For example, it is possible that depression, sell-blame, and feeling oneself to be a victim type are parts of a maladaptive behavior pattern that existed before the rape. Beck (1967, 1976) noted that negative thoughts such as self-blame and self-derogation are often associated with and can be causally related to depression. As such, the self-blame observed in our sample may be part

TABLE 12.5. Correlations Among Coping Factor Scores and Outcome Factor Scores

Coping factors	Outcome factors		
	Depression	Fear	Sexual dissatisfaction
Remain Home	.33**	.35**	.15
Withdraw	.56***	.08	.30*
Activity	.12	.07	.17
Precaution	.20′	−.03	−.29*
Suppression	−.12	−.03	.12
Minimization	.18	−.01	.02
Stress reduction	−.24*	−.23*	.03

* $p < .05$. ** $p < .01$. *** $p < .001$.

[1]Our figure of 50% comes from calculating the percentage of our subjects who mentioned an aspect of their personality or behavior in response to the open-ended question, "Explain the reasons you believe account for why you were raped." Had we calculated the number of women who responded affirmatively to at least one of our self-blame statements (items included on the factor scores Poor Judgment or Victim Type), the percentage would be higher.

of a preexisting pattern of negative thinking and depression.[2]

Arguing against this possibility is research showing that self-blame is not consistently associated with worse adjustment after a traumatic event. In fact, self-blame has been found to be adaptive among victims of severe accidents (Bulman & Wortman, 1977) and among parents of children with malignant diseases (Chodoff, Friedman, & Hamburg 1964), whereas it appears to have no clear impact on coping among breast cancer patients (Taylor, Lichtman, & Wood, 1984). Although it is possible that these contradictory findings result from methodological differences (e.g., different operational definitions of self-blame), we believe that self-blame may have a differential impact on traumatic adjustment, depending on the nature of the threatening event and the characteristics of the victim.

Fine (1983–1984) critically examined psychological theories that emphasize the adaptiveness of certain behaviors for achieving a sense of control. She suggested that different psychological processes may hold true when low-power individuals feel in control than when high-power individuals do. For example, she argues that gender be taken into consideration when generating predictions regarding self-blame and control. According to this line of thought, it may be that rape victims' acceptance of their assault has a different psychological meaning than other populations' acceptance of blame for different traumatic events. Because of cultural beliefs that women are not powerful and are "asking to be raped," women who blame themselves for a sexual assault might feel different than men who blame themselves for a freakish accident (as in Bulman & Wortman's 1977 study). Self-blame in rape victims may reflect acceptance views of women as "responsible victims," views that may erode a person's sense of mastery (cf. Taylor, 1983). Further research is needed in order to clarify these issues.

This study failed to identify a truly adaptive pattern of cause attributions for victims of rape. However, societal blame appears to be a blaming strategy preferable to self-blame for individuals in search of meaning. Blaming society for rape is compared with a sociological analysis of the social and political causes of rape, and has been advocated on these grounds (Brownmiller, 1975). Our data suggest that there may be clinical reasons to advocate a causal reattribution for rape from self-blame to societal blame. Studying whether such reattributions are actually therapeutic will clarify this point.

Other coping patterns in addition to self-blame were consistently associated with adjustment to rape. As in previous research (Burgess & Holmstrom, 1979), remaining at home and withdrawing from others were associated with less successful adjustment, especially depression. One cannot determine from the data whether these behaviors are methods of coping with the fear and shame that often follow rape or are symptoms of poor adjustment. As noted earlier, coping researchers have sometimes had difficulty distinguishing the consequences of a stressful event from coping efforts. We adopted the conventional resolution that designates active behavioral responses as coping efforts and emotional reactions as outcomes of the crisis (e.g., F. Cohen & Lazarus, 1979). However, the distinction between coping efforts and outcomes is sometimes difficult to maintain in specific cases, as it was in the case of these particular coping behaviors.

Another common response to rape is the use of precautional behavior strategies (e.g., locking doors carefully). Our results are not definitive in terms of whether this is associated with better postrape adjustment. There was no evidence that use of precautionary strategies reflects excessive fear and anxiety, as suggested by the work of Riger and Gordon (1979). In fact, the use of precautionary behavioral strategies is associated with fewer sexual problems after rape. It is possible that there is a complex relation between the use of precautionary strategies and postrape adjustment, depending on the particular type of precautionary strategy used.

Stress Reduction was the only coping strategy that was associated with fewer adverse consequences of rape. Women who used this strategy kept their minds on positive thoughts and used specific techniques designed to reduce stress. The correlational data do not indicate whether this coping behavior actually improves postrape adjustment, or whether both variables are influenced by a third variable (for example, prerape psychologi-

[2]Unfortunately there is no way of addressing this issue conclusively. Neither experimental nor longitudinal studies of spontaneous adjustment to rape are feasible. Consequently, this problem plagues all such studies of rape and of adjustment to any crisis with a low base rate.

cal adjustment or response biases such as social desirability). Future research is needed in order to tease apart confounding factors that contribute to the covariation observed between this coping style and postrape adjustment.

More information needs to be obtained about the coping behavior of rape victims who adjust successfully after the event. Items concerning exercise and meditation did not load on our Stress Reduction factor so women who claim to use stress reduction as a coping strategy are probably referring to other techniques. We know little about what these women are doing. It is possible that they are practicing their own forms of mental imagery, a coping technique that has been found to be adaptive for other stressful events (see Sheikh & Jordon, 1983). More precise information about the coping behaviors associated with positive adjustment in rape victims is clearly a promising field for future research. In any case, our results suggest that clinicians who counsel rape victims might consider using stress reduction techniques.

Before closing, two limitations of this study should be mentioned. First, the subject sample deserves consideration. Respondents in our study were recruited from rape crisis centers, which makes them different from rape victims recruited from emergency rooms or from rape victims who respond to public requests to participate in research. Specifically, the women in our sample may be more likely to use a psychological service for a crisis and may be more likely to seek help from professionals than other samples of rape victims would be. In this respect, our sample may be more comparable with victims seen in treatment than with research samples of rape victims recruited in other ways. How these sample differences would affect the results is not known. Our findings about rape victims are also limited because our sample did not include any of the large number of women who fail to report their rape to anyone. However, this criticism is equally true of other rape studies; no study of rape victims can generalize its results to the entire population of rape victims. By way of demonstrating comparability with other rape studies, it should be noted that demographic variables and characteristics of the assaults in this study were similar to those reported in previous research.

A second criticism of the study pertains to the use of factor analysis with so small a sample. Despite this problem, the factor analyses consistently produced factors that were interpretable and generally on the order of what had been predicted.[3] Moreover, the factor scores consistently had satisfactory convergent validity (when it could be assessed), and they uniformly had high internal consistency.

In summary, the results from this study suggest that different causal attributions and coping patterns are predictably associated with variations in the severity of women's reactions to rape. The most significant finding was that self-blame of any form is consistently related to poor adjustment in rape victims. The results have both theoretical and clinical implications. Theoretically, they imply that self-blame may not be a healthy response to victimization, as previous work has suggested (Bulman & Wortman, 1977; Janoff-Bulman, 1979). Clinically, they suggest that interventions that discourage self-blame in rape victims should be initiated and evaluated.

REFERENCES

Atkeson, B., Calhoun, K., Resick, P., & Ellis, B. (1982). Victims of rape: Repeated assessment of depressive symptoms. *Journal of Clinical and Consulting Psychology, 50,* 96–102.

Beck, A. T. (1967). *Depression: Clinical, experimental and theoretical aspects.* New York: Hocker.

Beck, A. T. (1976). *Cognitive therapy and the emotional disorders.* New York: International Universities Press.

Brownmiller, S. (1975). *Against our will: Men, women, and rape.* New York: Bantam Books.

Bulman, R., & Wortman, C. (1977). Attributions of blame and coping in the "real world": Severe accident victims react to their lot. *Journal of Personality and Social Psychology, 35,* 351–383.

Burgess, A., & Holmstrom, L. (1979). *Rape crisis and recovery.* Bowie, MD: Brady.

Chodoff, P., Friedman, S. B., & Hamburg, D. A. (1964). Stress, defenses and coping behavior: Observations in parents of

[3]Factor analysis of the attribution questions yielded three factors that were slightly different from what we had expected, but were nonetheless highly interpretable. In fact, the attribution factors, suggested by factor analysis, were more reflective of our data than were our original predictions, which had been made in advance of data. For example, we had expected that *too trusting* would be a measure of characterological self-blame, as proposed by Janoff-Bulman (1979). However, in their open-ended response, 46% of our sample claimed to have become more interpersonally cautious as a result of the rape, indicating that they believed that *too trusting* was a modifiable characteristic. Consequently, it made considerable sense for the causal attribution *too trusting* to load on our factor Poor Judgment (behavioral self-blame) rather than on Victim Type (characterological self-blame), as it did.

children with malignant diseases. *American Journal of Orthopsychiatry, 120,* 743–749.

Cohen, F., & Lazarus, R. S. (1979). Coping with the stress of illness. In G. Stone, F. Cohen, & N. E. Adler (Eds.), *Health psychology—A handbook* (pp. 217–254). San Francisco: Jossey-Bass.

Cohen, J. (1960). A coefficient of agreement for nominal scales. *Educational and Psychological Measurement, 20,* 37–46.

Ellis, E. M., Atkeson, B. M., & Calhoun, K. S. (1981). An assessment of long-term reaction to rape. *Journal of Abnormal Psychology, 90,* 263–266.

Feldman-Summers, S., Gordon, P. E., & Meagher, J. R. (1979). The impact of rape on sexual satisfaction. *Journal of Abnormal Psychology, 88,* 101–105.

Fine, M. (1983–1984). Coping with rape: Critical perspectives on consciousness. *Imagination, Cognition and Personality 3*(3), 249–267.

Frank, E., Turner, S. M., & Steward, B. D. (1980). Initial response to rape: The impact of factors within the rape situations. *Journal of Behavioral Assessment, 2,* 39–53.

Freedman, A., Kaplan, H., & Sadock, B. (Eds.). (1975). *Comprehensive textbook of psychiatry*. Baltimore: Williams and Wilkins.

Haan, N. (1977). *Coping and defending*. New York: Academic Press.

Hollingshead, A. B. (1975, June). Four factor index of social status. Unpublished manuscript. (Available from A. B. Hollingshead, P.O. Box 1965, Yale Station, New Haven, CT 06520)

Janoff-Bulman, R. (1979). Characterological versus behavioral self-blame: Inquiries into depression and rape. *Journal of Personality and Social Psychology, 37,* 1798–1809.

Katz, S., & Mazur, M. (1979). *Understanding the rape victim: A synthesis of research findings.* New York: Wiley

Kilpatrick, D. G., Resick, P. A., & Veronen, L. J. (1981). Effects of a rape experience. *Journal of Issues, 37*(4), 105–122.

Kilpatrick, D. G., Veronen, L. J., & Resick, P A. (1979). Assessment of the aftermath of rage: Changing patterns of fear. *Journal of Behavioral Assessment, 1,* 133–148.

Lazarus, R. S., & Launier, R. (1978). Stress-related transactions between person and environment. In L. A. Pavin & M. Lewis (Eds.), *Perspectives in interactional psychology* (pp. 287–327). New York: Plenum.

Libow, J. A., & Doty, D. W. (1979). An exploratory approach to self-blame and self-derogation by rape victims. *American Journal of Orthopsychiatry, 49,* 670–679.

Lipowski, Z. J. (1970). Physical illness, the individual and the coping process. *Psychiatry in Medicine, 1,* 91–102.

Miller, D. T., & Porter, C. A. (1983). Self-blame in victims of violence. *Journal of Social Issues, 39*(2), 139–152.

Norris, J., & Feldman-Summers, S. (1981). Factors related to the psychological impacts of rape on the victim. *Journal of Abnormal Psychology, 90,* 562–567.

Resick, P. A., Calhoun, K. S., Atkeson, B. M., & Ellis, E. M. (1981). Social adjustment in victims of sexual assault. *Journal of Clinical and Consulting Psychology, 19,* 705–712.

Riger, S., & Gordon, M. T. (1979). The structure of rape prevention beliefs. *Personality and Social Psychology Bulletin, 5,* 186–190.

Riger, S., & Gordon, M. T. (1981). The fear of rape: A study in social control. *Journal of Social Issues, 37*(4), 71–92.

Ruch, L. O., Chandlers, S. M., & Harter, R. A. (1980). Life change and rape impact. *Journal of Health and Social Behavior, 21*, 248–260.

Sheikh, A. A., & Jordon, C. S. (1983). Clinical uses of mental imagery. In A. A. Sheikh (Ed.), *Imagery: Current theory, research and applications* (pp. 391–435). New York: Wiley.

Silver, R. L., Boon, C., & Stones, M. H. (1977). Searching for meaning in misfortune: Making sense of incest. *Journal of Social Issues*, 39(2)81–102.

Taylor, S. E. (1983). Adjustment to threatening events: A theory of cognitive adapation. *American Psychologist, 38,* 1161–1174.

Taylor, S. E., Lichtman, R. R., & Wood, J. V. (1984). Attributions, beliefs about control, and adjustment to breast cancer. *Journal of Personality and Social Psychology, 46,* 489–502.

Taylor, S. E., Wood, J. V., & Lichtman, R. R. (1983). It could be worse. Selective evaluation as a response to victimization. *Journal of Social Issues, 39*(2), 19–40.

Vaillant, G. E. (1971). Theoretical hierarchy of adaptive ego mechanisms. *Archives of General Psychiatry, 24,* 107–118.

Veronen, L. J., & Kilpatrick, D. G. (1983). Rape: A precursor of change. In E. J. Callahan & McClusky (Eds.), *Life span developmental psychology: Nonnormative life events* (pp. 167–191). New York: Academic Press.

Worden, J. W., & Sobel, H. J. (1978). Ego strength and psychosocial adaptation to cancer. *Psychosomatic Medicine, 40,* 585–591.

READING 13

Attractiveness of the Underling: An Automatic Power → Sex Association and Its Consequences for Sexual Harassment and Aggression

John A. Bargh and Paula Raymond • New York University
John B. Pryor • Illinois State University
Fritz Strack • Universität Trier

One characteristic of men who sexually harass is that they are not aware that their actions are inappropriate or a misuse of their power (L. F. Fitzgerald, 1993a). We investigated the existence and automaticity of a mental association between the concepts of power and sex, and its consequences for sexual harassment tendencies. Using a subliminal priming paradigm, Experiment 1 demonstrated an automatic link between power and sex, and only for men high in the likelihood to sexually harass or aggress. In Experiment 2, male participants were unobtrusively primed with either power-related or neutral stimuli. For men likely to sexually aggress, but not other participants, attraction ratings of a female confederate were significantly higher in the power priming than the neutral priming condition.

Power is the ultimate aphrodisiac.
—Henry Kissinger

Sexual harassment can take two general forms (Fitzgerald, 1993b; MacKinnon, 1979; U.S. Equal Employment Opportunity Commission, 1980). One is quid pro quo harassment, in which the woman is coerced into having sex with her supervisor or coworker under the threat of job-related reprisals. The other form is hostile environment harassment, in which female employees are subjected to repeated offensive and denigrating sexual comments and behavior. In the recent U.S. Supreme Court case of *Harris v. Forklift Systems* (1993), the plaintiff accused the plant manager of making such remarks as "Let's go discuss your pay raise at the Holiday Inn."

Importantly, the manager of Forklift Systems did not make such comments to the male employees of the company. The definition of sexual harassment that is emerging from the U.S. Supreme Court is any sexually oriented speech or behavior that makes it more difficult for one gender than the other to perform in the work environment (Greenhouse, 1993a, 1993b). In short, sexual harassment is a form of gender-based discrimination.

Among forms of discrimination, it would be difficult to find one that affects a greater proportion of the population than sexual harassment. Based on her review of the available incidence data, including large-scale surveys of federal employees, trade union workshops, and universities, Fitzgerald (1993a, 1993b; see also Fitzgerald et al., 1988; Gutek, 1985) estimated that one of every two women will experience harassment in the work environment at some point in their careers. She concluded from this evidence that "the great majority of harassment is not physically violent but rather reflects intrusive, unwanted, and coercive sexual attention from which there is frequently no viable escape" (Fitzgerald, 1993b, p. 1071).

Until recently, explanations for sexual harassment have centered on reasons why men in general engage in such behavior. Feminist theorists have argued that sexual harassment and coercion are used by men to maintain their power advantage over women in society (e.g., Brownmiller, 1975; Farley, 1978; see also Bohner, Weisbrod, Raymond, Barzvi, & Schwarz, 1993). Sociologists have stressed the general tendency for those in a superior position of organizational power (i.e., men) to exploit subordinates (i.e., women; Tangri, Burt, & Johnson, 1982). In addition, some evolutionary psychologists have argued that rape is a sex-specific adaptation for men in general that is triggered by certain environmental cues (Thornhill & Thornhill, 1992).

However, only a minority of men who have power over women sexually harass them (Fitzgerald, 1993a)—the majority do not. Furthermore, some social situations are more likely to give rise to sexual harassment than others (Pryor, Giedd, & Williams, 1995; Pryor, LaVite, & Stoller, 1993). Thus, any account of harassment must first address and identify the characteristics of the harasser and of the situation in which harassment occurs (i.e., the person × situation interaction; Pryor et al., 1993).

Sexual Harassment as an Abuse of Power

We sought to understand better the reasons why some male supervisors so frequently give their female subordinates unwanted sexual attention in the form of comments, suggestions, and advances. Certainly the most insidious feature of harassment in the workplace is the lack of easy escape for the victimized woman from the situation: the threat of economic consequences (giving up the job means giving up one's income) and career-related sanctions (a poor or no letter of recommendation in the future) as consequences for noncompliance or filing an official complaint. If the harasser did not have considerable control over the woman's important outcomes at little or no cost to his own, she could engage in retribution or just walk away from the situation. Classic treatments of *social power* have defined it in terms of the ability of one person to affect the rewards and costs of another person without the latter having any reciprocal control (French & Raven, 1959; Russell, 1938; Thibaut & Kelley, 1959). Thus, sexual harassment can be conceptualized as a case of the misuse or abuse of power (Bargh & Raymond, 1995).

Similarities between sexual harassment and sexual aggression were first noted by Farley (1978) and Gutek and Morasch (1982). Both phenomena involve the application of greater power to get the woman to cooperate in fulfilling the man's sexual needs—the rapist uses superior physical power, whereas the harasser uses superior authority or organizational power, to obtain sex. More recently, the American Psychological Association's Task Force on Male Violence Against Women has "recognized that men's actual use of physical force against women lies on one end of a continuum of behaviors, all of which involve men's abuse of power (physical strength, economic resources, or employment status) over women who have less power" (Goodman, Koss, Fitzgerald, Russo, & Keita, 1993, p. 1054).

Power as a Sexual Motive in Rape

Research on men who have forced women to have sex with them has found both dominance and sexuality to motivate sexual aggression; that is, dominating a woman is sexually arousing to these men. Groth (1979) interviewed convicted rapists and found forcible rape to be motivated by power needs and anger as well as by sexuality, but with the need to dominate the most common motive (55%) among the rapists.

Malamuth (1986) studied sexual aggression in a nonincarcerated population. Responses to questions concerning dominance motivation, or "the degree to which feelings of control over one's partner motivate sexuality" (p. 956), correlated reliably with self-reported sexual aggression such as the use of force and rape. Moreover, self-reported arousal at thinking about forcible sex correlated reliably with both self-reported sexual aggression and with the dominance motivation scales, supporting the link between dominance and sexuality. That these responses were valid and not an artifact of the self-report format was indicated by a strong correlation between the self-report measure of arousal (a precursor of the Attractiveness of Sexual Aggression [ASA] scale; Malamuth, 1989a, 1989b) and the amount of penile tumescence that occurred while the participant read an account of a rape.

Power as a Sexual Motive in Harassment

Power and sex tend to be intertwined in sexual harassers as well as in rapists. A series of studies by Pryor and his colleagues (Pryor, 1987: Pryor et al., 1993; Pryor & Stoller, 1994) has shown that the mental concepts of power and sex are associated in men who are likely to sexually harass women. This research has used a self-report inventory called the Likelihood to Sexually Harass (LSH) scale (Pryor, 1987). The LSH scale consists of 10 different scenarios in which men are asked to imagine having some kind of leverage over an attractive woman. In one scenario, for example, the man is to imagine that he is the manager of a restaurant and has witnessed an attractive female waitress intentionally failing to charge her friends for their meals. For each scenario, the respondent rates the likelihood that he would use this leverage (e.g., the threat of firing the waitress) to gain sexual favors from the woman.

Three studies have demonstrated that men who are high on the LSH scale are more likely than other men to take sexual advantage of female underlings in laboratory settings. This behavioral tendency seems to occur especially under circumstances where such behavior seems condoned or permitted (Pryor, 1987; Pryor et al., 1993; Pryor & Stoller, 1994). For example, Pryor (1987, Study 3) found high-LSH men to take advantage of their assigned role as a "golf instructor" and to engage in more sexual contact with the attractive female "golf student" (actually a confederate) by, for example, enveloping her closely from behind while teaching her how to putt. Pryor et al. (1993) asked high- and low-LSH men to instruct and evaluate an attractive female secretarial trainee in a word-processing task. Half of the participants were exposed to a male authority figure (a graduate student experimenter) who openly sexually harassed the woman (a confederate), with harassment operationally defined as unsolicited sexual touching and other verbal sexual behavior. The other half were exposed to a role model who treated the woman in a friendly but professional manner. High-LSH men exposed to the harassing role model tended to do likewise, engaging in greater amounts of sexual touching and talk. Low-LSH men did not harass the woman when exposed to the harassing role model. Neither high- nor low-LSH men harassed when exposed to the professional role model condition. Thus, high-LSH men seem ready to take advantage of vulnerable women when the circumstances permit, behaving toward them in an overtly sexual manner.

Given these laboratory demonstrations of greater degree of sexual behavior toward women of relatively less power in the experimental situation by high- versus low-LSH men, the question becomes one of the process by which power features of a situation produce increased sexual behavior for certain men but not others. Pryor and Stoller (1994) investigated the cognitive mechanism behind the abuse of power advantages to gain sexual favors. They administered a paired-associates memory test to male participants, in which words related to power (e.g., *strong* and *boss*) and sex (e.g., *intercourse* and *fondling*) were presented in balanced combinations. Men who were likely to sexually harass women tended to overestimate the frequency with which power and sex-related words had co-occurred. They also indicated more confidence in their recognition of power-sex combinations than did low-LSH men. In other words, high-LSH men tended to perceive an illusory correlation between power and sex words. As the retrieval advantage of the power-sex combination can be taken as an indication of the operation of an efficient power-sex schema in memory, this finding suggests an association between the concepts of power and sex in men who are likely to be sexual harassers. The present research investigated the automaticity of this association.

Qualitative Differences Between Rapists and Harassers

Although rape and sexual harassment are similar in these respects, there do seem to be important differences as well. Sexual aggression in which physical force is used to have sex has been linked to different motivational sources than sexual exploitation in which no physical force is used. Lisak and Roth (1988) surveyed male undergraduates' sexual experiences and found that the need to feel more powerful than women, along with anger toward women and a disinhibition factor (primarily use of alcohol), consistently differentiated men who had sexually aggressed against a woman (i.e., sexual assault, attempted rape, or rape) from those who had manipulated or coerced a woman into having sex without the use of physical force. Lisak and Roth (1988) concluded that "the use of force may be a type of barrier that only men of certain characteristics are capable of crossing" (p. 801). Thus, we examined the potential mediating role of an automatic power → sex association separately for men likely to commit rape (as measured by the ASA) and for men likely to sexually harass (as measured by the LSH).

Moreover, based on the distinction drawn by Gutek and Morasch (1982) and Lisak and Roth (1988)—that rapists abuse physical power whereas sexual harassers abuse authority or organizational power—we distinguished these two different forms of power in our experimental stimuli. By doing so we were able to assess the possibility that one type of power would be more strongly associated with sexuality than the other, and also whether the concept of physical power would be linked to sex for those high in sexual aggression tendencies, whereas the concept of authority-based power would be linked to sex for those high in sexual harassment tendencies.

Automaticity of the Power → Sex Association

The apparent lack of comprehension shown by the Senate Judiciary Committee during Anita Hill's testimony of alleged sexual harassment by Judge Clarence Thomas prompted many observers to argue "men just don't get it" when it comes to their harassing behavior. At an individual level, Fitzgerald (1993a) noted that the majority of men who harass may not be aware that they are doing so.

One factor that may contribute to the prevalence of sexual harassment and to some men's lack of awareness of the harassing nature of their own behavior is the automaticity of a power–sex association. In other words, the association between the concepts of power and sex for men who sexually harass, evidenced in Pryor's (Pryor & Stoller, 1994) research, may be so strong as to cause the concept of sexuality to become active automatically and outside of awareness whenever the concept of power is activated. The consequence would be thinking or behaving in a sexualized manner without being aware of the role that power plays in the conceptualization of the situation in sexual terms.

For example, the male boss could be sexually attracted to the female subordinate by virtue of his power over her, but without awareness of the role this relative power plays in his perception of and feelings toward her. The power features of the situation would automatically and outside of his awareness activate the concept or schema of sexuality, causing him to be more likely to categorize and think of her in sexual terms (e.g., Bruner, 1957; Higgins & King, 1981). Because the activation and operation of the concept of sexuality by power features is hypothesized to occur in this preconscious fashion (see Bargh, 1994a, 1994b), opaque to conscious awareness, the boss will attribute his attraction to her features or his preferences for certain types of women—that is, his theory of what causes him to be attracted to women (see Nisbett & Wilson, 1977).

From Power Cues to Sexual Advances

The hypothesized sequence of this automatic process is that the presence of power features within a situation will cause the concept of power to become active in memory. These power features certainly include features of situations in which the man does have relative power, such as at the office, or at home in a traditional sex role family setting. And for some men, their greater physical power over most women may activate the concept of power and the hypothesized power–sex link.

For men who possess an automatic power–sex association, however, we assume that this activation of the power concept will spread automatically to the concept or schema of sexuality. This priming or greater accessibility of the concept of sexuality may cause the man to think of his female subordinates in sexual terms, perhaps misattributing these sexual thoughts as evidence of his attraction. And his behavior toward these women will be based on these feelings of attraction, causing unwanted sexual advances. He will be attracted to her in the sense of a behavioral predisposition to draw closer to her, to reduce the interpersonal distance, to engage in more touching, as Pryor's (e.g., 1987) several studies have previously demonstrated. Because of the nonconscious nature of the power influence, however, he will not be aware of the inappropriateness of this behavior because he does not consciously experience the power imbalance as part of his subjective field, only the woman's behavior (e.g., smiling and friendliness) and physical features (see Kipnis, 1976). However, as argued by Brewer (1982), the female employee understands the situation quite differently, in terms of the constraints imposed on her by his authority and power over her. Thus, she experiences the boss's sexually oriented behavior toward her as an overt power play.

In our view, these kinds of misperceptions and miscommunications are much more likely if the man has these sexual thoughts without having had the conscious intention to think of the woman in that way. These preconsciously driven, perceptually fluent thoughts will be experienced as a direct function of the environment because of the absence of any awareness of one's own cognitive involvement in producing them (see Bargh, 1989, 1994b; Jones & Nisbett, 1971). The male power holder will thus perceive his attraction and sexual thoughts toward the female subordinate as caused by her behavior (e.g., as flirtation instead of friendliness), sheer attractiveness, or both.

To reiterate, our experiments began with the observed fact of the sexual harasser's overt sexual behavior toward women when given relative power over them in experimental situations (Pryor, 1987; Pryor et al., 1993). The purpose of the experiments was not to provide another demonstration of these behavioral effects of power, but to test a mediational process model of them. Our hypothesis was that the effect of power on sexual harassment and aggression is mediated at least in part by an automatic power→sex association that causes men who possess it (i.e., high-LSH or high-ASA men) to be more attracted to women over whom they have some form of power or leverage, relative to the same women if they did not have a power advantage. We argue that men low in the tendency to harass or aggress (low-LSH or low-ASA men) do not possess this automatic power–sex association, so that their attraction toward a woman will not differ depending on whether or not they have power over her.

We conducted two experiments to test this model. Experiment 1 assessed whether an automatic power–sex association existed and whether only men who were likely to sexually harass possessed it. Experiment 2 unobtrusively primed participants with power-related stimuli to assess the effect of the mere activation of the power concept on participants' attraction toward a female confederate.

Experiment 1

Overview

In the first experiment, we used the sequential priming paradigm to assess the automaticity of the power–sex association in men. In this paradigm (Bargh, Chaiken, Govender, & Pratto, 1992; Fazio, Sanbonmatsu, Powell, & Kardes, 1986; Neely, 1977), participants respond as quickly as they can to a target word on each trial. Immediately before the target word on each trial, a prime word is presented subliminally—at a parafoveal location on the screen for a brief duration, and immediately masked (see Bargh, Bond, Lombardi, & Tota, 1986). To the extent that responses to the target are facilitated by the presentation of the prime (compared with a control or neutral prime condition), an automatic mental association must exist between the prime and target concepts because of both the subliminal nature of the prime presentation and the very brief interval before the presentation of the target. This interval is too brief for any strategic or conscious processing of the prime to occur even if participants are aware of the prime (Neely, 1977; Posner & Snyder, 1975).

Participants pronounced the target word on each trial as quickly as possible. The pronunciation task has been shown to be a sensitive measure of automatic mental associations in previous research (Balota & Lorch, 1986; Bargh, Chaiken. Raymond, & Hymes, 1996). Our hypothesis was that male participants who scored highly on the LSH and ASA scales would show an automatic, unidirectional power→sex association in memory, whereas men who were not likely to sexually harass or aggress against women would show no such connection between the concepts.

Method

Participants. A total of 74 male New York University undergraduates participated in the experiment in return for partial credit in an introductory psychology course. Data from four were excluded from the analyses because they learned English after the age of 15, and data from a further three were excluded because of a failure to follow instructions,[1] resulting in a final sample size of 67 participants.

Materials and apparatus. After greeting the participant, the male experimenter escorted him into the experimental room, and seated him in front of a CRT screen. This CRT display was under program control of an Apple II + microcomputer. Also on the table in front of the participant was a microphone connected to a Scientific Prototype Audio Threshold Detection Relay (Model 761G) that was in turn connected to the computer as an input device. The relay transformed the analog audio input (i.e., the participant speaking) from the microphone into a signal whenever the input reached the preset threshold, with the relay dropping back into readiness for the next signal when the participant completed saying the target word on each trial. In practice, this meant that the signal was sent each time the participant began to speak a target word so that we could measure the latency between the initial presentation of the target and the response onset.

We developed four types of stimuli, which were used both as primes and as target stimuli in the experimental task: physical power, authority power, ambiguous sexual, and neutral. To develop the two types of power stimuli, we included the six general dominance stimuli used by Pryor and Stoller (1994) in a pretest in which 39 male participants rated 102 potential power-related words on a –5 (*extremely related to authority-based power*) to +5 (*extremely related to physical power*) scale. Two sets of words most clearly differentiated between authority and physical power, with means below –2 and above 2.4, respectively. The resultant set of authority power stimuli consisted of *authority, executive, boss, influence, rich,* and *control,* whereas the set of physical power stimuli contained *mighty, strong, tough, macho, muscular,* and *boxer*.

We did not use the same set of sexual-related stimuli as used by Pryor and Stoller (1994) because of the potential for these words to cause embarrassment or surprise (e.g., intercourse or foreplay) and thereby distort pronunciation latencies (see Howes & Solomon, 1950). Thus we developed a set of "ambiguous sex-related" stimuli—words that have a sexual connotation but also a more common, nonsexual meaning. A separate group of 48 men rated each of 59 words as to their sexual content, from 0 (*not at all sexual*) to 5 (*extremely sexual*). Based on these ratings, we selected for the experiment six words with ratings around 3 (mean ratings ranged from 2.7 to 3.5): *bed, date, feel, hard, motel,* and *wet*. Also from these ratings we selected six neutral control stimuli, which were rated as unrelated to sexuality (mean ratings less than 0.8): *board, building, chalk, clock, coffee,* and *house.*

A total of 120 prime–target pairs were constructed. Each of the critical power- and sex-related stimuli appeared as a target word four times, preceded on different trials by each of the four types of prime: physical power, authority power, sex, and neutral. Because there were six instances of each type of stimuli, there were 72 trials on which a physical power, authority power, or sex-related word appeared as the target. On the remaining 48 trials a neutral word appeared as the target, preceded by one of the four types of primes equally often (neutral target response times were not analyzed). Two random orders of these prime-target pairs were constructed.

Participants completed both the LSH scale (Pryor, 1987) and the ASA scale (Malamuth, 1989a, 1989b) following the completion of the pronunciation task. The LSH scale consists of 10 scenarios in which the participant is to imagine he has a kind of leverage or control over an attractive woman and then estimates the likelihood (from 1, *not at all likely*; to 5, *very likely*) that he would take advantage of this opportunity to obtain sexual favors from the woman. For example, in one scenario the protagonist has an opportunity to offer a female computer salesperson a lucrative contract

[1]These participants did not pronounce the words as quickly as possible, as instructed. For each, over 25% of response times exceeded 1,000 ms. This rate of slow responding was more than 10 times that of the average of the remaining participants. However, the pattern of significant and nonsignificant results reported here is unchanged if data from these participants are included in the analyses.

in exchange for sexual favors; in another scenario the protagonist has the power to give a movie role to an aspiring actress if she sleeps with him. A given participant's LSH score is the sum of the ratings across the 10 scenarios and thus can range from 10 (*low likelihood of harassment*) to 50 (*high likelihood*). Pryor (1987, p. 275) reported a reliability coefficient (alpha) of .95 for the LSH: we obtained a split-half (odd–even) reliability coefficient of .85 across all participants in Experiment 1 and a coeffcient of .91 in Experiment 2.

The ASA scale inquires after the participant's sexual preferences, with the critical items having to do with the attractiveness of rape and of forcing a woman to do something sexual she does not want to do. These items are embedded in a questionnaire along with other items concerning conventional (e.g., heterosexual intercourse) and unconventional (e.g., group sex) sexual practices, homosexuality, deviance (e.g., pedophilia), and bondage. For each of these types of sexual activity the participant indicates whether he has ever thought of trying it (yes or no), how attractive he finds the idea of it (from 1 = *very unattractive* to 4 = *very attractive*), what percentage of men would find it attractive, how arousing he would find it if he engaged in it (from 1 = *not arousing* to 7 = *very arousing*), and how likely he would be to engage in it if he would in no way be punished for doing so (from 1 = *not at all likely* to 7 = *very likely*). Malamuth (1989a, pp. 37–38) reports an internal consistency (alpha) of .91 for the ASA scale, with a test-retest reliability coefficient of .76. For our purposes, a participant's ASA score was the sum of the attractiveness, arousal, and likelihood-of-doing items for the rape and using-force items (after transforming the attractiveness scale into the same metric as the others).[2] We obtained a split-half (rape vs. using-force items) reliability coefficient of .84 across all participants in our Experiment 1 and .79 in Experiment 2.

Procedure. Participants were tested individually. The experimenter showed the participant into the experimental room and rated him in front of the microphone and CRT screen. The participant was informed that he would be participating in two separate experiments, the first having to do with reading speed.

On each trial of the pronunciation task, three asterisks appeared in the center of the CRT display. The participant had been instructed to focus his attention on the asterisks at the start of each trial and to pronounce as quickly as possible the word that subsequently appeared at the same location as the asterisks. The prime word appeared 4 s later, centered either 2 cm above or 2 cm below (equally often, in a randomized sequence) the fixation point. The prime remained on the screen for 90 ms, followed by a masking string of letters for 10 ms (XRLMOZQAESB).[3] As the distance between the participant's eyes and the fixation point on the CRT screen was approximately 50 cm (with little variability due to the need to stay close to the microphone), this placed the priming stimuli at 2.3° of visual angle, within the participant's pararoveal visual field. Words presented to the parafoveal area (between 2° and 6° of visual angle) have been shown to activate their semantic representation in memory outside of conscious awareness (e.g., Rayner, 1978). Moreover, Rayner round that the minimum time needed for participants to make the saccadic jump from a fixation point to a parafoveally presented word was 140 ms, with an average of 190 ms. Thus our participants would not have been able to foveally process the primes even if they had looked toward their location: The prime and mask would have been erased, and the target word presented, before their eyes got there.[4] Thus, participants experienced the phenomenal appearance of the primes as hashes of light on the screen.

The target word then was presented in the center of the screen, overwriting the asterisks. It remained there until the participant began to pronounce the word: the participant's voice triggered the voice-activated relay, which sent a signal to the computer that stopped the timer and erased the target word from the screen. The computer re-

[2] Malamuth (1989a) also included the "thinking about" and percentage estimate items in the ASA composite score, but for our participants these items only moderately correlated with each other and the attractiveness, arousingness, and likelihood items (average r = .50). The attractiveness, arousingness, and likelihood items, on the other hand, intercorrelated highly (average r = .81). They are also conceptually closer to our focus on harassment behavior (as opposed to thought) tendencies, as Malamuth (1986) found the arousal self-report items to correlate significantly with self-reported acts of sexual aggression.

[3]Because of variability in the location of the CRT monitor's raster scan, the actual prime display times could vary from 73 to 107 (90 ± 17) ms (see Bargh et al., 1986, pp. 872–873).

[4]There is recent, somewhat controversial evidence of the existence of "express saccades" of 100 ms in humans (Fischer & Weber, 1993), but even these would take longer than the presentation time of the prime.

corded the pronunciation latency in ms on each trial. There was a 4-s pause before the next trial began (i.e., asterisks appeared in the middle of the screen).

Participants were given 10 practice trials using different prime and target stimuli from those used in the experimental trials, with the experimenter present to answer any questions and to ensure that the participants understood the procedure. After the practice trials, the experimenter started the program to run the experimental trials and left the room. When the participant had completed the 120 pronunciation task trials, the experimenter reentered the room and gave the participant an anagram task to work on for 5 min, as another ostensible language-ability-related task. This interpolated anagram task served to clear working memory prior to the administration of the LSH and ASA scales. Following completion of the anagram task, participants filled out a "Language and Cultural Diversity" questionnaire, which contained a question concerning the age at which the participant learned to speak English.

The experimenter informed the participant at this point that the first experiment was completed, and the participant's awareness of the nature of the light hashes (i.e., prime presentations) was probed. Only two participants showed any awareness that the flashes had actually been words, and neither could accurately report on the content of any specific word or on their general meaning (e.g., sex- or power-related words). At this point the participant was debriefed as to the purpose of the first experiment. He was informed that the hashes of light had been words and that we were interested in the existence of mental associations between the prime and target word on each trial.

The ostensible second experiment began with the experimenter handing the participant the LSH and the ASA questionnaires along with an envelope. The experimenter alerted the participant to the private and personal nature of the questions asked in the questionnaires and assured the participant of complete anonymity in his responses. The experimenter stressed that the questionnaires should be completed as honestly and completely as possible. The participant was told not to put his name or any other identifying information on the questionnaires and, after completing the questionnaires, to put them in the envelope, seal it, deposit it through a slot into a locked metal box in the corner of the room, and then come out of the room into the hallway. The experimenter left the room while the participant completed the questionnaires. When the participant came out of the room, the experimenter thanked him for his participation and informed him that the questionnaires were for a survey of interpersonal relationships.

Results

Following the criteria of Balota and Lorch (1986), target pronunciation latencies less than 300 ms or greater than 1,000 ms (2.6% of all latencies) were excluded from the analyses to reduce the distorting effect of outliers. For each participant, mean response times for the following prime→target combinations were computed: physical power→sex, authority power→sex, neutral→sex, sex→physical power, neutral→physical power, sex→authority power, and neutral→authority power. Next, facilitation scores were computed by subtracting each of the means involving power or sex primes from the corresponding neutral prime mean (e.g., the physical power→sex mean was subtracted from the neutral→sex mean). These facilitation scores thus represented the increase (or decrease, in the case of negative scores) in speed of responding to a particular set of target stimuli due to the presence of a particular type of prime.

We then conducted a multivariate analysis of variance (MANOVA) on the facilitation scores, with Power Type (physical vs. authority) and Direction (power→sex vs. sex→power) as within-subjects factors, and Predisposition to Harass (high vs. low) and Trial Order as the between-subjects factors. None of the reliable effects reported below were modified by the Trial Order factor (all *ps* > .25), and so it will not be discussed further.

The Predisposition Factor was determined by the LSH scale in one MANOVA and by the ASA scale in another. In each, we included data from participants who scored in either the upper or the lower quartile on that scale, following Pryor's (1987) procedure. For the LSH (minimum store = 10, maximum score = 50), the lower quartile consisted of scores below 13 ($N = 18$) and the upper quartile as scores greater than 25 ($N = 15$). For the ASA (minimum score = 6, maximum score = 30), the lower quartile score fell at 6 (the minimum possible score, $N = 27$) and the upper quartile scores were above 11.5 ($N = 17$).

The particular sets of participants who scored high or low on one scale were not the same as those who scored high or low on the other scale. Overall, the LSH and ASA scores correlated moderately, $r = .52$ ($p = .0001$). This is comparable to the correlation of .44 reported by Pryor (1987) between the LSH and an earlier version of the ASA, Malamuth's (e.g., 1986) Likelihood of Rape scale. Of the total of 35 participants who scored in the lowest quartile of either the LSH or ASA, the scores of only 9 (26%) fell into the lowest quartile of both scales; of the total of 32 participants whose scores were in the highest quartile of one or the other scale, only 10 (31%) scores were in the highest quartile of both scales.

LSH scores as predictors of automatic power→sex association. The MANOVA using LSH scores to create the Predisposition factor revealed only a reliable main effect of Predisposition, $F(1, 29) = 6.58, p = .016$, accounting for 5.0% of the total variance. Neither the Power Type nor the Directionality main effects proved reliable, nor did they interact with the Predisposition factor, all Fs < 1. Thus, participants who were highly likely to sexually harass, according to the LSH scale, were faster to pronounce the ambiguous sexual target words when they were preceded by power-related primes (either the physical- or authority-based power varieties) and were also faster to pronounce the power-related targets when they were preceded by the ambiguous sex-content primes, compared with the respective neutral prime conditions. The left half of Figure 13.1 depicts this bidirectional priming effect, with the means collapsed across the two types of power. Across all 67 participants in the experiment, LSH scores were found to correlate significantly with the mean power–sex facilitation score, collapsing across directionality ($r = .37, p = .002$); the higher the LSH score, the stronger the mental association between power and sex.

ASA scores as predictors of automatic power→sex association. The MANOVA using ASA scores to classify participants on the Predisposition factor revealed a reliable Predisposition × Directionality interaction, $F(1, 40) = 4.51, p = .04$, accounting for 4.0% of the total variance. This effect held equally for both types of power stimuli, three-way interaction $F < 1$, so again the means shown in the right half of Figure 13.1 collapse across the two types of power. As can be seen in the figure, participants likely to sexually aggress as determined by their ASA scores showed a reliable power→sex priming effect but no sign of a sex→power priming effect. Across all 67 participants, ASA scores correlated significantly with the mean power→sex priming effect, $r = .32, p = .008$. With the exception of a reliable main effect of Power Type, $F(1, 40) = 4.43, p = .04$ (2.1% of total variance), and a marginally reliable main effect of Predisposition, $F(1, 40) = 3.32, p = .08$ (1.7% of total variance), all other effects were unreliable at $p > .22$.

Absolute versus relative facilitation effects. The analyses reported thus far compare the mean facilitation scores of the high-LSH and high-ASA participants to those of the low-LSH and low-ASA participants, respectively. Although significant differences were obtained in these comparisons, this does not necessarily mean that there was absolute, greater-than-zero levels of facilitation in the high conditions and a lack of any significant facilitation in the low conditions. However, the pattern of means shown in Figure 13.1 does suggest that this was the case, and separate t tests comparing the facilitation means with zero confirm it. None of the means shown in Figure 13.1 for the low-LSH or low-ASA participants were different from zero, ts < 1. In other words, there was no sign of an automatic power→sex or sex→power association for these participants. For the high-LSH participants, on the other hand, the average of the power→sex and sex→power means was reliably greater than zero ($p = .013$, two-tailed), demonstrating an overall automatic power→sex association, and for the high-ASA participants the power→sex mean was reliably different from zero, $p < .03$, whereas the sex→power mean was not, $t < 1$.

Discussion

The left half of Figure 13.1 shows a bidirectional automatic power→sex association for participants likely to sexually harass, as measured by Pryor's (1987) LSH scale. The direction of the prime-target combination made no difference to the automatic facilitation effect; thus, this result is consistent with Pryor and Stoller's (1994) argument of a schematic fusion between the concepts in harassers.

The right half of Figure 13.1 tells a different story. When participants are differentiated using the ASA scale, an interaction is obtained, such that reliable facilitation occurred only for high scorers and only in the power→sex priming conditions. The low scorers on the ASA showed no evidence

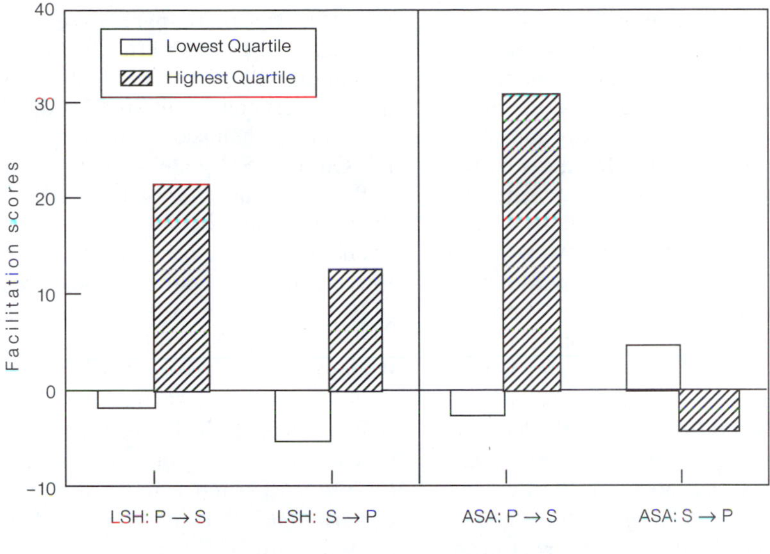

FIGURE 13.1 ■ Mean response time facilitation (in milliseconds) for participants scoring in the upper or lower 25% of the Likelihood to Sexually Harass (LSH) scale (left panel) or in the upper or lower 25% of the Attractiveness of Sexual Aggression (ASA) scale (right panel). Solid lines indicate power → sex prime–target conditions; dashed lines indicate sex → power conditions. P = physical power-related stimuli; S = sexuality-related stimuli.

of any automatic power→sex or sex→power association, and the high scorers' pronunciation times were not facilitated in the sex→power condition. Men who have a strong desire for forced sex possess a unidirectionally automatic mental association between the ideas of power and sex.

Note that of our 12 power-related stimuli, only three (*mighty, powerful,* and *authority*) had been used in the Pryor and Stoller (1994) study. Thus our finding of a power→sex association replicated theirs with considerably different power-related content. Also, the strength of the power→sex link is evidenced by the reliable power→sex priming effects (bidirectional in the case of the LSH; unidirectional in the case of the ASA) we obtained despite the fact that our sexual stimuli were only indirectly related to sexuality.

The results of Experiment 1 are consistent with the hypothesis that sexual harassers automatically think in terms of sex in situations in which they have power. The bidirectional priming effect found for participants who scored highly on the LSH scale, contrasted with the unidirectional priming effect for participants who scored highly on the ASA scale, points to potential differences between the cognitive dynamics of sexual harassment and of sexual aggression, to which we will return in the General Discussion section. Regardless of this difference, however, for both sexual harassers and sexual aggressors, activation of the concept of power resulted in automatic activation of the concept of sexuality.

Experiment 2 examined the consequences of the nonconscious activation of the sex concept for social interactions with female subordinates. One potential consequence is that the man will likely not be aware of the role that having power over the woman plays in his sexual feelings toward her. In the absence of this knowledge, he will tend to misattribute these feelings as being caused by qualities of the female target, as this is the only explanation he has consciously available. That is, "it's not that she works for me, I just find her very attractive."

Experiment 2

Overview

If the concept of sex is activated without the person realizing it, merely because of the presence of power cues or features in the environment, ambiguously sexual behavior of attractive subordinates may be interpreted in sexual terms. Just as primed or chronically accessible social constructs have been found to automatically categorize and disambiguate relevant social behavior (see Bargh et al., 1986), a male boss could categorize the friendly and deferential behavior of his attractive female subordinate as flirtation or sexually motivated because his concept of sexuality had been primed by activation spreading from his concept of power.

Male participants took part in an experiment on "visual illusions" along with a female confederate whom the men believed was another participant. Our prediction was that participants high in the likelihood of sexual harassment or sexual aggression (or both) would find the confederate to be more attractive if their concept of power had been primed than if it had not been. Participants low in sexual harassment or aggression tendencies would show no influence of the power priming. It is noteworthy that in this experiment the priming manipulation was unlike those used in most previous priming studies (see Devine, 1989, Experiment 2, for an exception) in that the concept assumed to become more accessible and to influence attraction (sexuality) was not directly primed. In previous priming studies, synonyms of a given trait (e.g., honesty or hostility) served as the priming stimuli, and impressions of a target person were shown to vary along that trait dimension. In Experiment 2, on the other hand, stimuli related to the concept of power served as the priming stimuli, so that the effect on attraction would occur only if activation automatically spread from the concept of power to that of sexuality.

To us, this second-level priming, compared with previous priming demonstrations in which stimuli directly related to the critical concept itself were presented, is a step closer to the experimental simulation of contextual effects on perception that occur in the natural environment. We theorized that the activation of the first-level mental concept, power, would spread to the closely associated, second-level mental concept, sex. Such a priming effect would demonstrate convincingly that environmental features can automatically activate concepts beyond the representations of those features themselves.

Method

Participants. A total of 112 male introductory psychology students participated in the experiment in return for partial credit for a course requirement. Data from five participants were excluded because they learned English after the age of 15. Of the remaining 107 participants, 69 had scores falling in the lowest quartile of the ASA distribution (score = 6), and 31 had scores in the highest quartile (> 10). On the LSH scale, 40 participants had scores in the lowest quartile (< 12), and 38 had scores in the highest quartile (> 25).

Of the 82 total participants who scored in the lowest quartile on either the ASA or LSH, only 28 (34%) had scores in the lowest quartile on both scales. Of the 53 total participants who scored in the highest quartile on either the ASA or LSH, only 13 (25%) had scores in the highest quartile on both scales. Thus, as in Experiment 1, it was not the case that the same group of participants generated both the ASA and LSH results; moreover, as in Experiment 1, the outcomes of the separate analyses were quite different.

Materials and apparatus. The experimental session was conducted in two adjoining 4.5 m × 3.5 m rooms. Each room had several chairs arranged to face a desk in the front of the room. In the connecting room an overhead projector was placed on the desk and was used to project standard visual illusions (e.g., Mueller-Lyer) onto the white wall in the front of the room.

The priming manipulation consisted of a 16-item word-fragment completion task, in which six of the items contained the critical priming words (in list positions 2, 4, 7, 11, 13, and 14). These were the same primes used in Experiment 1. For example, on the authority-power version, participants completed the fragments _NFLU_ _ _ E, AUT_ _ R _ T_, EXE_ _ _ _ VE, BO_S, R_ _ H, and _ _ NTROL. We took care in the development of the fragments so that participants would be able to produce all of the correct solutions. The remaining 10 items were neutral fillers, such as _ ON _ AY, PA_ _ R, and SAL _ D (in the neutral priming condition, all 16 items consisted of such fillers).

On the final questionnaire, titled "Impression Formation," the participant rated the attractiveness of the female confederate on six bipolar adjective rating scales and two questions concerning the desirability of future interaction with the confederate. In order to enhance the cover story that the experiment had to do with impressions of others and not exclusively with attraction per se, the participant first circled whether the "other participant" had been male or female. Next, he responded to each of the six trait scales by circling a number from 0 to 9, depending on the extreme to which he felt one or the other pole of the scale described the confederate. The scale of interest, Unattractive–Attractive, was embedded as the fifth scale along with others unrelated to our hypotheses and for which the participant had no basis for judgment (e.g., introverted–extraverted and unintelligent–intelligent).

Following these trait ratings came the other ratings of relevance to our hypotheses: how much the participant desired future contact with the confederate. The participant circled a number from 0 (*not at all*) to 9 (*very much*) indicating his level of interest in getting to know the confederate better, and on a separate scale, indicating whether he would be pleased if the confederate were to be assigned to work together with him on a task in a future experiment. We averaged these two ratings to form an index of how much the participant desired future interaction with the confederate (the two items correlated reliably at .67).

On the second page of this questionnaire was a series of items concerning the participant's reasons for his impression of the confederate. On separate 0 (*not at all*) to 9 (*very much*) scales, the participant rated the extent to which he believed his impression was due to the other participant's personality traits, her physical features and appearance, the participant's own preferences regarding people, and the kinds of things the participant did during the experiment.

Procedure. Participants were greeted by the experimenter (either male or female) and were shown into the experimental room where the confederate was already sitting (two different confederates were used). After an initial explanation to the two participants that the experiment concerned perception of visual illusions, the experimenter showed them into the adjacent room. They were seated being the front wall, onto which an overhead projector displayed a blank screen. The experimenter then turned off the room light and placed a transparency containing several standard visual illusions on the projector. The participants were instructed to each pick one of the illusions and to think about why the illusion occurred. After 1 min the participants were each given a form on which to explain the illusion. On this form the participant noted the number of the illusion in the display that he would be explaining and then gave his explanation for it in a free-response format.

The participants were given a few minutes to finish writing down their explanation for the chosen illusion (the confederate completed this task as if she were an actual participant). The experimenter then collected these forms and handed the word-fragment completion (priming) task to each participant to complete, with the instructions to complete all the words as quickly as possible. The participant was randomly assigned to one of the three priming conditions (neutral, authority power, or physical power), and both the confederate and experimenter were blind to this condition. The confederate completed the task at about the same pace and finished at the same time as the participant, but her view of the participant's form was blocked by the overhead projector so that she remained blind to the participant's priming condition. When the participant had finished the word-fragment completion task, the experimenter collected the sheets from both participants.

At this point, the experimenter explained that he or she was interested in the kinds of impressions people form of others with whom they have minimal interaction, such as when waiting together in a bank teller line. The participants were told that they were going to be asked questions about each other and that to ensure confidentiality they would complete the questionnaires in separate rooms. The experimenter then asked the confederate to follow him or her back into the adjacent room to fill out her questionnaire. When the experimenter returned, the participant was given the attraction questionnaire and asked to complete it in terms of his honest and objective opinion of the confederate; it was emphasized that she would never see his responses just as he would not see her ratings of him.

When the participant had completed the questionnaire, he was given 5 min to complete a list of anagrams, ostensibly as part of the visual imagery focus of the experiment (i.e., the earlier visual illusion task). The purpose of the anagram task was to minimize as much as possible any potential influence of the priming manipulation and the attraction ratings on responses to the ASA and LSH questionnaires, which followed. After the anagram task, the participant was informed that the experiment was over but was asked to complete a survey for an unrelated research project. As in Experiment 1, the participant was handed the LSH and ASA questionnaires and an envelope to place them in when finished. The participant placed the envelope in the locked metal box and opened the door to let the experimenter know he was finished.

The experimenter at this point probed for any suspiciousness concerning the content of the priming task and how it might have influenced the participant's responses on the attraction questionnaire; no participant showed any sign of awareness of a relation between the two tasks. Finally, the participant was debriefed in a general way such that the concept of contextual priming influences on judgment was described, but neither the specific focus on power and sexual concepts nor the use of the sexual harassment and aggression questionnaires as selection devices was described. The participant was thanked for his participation and shown out of the experimental room.

Results

There was no influence of the priming manipulation on the participants' responses to the LSH and ASA questionnaires; all *F*s < 1.

Attraction ratings. We conducted a MANOVA on the attraction ratings, with Prime Type (neutral, authority power, and physical power) and Predisposition to Harass (high vs. low) as the between-subjects factors, and Rating Type (attractiveness vs. get-to-know) the within-subjects factor. As in Experiment 1, the Predisposition factor was defined by the LSH scale in one MANOVA and by the ASA scale in the other.

In the MANOVA using LSH scores, there were no reliable main effects of Predisposition or Prime Type, nor was their interaction reliable, all *F*s < 1. Separate analyses of the attractiveness and get-to-know ratings also failed to reveal any reliable effects, all *ps* > .36. The attraction rating means for the high and low-LSH participants are presented in the left half of Figure 13.2. Across all participants in the experiment, LSH scores were uncorrelated with overall attraction scores (mean of the attractiveness and get-to-know ratings): $r = .14$ in the neutral priming condition ($N = 37$) and $r = .03$ in the two power priming conditions combined ($N = 70$), *ps* > .25.

The MANOVA using the ASA scores to distinguish high- and low-Predisposition participants revealed a reliable Predisposition × Prime Type interaction, $F(2, 94) = 3.07$, $p = .05$ (accounting for 5.1% of the total variance), which held across both rating scales (three-way interaction $F < 1$). The simple main effect of the power priming manipulation was reliable for the high-ASA participants, $F(1, 94) = 4.94$, $p < .03$, but not for the low-ASA participants, $F(1, 94) = 2.07$, $p > .15$. As predicted, high-ASA participants were more attracted to the confederate when their concept of power had been unobtrusively activated than when it had not been. Neither the Predisposition nor Prime Type main effects were reliable, *ps* > .21. The relevant attraction rating means are presented in the right half of Figure 13.2. Across all experimental participants, ASA scores were reliably negatively correlated with overall attraction ratings in the neutral priming condition, $r = .43$, $p < .01$, but uncorrelated with attraction in the two power prime conditions, $r = .07$, $p > .25$.

Attributions for attraction. Participants rated the extent to which their feelings of attraction toward the confederate could be attributed to each of four possible sources: her personality, her physical characteristics, the participant's personal preferences, and the experimental situation itself. We entered these ratings into a MANOVA with Predisposition to Harass and Prime Type the between-subjects factors, and Influence Type (the four attribution ratings) the repeated measures factor. As before, separate MANOVAs were conducted using the LSH and then the ASA scores to define high and low predisposition to harass.

The analysis involving the LSH scores revealed an overall main effect of Predisposition, $F(1, 72) = 5.13$, $p = .027$, such that participants likely to sexually harass rated each of the possible reasons as a stronger influence on their feelings ($M = 5.1$) than did low-predisposition participants ($M = 4.6$). There was also a reliable main effect of Influence Type, $F(3, 195) = 31.44$, $p < .001$. Participants in general rated the confederate's physical features ($M = 6.0$) and their own preferences ($M = 6.3$) as the most important reasons for their attractiveness ratings, with her personality ($M = 3.5$) and the experimental situation ($M = 3.5$) seen as much less important. This pattern of relative importance did not vary as a function of Predisposition or Prime Type, *F*s < 1.02.

The analysis utilizing the ASA scores produced the identical results: the same reliable main effects of Predisposition and of Influence Type, the same pattern of means, and no reliable qualifying interactions, *F*s < 1.

Discussion

The results of Experiment 2 supported the hypothesis that men who are likely to sexually aggress

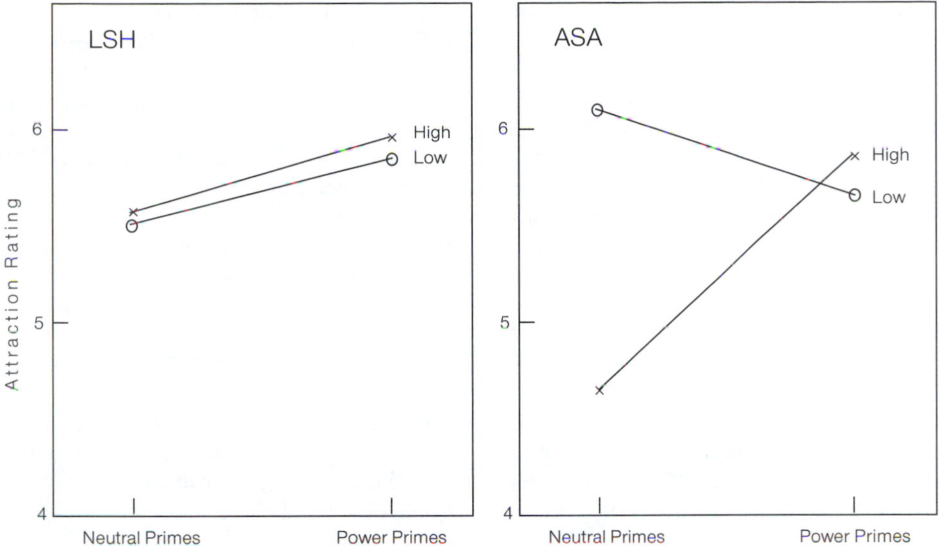

FIGURE 13.2 ■ Mean attraction ratings (1 = *not at all* and 9 = *very attracted*) of the participants toward the female confederate for those participants scoring in the upper or lower 25% of the Attractiveness of Sexual Aggression (ASA) scale (right panel), separately for the neutral priming and power priming conditions.

(high ASA) are more attracted to a woman if they have been primed with thoughts of power. Even though these participants were not aware of the influence of the activated concept of power, they were significantly more attracted to her and expressed a greater interest in getting to know her if their mental concept of power had been unobtrusively activated than if it had not.

In the absence of awareness of the influence of power on their feelings of attraction, the high-ASA participants (and participants in general) attributed their attraction mainly to the confederate's physical appearance and their own preferences. This is not surprising as all participants could do was use those elements of the situation of which they were consciously aware in accounting for their opinion, but it does demonstrate their lack of sensitivity or awareness of any felt special quality of the situation caused by the activated concept of power. Many theorists and researchers have argued that in the absence of internal cues or explanations for one's feelings and behavior, one looks to the external environment (Bem, 1972; Schachter & Singer, 1962; Zillman, 1978) or one's theory of what usually causes those feelings and behavior (Gazzaniga, 1985; Nisbett & Wilson, 1977) to find the reason.

Men who possess the automatic power→sex association, in our opinion, do not have access to the cause of their heightened attraction toward women over whom they have power. Hence, they will attribute their feelings and perceptions to features of the external environment (the woman's behavior and appearance) or to a plausible theory of what causes them to be attracted—which in this case is likely to amount to the same thing. The current findings show that for sexual aggressors, having relative power over a woman automatically increases her sexual attractiveness and also the strength of one's intention to interact with her.

Just as in Experiment 1, the results differed for the high-LSH and high-ASA participants. In the first experiment, only the high-ASA participants showed a unidirectional power→sex automatic association, and in the second experiment they were the only participants who were reliably influenced in their attraction ratings by the power priming manipulation. Clearly there are important differences between what is measured by the LSH and the ASA. The LSH scale is concerned with whether one would coerce a woman to have sex with him without using physical force (Pryor, 1987), whereas the ASA deals directly with the attractiveness of using physical force to gain sex (Malamuth, 1989a). Therefore, the different results using the two measures may be attributable to differences between men who would use physical force (i.e., rape) versus those who would not (see Gutek & Morasch, 1982; Lisak & Roth, 1988).

Interestingly, it is evident that the reliable interaction between priming and ASA level (Figure 13.2, right panel) is attributable to the low attraction ratings by the high-ASA participants in the neutral priming condition. When there are no power features of a situation for these men—as in situations where they do not have power over the woman—they are significantly less attracted to her than are other men. Note that there was a significant (negative) correlation over all participants between ASA scores and attraction toward the confederate only in the neutral priming condition; in the power priming condition all participants were equally attracted to the confederate regardless of ASA score. In other words, it is only when these men have relative power over a woman that they find her as attractive as do other men.

It might be argued that because high-ASA participants did not find the confederate more attractive than did low-ASA participants in the power prime condition of Experiment 2, the automatic power sex link cannot be an explanation for why high ASA men are more likely to abuse power to gain sexual favors from women. In other words, if high-ASA men are just as attracted to the confederate as are low-ASA men in the power prime condition, power is not having any differential effect on their attraction relative to other men. However, consider that for any individual, one is only aware of one's own feelings of relative attraction for the various potential partners of the opposite sex (or same sex depending on sexual preference) and so will be more likely to behave sexually toward those one feels most attracted to from among those possibilities. What is important, in other words, is the effect of power on the relative attractiveness of women within the group of men who are likely to sexually harass or aggress and the absence of any such effect of power on relative attractiveness among men who are not likely to harass or aggress against women.

General Discussion

The results of the experiments provide support for the existence of the automatic power→sex association in men who are likely to sexually harass or aggress and the consequences of the nonconscious and unintentional activation of the sex concept for feelings of attraction toward and desires to interact with women. It would appear that at least one contributing factor in the sexual exploitation of women by those with power over them is the nonconscious influence of that power on sexual feelings toward them.

Several important issues remain. One is the correlational nature of our observed link between the attractiveness of sexual aggression (ASA) and the automatic power→sex association. High-ASA men possess this automatic link, and their attraction toward women is increased by feelings of power, but did the automatic association cause the tendency to harass and the preference for aggressive sex, or vice versa? That is, does the automaticity of the power influence itself corrupt, or do already corrupt people develop the automatic power→sex link?

The Automatic Power→Sex Association: Cause or Symptom?

Cause. Although there is no way to answer this causal question from the present data alone, there exist arguments and evidence in support of both causal directions. We will first consider the possibility that the automatic link develops first and produces sexual harassment behavior. Another way of stating this case is that there is something about having power in a situation that produces the association with sex, which in turn leads to sexual harassment behavior.

The behavior of subordinates toward their superiors is different from their behavior toward people who do not have power over them (Jones, 1964): more deferential, friendly, appreciative, and hardly ever negative. Kipnis (1976) and Brewer (1982) have argued that the power holder comes to attribute these behaviors on the part of others to the greater import, value, and quality of his or her own ideas, contributions, and personality, and fails to recognize the critical constraining role played by his or her power on the subordinates' reactions to him or her. What is key for present purposes is that the power holder tends to make dispositional attributions for the subordinate's behavior toward him or her, not situational attributions that take into account their power differential (Gilbert, 1989; Jones & Nisbett, 1971; see also Fiske, 1993). Friendly, submissive, deferential behavior is attributed to the relationship between them as individuals, not as holders of different social roles.

Some men may interpret this friendly and appreciative behavior toward them as indicating attraction on the part of the woman because her behavior resembles what they would consider flirtation or attraction outside of their realms of power. Whether the man interpreted the behavior as friendliness or as flirtation or attraction would likely depend on the chronic accessibility of his constructs for friendliness and for attraction (e.g., Bargh et al., 1986). In our view, therefore, the more chronically accessible the individual's construct for attraction or sexual interest, the more likely he will interpret the woman's behavior in that manner. Over time, he would be likely to develop an automatic power→sex association because of the consistent covariation between having power and perceived sexual interest in him on the part of women.

Another possibility, one that Kissinger probably had in mind when he uttered his famous phrase, is that there are real—not just perceived—differences in the sexual interest shown by women in general to men in positions of power. (This also would produce, over time, the automatic association between having power and sexual interest from women.) It has been argued on evolutionary grounds (e.g., Buss, 1989; Buss & Schmitt, 1993) that women are generally attracted to men who have power. Men historically as well as today hold control over economic resources; therefore women could only secure such resources for themselves and for their children (more of a concern for women than for men; see Kenrick & Keefe, 1992) by allying themselves with powerful men. Those women who mated with powerful men were thus more likely to have children who had the power and resources to successfully mate, and so would be more likely to pass on these characteristics through the generations.

Thus, even if only some women are attracted to a man by virtue of his holding a position of power, the association between power and sex could be formed. This would set up a vicious cycle in which the sex concept would be primed by activation spreading from the concept of power, causing the man to interpret the ambiguously flirtatious behavior of other women as sexual, when in fact it is just friendly and deferential because of his power over her.

Symptom. Alternatively, it may be that the power→sex association develops from the belief that the use of power is necessary to gain sex. Several researchers have concluded that the abuse of power is an act of compensation for feelings of inadequacy and relative powerlessness. Lisak and Roth (1988) found that sexually aggressive men who had used force to gain sex from a woman were more likely than sexually nonaggressive men to have feelings of inadequacy and low power in relationships with women. They concluded that these men use greater force against women in an attempt to redress this perceived power imbalance. Bugental (1993), in a related discussion of why parents physically abuse their children, pointed out that these parents often feel that they are at a power disadvantage with respect to their children and (just like sexually aggressive men) are acting in an apparent attempt to counter that perceived power advantage.

In both these cases, the objectively powerful people (men and parents) paradoxically perceive themselves as having relatively less power and react by using their power against the objectively powerless people (women and children). Bugental (1993) has commented eloquently on this paradox:

> In following media coverage of interpersonal confrontations, we are amazed by the extent of force or violence that objectively powerful people often exert against the powerless, that is, against highly vulnerable victims. We are perplexed and appalled when a large group of police exercises excessive force against a lone individual. We are outraged when a powerful adult is violent towards a very small child or infant. Yet such individuals often recount that they felt at risk in such situations, as if the victim were in fact acting to threaten them. (pp. 288–289)

In terms of the present analysis of sexual harassment tendencies, it may be that those who develop automatic power sex associations see the use of power to gain sex as legitimate in that it is a reaction to the perceived use of power by women against them. In fact, Lisak and Roth (1988) did find that men who had sexually assaulted a woman were more likely than other men to report that women had tried to domineer and belittle them; they also believed that women consider themselves to be superior to men. Consistent with this interpretation of our results, high-ASA participants in our Experiment 2 were reliably less attracted to the confederate when the concept of power had not been primed; when it was primed they were as attracted to the confederate as were the other participants.

Harassment Versus Aggression

Another issue uncovered by our results is that men who engage in sexual coercion, as assessed by the LSH scale, do not show the same effect of power on attraction as do men who engage in sexual aggression, as tapped by the ASA scale. Those who would commit sexual blackmail (high-LSH participants) showed a bidirectional, schematic connection between the concepts of power and sex instead of the unidirectional, if-power-then-sex connection evidenced by sexual aggressors (high-ASA participants). Also unlike the high-ASA participants, high-LSH participants were not differentially attracted to the confederate in the power versus neutral priming conditions of Experiment 2.

This suggests to us that it is the unidirectional power→sex association that is critical for the nonconscious influence of power on attraction and resultant sexually oriented behavior toward female subordinates. Given the low attraction ratings of the confederate by the high-ASA men when their concept of power was not activated, it would seem that having power over a woman may even be a prerequisite for being sexually attracted to her. The high-LSH men, on the other hand, were able, like the other participants, to find the confederate moderately attractive regardless of whether their concept of power was activated. As argued by Pryor and Stoller (1994), because of the schematic, bidirectional power–sex association for these men, either having power or the presence of an attractive female (i.e., the confederate in Experiment 2) are sufficient to activate the sexual schema in an all-or-none fashion; one is not conditional on the other.

That attraction toward the confederate was dependent on activation of the power concept for high-ASA but not high-LSH men is consistent with Lisak and Roth's (1988) finding that the need to feel more powerful than women differentiated men who had gained sex by using physical force against a woman from men who had coerced a woman but had not used force.

Turning King Leers Into Prince Charmings

Although we have made the case for the importance of automatic associations between situational power features and the concept of sexuality in driving sexual harassment behavior, we do not mean to suggest that harassment is always or even usually unintended and innocent. As we have noted above, one likely route for the development of an automatic power→sex association is a preexisting insecurity or anger toward women (see also Bugental, 1993; Lisak & Roth, 1988; Malamuth, 1986). It would be naive to think that all people who abuse their official power for selfish ends do so without realizing it; one can hear the ghosts of Hobbes, Macchiavelli, and Nietzsche laughing uproariously at the thought.

Our point instead is that there are many men who behave in line with their sexual feelings toward female subordinates and so disturb and upset them without consciously realizing the influence of their power over their feelings and behavior (Fitzgerald, 1993a). That the victim of harassment, as well as objective outside observers, often see the behavior as the power play it is shows the blind spot these men have for the cause of their behavior. It is quite similar to well-publicized cases of blatant conflict of interest by public figures, who vigorously maintain the absence of any such conflict and seem genuinely puzzled by others' perception of one (see examples in Bargh & Raymond, 1995).

What can men do? Just as well-meaning people can be biased by the automatic operation of stereotypes but can control their influence if made aware of the possibility of such nonconscious bias (Bargh, 1992), and if they do not wish to be biased (Devine, 1989; Fiske, 1989), so too can men with power over women adjust and counteract the influence of that power if they are made aware of the possibility of the influence. If one was aware that one's power over a woman could cause attraction to her that would not occur in the absence of that power, they could correct their feelings accordingly (see Schwarz & Bless, 1992; Strack & Hannover, 1996). Once such consciousness raising has occurred, one can start to regain control over the automatic effects of power.

REFERENCES

Balota, D. A., & Lorch, R. F., Jr. (1986). Depth of automatic spreading activation: Mediated priming effects in pronunciation but not in lexical decision. *Journal of Experimental Psychology: Learning, Memory, and Cognition, 12,* 336–345.

Bargh, J. A. (1989). Conditional automaticity: Varieties of automatic influence in social perception and cognition. In J. S. Uleman & J. A. Bargh (Eds.), *Unintended thought* (pp. 3–51). New York: Guilford Press.

Bargh, J. A. (1992). Being unaware of the stimulus versus unaware of its effect: Does subliminality per se matter to social psychology? In R. Bornstein & T. Pittman (Eds.), *Perception without awareness* (pp. 236–258). New York: Guilford Press.

Bargh, J. A. (1994a). The Four Horsemen of automaticity: Intention, efficiency, awareness, and control as separate issues in social cognition. In R. S. Wyer & T. K. Srull (Eds.), *Handbook of social cognition* (2nd ed., Vol. 1. pp. 1–40). Hillsdale, NJ: Erlbaum.

Bargh, J. A. (1994b, June). *The preconscious in social interaction.* Invited address, Annual Convention of the American Psychological Society, Washington, DC.

Bargh, J. A., Bond. R. N., Lombardi, W. J., & Tota, M. E. (1986). The additive nature of chronic and temporary sources of construct accessibility. *Journal of Personality and Social Psychology, 50,* 869–878.

Bargh, J. A., Chaiken, S., Govender, R., & Pratto, F. (1992). The generality of the automatic attitude activation effect. *Journal of Personality and Social Psychology, 62,* 893–912.

Bargh, J. A., Chaiken. S., Raymond, P., & Hyme, C. (1996). The automatic evaluation effect: Unconditional automatic attitude activation with a pronunciation task. *Journal of Experimental Social Psychology, 32,* 104–128.

Bargh, J. A., & Raymond, P. (1995). The naive misuse of power. Nonconscious sources of sexual harassment. *Journal of Social Issues, 51,* 85–96.

Bem, D. J. (1972). Self-perception theory. *Advances in experimental social psychology, 6,* 1–62.

Bohner, G., Weisbrod, C., Raymond, P., Barzvi, A., & Schwarz, N. (1993). Salience of rape affects self-esteem: The moderating role of gender and rape myth acceptance. *European Journal Social Psychology, 23,* 561–579.

Brewer, M. B. (1982). Further beyond nine to five: An integration and future directions. *Journal of Social Issues, 38,* 149–158.

Brownmiller, S. (1975). *Against our will.* New York: Simon & Schuster.

Bruner, J. S. (1957). On perceptual readiness. *Psychological Review, 64,* 123–157.

Bugental, D. B. (1993). Perceived control and abuse. *American Behavioral Scientist, 45,* 294–304.

Buss, D. M. (1989). Sex differences in human mate preferences: Evolutionary hypotheses tested in 37 cultures. *Behavioral and Brain Sciences, 12,* 1–49.

Buss, D. M., & Schmitt, D. P. (1993). Sexual strategies theory: An evolutionary perspective on human mating. *Psychological Review, 100,* 204–232.

Devine, P. G. (1989). Stereotypes and prejudice: Their automatic and controlled components. *Journal of Personality and Social Psychology, 56,* 5–18.

Farley, L. (1978). *Sexual shakedown.* New York: McGraw-Hill.

Fazio, R. H., Sanbonmatsu, D. M., Powell, M. C., & Kardes, F. R. (1986). On the automatic activation of attitudes. *Journal of Personality and Social Psychology, 50,* 229–238.

Fischer, B., & Weber, H. (1993). Express saccades and visual attention. *Behavioral and Brain Sciences, 16,* 553–610.

Fiske, S. T. (1989). Examining the role of intent: Toward understanding its role in stereotyping and prejudice. In J. S. Uleman & J. A. Bargh (Eds.), *Unintended thought* (pp. 253–283). New York: Guilford Press.

Fiske, S. T. (1993). Controlling other people: The impact of power on stereotyping. *American Psychologist, 48,* 621–628.

Fitzgerald, L. F. (1993a, February). *The last great open secret: The sexual harassment of women in the workplace and academia.* Edited transcript of a Science and Public Policy Seminar presented by the Federation of Behavioral, Psychological, and Cognitive Sciences, Washington, DC.

Fitzgerald, L. F. (1993b). Sexual harassment: Violence against women in the workplace. *American Psychologist, 48,* 1070–1076.

Fitzgerald, L. F., Shullman, S. L., Bailey, N., Richards, M., Swecker, J., Gold, A., Ormerod, A. J., & Weitzman, L. (1988). The incidence and dimensions of sexual harassment in academia and the workplace. *Journal of Vocational Behavior, 32,* 152–175.

French, J. R. P., & Raven, B. (1959). The bases of social power. In D. Cartwright (Ed.), *Studies in social power.* Ann Arbor: Institute for Social Research.

Gazzaniga, M. S. (1985). *The social brain: Discovering the networks of the mind.* New York: Basic Books.

Gilbert, D. T. (1989). Thinking lightly about others: Automatic components of the social inference process. In J. S. Uleman & J. A. Bargh (Eds.), *Unintended thought* (pp. 189–211). New York: Guilford Press.

Goodman, L. A., Koss, M. P., Fitzgerald, L. F, Russo, N. F, Keita, G. P. (1993). Male violence against women: Current research and future directions. *American Psychologist, 4,* 1054–1058.

Greenhouse, L. (1993a, November 10). Court, 9–0, makes sexual harassment easier to prove. *New York Times,* pp. A1, 22.

Greenhouse, L. (1993b, October 14). Ginsburg at fore in court's give-and-take. *New York Times,* pp. A1, 88.

Groth, A. N. (1979). *Men who rape. The psychology of the offender.* New York: Plenum Press.

Gutek, B. (1985). *Sex and the workplace.* San Francisco: Jossey-Bass.

Gutek, B., & Morasch, B. (1982). Sex ratios, sex role spillover and sexual harassment of women at work. *Journal of Social Issues, 38,* 55–74.

Higgins, E. T. & King, G. A. (1981). Accessibility of social constructs: Information processing consequences of individual and contextual variability. In N. Cantor & J. F. Kihlstrom (Eds.), *Personality, cognition, and social interaction* (pp. 69–121). Hillsdale, NJ: Erlbaum.

Howes, D. H., & Solomon, R. L. (1950). A note on McGinnies' "Emotionality and perceptual defense." *Psychological Review, 57,* 229–234.

Jones, E. E. (1964). *Ingratiation.* New York: Appleton-Century-Crofts.

Jones, E. E., & Nisbett, R. E. (1971). The actor and the observer: Divergent perceptions of the causes of behavior. In E. E. Jones et al. (Eds.), *Attribution: Perceiving the causes of behavior* (pp. 79–94). Morristown, NJ: General Learning Press.

Kenrick, D. T., & Keefe, R. C. (1992). Age preferences in mates reflect sex differences in human reproductive strategies. *Behavioral and Brain Sciences, 1,* 75–92.

Kipnis, D. (1976). *The powerholders.* Chicago: University of Chicago Press.

Lisak, D., & Roth, S. (1988). Motivational factors in nonincarcerated sexually aggressive men. *Journal of Personality and Social Psychology, 55,* 795–802.

MacKinnon, C. A. (1979). *Sexual harassment of working women.* New Haven, CT: Yale University Press.

Malamuth, N. M. (1986). Predictors of naturalistic sexual aggression. *Journal of Personality and Social Psychology, 50,* 953–962.

Malamuth, N. M. (1989a). The attraction to sexual aggression scale: Part One. *Journal of Sex Research, 26,* 26–49.

Malamuth, N. M. (l989b). The attraction to sexual aggression scale: Part Two. *Journal of Sex Research, 26,* 324–354.

Neely, J. H. (1977). Semantic priming and retrieval from lexical memory: Roles of inhibitionless spreading activation and limited capacity attention. *Journal of Experimental Psychology: General, 106,* 226–254.

Nisbett, R. E., & Wilson, T. D. (1977). Telling more than we can know: Verbal reports on mental processes. *Psychological Review, 84,* 231–259.

Posner, M. I., & Snyder, C. R. R. (1975). Attention and cognitive control. In R. L. Solso (Ed.), *Information processing and cognition: The Loyola symposium* (pp. 55–85). Hillsdale, NJ: Erlbaum.

Pryor, J. B. (1987). Sexual harassment proclivities in men. *Sex Roles, 17,* 269–290.

Pryor, J. B., Giedd, J. L., & Williams, K. B. (1995). A social psychological model for predicting sexual harassment. *Journal of Social Issues, 51,* 69–84.

Pryor, J. B., LaVite, C. M., & Stoller, L. M. (1993). A social psychological analysis of sexual harassment: The person/situation interaction. *Journal of Vocational Behavior, 42,* 68–83.

Pryor, J. B., & Stoller, L. M. (1994). Sexual cognition processes in men who are high in the likelihood to sexually harass. *Personality and Social Psychology Bulletin, 20,* 163–169.

Rayner, K. (1978). Foveal and parafoveal cues in reading. In J. Requin (Ed.), *Attention and performance VIII* (pp. 149–161). Hillsdale, NJ: Erlbaum.

Russell, B. (1938). *Power: A new social analysis.* New York: Norton.

Schachter, S., & Singer, J. (1962). Cognitive, social, and physiological determinants of emotion. *Psychological Review, 69,* 379–399.

Schwarz, N., & Bless, H. (1992). Constructing reality and its alternatives: An inclusion/exclusion model of assimilation and contrast effects in social judgment. In L. L. Martin & A. Tesser (Eds.), *The construction of social judgments* (pp. 217–245). Hillsdale, NJ: Erlbaum.

Strack, F., & Hannover, B. (1996). Awareness of influence as a precondition for implementing correctional goals. In P. M. Gollwitzer & J. A. Bargh (Eds.), *The psychology of action* (pp. 579–596). New York: Guilford Press.

Tangri, S. S., Burt, M. R., & Johnson, L. B. (1982). Sexual harassment at work: Three explanatory models. *Journal of Social Issues, 38,* 33–54.

Thibaut, J. W., & Kelley, H. H. (1959). *The social psychology of groups.* New York: Wiley.

Thornhill, R., & Thornhill, N. W. (1992). The evolutionary psychology of men's coercive sexuality. *Behavioral and Brain Sciences, 15,* 363–421.

U. S. Equal Employment Opportunity Commission. (1980). Discrimination because of sex under Title VII of the 1964 Civil Rights Act as amended: Adoption of interim guidelines—Sexual harassment. *Federal Register, 45,* 25024–25025.

Zillman, D. (1978). Attribution and misattribution of excitatory reactions. In J. Harvey, W. Ickes, & R. F. Kidd (Eds.), *New directions in attribution research* (Vol. 2, pp. 335–368). Hillsdale, NJ: Erlbaum.

INTRODUCTION TO PART 7

Infidelity

The highly regarded sociological sexologist Ira Reiss (1986) concluded that sexual possessiveness and jealousy are found in all cultures, even though the forms and manifestations vary from one culture to another. This seeming universality suggests that the desire to have your mate be sexually faithful to you is a deeply rooted aspect of human nature. Yet it is also undeniably true that sexual infidelity has occurred to some extent throughout history and across most known cultures.

Two papers in this section approach the problem of infidelity. Buss, Larsen, Westen, and Semmelroth (1992) start from the presumption that the cross-cultural universality of sexual possessiveness indicates that people have probably been shaped by evolution to desire fidelity in their partners. They extend this reasoning in view of the different reproductive goals of men and women and propose that men and women will have different emphases in their possessiveness. Their findings suggest that men are more concerned about the physical aspects of sexual betrayal and object most strongly to their female partners having sexual intercourse with another man. Women, meanwhile, object more strongly to involvement in emotional intimacy than to the sex act per se.

The findings seem clear and provide valuable support for important aspects of evolutionary theorizing about sexual jealousy. Other authors have challenged them, however. Buunk, Angleitner, Oubaid, and Buss (1996) found that Dutch and German men expressed more distress over emotional than sexual infidelity, which points toward cultural relativity and thus may at least indicate that evolution is not the whole story. Harris (2000) conducted a series of replications of the Buss et al. (1992) paper and found results that were only partly consistent with what the original paper found. In her work, men exhibited more physiological arousal to sexual than emotional jealousy, but this appears to have been due to greater male arousal to sexual imagery in general: Men were equally aroused whether they imagined their partner having sex with another man or with themselves. Women did not show different responses to the two types of imagined infidelity. When turning from physiological measures to people's own self-reported feelings about sexual and emotional infidelity, Harris found that men were about equally divided, whereas most women said the emotional infidelity would be worse. Taken together, these results suggest that Buss et al. (1992) identified an important phenomenon—but one that is not as simple or consistent as you might think.

Although sexual infidelity is a popular theme in the mass media, in everyday life it turns out to be relatively rare, and the vast majority of people spend most of their married lives in complete fidelity. This presents something of a problem to researchers who wish to study infidelity, because it is difficult to find enough instances of infidelity to compose a statistically powerful sample. An interesting solution to that dilemma was developed by Hansen (1987), who lowered the criterion for infidelity: Instead of looking at sexual intercourse involving a married person and someone other than the spouse, he looked at lesser forms of sexual behavior and used dating couples instead of married couples. This enabled him to identify a large group of people who had ever necked or petted with someone other than their main dating partner at the time, and so the predictors of this relatively minor form of infidelity could be studied effectively.

Hansen's conclusions are similar to what has been found in larger investigations, such as Lawson's (1988) work and Blumstein and Schwartz's (1983) study. Infidelity seems to be linked to relationship problems, although the direction of causality is unclear: Do relationship problems cause infidelity, or does infidelity cause problems? Blumstein and Schwartz (1983) found, for example, that if either member of a couple had sexual relations with anyone other than the partner, the couple was more likely to break up than if both remained faithful. This was true even among couples who had reached an agreement or understanding to allow each other to have sex with other people. Lawson (1988) found that many people embarked on extramarital affairs with the firm initial belief that they would not allow the affair to affect their marriage, but some of these people were unable to maintain that separation. In particular, many people fall in love with their sex partners, and unfaithful spouses often develop strong, passionate feelings for their lovers. These feelings do sometimes cause people to break apart their marriages, although Lawson did not find any large pattern of people divorcing their spouses to marry their lovers. Until causal processes are better understood, the main conclusion that seems safe at present is that infidelity constitutes a significant risk factor for the survival of close relationships.

REFERENCES

Blumstein, P., & Schwartz, P. (1983). *American couples*. New York: Simon & Schuster (Pocket).

Buss, D. M., Larsen, R. S., Westen, D., & Semmelroth, J. (1992). Sex differences in jealousy: Evolution, physiology, and psychology. *Psychological Science, 3,* 251–255.

Buunk, B. P., Angleitner, A., Oubaid, V., & Buss, D. M. (1996). Sex differences in jealousy in evolutionary and cultural perspectives: Tests from the Netherlands, Germany, and the United States. *Psychological Science,* 7, 359–363.

Hansen, G. L. (1987). Extradyadic relations during courtship. *Journal of Sex Research, 23,* 382–390.

Harris, C. R. (2000). Psychophysiological responses to imagined infidelity: The specific innate modular view of jealousy reconsidered. *Journal of Personality and Social Psychology, 78,* 1082–1091.

Lawson, A. (1988). *Adultery: An analysis of love and betrayal*. New York: Basic Books.

Reiss, I. L. (1986). A sociological journey into sexuality. *Journal of Marriage and the Family, 48,* 233–242.

Discussion Questions

1. Could the findings of Buss et al. (1992)—namely, that men object more strongly to sexual infidelities, while women object more to emotional ones—be explained on the basis of social roles and cultural norms, rather than evolutionary theory?
2. In homosexuals, infidelity does not carry the danger of pregnancy that heterosexual infidelity does. How would this affect the gender differences in attitudes toward partner infidelity?
3. How reliable are answers to hypothetical questions such as "How would you feel if your partner formed a nonsexual but emotionally intimate relationship with someone else?"
4. Do you think that a really secure person would not mind having his or her romantic partner have a sexual relationship with someone else?
5. Given that people everywhere want their romantic partners to be faithful to them, why does infidelity occur as often as it does?
6. What are the best ways to keep a partner from being unfaithful?
7. Is infidelity ever justified?

Suggested Readings

Blumstein, P., & Schwartz, P. (1983). *American couples*. New York: Simon & Schuster (Pocket). This is one of the best books on close relationships. It reports the results of a large, thorough investigation of both heterosexual and homosexual couples, with special emphasis on sex, money, and power. The authors followed up their sample a year and a half later to see which couples had broken up and which remained together, and by going back to their extensive data on each couple they were able to identify the statistical predictors of breaking up.

Lawson, A. (1988). *Adultery: An analysis of love and betrayal*. New York: Basic Books. Lawson's work on adultery is long-winded but readable. She mixes statistical research findings with vivid stories about infidelity and its consequences.

Reiss, I. L. (1986). *Journey into sexuality: An exploratory voyage*. New York: Prentice-Hall. This important work provides an overview of the author's ground-breaking research.

READING 14

Sex Differences in Jealousy: Evolution, Physiology, and Psychology

David M. Buss, Randy J. Larsen, Drew Westen, and Jennifer Semmelroth
• University of Michigan

In species with internal female fertilization, males risk both lowered paternity probability and investment in rival gametes if their mates have sexual contact with other males. Females of such species do not risk lowered maternity probability through partner infidelity, but they do risk the diversion of their mates' commitment and resources to rival females. Three studies tested the hypothesis that sex differences in jealousy emerged in humans as solutions to the respective adaptive problems faced by each sex. In Study I, men and women selected which event would upset them more–a partner's sexual infidelity or emotional infidelity. Study 2 recorded physiological responses (heart rate, electrodermal response, corrugator supercilii contraction) while subjects imagined separately the two types of partner infidelity. Study 3 tested the effect of being in a committed sexual relationship on the activation of jealousy. All studies showed large sex differences, confirming hypothesized sex linkages in jealousy activation.

In species with internal female fertilization and gestation, features of reproductive biology characteristic of all 4,000 species of mammals, including humans, males face an adaptive problem not confronted by females—uncertainty in their paternity of offspring. Maternity probability in mammals rarely or never deviates from 100%. Compromises in paternity probability come at substantial reproductive cost to the male—the loss of mating effort expended, including time, energy, risk, nuptial gifts, and mating opportunity costs. A cuckolded male also loses the female's parental effort, which becomes channeled to a competitor's gametes. The adaptive problem of paternity uncertainty is exacerbated in species in which males engage in some postzygotic parental investment (Trivers, 1972). Males risk investing resources in putative offspring that are genetically unrelated.

These multiple and severe reproductive costs should have imposed strong selection pressure on males to defend against cuckoldry. Indeed, the literature is replete with examples of evolved anticuckoldry mechanisms in lions (Bertram, 1975), bluebirds (Power, 1975), doves (Erickson & Zenone, 1976), numerous insect species (Thornhill & Alcock, 1983), and nonhuman primates (Hrdy, 1979). Since humans arguably show more paternal investment than any other of the 200 species of primates (Alexander & Noonan, 1979), this selection pressure should have operated especially intensely on human males. Symons (1979); Daly, Wilson, and Weghorst (1982); and Wilson and Daly (1992) have hypothesized that male sexual jealousy evolved as a solution to this adaptive problem (but see Hupka, 1991, for an alternative view). Men who were indifferent to sexual contact between their mates and other men presumably experienced lower paternity certainty, greater investment in competitors' gametes, and lower reproductive success than did men who were motivated to attend to cues of infidelity and to act on those cues to increase paternity probability.

Although females do not risk maternity uncertainty, in species with biparental care they do risk the potential loss of time, resources, and commitment from a male if he deserts or channels investment to alternative mates (Buss, 1988; Thornhill & Alcock, 1983; Trivers, 1972). The redirection of a mate's investment to another female and her offspring is reproductively costly for a female, especially in environments where offspring suffer in survival and reproductive currencies without investment from both parents.

In human evolutionary history, there were likely to have been at least two situations in which a woman risked losing a man's investment. First, in a monogamous marriage, a woman risked having her male invest in an alternative woman with whom he was having an affair (partial loss of investment) or risked his departure for an alterative woman (large or total loss of investment). Second, in polygynous marriages, a woman was at risk of having her mate invest to a larger degree in other wives and their offspring at the expense of his investment in her and her offspring. Following Buss (1988) and Mellon (1981), we hypothesize that cues to the development of a deep emotional attachment have been reliable leading indicators to women of potential reduction or loss of their mate's investment.

Jealousy is defined as an emotional "state that is aroused by a perceived threat to a valued relationship or position and motivates behavior aimed at countering the threat. Jealousy is 'sexual' if the valued relationship is sexual" (Daly et al., 1982, p. 11; see also Salovey, 1991; White & Mullen, 1989). It is reasonable to hypothesize that jealousy involves physiological reactions (autonomic arousal) to perceived threat and motivated action to reduce the threat, although this hypothesis has not been examined. Following Symons (1979) and Daly et al. (1982), our central hypothesis is that the events that activate jealousy physiologically and psychologically differ for men and women because of the different adaptive problems they have faced over human evolutionary history in mating contexts. Both sexes are hypothesized to be distressed over both sexual and emotional infidelity, and previous findings bear this out (Buss, 1989). However, these two kinds of infidelity should be weighted differently by men and women. Despite the importance of these hypothesized sex differences, no systematic scientific work has been directed toward verifying or falsifying their existence (but for suggestive data, see Francis, 1977; Teismann & Mosher, 1978: White & Mullen, 1989).

Study 1: Subjective Distress over a Partner's External Involvement

This study was designed to test the hypothesis that men and women differ in which form of infidelity—sexual versus emotional—triggers more upset and subjective distress, following the adaptive logic just described.

Method

After reporting age and sex, subjects (N = 202 undergraduate students) were presented with the following dilemma:

> Please think of a serious committed romantic relationship that you have had in the past, that you currently have, or that you would like to have. Imagine that you discover that the person with whom you've been seriously involved became interested in someone else, what would distress or upset you more (*please circle only one*):
>
> (A) Imagining your partner forming a deep emotional attachment to that person.
>
> (B) Imagining your partner enjoying passionate sexual intercourse with that other person.

Subjects completed additional questions, and then encountered the next dilemma, with the same instructional set, but followed by a different, but parallel, choice:

> (A) Imagining your partner trying different sexual positions with that other person.
>
> (B) Imagining your partner falling in love with that other person.

Results

Shown in Figure 14.1 (upper panel) are the percentages of men and women reporting from distress in response to sexual infidelity than emotional infidelity. The first empirical probe, contrasting distress over a partner's sexual involvement with distress over a partner's deep emotional attachment, yielded a large and highly significant sex difference ($\chi^2 = 47.56$, $df = 3$, $p < .001$). Fully 60% of the male sample reported greater distress over their partner's potential sexual infidelity; in contrast, only 17% of the female sample chose that option, with 83% reporting that they would experience greater distress over a partner's emotional attachment to a rival.

This pattern was replicated with the contrast between sex and love. The magnitude of the sex difference was large, with 32% more men than women reporting greater distress over a partner's sexual involvement with someone else, and the majority of women reporting greatest distress over a partner's falling in love with a rival ($\chi^2 = 59.20$, $df = 3$, $p < .001$).

Study 2: Physiological Responses to a Partner's External Involvement

Given the strong confirmation of jealousy sex linkage from Study 1, we sought next to test the hypotheses using physiological measures. Our central measures of autonomic arousal were electrodermal activity (EDA), assessed via skin conductance, and pulse rate (PR). Electrodermal activity and pulse rate are indicators of autonomic nervous system activation (Levenson, 1988). Because distress is an unpleasant subjective state, we also included a measure of muscle activity in the brow region of the face—electromyographic (EMG) activity of the corrugator supercilii muscle. This muscle is responsible for the furrowing of the brow often seen in facial displays of unpleasant emotion or affect (Fridlund, Ekman, & Oster, 1987). Subjects were asked to image two scenarios in which a partner became involved with someone else—one sexual intercourse scenario and one emotional attachment scenario. Physiological responses were recorded during the imagery trials.

Subjects

Subjects were 55 undergraduate students, 32 males and 23 females, each completing a 2-hr laboratory session.

Physiological Measures

Physiological activity was monitored on the running strip chart of a Grass Model 7D polygraph and digitized on a laboratory computer at a 10-Hz

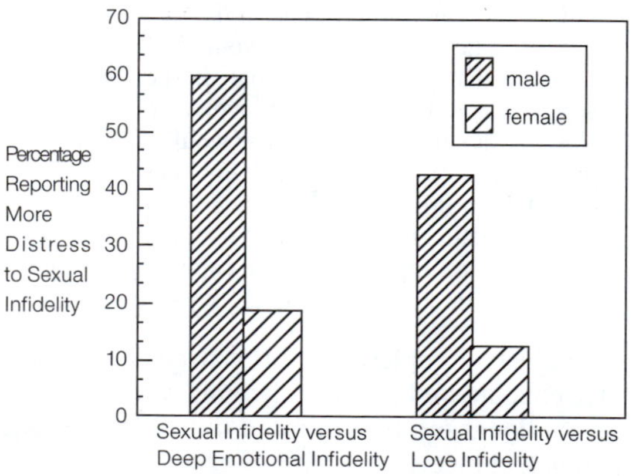

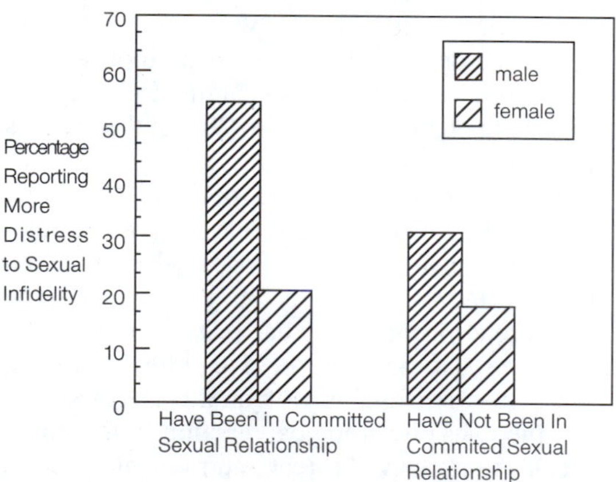

FIGURE 14.1 ■ Reported comparisons of distress in response to imagining a partner's sexual or emotional infidelity. The upper panel shows results of Study 1—the percentage of subjects reporting more distress to the sexual infidelity scenario than to the emotional infidelity (left) and the love infidelity (right) scenarios. The lower panel shows results of Study 3—the percentage of subjects reporting more distress to the sexual infidelity scenario than to the emotional infidelity scenario, presented separately for those who have experienced a committed sexual relationship (left) and those who have not experienced a committed sexual relationship (right).

rate, following principles recommended in Cacioppo and Tassinary (1990).

ELECTRODERMAL ACTIVITY

Standard Beckman Ag/AgCl surface electrodes, filled with a .05 molar NaCl solution in a Unibase paste, were placed over the middle segments of the first and third fingers of the right hand. A Wheatstone bridge applied a 0.5-V voltage to one electrode.

PULSE RATE

A photoplethysmograph was attached to the subject's right thumb to monitor the pulse wave. The signal from this pulse transducer was fed into a Grass Model 7P4 cardiotachometer to detect the rising slope of each pulse wave, with the internal circuitry of the Schmitt trigger individually adjusted for each subject to output PR in beats per minute.

ELECTROMYOGRAPHIC ACTIVITY

Bipolar EMG recordings were obtained over the corrugator supercilii muscle. The EMG signal was relayed to a wide-band AC-preamplifier (Grass Model 7P3), where it was band-pass filtered, full-wave rectified, and integrated with a time constant of 0.2 s.

Procedure

After electrode attachment, the subject was made comfortable in a reclining chair and asked to relax. After a 5-min waiting period, the experiment began. The subject was alone in the room during the imagery session, with an intercom on for verbal communication. The instructions for the imagery task were written on a form which the subject was requested to read and follow.

Each subject was instructed to engage in three separate images. The final image was designed to be emotionally neutral: "imagine a time when you were walking to class, feeling neither good nor bad, just neutral." The subject was instructed to press a button when he or she had the image clearly in mind, and to sustain the image until the experimenter said to stop. The button triggered the computer to begin collecting physiological data for 20 s, after which the experimenter instructed the subject to "stop and relax."

The next two images were infidelity images, one sexual and one emotional. The order of presentation of these two images was counterbalanced. The instructions for sexual jealousy imagery were as follows: "Please think of a serious romantic relationship that you have had in the past, that you currently have, or that you would like to have. Now imagine that the person with whom you're seriously involved becomes interested in someone else. *Imagine you find out that your partner is having sexual intercourse with this other person.* Try to feel the feelings you would have if this happened to you."

The instructions for emotional infidelity imagery were identical to the above, except the italicized sentence was replaced with *"Imagine that your partner is falling in love and forming an emotional attachment to that person."* Physiological data were collected for 20 s following the subject's button press indicating that he or she had achieved the image. Subjects were told to "stop and relax" for 30 s between imagery trials.

Results

PHYSIOLOGICAL SCORES

The following scores were obtained: (a) the amplitude of the largest EDA response occurring during each 20-s trial; (b) PR in beats per minute averaged over each 20-s trial: and (c) amplitude of EMG activity over the corrugator supercilii averaged over each 20-s trial. Difference scores were computed between the neutral imagery trial and the jealousy induction trials. Within-sex t tests revealed no effects for order of presentation of the sexual jealousy image, so data were collapsed over this factor.

JEALOUSY INDUCTION EFFECTS

Table 14.1 shows the mean scores for the physiological measures for men and women in each of the two imagery conditions. Differences in physiological responses to the two jealousy images were examined using paired-comparison t tests for each sex separately for EDA, PR, and EMG. The men showed significant increases in EDA during the sexual imagery compared with the emotional imagery ($t = 2.00$, $df = 29$, $p < .05$). Women showed significantly greater EDA to the emotional infidelity image than to the sexual infidelity image (t

TABLE 14.1. Means and Standard Deviations on Physiological Measures During Two Imagery Conditions

Measure	Imagery type	Mean	*SD*
	Males		
EDA	Sexual	1.30	3.64
	Emotional	−0.11	0.76
Pulse rate	Sexual	4.76	7.80
	Emotional	3.00	5.24
Brow EMG	Sexual	6.75	32.96
	Emotional	1.16	6.60
	Females		
EDA	Sexual	−0.07	0.49
	Emotional	0.21	0.78
Pulse rate	Sexual	2.25	4.68
	Emotional	2.57	4.37
Brow EMG	Sexual	3.03	8.38
	Emotional	8.12	25.60

Note. Measures are expressed as changes from the neutral image condition. EDA is in microsiemen units, pulse rate is in beats per minute, and EMG is in microvolt units.

= 2.42, df = 19, $p < .05$). A similar pattern was observed with PR. Men showed a substantial increase in PR to both images, but significantly more so in response to the sexual infidelity image (t = 2.29, df = 31, $p < .05$). Women showed elevated PR to both images, but not differentially so. The results of the *corrugator* EMG were similar, although less strong. Men showed greater brow contraction to the sexual infidelity image, and women showed the opposite pattern, although results with this nonautonomic measure did not reach significance (t = 1.12, df = 30, $p < .14$, for males; t = −1.24, df = 22, $p < .12$, for females). The elevated EMG contractions for both jealousy induction trials in both sexes support the hypothesis that the affect experienced is negative.

Study 3: Contexts that Activate the Jealousy Mechanism

The goal of Study 3 was to replicate and extend the results of Studies 1 and 2 using a larger sample. Specifically, we sought to examine the effects of having been in a committed sexual relationship versus not having been in such a relationship on the activation of jealousy. We hypothesized that men who had actually experienced a committed sexual relationship would report greater subjective distress in response to the sexual infidelity imagery than would men who had not experienced a high-investing sexual relationship, and that women who had experienced a committed sexual relationship would report greater distress to the emotional infidelity image than women who had not been in a committed sexual relationship. The rationale was that direct experience of the relevant context during development may be necessary for the activation of the sex-linked weighting of jealousy activation.

Subjects

Subjects for Study 3 were 309 undergraduate students, 133 men and 176 women.

Procedure

Subjects read the following instructions:

> Please think of a serious or committed romantic relationship that you have had in the past, that you currently have, or that you would like to have. Imagine that you discover that the person with whom you've been seriously involved became interested in someone else. What would distress or upset you more (*please circle only one*):
>
> (A) Imagining your partner falling in love and forming a deep emotional attachment to that person.
>
> (B) Imagining your partner having sexual intercourse with that other person.

Alternatives were presented in standard forced-choice format, with the order counterbalanced across subjects. Following their responses, subjects were asked: "Have you ever been in a serious or committed romantic relationship? (yes or no)" and "If yes, was this a sexual relationship? (yes or no)."

Results

The results for the total sample replicate closely the results of Study 1. A much larger proportion of men (49%) than women (19%) reported that they would be more distressed by their partner's sexual involvement with someone else than by their partner's emotional attachment to, or love for, someone else (χ^2 = 38.48, df = 3, $p < .001$).

The two pairs of columns in the bottom panel of Figure 14.1 show the results separately for those subjects who had experienced a committed sexual relationship in the past and those who had not. For women, the difference is small and not significant: Women reported that they would experience more distress about a partner's emotional infidelity than a partner's sexual infidelity, regardless of whether or not they had experienced a committed sexual relationship ($\chi^2 = 0.80$, $df = 1$, ns).

For men, the difference between those who had been in a sexual relationship and those who had not is large and highly significant. Whereas 55% of the men who had experienced committed sexual relationships reported that they would be more distressed by a partner's sexual than emotional infidelity, this figure drops to 29% for men who had never experienced a committed sexual relationship ($\chi^2 = 12.29$, $df = 1$, $p < .001$). Sexual jealousy in men apparently becomes increasingly activated upon experience of the relevant relationship.

Discussion

The results of the three empirical studies support the hypothesized sex linkages in the activators of jealousy. Study 1 found large sex differences in reports of the subjective distress individuals would experience upon exposure to a partner's sexual infidelity versus emotional infidelity. Study 2 found a sex linkage in autonomic arousal to imagined sexual infidelity versus emotional infidelity; the results were particularly strong for the EDA and PR. Study 3 replicated the large sex differences in reported distress to sexual versus emotional infidelity, and found a strong effect for men of actually having experienced a committed sexual relationship.

These studies are limited in ways that call for additional research. First, they pertain to a single age group and culture. Future studies could explore the degree to which these sex differences transcend different cultures and age groups. Two clear evolutionary psychological predictions are (a) that male sexual jealousy and female commitment jealousy will be greater in cultures where males invest heavily in children, and (b) that male sexual jealousy will diminish as the age of the male's mate increases because reproductive value decreases. Second, future studies could test the alternate hypothesis that the current findings reflect (a) domain-specific psychological adaptations to cuckoldry versus potential investment loss or (b) a more domain-general mechanism such that any thoughts of sex are more interesting, arousing, and perhaps disturbing to men, whereas any thoughts of love are more interesting, arousing, and perhaps disturbing to women, and hence that such responses are not specific to jealousy or infidelity. Third, emotional and sexual infidelity are clearly correlated, albeit imperfectly, and a sizable percentage of men in Studies 1 and 3 reported greater distress to a partner's emotional infidelity. Emotional infidelity may signal sexual infidelity and vice versa, and hence both sexes should become distressed at both forms (see Buss, 1989). Future research could profitably explore in greater detail the correlation of these forms of infidelity as well as the sources of within-sex variation. Finally, the intriguing finding that men who have experienced a committed sexual relationship differ dramatically from those who have not, whereas for women such experiences appear to be irrelevant to their selection of emotional infidelity as the more distressing event, should be examined. Why do such ontogenetic experiences matter for men, and why do they appear to be irrelevant for women?

Within the constraints of the current studies, we can conclude that the sex differences found here generalize across both psychological and physiological methods—demonstrating an empirical robustness in the observed effect. The degree to which these sex-linked elicitors correspond to the hypothesized sex-linked adaptive problems lends support to the evolutionary psychological framework from which they were derived. Alterative theoretical frameworks, including those that invoke culture, social construction, deconstruction. arbitrary parental socialization, and structural powerlessness, undoubtedly could be molded post hoc to fit the findings—something perhaps true of any set of findings. None but the Symons (1979) and Daly et al. (1982) evolutionary psychological frameworks, however, generated the sex-differentiated predictions in advance and on the basis of sound evolutionary reasoning. The recent finding that male sexual jealousy is the leading cause of spouse battering and homicide across cultures worldwide (Daly & Wilson, 1988a, 1988b) offers suggestive evidence that these sex differences have large social import and may be species-wide.

REFERENCES

Alexander, R. D., & Noonan, K. H. (1979). Concealment of ovulation, parental care, and human social evolution. In N. Chagnon & W. Irons (Eds.), *Evolutionary biology and human social behavior* (pp. 436–453). North Scituate, MA: Duxbury.

Bertram, B. C. R. (1971). Social factors influencing reproduction in wild lions. *Journal of Zoology, 177,* 463–482.

Buss, D. M. (1988). From vigilence to violence: Tactics of mate retention. *Ethology and Sociobiology, 9,* 291–317.

Cacioppo, J. T., & Tassinary, L. G. (Eds.). (1990). *Principles of psychophysiology: Physical, social, and inferential elements.* Cambridge, England: Cambridge University Press.

Daly, M., & Wilson, M. (1988a). Evolutionary social psychology and family violence. *Science, 242,* 519–524.

Daly, M., & Wilson, M. (1988b). *Homicide.* Hawthorne, NY: Aldine.

Daly, M., & Wilson, M., & Weghorst, S. J. (1982). Male sexual jealousy. *Ethology and Sociobiology, 3,* 11–27.

Erickson, C. J., & Zenone, P. G. (1976). Courtship differences in male ring doves: Avoidance of cuckoldry? *Science, 192,* 1353–1354.

Fridlund, A., Ekman, P., & Olster, J. (1987). Facial expressions of emotion. In A. Siegman & S. Feldstein (Eds.), *Nonverbal behavior and communications* (pp. 143–224). Hillsdale, NJ: Erlbaum.

Hrdy, S. B. G. (1979). Infanticide among animals: A review, classification, and examination of the implications for the reproductive strategies of females. *Ethology and Sociobiology, 1,* 14–40.

Hupka, R. B. (1991). The motive for the arousal of romantic jealousy: Its cultural origin. In P. Salovey (Ed.), *The psychology of jealousy and envy* (pp. 252–270). New York: Guilford Press.

Levenson, R. W. (1988). Emotion and the autonomic nervous system: A prospectus for research on autonomic specificity. In H. Wagner (Ed.), *Social psychophysiology: Theory and clinical applications* (pp. 17–42). London: Wiley.

Mellon, L. W. (1981). *The evolution of love.* San Francisco: W. H. Freeman.

Power, H. W. (1975). Mountain bluebirds: Experimental evidence against altruism. *Science, 189,* 142–143.

Salovey, P. (Ed.). (1991). *The psychology of jealousy and envy.* New York: Guilford Press.

Symons, D. (1979). *The evolution of human sexuality.* New York: Oxford University Press.

Teismann, M. W., & Mosher, D. L. (1978). Jealous conflict in dating couples. *Psychological Review, 42,* 1211–1216.

Thornhill, R., & Alcock, J. (1983). *The evolution of insect mating systems.* Cambridge, MA: Harvard University Press.

Trivers, R. (1972). Parental investment and sexual selection. In B. Campbell (Ed.), *Sexual selection and the descent of man, 1871–1971* (pp. 136–179). Chicago: Aldine.

White, G. L., & Mullen, P. E. (1989). *Jealousy: Theory, research, and clinical strategies.* New York: Guilford Press.

Wilson, M., & Daly, M. (1992). The man who mistook his wife for a chattel. In J. Barkow, L. Cosmides, & J. Tooby (Eds.), *The adapted mind: Evolutionary psychology and the generation of culture* (pp. 289–322). New York: Oxford University Press.

READING 15

Extradyadic Relations During Courtship

Gary L. Hansen • University of Kentucky

Although extramarital sex has been the focus of a considerable amount of study, sexual relations outside of other committed, intimate relationships have received little attention. A few researchers (e.g., Buunk, 1980; Thompson, 1984) have included cohabitors, but research is lacking on extradyadic relations during committed dating or courtship. I examined (a) the extent of extradyadic relations during courtship among a sample of college students and (b) the relationship between extradyadic behavior and possible associated variables. The dyad outside of which the "extra" relationship occurs I defined as a man and woman who are committed to dating only each other.

On the attitudinal level, premarital permissiveness has been found to be associated with extramarital permissiveness (Reiss, Anderson, & Sponaugle, 1980; Singh, Walton, & Williams, 1976; Weis & Jurich, 1985). On the behavioral level, premarital sexual activity is associated with both projected involvement in extramarital sex (Bukstel, Roeder, Kilmann, Laughlin, & Sotile, 1978) and actual involvement (Athanasiou & Sarkin, 1974; Kinsey, Pomeroy, Martin, & Gebhard, 1953). In this work, no distinction has been made between premarital sex with one's committed dating partner, premarital sex when not in a committed relationship, and extradyadic premarital sex. Since participants may be learning the sexual scripts they will take into marriage, involvement in these different types of premarital sexual activity may have differential impact on the likelihood of later extramarital involvement.

Therefore, it is important to examine extradyadic relations during courtship. Such study is also important because jealousy over the involvement of one's partner with another man or woman is a major spark of courtship violence (Makepeace, 1981).

Since religiosity is negatively related to both extramarital permissiveness (Glenn & Weaver, 1979; Medora & Burton, 1981; Singh et al., 1976; Weis & Jurich, 1985) and general sexual experience (Curran, Neff, & Lippold, 1973; Mahoney, 1980), I hypothesized that it would also be negatively associated with extradyadic relations during courtship.

Although many factors can cause inconsistency between attitudes and behavior (Fishbein & Ajzen, 1975), both orientation toward sexual expression and approval of extradyadic relations (permissiveness) may be associated with extradyadic behavior. Orientation toward sexual expression can be thought of as a continuum of sexual attitudes (Hudson, Murphy, & Nurius, 1983). At one end are those who feel that the expression of human sexuality should be open, free, and unrestrained, whereas those at the other end feel that sexual expression should be constrained and closely regulated. I hypothesized that more liberal sexual attitudes and extradyadic permissiveness are positively related to engaging in extradyadic relations.

Feminine sexuality has traditionally been conceptualized as passive, naive, and disinterested. An unmarried traditional woman learns either to deny sexual interests and desires and value virginity, or she links sex, love, and commitment. The modern view of female sexuality, however, stresses sexual interest, knowledge, assertiveness, and satisfaction. This view is more likely to predispose one to engage in extradyadic relations. Therefore, nontraditional gender-role orientation should be positively associated with extradyadic behavior for women. Since gender-role changes have not involved a reconceptualization of male sexuality to the extent that they have for female sexuality, I hypothesized no relationship between gender-role orientation and extradyadic relations for men.

Finally, the length of time one has been dating should be associated with extradyadic relations. Those who have had more dating experiences have simply had more opportunities to engage in such relations.

Method

Sample and Data Collection

Subjects were recruited from several sociology classes at a medium-sized southern university. They were told that the purpose of the research project was to study dating, sexuality, and gender roles among college students and that participation was voluntary. Of 245 people attending the classes, only one refused to participate. The anonymous questionnaires took approximately 20 minutes to complete and were administered during regular class periods. Since some dating couples take classes together, men and women were seated separately. Only data from subjects who had ever been in a committed dating relationship were analyzed. This resulted in a final sample of 215 respondents (93 men and 122 women). The mean age of subjects was 20.8 years. Most (80.9%) were White, and 85.6% had never been married.

Measures

Extradyadic relations were measured by asking subjects, "While in a committed dating relationship, have you ever engaged in the following with someone other then your dating partner?" Erotic kissing, petting,[1] and sexual intercourse were listed. Subjects responded either *yes* (scored 1) or *no* (scored 0) for each. An extradyadic relations score was computed by summing the three scores. This Guttman-type scale of extradyadic relations had a coefficient of reproducibility of .98.

Subjects who had engaged in any extradyadic behavior were asked if their dating partner knew they had sexual contact with someone else. If they had engaged in extradyadic sexual relations during more than one committed relationship, subjects were instructed to answer for the most recent relationship during which it occurred. Subjects were also asked if they had ever had a committed partner who engaged in erotic kissing, petting, or intercourse with someone else. Finally, they were asked about the impact of their own and their partner's extradyadic relations on their own dating relationship.

Religiosity was measured using two items. One asked subjects to indicate the influence of religion on their lives and was followed by five responses which ranged from *none* to *great*. The second item asked how often subjects attend church services, with response options from *never* to *once a week*. Both items were scored from 1 to 5 so that high scores indicated greater religiosity. Each subject's religiosity score was the total.

Sexual attitude was assessed by the 25-item scale developed by Hudson et al. (1983). The scale measures the extent to which an individual adheres to a liberal or a conservative orientation toward sexual expression. A 5-point, Likert-type response format was used, with the most liberal response being scored 5. Each subject's score was the total for the 25 items. The alpha reliability coefficient was .88.

Extradyadic permissiveness was determined by six items patterned after Reiss' extramarital permissiveness scale (Reiss & Miller, 1979). The first item stated, "It is acceptable for a male in a committed dating relationship to engage in erotic kissing with someone other than his dating partner." Two other items substituted "petting" and "full sexual intercourse" for "erotic kissing." The remaining three items asked about the same three sexual activities but substituted "female" for "male" and "her" for "his." A 5-point, Likert-type response format was used, with the most permissive response being scored 5. Each subject's extradyadic permissiveness score was the total for all six items. The alpha reliability coefficient was .93.[2]

[1]Subjects were informed. "Petting means sexually stimulating behavior more intimate then erotic kissing and simple hugging, but not including full sexual intercourse."

[2]The possibility was considered of treating extradyadic permissiveness for men and extradyadic permissiveness for women as two separate variables. Difference of means tests indicated that neither male nor female subjects scored significantly different on the items pertaining to men than they did on those pertaining to women. Since there is no indication of a double standard, all items were combined into one scale.

Gender-role orientation was assessed by 10 items from Brogan and Kutner's (1976) scale. The items were those with the highest item/total correlations as reported by Brogan and Kutner. A 5-point, Likert-type response format was used, with the most modern (nontraditional) response being scored 5. Each subject's score was the total for the 10 items. The alpha coefficient was .86.

TABLE 15.1. Frequency Distribution of Responses to Items Pertaining to Sexual Behavior for Men and Women

Item	Men (%)	Women (%)	χ^2
Erotic kissing with dating partner	(*n* = 91)	(*n* = 119)	
Yes	95.6	98.3	0.57
No	4.4	1.7	
Petting with dating partner	(*n* = 90)	(*n* = 118)	
Yes	94.4	88.1	1.75
No	5.6	11.9	
Intercourse with dating partner	(*n* = 90)	(*n* = 117)	
Yes	71.1	70.1	0.99
No	28.9	29.9	
Extradyadic erotic kissing	(*n* = 92)	(*n* = 119)	
Yes	65.2	39.5	12.72*
No	34.8	60.5	
Extradyadic petting	(*n* = 92)	(*n* = 119)	
Yes	46.7	18.5	18.16*
No	53.3	81.5	
Extradyadic intercourse	(*n* = 91)	(*n* = 118)	
Yes	35.2	11.9	14.92*
No	64.8	88.1	
Partner engaged in extradyadic erotic kissing	(*n* = 92)	(*n* = 117)	
Yes	43.5	42.7	0.00
No	56.5	57.3	
Partner engaged in extradyadic petting	(*n* = 89)	(*n* = 116)	
Yes	24.7	25.9	0.00
No	75.3	74.1	
Partner engaged in extradyadic intercourse	(*n* = 87)	(*n* = 117)	
Yes	12.6	21.4	2.05
No	87.4	78.6	
Partner know about extradyadic relations (most recent relationship during which it occurred)	(*n* = 53)	(*n* = 49)	
Certain knows	30.0	38.8	1.79
Fairly sure knows	11.7	6.1	
Not sure	10.0	10.2	
Fairly sure does not know	18.3	14.3	
Certain does not know	30.0	30.6	
Effect of own extradyadic relations on quality of dating relationship (most recent relationship during which it occurred)	(*n* = 53)	(*n* = 49)	
Improved a great deal	7.6	12.2	1.40
Improved somewhat	17.0	14.3	
Did not affect	35.9	32.7	
Hurt somewhat	30.2	26.5	
Hurt a great deal	9.3	14.3	
Effect of partner's extradyadic relations on quality of dating relationship (most recent relationship during which it occurred)	(*n* = 40)	(*n* = 50)	
Improved a great deal	2.5	4.0	2.36
Improved somewhat	5.0	8.0	
Did not affect	15.0	16.0	
Hurt somewhat	32.5	42.0	
Hurt a great deal	15.0	30.0	

Years dating was determined by asking subjects their age and the age they began to date. Years dating was the difference between the two. Since the difference between current age and the age one began to date would be meaningless for married subjects, this variable was calculated only for never-married subjects.

Results

Descriptive Analysis

Saunders and Edwards (1984) conclude that one should differentiate explicitly between men and women in any research having to do with extramarital permissiveness. Since this should also apply to extradyadic relations during courtship, hypothesized relationships were examined for men and women separately.

Frequency distributions of responses to extradyadic sexual behavior items are presented in Table 15.1. In order to have a point of comparison for extradyadic behavior, the frequency of engaging in erotic kissing, petting, and intercourse with one's committed dating partner are also included. As expected for a college-age sample, a large majority of subjects were sexually active with their dating partners. The sexual behavior of men and women in committed relationships did not differ significantly.

A substantial proportion of men had engaged in each type of extradyadic activity. Although significantly fewer women than men had engaged in extradyadic activities, the numbers are far from inconsequential. Approximately the same portion of subjects felt that their partner knew of their extradyadic behavior as felt that their partner did not know. When asked how their extradyadic behavior affected the quality of their dating relationship, more subjects thought it had hurt than improved the relationship; approximately a third believed that it had no effect.

More than two in five men and women knew that a committed dating partner had engaged in extradyadic erotic kissing. More than one in eight men and one in five women knew that a committed dating partner had engaged in extradyadic intercourse. A large majority felt that it had hurt the quality of their dating relationship.

In order to examine the relative impact of subjects' own versus partners' extradyadic relations on dating relationships, responses from subjects who both had themselves engaged in extradyadic and had a partner who had also done so were examined. These subjects thought that their partner's extradyadic behavior had hurt their dating relationship more than their own behavior had. This was the case for both men, $t(31) = -3.90, p < .001$, and women, $t(31) = -4.06, p < .001$.

Test of Hypothesized Relations

Correlation coefficients between predictor variables and extradyadic relations are presented in Table 15.2.[3] Extradyadic permissiveness and years dating are positively related to extradyadic relations for men. The relationship between religiosity and extradyadic relations is not significant.

[3]Being married can influence predictor variables such as sexual attitude and gender-role orientation. Since married or formerly married subjects were questioned not about their current attitudes but about behavior which occurred prior to marriage, further analysis was confined to never-married subjects. Since it is recommended for the regression analysis which follows, listwise deletion of missing data was also employed. These two procedures reduced the sample used in both the correlational and regression analyses.

TABLE 15.2. Zero-Order Correlations, Means, and Standard Deviations of Measures Included in the Analysis

	1.	2.	3.	4.	5.	6.	*M*	*SD*
1. Religiosity	—	−0.55***	−0.03	−0.30**	−0.10	−0.19	7.04	1.96
2. Sexual attitude	−0.36***	—	0.12	0.46***	0.22*	0.12	85.70	13.83
3. Extradyadic permissiveness	−0.08	0.19*	—	−0.11	0.16	0.48***	10.41	4.19
4. Gender-role orientation	−0.23**	0.43***	0.18*	—	0.23*	−0.02	30.21	7.46
5. Years dating	−0.24**	0.14	0.19*	0.11	—	0.33**	5.70	2.65
6. Extradyadic relations	−0.20*	0.25**	0.23*	0.18*	0.13	—	1.45	1.26
M	7.48	82.47	8.06	37.30	4.31	0.73		
SD	1.89	13.20	2.86	6.87	1.79	1.02		

Note. Men above the diagonal, women below the diagonal.
$^*p < .05$. $^{**}p < .01$. $^{***}p < .001$.

TABLE 15.3. Multiple Regression of Extradyadic Relations on Predictor Variables

	Men		
	Multiple R	R^2	Beta
Extradyadic permissiveness	.483	.233	.434
Years dating	.547	.300	.269
Religiosity	.567	.321	−.201
Sexual attitude	.572	.327	−.070
Gender-role orientation	.574	.330	−.057
	Women		
	Multiple R	R^2	Beta
Sexual attitude	.252	.064	.150
Extradyadic permissiveness	.311	.097	.171
Religiosity	.331	.110	−.105
Gender-role orientation	.335	.112	.057
Years dating	.338	.114	.048

Sexual attitude is not related to extradyadic relations.

Four of the five predicted relationships were supported for women. Extradyadic relations was negatively related to religiosity and positively related to liberal sexual attitude, extradyadic permissiveness, and nontraditional gender-role orientation. It was not related to years dating.

Multivariate Analysis

Results of a stepwise regression for both the male and female samples are presented in Table 15.3.[4] The variables accounted for 33.0% of the variance in extradyadic relations for men: Extradyadic permissiveness was the best predictor. The two variables with significant correlations with extradyadic relations (extradyadic permissiveness and years dating) accounted for 30.0% of the variance.

For women, the variables accounted for 11.4% of the variance, with sexual attitude being the best predictor. The four variables with significant correlations with extradyadic relations (religiosity, sexual attitude, extradyadic permissiveness, and gender-role orientation) accounted for 11.2% of the variance.

Discussion

Results for this sample of college students indicate that extradyadic relations during courtship are prevalent. If one considers either engaging in extradyadic relations or knowing that a committed dating partner has engaged in such relations as constituting direct experience, 70.9% of the men and 57.4% of the women in this study have had experience with some type of extradyadic relations. Most of these subjects had never been married. Many who have not experienced extradyadic relations may still do so before marrying. Instead of simply examining the relationship between general premarital sexual permissiveness or behavior and extramarital sexual behavior, future work should consider the differential impact of various types of experiences with extradyadic relations during courtship on extramarital relations.

In contrast to sexual behavior within committed dating relationships where no sex differences were found, more men than women had engaged in extradyadic behavior. For this sample, it appears that the traditional gap between male and female premarital sexual behavior is disappearing far more rapidly within the context of committed, intimate relations than outside such relations.

Even though a large proportion of subjects had experienced extradyadic relations, no evidence was found of widespread acceptance of them. Although men scored higher on extradyadic permissiveness

[4]Stepwise regression, which allows the variable that explains the most remaining criterion variance to enter the equation at each step, was used since there was no theoretical rationale for dictating the order of entry into the regression equations. Since no attempt was made to reduce the regression equation to the best *n* predictors, SPSS (Nie, Hull, Jenkins, Steinbrenner, & Bent, 1975) default values for the criteria for inclusion of variables were used. These values place little restriction on a stepwise regression.

than women, they can be described as moderately opposed to extradyadic relations; women were strongly opposed. In light of the sex differences in extradyadic behavior, it is noteworthy that no evidence was found of a double standard on the attitudinal level. Neither sex found extradyadic relations significantly more acceptable for men than for women.

The perception that the partner's extradyadic behavior was more harmful to the relationship than their own may be due to subjects being unwilling to acknowledge the negative impact of their own extradyadic relations or to the fact that the extradyadic behavior of some subjects may have been secretive, whereas all the subjects knew about their partners' extradyadic relations.

Although there is little evidence to suggest that extramarital sexual permissiveness predicts behaviors (Thompson, 1983), I found that extradyadic permissiveness is the best predictor of extradyadic relations during courtship for men. Permissiveness alone explains 23.3% of the variance in extradyadic relations. From these data it is impossible to determine the causal ordering of the two variables. Extradyadic permissiveness may indeed predispose one to engage in extradyadic relations. On the other hand, one may become more permissive after engaging in extradyadic relations. Years dating is also related to extradyadic relations for men. This indicates that greater experience and opportunity increase the chances that men will engage in extradyadic relations.

The variables included in the analysis explained less of the variance in extradyadic relations for women than for men (11.4% vs. 33.0%). It may be that college women are still operating according to a sexual script that includes passivity, particularly in the extradyadic area. If men are taking the lead in initiating their extradyadic relations and women are relatively passive in theirs, it is not surprising that attitudinal variables like permissiveness are less predictive of female than of male extradyadic relations. Extradyadic relations during courtship may be something that happens to women rather than something they consciously initiate.

Studies of extramarital relations have found that it is associated with low ratings of marital happiness (Bell, Turner, & Rosen, 1975) and being in inequitable/underbenefited relationships (Walster, Traupman, & Walster, 1978). Researchers should examine whether relationship quality also affects extradyadic relations during courtship. They should also consider how long individuals are in their dating relationships before extradyadic behavior occurs, how often they see their dating partners, how frequently extradyadic behavior occurs, and the impact of extradyadic relations upon both the individuals involved and their dating relationships.

REFERENCES

Athanasiou, R., & Sarkin, R. (1974). Premarital sexual behavior and postmarital adjustment. *Archives of Sexual Behavior, 3,* 207–225.

Bell, R. R., Turner, S., & Rosen, L. (1975). A multivariate analysis of female extramarital coitus. *Journal of Marriage and the Family, 37,* 375–384.

Brogan, D., & Kutner, N. G. (1976). Measuring sex-role orientation: A normative approach. *Journal of Marriage and the Family, 311,* 31–40.

Bukstel, L. H., Roeder, G. D., Kilmann, P. R., Laughlin, J., & Sotile, W. M. (1978). Projected extramarital sexual involvement in unmarried college students. *Journal of Marriage and the Family, 40,* 337–340.

Buunk, B. (1980). Extramarital sex in the Netherlands: Motivation in social and marital context. *Alternative Lifestyles, 3,* 11–39.

Curran, J. P., Neff, S., & Lippold, S. (1973). Correlates of sexual experience among university students. *The Journal of Sex Research, 9,* 124–131.

Fishbein, M., & Ajzen, I. (1975). *Belief, attitude, intention and behavior: An introduction to theory and research.* Reading, MA: Addison-Wesley.

Glenn, N. D., & Weaver, C. N. (1979). Attitudes toward premarital, extramarital, and homosexual relations in the U.S. in the 1970s. *The Journal of Sex Research, 15,* 108–118.

Hudson, W. W., Murphy, G. J., & Nurius, P. S. (1983). A short-form scale to measure liberal vs. conservative orientations toward human sexual expression. *The Journal of Sex Research, 19,* 258–272.

Kinsey, A. C., Pomeroy, W. B., Martin, C. E., & Gebhard, P. H. (1953). *Sexual behavior in the human female.* Philadelphia: Saunders.

Mahoney, E. R. (1980). Religiosity and sexual behavior among heterosexual college students. *The Journal of Sex Research, 16,* 97–113.

Makepeace, J. M. (1981). Courtship violence among college students. *Family Relations, 30,* 97–102.

Medora, N. P., & Burton, M. M. (1981). Extramarital sexual attitudes and norms of an undergraduate student population. *Adolescence, 16,* 251-262.

Nie, N. H., Hull, C. H., Jenkins, J. C., Steinbrenner, K., & Bent, D. H. (1975). *SPSS: Statistical package for the social sciences* (2nd ed.). New York: McGraw-Hill.

Reiss, I. L., Anderson, R. E., & Sponaugle, G. C. (1980). A multivariate model of the determinants of extramarital sexual permissiveness. *Journal of Marriage and the Family, 42,* 395–411.

Reiss, I. L., & Miller, B. C. (1979). Heterosexual permissiveness: A theoretical analysis. In W. R. Burr, R. Hill, F. I. Nye, & I. L. Reiss (Eds.), *Contemporary theories about the family* (Vol. 1, pp. 57–100). New York: Free Press.

Saunders, J. M., & Edwards, J. N. (1984). Extramarital sexuality: A predictive model of permissive attitudes. *Journal of Marriage and the Family, 46,* 825–835.

Singh, B. K., Walton, B. L., & Williams, J. S. (1976). Extramarital sexual permissiveness: Conditions and contingencies. *Journal of Marriage and the Family, 38,* 701–712.

Thompson, A. P. (1983). Extramarital sex: A review of the research literature. *The Journal of Sex Research, 19,* 1–22.

Thompson, A. P. (1984). Emotional and sexual components of extramarital relations. *Journal of Marriage and the Family, 46,* 35–42.

Walster, E., Traupman, J., & Walster, C. W. (1978). Equity and extramarital sexuality. *Archives of Sexual Behavior, 7,* 127–142.

Weis, D. L., & Jurich, J. (1985). Size of community of residence as a predictor of attitudes toward extramarital sexual relations. *Journal of Marriage and the Family, 47,* 173–178.

INTRODUCTION TO PART 8

Paraphilias

Although most sex acts are restricted to a fairly uniform set of activities, some people's sexual tastes take radically different forms. These unusual preferences have sometimes been stigmatized as "perversions," although more recently many researchers have adopted the more neutral term "paraphilias."

The causes of these unusual preferences remain shrouded in mystery. Many people seem to have discovered them early in childhood, although we still do not know whether that indicates the importance of childhood experiences or simply some inborn, genetic pattern that manifests itself early in life. They are quite resistant to change. Most paraphilias are more common in men than in women, but researchers do not know why men are more prone to adopt these unusual patterns.

Even the proper value judgments remain debatable. Some sexual inclinations seem harmless, others cause problems only to the people who have them, and others may affect multiple people and possibly in adverse ways. Should people with unusual tastes, or at least the ones who do not harm or inconvenience anyone but themselves, be tolerated with indulgence, be referred sympathetically to therapy that seeks to change them, or be condemned as sinners? Are people with such tastes "sick"? One wise solution was put forward by Sigmund Freud, who suggested that the label "perversion" (in its negative, pejorative sense) should be used if the person is unable to enjoy sex without it, but that the unusual sexual preference should be tolerated and accepted so long as it does not become indispensable to the person's sex life. In plain terms, it is OK to like spanking or have a "thing" for latex or rubber, as long as you can also enjoy sex without it, but you should worry about yourself if you start finding that you cannot experience arousal or orgasm any other way.

The one paper in this section addresses one of the most common paraphilias, namely masochism. Baumeister (1988a) drew on social psychology's theories about self-awareness to suggest that masochism is centrally concerned with allowing a person to escape awareness of self. In subsequent work, Baumeister (1991) concluded that many other activities are likewise attempts to escape from the self, including meditation, suicide, alcohol consumption, and binge eating. He also concluded that masochism itself seems relatively harmless. Unlike most sexual variations, masochism appears to be culturally and historically relative, being found mainly in the modern West and Japan. Masochism is thus more likely than other patterns of sexual behavior to be caused mainly by social and cultural factors.

Gender differences in masochism were addressed in a later paper by the same author. Baumeister (1988b) concluded that men and women have on average somewhat divergent tastes in their masochistic activities. Female masochism emphasizes mild pain, role-playing, and the embarrassment of being put on display naked for others to see. Male masochism emphasizes more severe pain, bondage, and degrading forms of humiliation (such as being treated like a dog). Men are more likely than women to engage in masochistic activity, although subsequent work has concluded that women are more likely than men to have masochistic fantasies and desires (Leitenberg & Henning, 1995). Neither gender is inherently "masochistic," however.

REFERENCES

Baumeister, R. F. (1988a). Masochism as escape from self. *Journal of Sex Research, 25,* 28–59. Uses social psychology's self-awareness theory to explain sexual masochism.

Baumeister, R. F. (1988b). Gender differences in masochistic scripts. *Journal of Sex Research, 25,* 478–499.

Baumeister, R. F. (1991). *Escaping the self: Alcoholism, spirituality, masochism, and other flights from the burden of selfhood.* New York: Basic Books.

Leitenberg, H., & Henning, K. (1995). Sexual fantasy. *Psychological Bulletin, 117,* 469–496.

Discussion Questions

1. Why do you think masochism has mainly been found in modern, Western cultures?
2. Many people have never tried masochism. What proportion do you think would enjoy it if they did ever give it a try?
3. Why do you think some people start off enjoying the masochistic, submissive role but then switch to begin preferring the dominant role?
4. Do you think sadomasochistic activities are more common or less common in homosexual relationships, as opposed to heterosexual ones? Why?
5. Are there any other sexual variations that might be explained on the basis of escape from self-awareness?

Suggested Readings

Baumeister, R. F. (1988). Gender differences in masochistic scripts. *Journal of Sex Research, 25,* 478–499. This article is a companion to the one in the reader. It describes the differences between male and female masochists.

Bullough, V. L. (1976). *Sexual variance in society and history.* Chicago, IL: University of Chicago Press. One of the most highly respected scholars on sexual history provides a fascinating tour through the history of sexual variations.

Laws, D. R., & O'Donohue, W. (1997). *Sexual deviance: Theory, assessment, and treatment*. This handbook is an excellent reference work on sexual deviance. It offers chapters dealing with many sexual variations, contributed by a broad assortment of experts in the field.

Scott, G. G. (1983). *Erotic power: An exploration of dominance and submission*. Secaucus, NJ: Citadel Press. This important and entertaining work describes the author's years of participant observation research on sadomasochism. The author joined S&M clubs, studied the providers of sexual services for pay, and pursued other experiences to offer a rich, insider's view of the world of sadomasochistic sexuality.

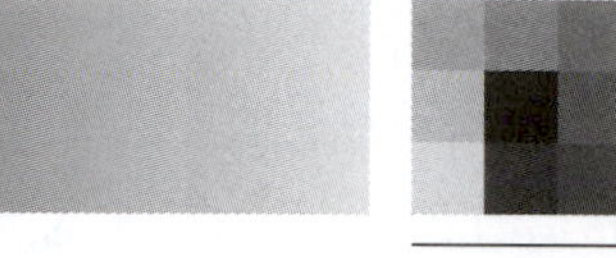

READING 16

Masochism as Escape from Self

Roy F. Baumeister • Case Western Reserve University

Recent theoretical advances from social psychology, especially self-awareness theory and action identification theory, are here applied to masochism. It is possible to consider masochism as neither a form of self-destruction nor a derivative of sadism. Instead, masochism may be a means of escaping from high-level awareness of self as a symbolically mediated, temporally extended identity. Such awareness is replaced by focus on the immediate present and on bodily sensations, and sometimes by a low-level awareness of self as an object. Evidence is reviewed indicating that the principal features of masochism (pain, bondage, and humiliation) help accomplish this hypothesized escape from high-level self-awareness. Historical evidence suggests that sexual masochism proliferated when Western culture became highly individualistic. This could mean that cultural emphasis on the autonomous, individual self increased the burdensome pressure of selfhood, leading to greater desires to escape from self masochistically.

The purpose of this manuscript is to articulate a new theory about masochism based on recent theoretical advances in social psychology, especially action identification theory (Vallacher & Wegner, 1985, 1986), levels of thinking (Pennebaker, 1985; Pennebaker, Hughes & O'Heeron, 1987; Pennebaker et al., 1986) and self-awareness theory (Carver, 1979; Carver & Sheier, 1981; Duval & Wicklund, 1972; Hull & Levy, 1979; Wicklund, 1975a). Weinberg's (1987) recent excellent review of the sociological literature on masochism cites the need for new theoretical work on the topic, and this paper is one response to that call. Strictly speaking, the present theory is offered as a companion rather than a rival to past views. Past theories have used models and concepts of psychopathology to account for masochistic activity among clinically deviant individuals, whereas the present paper attempts to use models and concepts of social psychology to explain masochism among normal, nonclinical people.

The central idea is that masochism is essentially an attempt to escape from self, in the sense of achieving a loss of high-level self-awareness. More precisely, awareness of self as a symbolic, schematic, choosing entity is removed and replaced with a low-level awareness of self as a physical body and locus of immediate sensations, or with a new identity with transformed symbolic meaning. Masochism may therefore be classed with physical exercise, intoxication, meditative techniques, and perhaps even being a fan or spectator, all of which facilitate escape from normal self-awareness. Masochism may differ from these in being an unusually powerful form of escape and in its link to sexual pleasure.

Why would anyone in today's self-seeking society want to escape from self? It is plausible that high-level self-awareness can lead to anxiety and discomfort under some circumstances. The requirements of making decisions under pressure or uncertainty of taking responsibility for actions that may disappoint or harm others, of maintaining a favorable public and private image of self despite all threats and challenges, and of asserting control over a recalcitrant social environment can become oppressive and stressful and can foster desires to escape. This burden of selfhood can be used to explain and predict the selective appeal of masochism. Additionally, masochism can serve as an effective deterrent to unwanted thoughts and feelings, perhaps especially feelings of guilt, anxiety, or insecurity.

Although the term "masochism" was coined to refer to a pattern of sexual behavior, it has been commonly used in a more generalized sense to describe nonsexual activities as well (e.g., Freud, 1938; see also Cowan, 1982; Franklin, 1987; Panken, 1983; Shainess, 1984). Such generalizations, however, will necessarily be inaccurate if they are based on a false understanding of the sexual behavior, which constitutes the original and prototypical masochism. Discussion of nonsexual masochism must be postponed until a proper understanding of purely sexual masochism is available.

Evidence

At present, *all* sources of empirical evidence concerning masochism have serious flaws. Probably the best approach currently viable is to look for converging patterns among the different sources of evidences, with clear awareness of the limitations and qualifications inherent in each type. The present work draws on survey data (e.g., Spengler, 1977), participant observation studies (e.g., Scott, 1983; Lee, 1983), firsthand reports by nonscientists (e.g., Greene & Greene, 1974), and historical patterns (e.g., Bullough, 1976a; Tannahill, 1980). In addition, I assembled a sample of anonymous letters to a sex-oriented magazine (*Variations*) reporting masochistic experiences.[1] These letters include some outright fantasies, presumably many real experiences embellished by fantasy, and perhaps some accurate reports of actual experiences. They cannot be regarded as behavioral self-reports, but they probably do embody the scripts and schemas that shape the masochistic imagination. Sampling biases include an editorial policy of deleting references to illegal activities and presumably a tendency for authors to report favorite experiences rather than disappointing or unpleasant ones (thus yielding a bias opposite to that in clinical observations, which overrepresent troubled and unhappy masochists; cf. Reik, 1941).

Once again, there is no source of empirical evidence about masochism that is free of flaws. Confirmation through converging evidence is necessary in order to obtain a reliable picture. Still, it will become apparent that the conclusions suggested by these letters are consistent with the implications of other empirical observations, so one may be cautiously confident that they are valid.

Psychopathology

Masochistic sexual practices have long been regarded as pathological. Freud (1938) described masochism as a perversion. Stekel (1953) linked masochism to cannibalism, criminality, vampirism, mass murder, necrophilia, epilepsy, pederasty, and the like. He actually said that all sadists (and therefore all masochists, who are all sadists in his view) are murderers, and in a temporary lapse of therapeutic fervor he described their company as the "kingdom of Hell" (Vol. II, p. 409). Reik said that all neurotics are masochists (1941, pp. 368–372). In DSM-III (American Psychiatric Association, 1980), masochism is listed as a psychosexual disorder. In short, clinical perspectives have regarded masochists as seriously disturbed.

Recent empirical studies furnish a surprisingly different picture. Empirical observers describe practicing masochists as remarkably normal, at least with respect to their nonsexual activities. Scott (1983) describes participants in the female-domination subculture groups on the West Coast as "better educated and from higher income and occupational brackets than the average American" (p. 6). Spengler's (1977) sample of German sadomasochists likewise portrays them as upper-class, successful individuals. Janus, Bess, and Saltus' (1977) well-known "sexual profile of men in power" found, to the researchers' extreme surprise, a high quantity of masochistic sexual activity among successful politicians and other powerful figures. Prostitutes catering to such clients administered more sexual domination than any other sexual service or act.

As argued earlier, clinical samples are likely to

[1]Interrater agreement was .933, based on a subsample of letters. Discrepancies were caused by simple oversights, differential interpretation of scoring rules, and ambiguity of some letters. Brief discussion raised agreement to 100%.

be the least well adjusted of masochists. Even so, some clinical observers have found masochists to be relatively normal. Cowan (1982) describes her masochistic therapy patients as "successful by social standards: professionally, sexually, emotionally, culturally, in marriage or out. They are frequently individuals of admirable inner strength of character, possessed of strong 'coping egos' and with an ethical sense of individual responsibility" (p. 31). Even Stekel (1953) says that "masochists represent often ideal whole men" (p. 51).

Thus, whether sexual masochism is pathological depends on whether one accepts the sexual practices per se as symptoms. If one defines the fact of masochistic sex as sufficient evidence of pathology, then (obviously) these people are sick. If one does not judge the sexual patterns alone, then the majority of these people appear normal and healthy. It appears that participating in sadomasochistic sex practices is compatible with an otherwise normal, sane, and even successful life.

If masochism does occur among nonclinical populations, then it is an appropriate topic for study by social psychologists. Theories based on clinical populations, although presumably quite valid for clinical populations, may not apply to nonclinical populations, for the appeal of these deviant sexual activities could well differ between normal and mentally ill individuals. The purpose of this paper is to use models and findings of social psychology to delineate a way of understanding masochism without invoking psychopathology or irrationality.

Primacy of Masochism

The prevailing theoretical position since Freud (1938) has been that masochism is derived from sadism. In clinical samples, sadism may perhaps be the main attraction, for it is plausible that the mentally ill are drawn to inflicting cruelty more than to receiving it. Most theorists (e.g., Stekel, 1953) have assumed a strong link between sadism and masochism and have emphasized sadism, because it is presumably the more important and fundamental pattern.

Abundant evidence contradicts this view, at least among normals. In the first place, masochism is apparently far more common than sadism. In the present sample of letters, there were far more written by submissives (158) than by dominants (64). (An additional few described episodes in which the partners exchanged roles.) An independent sample of writings on lesbian sadomasochism likewise included a predominance of writings from the submissive perspective: three dominant and 11 submissive (also two in third person and five with role exchange) (Samois, 1982). Friday (1980) has devoted much of her journalistic career to collecting sexual fantasies, and she notes that masochistic fantasies outnumber sadistic ones by about four to one (p. 485). Xaviera Hollander, media spokesperson for prostitutes, claims that roughly 90% of the clients who purchase sadomasochistic services preferred the submissive role (Greene & Greene, 1974). Janus, Bess, and Saltus (1977) reported that among prostitutes catering to rich and powerful clients in Washington, D.C., requests to be beaten outnumbered requests to inflict beatings about eight to one. Scott (1983) reports that membership in West Coast S&M clubs showed a preponderance of submissives, ranging from double to quadruple. She also records that a common pattern in couples occurs when one partner wants to submit masochistically but the other partner is reluctant to take the dominant role. The reverse pattern, in which one partner wants to dominate but the other is reluctant to submit, apparently is quite rare. The only study that failed to find a hefty majority of submissives was one done by mail in Germany, which found about equal numbers (Spengler, 1977).

Further evidence for the primacy of masochism comes from Kamel's (1983) study of participation in the sadomasochistic subculture among male homosexuals. He found that nearly all participants began as submissives, and some later took on the dominant role. This pattern is confirmed by Lee (1983) for male homosexuals, by Scott (1983) for heterosexuals, and by Califia (1983) for lesbians. Thus, behavioral evidence suggests that masochism comes first, and sadistic or dominant role-taking comes only later if at all. If masochism always precedes sadism, it is implausible to argue that masochism is derived from sadism. Rather, sadism must be the secondary, derivative pattern.

In short, the weight of empirical evidence does not support the argument that masochism is derived from sadism. It seems possible that masochism often occurs without any clear sadistic aspect or motivation. When sadism and masochism are both in evidence, masochism appears to come first. Thus, masochism is more common and more fundamental than sadism, and it deserves primary emphasis in theoretical treatments.

Masochism as Self-Destructiveness

Many attempts to generalize masochism to nonsexual behavior have taken self-destructive intentions as the defining feature of masochism (e.g., Franklin, 1987; Lewin, 1980; Shainess, 1984; Stekel, 1953). In that view, masochism is fundamentally the desire for harm to self. It is quite apparent that masochists seek pain, and pain serves as a biological warning of harm or injury. In experience, pain and injury are highly correlated, so one may ask whether it is the pain or the injury that is the masochist's primary desire.

Recent evidence suggests that masochists do not seek failure, harm, or, injury. It appears that masochists persistently seek pain but carefully avoid injury. Rubin (1982) reports that dominant partners in sadomasochistic subcultures compete to be the safest. Other observers report that any person who injures a partner during sadomasochistic sex is avoided by other potential lovers (e.g., Kamel, 1980; Scott, 1983). Scott's (1983) account of West Coast sadomasochists emphasizes that their pursuit of pain was accompanied by extreme care to avoid any sort of harm. Manuals and workshops explaining how to perform sadomasochistic sex have as their main theme instruction in how to inflict pain without causing injury (e.g., Bellwether, 1982; also see Greene & Greene, 1974).

It appears plausible, therefore, that masochism does not involve seeking harm to self.[2] Pain is often sought, but injury is widely and carefully avoided. The evidence of the frequently successful and competent nature of masochists' daily lives suggests that masochistic sexuality has no correlate of self-defeating conduct in everyday life, although evidence on this is not conclusive. Another reason to doubt that explanation of masochism as self-destructiveness is the fact that decades of behavioral research with normal individuals have failed to yield any clear evidence of deliberate self-destructive tendencies or motivations (Baumeister & Scher, 1988).

Important consequences follow from recognizing that masochism is not normally self-destructive. The masochist's quest for pain must be understood as arising from motives other than the desire for harm and injury. Moreover, the recent controversy over whether perennial victims or abused wives are masochistic (e.g., Caplan, 1984; Franklin, 1987) can easily be resolved in the negative, for as soon as there is evidence of injury then it is no longer appropriate to speak of masochism. Battered wives should not be mistaken for sexual masochists.

Self and the Paradox of Masochism

Although at present no single, unified theory of self is available, several generalizations can be made based on a substantial body of research. Most psychological theorists would probably agree that the self develops originally to facilitate the organism's quest for happiness and avoidance of suffering. In order to accomplish these goals, the self is oriented toward controlling the environment. Indeed, the self seeks both to control the environment and to perceive itself as having control. Lastly, the self desires to maintain a positive evaluation, both in its view of self and in others' perception. People desire to avoid loss of esteem and they desire to increase esteem, both publicly and privately.

In the context of current theory about the self, then, masochism presents a challenging paradox. Whereas the self seeks to avoid pain, masochists seek pain. Whereas the self strives for control, masochists relinquish control. Whereas the self seeks to maintain and increase esteem, masochists seek humiliation.

My central argument is that this paradox is not misleading; rather, it indicates the essential nature of masochism. Masochism represents a systematic attempt to eradicate (temporarily) the main features of the self. The self as active agent who makes choices and takes initiative, and the self as evaluatively toned concept, are eliminated in masochism.

---

[2]It must be acknowledged that some psychodynamic approaches emphasize symbolic self-destruction rather than actual physical harm. Evidence reported here denies that masochists seek actual harm to self, but it is difficult or impossible to evaluate the hypothesis that they unconsciously desire subtle, vague, possible disadvantages. As far as I can ascertain, the evidence that masochists (or others) desire subtle self-destruction consists of questionable interpretations of highly ambiguous actions. Research has failed to show harm to self as a primary goal or motive among nonclinical samples (Baumeister & Scher, 1988).

Burden of Selfhood

Why would people want to escape from self or remove awareness of self? It is plausible that the self can become burdensome and that self-awareness can therefore become aversive.

Aversiveness was one feature of the original theory of objective self-awareness (Duval & Wicklund, 1972). Subsequent research has suggested that sometimes people enjoy self-awareness, but there is ample evidence that people wish to escape and avoid self-awareness under some circumstances, such as after receiving an unfavorable evaluation (Duval & Wicklund, 1972), after finding out that they will probably be unable to improve or succeed on an important matter (Steenbarger & Aderman, 1979), after experiencing an interpersonal rejection or putdown (Gibbons & Wicklund, 1976), and after performing actions that contradict their personal attitudes (Greenberg & Musham, 1981). Wicklund (1975a) argued that people are generally unable to live up to their ideals and goals, so the desire to escape from self-awareness may be very common.

Desire to escape from self-awareness has been linked to alcohol use (e.g., Hull, 1981; Hull & Young, 1983; Hull, Young & Jouriles, 1986), as well as cigarette smoking (Wicklund, 1975b; see also Liebling, Seiler & Shaver, 1974). It is plausible that escape from self-awareness is an underlying goal in other recreational activities, including spectator sports, watching movies, and taking drugs.

Requirements for many choices and decisions entail a demand for autonomy and initiative that can be burdensome. Part of the impact of Brady's (1958) executive monkey experiment was the intuitive appeal that having to make many decisions was stressful. Although later studies suggested that Brady's results were confounded, Weiss (1971a) showed that having to make many responses was indeed a cause of stress. Other studies showed that exerting control becomes especially stressful under various conditions (Weiss, 1971b, 1971c). In short, subjects may generally prefer control, but exerting control has its psychological costs.

The potentially burdensome nature of pressures and responsibilities has been documented in a very different context by Spence and Sawin (1984). These researchers found that men's greatest complaint about the male role was occupational demands, particularly the pressures to be successful and the weight of responsibility. Pennebaker et al. (1986) showed that people who had control over a noise stressor thought at higher levels and experienced more negative affect than people who had no control. Thus, having control prevented people from escaping negative affect by shifting to lower levels of thinking.

A successful self in particular becomes the focus of others' high expectations, which can also be burdensome. Others' expectations for continued success can cause aversive, performance-inhibiting pressure (e.g., Baumeister, Hamilton, & Tice, 1985), leading to strategic and even potentially self-harmful behaviors to escape such pressures (Jones & Berglas, 1978). Trying to maintain a high level of personal esteem in the face of all challenges and threats can be difficult and wearisome. Indeed, aversive states of high self-awareness have been shown to cause individuals to desire relief so strongly that they ignore or accept risks, costs, and even harm to the self (Baumeister & Scher, 1988).

In short, there is ample empirical and theoretical precedent for the suggestion that some people may want to escape from self-awareness on occasion. Exerting responsibility and maintaining esteem may become emotionally draining, yet the self that is identified with agency and esteem cannot easily relinquish them. There may even be a cyclic escalation, in which the more responsibility and esteem the individual accumulates, the more difficult and exhausting it is to sustain them. Such a suggestion would explain why masochism was so popular among the most esteemed and powerful men studied by Janus et al. (1977). High levels of esteem and agency (or responsibility) produce the most complex and elaborate selves, which may also be the most burdensome selves. As a result, such individuals may seek the strongest modes of escape—such as masochism.

Levels of Selfhood

The central argument of this article is that masochism provides a powerful method of removing high-level, abstract self-awareness. An appreciation of different levels of selfhood is crucial to understanding the present view of masochism. Masochistic practices appear to thwart and conceal the higher levels of selfhood, while focusing attention on the lowest possible levels. This fits well with the preceding argument, for it is principally the high levels of selfhood that become burdensome.

Masochism seeks to escape the normal, familiar self, as defined in a symbolic, high-level, long-term manner. Two important ways of accomplishing this are to re-focus awareness on the self in a physical, low-level immediate manner, and to create a new, fantasized identity that is fundamentally different from the self that is escaped. To explain this point, it will be necessary to summarize some recent theoretical developments.

Action Identification and Self-awareness

Vallacher and Wegner (1985, 1986) have proposed a theory of action identification which emphasizes that the same action can be understood at different levels of abstraction and meaning. High levels involve symbolism, abstraction, and temporal extension (e.g., pursuing career ambitions); in contrast, low levels emphasize temporal and physical immediacy (e.g., muscle movements). These authors argue that people in general prefer to be aware of their acts in high-level terms. However, stress or failure motivates people to shift to lower levels in order to escape negative affect. Moreover, change of meaning is accomplished by dropping to a low level and then moving up to a new, different high-level identification.

Carver and Scheier (1981) have proposed a hierarchical model of self-awareness (also see Powers, 1973). One can be aware of oneself at various levels, again ranging from the long-term, abstract manner characteristic of high levels down to the immediate, concrete nature of low levels. Carver and Scheier suggest that failure or blockage at a high level causes self-awareness to shift to lower levels.

Combining these two views, one may suggest that one's ordinary identity involves a high-level awareness of self, using a broad perspective on one's activities. The person is aware of self as involved in various projects and relationships, with multiple ambitions, goals, responsibilities, and so forth. This definition extends far into the past and future, and it is highly symbolic and interpretive.

In contrast, it is possible to be aware of oneself at a low level, as a mere body experiencing sensations and movements. Symbolic interpretation is largely irrelevant to awareness of movement and sensation, and the temporal focus is on the immediate present, without clear connection to the past and future. The low-level emphasis on movement and sensation makes it an attractive escape from aversive emotion and from awareness of undesirable features of oneself (or of one's actions).

At this point, it will be useful to examine the principal masochistic practices to show how they deny or remove high-level self-awareness while promoting low-level self-awareness. The principal features of masochism can be covered under the headings of pain, loss of control, and humiliation.

Pain

Pain is not universal in masochistic experiences (e.g., Reik, 1941; Weinberg, 1987), but it is common. Among the letters in the present sample, pain was administered chiefly by spanking, paddling, or (typically mild) whipping, usually on the buttocks. A few letters referred to using clothespins or clamps to pinch the skin, and to slapping the face. Any other methods of inflicting pain (e.g., dripping hot wax from a candle onto the submissive's skin; Kamel, 1980) are apparently uncommon,

It is important to recognize that the doses of pain in masochistic sex seem to be carefully limited. There is a theoretical rumor, implicit in some masochistic fantasies, that intense pain becomes indistinguishable from pleasure. Even if true, this may be quite irrelevant to masochism, because masochists apparently take their pain in small doses. Masochistic pain is genuine pain, if generally not severe pain.

How much does the pain hurt? Reik (1941) noted that the pain is experienced as aversive by the masochist even during the experience. Moreover, masochists apparently dislike headaches and dental work as much as anyone else (e.g., Scott, 1983; Weinberg, Williams, & Moser, 1984). If the sensation of pain never becomes pleasant, then masochists presumably seek pain for something other than the sensation itself: either the *meaning* of the sensation or the *effects* of the sensation. The present focus is on the effects of the sensation on meaning.

Pain can facilitate escape from high-level self-awareness. Scarry's (1985) recent analysis proposes that the sensation of pain removes broader awareness of self and world. Using a sample of accounts of torture, Scarry argues that bodily pain supersedes the awareness of self as a symbolic being with interpersonal and ideological commitments. She notes that pain gradually obliterates psychological content, eventually leaving only the awareness of pain. One's knowledge of the world is temporarily forgotten, and attention is narrowed to the immediate present, both spatially and temporally. She says that pain destroys meaning, in the sense that pain banishes abstract meanings and symbols from awareness. A similar conclusion is reached from quite different sources by Goleman (1985), who uses clinical observations and physiological research to argue that pain effects a "dimming of attention."

One implication of Scarry's argument is that pain has great potential as a narcotic, in that it blots out higher-order thought and complex or symbolic self-awareness. She emphasizes that pain shrinks the world to the immediate temporal and spatial present; other places, other ideas, and other meanings of self cease to seem real. The main drawbacks to using pain as narcotic are that pain is inherently unpleasant and that pain usually comes with injury (which has practical consequences). But as argued earlier, masochists obtain pain without injury, and they seek carefully controlled doses of pain administered by an intimate partner, so the aversiveness is kept within acceptable bounds. There is also some evidence that many masochists emphasize the anticipation and suspense rather than the actual pain (Reik, 1941; Weinberg & Kamel, 1983). Either way, pain may be an effective means of removing unwanted thoughts and self-images from awareness. Califia (1983) expresses the effectiveness of the mere sight of a whip on a masochist: "A whip is a great way to get someone to be here now. They can't look away from it, and they can't think about anything else" (p. 134). Thus, masochists circumvent the drawbacks of pain, presumably enabling them to benefit from pain's narcotic effects.

On the other hand, pain undeniably focuses attention on the physical self, at least the body part where the pain is located (Scarry, 1985). Moreover, a standard philosophical argument emphasizes the incorrigibility of pain (i.e., it is impossible to be mistaken about being in pain), from which it may follow psychologically that pain furnishes the self with minimal proof of its existence (cf. Sartre, 1949). Thus, although pain obliterates broader, long-term, and symbolic aspects of self, it may contribute to a low-level awareness of oneself existing as a physical body.

To sum up: Masochistic pain may function as a technique for removing higher-level self-awareness, while promoting a low-level awareness of self as physical object.[3] Pain brings self-awareness down from symbolic identity to physical body.

Bondage

Many masochists report experiences of being bound or restrained in an impressive variety of ways. Many letters in the present sample went into extensive detail about each rope and knot used to restrain the masochist. Masochists described being restrained with ropes, scarves, neckties, stockings, handcuffs, blindfolds, gags, and more elaborate devices.

There is little mystery about the effects of bondage. Freedom of action and initiative are eliminated. The masochist is left completely helpless and is thereby required to be a fully passive participant in whatever activities the dominant partner chooses. Apparently, this situation of utter helplessness and vulnerability is tremendously appealing to many otherwise normal people.

It is reasonable to infer that the appeal of restraint is that the individual is freed from initiative and choice. One consequence is that the person is freed from responsibility for sex acts that might otherwise involve conflict. Thus, one masochistic lesbian suggested that being tied up removed guilt: " . . . it gives you a chance to be sexual without any responsibility for your sexy feelings . . . 'it's not my fault, Mommy.'" (Zoftig, 1982, pp. 88–89). More broadly, it is plausible that when people come to regard efficacy, control, and responsibility as burdensome, they may enjoy masochistic interludes of escape. Some findings are consistent with this speculation. Scott (1983) reports that among couples who exchange dominant and submissive roles, individuals prefer not to take the dominant role sexually if they have had a demanding day at work. Janus et al. (1977) report that powerful, successful men are especially drawn to masochistic sex. Still, this evidence is more suggestive than conclusive. Further research

[3]This is not to deny the symbolic functions of pain, as evidence of submission and possible love (e.g., Weinberg, 1987). The purely symbolic uses of pain are irrelevant to the present argument, but are not contradicted by it.

is needed to establish whether prolonged experiences of power, responsibility, or choice can lead generally to an aversive self-awareness or to a desire to be passive—and, specifically, to masochism.

Thus, the responsible, decision-making aspect of the self is prevented by bondage and blindfolding. An important feature of the self is denied at high levels. Is there any reason to think that this loss of control would foster *low* levels of awareness? Being tied up may conceivably promote low-level, immediate self-awareness by focusing attention on one's helplessness and vulnerability, although direct evidence for this point is lacking, Theoretical and empirical precedents exist for this argument. Carver and Scheier (1981) proposed that loss of high-level efficacy promotes low-level self-awareness, so bondage may foster low-level awareness in the masochist. Pennebaker et al. (1986) provide evidence that people move to lower levels of thinking when deprived of control; the low levels reduce both self-awareness and negative affect, which may explain the appeal of bondage as escape.

One sign of low-level agency comes from data on oral sex. Submissives typically perform oral sex on their dominant partners. Performance of oral sex by the submissive was modal in all categories of letters; the frequency of this activity reached 84% among letters written by female dominants. Indeed, submissives in this sample were three times as likely as dominants to perform oral sex, $chi^2(1) = 91.23$, $p < .001$. During oral sex, the (submissive) performer is active, while the dominant is passive. Although performing oral sex does not require high-level choice or abstract, complex thought, there is some degree of initiative involved in moving one's mouth and so forth. Thus, personal agency, while denied at high levels by masochistic bondage and obedience, is retained and even promoted at low levels of action identification. The focus is on pleasing and satisfying the partner, usually at the dominant partner's initiative, in a specific, immediate, limited fashion. The submissive ceases to be a responsible planner or decision-maker, becoming instead an active mouth.

Humiliation

The pursuit of humiliation is a major theme in masochism. Considerable effort and imagination go into devising humiliations to undergo. And, again, much of this effort and imagination is on the part of the masochist. Indeed, prostitutes report that many clients come with detailed, precise scripts for the prostitute to use in humiliating them (e.g., Juliette, 1983). Thus, it would be wrong to view the humiliation in sadomasochism as purely a product of the dominants' efforts to enforce their superior status, for masochists seem to desire these humiliating activities at least as much as their partners.

It seems likely that these humiliations temporarily render the maintenance of dignity and even identity impossible. Being dressed up in brassiere and panties, handcuffed to a bed, and spanked, afterwards licking a prostitute's feet or genitals, is simply incompatible with one's identity as a male U.S. Senator, for example (Janus et al., 1977). This may indeed form part of the appeal of such activities: Participating in them temporarily removes that identity. Likewise, the feminine fantasy of being displayed naked is probably contrary to normal practices. As Reik (1941) noted, women are brought up to be sexually modest, to prevent others from seeing their genitals or underwear. Lying naked on a table with one's legs spread, in a roomful of strangers, would thus be incompatible with the woman's normal self. Moreover, it emphasizes her bodily self as a sex object, instead of her symbolic and interpersonal self.

Perhaps the clearest evidence that humiliation denies identity is the standard assimilation of masochist to slave. Masochists frequently define themselves as slaves during their sex games; indeed, "slave" was the most common designation for the masochists in this sample, and nearly all sources report similar patterns. The inherent, fundamental meaning of slavery is loss of personhood. Slavery originated as a substitute for being killed in war, and it has always involved some form of *social death* symbolizing physical death (Patterson, 1982). The slave's identity is nullified, and slaves are treated as if they lack social rank or status, family ties, ideology, opinions, rights, ancestors, and so forth. In short, the predominant model of masochism is a condition (slavery) in which one's social identity is removed.

Yet, masochistic humiliation may also promote self-awareness at a low level of action identification. Humiliation provides embarrassment and is thus linked to self-awareness (Modigliani, 1968, 1971; Baumeister, 1982). Pain promotes awareness of one's body by forcing attention to sensations. Similarly, for a woman to display her nude genitals to others would focus attention on herself as a body, as an immediate object of sexual desire. As noted earlier, such display may run contrary to her normal self and behavior patterns. Thus, masochistic display replaces her ordinary identity with that of a set of genitals to be viewed and desired.

Use of mirrors or even audiences in S&M probably also intensifies the immediate, low-level awareness of self. Through the mirror or audience, the masochist's attention is drawn to his or her immediate condition and predicament. Mirrors and audiences are used to intensify embarrassment and humiliation. Such feelings can be regarded as an immediate focus on the present self. In an important sense, having a witness to one's degradation may facilitate the feeling that the normal identity has been removed and destroyed. One is seen as a slave, pet, or sex object; the witness confirms the loss of self by conferring social reality (Wicklund & Gollwitzer, 1982). If the male Senator in the above example were to desire an audience, it would not be for the sake of restoring his Senatorial identity, but rather for the sake of confirming the *negation* of that identity.

Summary of Escape Theory

To summarize the preceding discussion of masochistic practices: First, pain (including even the fantasy or threat of pain) blots out broader self-awareness, focusing the person narrowly on the here and now. Bondage makes it impossible for the self to exert initiative or control or to take responsibility for actions and decisions. Humiliation makes it impossible to sustain one's dignity and self-esteem and even one's social identity. (Emotional humiliation may, like pain, prevent certain types of higher cognitive activity, focusing the mind instead on the immediate circumstances.) Masochistic activity, in other words, is a concerted and multifaceted attack on the high-level aspects of the self. The self as a symbolic entity, extended in time, capable of planning and executing high-level action, and sustaining a certain level of self-worth and dignity, is systematically denied.

At the same time, awareness of self is focused on the lowest possible levels. Attention is drawn to the self as a body, as a locus of sensation, as a helpless and vulnerable being deprived of dignity and esteem, as a mere sex object or subhuman creature. Initiative is reduced to the level of moving one's mouth or limbs in response to external commands, and pride is reduced to the satisfaction of being a good slave. Self is reduced to the here-and-now bare minimum.

The present argument is that the movement to low levels is motivated by a desire to escape from the high levels of self-awareness. It is at high levels that selves become burdensome. (Indeed, if the low-level self is burdensome—for example, if the person is physically tired—he or she is not likely to be inclined toward masochistic indulgence; Scott, 1983.) Masochism is an escape *from* identity to body.

The shift to low levels of awareness has one further important consequence, however. Low levels facilitate transformation, fantasy, and the elaboration of new high-level identities (Vallacher & Wegner, 1985).

Transformation of Identity: The Ultimate Escape

Once the self is brought down to a low level, it is capable of being transformed (Vallacher & Wegner, 1985, 1986). Scarry (1985) likewise emphasizes the power of bodily pain for facilitating fictional, transforming interpretations. Pain makes reality malleable, in her view, and she supports her thesis with a compelling account of the fictionalization common to torture practices (e.g., pretext of interrogation, perversion of medical and legal functions). Insofar as masochistic practices involve pain and low levels of action identification, masochism may facilitate the acquisition (at least temporarily, or in fantasy) of new identities.

Becoming someone different is a further step in escape from self. Indeed, one could argue that changing one's identity is the ultimate fulfillment of masochistic desires to be rid of one's ordinary self: One *becomes someone else.* Becoming a full-time slave was a reasonably common ending among the present sample of letters (44%). In contrast, empirical observations of actual behavior show full-time slavery to be relatively uncommon, although it is frequently desired (e.g., Scott, 1983). The implication is that permanent transformation of one's normal identity is an important part of masochistic fantasy, although it is impractical in real life. People do not actually change their identities through sex games, but the masochistic desire to escape from self can fantasize identity change as a form of fulfillment.

The interest in display humiliation and in having audiences may be understood as connected with the transformation of self. Wicklund and Gollwitzer (1982; also Gollwitzer, 1986) have argued that the acquisition of identity requires *social reality*, that is, acknowledgement by others. The other people are apparently interchangeable to a large extent; in other words, it does not seem to matter who sees the person as having this identity, as long as someone does.

Evidence from the present sample is consistent with the hypothesis that masochists desire audiences to confer social reality on their identity transformations. First, it is obvious that the presence of an audience enhances humiliation. Secret humiliations are not effective, and embarrassments require audiences (e.g., Modigliani, 1971). Letters by submissives were twice as likely as letters by dominants to report the presence of additional people, constituting audiences, $chi^2(1, N = 219) = 6.50$, $p < .02$. It appears that audiences are of greater interest to submissives than to dominants; it is the masochists who want audiences.

On the other hand, as reported in the letters, it was generally the dominant partner who was acquainted with the audience. Dominant partners were reasonably well acquainted with the third parties in 79 (89%) of the 89 letters that reported audiences, whereas submissives were acquainted with the audience in only 19 (21%). The difference is significant, chi^2 (1, N = 178) = 81.73, $p < .001$. Thus, although it may be the masochists who desire the audiences, they desire audiences who are unknown to them. Neighbors, relatives, family, colleagues at work were only rarely mentioned as witnesses. To be sure, the stigma of masochistic sex would create practical drawbacks to having one's submission witnessed by acquaintances. Still, the data seem to suggest not only a lack of desire for acquaintances to witness one's humiliation, but even an actual (and substantial) preference for strangers. Fantasies also could involve acquaintances, but the majority of fantasies with audiences also seem to emphasize audiences of strangers (although data are insufficient for statistical analysis). Friends, colleagues, and neighbors appear in fantasies as co-participants, but not as audiences.

In short, it appears that many masochists desire to be watched by strangers. Audiences can promote self-awareness, but they only promote the person's awareness or his or her normal identity if they know who the person is. The desire to be watched by strangers suggests instead that masochists seek to be aware of a transformed self with the new identity as sexual slave.

Scott's (1983) observations, although impressionistic on this matter, are consistent with the present findings. She reports that masochists carefully avoid letting their acquaintances find out about their activities, but they do enjoy the company of others, including spectators. Again, practical concerns explain the avoidance of acquaintances but not the positive desire to be seen by strangers.

The implication is that masochists desire to exclude the normal social world. The adoption of a new identity is reinforced and affirmed by the presence of witnesses (Wicklund & Gollwitzer, 1982), but witnesses who would remind one of one's normal, everyday identity would probably hamper the transformation. As in brainwashing, identity change is facilitated by the removal of all social support for the to-be-discarded identity and replacement of them with witnesses who know only the new, transformed identity (Cf. Baumeister, 1986).

Relation to Everyday Power Dynamics

The argument that masochism is escape from normal self and everyday social reality has important implications for the recent debates about the politics of masochism. In particular, feminist (and other) critiques of sadomasochistic practices (e.g., Linden, 1982) are based on viewing these sexual activities as endorsement of oppression and violence, including Nazi brutality, genocide, medieval tortures, rape, wife-battering, and more. If the present thesis is correct, these critiques are unfounded. Sadomasochistic sex does not re-enact or endorse genuine oppression; it simply uses obsolete symbols to enact escape and fantasy. People who have really suffered victimization or cruelty would not want to re-enact such things in sexual games.

Moreover, masochists sometimes defend their practices by claiming that their games permit insights into the nature of power relationships in normal life (Califia, 1982, 1983; see also Weeks, 1985). If the present theory is correct, these defenses of masochistic activity are no more valid than the critiques, for masochistic sexuality bears no viable relationship to genuine political dynamics.

One way to assemble data on the relationship of masochism to political structures is to examine the sociopolitical distribution of masochism. If masochists are indeed re-enacting oppression and suffering from their experiences, then people who have experienced the most oppression should be the most masochistic. In contrast, if masochism is an *escape* from reality, then it should appeal mainly to those who have not been exploited or oppressed. Evidence supports the latter hypothesis. Masochism appears to be more common among whites than blacks, more common among men than women, and (most important) more common among the upper socioeconomic classes than among the lower ones (Scott, 1983; also Spengler, 1977; Symanski, 1981). Although these data are not fully conclusive, they are corroborated by comparison with studies of prostitutes. Working-class users of prostitutes purchase mainly fellatio and normal intercourse (e.g., Diana, 1985), whereas upper-class clients frequently request to be sexually dominated (e.g., Janus et al., 1977; also Symanski, 1981). Thus, the weight of the evidence suggests that society's real victims are underrepresented among masochists. That supports the escape hypothesis. Sexual masochism does not reproduce familiar or actual experiences; rather, it apparently enacts fantasies that are radically divorced from normal reality.

Self and Opponent Processes

Solomon and Corbit (1974) proposed that many psychological phenomena can be explained on the basis of opponent processes. That is, each response is accompanied by a second, opposite response that is slower to take effect. They suggested that masochistic phenomena might involve opponent processes.

Although direct evidence is lacking, opponent processes could plausibly explain the appeal of the masochistic escape from self. Each of the three essential features of masochism might be associated with an opponent process, and their combination might produce a very appealing subjective state. The masochist experiences pain: an opponent process might produce a feeling of euphoria and well-being after the cessation of pain. The masochist experiences helplessness and loss of control; an opponent process might produce a feeling of self-efficacy, power, responsibility, and capability. The masochist experiences humiliation and degradation; and opponent process might produce a feeling of self-worth, pride, and self-respect.

Some observers have suggested that masochistic episodes produce subsequent feelings of energy, fulfillment, and willingness to take on major challenges (e.g., Smith & Cox, 1983, p. 82; Scott, 1983, p. 4). These observations are far from conclusive, however, and clinical observers tend to report the opposite result, namely that masochists feel wretched and guilty afterwards (e.g., Cowan, 1982; Stekel, 1953). (The difference may be one of sampling bias, for masochists who feel wretched are more likely to seek therapy than masochists who feel euphoric.)

Thus, opponent process theory augments the idea that masochism provides an escape from high-level self-awareness, for it suggests that after the masochistic escape would follow a period of highly positive, euphoric self-awareness. This might substantially enhance the appeal of the escape. Although the arguments are plausible and appealing, however, they are best considered very tentative until some form of direct evidence becomes available.

Relation to Sexual Arousal

The argument thus far has been that masochism is an attempt to escape from high-level, symbolic, temporally extended self-awareness. It is reasonable to ask how this might contribute to sexual excitement. Although the appeal of masochism may extend beyond sex, it must include sexual pleasure.

The causes of sexual excitement are not fully understood, but there is sufficient evidence to justify some speculative hypotheses about masochism. For present purposes, the most important notion is that self-awareness can be detrimental to sexual excitement and pleasure. Some evidence suggests that full sexual pleasure can be experienced only when one has set aside one's awareness of self as a separate, autonomous, esteem-maintaining being. Self-oriented approaches to sex, such as viewing sex as a performance or a conquest, may detract from sexual enjoyment and impair sexual functioning (LoPiccolo, 1978).

Masters and Johnson's (1970) work preceded

social psychology's study of self-attention, but many of their findings appear to involve self-awareness. They propose that "fear of sexual inadequacy is the greatest known deterrent to effective sexual functioning" (p. 12). They describe these fears in terms reminiscent of self-awareness theory, especially comparison of self with socially approved standards of masculinity and femininity. They say that sexual dysfunction often results when the individual becomes a demanding, evaluative "spectator" of his or her own sexual response. Thus, self-evaluation during sex is "the all-important factor in both onset of and reversal of sexual inadequacy" (p. 197). If evaluative self-attention impairs sexual functioning, then it is plausible that masochism may enhance sexual arousal by removing such self-awareness.

Indeed, the techniques of sex therapy proposed by Masters and Johnson (1970) have important parallels in masochistic activities. First, the emphasis on socially isolating the sexual partners from the demands of their everyday worlds (e.g., having them stay at a motel during the therapy, even if they live nearby) is reminiscent of the masochistic attempt to remove the everyday world from awareness through pain and fantasy. Second, what Masters and Johnson call the "sensate focus" involves directing attention to immediate sensations, which appears to be the same focus brought on by masochistic submission (including pain). Third, the therapeutic emphasis on the couple rather than the individual parallels the masochistic emphasis on the relationship context for sexuality. Fourth, the therapeutic use of permission (i.e., couples are told to refrain from sex, and their sexual activities are restricted and directed by the therapist) resembles the restrictions and commands that characterize masochistic sex games. Indeed, a substantial number of letters in the present sample referred to commands that restricted sexual activity, including requiring the masochist to request permission to have an orgasm (and punishment for violations). Fifth, in order to teach the male therapy patient that he cannot will himself to have an erection, Masters and Johnson advocate teaching him an enforcedly passive role in sex, similar to the enforced passivity of the masochist.

Although parallels between sex therapy and masochism should not be overstated, it is apparent that masochism does resemble many practices that therapists use to treat sexual dysfunction. It is therefore plausible that masochism can enhance sexual response. Masochism may consequently appeal to individuals who desire such enhancement, presumably including both sexually insecure individuals and people who desire unusually intense sensations and experiences.

It is plausible that masochism enhances sexual arousal in other ways. Spanking allegedly produces a temporary warmth and redness on the skin of the buttocks, called reactive hyperemia. Given the proximity of the buttocks to the genitals, this hyperemia may contribute to sexual warmth (Reik, 1941). Also, the typical brevity of normal foreplay may prevent full sexual enjoyment in many cases, perhaps especially among women (e.g., Gebhard, 1978). Sadomasochistic sex games typically last much longer than conventional foreplay, however, and the period of nudity and bodily contact may allow sexual arousal to reach higher levels. One theorist has proposed that sadomasochism be regarded simply as prolonged foreplay (Lee, 1983; see also Reik, 1941, p. 60). Although these arguments are plausible, it seems likely that a principal contribution of masochistic activity to sexual enjoyment is the escape from self-awareness.

Historical Pattern

Researchers have difficulty knowing for certain what the sexual habits of modern couples are. These difficulties are compounded when one desires to know the sexual practices of long-dead individuals, for one does not even have self-report or survey data. Still, much has been written about sex through the ages, and modern scholars have found it possible to make reasonably educated guesses about the sex lives of our ancestors. A handful of important works have surveyed sexual practices across cultural and historical boundaries.

Such evidence provides a possibility for testing the present hypothesis about masochism. If masochistic desires arose from the wish to escape the burdens of self, then masochistic sex should have been most common when these burdens were greatest and most oppressive.

In previous work, I have argued that individuality became a dominant value and pattern in Western culture during the early modern period, from 1500–1800 (Baumeister, 1986, 1987, also see Trilling, 1971, and Weintraub, 1978). In other words, it was during that period that the culture began to require each person to maintain a unique, separate, autonomous, positively valued self, with its own distinct goals and potentiality. The increased emphasis on individuality would presumably increase the burden of selfhood, and so one may predict that sexual masochism would have increased greatly during the early modern period.

The evidence supports the hypothesis. It appears that most sexual practices have been known and enjoyed throughout history, but masochism is a rare exception. Masochism appears to be mainly a modern pattern, which spread through Western society during the early modern period.

The most comprehensive histories of sex are provided by Bullough (1976a) and Tannahill (1980), Tannahill records extensive varieties of sexual practices, including many atypical or deviant activities, occurring throughout the ancient and medieval world (as well as in other cultures). In her account, however, masochism does not appear until the 18th century, when it suddenly became widely evident in Europe. She notes that the sex manuals of some ancient civilizations were remarkably complete by modern standards, covering all the variations known today—except masochism, which she says is conspicuous by its absence. Likewise, masochism does not appear in Bullough's (1976a) history until the early modern period, with one exception: He suggests briefly that masochism is evident in the self-mutilation that occurred during some ancient Greek religious ceremonies. Probably it is a mistake to regard those activities as masochistic. In the first place, sex and religion provide radically different contexts, and it seems unwarranted to assume that activities have the same meaning in religious ritual as they have in sexual play. In the second place, as noted earlier, masochists do not engage in self-mutilation anyway. Probably Bullough was misled by the Freudian suggestion that masochism is aggression directed toward the self. In any case, his account shows no signs of explicitly sexual masochism until the early modern period.

Other historians confirm these patterns.[4] Licht (1934) documents the extensive sex scenes in ancient Greek literature, but there was apparently no sadomasochistic sexual activity depicted. Ellis (1936) reports their absence in ancient Latin (Roman) literature. Taylor (1970) again describes some religious activities as masochistic, but he reports no evidence of masochistic sex until the eighteenth century.

The Middle Ages left extensive writings about sex, especially in the Christian Church's theological discussions about the relative immorality of various practices (Bullough & Brundage, 1982). Homosexuality, bestiality, masturbation, abortion, contraception, adultery, coprophilia, prostitution, anal sex, transvestism, and a variety of other practices were discussed and debated, but apparently there was no mention of masochism. Given Christianity's profound negativity toward sexual activities (Bullough, 1976a; Tannahill, 1980), it is extremely implausible that the Church theologians had simply decided to tolerate masochistic sex without comment. Rather, it seems most likely that the lack of reference to masochism indicates a lack of masochistic sexual activity. Possibly masochism was completely unheard of.

Ellis (1936) conducted a thorough search for historical references to explicitly sexual masochism. He concluded that the earliest mention of it—a secondhand rumor about a man who supposedly enjoyed flagellation—occurred just before the start of the sixteenth century, and that such evidence did not become common until the 18th century.

Written and literary discussions of masochism first appeared in the 17th century (Bullough, 1976a; Taylor, 1970). Two fictional works of that century included flogging scenes. Pornography devoted to flogging appeared in the eighteenth century and soon became widespread (Bullough, 1976a; Tannahill, 1980). By the end of the eighteenth century, there were many such writings, as well as private clubs apparently devoted to masochistic practices (Faulk & Weinberg, 1983). The abundant evidence of masochistic activity beginning in the eighteenth century contrasts sharply with the lack of any record of such activities prior to the Renaissance.

Another source of evidence is provided by histories of prostitution. It appears that prostitutes have long catered to various sexual tastes, but the earliest evidence of masochistic clients comes around the 18th century. Thus, in the ancient Middle East, there were heterosexual and homo-

[4]Bullough (1976b) found one piece of evidence that ancient Egyptian mythology regarded anal sex as a symbolic expression of dominance, but it appears that interest in that symbolism arose only out of the desire to dominate, not to submit. Thus, there is a weak suggestion of sadism, but no indication of masochism. If sadism is historically older than masochism, as I suspect, this casts further doubt on the link postulated by past theories between masochism and sadism.

sexual prostitutes, as well as "animal prostitutes" catering to clients with a desire for bestiality, but there is no sign of professional dominatrices (Benjamin & Masters, 1965). Ancient Greece and Rome likewise had both heterosexual and homosexual prostitutes, and it appears that there were Roman prostitutes who catered to special tastes for pederasty and fellatio, but again there is no reference to sadomasochism.

Medieval prostitution was vaguely tolerated by the Church as a necessary evil, although gradually the Church became intolerant of sexual practices it regarded as unnatural—including homosexuality, bestiality, concubinage, and adultery (Otis, 1985). But there was apparently no discussion of prostitutes providing sadomasochistic services.

In the historical evidence from the 18th century, there are numerous references to prostitutes specializing in flagellation (Benjamin & Masters, 1965; Tannahill, 1980). By the nineteenth century, most major brothels had such a specialist, and in large cities there were entire brothels devoted solely to flagellation (Tannahill, 1980). Bullough & Bullough (1964) provide a detailed anecdotal history of prostitution, in which the first references to flogging come in the early 19th century.

Thus, the evidence from histories of prostitution confirms the impression that sexual masochism appeared in our culture roughly around 1700, It would be incautious to conclude from the lack of indications that masochism was completely unknown before then. But there is no disputing the contrast between the abundant evidence of masochism after 1700 and the paucity of such evidence before 1600. It seems safe to conclude that sexual masochism underwent a dramatic increase in Western culture late in the early modern period.

Thus, in Western history, the spread of sexual masochism coincided with the increased emphasis on individuality. Just when the individual self took on a vastly augmented scope and importance, evidence of masochistic sexuality proliferated. It seems quite plausible that the new emphasis on individuality increased the burden of selfhood, and that not everyone would be fully comfortable with the new demands for autonomy, uniqueness, and self-promotion. As a result, people may have been increasingly drawn to a form of sexual play based on a powerful (if temporary) way of escaping the self.

There are valid reasons for caution in drawing conclusions from historical evidence about sexuality. Not only are there questions about the validity and exhaustiveness of the available evidence, but the innate complexity of social change makes it difficult to make simple causal inferences. Western society changed in numerous ways from 1500 to 1800, and it is quite conceivable that factors other than the increasing individuality could have contributed to promoting masochistic sex. Still, the evidence is at least entirely consistent with the hypothesis that masochism arises from the desire to escape from high-level self-awareness. As noted earlier, the best approach to masochism that is currently viable is to look for converging patterns among different sources of evidence, each with its own flaws. The historical evidence provides a welcome corroboration of the empirical sources cited earlier. This convergence strengthens the case for the hypothesis that masochism is escape from self.

Escape or Therapy?

Before concluding, it is useful to consider the related hypothesis that masochism is therapeutic. Cowan (1982) argues that masochism improves self-knowledge. She is not specific about what is learned or about how masochism improves self-knowledge. At several points she seems to argue that self-knowledge often hurts, so hurting may promote self-knowledge (a non sequitur). More important, she says masochistic suffering can be beneficial in that it involves letting go of "old, worn-out self-images and attitudes" and promotes "loss of old ego-constructs" (p. 50). She also suggests that masochism is based on punishment and retribution for the sin of pride, basing her discussion on the Jungian equation of religious spirituality with psychotherapy.

The alleged therapeutic benefits of masochism have been touted by masochists themselves, possibly as a means of justifying their sexual activities (cf. Weeks, 1985, pp. 238–239). Califia (1983) characterizes masochistic submission as "a healing process" (p. 134), arguing vaguely that it remedies "old wounds" and leads beyond orgasm to catharsis. Several masochists interviewed by Janus et al. (1977, p. 102) likewise used the term "cathartic" to describe the effects of being whipped. Lucy (1982) claims she learned about herself "emotionally and physically" (p. 35) from participating in masochistic sex. She too describes it as cathartic and healing, and she claims it reduced her chronic anxiety levels and improved her ability to communicate with others.

Thus, improved self-knowledge and catharsis are the principal claims made by the proponents of the therapeutic hypothesis. It is troubling that no specific insights into self are cited (except for the insight that one enjoys masochistic sex), and that insight and catharsis are not generally considered sufficient for therapeutic improvement. The present sample of epistolary self-reports was generally devoid of therapeutic claims and even of claims of improved self-knowledge, except for the realization that the person was a masochist.

Healing the self and escaping the self are not completely different, so some of the claims for therapeutic efficacy are compatible with the view espoused here. Both escape and therapy remove bothersome aspects of the self, and both may be sought when one feels guilty, overburdened, or dissatisfied with the self. The main difference is presumably that a therapeutic effect is a lasting transformation, whereas an escape is a temporary distraction. Therapy and escape thus differ in their aftereffects. A useful analogy contrasts medicine with narcotic. With medicine, one takes it, one gets better, and one stops taking it. With a narcotic, one takes it, one feels better, and when it wears off one soon wants to take it again.

The weight of evidence about patterns of masochistic sexual behavior appears more consistent with the escape hypothesis than with the therapy hypothesis. There is almost no evidence that masochistic experiences bring about some healing transformation that ends the need for such "therapy." Instead, the predominant pattern appears to be that masochists increase their interest and participation in sexual submission. Spengler (1977) found that the most common reaction to one's first masochistic experience was a desire to have more such experiences. The accounts of people's encounters with masochism (Califia, 1983; Kamel, 1983; Lee, 1983; Scott, 1983) all portray the general pattern as one of escalating involvement. In the present sample, 88% of the letters indicated that there would be future contacts involving sadomasochistic activities, in contrast with the 3% who projected a relationship with that partner continuing without such activities. The standard pattern of increasing, escalating involvements has led some theorists to characterize masochism as an addiction (e.g., Mass, 1983).

In short, where the escape and therapy hypotheses differ, the evidence appears to favor the escape hypothesis. Evidence for the therapeutic value of masochism is lacking, and patterns of masochistic activity appear to resemble patterns of narcotic use more than of medicine use. Masochism does not effect a permanent transformation of the self that cures its problems. Rather, masochism effects a temporary transformation or concealment of the self that enables the individual to forget his or her problems.

Conclusion

To summarize: Masochism should not automatically be regarded as a symptom of mental illness, for it appears to occur most commonly among normal and successful persons. It should not be regarded as derived from sadism, for it is more common than sadism, and where both patterns are found the masochism generally comes first. It should not be confused with self-destructive behavior, for masochists apparently are quite careful to avoid harm to themselves.

Rather, masochism can be understood as a way of providing a temporary and powerful escape from high-level awareness of self as an abstract, temporally extended, symbolically constructed identity. Masochistic practices replace this self-awareness with a low-level, temporally constricted awareness of self as a physical body, focusing on immediate sensations (both painful and pleasant) and on being a sexual object. In particular, masochism removes two fundamental aspects of the self, namely the orientation toward control and the motive to maximize esteem. Some masochists carry the escape one step further and in fantasy adopt a totally new identity, such as that of a slave. The escape from high-level self-awareness may appeal to individuals burdened with the demands of autonomous selfhood, and it may facilitate sexual response.

Further study with masochists is warranted (cf. Weinberg, 1987). If the present theory is correct, masochistic activity may often be precipitated by events that make the self burdensome. Masochistic desires should increase after severe external demands for autonomy, responsibility, decisions, self-assertion, and esteem maintenance. The resemblance (and relation) of masochism to narcotic use and other addictive patterns deserves investigation. Personality traits such as locus of control and self-consciousness should predict involvement in masochism.

If the present theory is correct, then masochism can be understood as a means of escaping high-level self-awareness and can be grouped together with other such escapes, presumably including skydiving, mountain climbing, alcohol intoxication, and so forth. Future investigations may examine the question of why some people choose masochism over alternative escapes. The question of why someone comes to prefer masochism over mountain climbing may be comparable to the question of why someone comes to prefer skydiving over mountain climbing; accidents of habit, opportunity, and association may play key causal roles. Possibly the link to sexual pleasure makes masochism stand out above other forms of escape. That is, sexual desire (as a biological need) may arise on a regular basis, and if it arises simultaneously with desires for escape, the two may become linked—or, more likely, if a link is established fortuitously, the colinked occurrence may strengthen that link. Further, if escape from self-awareness increases sexual pleasure, some people may find masochism a reliable way of enhancing sex. Possibly some important experience enables the individual to discover the appeal of masochism, so that later desires for escape take the form of masochistic desires. (For example, a few experiences that associate mild pain or humiliation with intimacy or sexual pleasure may create a readiness to formulate desires for escape in masochistic terms.)

If masochism centers around escape from one's normal identity, then attempts to establish a full-time identity as a masochist may ultimately be self-defeating. Sociological studies of identification with masochistic subcultures (see Weinberg, 1987) may explore what happens when the individual comes to identify him or herself so strongly with these groups and activities that this identity comes to predominate, indicated perhaps by a desire to come out of the closet and be generally recognized as a masochist. At this point, obviously, masochism would cease to be an escape from self. If the present theory is correct, one of two consequences should occur: Either the person should shift his or her main involvement from the submissive to the dominant role, or the person should gradually lose interest and enjoyment, because masochism can no longer function as an effective escape. This may explain why masochists, unlike homosexuals, have not developed into public figures and activists. Califia (1983), one of the few who has come out of the closet to campaign for S&M liberation, shifted her main sexual role preference from submissive to dominant.

I do not mean to stigmatize or condemn masochism by treating it as an escape or comparing it to a narcotic. Many individuals seem to make use of some form of escape from their everyday, high-level awareness of who they are. As escapes go, masochism appears to be relatively harmless, and if the self-reports are to be believed, the yield of pleasure is often substantial. Masochism seems to form one of the more extreme forms of escape, providing more powerful experiences then a game of checkers or a movie. Thus, it may appeal to people who desire or require especially powerful means to achieve a successful escape from self.

REFERENCES

American Psychiatric Association. (1980). *Diagnostic and statistical manual of mental disorders* (3rd ed.). Washington, DC: Author.

Baumeister, R. F. (1982). A self-presentational view of social phenomena. *Psychological Bulletin, 91,* 3–25.

Baumeister, R. F. (1986). *Identity: Cultural change and the struggle for self.* New York: Oxford University Press.

Baumeister, R. F. (1987). How the self became a problem: A psychological review of historical research. *Journal of Personality and Social Psychology, 52,* 163–176.

Baumeister, R. F., Hamilton, J. C., & Tice, D. M. (1985). Public versus private expectancy of success: Confidence booster or performance pressure? *Journal of Personality and Social Psychology, 48,* 1447–1457.

Baumeister, R. F., & Scher, S. J. (1988). Self-defeating behavior patterns among normal individuals: Review and analysis of common self-destructive tendencies. *Psychological Bulletin, 104,* 3–22.

Bellweather, J. (1982). Love means never having to say oops: A lesbian's guide to s/m safety. In Samois, *Coming to power* (pp. 69–79). Boston, MA: Alyson.

Benjamin, H., & Masters, E. L. (1965). *Prostitution and morality.* London: Souvenir Press.

Brady, J. V. (1958). Ulcers in "executive" monkeys. *Scientific American, 199,* 95–100.

Bullough, V. L. (1976a). *Sexual variance in society and history.* Chicago, IL: University of Chicago Press.

Bullough, V. L. (1976b). *Sex, society, and history.* New York: Science History Publications.

Bullough, V. L., & Brundage, J. (1982). *Sexual practices and the medieval church.* Buffalo, NY: Prometheus.

Bullough, V. L., & Bullough, B. L. (1964). *The history of prostitution*. New Hyde Park, NY: University Books.

Califia, P. (1982). A personal view of the history of the lesbian S/M community and movement in San Francisco. In Samois, *Coming to power* (pp. 243–287). Boston, MA: Alyson.

Califia, P. (1983). A secret side of lesbian sexuality. In T. Weinberg & G. Kamel (Eds.), *S and M: Studies in sadomasochism* (pp. 129–136). Buffalo, NY: Prometheus.

Caplan, P. (1984). The myth of women's masochism. *American Psychologist, 39,* 130–139.

Carver, C. S. (1979). A cybernetic model of self-attention processes. *Journal of Personality and Social Psychology, 37,* 1251–1281.

Carvcr, C. S., & Scheier, M. F. (1981). *Attention and self-regulation: A control-theory approach to human behavior.* New York: Springer-Verlag.

Cowan, L. (1982). *Masochism: A Jungian view.* Dallas, TX: Spring Publications.

Diana, L. (1985). *The prostitute and her clients*. Springfield, IL: Thomas.

Duval, S., & Wicklund, R. A. (1972). *A theory of objective self-awareness*. New York: Academic Press.

Ellis, H. (1936). *Studies in the psychology of sex.* (Vol 1). New York: Random House. Original work published in 1905.

Faulk, G., & Weinberg, T. S. (1983). Sadomasochism and popular Western culture. In T. Weinberg & G. Kamel (Eds.), *S and M: Studies in sadomosochism* (pp. 137–144). Buffalo, NY: Prometheus.

Franklin, D. (1987). The politics of masochism. *Psychology Today, 21*(No. 1), 52–57.

Freud, S. (1938). Sadism and masochism. From A. A. Brill (trans.), *Basic writings of Sigmund Freud,* New York: Modern Library. Reprinted in Kamel & Weinberg (Eds.), *S and M* (pp. 30–32). Buffalo, NY: Prometheus.

Friday, N. (1980). *Men in love.* New York: Dell.

Gebhard, P. H. (1978). Factors in marital orgasm. In J. LoPiccolo & L. LoPiccolo (Eds.), *Handbook of sex therapy* (pp. 167–174). New York: Plenum.

Gibbons, F. X., & Wicklund, R. A. (1976). Selective exposure to self. *Journal of Research in Personality, 14,* 98–106.

Goleman, D. (1985). *Vital lies, simple truths: The psychology of self-deception.* New York: Simon & Schuster.

Gollwitzer, P. M. (1986), Striving for specific identities: The social reality of self-symbolizing. In R. Baumeister (Ed.), *Public self and private self* (pp. 143–159). New York: Springer-Verlag.

Greenberg, J., & Musham, C. (1981). Avoiding and seeking self-focused attention. *Journal of Research in Personality, 15,* 191–200.

Greene, G., & Greene, C. (1974). *S-M: The last taboo.* New York: Grove Press.

Hull, J. G. (1981). A self-awareness model of the causes and affects of alcohol consumption. *Journal of Abnormal Psychology, 94,* 586–600.

Hull, J. G., & Levey, A. S. (1979). The organizational functions of the self: An alternative to the Duval and Wicklund model of self-awareness. *Journal of Personality and Social Psychology, 37,* 756–768.

Hull, J. G., & Young, R. D. (1983). Self-consciousness, self-esteem, and success-failure as determinants of alcohol consumption in male social drinkers. *Journal of Personality and Social Psychology, 44,* 1087–1109.

Hull, J. G., Young, R. D., & Jouriles, E. (1986). Applications of the self-awareness model of alcohol consumption: Predicting patterns of use and abuse. *Journal of Personality and Social Psychology, 51,* 790–796.

Janus, S., Bess, B., & Saltus, C. (1977). *A sexual profile of men in power.* Englewood Cliffs, NJ: Prentice-Hall.

Jones, E. E., & Berglas, S. C. (1978). Control of attributions about the self through self-handicapping strategies: The appeal of alcohol and the role of underachievement. *Personality and Social Psychology Bulletin, 4,* 200–206.

Juliette, (1983). Autobiography of a dominatrix. In T. Weinberg & G. W. L. Kamel (Eds.), *S and M: Studies in sadomasochism* (pp. 87–93). Buffalo. NY: Prometheus.

Kamel, G. W. L. (1980). Leathersex: Meaningful aspects of gay sadomasochism. *Deviant Behavior, 1,* 171–191.

Kamel, G. W. L. (1983). The leather career: On becoming a sadomasochist. In T. Weinberg & G. Kamel (Eds.), *S and M: Studies in sadomasochism* (pp. 73–79). Buffalo, NY: Prometheus.

Lee, J. A. (1983). The social organization of sexual risk. In T. Weinberg & G. Kamel (Eds.), *S and M: Studies in sadomasochism* (pp. 178–199). Buffalo, NY: Prometheus.

Lewin, K. K. (1980). *Sexual self-destruct: Conscience of the West.* St. Louis, MO: Green.

Licht, H. (1934). *Sexual life in ancient Greece.* New York: Dutton.

Liebling, B. A., Seiler, M., & Shaver, P. (1974), Self-awareness and cigarette smoking behavior. *Journal of Experimental Social Psychology, 10,* 325–332.

Linden, R. R. (1982). *Against sadomasochism: A radical feminist analysis.* East Palo Alto, CA: Frog in Well Press.

LoPiccolo, J. (1918). Direct treatment of sexual dysfunction. In J. LoPiccolo & L. LoPiccolo (Eds.), *Handbook of sex therapy* (pp. 1–18). New York: Plenum.

Lucy, J. (1982). If I ask you to tie me up, will you still want to love me? In Samois, *Coming to power* (pp. 29–40). Boston, MA; Alyson.

Mass, L. (1983). Coming to grips with sadomasochism. In T. Weinberg & G. Kamel (Eds.), *S and M: Studies in sadomasochism* (pp. 15–66), Buffalo, NY: Prometheus.

Masters, W. H., & Johnson, V. E. (1970). *Human sexual inadequacy.* Boston, MA; Little, Brown & Co.

Modigliani, A. (1968). Embarrassment and embarrassability. *Sociometry, 31,* 313–326.

Modigliani, A. (1971). Embarrassment, facework, and eye contact: Testing a theory of embarrassment. *Journal of Personality and Social Psychology, 16,* 15–24.

Otis, L. I. (1986). *Prostitution in medieval society.* Chicago, IL: University of Chicago Press.

Panken, S. (1983). *The joy of suffering: Psychoanalytic theory and therapy of masochism.* New York: Aronson.

Patterson, O. (1982). *Slavery and social death.* Cambridge, MA: Harvard University Press.

Pennebaker, J. W. (1985). Traumatic experience and psychomatic disease: Exploring the roles of behavioral inhibition, obsession, and confiding. *Canadian Psychology, 26,* 82–95.

Pennebaker, J. W., Hughes, C., & O'Heeron, R. C. (1987). The psychophysiology of confession: Linking inhibitory and psychomatic processes. *Journal of Personality and Social Psychology, 52,* 781–793.

Pennebaker, J. W., Brumbelow, S., Cropanzano, R., Czajka, J., Ferrara, K., Thompson, R., & Thyssen, T. (1986). Levels of thinking. Unpublished manuscript, Southern Methodist University.

Powers, W. T. (1973). *Behavior: The control of perception.* Chicago, IL: Aldine.

Reik, T. (1957/1941). *Masochism in modern man* (tr. M. H. Beigel & G. M. Kurth). New York: Grove Press.

Rubin, G. (1982). The leather menace: Comments on politics and S/M. In Samois, *Coming to power* (pp. 192–227). Boston, MA: Alyson.

Samois. (1982). *Coming to power*. Boston, MA: Alyson.

Sartre, J.-P. (1949). *Nausea.* (L. Alexander, tr.). New York: New Directions. (Original work published 1938)

Scarry, E. (1985). *The body in pain: The making and unmaking of the world.* New York: Oxford University Press.

Scott, G. G. (1983). *Erotic power: An exploration of dominance and submission.* Secaucus: NJ: Citadel Press.

Shainess, N. (1984). *Sweet suffering: Woman as victim.* New York: Simon & Schuster.

Smith, H. & Cox, C. (1983). Dialogue with a dominatrix. In T. Weinberg & G. Kamel (Eds.), *S and M: Studies in sadomasochism* (pp. 80–86). Buffalo, NY: Prometheus.

Solomon, R. L., & Corbit, J. D. (1974). An opponent-process theory of motivation: I. Temporal dynamics of affect. *Psychological Review, 81,* 119–145.

Spence, J. T., & Sawin, L. L. (1984). Images of masculinity and femininity: A reconceptualization. In V. O'Leary, R. Unger, & B. Wallston (Eds.), *Sex, gender, and social psychology* (pp. 35-66). Hillsdale, NJ: Erlbaum.

Spengler, A. (1977). Manifest sadomasochism of males: Results of an empirical study. *Archives of Sexual Behavior, 6,* 441–456.

Steenbarger, B. N., & Aderman, D. (1979). Objective self-awareness as a nonaversive state: Effect of anticipating discrepancy reduction. *Journal of Personality, 47,* 330–339.

Stekel, W. (1953). *Sadism and masochism: The psychology of hatred and cruelty* (tr. E. Gutheil). Volume 1 and 2. New York: Liveright. (Original work published 1929)

Symanski, R. (1981). *The immoral landscape: Female prostitution in Western societies.* Toronto, Canada: Butterworth & Co.

Tannahill, R. (1980). *Sex in history.* New York: Stein and Day.

Taylor, G. R. (1970). *Sex in history.* New York: Harper & Row. (Original work published 1954)

Trilling, L. (1971). *Sincerity and authenticity.* Cambridge, MA: Harvard University Press.

Vallacher, R. R., & Wegner, D. M. (1985). *A theory of action identification.* Hillsdale, NJ: Erlbaum.

Vallacher, R. R., & Wegner, D. M. (1986). What do people think they're doing? Action identification and human behavior. *Psychological Review.*

Weeks, J. (1985). *Sexuality and its discontents: Meanings, myths, and modern sexualities.* London: Routledge & Kegan Paul.

Weinberg, M. S., Williams, C. J., & Moser, C. (1984). The social constituents of sadomasochism. *Social Problems, 31,* 379–389.

Weinberg, T. S. (1987). Sadomasochism in the United States: A review of recent sociological literature. *Journal of Sex Research, 23,* 50–69.

Weinberg, T., & Kamel, W. L. (Eds.). (1983). *S and M: Studies in sadomasochism.* Buffalo, NY: Prometheus.

Weintraub, K. J. (1978). *The value of the individual: Self and circumstances in autobiography.* Chicago, IL: University of Chicago Press.

Weiss, J. M. (1971a). Effects of coping behavior in different warning signal conditions on stress pathology in rats. *Journal of Comparative and Physiological Psychology, 77,* 1–13.

Weiss, J. M. (1971b). Effects of punishing the coping response (conflict) on stress pathology in rats. *Journal of Comparative and Physiological Psychology, 77,* 14–21.

Weiss, J. M. (1971c). Effects of coping behavior with and without a feedback signal on stress pathology. *Journal of Comparative and Physiological Psychology, 77,* 22–30.

Wicklund, R. A. (1975a). Objective self-awareness. In L. Berkowitz (Ed.), *Advances in experimental social psychology,* Vol. 8 (pp. 233–275). New York: Academic Press.

Wicklund, R. A. (1975b). Discrepancy reduction or attempted distraction? A reply to Liebling, Seiler & Shaver. *Journal of Experimental Social Psychology, 11,* 78–81.

Wicklund, A., & Gollwitzer, P. M. (1982). *Symbolic self-completion.* Hillsdale, NJ: Erlbaum.

Zoftig, S. (1982). Coming out. In Samois, *Coming to power* (pp. 86–96). Boston, MA: Alyson.

INTRODUCTION TO PART 9

Pornography and Desire

Nearly all studies find that men spend more time and money obtaining pornography than do women. Indeed, women report that they enjoy pornography less than men (e.g., Kinsey et al., 1953). But those differences do not guarantee that women actually would enjoy pornography less than men.

In the following article, Fisher and Byrne (1978) conducted an experimental test of responses to pornography. They began with multiple theories about how men and women would respond differently. Fortunately, their research design was fairly thorough, because it enabled them to reach conclusions they had not anticipated. They found that men and women enjoyed pornography almost equally, and that men and women had roughly similar tastes in the thematic content: Both men and women preferred the theme of first-time sex between people who had just met over either a love or lust theme, even though people were watching exactly the same tape.

Fisher and Byrne's work calls attention to the importance of the story line in erotica, and this is something that the pornography industry has not seemed to grasp fully. Most purveyors of pornographic products emphasize providing explicit depictions of sexual activity, often featuring closeup shots of the nude genital organs. Yet Fisher and Byrne found that the degree of explicitness of the depictions had no effect on the arousal level: People were just as turned on by watching couples who kept their underwear on as they were by full nudity and explicit depictions of sex acts.

All of this confirms the importance of the brain as a major sex organ. People's sexual arousal was less influenced by the degree of visual explicitness than by what they thought was happening in the minds and emotions of the characters. This was true for both men and women, whose responses to pornography in this research seemed surprisingly similar. More generally, it may well be true that sex is not just a matter of bodies and senses but also one of social context and interpretation.

REFERENCES

Fisher, W. A., & Byrne, D. (1978). Sex differences in response to erotica: Love versus lust. *Journal of Personality and Social Psychology, 36,* 117–125.

Kinsey, A. C., Pomeroy, W. B., Martin, C. E., & Gebhard, P. H. (1953). *Sexual behavior in the human female*. Philadelphia: Saunders.

Discussion Questions

1. If women enjoy pornography just as much as men, why do women spend less time and money obtaining pornography?
2. Do you think the pornography industry has made a serious effort to attract female customers?
3. Prior to 1970, pornography was rare and expensive. How do you think the vastly increased availability of sexually explicit materials will affect society?
4. Is pornography an ideal form of "safe sex" that society should encourage?
5. Why does our society permit movies to show killing and bloodshed, even for children, whereas depictions of sex are considered more dangerous?
6. Do you think some or all forms of pornography have harmful effects? What are they?

Suggested Readings

Cowan, G., & Dunn, K. F. (1994). What themes in pornography lead to perceptions of the degradation of women? *Journal of Sex Research, 31,* 11–21. An empirical study of men's and women's responses to pornography. The results may surprise you as they surprised the authors!

Donnerstein, E., & Berkowitz, L. (1981). Victim reactions in aggressive erotic films as a factor in violence against women. *Journal of Personality and Social Psychology, 41,* 710–724. Although many studies have suggested that pure erotica produces no increase in aggressive behavior, aggressive pornography is quite another matter. In this pair of studies, viewing violent pornography caused men to retaliate very aggressively toward a woman who insulted them.

Mann, J., Berkowitz, L., Sidman, J., Starr, S., & West, S. (1974). Satiation of the transient stimulation effect of erotic films. *Journal of Personality and Social Psychology, 30,* 729–735. This well-designed study examined the effects of viewing pornography on sexual behavior. Its longitudinal design enabled it to learn about not only the immediate effects but the lasting changes in behavior.

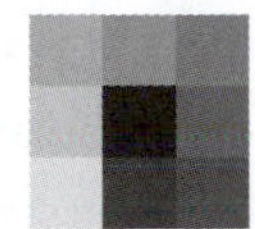

READING 17

Sex Differences in Response to Erotica? Love Versus Lust

William A. Fisher and Donn Byrne • Purdue University

The current research examined gender differences in response to varying erotic themes. In Experiment 1, unmarried male (n = 30) and female (n = 32) subjects viewed an erotic film portraying petting; this film was prefaced with instructional sets that established either a love theme (affectionate marital sex) or a lust theme (unemotional sex with a prostitute). In Experiment 2, 36 married couples viewed either a petting erotic film or one depicting coitus; these films were prefaced with instructional sets that established either the love or lust themes or a casual-sex theme (a chance sexual encounter). Arousal, affective, and evaluative responses to these stimuli were assessed. Results of Experiment 1 confirmed the effectiveness of the thematic manipulation and indicated that males and females were not differentially responsive to the love or lust themes along any of the response dimensions. Results of Experiment 2 replicated this finding and indicated that both men and women were more sexually aroused by the casual-sex theme than by those involving love or lust. Apparently, romantic or affectional emphasis is not a precondition for female arousal by erotica. Methodological and conceptual issues relating to the discrepancy between the often-cited female indifference to erotica and the present findings for equal male–female arousal responses are discussed.

It has long been believed that females are less aroused by erotica than are males, and survey research has consistently corroborated this assumption. Unlike males, females interviewed by Kinsey and his associates (Kinsey, Pomeroy, Martin, & Gebhard, 1953) reported that they were not aroused by erotic depictions, and surveys conducted nearly two decades later continue to indicate that this situation has not appreciably changed (Abelson, Cohen, Heaton, & Suder, 1971). Too, field research has documented the fact that women rarely frequent adult bookstores or pornographic movies, and they are not large-scale consumers of erotica (Nawy, 1971). In fact, the assumption that males and females are differentially aroused by erotica was not seriously questioned until quite recently.

EXPERIMENTAL RESEARCH RAISES QUESTIONS

Experimental investigations of actual male and female responses to erotic stimuli have been conducted only in the past few years, but from its inception this research has created doubts concerning female indifference to erotica. Among both married and unmarried individuals in the United States and in Europe, gender differences in sexual arousal following exposure to erotica have been quite limited (Byrne & Lamberth, 1971; Griffitt,

1973; Schmidt, 1975). In addition, approximately the same percentage of males and females report physiological responses to erotic stimuli (Schmidt & Sigusch, 1970), and males and females evidence similar slight increases in sexual activity following exposure to erotica (Schmidt, 1975). Despite these striking similarities, however, men and women do seem to differ with respect to the quality of their affective and evaluative responses to erotica. Results indicate a tendency for females to respond to erotic depictions with more negative affect than do males and to evaluate erotic stimuli more negatively (Byrne, Fisher, Lamberth, & Mitchell, 1974; Griffitt, 1973; Schmidt & Sigusch, 1970).

EXPLAINING EXPERIMENTAL–SURVEY RESEARCH INCONSISTENCIES

It is suggested that social desirability considerations may account for much of the discrepancy between survey and experimental findings with respect to sex differences in erotica-induced arousal. In particular, since interest in erotica seems to be socially proscribed for females in our culture, women may be reluctant to report that they have been aroused by such stimuli (Gebhard, 1973). In laboratory situations, however, the onus is on the experimenter; he or she is responsible for one's contact with erotica, and this seems to facilitate "admission" of arousal and other responses. Too, survey questions concerning whether or not an individual has been aroused by erotica have not taken into account likely sex differences in the kind or amount of erotica one has encountered. In consequence, females may report that they have not been aroused by erotica on the basis of the fact that they have had relatively little experience with such material and not because they are unresponsive to it (Gebhard, 1973; Sigusch, Schmidt, Reinfeld, & Wiedemann-Sutor, 1970). Hence, it seems inappropriate to generalize from survey data concerning whether or not women *have* been aroused by erotica to assumptions that they are unable to respond in such a way. For these reasons, experimental studies involving exposure of males and females to identical erotic stimuli and assessment of their reactions would seem to be the most suitable procedures for investigating sex differences in response to erotica.

THE ROLE OF AFFECTION AND ROMANCE

While experimental investigations do not tend to indicate sex differences in arousal responses to erotica per se, many have assumed that females are more aroused by affectional romantic erotic themes, while males are aroused by purely libidinous, unemotional erotica (Kinsey et al., 1953; Shope, 1975). Investigating gender differences in arousal responses to varying erotic themes, Sigusch and his associates (Sigusch et al., 1970) reported that females were more aroused by affectional and males were more aroused by purely libidinous erotica. In contrast, Schmidt, Sigusch, and Schäffer (1973) found no sex differences in arousal responses to these varying erotic themes, while Jakobovits (1965) reported that females were *more* aroused by "hard-core obscenity" than by "erotic realism" stimuli containing libidinous detail together with nonerotic elements.

SIMPLIFYING A METHODOLOGICAL IMBROGLIO

The inconsistent nature of these findings with respect to erotic theme may be accounted for by a methodological difficulty associated with research in this area. The erotic stimuli employed in such experiments have differed from one another in many ways in addition to intended thematic differences. Variations in theme have been confounded with differences in length, coarseness of language, the specific sexual acts and characters involved in erotic interaction, and a plethora of other differences, making interpretation of results ambiguous. In order to satisfactorily examine sex differences in response to varying themes, the current research employs a methodology that permits manipulation of the theme of an erotic stimulus unconfounded by differences along any other dimension.

In Experiment 1, unmarried subjects viewed an explicit erotic film prefaced with either an affectional and romantic or a purely libidinous, unemotional instructional set. Arousal, affective, and evaluative responses to these stimuli were assessed, as well as background variables pertaining to sexual socialization experiences and sex- and erotica-related beliefs. Experiment 2 was in general similar to Experiment 1, but involved married subjects and a wider range of erotic stimuli in an attempt to extend the generality of this research.

Experiment 1

Method

Subjects were students in undergraduate abnormal psychology classes at Purdue University (30 males, 32 females, all unmarried) who received extra course credit for voluntary participation. All subjects completed an informed consent document well in advance of the study and subjects' anonymity was preserved throughout these procedures. The experimental design was a 2 × 2 (Male Versus Female Subjects × Affectional Versus Libidinous Theme of an Erotic Movie) between-groups factorial.

After granting informed consent but before the actual experiments, subjects completed a 69-item background questionnaire tapping sexual socialization variables and sex- and erotica-related beliefs. Subjects were run in small same-sex groups in sessions conducted by one male and one female experimenter. Following introductory remarks, subjects completed the Bentler Sexual Experience Inventory (Bentler, 1968a, 1968b), assessing heterosexual experience. Subjects then rated their premanipulation feelings of sexual arousal on a self-report grid that allowed for multiple ratings on a 6-point scale (from "not sexually aroused" to "highly sexually aroused") and received a handout containing background information about the movie, as follows:

> Now, you are going to see a portion of a movie which was recently filmed in Denmark. As part of a research project dealing with X-rated movies, your cooperation will be extremely helpful. The dubbing of the dialogue in English has not yet been completed, so you will see a version of the film without a sound track.

These general remarks were followed by differential instructions intended to manipulate the affectional versus libidinous theme.

Love (Affectional) Theme:

> The scene to be presented takes place in a small apartment in Copenhagen. A young working man and his wife, recently married and very much in love are just returning from a dance. They are eager to express their love for one another.

Lust (Libidinous) Theme:

> The scene to be presented takes place in a small apartment in Copenhagen. A young working man has been approached by a prostitute at a dance and has agreed to purchase her services for the evening. They are just returning from the dance. He is eager to obtain what he has bought, and she is quite willing to fulfill her part of the bargain. At this juncture the erotic film, about 10 minutes long, was shown. A silent 16 mm color production, the film depicts a heterosexual interaction in which "both partners undress completely and pet (manual–genital contacts, cunnilingus, and fellatio) reaching orgasm" ("Petting II," Schmidt & Sigusch, 1970, p. 268).

After viewing the film, subjects indicated how sexually aroused they were on a sexual arousal self-report grid, and responded to the 11-item Feelings Scale (Byrne & Sheffield, 1965), which tapped positive and negative affective reactions to the movie. On the male and female versions of the Self Report of Sexual–Physiological Reactions (Schmidt & Sigusch, 1970), subjects were asked if and to what extent they experienced various physiological reactions to the movie (i.e., for males, erection, pre-ejaculatory emission, and "physical excitement"; for females, breast and genital sensations, vaginal lubrication, and "physical excitement"). Questionnaire items tapping evaluative responses to the film and evaluations of the male and female characters in the film were then completed, as well as the Interpersonal Judgment Scale (Byrne, 1971), assessing attraction to the male and female film characters. An explanatory debriefing terminated each experimental session.

Results

Manipulation Check

A 2 × 2 (Sex of Subject × Love Versus Lust Theme of an Erotic Movie) between-groups analysis of variance examined subjects' evaluations of the extent to which the characters in the film cared for one another. Compared to lust-theme subjects, love-theme subjects rated the characters as caring for one another more, $F(1, 58) = 120.20, p < .0001$; thus, the desired thematic differentiation was obtained.[1]

---

[1]This effect was qualified by a Sex of Subject × Movie Theme interaction, $F(1, 58) = 9.60, p < .004$. Simple effects tests (Winer, 1971) revealed that male and female love (versus lust) theme subjects rated the film couple as caring for one another more, $F(1, 58) = 30.95, p < .001$; $F(1, 58) = 98.89, p <$

TABLE 17.1. Mean Postexposure Sexual Arousal and Physical Excitement by Sex of Subject and Movie Theme

Subjects	Love theme	Lust theme
Male		
Sexual arousal	4.29	4.00
Physical excitement	3.29	3.08
Females		
Sexual arousal	4.06	3.93
Physical excitement	3.06	3.00

Note. Mean sexual arousal is computed on the basis of responses to a 6-point scale (1 = "not sexually aroused," 6 = "highly sexually aroused"). Mean physical excitement is computed on the basis of responses to a 5-point scale (1 = "not at all physically excited," 5 = "very much physically excited").

A one-way repeated-measures analysis of variance (preexposure versus postexposure) examined self-reports of sexual arousal. Results showed a pre- to postexposure increase in sexual arousal, $F(1, 61) = 258.33, p < .0001$ (*M* prearousal = 1.92, *M* postarousal = 4.08; 1 = "not sexually aroused," 6 = "highly sexually aroused"); hence, the erotic film elicited a significant increase in sexual arousal.

AROUSAL RESPONSES

A 2 × 2 (Sex of Subject × Love Versus Lust Theme) multivariate analysis of covariance using the preexposure measure of sexual arousal as a covariate examined self-reported postexposure sexual arousal and physical excitement. No main effects or interactions attained significance for these variables: all multivariate $Fs(2, 56) < 1$, ns; all univariate $Fs(1, 57) < 1$, ns (see Table 17.1). Hence, males and females did not report differential arousal responses to love- or lust-theme erotica.

Correlational analyses revealed that self-reports of sexual arousal and physical excitement were related to one another and to self-reports of erection for males and vaginal-lubrication and breast and genital sensations for females (see Table 17.2.). One-way analyses of variance (love versus lust theme for male and female subjects separately) were performed on data from the Self-Reports of Sexual–Physiological Reactions; no differential effects of movie theme were observed for any of the gender-specific physiological reactions to the movie (see Table 17.3 for cell means and *F* ratios).

AFFECTIVE AND EVALUATIVE RESPONSES

Affective and evaluative responses to the erotic film were examined with a 2 × 2 (Sex of Subject × Love Versus Lust Theme) analysis of variance. Male (versus female) and love (versus lust) theme subjects did not differ with respect to positive affective responses, $F(1, 58) < 1$, ns; $F(1, 58) = 1.90$, ns; and the interaction of these factors was not significant, $F(1, 58) = 2.09$, ns. Too, male (versus female) and love (versus lust) theme subjects did not differ with respect to negative affective responses, $F(1, 58) = 1.58$, ns; $F(1, 58) < 1$, ns; and the interaction was again nonsignificant, $F(1, 58) < 1$.

Compared to lust-theme subjects, love-theme subjects evaluated the male and female film char-

TABLE 17.2. Correlations of Self-Reported Sexual Arousal, Physical Excitement, and Physiological Reactions

Subjects	Sexual arousal (not at all–highly)	Sexual excitement (not at all–highly)
Males[a]		
Erection (none–full)	.50***	.72***
Physical excitement (not at all–highly)	.73***	—
Females		
Vaginal lubrication (none–much)	.46***	.58***
Breast sensations (none–many)	.36**	.53***
Genital sensations (none–many)	.25*	.58***
Physical excitement (not at all–highly)	.55***	—

Note. For males, *df* = 28; for females, *df* = 30.
[a] Because there was no variance for self-reports of pre-ejaculatory emission, correlations could not be computed for this variable.
* $p < .10$.
** $p < .05$.
*** $p < .01$.

.0001. Male (versus female) love-theme subjects rated the film couple as caring for one another less, $F(1, 58) = 6.98, p < .02$, while male and female lust-theme subjects' evaluations did not differ, $F(1, 58) = 3.03$, ns. Although this interaction was not anticipated, it does not pose any particular problems for this experiment. Mean caring ratings by both male and female love-theme subjects were well above the midpoint of the scale range, while both male and female lust-theme subjects' ratings fell well below the midpoint. Thus, the manipulation was successful.

acters more positively, $F(1, 57)$ 7.49, $p < .009$; $F(1, 58) = 17.03$, $p < .0004$, and Interpersonal Judgment Scale scores indicated that love (versus lust) theme subjects were more attracted to these characters, $F(1, 57) = 5.93$, $p < .02$; $F(1, 57) = 5.41$, $p < .03$. In addition, females (compared to males) were more likely to rate the stimuli as pornographic, $F(1, 58) = 6.07$, $p < .02$, and were more in favor of restrictions on the production and display of the stimuli and other, similar material, $F(1, 57) = 8.60$, $p < .006$.

BACKGROUND VARIABLES

One-way analyses of variance (male versus female subjects) examined background questionnaire data pertaining to sexual socialization experiences and sex- and erotica-related beliefs. Compared to males, females were younger, $F(1, 59) = 15.66$, $p < .0005$ (M male age = 20.47 years, M female age = 19.42 years), and reported that they had seen less erotica, $F(1, 60) = 16.26$, $p < .0005$, and were generally less aroused by erotica, $F(1, 60) = 11.94$, $p < .002$. Too, females (versus males) reported that they masturbated less frequently, $F(1, 59) = 14.84$, $p < .0006$, and enjoyed (or would enjoy) oral–genital stimulation of or by their partner less, $F(1, 54) = 21.51$, $p < .0002$; $F(1, 55) = 7.63$, $p < .008$. Despite these differences in masturbatory experience, contact with erotica, and attitudes about fellatio and cunnilingus, data from the Bentler Sexual Experience Inventory indicated similar levels of heterosexual experience for males and females, $F(1, 60) < 1$, ns. Compared to males, females were less likely to indicate the belief that Supreme Court censorship decisions have been too restrictive, $F(1, 57) = 6.32$, $p < .02$, and females were also less in favor of the free availability of erotica for adults, $F(1, 60) = 8.29$, $p < .006$.

Experiment 2

In order to explore the generality of these findings across differing subject samples and erotic stimuli, additional research was conducted. In Experiment 2, mixed-sex groups of married couples viewed an erotic film either depicting petting and partial nudity or depicting coitus. These films were prefaced with instructional sets manipulating either love or lust theme (as in Experiment 1), or a casual-sex theme describing a chance sexual encounter. The casual-sex theme was introduced to provide a more socially acceptable scenario than the prostitute–client lust theme, but one which was still purely libidinous and unemotional. Arousal, affective, and evaluative responses to these stimuli were assessed, as well as background variables pertaining to sexual socialization experiences and sex- and erotica-related beliefs.

TABLE 17.3. Mean Physiological Response by Sex of Subject and Movie Theme

Subjects	Love theme	Lust theme	*df*	*F*
Males				
Erection (1 = none, 3 = full)	1.82	1.69	1, 28	<1, *ns*
Pre-ejaculatory emission (1 = no, 2 = yes)	1.00	1.00	1, 27	<1, *ns*
Females				
Vaginal lubrication (1 = none, 5 = much)	2.44	2.43	1, 30	<1, *ns*
Breast sensations (1 = none, 5 = many)	1.39	1.93	1, 30	2.07, *ns*
Genital sensations (1 = none, 5 = many)	3.06	3.43	1, 30	1.08, *ns*

Method

Procedures of Experiment 2 were similar to those of Experiment 1, with several exceptions. Subjects were 36 volunteer married couples in their mid-20s who responded to advertisements in the local newspaper and notices posted in the campus community; at least one member of the majority of these couples was a student at Purdue University. Subjects were run in small mixed-sex groups of couples. In addition to love and lust themes, a casual-sex theme was manipulated by giving subjects differential instructions, as follows.

Casual-Sex Theme:

> The scene to be presented takes place in a small apartment in Copenhagen. A young working man has met a girl at a dance, and they were sexually attracted to one another almost immediately. They are just returning from the dance and are eager to enjoy the sexual exploration which each is anticipating.

An erotic film portraying petting and partial nudity was shown in Experiment 2; this film depicts a heterosexual interaction in which "both partners undress to their underwear and pet (manual–genital contacts) without reaching orgasm" ("Petting I," Schmidt & Sigusch, 1970, p. 268). In addition, an erotic film portraying coitus was presented; this film consists of a heterosexual interaction involving "foreplay with manual–genital contacts, cunnilingus, and fellatio; coitus in different positions" ("Coitus II," Schmidt & Sigusch, 1970, p. 270). The experimental design was a 2 × 2 × 3 (Sex of Subject × Petting Versus Coitus Erotic Movie × Love Versus Casual-Sex Versus Lust Theme) between-groups factorial.

Results

AROUSAL RESPONSES

A 2 × 2 × 3 × 2 (Sex of Subject × Petting Versus Coitus Movie × Love Versus Casual-Sex Versus Lust Theme × Preexposure Versus Postexposure) three-between, one-within analysis of variance examined self-reported sexual arousal. Results indicated a pre- to postexposure increase in sexual arousal, $F(1, 60) = 182.16$, $p <.0001$ (M prearousal = 1.39, M postarousal = 3.56: 1 = "not sexually aroused," 6 = "highly sexually aroused"), while the main effect for sex of subject was not significant, $F(1, 60) = 1.35$, ns. A main effect for theme of the erotic stimuli was also observed, $F(2, 60) = 4.39$, $p <. 02$. Newman-Keuls procedures (Winer, 1971) revealed that the casual-sex theme (M = 2.92) was more arousing than either the love (M = 2.19) or lust (M = 2.31) themes, which were equally arousing (all $ps < .05$: see Table 17.4). Correlational analyses revealed that self-reported sexual arousal was significantly related to self-reports of erection, $r(33) = .60$, $p < .001$, and pre-ejaculatory emission, $r(33) = .36$, $p < .02$ (for males), and vaginal lubrication. $r(34) = .35$, $p < .02$, and breast sensations, $r(34) = .53$, $p < .001$ (for females). A series of 2 × 3 (Petting Versus Coitus Movie × Love Versus Casual-Sex Versus Lust Theme) analyses of variance performed separately for male and female subjects examined self-reported physiological reactions to the erotic stimuli. A main effect of erotic theme was observed for self-reports of erection, $F(2, 29) = 3.86$, $p < .04$. Newman-Keuls procedures revealed that the casual-sex theme (M = 1.25; 0 = no erection, 1 = semi-erection, 2 = full erection) elicited a stronger erectile response than the lust theme (M = .83; $p < .05$), while the love (M = 1.00) and casual-sex themes, and love and lust themes were equally arousing. Too, a main effect of petting versus coitus erotic movie was observed for self-reported vaginal lubrication, $F(1, 30) = 4.76$, $p < .04$: compared to females who viewed the petting film (M = 1.00; 0 = no vaginal lubrication, 1 = unsure, 2 = vaginal lubrication, those who viewed the coitus movie (M = 1.61) reported more vaginal lubrication. No other main effects or interactions were observed for gender-specific physiological reactions (see Table 17.5 for cell means and F ratios).

TABLE 17.4. Mean Pre- and Postexposure Sexual Arousal by Sex of Subject, Content of Erotic Movie, and Movie Theme

Variable	Subjects	
	Males	Females
Petting movie		
Love theme		
Preexposure	1.33	1.17
Postexposure	3.50	3.17
Causal-sex theme		
Preexposure	1.33	1.50
Postexposure	4.17	3.33
Lust theme		
Preexposure	1.00	1.00
Postexposure	2.83	4.33
Coitus movie		
Love theme		
Preexposure	1.00	1.17
Postexposure	3.00	3.17
Causal-sex theme		
Preexposure	1.50	2.33
Postexposure	4.00	5.17
Lust theme		
Preexposure	1.50	1.83
Postexposure	3.00	3.00

Note. Means are computed on the basis of responses to a 6-point scale (1 = "not sexually aroused," 6 = "highly sexually aroused").

AFFECTIVE AND EVALUATIVE RESPONSES

Affective and evaluative responses to the stimuli were examined with a 2 × 2 × 3 (Sex of Subject × Petting Versus Coitus Movie × Love Versus Casual-Sex Versus Lust Theme) analysis of variance. Subjects who viewed the coitus (versus petting) movie responded with more positive affect, F(1,

60) = 11.48, $p < .002$, and evaluated it as more pornographic, $F(1, 60) = 17.00$, $p < .0004$.

BACKGROUND VARIABLES

One-way analyses of variance (male versus female subjects) examined questionnaire data pertaining to sexual socialization experiences and sex-related beliefs. Compared to males, females reported having been less aroused by erotica in the past, $F(1, 70) = 11.73$, $p < .002$, and were more likely to indicate that guilt had inhibited their free sexual expression, $F(1, 69) = 3.92$, $p < .05$. Females (versus males) reported having had fewer premarital sex partners, $F(1, 69) = 6.04$, $p < .02$, and reported enjoying intercourse less $F(1, 70) = 5.21$, $p < .03$. Too, females (more than males) endorsed the belief that sex should be accompanied by a love relationship, $F(1, 70)$ 7.33, $p < .009$, and were more opposed to extramarital sex, $F(1, 69) = 5.76$, $p < .02$.

General Discussion

Results of Experiment 1 demonstrated that the thematic manipulation was quite successful. Erotic theme did not, however, interact with sex of subject to result in differential arousal, affective, or evaluative responses to the stimuli. Along the dimensions measured, females were not more responsive to love-theme erotica and males were not more responsive to lust-theme erotica. Experiment 2 replicated these findings and further indicated that *both* males and females were more aroused by the casual-sex theme than by the love or lust themes, which were equally arousing. Apparently, the prospect of a chance sexual encounter was more exciting to both men and women than either marital sex or sex with a prostitute. The results strongly suggest that affectional or romantic emphasis is not a precondition for female arousal by erotica.

Consistent with earlier experimental findings (Byrne et al., 1974; Grifitt, 1973; Schmidt, 1975; Schmidt & Sigusch, 1970), females were more likely than males to rate the erotic stimuli as pornographic and were more in favor of restrictions on such material. And, in line with survey data (Abelson et al., 1971; Kinsey et al., 1953), females, compared to males, reported having been less aroused in the past by erotica, having had less contact with erotica, and having engaged in less frequent masturbation. They also indicated more negative beliefs about erotica and certain sexual acts. In spite of these differences, however, the data from two experiments indicate that females were as aroused by the erotic stimuli as were males.

In view of societal proscriptions on erotica for women, questions may be raised with respect to the representativeness of the females who took part

TABLE 17.5. Mean Physiological Responses by Content of Erotic Movie and Movie Theme

	Petting			Coitus		
Subjects	Love	Casual sex	Lust	Love	Casual sex	Lust
Males						
Erection[a]						
F(2, 29) = 3.86, *p* < .04; *F*(1.29) < 1, *ns.*	1.00	1.33	.83	1.00	1.17	.83
Pre-ejaculatory emission[b]						
F(2, 29) = 1. 43, *ns; F*(1, 29) < 1, *ns.*	.00	.33	.33	.20	.67	.17
Females						
Vaginal lubrication[b]						
F(2, 30) <1, *ns; F*(1, 30) = 4.76, *p* < .04.	1.00	.83	1.17	1.67	1.83	1.33
Genital sensations[b]						
F(2, 30) < 1, *ns; F*(1, 30) < 1, *ns.*	1.67	1.67	2.00	2.00	2.00	1.33
Breast sensations[b]						
F(2, 30) < 1.13, *ns; F*(1, 30) = 2.00, *ns.*	.33	.33	.67	.33	1.33	1.00

Note. F ratios below each variable represent main effects of erotic theme and content of erotic movie, in this order. For interaction terms, all *F*s < 1, ns, except for genital sensations, *F*(2, 30) = 2.50, *ns*.
[a]0 = none, 1 = partial, 2 = full.
[b]0 = no, 1 = unsure, 2 = yes.

in these experiments. In particular, it may be speculated that these women were more sexually liberal than other females. The fact that females who participated in this research expressed more negative sex- and erotica-related beliefs than did males and reported less prior contact with erotica, however, suggests that the current samples of women were not unrepresentative. In essence, differences in attitudes toward and experience with erotica that are assumed to characterize men and women in general were rejected in the present samples. In an attempt to evaluate the representativeness of the females who participated in this research, they were compared along several key dimensions with representative groups of women. Females in Experiment 1 were compared with a sample of 32 undergraduate women who took part in a pretesting procedure associated with an introductory psychology course: this pretesting session was designed specifically so as to minimize self-selection bias. Subjects were informed that the pretesting would involve a series of general questionnaires covering a wide variety of issues, including sex; while subjects were informed that they could choose not to answer these items, virtually the entire sample completed all questions. Results show that females in Experiment 1 and those in the pretesting group did not differ with respect to virginity, $F(1, 62) = 1.57$, ns, nor age of first intercourse, $F(1, 33) = 1.08$, ns. The married women in Experiment 2 were compared to a national sample of women (Hunt, 1974) concerning premarital coital experience and masturbation. Females from Experiment 2 did not differ from those in the national sample with respect to having had premarital intercourse, $z = .53$, ns, or having ever masturbated, $z = .12$, ns. These data further suggest the representativeness of the current samples of women and are consistent with findings reported by Kaats and Davis (1971), which indicate that factors other than sexual liberalness may determine volunteering for sex research.

It may be relevant to mention that procedures for collecting arousal and other data—which are clearly not part of the usual context for viewing erotica—may have introduced certain demand characteristics. While it is difficult to gauge the impact of these measurement procedures on subjects' responses, there appears to be no reason to anticipate differential effects on males and females. The findings for equal male–female arousal responses were consistent across a range of sexually explicit films and a variety of erotic themes; they did not differ as a function of single versus married status, or conducting the experiment with same-sex versus mixed-sex groups. While the current experiments did not involve exposing subjects individually to erotic stimuli, previous research employing such procedures has also reported no sex differences in arousal responses to erotica (Schmidt, 1975). And, although a nonerotic film control condition was not employed in these experiments, previous research (Miller, 1977) has revealed that even subjects who expected to see erotic stimuli, but who instead viewed nonerotic control material, did not report that they were sexually aroused. Thus, the mere fact that subjects are asked about their sexual arousal does not appear to elicit such responses.

With respect to ratings of sexual arousal, questions may be raised concerning the equivalence of male–female self-reports; it may be speculated that men and women have different interpretations of "sexual arousal" and "physical excitement." Within-sex correlation results, however, show that self-reported sexual arousal was significantly related to reports of physiological reactions and physical excitement for both men and women. These findings are in accord with data reported by Wincze, Hoon, and Hoon (1977), which suggest a strong association between direct physiological and subjective measures of sexual arousal. The question of whether males and females (or for that matter, any different individuals) attach the same meanings to subjective ratings of sexual arousal is impossible to resolve definitively. For each sex, however, self-reports of sexual arousal do seem to reflect physiological indicators of arousal. Hence, there seems to be some basis for comparison of males' and females' self-reported sexual arousal.

The current findings suggest that men and women may not be differentially aroused by a variety of erotic themes and indicate that there may be no *inherent* obstacles to female stimulation by erotica. Females' expressions of disinterest in erotica were in sharp contrast to the fact that they were not less aroused by it than were males. Social proscription of female interest in erotica may promote espousal of indifference, which is not present when arousal responses to specific erotic stimuli are examined.

Conclusions

The current research considered gender differences in response to varying erotic themes in order to refine more general notions concerning sex differences in response to erotica per se. Prefacing sexually explicit films with differential instructional sets permitted manipulation of erotic theme unconfounded by differences along other stimulus dimensions. Results of two experiments indicated that affectional or romantic emphasis is not a prerequisite for female arousal by erotica. Culturally imposed considerations of social desirability, it is suggested, may account for females' expressed disinterest in erotica even though they do not appear to be less aroused by actual erotic stimuli than are males.

REFERENCES

Abelson, H., Cohen, R., Heaton, E., & Suder, C. (1971). National survey of public attitudes toward and experience with erotic materials. In *Technical report of the Commission on Obscenity and Pornography* (Vol. 6). Washington, DC: U.S. Government Printing Office.

Bentler, P. M. (1968). Heterosexual behavior assessment—I. Males. *Behaviour Research and Therapy, 6,* 21–25. (a)

Bentler, P. M. (1971). Heterosexual behavior assessment—II. Females. *Behaviour Research and Therapy, 6, 27–30.* (b)

Byrne, D. (1971). *The attraction paradigm.* New York: Academic Press.

Byrne, D., Fisher, J. D., Lamberth, J., & Mitchell, H. E. (1974). Evaluations of erotica: Facts or feelings? *Journal of Personality and Social Psychology, 19,* 111–116.

Byrne, D., & Lamberth, J. (1971). The effect of erotic stimuli on sex arousal, evaluative responses, and subsequent behavior. In *Technical report of the Commission on Obscenity and Pornography* (Vol. 8). Washington, DC: U.S. Government Printing Office.

Byrne, D., & Sheffield, J. (1965). Response to sexually arousing stimuli as a function of repressing and sensitizing defenses. *Journal of Abnormal Psychology, 70,* 114–118.

Gebhard, P. H. (1973). Sex differences in sexual response. *Archives of Sexual Behavior, 2,* 201–203.

Griffitt, W. (1973). Response to erotica and the projection of response to erotica in the opposite sex. *Journal of Experimental Research in Personality, 6,* 330–338.

Hunt, M. (1974). *Sexual behavior in the 1970's.* Chicago: Playboy Press.

Jakobovits, L. A. (1965). Evaluational reactions to erotic literature. *Psychological Reports, 16,* 985–991.

Kaats, G. R., & Davis, K. E. (1971). Effects of volunteer biases in studies of sexual behavior and attitudes. *Journal of Sex Research, 7,* 26–34.

Kinsey, A. C., Pomeroy, W. B., Martin, C. E., & Gebhard, P. H. (1953). *Sexual behavior in the human female.* Philadelphia: Saunders.

Miller, C. T. (1977). *Generalizability of the facilitating effect of anger on sexual arousal.* Unpublished master's thesis. Purdue University.

Nawy, H. (1971). The San Francisco erotic marketplace. In *Technical report of the Commission on Obscenity and Pornography* (Vol. 4). Washington, DC: U.S. Government Printing Office.

Schmidt, G. (1975). Male–female differences in sexual arousal and behavior during and after exposure to sexually explicit stimuli. *Archives of Sexual Behavior, 4,* 353–364.

Schmidt, G., & Sigusch, V. (1970). Sex differences in responses to psychosexual stimulation by films and slides. *Journal of Sex Research, 6,* 268–283.

Schmidt, G., Sigusch, V., & Schäfer, S. (1973). Responses to reading erotic stories: Male–female differences. *Archives of Sexual Behavior, 2,* 181–199.

Shope, D. F. (1975). *Interpersonal sexuality.* Philadelphia: Saunders.

Sigusch, V., Schmidt, C., Reinfeld, A., & Wiedemann-Sutor, I. (1970). Psychosexual stimulation: Sex differences. *Journal of Sex Research, 6,* 10–24.

Wincze, J. P., Hoon, P., & Hoon, E. F. (1977). Sexual arousal in women: A comparison of cognitive and physiological responses by continuous measurement. *Archives of Sexual Behavior, 6,* 121–133.

Winer, B. J. (1971). *Statistical principles in experimental design.* New York: McGraw-Hill.

Appendix: How to Read a Journal Article in Social Psychology

Christian H. Jordan and Mark P. Zanna • University of Waterloo

How to Read a Journal Article in Social Psychology

When approaching a journal article for the first time, and often on subsequent occasions, most people try to digest it as they would any piece of prose. They start at the beginning and read word for word, until eventually they arrive at the end, perhaps a little bewildered, but with a vague sense of relief. This is not an altogether terrible strategy; journal articles do have a logical structure that lends itself to this sort of reading. There are, however, more efficient approaches–approaches that enable you, a student of social psychology, to cut through peripheral details, avoid sophisticated statistics with which you may not be familiar, and focus on the central ideas in an article. Arming yourself with a little foreknowledge of what is contained in journal articles, as well as some practical advice on how to read them, should help you read journal articles more effectively. If this sounds tempting, read on.

Journal articles offer a window into the inner workings of social psychology. They document how social psychologists formulate hypotheses, design empirical studies, analyze the observations they collect, and interpret their results. Journal articles also serve an invaluable archival function: They contain the full store of common and cumulative knowledge of social psychology. Having documentation of past research allows researchers to build on past findings and advance our understanding of social behavior, without pursuing avenues of investigation that have already been explored. Perhaps most importantly, a research study is never complete until its results have been shared with others, colleagues and students alike. Journal articles are a primary means of communicating research findings. As such, they can be genuinely exciting and interesting to read.

That last claim may have caught you off guard. For beginning readers, journal articles may seem anything but interesting and exciting. They may, on the contrary, appear daunting and esoteric, laden with jargon and obscured by menacing statistics. Recognizing this fact, we hope to arm you, through this paper, with the basic information you will need to read journal articles with a greater sense of comfort and perspective.

Social psychologists study many fascinating topics, ranging from prejudice and discrimination, to culture, persuasion, liking and love, conformity and obedience, aggression, and the self. In our daily lives, these are issues we often struggle to understand. Social psychologists present systematic observations of, as well as a wealth of ideas about, such issues in journal articles. It would be a shame if the fascination and intrigue these topics have were lost in their translation into journal publications. We don't think they are, and by the end of this paper, hopefully you won't either.

Journal articles come in a variety of forms, including research reports, review articles, and theoretical articles. Put briefly, a *research report* is a formal presentation of an original research study, or series of studies. A *review article* is an evaluative survey of previously published work, usually organized by a guiding theory or point of view. The author of a review article summarizes previous investigations of a circumscribed problem, comments on what progress has been made toward its resolution, and suggests areas of the problem that require further study. A *theoretical article* also evaluates past research, but focuses on the development of theories used to explain empirical findings. Here, the author may present a new theory to explain a set of findings, or may compare and contrast a set of competing theories, suggesting why one theory might be the superior one.

This paper focuses primarily on how to read research reports, for several reasons. First, the bulk of published literature in social psychology consists of research reports. Second, the summaries presented in review articles, and the ideas set forth in theoretical articles, are built on findings presented in research reports. To get a deep understanding of how research is done in social psychology, fluency in reading original research reports is essential. Moreover, theoretical articles frequently report new studies that pit one theory against another, or test a novel prediction derived from a new theory. In order to appraise the validity of such theoretical contentions, a grounded understanding of basic findings is invaluable. Finally, most research reports are written in a standard format that is likely unfamiliar to new readers. The format of review and theoretical articles is less standardized, and more like that of textbooks and other scholarly writings, with which most readers are familiar. This is not to suggest that such articles are easier to read and comprehend than research reports; they can be quite challenging indeed. It is simply the case that, because more rules apply to the writing of research reports, more guidelines can be offered on how to read them.

The Anatomy of Research Reports

Most research reports in social psychology, and in psychology in general, are written in a standard format prescribed by the American Psychological Association (1994). This is a great boon to both readers and writers. It allows writers to present their ideas and findings in a clear, systematic manner. Consequently, as a reader, once you understand this format, you will not be on completely foreign ground when you approach a new research report—regardless of its specific content. You will know where in the paper particular information is found, making it easier to locate. No matter what your reasons for reading a research report, a firm understanding of the format in which they are written will ease your task. We discuss the format of research reports next, with some practical suggestions on how to read them. Later, we discuss how this format reflects the process of scientific investigation, illustrating how research reports have a coherent narrative structure.

TITLE AND ABSTRACT

Though you can't judge a book by its cover, you can learn a lot about a research report simply by reading its title. The title presents a concise statement of the theoretical issues investigated, and/or the variables that were studied. For example, the following title was taken almost at random from a prestigious journal in social psychology: "Sad and guilty? Affective influences on the explanation of conflict in close relationships" (Forgas, 1994, p.

56). Just by reading the title, it can be inferred that the study investigated how emotional states change the way people explain conflict in close relationships. It also suggests that when feeling sad, people accept more personal blame for such conflicts (i.e., feel more guilty).

The abstract is also an invaluable source of information. It is a brief synopsis of the study, and packs a lot of information into 150 words or less. The abstract contains information about the problem that was investigated, how it was investigated, the major findings of the study, and hints at the theoretical and practical implications of the findings. Thus, the abstract is a useful summary of the research that provides the gist of the investigation. Reading this outline first can be very helpful, because it tells you where the report is going, and gives you a useful framework for organizing information contained in the article.

The title and abstract of a research report are like a movie preview. A movie preview highlights the important aspects of a movie's plot, and provides just enough information for one to decide whether to watch the whole movie. Just so with titles and abstracts; they highlight the key features of a research report to allow you to decide if you want to read the whole paper. And just as with movie previews, they do not give the whole story. Reading just the title and abstract is never enough to fully understand a research report.

INTRODUCTION

A research report has four main sections: introduction, method, results, and discussion. Though it is not explicitly labeled, the introduction begins the main body of a research report. Here, the researchers set the stage for the study. They present the problem under investigation, and state why it was important to study. By providing a brief review of past research and theory relevant to the central issue of investigation, the researchers place the study in an historical context and suggest how the study advances knowledge of the problem. Beginning with broad theoretical and practical considerations, the researchers delineate the rationale that led them to the specific set of hypotheses tested in the study. They also describe how they decided on their research strategy (e.g., why they chose an experiment or a correlational study).

The introduction generally begins with a broad consideration of the problem investigated. Here, the researchers want to illustrate that the problem they studied is a real problem about which people should care. If the researchers are studying prejudice, they may cite statistics that suggest discrimination is prevalent, or describe specific cases of discrimination. Such information helps illustrate why the research is both practically and theoretically meaningful, and why you should bother reading about it. Such discussions are often quite interesting and useful. They can help you decide for yourself if the research has merit. But they may not be essential for understanding the study at hand. Read the introduction carefully, but choose judiciously what to focus on and remember. To understand a study, what you really need to understand is what the researchers' hypotheses were, and how they were derived from theory, informal observation, or intuition. Other background information may be intriguing, but may not be critical to understand what the researchers did and why they did it.

While reading the introduction, try answering these questions: What problem was studied, and why? How does this study relate to, and go beyond, past investigations of the problem? How did the researchers derive their hypotheses? What questions do the researchers hope to answer with this study?

METHOD

In the method section, the researchers translate their hypotheses into a set of specific, testable questions. Here, the researchers introduce the main characters of the study—the subjects or participants—describing their characteristics (gender, age, etc.) and how many of them were involved. Then, they describe the materials (or apparatus), such as any questionnaires or special equipment, used in the study. Finally, they describe chronologically the procedures of the study; that is, how the study was conducted. Often, an overview of the research design will begin the method section. This overview provides a broad outline of the design, alerting you to what you should attend.

The method is presented in great detail so that other researchers can recreate the study to confirm (or question) its results. This degree of detail is normally not necessary to understand a study, so don't get bogged down trying to memorize the particulars of the procedures. Focus on how the independent variables were manipulated (or measured) and how the dependent variables were measured.

Measuring variables adequately is not always an easy matter. Many of the variables psychologists are interested in cannot be directly observed, so they must be inferred from participants' behavior. Happiness, for example, cannot be directly observed. Thus, researchers interested in how being happy influences people's judgments must infer happiness (or its absence) from their behavior—perhaps by asking people how happy they are, and judging their degree of happiness from their responses; perhaps by studying people's facial expressions for signs of happiness, such as smiling. Think about the measures researchers use while reading the method section. Do they adequately reflect or capture the concepts they are meant to measure? If a measure seems odd, consider carefully how the researchers justify its use.

Oftentimes in social psychology, getting there is half the fun. In other words, how a result is obtained can be just as interesting as the result itself. Social psychologists often strive to have participants behave in a natural, spontaneous manner, while controlling enough of their environment to pinpoint the causes of their behavior. Sometimes, the major contribution of a research report is its presentation of a novel method of investigation. When this is the case, the method will be discussed in some detail in the introduction.

Participants in social psychology studies are intelligent and inquisitive people who are responsive to what happens around them. Because of this, they are not always initially told the true purpose of a study. If they were told, they might not act naturally. Thus, researchers frequently need to be creative, presenting a credible rationale for complying with procedures, without revealing the study's purpose. This rationale is known as a *cover story,* and is often an elaborate scenario. While reading the method section, try putting yourself in the shoes of a participant in the study, and ask yourself if the instructions given to participants seem sensible, realistic, and engaging. Imagining what it was like to be in the study will also help you remember the study's procedure, and aid you in interpreting the study's results.

While reading the method section, try answering these questions: How were the hypotheses translated into testable questions? How were the variables of interest manipulated and/or measured? Did the measures used adequately reflect the variables of interest? For example, is self-reported income an adequate measure of social class? Why or why not?

RESULTS

The results section describes how the observations collected were analyzed to determine whether the original hypotheses were supported. Here, the data (observations of behavior) are described, and statistical tests are presented. Because of this, the results section is often intimidating to readers who have little or no training in statistics. Wading through complex and unfamiliar statistical analyses is understandably confusing and frustrating. As a result, many students are tempted to skip over reading this section. We advise you not to do so. Empirical findings are the foundation of any science and results sections are where such findings are presented.

Take heart. Even the most prestigious researchers were once in your shoes and sympathize with you. Though space in psychology journals is limited, researchers try to strike a balance between the need to be clear and the need to be brief in describing their results. In an influential paper on how to write good research reports, Bem (1987) offered this advice to researchers:

> No matter how technical or abstruse your article is in its particulars, intelligent nonpsychologists with no expertise in statistics or experimental design should be able to comprehend the broad outlines of what you did and why. They should understand in general terms what was learned. (p. 74)

Generally speaking, social psychologists try to practice this advice.

Most statistical analyses presented in research reports test specific hypotheses. Often, each analysis presented is preceded by a reminder of the hypothesis it is meant to test. After an analysis is presented, researchers usually provide a narrative description of the result in plain English. When the hypothesis tested by a statistical analysis is not explicitly stated, you can usually determine the hypothesis that was tested by reading this narrative description of the result, and referring back to the introduction to locate an hypothesis that corresponds to that result. After even the most complex statistical analysis, there will be a written description of what the result means conceptually. Turn your attention to these descriptions. Focus on the conceptual meaning of research findings, not on the mechanics of how they were obtained (unless you're comfortable with statistics).

Aside from statistical tests and narrative descriptions of results, results sections also frequently contain tables and graphs. These are efficient summaries of data. Even if you are not familiar with statistics, look closely at tables and graphs, and pay attention to the means or correlations presented in them. Researchers always include written descriptions of the pertinent aspects of tables and graphs. While reading these descriptions, check the tables and graphs to make sure what the researchers say accurately reflects their data. If they say there was a difference between two groups on a particular dependent measure, look at the means in the table that correspond to those two groups, and see if the means do differ as described. Occasionally, results seem to become stronger in their narrative description than an examination of the data would warrant.

Statistics *can* be misused. When they are, results are difficult to interpret. Having said this, a lack of statistical knowledge should not make you overly cautious while reading results sections. Though not a perfect antidote, journal articles undergo extensive review by professional researchers before publication. Thus, most misapplications of statistics are caught and corrected before an article is published. So, if you are unfamiliar with statistics, you can be reasonably confident that findings are accurately reported.

While reading the results section, try answering these questions: Did the researchers provide evidence that any independent variable manipulations were effective? For example, if testing for behavioral differences between happy and sad participants, did the researchers demonstrate that one group was in fact happier than the other? What were the major findings of the study? Were the researchers' original hypotheses supported by their observations? If not, look in the discussion section for how the researchers explain the findings that were obtained.

DISCUSSION

The discussion section frequently opens with a summary of what the study found, and an evaluation of whether the findings supported the original hypotheses. Here, the researchers evaluate the theoretical and practical implications of their results. This can be particularly interesting when the results did not work out exactly as the researchers anticipated. When such is the case, consider the researchers' explanations carefully, and see if they seem plausible to you. Often, researchers will also report any aspects of their study that limit their interpretation of its results, and suggest further research that could overcome these limitations to provide a better understanding of the problem under investigation.

Some readers find it useful to read the first few paragraphs of the discussion section before reading any other part of a research report. Like the abstract, these few paragraphs usually contain all of the main ideas of a research report: What the hypotheses were, the major findings and whether they supported the original hypotheses, and how the findings relate to past research and theory. Having this information before reading a research report can guide your reading, allowing you to focus on the specific details you need to complete your understanding of a study. The description of the results, for example, will alert you to the major variables that were studied. If they are unfamiliar to you, you can pay special attention to how they are defined in the introduction, and how they are operationalized in the method section.

After you have finished reading an article, it can also be helpful to reread the first few paragraphs of the discussion and the abstract. As noted, these two passages present highly distilled summaries of the major ideas in a research report. Just as they can help guide your reading of a report, they can also help you consolidate your understanding of a report once you have finished reading it. They provide a check on whether you have understood the main points of a report, and offer a succinct digest of the research in the authors' own words.

While reading the discussion section, try answering these questions: What conclusions can be drawn from the study? What new information does the study provide about the problem under investigation? Does the study help resolve the problem? What are the practical and theoretical implications of the study's findings? Did the results contradict past research findings? If so, how do the researchers explain this discrepancy?

Some Notes on Reports of Multiple Studies

Up to this point, we have implicitly assumed that a research report describes just one study. It is also quite common, however, for a research report to describe a series of studies of the same problem in a single article. When such is the case, each study reported will have the same basic structure (introduction, method, results, and discussion sections) that we have outlined, with the notable exception that sometimes the results and discussion section for each study are combined. Combined "results and discussion" sections contain the same information that separate results and discussion sections normally contain. Sometimes, the authors present all their results first, and only then discuss the implications of these results, just as they would in separate results and discussion sections. Other times, however, the authors alternate between describing results and discussing their implications, as each result is presented. In either case, you should be on the lookout for the same information, as outlined above in our consideration of separate results and discussion sections.

Reports including multiple studies also differ from single study reports in that they include more general introduction and discussion sections. The general introduction, which begins the main body of a research report, is similar in essence to the introduction of a single study report. In both cases, the researchers describe the problem investigated and its practical and theoretical significance. They also demonstrate how they derived their hypotheses, and explain how their research relates to past investigations of the problem. In contrast, the separate introductions to each individual study in reports of multiple studies are usually quite brief, and focus more specifically on the logic and rationale of each particular study presented. Such introductions generally describe the methods used in the particular study, outlining how they answer questions that have not been adequately addressed by past research, including studies reported earlier in the same article.

General discussion sections parallel discussions of single studies, except on a somewhat grander scale. They present all of the information contained in discussions of single studies, but consider the implications of all the studies presented together. A general discussion section brings the main ideas of a research program into bold relief. It typically begins with a concise summary of a research program's main findings, their relation to the original hypotheses, and their practical and theoretical implications. Thus, the summaries that begin general discussion sections are counterparts of the summaries that begin discussion sections of single study reports. Each presents a digest of the research presented in an article that can serve as both an organizing framework (when read first), and as a check on how well you have understood the main points of an article (when read last).

Research Reporting as Story Telling

A research report tells the story of how a researcher or group of researchers investigated a specific problem. Thus, a research report has a linear, narrative structure with a beginning, middle, and end. In his paper on writing research reports, Bem noted that a research report:

> . . .is shaped like an hourglass. It begins with broad general statements, progressively narrows down to the specifics of [the] study, and then broadens out again to more general considerations. (1987, p. 175)

This format roughly mirrors the process of scientific investigation, wherein researchers do the following: (1) start with a broad idea from which they formulate a narrower set of hypotheses, informed by past empirical findings (introduction); (2) design a specific set of concrete operations to test these hypotheses (method); (3) analyze the observations collected in this way, and decide if they support the original hypotheses (results); and (4) explore the broader theoretical and practical implications of the findings, and consider how they contribute to an understanding of the problem under investigation (discussion). Though these stages are somewhat arbitrary distinctions—research actually proceeds in a number of different ways—they help elucidate the inner logic of research reports.

While reading a research report, keep this linear structure in mind. Though it is difficult to remember a series of seemingly disjointed facts, when these facts are joined together in a logical, narrative structure, they become easier to comprehend and recall. Thus, always remember that a research report tells a story. It will help you to organize the information you read, and remember it later.

Describing research reports as stories is not just a convenient metaphor. Research reports are stories. Stories can be said to consist of two components: A telling of what happened, and an explanation of why it happened. It is tempting to view science as an endeavor that simply catalogues facts, but nothing is further from the truth. The goal of science, social psychology included, is to *explain* facts, to explain *why* what happened happened. Social psychology is built on the dynamic interplay of discovery and justification, the dialogue between systematic observation of relations and their theoretical explanation. Though research reports do present novel facts based on systematic observation, these facts are presented in the service of ideas. Facts in isolation are trivia. Facts tied together by an explanatory theory are science. Therein lies the story. To really understand what researchers have to say, you need consider how their explanations relate to their findings.

The Rest of the Story

> There is really no such thing as research. There is only search, more search, keep on searching. (Bowering, 1988, p. 95)

Once you have read through a research report, and understand the researchers' findings and their explanations of them, the story does not end there. There is more than one interpretation for any set of findings. Different researchers often explain the same set of facts in different ways.

Let's take a moment to dispel a nasty rumor. The rumor is this: Researchers present their studies in a dispassionate manner, intending only to inform readers of their findings and their interpretation of those findings. In truth, researchers aim not only to inform readers, but also to *persuade* them (Sternberg, 1995). Researchers want to convince you their ideas are right. There is never only one explanation for a set of findings. Certainly, some explanations are better than others; some fit the available data better, are more parsimonious, or require fewer questionable assumptions. The point here is that researchers are very passionate about their ideas, and want you to believe them. It's up to you to decide if you want to buy their ideas or not.

Let's compare social psychologists to salesclerks. Both social psychologists and salesclerks want to sell you something; either their ideas, or their wares. You need to decide if you want to buy what they're selling or not—and there are potentially negative consequences for either decision. If you let a sales clerk dazzle you with a sales pitch, without thinking about it carefully, you might end up buying a substandard product that you don't really need. After having done this a few times, people tend to become cynical, steeling themselves against any and all sales pitches. This too is dangerous. If you are overly critical of sales pitches, you could end up foregoing genuinely useful products. Thus, by analogy, when you are too critical in your reading of research reports, you might dismiss, out of hand, some genuinely useful ideas—ideas that can help shed light on why people behave the way they do.

This discussion raises the important question of how critical one should be while reading a research report. In part, this will depend on why one is reading the report. If you are reading it simply to learn what the researchers have to say about a particular issue, for example, then there is usually no need to be overly critical. If you want to use the research as a basis for planning a new study, then you should be more critical. As you develop an understanding of psychological theory and research methods, you will also develop an ability to criticize research on many different levels. And *any* piece of research can be criticized at some level. As Jacob Cohen put it, "A successful piece of research doesn't conclusively settle an issue, it just makes some theoretical proposition to some degree more likely" (1990, p. 1311). Thus, as a consumer of research reports, you have to strike a delicate balance between being overly critical and overly accepting.

While reading a research report, at least initially, try to suspend your disbelief. Try to understand the researchers' story; that is, try to understand the facts—the findings and how they were obtained—and the suggested explanation of those facts—the researchers' interpretation of the findings and what they mean. Take the research to task only after you feel you understand what the authors are trying to say.

Research reports serve not only an important archival function, documenting research and its findings, but also an invaluable stimulus function. They can excite other researchers to join the investigation of a particular issue, or to apply new methods or theory to a different, perhaps novel, issue. It is this stimulus function that Elliot Aronson, an eminent social psychologist, referred to when he admitted that, in publishing a study, he hopes his colleagues will "look at it, be stimulated by it, be provoked by it, annoyed by it, and then go ahead and do it better.... That's the exciting thing about science; it progresses by people taking off on one another's work" (1995, p. 5). Science is indeed a cumulative enterprise, and each new study builds on what has (or, sometimes, has not) gone before it. In this way, research articles keep social psychology vibrant.

A study can inspire new research in a number of different ways, such as: (1) it can lead one to conduct a better test of the hypotheses, trying to rule out alternative explanations of the findings; (2) it can lead one to explore the limits of the findings, to see how widely applicable they are, perhaps exploring situations to which they do not apply; (3) it can lead one to test the implications of the findings, furthering scientific investigation of the phenomenon; (4) it can inspire one to apply the findings, or a novel methodology, to a different area of investigation; and (5) it can provoke one to test the findings in the context of a specific real world problem, to see if they can shed light on it. All of these are excellent extensions of the original research, and there are, undoubtedly, other ways that research findings can spur new investigations.

The problem with being too critical, too soon, while reading research reports is that the only further research one may be willing to attempt is research of the first type: Redoing a study better. Sometimes this is desirable, particularly in the early stages of investigating a particular issue, when the findings are novel and perhaps unexpected. But redoing a reasonably compelling study, without extending it in any way, does little to advance our understanding of human behavior. Although the new study might be "better," it will not be "perfect," so *it* would have to be run again, and again, likely never reaching a stage where it is beyond criticism. At some point, researchers have to decide that the evidence is compelling enough to warrant investigation of the last four types. It is these types of studies that most advance our knowledge of social behavior. As you read more research reports, you will become more comfortable deciding when a study is "good enough" to move beyond it. This is a somewhat subjective judgment, and should be made carefully.

When social psychologists write up a research report for publication, it is because they believe they have something new and exciting to communicate about social behavior. Most research reports that are submitted for publication are rejected. Thus, the reports that are eventually published are deemed pertinent not only by the researchers who wrote them, but also by the reviewers and editors of the journals in which they are published. These people, at least, believe the research reports they write and publish have something important and interesting to say. Sometimes, you'll disagree; not all journal articles are created equal, after all. But we recommend that you, at least initially, give these well-meaning social psychologists the benefit of the doubt. Look for what they're excited about. Try to understand the authors' story, and see where it leads you.

Author Notes

Preparation of this paper was facilitated by a Natural Sciences and Engineering Research Council of Canada doctoral fellowship to Christian H. Jordan. Thanks to Roy Baumeister, Arie Kruglanski, Ziva Kunda, John Levine, Geoff MacDonald, Richard Moreland, Ian Newby-Clark, Steve Spencer, and Adam Zanna for their insightful comments on, and appraisals of, various drafts of this paper. Thanks also to Arie Kruglanski and four anonymous editors of volumes in the series, *Key Readings in Social Psychology* for their helpful critiques of an initial outline of this paper. Correspondence concerning this article should be addressed to Christian H. Jordan, Department of Psychology, University of Waterloo, Waterloo, Ontario, Canada N2L 3G1. Electronic mail can be sent to chjordan@watarts.uwaterloo.ca

REFERENCES

American Psychological Association (1994). *Publication manual* (4th ed.). Washington, D.C.

Aronson, E. (1995). Research in social psychology as a leap of faith. In E. Aronson (Ed.), *Readings about the social animal* (7th ed., pp. 3–9). New York: W. H. Freeman and Company.

Bem, D. J. (1987). Writing the empirical journal article. In M. P. Zanna & J. M. Darley (Eds.), *The compleat academic: A practical guide for the beginning social scientist* (pp. 171–201). New York: Random House.

Bowering, G. (1988). *Errata*. Red Deer, Alta.: Red Deer College Press.

Cohen, J. (1990). Things I have learned (so far). *American Psychologist, 45*, 1304–1312.

Forgas, J. P. (1994). Sad and guilty? Affective influences on the explanation of conflict in close relationships. *Journal of Personality and Social Psychology, 66*, 56–68.

Sternberg, R. J. (1995). *The psychologist's companion: A guide to scientific writing for students and researchers* (3rd ed.). Cambridge: Cambridge University Press.

Author Index

C

Subject Index